Windows® Security Monitoring

Windows® Security Monitoring

Scenarios and Patterns

Andrei Miroshnikov

WILEY

Windows® Security Monitoring: Scenarios and Patterns

Published by
John Wiley & Sons, Inc.
10475 Crosspoint Boulevard
Indianapolis, IN 46256
www.wiley.com

Copyright © 2018 by John Wiley & Sons, Inc., Indianapolis, Indiana
Published simultaneously in Canada

ISBN: 978-1-119-39064-0
ISBN: 978-1-119-39089-3 (ebk)
ISBN: 978-1-119-39087-9 (ebk)

Manufactured in the United States of America

10 9 8 7 6 5 4 3 2 1

For general information on our other products and services please contact our Customer Care Department within the United States at (877) 762-2974, outside the United States at (317) 572-3993 or fax (317) 572-4002.

Wiley publishes in a variety of print and electronic formats and by print-on-demand. Some material included with standard print versions of this book may not be included in e-books or in print-on-demand. If this book refers to media such as a CD or DVD that is not included in the version you purchased, you may download this material at http://booksupport.wiley.com. For more information about Wiley products, visit www.wiley.com.

Library of Congress Control Number: 2017962214

I dedicate this book to those who always wants to know more and seek new information and experience every day.

—Andrei

About the Author

Andrei Miroshnikov graduated at Irkutsk State University (Russia) with a Master Degree in Computer Science. With more than 9 years of experience in the Information Security field, he is an author and organizer for Forensics CTF for the DEFCON 24 conference. He authored "Windows 10 and Windows Server 2016 security auditing and monitoring reference," which is a part of Microsoft TechNet. Andrei is a speaker for Microsoft BlueHat and Positive Hack Days conferences.

About the Technical Editor

Roger A. Grimes, Microsoft, Principal Security Architect, is a 30-year computer security consultant specializing in host security, advanced persistent threat, IdM, and other defenses. Roger has written 9 books and over 1,000 magazine articles on computer security. He is a frequent guest speaker at national security conferences.

Credits

Project Editor
Tom Dinse

Technical Editor
Roger A. Grimes

Production Editor
Barath Kumar Rajasekaran

Copy Editor
Kimberly A. Cofer

Production Manager
Katie Wisor

Manager of Content Development and Assembly
Pete Gaughan

Marketing Manager
Christie Hilbrich

Business Manager
Amy Knies

Executive Editor
Jim Minatel

Project Coordinator, Cover
Brent Savage

Proofreader
Nancy Bell

Indexer
Johnna VanHoose Dinse

Cover Designer
Wiley

Cover Image
©traffic_analyzer/Getty Images

Acknowledgments

I would like to say thank you to my wife, Anna, for supporting me during the year I spent working on this book. She was taking care of our home and kids to give me more time to spend on the book.

Thank you to my mother, Natalia Miroshnikova, and father, Sergey Miroshnikov, who invested their time in me from the moment I was born. I owe them a lot.

Thank you to my technical editor, Roger A. Grimes, who supported me from the beginning of this process till the end.

Thank you to my friends Lucine Wang and Jon DeHart for a good time we spent together; this helped me to get some small breaks during my tight schedule.

Thank you to John Wiley & Sons for giving me the opportunity to write my own book. It is a great company to work with. I would like to also say a personal thank you to Tom Dinse, Jim Minatel, and Kim Cofer for their help editing the book and coordinating all work related to its creation.

Contents at a glance

Contents

Introduction

In this book I share my experience and the results of my research about the Microsoft Windows security auditing subsystem and event patterns. This book covers the Windows Security auditing subsystem and event logs for Windows systems starting from Windows 7 through the most recent Windows 10 and Windows Server 2016 versions.

Many IT Security/Infrastructure professionals understand that they should know what is going on in their company's infrastructure—for example, is someone using privileged accounts during nonworking hours or trying to get access to resources he or she shouldn't have access to? Looking for activities like these is critical to all organizations. To help with this, this book provides technical details about the most common event patterns for Microsoft Windows operating systems. It is a great source of information for building new detection methods and improving a company's Security Logging and Monitoring policy.

The primary goal of this book is to explain Windows security monitoring scenarios and patterns in as much detail as possible. A basic understanding of Microsoft Active Directory Services and Microsoft Windows operational systems will be helpful as you read through the book.

The following areas are covered:

- Implementation of the Security Logging and Monitoring policy
- Technical details about the Windows security event log subsystem
- Information about most common monitoring event patterns related to operations and changes in Microsoft Windows operating systems

The following software and technologies are covered:

- Microsoft Windows security event logs
- Microsoft Windows security auditing subsystem

- Microsoft Windows Active Directory Services
- Microsoft AppLocker
- Microsoft Windows event logs (Application, System, NTLM, and others)
- Microsoft Windows 7, 8, 8.1, 10
- Microsoft Windows Server 2008 R2, 2012, 2012 R2, 2016
- Microsoft PowerShell
- Microsoft Windows Sysinternals tools
- Third-party tools

You will find detailed explanations for many event patterns, scenarios, technologies, and methods, and it is my hope that you will find that you've learned a lot, and will start using this book every day. This book is intended as a reference that you will return to many times in your career.

Who This Book Is For

This book is best suited for IT security professionals and IT system administrators. It will be most valuable for IT security monitoring teams, incident response teams, data analytics teams, and threat intelligence experts.

The best way to use this book is as a reference and source of detailed information for specific Windows auditing scenarios.

What This Book Covers

One of the main goals of this book is to help you create a Security Logging and Monitoring (SL&M) standard for your company. At the beginning of the book I cover what this standard is about, which sections it has, and discuss best practices for creating this document.

Before jumping into the world of event logs, you need to understand how the Windows Auditing Subsystem works and which components and settings belong to this system. I cover security best practices for the Windows security auditing subsystem, its components, and internal data flows.

There are multiple event logs in Windows systems besides the Security log, and many of these logs contain very useful information. It's important to know which subsystems have which event logs, the purpose of these event logs, and the type of information collected in these logs. This information is also present in this book.

I think the most interesting part of the book deals with security monitoring scenarios and patterns. Based on these scenarios, security managers, analysts, engineers, and administrators will be able to improve security monitoring policies and build new or improve existing detection methods.

How This Book Is Structured

This book consists of 15 chapters and three appendixes. The first three chapters cover general information about the Windows auditing subsystem and security monitoring policy. The remaining chapters go deeper in to different monitoring scenarios and event patterns.

Chapter by chapter, this book covers:

- **Windows Security Logging and Monitoring Policy (Chapter 1)**—This chapter guides you through the sections of the Security Logging and Monitoring (SL&M) standard and provides the basic information you need to create your own version of it.

- **Auditing Subsystem Architecture (Chapter 2)**—In this chapter you will find information about Legacy Auditing and Advanced Auditing settings, Windows auditing group policy settings, auditing subsystem architecture, and security event structure.

- **Auditing Subcategories and Recommendations (Chapter 3)**—In this chapter you will find descriptions for each Advanced Auditing subcategory and recommended settings for domain controllers, member servers, and workstations.

- **Account Logon (Chapter 4)**—This chapter contains information about Windows logon types and the events generated during each of them.

- **Local User Accounts (Chapter 5)**—In this chapter you will find information about different built-in local user accounts on Microsoft Windows operating systems and specific monitoring scenarios for the most important operations/changes done to local user accounts.

- **Local Security Groups (Chapter 6)**—In this chapter you will learn about different scenarios related to local security groups, such as security group creation, deletion, and modification, and so on.

- **Microsoft Active Directory (Chapter 7)**—In this chapter you will find information about the most common monitoring scenarios for Active Directory, such as user or computer account creation, operations with groups, operations with trusts, and so on.

- **Active Directory Objects (Chapter 8)**—This chapter contains detailed information about monitoring Active Directory changes and operations with objects, such as group policy creation, organization unit modification, and so on.

- **Authentication Protocols (Chapter 9)**—In this chapter you will find information about how the LM, NTLM, NTLMv2, and Kerberos protocols work and how to monitor the most common scenarios involving these protocols.

- **Operating System Events (Chapter 10)**—This chapter contains information about the different system events that might indicate malicious activity performed on the system.

- **Logon Rights and User Privileges (Chapter 11)**—In this chapter you will find detailed information about how to monitor logon rights and user privileges policy changes, user privileges use, and use of backup and restore privileges.

- **Windows Applications (Chapter 12)**—It is important to monitor the use of applications on the host, activities such as application installation, removal, execution, application crushes, application block events by the AppLocker component, and so on. In this chapter you will find detailed information about monitoring these scenarios and more.

- **Filesystem and Removable Storage (Chapter 13)**—This chapter is probably one of the most interesting chapters in the book, because it covers some of the most common questions you'll have or hear during incident investigation procedures: Who deleted the file? Who created the file? How this file was accessed? Using which tool/application?

  Some of these questions are easy to answer, but some of them are not. In this chapter you will find information about monitoring recommendations for the most common scenarios related to Windows filesystem and removable storage objects.

- **Windows Registry (Chapter 14)**—This chapter contains information about Windows registry operations and monitoring scenarios.

- **Network File Shares and Named Pipes (Chapter 15)**—In this chapter you will find information about monitoring scenarios for actions related to network file shares and named pipes.

What You Need to Use This Book

This book requires that you have Windows 10 (build 1511 or higher) installed to open the .evtx files included in this book's download materials.

Conventions

To help you get the most from the text and keep track of what's happening, we've used a number of conventions throughout the book.

NOTE Notes, tips, hints, tricks, and asides to the current discussion look like this.

As for styles in the text:

- We *italicize* new terms and important words when we introduce them.
- We show keyboard strokes like this: Ctrl+A.
- We show filenames, URLs, and code within the text like so: `persistence.properties`.

We present code and event listings in two different ways:

```
We use a monofont type with no highlighting for most code and event
examples.
```

```
We use bold type to emphasize code or events of particularly importance
in the present context.
```

What's on the Website

All of the event examples used in this book are available for download at `www.wiley.com/go/winsecuritymonitoring` as `.evtx` files. These files can be opened by the built-in Windows 10 or Windows Server 2016 Event Viewer application. You will find references to these event log files in each section of every chapter that has event samples in it.

Introduction to Windows Security Monitoring

Windows Security Logging and Monitoring Policy

The purpose of the Security Logging and Monitoring (SL&M) policy is to ensure the confidentiality, integrity, and availability of information by specifying the minimum requirements for security logging and monitoring of company systems.

It is recommended to have such a policy defined and published in order to standardize security logging and monitoring requirements.

This chapter guides you through the sections of the SL&M policy and provides basic information for creating your own version.

Security Logging

This section outlines the requirements for what needs to be logged and how logs need to be managed.

Security logs provide vital information about system events that may, when correlated with other events or used independently, indicate a breach or misuse of resources. When configured and managed properly, logs are key in establishing accountability and attribution for any event. They provide answers to the critical questions about security events: who is involved, what happened, when and where it happened, and how it happened.

Companies should ensure that information passing through their systems, including user activities such as web sites visited and servers accessed, is logged, reviewed, and otherwise utilized.

Implementing the recommendations in this section can mitigate the risk of an attacker's activities going unnoticed and enhance a company's ability to conclude whether an attack led to a breach.

Security Logs

Information systems should enable and implement logging, also referred to as audit logging. Activities that should be logged may include the following:

- All successful and unsuccessful logon attempts
- Additions, deletions, and modifications of local and domain accounts/ privileges
- Users switching accounts during an active session
- Attempts to clear audit logs
- Activity performed by privileged accounts, including modifications to system settings
- Access to restricted data additions, deletions, and modifications to security/audit log parameters
- User account management activities
- System shutdown/reboot
- System errors
- New system service creation
- Application shutdown/restart
- Application errors/crashes
- Process creation/termination
- Registry modification(s)
- Local security policy modifications
- GPO-based security policy modifications
- Use of administrator privileges
- File access
- Critical process manipulation (LSASS.exe)
- System corruption (for example, audit pipeline failure, LPC impersonation, and so on)

All of these items are discussed in more detail in this book.

You should also think about where and how to store system events that are used to detect system attack attempts. These events also represent evidence for incident follow-up.

System Requirements

Here are the basic requirements for monitoring an information system. An information system should:

- Initiate session audits at system start-up. It should provide the capability to log all events related to an account's sessions, and the capability to remotely access these events.
- Utilize methods to ensure auditing services continue to run or restart in the event of a system failure or unexpected stop.
- Provide an alternate audit capability in the event of a failure in primary audit capability.
- Employ methods for coordinating audit information among external organizations when audit information is transmitted across organizational boundaries.
- Preserve the identity of individuals in case of cross-organizational audit trails.

PII and PHI

Information systems handling Personally Identifiable Information (PII) and Protected Health Information (PHI) should also log the following information about the data:

- Information type
- Date
    - Date when operation with the data has been performed
- Time
    - Time when operation with the data has been performed
- Identities of the receiving party
- Identities of the releasing party

Availability and Protection

Logging should be active at all times and protected from unauthorized access, modification, and accidental or deliberate destruction on all company information resources.

Configuration Changes

Company employees should not disable audit logs or make system configuration changes that conflict with approved baselines or services without prior authorization from the internal information security team. All changes must create auditable events themselves for tracking purposes.

Secure Storage

Logs should be stored in such a way that they cannot be tampered with, or that tampering can be detected and corrected. You cannot trust the log if you do not control the log's integrity.

Access to view the logs should be limited to only those staff members with a job responsibility to analyze the log data. This requirement applies to local logs as well as centralized storage.

Security log storage should have adequate capacity and mechanisms to recycle logs, ensuring that logs will not exhaust the available storage space in an unreasonable amount of time.

Centralized Collection

The company's information security team should provide for the central collection of security logs from systems throughout the environment.

The centralized log collection and analysis tool should meet the following requirements:

- The log management infrastructure (central log collection system) should have built-in resilience to ensure high availability.
- Monitoring controls should be implemented to ensure that the log management infrastructure (central log collection system and agent or agentless host/devices) is available at all times, and any issues that impact the logging infrastructure must generate an alert for the operational security team to review and respond.
- Security logs should be protected both in transit and at rest with approved secure transmission protocol and encryption technologies.

Centralized logging servers should be considered critical assets and be protected in accordance with corporate standards for confidential information. Systems that cannot be configured to log to a centralized or consolidated log system should have appropriate access controls for access to log data.

These requirements can be achieved using the built-in Windows Event Forwarding (WEF) feature, which is included in all Windows operating systems starting from Windows XP SP2 and Windows Server 2003 SP1. WEF is out of scope for this book, but there is a lot of information about this feature on the Internet.

Backup and Retention

An event log retention policy should be defined for both local and centralized collection storage. For example, the company should retain security logs for at least 30 days short term in the Security Information and Event Manager (SIEM) and 90 days long term in the long-term storage. Company policy, and legal and regulatory requirements, should be taken into consideration when defining the policy.

Chapter 2 contains detailed information about the Microsoft Windows auditing subsystem's group policy settings, which allow you to specify security event log maximum size, retention policy, event log file location, and so on.

Periodic Review

Security analysts should regularly review and analyze the collected logs according to a documented and approved schedule to ensure relevancy and adequacy of collected information. Out of date, deprecated, redundant, or superfluous logs should be removed from the central collection system to ensure positive system performance and to reduce the occurrence of false positives.

Security Monitoring

This section describes what needs to be monitored. It includes requirements for monitoring of logs, intrusion detection systems, and internal communications, as well as mandates for performance review of monitoring systems.

Implementing the recommendations in this section reduces the risk of failure to monitor for security events. Such failure can result in unsuccessful detection or slowed reaction to potential intrusions or misuse of corporate systems.

Companies should implement security monitoring processes and technologies to ensure timely detection and response to security events.

Security logs collected from disparate information systems must be aggregated and analyzed in a timely manner to quickly detect possible unauthorized user activities, misuse, compromise, or attack.

Standard operating procedures should be established and followed by the Security Operations staff to perform analysis and detection activities including, but not limited to, the following:

- Perform monitoring of company's systems for incidents
- Identify and document incidents as they occur

- Classify incidents into common incident categories, accounting for the fact that some incidents may fit into more than one category
- Analyze and prioritize incidents based on criticality and severity
- Notify appropriate parties (internal or external)

Communications

Electronic communication and all content, voicemail, and any other data of any kind stored or transmitted by company-owned or leased equipment, is the property of the company, and the company may access, monitor, intercept, and/or retain this data at any time without further notice.

Internal communications monitoring should include e-mail, tracking the websites that personnel visit, monitoring internal chat groups, social networks and newsgroups, reviewing material downloaded or uploaded, and voice communications.

Audit Tool and Technologies

Security monitoring and auditing tools and technologies (for example, intrusion detection systems, network scanning tools, and so on) should be deployed and used to monitor company assets. Without proper automation, security monitoring may be a really hard task.

Network Intrusion Detection Systems

Network-based Intrusion Detection Systems (NIDS) are designed to provide monitoring and support of network intrusion detection across a variety of platforms and technologies and should not be used for any other purpose.

The department charged with ensuring information security should be responsible for approving all Network Intrusion Detection Systems for use on managed networks and systems.

Host-based Intrusion Detection Systems

Host-based Intrusion Detection System (HIDS) should be capable of performing file integrity monitoring for critical content files, system files, and configurations, and alerting when attempts to modify the system are detected.

Host-based intrusion detection capabilities should be deployed on all the information resources where sensitive data is stored and potential for damage is high.

HIDS should be configured to perform file integrity comparisons to known good versions on a regular schedule.

Data fields logged by host-based IDS may include the following:

- Timestamp (date and time)
- Event or alert type
- Rating (priority, severity, impact, confidence, and so on)
- Event details specific to the type of event (IP address, port information, application information, filenames and paths, and user accounts)

System Reviews

The department charged with ensuring for information security should perform periodic reviews to ensure the company's monitoring systems are successful in detecting unauthorized attempts to access information resources.

Reporting

Any computer security event deemed suspicious or malicious and critical or high priority should be reported immediately with all relevant details and logs.

Part

II

Windows Auditing Subsystem

In This Part

Auditing Subsystem Architecture

The Windows auditing subsystem was introduced in the earliest Microsoft Windows versions. It provides the ability to report auditing events for kernel- and user-mode applications and components.

In this chapter you will find information about legacy and advanced auditing settings, Windows auditing group policy settings related to auditing, auditing subsystem architecture, and security event structure.

Legacy Auditing Settings

Legacy auditing was the only available security auditing mechanism on pre-Vista Windows systems. It was not as agile as the new advanced auditing introduced in Windows Vista, but still was able to perform its function.

Legacy auditing settings can be configured using Windows group policy settings. No built-in command-line tools, such as `auditpol`, were available in the pre-Vista systems for configuring local auditing settings. But the `auditpol` tool was a part of the Windows 2000, XP, and 2003 resource kits. The `auditusr` command-line tool was included in pre-Vista operating systems, but it was a tool for configuring per-user auditing settings only. See Chapter 10 for more information about per-user auditing.

Group policy settings for legacy auditing categories are located under the `Computer Configuration\Windows Settings\Security Settings\Local Policies\Audit Policy\` node. You can view and edit local group policy settings using the `gpedit.msc` management console. Figure 2-1 shows an example of legacy auditing group policy settings.

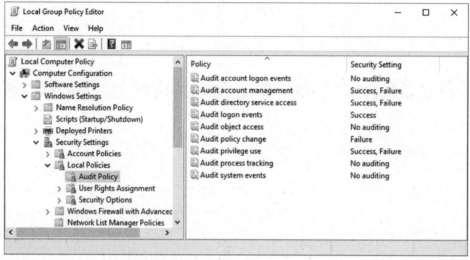

Figure 2-1: Legacy auditing group policy settings

Table 2-1 shows available legacy auditing categories and their descriptions.

Table 2-1: Legacy Auditing Categories

CATEGORY NAME	DESCRIPTION
Audit account logon events	Audit NTLM-family and Kerberos protocols credential validation operations. On domain controllers this category enables Kerberos AS_REQ, TGS_REQ, and AP_REQ requests auditing.
Audit account management	Audit user, computer, security group, distribution group, and Authorization Manager (AzMan) application group management operations. This category also provides monitoring of password hash import operations during Active Directory account migration and Password Policy Check API calls.
Audit directory services access	Audit Active Directory object modifications, object access attempts, and replication operations.
Audit logon events	Audit account logon, logoff, and lockout events. Provides detailed auditing for IPsec modes. Audit logon events for members of special groups (see Chapter 4 for more details) and special privileges owners (Chapter 11). Audit workstation lockouts, terminal session connections, and screensaver operations. Also enables auditing on Network Policy Servers (NPS).

CATEGORY NAME	DESCRIPTION
Audit object access	Audit filesystem, registry, kernel objects, handles, file shares, and filtering platform operations. Also enables auditing for Active Directory Certificate Services role operations.
Audit policy change	Audit authorization, authentication, filtering platform, audit and Windows firewall policy changes.
Audit privilege use	Audit use of sensitive and nonsensitive privileges.
Audit process tracking	Audit process creation, termination, and Data Protection API (DPAPI) operations.
Audit system events	Audit security-related changes and operations, IPsec driver events, Windows firewall service and driver events, Windows startups, and system time changes.

Auditing settings are stored in the Local Security Authority (LSA) policy database. The LSA policy database is located in the `HKLM\SECURITY\Policy` registry key. Auditing settings are stored in the `Default` value of the `HKLM\SECURITY\Policy\PolAdtEv` registry key. These settings can be configured locally or through Active Directory group policy, if the machine is joined to the domain.

Events generated in the Windows security event log by legacy auditing categories have ID numbers that are between 500 and 900. Legacy auditing events are available only in pre-Vista Windows operating systems. In more recent Windows versions, legacy events are replaced by new events with event ID numbers between 4000 and 7000.

Legacy auditing policies can be set to one of the following states:

- **Success:** Only `Audit Success` events are generated.

- **Failure:** Only `Audit Failure` events are generated.

- **Success, Failure:** Both `Audit Success` and `Audit Failure` events are generated.

- **No auditing:** In legacy audit policy settings, "No auditing" is not the same as "No Auditing" in advanced audit policy settings. In the legacy audit settings, No auditing means "Not Configured." That means that you have not set a value for that audit setting. For example, if you set a setting to Success and later switch to "No auditing," the value will still be the same as before switching to "No auditing" (that is, it will be Success).

Legacy auditing settings "tattoo" the registry, which means that they are applied directly to auditing subsystem registry keys, not to temporal group policy keys.

This book does not go any deeper into legacy auditing settings and events because modern Windows systems have advanced auditing settings available, which allows for configuring more granular auditing settings using subcategories. There is no real value in using legacy audit settings on modern Windows versions.

Later in this book you will find information about relationships between legacy and advanced auditing settings on modern Windows systems and how they affect each other.

Advanced Auditing Settings

Prior to Windows Server 2008 and Windows Vista it was difficult to exclude unneeded events from auditing. This was because auditing included nine categories and, for example, if you enabled Object Access auditing it would start to collect data for registry, file system, file share, and other object operations. However, in most cases you don't need to audit all of those.

Advanced audit introduced subcategories for each of the nine legacy categories, and you can configure them to include or exclude security events. The general category names were also changed in comparison with legacy auditing.

Advanced audit settings can be configured using group policy settings for operating system versions starting from Windows 7 or Windows Server 2008 R2. Auditing settings can also be configured using the built-in auditpol application, which was included in all operating systems by default starting from Windows Vista and Windows Server 2008. The auditpol tool is the only available option to configure advanced audit settings on the Windows Vista and Windows Server 2008 operating systems. The auditpol tool is the only method to directly read audit settings from the Local Security Authority database.

Group policy settings for advanced audit categories were first introduced for Windows 7 and Windows Server 2008 R2 systems. They are located under the Computer Configuration\Windows Settings\Security Settings\Advanced Audit Policy Configuration\Audit Policies\ node. Figure 2-2 shows an example of advanced audit group policy settings.

You will find detailed explanations of each advanced audit subcategory and recommendations for workstations, servers, and domain controllers in Chapter 3.

Advanced audit subcategories can be set to one of the following states:

- **Success:** Only Audit Success events are generated.
- **Failure:** Only Audit Failure events are generated.
- **Success, Failure:** Both Audit Success and Audit Failure events are generated.
- **No Auditing:** Auditing for the subcategory is disabled. No events will be generated.
- **Not Configured:** No changes are made to the advanced audit policy. The host will use previously applied settings.

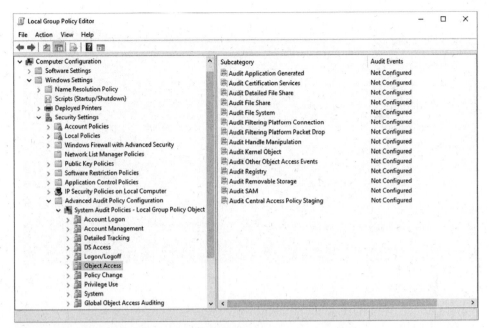

Figure 2-2: Advanced audit group policy settings

Each advanced audit category and subcategory has its own global unique identifier (GUID). These GUIDs are consistent among all Microsoft Windows versions. All GUIDs have the following format:

- **Category:** *XXXXXXXX*-797A-11D9-BED3-505054503030, where *XXXXXXXX* is different for each category.

- **Subcategory:** *XXXXXXXX*-69AE-11D9-BED3-505054503030, where *XXXXXXXX* is different for each subcategory.

To view all GUIDs for categories and subcategories use the following command in the Administrator ➪ Command Prompt window: `auditpol /list /subcategory:* /v`. Figure 2-3 shows an example of the `auditpol /list` command output.

The Windows group policy editor (`gpedit.msc`) has the ability to import and export advanced audit policy settings. Import and export menu items are available in the context menu of the `Computer Configuration\Windows Settings\Security Settings\Advanced Audit Policy Configuration\Audit Policies\` node.

The following sections cover different methods for configuring advanced audit settings on a machine.

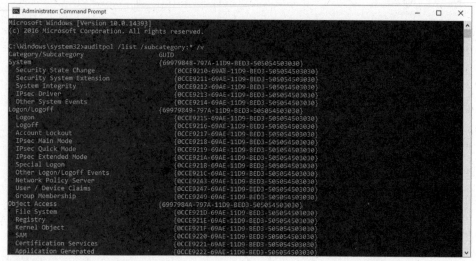

Figure 2-3: Listing auditing categories and subcategories GUIDs using the auditpol command-line tool

Set Advanced Audit Settings via Local Group Policy

If advanced audit settings are changed in the local group policy, the following file is modified:

```
%WINDIR%\system32\grouppolicy\machine\microsoft\windows nt\audit\
audit.csv
```

If no advanced audit settings were applied to the system before, the audit.csv file will be created. The \grouppolicy folder is hidden. To view it in the Windows File Explorer, enable the "Show hidden files, folders, and drives" option in the Folder Options.

Figure 2-4 shows an example of the audit.csv file content.

Machine Name	Policy Target	Subcategory	Subcategory GUID	Inclusion Setting	Exclusion	Setting Value
	System	Audit Authentication Policy Change	{0cce9230-69ae-11d9-bed3-505054503030}	No Auditing		0
	System	Audit Authorization Policy Change	{0cce9231-69ae-11d9-bed3-505054503030}	Success		1
	System	Audit Filtering Platform Policy Change	{0cce9233-69ae-11d9-bed3-505054503030}	Failure		2
	System	Audit MPSSVC Rule-Level Policy Change	{0cce9232-69ae-11d9-bed3-505054503030}	Success and Failure		3

Figure 2-4: Audit.csv file content example

The Machine Name column should always be empty.

The Inclusion Settings column shows which auditing settings are set for a specific subcategory.

The Exclusion column was designed for use with per-user auditing policies, but because per-user policies don't have group policy settings to configure them, this column is always empty.

The `Setting Value` column shows a numeric value associated with the `Inclusion Setting` column value:

- **0:** No Auditing
- **1:** Success
- **2:** Failure
- **3:** Success and Failure

After the `audit.csv` file is created/modified, it is merged with the local advanced audit settings in the Local Security Authority (LSA) policy database. LSA policy database is located in the `HKLM\SECURITY\Policy` registry key. Auditing settings are stored in the `Default` value of the `HKLM\SECURITY\Policy\PolAdtEv` registry key. The existing setting for the subcategory will be replaced by the settings from the local group policy, except those set to "Not Configured" in group policy.

Set Advanced Audit Settings via Domain Group Policy

Advanced audit settings modification using domain group policy is similar to the process for local group policy that was explained in the previous section. After domain policy is applied, group policy settings are copied locally to the `%WINDIR%\GroupPolicy\DataStore\0\sysvol\DOMAIN_NAME\Policies\` folder. Each group policy has its own folder in this directory, named by its group policy GUID. The group policy folder, if any advanced audit settings were enabled, has a `group_policy_folder\machine\microsoft\windows nt\audit\audit.csv` file in it. Here is an example of the `audit.csv` path for one of the group policies applied to the machine in the lab domain:

```
C:\Windows\System32\GroupPolicy\DataStore\0\sysvol\hqcorp.local\
Policies\{6AC1786C-016F-11D2-945F-00C04fB984F9}\Machine\Microsoft\
Windows NT\Audit\audit.csv
```

The `audit.csv` file has the same structure as discussed in the "Set Advanced Audit Settings via Local Group Policy" section.

After the `audit.csv` file is created/modified, it is also merged with the local advanced audit settings in the Local Security Authority (LSA) policy database. The process is the same as for local group policy.

Set Advanced Audit Settings in the Local Security Authority (LSA) Policy Database

The only way to modify advanced audit settings in the LSA Policy Database using built-in Windows tools is to use `auditpol`, which directly communicates with it.

To modify auditing settings for a subcategory, you need to execute the following command:

```
auditpol /set /subcategory:SUBCATEGORY_GUID_OR_NAME {options}
```

This command should be executed in an elevated command-line processor, not PowerShell. You already know how to find a GUID for a subcategory. The {options} section can have two parameters:

- **/success:** Enable success auditing setting
- **/failure:** Enable failure auditing setting

These two parameters may have one of the following two values assigned:

- **enable:** Enable setting
- **disable:** Disable setting

For example, if you need to enable Success auditing and disable Failure auditing (assuming it was enabled) for the Logoff subcategory, you may use one of the following commands:

- `auditpol /set /subcategory:{0CCE9216-69AE-11D9-BED3-505054503030} /success:enable /failure:disable`
- `auditpol /set /subcategory:"Logoff" /success:enable /failure:disable`

It is also possible to change settings for multiple subcategories by listing them one after another, separated by a comma: `/subcategory:{0CCE9216-69AE-11D9-BED3-505054503030},{0CCE9240-69AE-11D9-BED3-505054503030}`. This works only for GUIDs, not for subcategory names.

Read Current LSA Policy Database Advanced Audit Policy Settings

The only way to get current advanced audit settings directly from a local LSA Policy Database using built-in Windows tools is to use the `auditpol` tool, which directly queries information from it.

You can use the following command to get current settings:

```
auditpol /get /category:*
```

Advanced Audit Policies Enforcement and Legacy Policies Rollback

The new "Audit: Force audit policy subcategory settings (Windows Vista or later) to override audit policy category settings" group policy setting was introduced for the Windows Vista and Windows Server 2008 operating systems, which enforce the use of new advanced audit subcategories instead of legacy categories.

This group policy setting is located under the `Computer Configuration\ Windows Settings\Security Settings\Local Policies\Security Options\` group policy path. If it is enabled, legacy audit settings do not affect advanced audit subcategories settings. This group policy setting is enabled by default. It modifies the `HKEY_LOCAL_MACHINE\SYSTEM\CurrentControlSet\Control\Lsa` registry key's `scenoapplylegacyauditpolicy` value.

Possible values:

- **0:** Disabled
- **1:** Enabled

Table 2-2 contains a dependency scheme between legacy and advanced audit categories for operating systems starting from Windows Vista and Windows Server 2008.

Table 2-2: Dependency between Legacy Audit and Advanced Audit Categories

LEGACY CATEGORY	ADVANCED CATEGORY
Audit account logon events	Account Logon
Audit account management	Account Management
Audit directory services access	DS Access
Audit logon events	Logon/Logoff
Audit object access	Object Access
Audit policy change	Policy Change
Audit privilege use	Privilege Use
Audit process tracking	Detailed Tracking
Audit system events	System

For example, if the "Audit policy change" category is enabled for Success in legacy audit settings and some additional requirements (discussed in the following section) are met to permit the use of legacy settings, then all subcategories under the Policy Change advanced category will be enabled for Success auditing.

Switch from Advanced Audit Settings to Legacy Settings

Two main requirements must be satisfied to switch from advanced audit back to legacy audit:

- Disable the "Audit: Force audit policy subcategory settings (Windows Vista or later) to override audit policy category settings" group policy setting.
- Delete the `Audit.csv` file in the local group policy folder (`%WINDIR%\ system32\grouppolicy\machine\microsoft\windows nt\audit\`).

THE "NO AUDITING" SETTING IN LEGACY AND ADVANCED AUDIT

Keep in mind that the "No auditing" setting in the legacy audit group policy settings is equal to the "Not Configured" setting in advanced audit—it does not change any policy. That is why after you switch back to the legacy audit settings and set any legacy audit category to "No auditing," your computer will still have the previous settings applied. Using the legacy audit group policy setting it is not possible to set any category and nested subcategories to the state when auditing is completely disabled.

If you need to set a subcategory to the "disabled state", you can use one of the following options:

- Use the advanced audit "No Auditing" group policy setting value.
- Use the `auditpol /set /subcategory:SUBCATEGORY_GUID_OR_NAME / failure:disable /success:disable` command to disable success and failure auditing for a specific subcategory.
- Use the `auditpol /clear` command to set all subcategories to the "disabled" state.

Switch from Legacy Audit Settings to Advanced Settings

To switch from legacy audit back to advanced audit, perform the following steps:

- Enable the "Audit: Force audit policy subcategory settings (Windows Vista or later) to override audit policy category settings" group policy setting.
- The `Audit.csv` file in the local group policy folder (`%WINDIR%\system32\ grouppolicy\machine\microsoft\windows nt\audit\`) must exist. It can even be an empty file.

Windows Auditing Group Policy Settings

Multiple additional group policy settings are related to the Windows auditing subsystem. In this section you will find detailed information about them.

Manage Auditing and Security Log

The "Manage auditing and security log" group policy setting controls the `SeSecurityPrivilege` user privilege assignment . If an account or group is added to this group policy setting, the account or group members will have `SeSecurityPrivilege` user privilege on the host.

`SeSecurityPrivilege` allows managing the security event log, which allows viewing the log, changing the size of the log, clearing the log, and so on. It also allows viewing or setting an object's System Access Control List (SACL). SACL is used to store auditing settings for an object. The object in this case is any auditable object, such as registry keys, files or folders, processes, threads, and so on.

This group policy setting is located at the following path: `Computer Configuration\Windows Settings\Security Settings\Local Policies\ User Rights Assignment\`.

See Chapter 11 for more information about user rights and privileges.

Generate Security Audits

The "Generate security audits" group policy setting controls the `SeAuditPrivilege` user privilege assignment to the accounts on the machine.

`SeAuditPrivilege` allows adding records to the security event logs. This privilege is required to use the `ReportEvent()` function from `AdvApi32.dll`. Event reporting functions are discussed in the "Windows Auditing Event Flow" section later in this chapter.

This group policy setting is located at the following path: `Computer Configuration\Windows Settings\Security Settings\Local Policies\ User Rights Assignment\`.

Security Auditing Policy Security Descriptor

Security auditing policy has its own security descriptor that controls access to it. To view it, use the `auditpol /get /sd` command. The security descriptor is stored as a Security Descriptor Definition Language (SDDL) string. It contains only Discretionary Access Control List (DACL) Access Control Entries (ACEs) (`D:` section). DACL contains information about access permissions set on an object. See Chapter 10 for more information about SDDL. Here is an example of an audit policy security descriptor for Windows 10:

`D:(A;;DCSWRPDTRC;;;BA)(A;;DCSWRPDTRC;;;SY)`

- **A:** Allow access ACE type
- **DCSWRPDTRC:**
  - **DC:** Delete All Child Objects
  - **SW:** All Validated Writes
  - **RP:** Read All Properties
  - **DT:** Delete Subtree
  - **RC:** Read Permissions
- **BA:** BUILTIN\Administrators group
- **SY:** Local System account

By default, the preceding security descriptor is set for the local security auditing policy on all Windows versions starting with Windows Vista.

You can set the security descriptor for the local auditing policy using the `auditpol /set /sd:DESCRIPTOR_SDDL_STRING` command.

To view or set the security descriptor for the local auditing policy using the `auditpol` tool, the account must have the `SeSecurityPrivilege`.

There is no group policy setting you can use to set the local auditing policy security descriptor. It is stored in the following registry key: `HKEY_LOCAL_MACHINE\ SYSTEM\CurrentControlSet\Control\Lsa\Audit\AuditPolicy`, with a value of `AuditPolicySD`.

Group Policy: "Audit: Shut Down System Immediately If Unable to Log Security Audits"

If this group policy setting is enabled, it causes the system to stop if a security audit event cannot be logged for any reason. It is a requirement for Trusted Computer System Evaluation Criteria (TCSEC)-C2 and Common Criteria certification to prevent auditable events from occurring if the audit system is unable to log them.

This policy modifies the following registry key: `HKEY_LOCAL_MACHINE\SYSTEM\ CurrentControlSet\Control\Lsa`, with a value of `crashonauditfail`. Possible values are:

- `0`: Disabled
- `1`: Enabled

It is also possible to modify the `crashonauditfail` value using the `auditpol` command:

- **Disable:** `auditpol /set /option:CrashOnAuditFail /value:disable`
- **Enable:** `auditpol /set /option:CrashOnAuditFail /value:enable`

If the `crashonauditfail` registry key value is modified, the event shown in Listing 2-1 is generated in the security event log.

Listing 2-1: ID 4906: The CrashOnAuditFail value has changed.

```
Log Name: Security
Source: Security-Auditing
Level: Information

New Value of CrashOnAuditFail:  1
```

NOTE The event described in Listing 2-1 is available on the book's website, in the `CrashOnAuditFail.evtx` file.

The 4906 event shows the new value for the `crashonauditfail` registry key value.

If, for example, `crashonauditfail` is set to `1` and the security event log retention method is set to "Do not overwrite events (Clear logs manually)," and the event log reaches its maximum size, then the system will stop and the screen shown in Figure 2-5 will appear (Windows Server 2016).

Figure 2-5: Windows Server 2016 CrashOnAuditFail blue screen

Stop code 0xc0000244 has the following meaning: {Audit Failed} An attempt to generate a security audit failed.

The group policy setting path is `Computer Configuration\Policies\Windows Settings\Security Settings\Local Policies\Security Options`.

Group Policy: Protected Event Logging

Protected Event Logging is a new feature that allows Windows components and applications to encrypt their event logs using the Cryptographic Message Syntax (CMS) standard and asymmetric cryptography. For now the only application that supports protected event logging in Windows is PowerShell v5 and higher. Using this feature, PowerShell can write encrypted events in the PowerShell event log.

To enable this feature, you need to provide a certificate with a public key that will be used for encryption. Then you can use the `Unprotect-CmsMessage` PowerShell cmdlet to decrypt the event log.

The "Protected Event Logging" group policy setting is supported only by Windows 10 and Windows Server 2016. It is located at the following group policy path: `Computer Configuration\Policies\Administrative Templates\ Windows Components\Event Logging`.

Group Policy: "Audit: Audit the Use of Backup and Restore Privilege"

The "Audit: Audit the use of Backup and Restore privilege" group policy setting allows you to enable full privilege use auditing, which includes the

`SeBackupPrivilege` and `SeRestorePrivilege` privileges. Enabling it can cause a lot of heavy event logging. This group policy setting is explained in more detail in Chapter 11.

The associated registry value is `HKEY_LOCAL_MACHINE\SYSTEM\ CurrentControlSet\Control\Lsa, fullprivilegeauditing`. Possible values:

- `40`: Disabled
- `41`: Enabled

The group policy setting path is `Computer Configuration\Policies\Windows Settings\Security Settings\Local Policies\Security Options`.

Group Policy: "Audit: Audit the Access of Global System Objects"

The "Audit: Audit the access of global system objects" group policy setting works in conjunction with the "Audit object access" auditing subcategory setting. It enables default SACL on global system objects.

Global system objects are temporary kernel objects that have had names assigned to them by the application or system component that created them. These objects are most commonly used to synchronize multiple applications or multiple parts of a complex application. Because they have names, these objects are global in scope and, therefore, visible to all processes on the device. These objects all have a security descriptor; but typically, they do not have a SACL assigned. If you enable this policy setting and it takes effect at startup time, the kernel assigns a SACL to these objects when they are created. This policy setting does not affect container objects.

Usually, detailed access monitoring of access requests to global system objects, such as mutexes and semaphores, is not required and also generates a high volume of events.

This group policy setting is located at the following path: `Computer Configuration\Windows Settings\Security Settings\Local Policies\ Security Options\`.

The associated registry value is `HKEY_LOCAL_MACHINE\SYSTEM\ CurrentControlSet\Control\Lsa, auditbaseobjects`. Possible values are:

- `0`: Disabled
- `1`: Enabled

Audit the Access of Global System Container Objects

The "Audit: Audit the access of global system objects" policy setting discussed earlier does not enable auditing for global system container objects. Container objects might contain other global system objects. You can modify the HKEY_LOCAL_MACHINE\ SYSTEM\CurrentControlSet\Control\Lsa, auditbasedirectories registry key value in order to enable this default SACL on global system container objects. Possible values for this key are:

- 0: Disabled
- 1: Enabled

Windows Event Log Service: Security Event Log Settings

The Windows Event Log service has its own settings for the security event log. These settings are stored in the local registry under the HKEY_LOCAL_MACHINE\ SYSTEM\CurrentControlSet\Services\EventLog\Security\ registry key. Some of the settings also have group policy settings associated with them and can be configured using event log properties in the Event Viewer application (Figure 2-6).

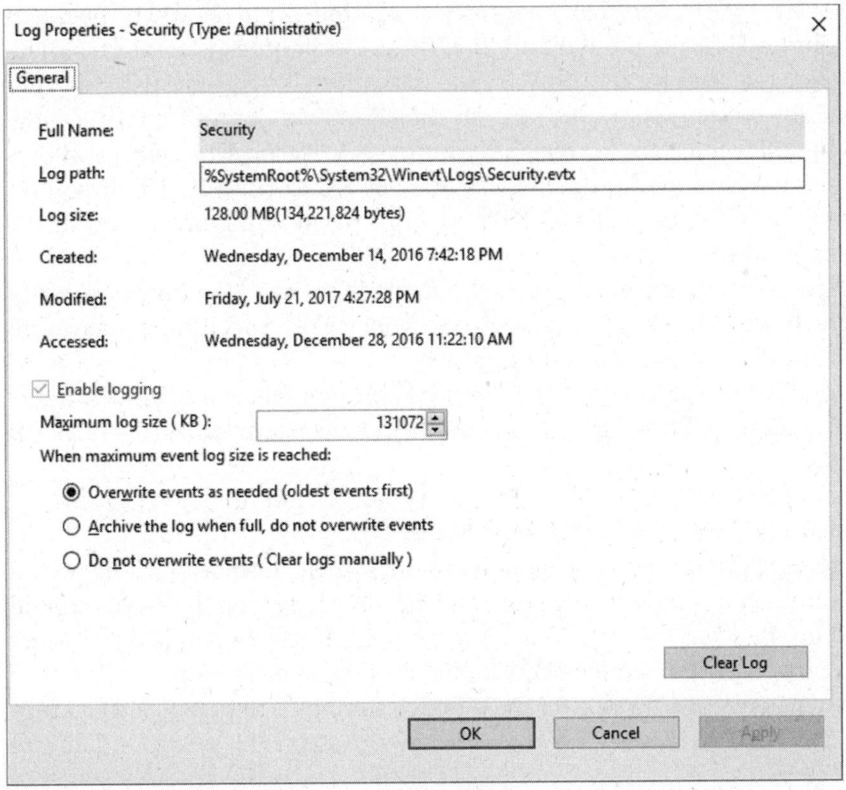

Figure 2-6: Event Viewer security event log settings

The group policy settings are located under the following group policy path: `Computer Configuration\ Policies\Administrative Templates\Windows Components\Event Log Service\Security`.

The following sections discuss the most common security event log settings.

Changing the Maximum Security Event Log File Size

You can use two group policy settings to change the maximum security event log file size:

- `Computer Configuration\Policies\Administrative Templates\Windows Components\Event Log Service\Security\Specify the maximum log file size (KB)`

- `Computer Configuration\Policies\Windows Settings\Security Settings\Event Log\Maximum security log size`

These group policy settings allow you to configure the maximum size of the security event log file. The size is specified in kilobytes and should be between 1,028 kilobytes (1.07 megabyte) and 2,147,483,647 kilobytes (2 terabytes). The group policy interface for the "Specify the maximum log file size (KB)" setting does not allow you to set a value smaller than 20,480 kilobytes for this setting. The group policy interface for the "Maximum security log size" setting allows you to specify the range for the log size from 64 KB to 4,194,240 KB. If you set the size to any value between 64 KB and 1,028 KB, it will be recorded in the registry as 1,028 KB.

If both the "Specify the maximum log file size (KB)" and "Maximum security log size" settings are set in the same group policy, the "Specify the maximum log file size (KB)" setting has higher priority.

The default security event log size for Windows Server 2016, Windows Server 2012 R2, Windows Server 2012, and Windows Server 2008 R2 is 128 MB (131,072 KB).

The default security event log size for Windows Server 10, Windows 8.1, Windows 8, and Windows 7 is 20 MB (20,480 KB).

These defaults are usually not enough to store security events for a long period of time. Your security monitoring policies determine how long the events should be stored on the machine after they are generated. It also depends on whether you are using a centralized event collection and storage solution.

The associated registry value for these policy settings is `HKEY_LOCAL_MACHINE\ SYSTEM\CurrentControlSet\Services\EventLog\Security, MaxSize`. The size specified in bytes.

The associated event log properties setting is `Log size` (refer to Figure 2-6).

Group Policy: Control Event Log Behavior When the Log File Reaches Its Maximum Size

This group policy setting allows you to configure overwrite policy for events in the security event log. By default new events overwrite the oldest events in the log, but you can change this behavior and control it by enabling this policy setting.

The associated registry value is `HKEY_LOCAL_MACHINE\SYSTEM\CurrentControlSet\Services\EventLog\Security`, `Retention`. Possible values are:

- `0`: Disabled
- `0xffffffff`: Enabled

The path to this group policy setting is `Computer Configuration\Policies\Windows Settings\Security Settings\Event Log\`.

If this policy is disabled, new security events overwrite the oldest events. This is the default setting for all recent Windows versions.

If this policy is enabled, then depending on the "Back up log automatically when full" group policy setting (`AutoBackupLogFiles` registry key value), the `AutoBackupLogFiles` security event log retention method will be configured (refer to Figure 2-6):

- `AutoBackupLogFiles = 1`: After the event log file is full, it is automatically archived and the current security log is cleared.

  The associated event log properties setting is "Archive the log when full, do not overwrite events".

- `AutoBackupLogFiles = 0`: After the event log file is full, all new events will be lost.

  The associated event log properties setting is "Do not overwrite events (Clear logs manually)".

Group Policy: Back Up Log Automatically When Full

This group policy setting allows the Windows event log service to back up a security event log file after the current file reaches its maximum size. For this policy setting to take effect, the "Control event log behavior when the log file reaches its maximum size" group policy setting should be enabled.

Archived security event log files are stored at the same location as the original file and named using the following convention:

`Archive-FILENAME-YYYY-MM-DD-hh-mm-ss-msec`, where:

- `FILENAME` is the name of the original log file without a file type extension.
- `msec` is the first three digits of the number of milliseconds in the file's creation timestamp.

The `YYYY-MM-DD-hh-mm-ss-msec` expression shows the time when event log file was archived. The time used in the filename is always in UTC+0/GMT time zone. Here is an example of archived log file name: `Archive-Secur ity-2017-07-22-10-20-21-127.evtx`.

Each time the event log is archived, it is cleared and the event shown in Listing 2-2 is recorded in the log right after it was archived.

Listing 2-2: ID 1105: Event log automatic backup

```
Log Name: Security
Source: Eventlog
Level: Information

Log:  Security
File: C:\Windows\System32\Winevt\Logs\
   Archive-Security-2017-07-22-11-01-32-194.evtx
```

NOTE The event described in Listing 2-2 is available on the book's website, in the `Event Log Archived.evtx` **file.**

The 1105 event shows the name of the log that was archived (`Log`) and the full path for the archive file (`File`).

The associated registry value is `HKEY_LOCAL_MACHINE\SYSTEM\ CurrentControlSet\Services\EventLog\Security, AutoBackupLogFiles`. Possible values are:

- `0`: Disabled
- `1`: Enabled

The associated event log properties setting is the `Log path` (refer to Figure 2-6).

The path to this group policy setting is `Computer Configuration\Policies\ Windows Settings\Security Settings\Event Log\`.

Group Policy: Control the Location of the Log File

This group policy setting allows you to specify the path and filename for a security log file. If this setting is disabled or not configured, the file is stored in the default location: `%SystemRoot%\System32\Winevt\Logs\Security.evtx`.

It is recommended that you use the standard `.evtx` extension in the filename, but the file extension can be set to any value—even a file without an extension can be specified.

Only local filesystem paths are allowed; any UNC (\\) or `File:\\` paths will be ignored and the default path will be used.

The associated registry value is `HKEY_LOCAL_MACHINE\SYSTEM\ CurrentControlSet\Services\EventLog\Security, File`.

The associated event log properties setting is "Archive the log when full, do not overwrite events" (refer to Figure 2-6).

The path to this group policy setting is `Computer Configuration\Policies\ Windows Settings\Security Settings\Event Log\`.

Security Event Log Security Descriptor

Security event log security descriptor can be configured using the "Configure log access" group policy setting. But starting from Windows 10 and Windows Server 2016 the new "Configure log access (legacy)" policy setting was introduced. The path to this group policy setting is `Computer Configuration\Policies\Windows Settings\Security Settings\Event Log\`.

Table 2-3 shows differences between operating system versions for security event access control settings.

Table 2-3: Security Event Log Access Control Policies

OPERATING SYSTEM	"CONFIGURE LOG ACCESS" REGISTRY VALUE	"CONFIGURE LOG ACCESS (LEGACY)" REGISTRY VALUE
Pre-Windows 10 and pre-Windows Server 2016	`HKLM\Software\Policies\Microsoft\Windows\EventLog\Security, ChannelAccess`	Group policy setting does not exist
Windows 10 and Windows Server 2016	`HKLM\Software\Policies\Microsoft\Windows\EventLog\Security, ChannelAccess`	`HKLM\System\CurrentControlSet\Services\EventLog\Security, CustomSD`

For Windows 10 and Windows Server 2016 it is recommended to set both policies for maximum application compatibility.

The "Configure log access" and "Configure log access (legacy)" group policy settings allow you to modify access rights for the security event log. The value for these group policy settings should be in Security Descriptor Definition Language (SDDL) format. SDDL format is described in Chapter 10.

To view current security event log security descriptor on the machine, use the `wevtutil gl security` command. The parameter that contains the SDDL string for the security descriptor is `channelAccess`. Figure 2-7 shows an example of the output for the `wevtutil gl security` command on a Windows Server 2016 machine.

Let's decode the SDDL string shown in Figure 2-7: `O:BAG:SYD:(A;;0xf0005;;;SY)(A;;0x5;;;BA)(A;;0x1;;;S-1-5-32-573)`

- `O:BA:` Owner of the object (security event log) is Built-in Administrators (BA) group
- `G:SY:` Primary group is Local System (SY)
- `D::` The beginning of DACL section
- `(A;;0xf0005;;;SY)`
  - `A:` Allow access ACE type

- ■ `0xf0005`: Full access
  - ■ `SY`: Local System account
- ■ `(A;;0x5;;;BA)`
  - ■ `A`: Allow access ACE type
  - ■ `0x5`: Read, Clear
  - ■ `BA`: BUILTIN\Administrators group
- ■ `(A;;0x1;;;S-1-5-32-573)`
  - ■ `A`: Allow access ACE type
  - ■ `0x1`: Read
  - ■ `S-1-5-32-573`: BUILTIN\Event Log Readers group

Figure 2-7: View current security event log access rights using the wevtutil tool

Table 2-4 contains information about event log access permissions that may help you to understand SDDL ACEs.

Table 2-4: Event Log Access Rights

HEXADECIMAL VALUE	ACCESS RIGHT
0x1	Read
0x2	Write
0x4	Clear
0xf0000	Full Access

The default value for security event log security descriptor depends on the operating system version. For all Windows versions starting from Windows Vista and Windows Server 2008 the default security descriptor is always the same as shown in Figure 2-7:

- **Local System:** Full access
- **Built-in Administrators:** Read, Clear
- **Event Log Readers:** Read

Any Write (0x2) access permissions in the security event log security descriptor are ignored, because write access to the security event log is controlled by the SeAuditPrivilege ("Generate security audits" group policy setting).

Guest and Anonymous Access to the Security Event Log

The registry key value HKEY_LOCAL_MACHINE\SYSTEM\CurrentControlSet\ Services\EventLog\Security, RestrictGuestAccess is used to allow or deny security event log Read access for Guests group members and the ANONYMOUS account. This registry key can be configured using the "Prevent local guests group from accessing security log" group policy setting, which is located in the Computer Configuration\Policies\Windows Settings\Security Settings\Event Log group policy path. This group policy modifies the RestrictGuestAccess registry key value, but this change has no effect on systems beginning with Windows Vista and Windows Server 2008. The security descriptor for the security event log does not change on these systems when the RestrictGuestAccess registry key value is modified.

Windows Auditing Architecture

The Windows auditing subsystem is distributed between Windows kernel-mode and user-mode components. Both modes have components that report auditing events, which is why the auditing subsystem is present in both modes—this prevents switching between modes.

Two main flows in the auditing subsystem involve multiple components to support main auditing functionality:

- **Policy flow:** Operations with auditing policy, such as getting current auditing policy settings or changing the settings.
- **Event flow:** Event reporting and recording.

The following sections discuss the event and policy flow components.

Windows Auditing Policy Flow

Figure 2-8 shows the policy flow components and interactions between them. The numbers in the figure match the step numbers in the discussions that follow.

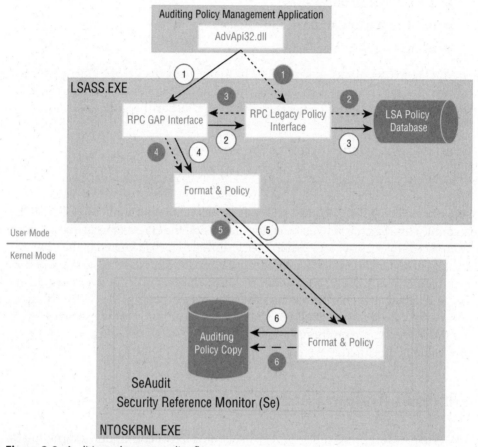

Figure 2-8: Auditing subsystem policy flow

An auditing policy management application, such as auditpol.exe, Group Policy Editor (gpedit.msc), or domain policy processing (Group Policy Client service), invokes auditing-related functions in advapi32.dll (Advanced API) to set or read auditing policy settings. The following functions might be used to set or get current auditing policy settings:

- **LsaSetInformationPolicy (PolicyAuditEventsInformation):** Set auditing settings for the host.

- **LsaQueryInformationPolicy (PolicyAuditEventsInformation):** Get current auditing settings for the host.

- `AuditSetPolicy:` Set auditing settings for the host.
- `AuditQueryPolicy:` Get current auditing settings for the host.

Some differences in the process take place prior to Step 1 related to processing of legacy and advanced audit policies involving the `audit.csv` file. These differences are explained later in this section.

LsaSetInformationPolicy and LsaQueryInformationPolicy Functions Route

This route is shown as a dotted line and filled circles in Figure 2-8.

Step 1. The `LsaSetInformationPolicy` and `LsaQueryInformationPolicy` functions interact with the RPC legacy policy interface in the `LSASS.exe` process to perform a function call.

Step 2. Changes or information queries are performed against the LSA policy database through the RPC legacy policy interface. The LSA policy database is located in the `HKLM\SECURITY\Policy` registry key. Auditing settings are stored in the `Default` value of the `HKLM\SECURITY\Policy\PolAdtEv` registry key.

Step 3. Policy changes are then sent to the RPC GAP interface which, as part of **Step 4**, informs the Format & Policy component about the change.

Step 5. The Format & Policy component acts as an intermediate agent between LSASS (user mode) and another Format & Policy component in the NTOSKRNL process. Communications between them are performed via Asynchronous Local Inter-Process Communication (ALPC) tunnels, which are discussed in Chapter 4. At this step, the LSASS process informs the NTOSKRNL process about policy changes.

`NTOSKRNL.exe`, also known as the System process, contains Windows kernel functions. Inside of this process there is a Security Reference Monitor (Se) module, which provides security-related routines, such as `SeAccessCheck` and `SeAudit`. The `SeAudit` routine implements audit and alarm procedures and contains the Format & Policy component.

Step 6. Changes are replicated to the kernel mode cached copy of the auditing settings (PolAdtEv key) from the LSA Policy Database.

AuditSetPolicy and AuditQueryPolicy Functions Route

This route is shown as a solid line and white circles in Figure 2-8.

Step 1. The `AuditSetPolicy` and `AuditQueryPolicy` functions interact with the RPC GAP interface in the `LSASS.exe` process to perform a function call.

Steps 2–3. A change request or information query is sent to the LSA Policy Database through RPC legacy policy interface.

Steps 4–6. These steps are the same as steps 4–6 for the `LsaSetInformationPolicy` and `LsaQueryInformationPolicy` functions.

Windows Auditing Event Flow

Figure 2-9 shows the event flow components and interactions between them.

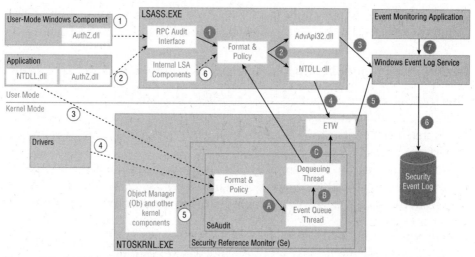

Figure 2-9: Auditing subsystem event flow

Multiple components report security events in both kernel and user modes. In Figure 2-9 these reporting methods and components are numbered using white circles and dotted lines:

1. **User-Mode Windows Components:** Multiple Windows components use private APIs from the Authz.dll library to report a security event. LSASS.exe has the RPC audit interface, which handles requests from these functions.

2. **Applications (User Mode):** Windows applications may use multiple public Authz.dll functions, such as the AuthzReportSecurityEvent or AuthzReportSecurityEventFromParams functions, to report a security event. LSASS.exe has the RPC audit interface, which handles requests from these functions.

3. **Applications (reporting event for Kernel Mode):** User-mode applications can also trigger security events by calling NTDLL.dll NT*AuditAlarm functions, such as NtOpenObjectAuditAlarm or NtPrivilegeObjectAuditAlarm. These function calls are handled by the Format & Policy component in the Security Reference Monitor's SeAudit routine.

4. **Drivers:** Drivers report events in the kernel mode using kernel routines such as SeReportSecurityEvent or SeReportSecurityEventWithSubCategory. These routine calls are handled by the Format & Policy component in the Security Reference Monitor's SeAudit routine.

5. **Object Manager and other kernel components:** Kernel components use private kernel-mode audit APIs to report a security event.

6. **Internal LSA components:** Internal LSA components may also report a security event using internal LSA audit APIs.

There are two main event flows: events reported to LSASS.exe and events reported to NTOSKRNL.exe. The following sections discuss both of them.

LSASS.EXE Security Event Flow

User-mode Windows components and regular applications report security events using Authz.dll functions. These functions invoke the RPC audit interface in the LSASS process. The steps that occur after RPC audit interface receives a call from one of the Autz.dll functions are shown in Figure 2-9 using dark circles with numbers inside.

Step 1. The RPC audit interface redirects requests to the Format & Policy module, which was discussed earlier.

Step 2. There are two main methods that LSASS may use to send an event to the Windows Event Log service for further processing:

- **Step 3:** AdvApi32.dll uses the ReportEvent() function.
- **Step 4:** NTDLL.dll uses Event Tracing for Windows (ETW) user-mode private APIs to send an event to the kernel-mode ETW component for further processing.

Step 5. Event Tracing for Windows (ETW) provides a mechanism to trace and log events that are raised by user-mode applications and kernel-mode drivers. ETW is implemented in the Windows operating system and provides developers a fast, reliable, and versatile set of event tracing features. ETW functionality is implemented as a kernel-mode component of the NTOSKRNL.exe process. ETW queues events and spools them to the Windows Event Log service as fast as the service will accept them.

Step 6. The Windows Event Log service writes events to the security event log.

Step 7. Event monitoring applications, such as Windows Event Viewer, may use public AdvApi32.dll APIs, such as the OpenEventLog and ReadEventLog functions, to query the security event log through the Windows Event Log service.

NTOSKRNL.EXE Security Event Flow

Kernel-mode security event reporting functionality is implemented in the NTOSKRNL.EXE process. This section discusses the steps that occur after the Format & Policy kernel component receives a call from one of the functions. These steps are shown in Figure 2-9 using dark circles with letters inside.

Step A. An audit event generation call is sent to the event queue. The event queue is implemented as a separate thread and performs event generation. If the queue is full, the component that sent an event generation call will be blocked until the queue can process new events.

Step B. After an event is processed it goes to the separate dequeuing thread.

Step C. The dequeuing thread sends the event to ETW or LSASS for further processing. Most of the time ETW is used, which does not require switching between kernel and user modes.

Security Event Structure

Each security event has the following XML structure:

```
<Event xmlns="http://schemas.microsoft.com/win/2004/08/events/event">
  <System>
    <Provider Name=" " Guid="" />
    <EventID></EventID>
    <Version></Version>
    <Level></Level>
    <Task></Task>
    <Opcode></Opcode>
    <Keywords></Keywords>
    <TimeCreated SystemTime="" />
    <EventRecordID></EventRecordID>
    <Correlation />
    <Execution ProcessID="" ThreadID="" />
    <Channel> </Channel>
    <Computer> </Computer>
    <Security />
  </System>
  <EventData>
    <Data Name=""> </Data>
  </EventData>
</Event>
```

The root `<Event>` section contains all elements of the event schema and the `xmlns` parameter that contains the version of the event's schema. All recent Windows operating system versions have the `schemas.microsoft.com/win/2004/08/events/event` schema version.

Within the `<Event>` section there are two main elements:

■ `<System>`: Contains a list of elements defined in the event's schema for this section. The elements within the `<System>` section are the same for all events with the `schemas.microsoft.com/win/2004/08/events/event` schema version. You will find detailed information for each element within this section later in this section.

- **`<EventData>`:** Contains various `<Data></Data>` elements that define event-specific data fields. Each event has its own set of `<Data></Data>` elements:
  - The `<Data></Data>` element defines a data field within an event. The `Name` parameter contains a data field name. The value of the parameter is shown within the `<Data></Data>` element. For example, `Security ID parameter` from Subject section with value S-1-5-18 is defined in the event as `<Data Name="SubjectUserSid">S-1-5-18</Data>`.

The remainder of this section discusses each event's element.

The `<Provider />` section contains information about the Event Tracing for Windows (ETW) provider that reported this security event. Event providers publish events to event logs. Providers are registered with the ETW subsystem, which handle all events and publishes requests from them. The `<Provider />` section has two parameters:

- **Name:** Name of the provider.
- **Guid:** GUID of the provider.

Each event Provider has a name and unique identifier (GUID) associated to it. To list all event Providers registered with the ETW subsystem you can use the following command: `logman query providers`. Figure 2-10 shows an example of the output of this command.

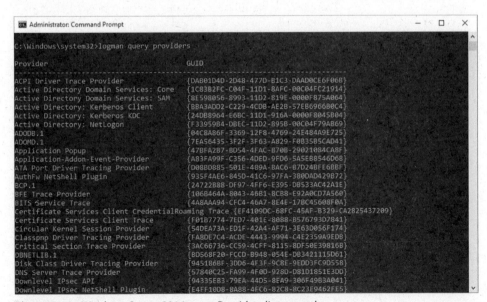

Figure 2-10: Windows Server 2016 event Providers list example

The default Windows security auditing provider is Microsoft-Windows-Security-Auditing. Its GUID is {54849625-5478-4994-A5BA-3E3B0328C30D}.

The `<EventID></EventID>` section contains the event ID number.

The `<Version></Version>` section contains a version number of the event. If the schema of the specific event was changed, a new version of the event is created with a new version number. Previous event versions are stored for backward compatibility. The event version number starts with 0. Table 2-5 contains Windows 10 and Windows Server 2016 security events that have more than one version.

Table 2-5: Security Events with Version 1 and Version 2

EVENT ID	VERSION	NEW VERSION INTRODUCED	CHANGES SINCE PREVIOUS VERSION
5140	1	Windows Server 2008 R2, Windows 7	Added `Object Type` field Added `Share Path` field Added `Accesses` field
4656	1	Windows Server 2012, Windows 8	Added `Resource Attributes` field Added `Access Reasons` field
4663	1	Windows Server 2012, Windows 8	Added `Resource Attributes` field
5156	1	Windows Server 2008 R2, Windows 7	Added `RemoteUserID` field Added `RemoteMachineID` field
5157	1	Windows Server 2008 R2, Windows 7	Added `RemoteUserID` field Added `RemoteMachineID` field
4616	1	Windows Server 2008 R2, Windows 7	Added `Process Information` section
6416	1	Windows Server 2016, Windows 10 [Build 1511]	Added `Device ID` field Added `Device Name` field Added `Class Name` field
5632	1	Windows Server 2008 R2, Windows 7	Added `EAP Reason Code` field Added `EAP Root Cause String` field Added `EAP Error Code` field
4688	1	Windows Server 2012 R2, Windows 8.1	Added `Process Command Line` field

EVENT ID	VERSION	NEW VERSION INTRODUCED	CHANGES SINCE PREVIOUS VERSION
	2	Windows Server 2016, Windows 10	`Subject` section renamed to `Creator Subject`
			Added `Target Subject` section
			Added `Mandatory Label` field
			Added `Creator Process Name` field
4624	1	Windows Server 2012, Windows 8	Added `Impersonation Level` field
	2	Windows Server 2016, Windows 10	Added `Logon Information` section
			`Logon Type` field moved to `Logon Information` section
			Added `Restricted Admin Mode` field
			Added `Virtual Account` field
			Added `Elevated Token` field
			Added `Linked Logon ID` field
			Added `Network Account Name` field
			Added `Network Account Domain` field

Security events that are not listed in Table 2-5 have only one version: 0.

The `<Level></Level>` section contains the event priority-level code. Table 2-6 contains a list of available event priority-level codes.

Table 2-6: Event Priority Level Codes

LEVEL NAME	VALUE	DESCRIPTION
Verbose	5	Identifies a detailed trace event
Informational	0 or 4	Identifies a nonerror event such as dynamic link library loading
Warning	3	Identifies a warning event such as long group policy processing time
Error	2	Identifies a severe error event
Critical	1	Identifies an abnormal exit or termination event

The `<Task></Task>` section contains the decimal code of the task category (auditing subcategory) to which the generated event belongs. Table 2-7 contains a list of task codes for all advanced audit subcategories.

Table 2-7: Advanced Auditing Subcategories Task Category Numbers

CATEGORY	SUBCATEGORY	DECIMAL	HEX
System	Security State Change	12288	0x3000
	Security System Extension	12289	0x3001
	System Integrity	12290	0x3002
	IPsec Driver	12291	0x3003
	Other System Events	12292	0x3004
Logon/Logoff	Logon	12544	0x3100
	Logoff	12545	0x3101
	Account Lockout	12546	0x3102
	IPsec Main Mode	12547	0x3103
	Special Logon	12548	0x3104
	IPsec Extended Mode	12549	0x3105
	IPsec Quick Mode	12550	0x3106
	Other Logon/Logoff Events	12551	0x3107
	Network Policy Server	12552	0x3108
	User/Device Claims	12553	0x3109
	Group Membership	12554	0x310A
Object Access	File System	12800	0x3200
	Registry	12801	0x3201
	Kernel Object	12802	0x3202
	SAM	12803	0x3203
	Other Object Access Events	12804	0x3204
	Certification Services	12805	0x3205
	Application Generated	12806	0x3206
	Handle Manipulation	12807	0x3207
	File Share	12808	0x3208
	Filtering Platform Packet Drop	12809	0x3209
	Filtering Platform Connection	12810	0x320A

CATEGORY	SUBCATEGORY	DECIMAL	HEX
	Detailed File Share	12811	0x320B
	Removable Storage	12812	0x320C
	Central Policy Staging	12813	0x320D
Privilege Use	Sensitive Privilege Use	13056	0x3300
	Non Sensitive Privilege Use	13057	0x3301
	Other Privilege Use Events	13058	0x3302
Detailed Tracking	Process Creation	13312	0x3400
	Process Termination	13313	0x3401
	DPAPI Activity	13314	0x3402
	RPC Events	13315	0x3403
	Plug and Play Events	13316	0x3404
	Token Right Adjusted Events	13317	0x3405
Policy Change	Audit Policy Change	13568	0x3500
	Authentication Policy Change	13569	0x3501
	Authorization Policy Change	13570	0x3502
	MPSSVC Rule-Level Policy Change	13571	0x3503
	Filtering Platform Policy Change	13572	0x3504
	Other Policy Change Events	13573	0x3505
Account Management	User Account Management	13824	0x3600
	Computer Account Management	13825	0x3601
	Security Group Management	13826	0x3602
	Distribution Group Management	13827	0x3603
	Application Group Management	13828	0x3604
	Other Account Management Events	13829	0x3605
DS Access	Directory Service Access	14080	0x3700
	Directory Service Changes	14081	0x3701
	Directory Service Replication	14082	0x3702
	Detailed Directory Service Replication	14083	0x3703
Account Logon	Credential Validation	14336	0x3800
	Kerberos Service Ticket Operations	14337	0x3801
	Other Account Logon Events	14338	0x3802
	Kerberos Authentication Service	14339	0x3803

The `<Opcode></Opcode>` section contains an opcode decimal code that iden-tifies an operation within the task (`<Task>`) or one of the predefined global opcodes listed in Table 2-8. Advanced audit tasks do not have any opcodes defined within them.

Table 2-8: Global System Opcodes

VALUE	SYMBOL	DESCRIPTION
0	WINEVENT_OPCODE_INFO	An informational event
1	WINEVENT_OPCODE_START	An event that represents starting an activity
2	WINEVENT_OPCODE_STOP	An event that represents stopping an activity
3	WINEVENT_OPCODE_DC_START	An event that represents data collection starting
4	WINEVENT_OPCODE_DC_STOP	An event that represents data collection stopping
5	WINEVENT_OPCODE_EXTENSION	An extension event
6	WINEVENT_OPCODE_REPLY	A reply event
7	WINEVENT_OPCODE_REPLY	An event that represents an activity resuming after being suspended
8	WINEVENT_OPCODE_REPLY	An event that represents the activity being suspended pending another activity's completion
9	WINEVENT_OPCODE_REPLY	An event that represents transferring an activity to another component
240	WINEVENT_OPCODE_REPLY	An event that represents receiving an activity transfer from another component

The `<Keywords></Keywords>` element contains additional keywords for the generated event. For security events this element may have the following values:

- **0x8010000000000000:** Audit Failure
- **0x8020000000000000:** Audit Success

The `<TimeCreated />` element contains the `SystemTime` parameter, which shows the local machine time when the event was generated. The time shows as the UTC+0 time zone (Zulu time). `2017-07-26T20:32:31.805159100Z` is an example of the `SystemTime` parameter value.

The `<EventRecordID></EventRecordID>` element contains a unique identifier (number) of the event within specific event log. Numbering starts from 1 after operating system is installed and increments by 1 for each new event. If the event log is cleared the number continues without resetting to 1. Each event log has its own numbering.

The `<Correlation />` element provides information for events correlation if the events are, somehow, connected to each other. For example, they might be part of the same Active Directory operation/transaction or part of the specific account's logon activity. If an event is a part of any transaction, the `<Correlation />` element might have the `ActivityID` parameter present with the GUID of the transaction/activity. All members of this transaction/activity will have the same value for the `ActivityID` parameter. For example, the following account logon–related events usually have the same `ActivityID` GUID for the same account:

- **4672:** Special privileges assigned to new logon.
- **4624:** An account was successfully logged on.
- **4627:** Group membership information.

It is the responsibility of the reporting component to mark events as part of the same transaction. This is not always done, so you may find that some events that look like part of the same transaction don't have any value in the `<Correlation />` element.

The `<Execution />` element contains the following two parameters:

- **ProcessID:** PID of the process that reported the event. You already know that a security event can be reported by the `lsass.exe` or `ntoskrnl.exe` processes (refer to Figure 2-9):
  - If an event is reported by the `ntoskrnl.exe` (System) process, this parameter's value will be 4.
  - If an event is reported by the `lsass.exe` process, this parameter will have a value of the `lsass.exe` process's ID (PID).

  The `ProcessID` parameter for nonsecurity events may contain PIDs for any process that invoked the event-reporting APIs.

- **ThreadID:** ID of the thread that was used to report the event within the process reported the event (for example, within `lsass.exe` or `ntoskrnl.exe` (System) process).

The `<Channel></Channel>` section contains the name of a channel where the event is written. A *channel* is a pathway that events take between an event publisher and a log file. Usually each channel has a single log file associated with it. There are four primary channels in Windows: System, Application, Setup, and Security. All security events, for example, should be sent to the Security channel to be written in the security event log.

The `<Computer></Computer>` element contains the name of the computer on which the event is generated. It may have the following formats:

- **Domain joined machine:** Computer DNS name, such as 2016dc.hqcorp.local
- **Non-domain–joined machine:** Computer NetBIOS name, such as Win10

The `<Security />` element is not usually used by security event log events, but it might be used by another event log's events to specify additional security information. For example, this element may contain a `UserID` parameter that contains a security identifier (SID) of the account that reported the event or that performed the action. The element will look like this: `<Security UserID="S-1-5-19" />`.

Auditing Subcategories and Recommendations

Advanced Auditing Policies functionality was introduced in Windows Vista/ Windows Server 2008 and at the time this book was written contains 59 subcategories.

In this chapter you will find descriptions for each Advanced Auditing subcategory and recommended settings for domain controllers, member servers, and workstations.

Account Logon

This category contains subcategories for the LAN Manager family of protocols (LM, NTLM, NTLMv2) and Kerberos protocol auditing.

Audit Credential Validation

The following event is reported by this subcategory:

ID	NAME	SUCCESS	FAILURE	DESCRIPTION
4776	The computer attempted to validate the credentials for an account	Yes	Yes	Host performed validation of account's credentials, which were received by Lan Manager family protocol.

This subcategory contains successful and failed Lan Manager family protocol credential validation events. Lan Manager family protocols include LM, NTLM, and NTLMv2 protocols. Events from this subcategory occur only on the host that stores the account's credentials.

NOTE In this chapter NTLM refers to all three protocols: LM, NTLM, and NTLMv2.

There are two main scenarios for NTLM credentials validation: local account authentication and domain account authentication.

Domain computer accounts and user accounts both can be authenticated using the NTLM authentication protocol. Credential validation for domain accounts always occurs on a domain controller. Figure 3-1 shows an example of NTLM authentication for a user account tries to access a server from a workstation host.

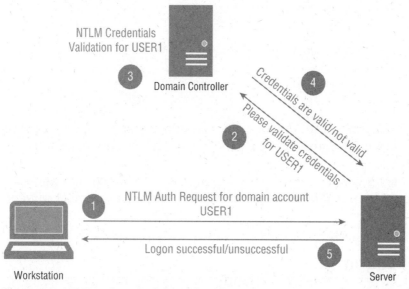

Figure 3-1: NTLM credential validation for a domain user account

Here is a brief explanation of the NTLM authentication flow shown in Figure 3-1:

1. NTLM authentication is performed from the workstation host to the server for the USER1 domain user account.

2. The server cannot validate the credentials for the domain account USER1 because it does not own them. The server sends the authentication data (credentials for USER1), which was received from the workstation, to the domain controller for validation.

3. The domain controller performs credential validation for USER1. This is when Audit Credential Validation events (4776) occur on the domain controller.

4. The domain controller sends the credential validation results back to the server.

5. The server lets the user log on or declines the user's logon attempt.

As you can see, even though the authentication attempt is going from client to server, the credential validation is performed on the domain controller, because only domain controllers store credentials for domain accounts. The Audit Credential Validation subcategory allows you to monitor NTLM credential validations on domain controllers for domain accounts. See Chapter 9 for more information about NTLM authentication.

Local user accounts are always authenticated using NTLM. Figure 3-2 shows an example of a logon from a workstation to a server using a local user account stored on the server.

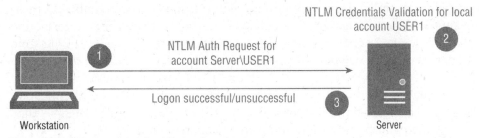

Figure 3-2: NTLM credential validation for a local user account

The following briefly explains the NTLM authentication flow for local user accounts:

1. NTLM authentication is performed from the workstation host to the server for the USER1 local user account stored on the server.

2. The server performs credential validation for USER1. This is when Audit Credential Validation events occur on the server.

3. The server lets the user log on or declines the user's logon attempt.

For both domain and local accounts, Audit Credential Validation events are generated on the host on which credential validation is performed. The host is where the account's credentials are stored.

On workstations and member servers the Audit Credential Validation subcategory allows you to track successful and failed authentication attempts using local accounts. The Audit Logon subcategory (part of the Logon/Logoff category) also provides information about local account logons, but to find out whether the account is local, you need to validate the account's domain information. Enabling Audit Credential Validation events on member servers and workstations may help you to easily track local account authentications, but provides less information than Audit Logon subcategory events. The volume of Audit Credential Validation events on workstations and member servers depends on the frequency of local account credential validation attempts, but it is usually low. Based on the low volume and usefulness for local account tracking, it is recommended that you enable both `Audit Success` and `Audit Failure` settings for the Audit Credential Validation subcategory on workstations and member servers.

On domain controllers the events volume for the Audit Credential Validation subcategory is usually high, but it depends on the amount of NTLM authentications in the domain. These events may help you to monitor accounts that still use NTLM, but other methods, such as Restrict NTLM policies (covered in Chapter 9), provide more detailed information.

The Audit Credential Validation subcategory events on domain controllers provide a centralized way to monitor account logons in the domain, but these events don't provide enough details, especially because there is no information about the logon destination host. Collecting Audit Logon subcategory events from all domain hosts is a better option for monitoring account usage in the domain.

The only unique scenario that the Audit Credential Validation subcategory events may help you with is monitoring unsuccessful NTLM authentication attempts in the domain. But these events still have a big disadvantage—they do not have information about the authentication destination host.

Read Chapter 9 for a better understanding of Lan Manager family protocol authentication flow and security events.

Based on this information, for domain controllers it is recommended that you enable only the `Audit Failure` setting for the Audit Credential Validation subcategory, and only if you need to monitor unsuccessful NTLM authentication attempts in the domain. For all other scenarios, such as general NTLM authentication monitoring in the domain or account logon monitoring, other methods (covered in Chapters 4 and 9) provide more detailed information than Audit Credential Validation events.

Audit Kerberos Authentication Service

The following events are reported by this subcategory.

ID	NAME	SUCCESS	FAILURE	DESCRIPTION
4768	A Kerberos authentication ticket (TGT) was requested	Yes	Yes	Kerberos TGT successfully issued or TGT issuance failed for some reason.

ID	NAME	SUCCESS	FAILURE	DESCRIPTION
4771	Kerberos pre-authentication failed	No	Yes	Kerberos pre-authentication data validation failed.

The Audit Kerberos Authentication Service subcategory provides detailed monitoring of Kerberos AS_REQ requests, which are used to request Kerberos Ticket-granting Tickets (TGTs). Only Active Directory domain controllers can issue Kerberos tickets and handle AS_REQ because they act as Kerberos Distribution Centers (KDCs). Figure 3-3 shows when Audit Kerberos Authentication Service events are triggered. You can find more detailed information about the Kerberos protocol in Chapter 9.

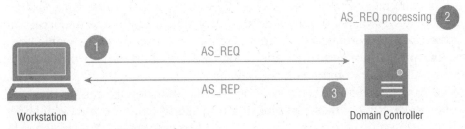

Figure 3-3: Kerberos AS_REQ request

Here is a brief explanation of the Kerberos AS_REQ flow:

1. A workstation sends AS_REQ to the domain controller in order to get a TGT for itself (computer account authentication).

2. The domain controller performs AS_REQ validation. This is when Audit Kerberos Authentication Service events occur.

3. Depending on AS_REQ validation results, the domain controller sends an AS_REP message with the issued TGT or an error/failure code.

Audit Kerberos Authentication Service subcategory events show both successful TGT issuance events and unsuccessful events (when for some reason a TGT was not issued).

There is no reason to turn on Kerberos AS_REQ request auditing on hosts that are not domain controllers. For workstations and member servers it is recommended that you set this subcategory setting to "No Auditing."

There are multiple scenarios for which AS_REQ request auditing might need to be enabled on domain controllers.

The most common scenario for this subcategory is centralized auditing of successful and unsuccessful account logons using Kerberos. One disadvantage of Audit Kerberos Authentication Service subcategory events is that they don't contain the source hostname from which the AS_REQ request was sent; they only contain the source host's IP address. Another specific of AS_REQ request auditing is that it captures requests for both user and computer accounts. If you are not interested in computer accounts, you will need to filter them out.

Do not forget that this subcategory only reports Kerberos authentication attempts. If you want to have a complete picture of account authentications within an Active Directory domain you will also need to collect information about Lan Manager family protocol authentication attempts (Audit Credential Validation subcategory).

Overall, depending on the volume of Kerberos AS_REQ requests in your Active Directory environment, you might decide not to put all Audit Kerberos Authentication Service events in long-term storage. For example, AS_REQ requests sent for computer accounts can be filtered by excluding all account names that end with a $ character. If you want to control all successful and unsuccessful Kerberos AS_REQ requests within an Active Directory domain, enable both Success and Failure auditing options for the Audit Kerberos Authentication Service subcategory on domain controllers.

The Audit Kerberos Authentication Service subcategory can be used for Kerberos AS_REQ requests troubleshooting. Audit Failure events will show you the result code with the reason the AS_REQ request failed. You will need to set the Audit Kerberos Authentication Service subcategory setting to Failure on domain controllers if you want to use it for Kerberos AS_REQ troubleshooting.

Another scenario for which AS_REQ auditing can be useful is centralized monitoring for account logons using the wrong password. This information is provided by a 4771 event. You will need to set Audit Kerberos Authentication Service subcategory setting to Failure for this scenario.

This subcategory will also help you find accounts that are not compliant with your organization's security standards. For example, you can find all accounts that use DES encryption in AS_REQ requests or accounts that don't use Kerberos pre-authentication. Enable both Success and Failure event auditing to collect all AS_REQ messages.

Events from this subcategory provide some additional information about a smart card certificate being used for authentication and also may help to troubleshoot some smart card authentication issues. For smart card troubleshooting enable Failure event auditing. To collect extended information about all smart card logons, enable both Success and Failure auditing.

To make a decision about which settings to set for this subcategory, read Chapter 9 to get more information about Kerberos AS_REQ events and then, based on the scenarios discussed earlier, make a decision about which settings you should enable. As a general recommendation, do not make a decision to enable or disable this subcategory if you don't know which events are generated by this subcategory and how useful the information from these events is.

This subcategory gives you detailed information about Kerberos AS_REQ requests. You need to decide which events you will put into long-term event storage; for example, you may want to store successful and unsuccessful AS_REQ events for user accounts only, excluding computer accounts. You also need to decide which events you want to alert on; for example, AS_REQ with DES encryption algorithms. Chapter 9 has more detailed recommendations.

Audit Kerberos Service Ticket Operations

The following events are reported by this subcategory.

ID	NAME	SUCCESS	FAILURE	DESCRIPTION
4769	A Kerberos service ticket was requested	Yes	Yes	This event shows you successful and unsuccessful TGS_REQ or AP_REQ requests to a domain controller.
4770	A Kerberos service ticket was renewed	Yes	No	Domain controller received TGS_REQ to renew a Kerberos TGT ticket.

This subcategory provides monitoring of Kerberos TGS_REQ and AP_REQ requests sent to a domain controller. It also contains a dedicated event (4770) for Kerberos ticket renewal requests.

Using this subcategory you can track TGS ticket requests sent by hosts to domain controllers. This information shows access attempts made by domain users or computer accounts.

There is no reason to turn on Kerberos TGS_REQ request auditing on hosts that are not domain controllers. For workstations and member servers it is recommended to set this subcategory setting to "No Auditing."

If you need to track all possible TGS requests performed by computer and/or user accounts using Kerberos, this subcategory will provide this information. It does not show all possible authentication requests in the domain, because it does not monitor NTLM authentication requests. This subcategory usually generates a high volume of events. Also, if you need to monitor all account logon activities in your environment, centralized collection of Audit Logon subcategory events will provide more detailed information.

Audit Kerberos Service Ticket Operations subcategory unsuccessful events are useful for Kerberos TGS_REQ requests troubleshooting.

Kerberos TGT ticket renewal events are informational and might be used for Kerberos protocol troubleshooting or monitoring. These events usually don't provide any useful information during security incident response.

To summarize, this subcategory is more useful for Kerberos TGS_REQ troubleshooting than for security monitoring. It is not recommended to enable it on domain controllers due the high volume of events generated and low usefulness in security incidents. But this subcategory provides information about access attempts performed by Active Directory accounts, which may help to detect unauthorized access attempts.

Read Chapter 9 for more information about Kerberos TGS_REQ and AP_REQ events and then, based on the scenarios discussed earlier in this chapter, make a decision about which settings you should enable. As a general recommendation, do not enable this subcategory if you don't know how you will use the collected events.

Audit Other Account Logon Events

This subcategory, currently, does not generate any security events. It is recommended to set it to "No Auditing" for all types of hosts.

Account Management

This category contains subcategories that show activities related to Microsoft Authorization Manager (AzMan) application groups, Windows security groups, Windows distribution groups, computer accounts, and user accounts.

Audit Application Group Management

This subcategory shows changes to Microsoft Authorization Manager's (AzMan) basic and LDAP query application groups. It works only for Active Directory Domain Services and Lightweight Directory Domain Services type authorization stores.

There is no reason to turn on AzMan application group auditing on hosts that are not domain controllers, because only Active Directory authorization stores can be monitored by this subcategory. For workstation and member servers it is recommended to set this subcategory to "No Auditing."

This subcategory reports only Audit Success events. It is recommended to turn on Success auditing for this subcategory on domain controllers if you use AzMan with Active Directory authorization stores in your company and want to monitor operations with AzMan application groups.

Audit Computer Account Management

The following events are reported by this subcategory:

ID	NAME	SUCCESS	FAILURE	DESCRIPTION
4741	A computer account was created	Yes	No	New Active Directory computer account object is created.
4742	A computer account was changed	Yes	No	Active Directory computer account object is modified.
4743	A computer account was deleted	Yes	No	An Active Directory computer account object is deleted.

This subcategory allows monitoring of Active Directory computer account creation, deletion, and modification operations. It contains only `Audit Success` events.

This subcategory generates events only on domain controllers. Set it to "No Auditing" on member servers and workstations.

On domain controllers this subcategory does not typically generate a high volume of events. It might be useful to capture computer account management events because they might provide information about who deleted specific computer objects or when a computer object was modified. Enable the Success setting for this subcategory on domain controllers.

Audit Distribution Group Management

This subcategory provides the ability to monitor operations with Active Directory distribution groups, such as group creation, deletion, modification, and member add/remove operations.

This subcategory can trigger events only on domain controllers. Set it to "No Auditing" on member servers and workstations.

If you want to monitor for any operation with distribution groups in the domain, enable the Success setting for this subcategory on all domain controllers. Depending on how often and how many members are added or removed from distribution groups, this subcategory might generate a low to medium volume of events. You can find more detailed information about distribution group monitoring in Chapter 7.

This subcategory reports only `Audit Success` events.

Audit Other Account Management Events

The following events are reported by this subcategory:

ID	NAME	SUCCESS	FAILURE	DESCRIPTION
4782	The password hash an account was accessed	Yes	No	Account's password hash was imported during account migration.
4793	The Password Policy Checking API was called	Yes	No	Generates when `NetValidatePasswordPolicyFree` or `NetValidatePasswordPolicy` Password Policy Checking API functions are invoked.

This subcategory provides the ability to monitor the use of Password Policy Checking API functions and Active Directory account hash import operations during account migration.

The Password Policy Checking API allows applications to verify that passwords meet the complexity, aging, minimum length, and history reuse requirements of a computer's password policy. It has two main functions that can be used to perform password validation: `NetValidatePasswordPolicyFree` and `NetValidatePasswordPolicy`. Each time these functions are invoked, an event is recorded in the security event log, which shows some details about the validation request and its results (status code). Password Policy Checking API functions can be used by any application and the volume of events can be high, depending on how often the functions are invoked. Password Policy Checking API events usually have little to no security relevance and are mainly used for Password Policy Checking API troubleshooting.

Active Directory accounts can be migrated from one domain to another using, for example, the Active Directory Migration Toolkit (ADMT) with the Password Export Server service component. As one of the options, the account's password hash can also be migrated. If such an operation is performed, an event is generated in the security event log on the destination domain controller, showing which account's hash was imported. The 4782 event is only generated when the ADMT DLL `RetrieveEncrytedSourcePasswords` function is used on destination domain controller to decrypt encrypted account passwords received by Password Export Server service. This does not generate for any other hash check, so it's not useful for alerting on pass-the-hash attacks. You can find more information about Active Directory account migration audit in Chapter 7.

On member servers and workstations only the 4793 event is generated in this subcategory. As explained earlier, this event is usually used for Password Policy Checking API troubleshooting. It is recommended that you set this subcategory setting to "No Auditing" on member servers and workstations, unless you have a reason to monitor Policy Checking API calls.

On domain controllers it is useful to track any unauthorized use of the RetrieveEncrytedSourcePasswords function. Enable the Success setting for this subcategory on domain controllers.

Audit Security Group Management

The Audit Security Group Management subcategory allows monitoring for security group operations such as group creation, modification, deletion, and member add/remove operations. It also allows tracking group type changes and security group membership enumeration operations. This subcategory covers both local and Active Directory security groups.

This subcategory is important to monitor on any host type: domain controllers, member servers, and workstations. Security groups are a main access control mechanism in the Windows operating system. Any operations related to security groups should be monitored. Enable the Success setting for this subcategory on the host types just mentioned.

You can find more detailed information about security group monitoring in Chapters 6 and 7. This subcategory reports only `Audit Success` events.

Audit User Account Management

This subcategory provides information about the following activities:

- Operations with local and Active Directory user accounts, such as account creation, modification, deletion, password reset, password change, account name change, and so on
- Adding Security Identifier (SID) history to the account
- Directory Services Restore Mode (DSRM) account's password modifications
- Windows Credential Manager backup and restore operations
- Blank password queries for an account (Windows 10 and Windows Server 2016 only)

Almost all events in this subcategory are important to monitor. Events in this subcategory, for example, may help you find who deleted a specific user account, who reset a user account's password, when an account was locked out, who changed the DSRM account's password and when it was changed, and so on.

It is recommended that you enable both Success and Failure settings for this subcategory on domain controllers, member servers, and workstations.

You can find more detailed information about user account monitoring in Chapters 5 and 7.

This subcategory reports both `Audit Success` and `Audit Failure` events.

Detailed Tracking

This category contains subcategories that provide information about Data Protection API (DPAPI) operations, Plug & Play (PNP) device operations, process creation, and termination operations.

Audit DPAPI Activity

This subcategory is mainly used for Data Protection API (DPAPI) troubleshooting. Also, if an unprotect or protect operation was performed with data protected by the `CryptProtectData` DPAPI function with the `CRYPTPROTECT_AUDIT` flag (`dwFlags`) set, then an audit event (event ID 4694 or 4695) will be triggered.

It is recommended that you enable both Success and Failure settings for this subcategory on all host types. The main reason for this is to audit use of `CryptUnprotectData` and `CryptProtectData` DPAPI functions against auditable data. This subcategory usually generates a very low volume of events.

This subcategory reports both `Audit Success` and `Audit Failure` events.

Audit PNP Activity

This subcategory was first introduced in Windows 10 and contains events that inform you about the following operations:

- New (Plug & Play) PNP device is connected to the system
- Device was disabled or enabled
- Device Installation Restriction policies events

The volume of events generated by this subcategory is usually low. It is important to monitor any new PNP device initialization. For example, if a virus infected the system via an attached USB drive, you will be able to find when the device was connected and additional details about the device. Enable the Success setting for this subcategory on all host types.

This subcategory contains only `Audit Success` events.

Audit Process Creation

The following events are reported by this subcategory:

ID	NAME	SUCCESS	FAILURE	DESCRIPTION
4688	A new process has been created	Yes	No	New process was created.

ID	NAME	SUCCESS	FAILURE	DESCRIPTION
4696	A primary token was assigned to process	Yes	No	This event generates every time a process runs using the noncurrent access token; for example, User Account Control (UAC) elevated token, RUN AS different user actions, scheduled task with defined user, services, and so on. This event was deprecated in Windows 7 and Windows 2008 R2.

This subcategory is very important to enable, because it shows you detailed information about any processes that have started in the system. This information is critical during incident response and forensics procedures. It is recommended to enable the Success setting for this subcategory on domain controllers, member servers, and workstations.

You can find more detailed information about process creation monitoring in Chapter 12.

Audit Process Termination

The following event is reported by this subcategory:

ID	NAME	SUCCESS	FAILURE	DESCRIPTION
4689	A process has exited	Yes	No	Triggers when the process is exited or terminated.

This subcategory provides information about process exit events, when a process was terminated or exited. This information is important for scenarios when you need to know when and by which account a process was terminated. The volume of events for this subcategory is typically low to medium, and depend on how often processes are exited in the system. It is recommended that you enable the Success setting for this subcategory on domain controllers, member servers, and workstations, if you need to track when the process was exited, for how long it was running, and which account was used to terminate/exit the process.

You can find more detailed information about process termination monitoring in Chapter 12.

Audit RPC Events

This subcategory, currently, does not generate any events. It is recommended to set it to "No Auditing" for all types of hosts.

DS Access

This category contains subcategories with information about Active Directory replication, object access attempts, and object changes.

Audit Detailed Directory Service Replication

The main purpose of this subcategory is Active Directory replication troubleshooting. It might generate a very high volume of events depending on replication scope. This subcategory only works on domain controllers and it is recommended you enable it only if you perform Active Directory replication troubleshooting or detailed monitoring.

This subcategory reports both `Audit Success` and `Audit Failure` events.

Audit Directory Service Access

The following event is reported by this subcategory:

ID	NAME	SUCCESS	FAILURE	DESCRIPTION
4662	An operation was performed on an object	Yes	Yes	Indicates an operation preformed on an Active Directory object.

This subcategory reports access attempts performed on Active Directory objects, such as organizational unit, user, contact, computer, and so on. Events are generated only for objects that have System Access Control List (SACL) Access Control Entries (ACEs) set for specific access attempts. The events are generated when specific access permissions were requested for an Active Directory object and provide the result of the request: were permissions granted or was access denied.

This subcategory is the only way to audit unsuccessful access attempts for Active Directory objects.

Also, while the subcategory covered in the following section (Audit Directory Service Changes) covers Active Directory object modification, creation, deletion, movement, and undelete operations, the Audit Directory Service Access category provides the ability to audit other operations, such as property read or Discretionary Access Control List (DACL) read operations. You can find more information about Active Directory object access auditing in Chapter 8.

This subcategory only works on domain controllers. If you need to audit unsuccessful access attempts to Active Directory objects, enable the Failure setting for this subcategory on all domain controllers. The "Audit Handle Manipulation" subcategory is not required to be enabled to get 4662 events.

To help you make a decision about whether you need to enable the Success or Failure setting for this subcategory, read Chapter 8 to get more information about Active Directory object access events. As a general recommendation, do not enable this subcategory if you don't know how you will use the collected events.

Audit Directory Service Changes

This subcategory reports Active Directory object change events, such as Active Directory object modification, creation, deletion, movement, and undelete operations. It only reports actual modifications, not Read operations.

It is important to enable the Success setting for this subcategory if you perform any object-level auditing on Active Directory objects. This subcategory only works on domain controllers.

To make a decision about whether you need to enable the Success setting for this subcategory, read Chapter 8 to get more information about Active Directory object change events. As a general recommendation, do not enable this subcategory if you don't know how you will use the collected events.

This subcategory contains only `Audit Success` events.

Audit Directory Service Replication

This subcategory, as well as the Audit Detailed Directory Service Replication subcategory mentioned earlier in this chapter, is mostly useful for Active Directory replication troubleshooting and monitoring. It has little to no security relevance. This subcategory only works on domain controllers and it is recommended that you enable it only if you perform Active Directory replication troubleshooting or detailed monitoring.

This subcategory has both `Audit Success` and `Audit Failure` events.

Logon and Logoff

This category contains subcategories with information about account lockout operations, user and device claims assigned to a logon session, group membership information for new account logons, IPsec negotiations, logon and logoff activities, Network Policy Server (NPS) operations, special groups and special privileges assigned to new logons, workstation lockout/unlock operations, and so on. In general, it contains events related to account logon and logoff activities.

Audit Account Lockout

The following event is reported by this subcategory:

ID	NAME	SUCCESS	FAILURE	DESCRIPTION
4625	An account failed to log on	No	Yes	This event generates when an account was locked out after a logon attempt or when logon attempt was performed for a locked out account.

This subcategory informs you when an account is locked out after a logon attempt or when a logon attempt was performed for a locked out account. This subcategory reports account lockouts for both local and Active Directory accounts. The 4625 event is the only event in this subcategory and it is generated on the machine where the unsuccessful logon attempt was performed.

If you need to monitor logon events for locked out accounts or logon events after which an account was locked out, enable the Failure setting for this subcategory. It is recommended to enable the Failure setting for this subcategory on domain controllers, member servers, and workstations because the account lockout information might be useful during incident investigations and also due to the low volume of events generated.

You can find more detailed information about account lockout logons in Chapter 4.

Audit User/Device Claims

The following event is reported by this subcategory:

ID	NAME	SUCCESS	FAILURE	DESCRIPTION
4626	User/Device claims information	Yes	No	Shows associated user or device claims for a new logon session

This subcategory generates an event for each account logon on a host showing user and device claims associated with a logged-in account logon session. If an account does not have any claims, no events are generated.

It is recommended to enable the Success setting for this subcategory for domain controllers, member servers, and workstations. Even if you haven't yet configured any claims in your Active Directory environment it is still recommended to enable it. With the Success setting enabled, user or device claims are captured by the security event log, so you will be informed that claims are in use in your Active Directory environment. The volume of events is the same as or lower than the volume of logon events.

You can find more detailed information about user and device claims in Chapter 4.

Audit Group Membership

The following event is reported by this subcategory starting from Windows 10 and Windows Server 2016:

ID	NAME	SUCCESS	FAILURE	DESCRIPTION
4627	Group membership information	Yes	No	Shows group membership information for a logged-in account.

This subcategory was first introduced in Windows 10 and generates an event for each account logon on a host showing group membership information for a logon session.

It is recommended to enable the Success setting for this subcategory for domain controllers, member servers, and workstations to have extended information about logged-in accounts. The 4627 event shows an account's group membership information for the time an account logged in, which may be useful to capture. The volume of events is the same as the volume of logon events, which might be high on domain controllers.

You can find more detailed information about event 4627 in Chapter 4.

Audit IPsec Extended Mode/Audit IPsec Main Mode/Audit IPsec Quick Mode

Audit IPsec subcategories are designed to be used for IPsec extended, quick, and main modes troubleshooting. Enable Success and Failure settings for these subcategories if you need to troubleshoot IPsec communications.

Audit Logoff

The following events are reported by this subcategory:

ID	NAME	SUCCESS	FAILURE	DESCRIPTION
4634	An account was logged off	Yes	No	Account logoff for accounts that do not initiate logoff using the `ExitWindowsEx` function reported by event 4647. This event is typically generated for all logon types except Interactive and RemoteInteractive.
4647	User initiated logoff	Yes	No	Indicates user initiated logoff typical for Interactive and RemoteInteractive logon types. This event is invoked as part of the `ExitWindowsEx` function.

This subcategory provides information about when an account was logged off. Events generate locally on the host where an account was logged off. In addition to revealing when an account was logged off, the information generated by these events can be used for calculation of how long an account was logged in. It is important to note that some logoff operations, such as those related to Network logons, occur after a session is expired or timed out. For such scenarios, logoff events do not provide an accurate time when the user stopped using the session. Also, in some scenarios, such as unexpected shutdown, logoff events are not recorded at all.

It is recommended that you enable the Success setting for this subcategory on member servers and workstations, because the volume of logoff operations is usually low. The volume of logoff events on domain controllers might be high, depending on how many user and computer accounts connect to them. In general, it is recommended to also enable it on domain controllers, but that is not as important as, for example, account logon events.

You can find more detailed information about account logoff events in Chapter 4.

Audit Logon

The following events are reported by this subcategory:

ID	NAME	SUCCESS	FAILURE	DESCRIPTION
4624	An account was successfully logged on	Yes	No	Account successfully logged on to the host.
4625	An account failed to log on	No	Yes	Account failed to log on to the host.
4648	A logon was attempted using explicit credentials	Yes	No	Shows when an account invoked a logon operation for another account.
4675	SIDs were filtered	Yes	No	Invoked when SIDs were filtered for an account that came from an Active Directory trust with the SID filtering feature enabled.

This subcategory is probably one of the most important and useful for incident response and forensics processes. It shows when an account was logged in to the host or failed to logon.

Events from this subcategory are triggered on the host on which the logon was performed. These events provide details about which user logged on to the host, using which logon type, when, from which IP address the connection was initiated, and so on. All this information is important to know when there's a security incident. A failed logon event shows you information about an account for which logon failed and the reason code for why it failed.

It is recommended to enable Success and Failure settings for this subcategory on member servers and workstations. The volume of logon events on domain controllers might be high, depending on how many user and computer accounts log on to them. In general, it is recommended to also enable them on domain controllers, but you need to verify that a local security event log is capable of holding all these events to be compliant with your security monitoring policy.

Otherwise you should apply proper filtering for these events—for example, send only events with specific logon types to the centralized event collector.

You can find more detailed information about account logon events in Chapter 4.

Audit Network Policy Server

This subcategory contains events related to the Network Policy Server (NPS) role for Windows server operating systems. It informs you when access is granted or denied for an account, a user is quarantined, a user is locked or unlocked, and so on.

Enable Success and Failure settings for this subcategory on servers with an NPS role installed if you need to monitor NPS operations. Enable the "No Auditing" setting for this subcategory on workstations, because an NPS role cannot be installed on nonserver operating systems.

Audit Other Logon/Logoff Events

This subcategory contains events for terminal session reconnect/disconnect, workstation lock/unlock, and screensaver invoke/dismiss operations. It also contains information about wireless and wired network 802.1x authentications and failed Credential Security Support Provider (CredSSP) credential delegation requests.

The volume of events produced by this subcategory is usually low. Screensaver invoke/dismiss operation monitoring is not usually needed, because such information is not required during the incident response process and has little to no security relevance. Session disconnect/reconnect and workstation lock/unlock operations are also not often useful during an investigation, but for some incidents they might provide useful information. For example, if a user's account was used to perform malicious actions from the user's machine, and the user tells you that he/she was in a meeting at this time and locked out of his machine, you can verify whether his/her machine was locked out using the security event log.

If you have any CredSSP delegation policies configured on a host, this subcategory will generate an event if CredSSP disallows a delegation request.

802.1x authentication events provide extended information about wireless or wired authentications performed by the host or user on the host. This information, for example, might help you to find out that the host was connected to an unauthorized wireless access point.

It is recommended to enable Success and Failure settings for this subcategory on domain controllers, member servers, and workstations.

This subcategory has both `Audit Success` and `Audit Failure` events.

Audit Special Logon

The following events are reported by this subcategory:

ID	NAME	SUCCESS	FAILURE	DESCRIPTION
4964	Special groups have been assigned to a new logon	Yes	No	Indicates when a member of special group logged in to the host.
4672	Special privileges assigned to new logon	Yes	No	Indicates when a special user privilege was assigned to the logged-in account.

This subcategory can inform you about logon of an account that was added to the list of accounts for monitoring by the "Special groups" Windows feature. "Special groups" is a Windows feature that allows you to generate additional events in the security event log if a member of a specified group/groups is logged in on the machine. If you use the "Special groups" feature, enable the Success setting for this subcategory on hosts where special groups are configured. You can find more information about the special groups feature in Chapter 4.

There is a predefined list of special user privileges, such as SeTcbPrivilege or SeAuditPrivilege, in the Windows operating system. These privileges are considered the most important to monitor. The Audit Special Logon subcategory generates an event in the Windows security event log every time one or more special privileges are assigned to a new logon session. Enable the Success setting for this subcategory to track logons for accounts with special privileges only if you will use this information in your monitoring use cases (scenarios). You can find more information about special user privileges in Chapter 11.

The volume of events for this subcategory depends on the number of account logons that have special privileges assigned and on the "Special groups" feature configuration.

Object Access

This category contains subcategories to audit operations related to Microsoft Authorization Manager (AzMan) applications, Active Directory Certificate Services (ADCS) components, network file shares, filesystem objects, Windows Filtering Platform, object handles, kernel objects, scheduled tasks, COM+ objects, registry keys, removable storage objects, SAM database objects, and Dynamic Access Control central policies.

Audit Application Generated

This subcategory contains events related to Microsoft Authorization Manager (AzMan) applications operations, such as application initialization, access checks, and application context creation. If you need to monitor AzMan applications, enable the Success setting for this subcategory.

This subcategory contains only `Audit Success` events.

Audit Certification Services

This subcategory allows you to audit Active Directory Certificate Services (ADCS) role operations, such as certificate revocation or service backup and restore operations. Enable Success and Failure settings for this subcategory on servers with the ADCS role installed to be able to monitor ADCS service operations and service state changes.

Audit Detailed File Share

The following event is reported by this subcategory:

ID	NAME	SUCCESS	FAILURE	DESCRIPTION
5145	A network share object was checked to see whether client can be granted desired access	Yes	Yes	This event provides detailed information about access attempts to files and folders on a network share.

If you need to audit each successful and unsuccessful access attempt to any file and folder on all network file shares on the host, you should enable the Success and Failure audit settings for this subcategory.

It is not possible to configure which files or folders and which access types should be audited by this subcategory. If you enable this subcategory, "Full Control" SACL is enabled on a network share level for all files and folders on all file shares. On file servers and domain controllers the event volume can be very high.

You can find more detailed information about detailed file share auditing in Chapter 15.

Audit File Share

This subcategory generates security events when a network share is added, deleted, or modified. It also alerts you about network share access attempts, but only shows information about the initial access to a share, not going into detailed file or folder access attempts alerting. Lastly, this subcategory contains an event that allows you to track Service Principal Name (SPN) check validation failures for the Server Message Blocks (SMB) protocol.

It is important to set this subcategory to the Success setting if you want to know any network file share creation, deletion, or modification operations. It is recommended to monitor these operations on all host types.

If you want to monitor every successful or failed connection to a network file share on a host, enable the Success and Failure settings for this subcategory. The number of events in this subcategory is much lower than in the Audit Detailed File Share subcategory, but it still might be high on domain controllers and file servers. If you need to monitor only failed access attempts, enable only the Failure setting.

SPN validation failures might help you to troubleshoot SMB connection problems. SPN validation, for example, may fail if an SMB server requires SPN validation and a client uses the NTLMv1 protocol, which does not support it.

Chapter 15 provides more detailed information about file share auditing and will help you gain a better understanding about which policy setting you need to enable on hosts in your environment.

This subcategory has both `Audit Success` and `Audit Failure` events.

Audit File System

If you need to perform filesystem operations monitoring, such as file modifications, deletions, permission changes, and so on, you need to enable this subcategory. Depending on the type of access you need to monitor—`Audit Success`, `Audit Failure`, or both—you need to enable appropriate settings for this subcategory's group policy setting.

To enable file handle related events (4656 and 4658) in this subcategory, the Audit Handle Manipulation subcategory also should be enabled.

Read Chapter 13 for a better understanding of how filesystem auditing works.

You can find a complete list of events for this subcategory on official Microsoft sites. This subcategory has both `Audit Success` and `Audit Failure` events.

Audit Filtering Platform Connection

Many times this subcategory is treated as though it monitors the Windows firewall. That is not true. The Windows firewall is just an application that allows you to configure Windows Filtering Platform (WFP) settings using WFP APIs. WFP is a framework that enables you to configure TCP/IP level rules, network authorization rules, and so on. It is a platform that allows applications to implement firewall, intrusion detection, network monitoring, and other network-related security functions.

This subcategory is designed for WFP connections monitoring. It contains events related to incoming network connections, local port bindings by applications, and port listening operations. Both `Audit Success` and `Audit Failure` events exist in this subcategory.

Usually, this subcategory generates a high volume of events, especially on hosts with a high number of network communications. Enable the Failure setting for this subcategory on member servers, domain controllers, and workstations if, for example, you want to monitor unsuccessful connections to a host. The number of `Audit Failure` events in this subcategory is usually much lower than `Audit Success` events.

Enable the Success setting for this subcategory only if you know that it is useful to collect such information in your environment or if it is required to be collected by internal monitoring software.

Audit Filtering Platform Packet Drop

The following events are reported by this subcategory:

ID	NAME	SUCCESS	FAILURE	DESCRIPTION
5152	The Windows Filtering Platform blocked a packet	No	Yes	This event is generated for each blocked inbound or outbound network packet.
5153	A more restrictive Windows Filtering Platform filter has blocked a packet	Yes	No	This event is logged if a more restrictive Windows Filtering Platform filter has blocked a packet.

This subcategory generates an alert on each network packet blocked by WFP. 5152 and 5153 events are primarily used for WFP troubleshooting. The volume of events can be very high. It is recommended to set this subcategory value to "No Auditing" unless you need to perform WFP troubleshooting or detailed monitoring for each blocked packet.

Audit Handle Manipulation

The following event is reported by this subcategory:

ID	NAME	SUCCESS	FAILURE	DESCRIPTION
4690	An attempt was made to duplicate a handle to an object	Yes	No	This event generates when an object's handle gets duplicated.

This subcategory works in conjunction with some other subcategories, such as Audit File System, and enables handle manipulation events for them. At the same time it has its own event, 4690, which is not very informative and usually has no security relevance.

Table 3-1 contains the list of subcategories with events that depend on the Audit Handle Manipulation subcategory.

Table 3-1: Subcategories with Events That Are Dependent on the Audit Handle Manipulation Subcategory

SUBCATEGORY	EVENT ID	SUCCESS	FAILURE
Audit SAM	4661	Yes	Yes
Audit File System	4656	Yes	Yes
	4658	Yes	No
Audit Kernel Object	4656	Yes	Yes
	4658	Yes	No
Audit Other Object Access Events	4658	Yes	No
Audit Registry	4656	Yes	Yes
	4658	Yes	No
Audit Removable Storage	4656	Yes	Yes
	4658	Yes	No

Enable this subcategory only if you need to monitor for any of the events listed in Table 3-1. You will also need to enable the subcategory these events belong to. For example, if you want to enable 4661 Audit Failure events in the Audit SAM subcategory, you will need to set both Audit SAM and Audit Handle Manipulation subcategories to the Failure setting.

Audit Kernel Object

This subcategory contains events for internal system objects such as symbolic links, named pipes, and desktops. Also, if, as mentioned in Chapter 2, the `audit-baseobjects` and/or `auditbasedirectories` registry key values are set to 1, this subcategory will report additional events.

To enable handle operations events (4656 and 4658) in this subcategory, the Audit Handle Manipulation subcategory also should be enabled.

This subcategory generates a very high number of events and these events are difficult to use during incident response or investigation procedures. Events in this subcategory usually contain operating system level information that has little to no security relevance. It is recommended to set this subcategory setting to "No Auditing" on all categories of hosts, unless you are required to perform monitoring of system object operations such as unsuccessful named pipe access attempts.

Audit Other Object Access Events

This subcategory reports when a Windows scheduled task is created, deleted, modified, enabled, or disabled. It also shows changes to COM+ objects, as well as COM+ object deletion and creation operations.

If you need to monitor for operations related to COM+ objects, set this subcategory group policy setting to Success.

It is recommended to monitor scheduled task operations. For example, any creation of a new scheduled task on a critical server should be monitored. Such information can be used as an atomic event. This information also can be used as part of an investigation and may help, for example, to find which account modified a specific scheduled task. Chapter 10 contains detailed information about scheduled task related events.

It is recommended that you set the group policy setting value for this subcategory to Success on domain controllers, member servers, and workstations to be able to track activity related to scheduled tasks.

There are just two `Audit Failure` events in this subcategory:

- **5148:** The Windows Filtering Platform has detected a DoS attack and entered a defensive mode; packets associated with this attack will be discarded.
- **5149:** The DoS attack has subsided and normal processing is being resumed.

It is not clear what the requirements are for the preceding `Audit Failure` events to be generated. Enable the Failure group policy setting for this subcategory and monitor for any 5148 and 5149 events on all hosts in your environment.

To enable the 4658 "handle close" event in this subcategory, the Audit Handle Manipulation subcategory also should be enabled.

You can find a complete list of events for this subcategory on official Microsoft sites. This subcategory has both `Audit Success` and `Audit Failure` events.

Audit Registry

If you need to perform registry keys auditing for registry key value modifications, registry key deletions, registry key permission changes, and so on, you need to enable this subcategory. Depending on the type of access you need to monitor—`Audit Success`, `Audit Failure`, or both—you need to set appropriate settings for this subcategory's group policy setting.

To enable registry key handle–related events (4656 and 4658) in this subcategory, the Audit Handle Manipulation subcategory also should be enabled.

Read Chapter 14 for a better understanding of how registry key auditing works.

Audit Removable Storage

The Audit Removable Storage subcategory enables "Full Control" SACL on all files and folders located on removable devices, such as DVDs and flash drives.

If you need to track all access requests to files and folders located on removable storage, enable this subcategory's group policy settings for Success and Failure. If you need to monitor only for unsuccessful access attempts, enable only the Failure setting.

The volume of events might be high if the host has permanently connected removable storage that is often in use by the system. It is recommended to test the impact of this subcategory being enabled prior deploying it widely.

This subcategory, when enabled for `Audit Success` events and when the Audit Handle Manipulation subcategory is also enabled, might generate routine handle request events (4656, 4658) to CD-ROM, DVD-ROM, or other removable media volumes. These events appear even if there is no media inserted.

To enable file handle–related events (4656 and 4658) in this subcategory, the Audit Handle Manipulation subcategory also should be enabled.

Read Chapter 13 to get a better understanding of how removable storage auditing works.

Audit SAM

The following event is reported by this subcategory:

ID	NAME	SUCCESS	FAILURE	DESCRIPTION
4661	A handle to an object was requested	Yes	Yes	Shows successful or unsuccessful access attempts to a SAM object.

This subcategory shows access attempts performed on Security Account Manager (SAM) objects. SAM is a system component that is responsible for managing the local security database (SAM database). The SAM database contains multiple objects, such as user accounts, security groups, computer settings, and so on. Each time any of the SAM database objects are accessed, an event is generated in the Windows security event log if the Audit SAM subcategory is enabled for Success, Failure, or both.

To enable SAM object handle 4661 events in this subcategory, the Audit Handle Manipulation subcategory should also be enabled.

Most operations with SAM database objects also invoke other events from other subcategories. For example, user account modification operations also trigger an event from the Audit User Account Management subcategory. Usually there is not much benefit in enabling this subcategory because the most important events are covered by other subcategories. Enable it only if you need detailed auditing for SAM database object operations.

Although there is no dedicated chapter in this book about SAM events, events from this subcategory are mentioned in many chapters.

Audit Central Policy Staging

The following event is reported by this subcategory:

ID	NAME	SUCCESS	FAILURE	DESCRIPTION
4818	Proposed Central Access Policy does not grant the same access permissions as the current Central Access Policy	Yes	No	Informs you about proposed central access policy access validation results.

This subcategory is related to Dynamic Access Control feature auditing. It shows you which Proposed Central Access Policy rules deny access to the resource in comparison to Current Central Access Policy. Enable this subcategory's group policy setting for Success if you need to monitor how staging policies will affect access to resources.

Policy Change

This category contains subcategories that inform you about machine configuration, settings, and policies changes.

Audit Policy Change

This subcategory contains events showing changes to machine local auditing policy and auditing settings (SACL) for securable objects, such as files, registry keys, named pipes, and so on. Here are some of the examples of activities monitored by this subcategory:

- Per-user audit
- Local auditing policy settings changes
- Registering and unregistering security event sources
- Local auditing policy changes

It is recommended to set this subcategory's group policy setting to Success on domain controllers, member servers, and workstations. The volume of events is typically low.

There is no dedicated chapter in this book about Policy Change events, but events from this subcategory are mentioned in many chapters.

You can find a complete list of events for this subcategory on official Microsoft sites. This subcategory contains only Audit Success events.

Audit Authentication Policy Change

This subcategory contains events related to operations with Active Directory trusts, Kerberos group policy settings, account lockout and password policies, and logon rights policies.

It is important to set this group policy setting to Success on domain controllers to be able to monitor Active Directory trust operations.

It is also important to monitor changes to local logon rights, and password and account lockout group policy settings for all categories of hosts.

There is no dedicated chapter about Authentication Policy Change events, but events from this subcategory are mentioned in many chapters in this book.

You can find a complete list of events for this subcategory on official Microsoft sites. This subcategory contains only Audit Success events.

Audit Authorization Policy Change

This subcategory informs you about changes to local user rights group policy settings, adjustments to the active account's session user rights, changes to object permissions and dynamic access control (DAC) resource attributes, and changes to applied central access policies for filesystem objects.

Enable this subcategory for Audit Success events if you need to monitor when dynamic access control central access policy is applied to the filesystem object or when the filesystem object resource attribute is changed.

It is important to monitor changes to local user rights group policy settings for all categories of hosts.

Also, object permissions changes (DACL), such as file or registry key access permissions changes, are important to monitor. The volume of events is typically low to medium. A 4670 event in this subcategory does not depend on the subcategory's setting; it will be triggered no matter what the setting is.

A 4703 "A user right was adjusted" event generated by this category might be really noisy and does not typically contain any important information from a security point of view. Some important user privileges, such as SeDebugPrivilege, are recommended to monitor when they are enabled in the session's token. You can find more information about user privileges in Chapter 11.

There is no dedicated chapter about Authorization Policy Change events, but events from this subcategory are mentioned in many chapters in this book.

You can find a complete list of events for this subcategory on official Microsoft sites. This subcategory contains only Audit Success events.

Audit Filtering Platform Policy Change

This subcategory contains events for IPsec service state and IPsec settings monitoring. It also contains events for Windows Filtering Platform callouts, filters, providers, and sub-layers, as well as PAStore engine events.

Enable this subcategory if you need to monitor or perform troubleshooting of these Windows components.

You can find a complete list of events for this subcategory on official Microsoft sites. This subcategory reports both Audit Success and Audit Failure events.

Audit MPSSVC Rule-Level Policy Change

This subcategory contains events for monitoring the Windows Firewall component. It shows Windows Firewall policy changes, rules addition/creation/deletion operations, rules processing errors, and more. This subcategory, usually, does not generate many events and it is recommended to set its group policy setting to Success and Failure for domain controllers, member servers, and workstations to have an audit trail of changes performed with Windows Firewall settings and rules.

You can find a complete list of events for this subcategory on official Microsoft sites. This subcategory reports both Audit Success and Audit Failure events.

Audit Other Policy Change Events

This subcategory contains events for monitoring Encrypted File System (EFS) data recovery agent policy changes, dynamic access control central access policies changes, boot configuration data (BCD) startup settings, Windows Filtering Platform (WPF) filter changes, group policy update operations, and Cryptographic Next Generation (CNG) operations.

This subcategory usually generates a low number of events. It is recommended to set its group policy setting to Success and Failure for domain controllers, member servers, and workstations.

You can find a complete list of events for this subcategory on official Microsoft sites. This subcategory has both Audit Success and Audit Failure events.

Privilege Use

This category contains subcategories that inform you about user privilege use attempts performed on a host.

Audit Non Sensitive Privilege Use

This subcategory generates an event when an attempt is made to use one of the following user privileges:

- Access Credential Manager as a trusted caller (SeTrustedCredManAccessPrivilege)
- Add workstations to domain (SeMachineAccountPrivilege)
- Adjust memory quotas for a process (SeIncreaseQuotaPrivilege)
- Bypass traverse checking (SeChangeNotifyPrivilege)
- Change the system time (SeSystemtimePrivilege)
- Change the time zone (SeTimeZonePrivilege)
- Create a page file (SeCreatePagefilePrivilege)
- Create global objects (SeCreateGlobalPrivilege)
- Create permanent shared objects (SeCreatePermanentPrivilege)
- Create symbolic links (SeCreateSymbolicLinkPrivilege)
- Force shutdown from a remote system (SeRemoteShutdownPrivilege)
- Increase a process working set (SeIncreaseWorkingSetPrivilege)
- Increase scheduling priority (SeIncreaseBasePriorityPrivilege)
- Lock pages in memory (SeLockMemoryPrivilege)
- Modify an object label (SeRelabelPrivilege)
- Perform volume maintenance tasks (SeManageVolumePrivilege)
- Profile single process (SeProfileSingleProcessPrivilege)
- Profile system performance (SeSystemProfilePrivilege)
- Remove computer from docking station (SeUndockPrivilege)
- Shut down the system (SeShutdownPrivilege)
- Synchronize directory service data (SeSyncAgentPrivilege)

When enabled, this subcategory usually generates a high number of events.

To make a decision about whether you need to enable Success and/or Failure settings for this subcategory, read Chapter 11 to get more information about user privileges events.

Audit Other Privilege Use Events

This subcategory, currently, does not generate any security events. It is recommended to set it to "No Auditing" for all types of hosts.

Audit Sensitive Privilege Use

This subcategory generates an event when an attempt is made to use one of the following user privileges:

- Act as part of the operating system (SeTcbPrivilege)
- Create a token object (SeCreateTokenPrivilege)
- Debug programs (SeDebugPrivilege)
- Enable computer and user accounts to be trusted for delegation (SeEnableDelegationPrivilege)
- Generate security audits (SeAuditPrivilege)
- Impersonate a client after authentication (SeImpersonatePrivilege)
- Load and unload device drivers (SeLoadDriverPrivilege)
- Manage auditing and security log (SeSecurityPrivilege)
- Modify firmware environment values (SeSystemEnvironmentPrivilege)
- Replace a process-level token (SeAssignPrimaryTokenPrivilege)
- Take ownership of files or other objects (SeTakeOwnershipPrivilege)
- Back up files and directories (SeBackupPrivilege)
- Restore files and directories (SeRestorePrivilege)

These privileges are considered to be the most sensitive and are recommended to be monitored.

If enabled, this subcategory usually generates a high number of events, especially during backup procedures when the "Audit: Audit the use of Backup and Restore privilege" group policy setting is enabled.

To make a decision about whether you need to enable Success and/or Failure setting for this subcategory, read Chapter 11 to get more information about user privileges events.

System

This category contains subcategories for IPsec driver events, system events, security extensions, and system integrity related events.

Audit IPsec Driver

This subcategory performs monitoring of IPsec service shutdown and startup operations, network packet drops by the IPsec subsystem, and other IPsec-related events.

It is recommended to set this subcategory's group policy setting to both Success and Failure for all types of hosts. It will show you when the IPsec service is started/stopped and any packet drops or service failures. The volume of events generated by this subcategory is usually low.

You can find a complete list of events for this subcategory on official Microsoft sites. This subcategory has both Audit Success and Audit Failure events.

Audit Other System Events

This subcategory provides the following monitoring capabilities:

- Windows Firewall service shutdown and startup operations and any operations issues experienced by the service
- BranchCache service errors and issues
- Key Storage Provider (KSP) operations

It is recommended to set this subcategory's group policy setting to both Success and Failure for all types of hosts. It will show you when the Windows Firewall service is started/stopped and any issues during its operations. If you have the BranchCache component enabled this subcategory will help to monitor issues related to it. The volume of events generated by this subcategory is usually low.

You can find a complete list of events for this subcategory on official Microsoft sites. This subcategory has both Audit Success and Audit Failure events.

Audit Security State Change

This subcategory provides the following monitoring capabilities:

- Auditing subsystem initialization
- System time changes

Every time the system time is changed, an event is generated in the security event log if this subcategory is enabled for Audit Success events. This subcategory also enables the 4608 event, which informs you that LSASS.exe starts and the auditing subsystem is being initialized.

Both auditing subsystem initialization and system time change events might be useful during incident response and forensics procedures. It is recommended to set this subcategory's group policy setting to Success on domain controllers, member servers, and workstations. The volume of events is typically low.

Chapter 10 contains additional information about events from this subcategory.

Audit Security System Extension

This subcategory provides the following monitoring capabilities:

- Local Security Authority (LSA) operations related to authentication packages, notification packages, security processes, and trusted logon processes
- System service installation

It is important to monitor for system service installations on any host. It is recommended to set this subcategory's group policy setting to Success on domain controllers, member servers, and workstations. The volume of events is typically low.

Chapter 10 contains additional information about service installation events. Chapter 4 contains information about LSA operations.

You can find a complete list of events for this subcategory on official Microsoft sites. This subcategory contains only `Audit Success` events.

Audit System Integrity

This subcategory provides the following monitoring capabilities:

- Audit subsystem resources exhaust alerting
- Events generated using `AuthziGenerateAdminAlertAudit` function
- Remote Procedure Call (RPC) integrity violations
- Cryptographic Next Generation (CNG) cryptographic operations
- Key Storage Provider (KSP) cryptographic operations
- Code integrity violations

Usually this subcategory does not generate many events. Some of the events, such as code integrity violation events, might be useful for security investigations. It is recommended to set this subcategory's group policy setting to Success on domain controllers, member servers, and workstations.

You can find a complete list of events for this subcategory on official Microsoft sites. This subcategory has both `Audit Success` and `Audit Failure` events.

Security Monitoring Scenarios

In This Part

Account Logon

User and computer account logon information is one of the most common sources of the information about who, when, and how a specific host was accessed. In this chapter you will find information about how the Windows authentication subsystem works and how to monitor different account logon scenarios.

Microsoft Windows operating systems have thirteen default logon types. One logon type is assigned to each logon request and each type is handled differently by the operating system. Table 4-1 contains all Windows logon types and their descriptions.

Table 4-1: Windows Logon Types

CONSTANT	NAME	DESCRIPTION
0	System	Local System account logon. (See the "Interactive Logon" section in this chapter.)
2	Interactive	Regular local logon where the account logs on using an interactive logon method. (See the "Interactive Logon" section in this chapter.)
3	Network	Network logon from another computer. (See the "Network Logon" section in this chapter.)

Continues

Table 4-1 (*continued*)

CONSTANT	NAME	DESCRIPTION
4	Batch	Batch job logon. Commonly used by Windows scheduled tasks. (See the "Batch and Service Logon" section in this chapter.)
5	Service	Used by Windows services. (See the "Batch and Service Logon" section in this chapter.)
6	Proxy	Proxy logon.
7	Unlock	A specific logon type for operating system Interactive or RemoteInteractive session unlock operations. (See the "Interactive and RemoteInteractive Session Lock Operation and Unlock Logon Type" section in this chapter.)
8	NetworkCleartext	Similar to the Network logon type, but using cleartext/encoded credentials instead of NTLM or Kerberos authentication. (See the "NetworkCleartext Logon" section in this chapter.)
9	NewCredentials	A specific logon type designed to be used in combination with the "Secondary Logon" Windows service to provide the ability to run local applications using the logged-in account's credentials, but perform network activity using another account's credentials. (See the "NewCredentials Logon" section in this chapter.)
10	RemoteInteractive	Terminal Services or Remote Desktop Services logon. (See the "RemoteInteractive Logon" section in this chapter.)
11	CachedInteractive	Interactive logon using cached credentials. (See the "Interactive Logon" section in this chapter.)
12	CachedRemoteInteractive	RemoteInteractive logon using cached credentials. (See the "RemoteInteractive Logon" section in this chapter.)
13	CachedUnlock	Interactive or RemoteInteractive Session session unlocked using cached credentials. (See the "Interactive and RemoteInteractive Session Lock Operation and Unlock Logon Type" section in this chapter.)

Further in this chapter you will find detailed information about each logon type mentioned in Table 4-1.

Interactive Logon

This section provides detailed information about the many scenarios in which the interactive logon type is used.

Successful Local User Account Interactive Logon

Interactive logon authentication flow for local user account logon is shown in Figure 4-1. This flow is a visualization of the authentication flow that happens every time a user logs on locally to the machine (regular local logon).

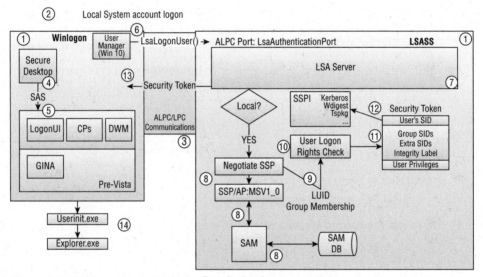

Figure 4-1: Windows interactive logon flow for local user account

The step numbers in this section refer to the numbers in this figure. (Note that there are two Steps 1. That's intended—both steps are performed at the same time. The first part initializes Winlogon and the second initializes the Local Security Authority Subsystem Service (LSASS).

> **NOTE** The event logs described in this section are available in this chapter's downloads, in the `Successful Local User Account Interactive Logon.evtx` file.

Step 1: Winlogon Process Initialization

In the first part of Step 1, Winlogon is initialized. Winlogon is a system component (it's a process) that acts as a proxy component between the user and Windows authentication subsystem internals. It is also responsible for switching

Windows desktops and handling the Secure Attention Sequence (SAS), which are discussed more fully in Step 4.

SAS is registered by Winlogon during system startup. Winlogon registers itself as a primary process responsible for handling SAS. This guarantees that Winlogon will receive SAS command signal before all other system processes. The default SAS sequence is Alt + Ctrl + Delete.

During operating system startup, the Winlogon process initializes multiple default desktops. Each modern Windows system has three default desktops:

- **Secure desktop:** This is a default desktop (aka logon screen) that is shown right after the operating system is initialized. This desktop is also activated when a user invokes the SAS sequence or when the User Account Control privilege escalation dialog appears. The secure desktop is controlled only by the Winlogon process. When the system starts, Winlogon sets the secure desktop as the current active desktop.

- **User desktop:** Created when a user interactive session is successfully created. The user desktop is the "normal" desktop used after a user logs on to the host.

- **Screensaver desktop:** This desktop shows when a screensaver is activated.

In an interactive logon scenario, the main responsibilities of Winlogon process are:

1. Initialize the secure desktop.
2. Get authentication data from the user.
3. Pass it to the internal Windows authentication subsystem.
4. Load the user's desktop or request that the user input authentication data again.

You will find more information about these steps later in this section.

The event shown in Listing 4-1 is generated in the Windows security event log at this stage.

Listing 4-1: Event ID 4688: A new process has been created.

```
Task Category: Process Creation
Keywords: Audit Success
Creator Subject:
        Security ID:            S-1-5-18 (SYSTEM)
        Account Name:           -
        Account Domain:         -
        Logon ID:               0x3E7
Target Subject:
        Security ID:            S-1-0-0 (NULL SID)
        Account Name:           -
        Account Domain:         -
        Logon ID:               0x0
Process Information:
        New Process ID:         0x2b4
        New Process Name:       C:\Windows\System32\winlogon.exe
```

```
Token Elevation Type:    %%1936 (TokenElevationTypeDefault (1))
Mandatory Label:         S-1-16-16384
                         (Mandatory Label\System Mandatory Level)
Creator Process ID:      0x24c
Creator Process Name:    C:\Windows\System32\smss.exe
Process Command Line:
```

This event shows that smss.exe (Session Management Subsystem) created winlogon.exe. smss.exe is also responsible for creating the virtual memory paging file, environmental variables, and some other actions that are beyond the scope of this discussion.

Process creation was invoked by the SYTEM (Local System) account and the new process will be running under the same account. This is indicated by NULL SID in the Target Subject\Security ID field, which means that the new process will run under the same account as the account that created the process.

See Chapter 12 for more information about process creation events.

Step 1: LSASS Initialization

In the second part of Step 1, the Local Security Authority Subsystem Service (LSASS) process is initialized. The LSASS component is a process that contains components of the Windows security subsystem. The most interesting component of LSASS is the Local Security Authority (LSA) server. Main functions of the LSA server are:

- Validates local account's credentials
- Generates security tokens for account sessions
- Manages local security policies
- Manages local security audit policies and settings

LSA server logic is discussed in Steps 7 through 12.

LSASS also contains other components, such as Security Support Providers (SSPs) and Authentication Packages (APs), which are also discussed in Step 8.

Before lsass.exe is started, smss.exe creates the wininit.exe process. wininit.exe is responsible for operating system initialization at startup. The event in Listing 4-2 is generated in the Windows security event log at this stage.

Listing 4-2: Event ID 4688: A new process has been created.

```
Task Category: Process Creation
Keywords: Audit Success
Creator Subject:
       Security ID:        S-1-5-18 (SYSTEM)
       Account Name:       -
       Account Domain:     -
       Logon ID:           0x3E7
```

```
Target Subject:
        Security ID:          S-1-0-0 (NULL SID)
        Account Name:         -
        Account Domain:       -
        Logon ID:             0x0
Process Information:
        New Process ID:       0x334
        New Process Name:     C:\Windows\System32\lsass.exe
        Token Elevation Type: %%1936 (TokenElevationTypeDefault (1))
        Mandatory Label:      S-1-16-16384
                              (Mandatory Label\System Mandatory Level)
        Creator Process ID:   0x2b4
        Creator Process Name: C:\Windows\System32\wininit.exe
        Process Command Line:
```

This event shows that `wininit.exe` created `lsass.exe`.

Process creation was invoked by the SYTEM (Local System) account and the new process will be running under the same account. This is indicated by NULL SID in the `Target Subject\Security ID` field, which means that the new process will run under the same account as the account that created the process.

See Chapter 12 for more information about process creation events.

Step 2: Local System Account Logon

Even though the Local System account is a built-in special account which represents the machine itself, it also performs its logon to the system. You will see the events shown in Listing 4-3 and Listing 4-4 in the Windows security event log associated to this logon event.

Listing 4-3: Event ID 4624: An account was successfully logged on.

```
Task Category: Logon
Keywords: Audit Success
Subject:
        Security ID:          S-1-0-0 (NULL SID)
        Account Name:         -
        Account Domain:       -
        Logon ID:             0x0
Logon Information:
        Logon Type:           0
        Restricted Admin Mode: -
        Virtual Account:      %%1843 (No)
        Elevated Token:       %%1842 (Yes)
Impersonation Level:          -
New Logon:
        Security ID:          S-1-5-18 (SYSTEM)
        Account Name:         SYSTEM
        Account Domain:       NT AUTHORITY
```

```
        Logon ID:               0x3E7
        Linked Logon ID:        0x0
        Network Account Name:   -
        Network Account Domain: -
        Logon GUID:             {00000000-0000-0000-0000-000000000000}
Process Information:
        Process ID:             0x4
        Process Name:
Network Information:
        Workstation Name:       -
        Source Network Address: -
        Source Port:            -
Detailed Authentication Information:
        Logon Process:          -
        Authentication Package: -
        Transited Services:     -
        Package Name (NTLM only): -
        Key Length:             0
```

This event is a unique type 0 (Logon Type) logon, which is a specific logon type for the Local System account.

No account requests the initial logon for the SYSTEM account, which is why Subject\Security ID has an S-1-0-0 (NULL SID) value.

There is also no Network Information, because it's always a local logon, and no Detailed Authentication Information, because neither Kerberos nor NTLM is used for SYSTEM account logon.

The SYSTEM account is not a Managed Account or Group Managed Account, which is why the Virtual Account field equals No.

The SYSTEM session is an administrative session, which means it has an elevated token assigned to the session (Elevated Token).

The Logon ID (Locally Unique Identifier/LUID) for the SYSTEM account is always 0x3E7.

The Process ID equals 0x4, which is always associated with the System process (ntoskrnl.exe). The Process Name field for the System process is always empty.

The Account Domain for all built-in system accounts, such as System, Local Service, and Network Service, has a value of NT AUTHORITY.

The Restricted Admin Mode field is applicable only to the RemoteInteractive and CachedRemoteInteractive logon types.

All other fields are discussed later in this chapter.

The 4627 event (shown in Listing 4-4) contains group membership information for the recently logged in account. The corresponding 4624 logon event has the same value for the Logon ID field.

Listing 4-4: Event ID 4627: Group membership information.

```
Task Category: Group Membership
Keywords: Audit Success
Subject:
        Security ID:         S-1-5-7 (ANONYMOUS LOGON)
        Account Name:        ANONYMOUS LOGON
        Account Domain:      NT AUTHORITY
        Logon ID:            0x0
Logon Type:                  0
New Logon:
        Security ID:         S-1-5-18 (SYSTEM)
        Account Name:        SYSTEM
        Account Domain:      NT AUTHORITY
        Logon ID:            0x3E7
Event in sequence:           1 of 1
Group Membership:
        %{S-1-5-32-544}  (BUILTIN\Administrators)
        %{S-1-1-0}       (Everyone)
        %{S-1-5-11}      (NT AUTHORITY\Authenticated Users)
        %{S-1-16-16384}  (Mandatory Label\System Mandatory Level)
```

The `Subject\Security ID` is `ANONYMOUS LOGON`, because, as you saw in the 4624 event in Listing 4-3, no account invoked logon for the SYSTEM account.

The `Event in sequence` field shows you the sequence number of the event, if the list of the account's groups exceeds a limit of one event. If the list of groups is too long, multiple 4627 events will be created. All of them will have the same values for the `Subject` and `New Logon` section fields.

The `Group Membership` field contains a list of security group SIDs included in the account's logon session security token.

In the current example you see that the SYSTEM account is, by default, has the following groups in the session's security token:

- BUILTIN\Administrators
- Everyone
- NT AUTHORITY\Authenticated Users
- Mandatory Label\System Mandatory Level

The last group, `Mandatory Label\System Mandatory Level`, is not really a group; it is a session integrity level label. Each logon session is assigned an integrity level label at logon, based on which groups this account is a member of. Table 4-2 contains a list of default integrity level labels, which can be assigned to the user's session security token.

Table 4-2: Logon Session Default Integrity Level SIDs

SID	INTEGRITY LEVEL
S-1-16-0	Mandatory Label\Untrusted Mandatory Level
S-1-16-4096	Mandatory Label\Low Mandatory Level

SID	INTEGRITY LEVEL
S-1-16-8192	Mandatory Label\Medium Mandatory Level
S-1-16-12288	Mandatory Label\High Mandatory Level
S-1-16-16384	Mandatory Label\System Mandatory Level

Based on the account's group membership, the highest integrity level label applies to the session. The integrity level label that is applied to the session also depends on the session's security token type. User Account Control (UAC) mechanism, if enabled, creates two logon sessions, elevated and non-elevated, which have different integrity level labels. The integrity level labels in Table 4-3 apply to the logon session, based on a group membership or account type.

Table 4-3: Integrity Level Labels Associated with Security Groups and Accounts

ACCOUNT/GROUP	INTEGRITY LEVEL LABEL
SYSTEM	System Mandatory Level
LOCAL SERVICE	System Mandatory Level
NETWORK SERVICE	System Mandatory Level
Administrators	High Mandatory Level
Backup Operators	High Mandatory Level
Network Configuration Operators	High Mandatory Level
Cryptographic Operators	High Mandatory Level
Authenticated Users	Medium Mandatory Level
Everyone	Low Mandatory Level
Anonymous	Untrusted Mandatory Level

The main idea behind integrity level labels is that within a logon session no created processes can have an integrity level higher than the level of the current logon session. You can access resources with higher integrity levels by elevating your token with UAC, aka switching to an elevated session. For each process assigned an integrity level, that integrity level is also assigned to many securable objects, such as files and registry keys. By default, a process can modify only objects with the same or lower integrity level.

NOTE Chapters 13 and 14 provide more information about an object's integrity levels. Chapter 12 has additional information about integrity labels for processes.

Step 3: ALPC Communications between Winlogon and LSASS

Winlogon and LSASS, which need to communicate with each other, use Asynchronous Local Inter-Process Communication (ALPC) calls to accomplish this goal.

ALPC is a method of communication between processes within the same host. The two main types of ALPC communications are:

- **ALPC Message Buffer:** Uses built-in ALPC message buffer
- **Shared memory:** Shared memory that is mapped to memory spaces of both processes

ALPC communications are done by accessing the target's (server) ALPC ports. LSASS has LsaAuthenticationPort port registered for all ALPC communications.

Pre-Vista systems implement a previous version of ALPC, called Local Inter-Process Communication (LPC). The main difference between these versions is that LPC does not support asynchronous communications.

Step 4: Secure Desktop and SAS

After the operating system is initialized, the secure desktop is created and set as the current active desktop. This is the desktop you see when the system is loaded and waiting for you to input authentication information. After the system receives SAS, it displays the authentication window. In recent Windows versions such as Windows 10 or Windows 8.1, SAS is not required to invoke the authentication window. The authentication window can be invoked by pressing any keyboard key or clicking a mouse button.

Step 5: Authentication Data Gathering

The system must somehow get authentication data (user credentials) from the user. Starting from Windows Vista this task is performed by the LogonUI process and Credential Providers (CPs).

LogonUI's purpose is to collect user credentials and pass them to LSASS for validation. LogonUI is invoked by Winlogon each time authenticated data needs to be collected/gathered from a user. After LogonUI gets a user's credentials and passes them to LSASS, it terminates.

Users can have multiple types of credentials to authenticate: username and password, smartcard, biometric data, and so on. To gather these types of user credentials, modules called Credential Providers (CPs) are used.

CPs are modules that have code implemented to work with specific types of credentials. They know how to collect specific types of credentials from the user and how to handle these credentials. The most common examples of CPs are passwords and smart cards. Figure 4-2 shows a classic Windows 10 logon screen offering options to choose between password and smart card CPs.

Figure 4-2: Windows 10 Credential Providers

When LogonUI starts it enumerates all available CPs and displays additional UI elements for these CPs, as shown in Figure 4-2.

You can find a list of all available CPs on a system in the following registry key: `HKEY_LOCAL_MACHINE\SOFTWARE\Microsoft\Windows\CurrentVersion\Authentication\Credential Providers`.

Pre-Vista Windows operating systems used Microsoft Graphical Identification and Authentication (GINA) dynamic-link library (`MSGina.dll`) instead of LogonUI. Legacy systems don't have credential providers; all this functionality is embedded/hardcoded in GINA. The main disadvantage of GINA is a lack of flexibility and extensibility: for each new credentials type GINA must be replaced by a new version. LogonUI just needs a new credential provider module.

Pre-Vista Windows operating systems also work with notification packages—DLLs—which are registered to handle specific notification events generated by Winlogon, such as Shutdown or Logon events notifications. Notification packages can perform additional actions when they receive specific notifications from Winlogon. To implement similar functionality in Windows Vista and newer operating system versions developers should use Service Control Manager (SCM) notifications or System Event Notification Service (SENS).

The events in Listing 4-5 are related to this phase.

Listing 4-5: Event ID 4688: A new process has been created.

```
Task Category: Process Creation
Keywords: Audit Success
Creator Subject:
      Security ID:          S-1-5-18 (SYSTEM)
      Account Name:         DESKTOP-OIUVHRF$
```

```
        Account Domain:         WORKGROUP
        Logon ID:               0x3E7
Target Subject:
        Security ID:            S-1-0-0 (NULL SID)
        Account Name:           -
        Account Domain:         -
        Logon ID:               0x0
Process Information:
        New Process ID:         0x270
        New Process Name:       C:\Windows\System32\LogonUI.exe
        Token Elevation Type: %%1936
        Mandatory Label:        S-1-16-16384
                                (Mandatory Label\System Mandatory Level)
        Creator Process ID:     0x2e4
        Creator Process Name:   C:\Windows\System32\winlogon.exe
        Process Command Line:   "LogonUI.exe" /flags:0x0 /state0:0xa3bc9855
                                /state1:0x41c64e6d
```

This is a LogonUI process creation event.

The process creation was initialized by the SYSTEM account. LogonUI will run under the SYSTEM account as well, because NULL SID means the same account as the Creator Subject.

See Chapter 12 for more information about process creation events.

At this stage you will also see multiple 4624 logon events for SYSTEM, NETWORK SERVICE, or LOCAL SERVICE accounts (New Logon field) that were invoked by services.exe—these are logons for multiple system services.

Step 6: Send Credentials from Winlogon to LSASS

After a credential provider gets authentication data from the user, Winlogon invokes the LsaLogonUser function to pass authentication data to LSASS. The LsaLogonUser function uses LsaAuthenticationPort, LSASS's ALPC port for communications.

Starting from Windows 10 and Windows Server 2016 this process was changed a little bit. A new User Manager system service was introduced in the operating system. This service provides the runtime components required for multi-user interaction and also is responsible for interactive logons. The User Manager service runs under svchost.exe. Starting from Windows 10 and Windows Server 2016, the User Manager service sends the user's credentials to lsass.exe instead of winlogon.exe as was the case previously.

The events in Listing 4-6 are related to this phase.

Listing 4-6: Event ID 4673: A privileged service was called.

```
Task Category: Sensitive Privilege Use
Keywords: Audit Success
Subject:
        Security ID:            S-1-5-18 (SYSTEM)
        Account Name:           DESKTOP-OIUVHRF$
```

```
        Account Domain:         WORKGROUP
        Logon ID:               0x3E7
Service:
        Server:                 NT Local Security Authority
                                / Authentication Service
        Service Name:           LsaRegisterLogonProcess()
Process:
        Process ID:             0x338
        Process Name:           C:\Windows\System32\lsass.exe
Service Request Information:
        Privileges:             SeTcbPrivilege
```

The LsaRegisterLogonProcess() function is invoked by the SYSTEM account using LSASS.

The LsaRegisterLogonProcess() function must be called to register the new logon process, which is able to perform user authentication and submit the logon request to LSASS. An example of such a logon process is Winlogon; it needs to be registered using LsaRegisterLogonProcess() before performing authentication functions. The account calling this function must have the SeTcbPrivilege privilege enabled.

You also can see in the Privileges field that SeTcbPrivilege was used for this call.

As a result of a successful LsaRegisterLogonProcess() function call, the 4611 event shown in Listing 4-7 is generated. This logon process is now trusted to submit logon requests.

Listing 4-7: Event ID 4611: A trusted logon process has been registered with the Local Security Authority.

```
Task Category: Security System Extension
Keywords: Audit Success
Subject:
        Security ID:            S-1-5-18 (SYSTEM)
        Account Name:           DESKTOP-OIUVHRF$
        Account Domain:         WORKGROUP
        Logon ID:               0x3E7
Logon Process Name:             Winlogon
```

This event contains the name of a logon process (Logon Process Name) that was successfully registered using LsaRegisterLogonProcess().

For Windows 10 and Windows Server 2016 this event will contain UserManager in the Logon Process Name field instead of WinLogon.

Step 7: LSA Server Credentials Flow

When credentials get to the LSA Server module of the LSASS process, the LSA Server makes a decision where to pass these credentials for further processing, based on the user account type.

As a first step of the verification algorithm, the LSA Server detects whether the account that tries to log in is a local account or domain account.

Step 8: Local User Scenario

If the account is a local user account, the user's credentials are passed to the Negotiate Security Support Provider (SSP), which then passes them to the MSV1_0 security support provider/authentication package (SSP/AP). Negotiate SSP selects between Kerberos SSP/AP and MSV1_0 SSP/AP. For local account interactive logons, MSV1_0 SSP/AP is selected.

NOTE Starting with Windows 7, Negotiate SSP is extended by NegoExtender SSP, which is an additional SSP that Negotiate SSP can select. NegoExtender SSP allows additional SSPs for Negotiate SSP to select from, and also adds PKU2U SSP as an additional option.

An authentication package (AP) is a DLL containing a set of authentication protocols implementations that usually belongs to the same authentication protocol family. An AP also has multiple credential verification algorithms implemented. One of the AP examples is an MSV1_0 authentication package (which is also an SSP; this will be explained shortly), which contains implementations of LM, NTLM, and NTLMv2 authentication protocols and also performs credential validation using the local Security Account Manager (SAM) database.

Another important characteristic of an authentication package is the requirement to be able to handle/reply to requests from the LSASS `LsaLookupAuthenticationPackage()` function.

Authentication packages are used by all types of local logons, including Interactive, Batch, and Service logons.

The Security Support Provider (SSP) is a DLL that implements the Security Support Provider Interface (SSPI) model. The SSPI model is a unified abstract layer that applications can use for authentication, integrity control, and encryption functions. Application developers don't need to create their own NTLM or Kerberos implementation in their applications; they can use NTLM SSP or Kerberos SSP, which are built-in in Windows and also support encryption and integrity control. Basically, SSPI defines rules that all SSPs should follow. You can think of SSPI as a framework.

SSPI provides the following functions:

- **Message integrity and privacy:** Allows encrypting and signing communications between server and client.

- **Security package management:** Allows you to select appropriate SSP for communications between server and client.

- **Credential management:** Allows you to work with credentials and supports authentication functions.

Each SSP must implement all SSPI model requirements. SSPs also contain implementation of specific authentication protocols. For example, SSP contains an implementation of Kerberos v5. NTLM SSP (MSV1_0 SSP/AP) contains an implementation of the LM, NTLM, and NTLMv2 protocols along with NTLM Session Security. SSPs are mainly used by non-interactive logons by applications.

MSV1_0 is an SSP/AP security package, which means it acts as an SSP and AP at the same time.

After MSV1_0 receives a user's credentials, it generates a hash (LM or NTLM depending on the local security policy setting) out of the user's password. Then, it sends a request to a Security Account Manager (SAM) for credentials verification. The SAM manager extracts this information from the SAM database, where all local user account information is stored, and sends this information back to LSASS.

The SAM database contains the following information about local user accounts:

- Local group membership information for each account

- Account password hashes (LM, NTLM, or both, depending on the local security policy setting)

- Account settings

If the account is disabled or locked out, the SAM manager replies to the LSASS with this information and the logon will not succeed.

The events shown in Listing 4-8 are related to this phase.

Listing 4-8: Event ID 4622: A security package has been loaded by the Local Security Authority.

```
Task Category: Security System Extension
Keywords: Audit Success
Security Package Name:   C:\Windows\system32\lsasrv.dll : Negotiate
```

You will find multiple 4622 events that inform you that `lsass.exe` loaded a specific security package (SSP/AP). The `Security Package Name` has the following format: `Package DLL Location : Package Name`.

Table 4-4 contains default Windows 10 (Build 1703) security packages.

Table 4-4: Default Windows 10 (Build 1703) Security Packages (SSP/AP)

NAME	DLL	DESCRIPTION
Negotiate	`C:\Windows\system32\lsasrv.dll`	Negotiation package to negotiate between Kerberos and NTLM security packages
NegoExtender	`C:\Windows\system32\negoexts.DLL`	NegoEx SSP provides an extension for Negotiate SSP to negotiate authentication with additional SSPs, not only MSV1_0 and Kerberos
Kerberos	`C:\Windows\system32\kerberos.DLL`	Contains an implementation of the Kerberos v5 authentication protocol
NTLM	`C:\Windows\system32\msv1_0.DLL`	Contains an implementation of the NTLM-family of authentication protocols
TSSSP	`C:\Windows\system32\tspkg.DLL`	Security package that contains CredSSP, a single sign-on SSP for Terminal Services and Remote Desktop sessions
pku2u	`C:\Windows\system32\pku2u.DLL`	Peer-to-peer authentication SSP; Windows Homegroups is a feature that uses PKU2U SSP
CloudAP	`C:\Windows\system32\cloudAP.DLL`	SSP for cloud (Microsoft Azure) authentication
WDigest	`C:\Windows\system32\wdigest.DLL`	Implements digest authentication, which can be used, for example, in HTTP digest authentication or LDAP authentication
Schannel	`C:\Windows\system32\schannel.DLL`	Implements SSL, PCT, and TLS authentication protocols
Microsoft Unified Security Protocol Provider	`C:\Windows\system32\schannel.DLL`	Contains the Microsoft Unified Security Protocol Provider

The event in Listing 4-9 informs you that a new authentication package was loaded by LSASS. MICROSOFT_AUTHENTICATION_PACKAGE_V1_0 is the only default authentication package loaded by Windows 10.

Listing 4-9: Event ID 4610: An authentication package has been loaded by the Local Security Authority.

```
Task Category: Security System Extension
Keywords: Audit Success
Authentication Package Name: C:\Windows\system32\msv1_0.DLL :
MICROSOFT_AUTHENTICATION_PACKAGE_V1_0
```

Step 9: Local User Logon: MSV1_0 Answer

After MSV1_0 gets a user's account hash from the SAM manager, it compares it with a hash generated from the user's supplied credentials. If both hashes are the same, MSV1_0 creates locally unique identifier (LUID) for the user's logon session. LUID is also called Logon ID and uniquely identifies a session within a host. This information is then passed to the LSASS process and used to create a session's security token.

The events in Listing 4-10 are related to this phase.

Listing 4-10: Event ID 4776: The computer attempted to validate the credentials for an account.

```
Task Category: Credential Validation
Keywords: Audit Success
Authentication Package:        MICROSOFT_AUTHENTICATION_PACKAGE_V1_0
Logon Account:                 Andrei
Source Workstation:            DESKTOP-OIUVHRF
Error Code:                    0x0
```

Each authentication attempt using the MSV1_0 authentication package (LM, NTLM, or NTLMv2 authentication protocol) generates a 4776 event on the machine where the credentials of the account, for which authentication is performed, are stored.

You can see that credentials for user Andrei were successfully validated. The authentication request came from the DESKTOP-OIUVHRF host, which is the local machine name.

See Chapter 9 for more information about Kerberos and NTLM authentication protocols events.

The event in Listing 4-11 shows the logon initiation attempt for a normal interactive logon. It is initiated by the local SYSTEM account.

Listing 4-11: Event ID 4648: A logon was attempted using explicit credentials.

```
Task Category: Logon
Keywords: Audit Success
Subject:
        Security ID:           S-1-5-18 (SYSTEM)
        Account Name:          DESKTOP-OIUVHRF$
        Account Domain:        WORKGROUP
        Logon ID:              0x3E7
        Logon GUID:            {00000000-0000-0000-0000-000000000000}
Account Whose Credentials Were Used:
        Account Name:          Andrei
        Account Domain:        DESKTOP-OIUVHRF
        Logon GUID:            {00000000-0000-0000-0000-000000000000}
Target Server:
        Target Server Name:    localhost
        Additional Information:localhost
```

```
Process Information:
        Process ID:            0x1e8
        Process Name:          C:\Windows\System32\svchost.exe
Network Information:
        Network Address:       127.0.0.1
        Port:                  0
```

`Account Whose Credentials Were Used\Account Name` contains the name of the account for which new logon is initiated, and `Account Domain` contains a domain (hostname for local accounts or domain name for domain accounts) to which the account belongs.

`Logon GUID` can be correlated to the 4769 Kerberos Distribution Center (KDC) event on the domain controller. It is explained in more detail in Chapter 9.

The `Target Server` section contains information about the target host for which the authentication attempt is performed. For local authentication, the `Target Server Name` will usually have a value of `localhost`.

`Target Server Name` may contain, but is not limited to, values with the following formats:

- localhost - local authentication
- Host's DNS-name
- Host's NetBIOS name
- Host's NetBIOS name with $ at the end, such as `myhost$`
- User Principal Name (UPN), which may be used by peer-to-peer applications such as Microsoft Skype for Business. An example is `myuser@domain.com`.

`Target Server\Additional Information` contains a target service principal name (SPN), which is used in Kerberos authentication, if it was defined at logon. If no SPN was defined or NTLM authentication performed, the `Additional Information` field will contain the same information as the `Target Server Name` field. The SPN is a unique identifier for a service instance and has the following format: *service_name/target_host_name*. Some examples of SPNs are:

- `cifs/myserver`
- `http/myserver.domain.local`
- `host/printserver01`

The `Process Information` section contains a name and PID of the process that called a logon function. For pre-Windows 10/Server 2016 systems, interactive logon attempts are made by `winlogon.exe`. Newer systems use the User Manager system service, which runs under the `svchost.exe` process.

The `Network Information` section contains network information about the authentication source from which the authentication request was received. For interactive logons, the `Network Address` and `Port` fields values depend on the request. The svchost.exe and winlogon.exe processes usually report Network Address = 127.0.0.1 and Port = 0 for all interactive logons.

Listing 4-12 shows a successful logon attempt, which always invokes a 4624 event.

Listing 4-12: Event ID 4624: An account was successfully logged on.

```
Task Category: Logon
Keywords: Audit Success
Subject:
        Security ID:            S-1-5-18 (SYSTEM)
        Account Name:           DESKTOP-OIUVHRF$
        Account Domain:         WORKGROUP
        Logon ID:               0x3E7
Logon Information:
        Logon Type:             2
        Restricted Admin Mode:  -
        Virtual Account:        %%1843 (No)
        Elevated Token:         %%1842 (Yes)
Impersonation Level:            %%1833 (Impersonation)
New Logon:
        Security ID:            S-1-5-21-3560676733-2118901975-1824268897-
                                1001
        Account Name:           Andrei
        Account Domain:         DESKTOP-OIUVHRF
        Logon ID:               0x3EA5D
        Linked Logon ID:        0x3EA8B
        Network Account Name:   -
        Network Account Domain: -
        Logon GUID:             {00000000-0000-0000-0000-000000000000}
Process Information:
        Process ID:             0x1e8
        Process Name:           C:\Windows\System32\svchost.exe
Network Information:
        Workstation Name:       DESKTOP-OIUVHRF
        Source Network Address: 127.0.0.1
        Source Port:            0
Detailed Authentication Information:
        Logon Process:          User32
        Authentication Package: Negotiate
        Transited Services:     -
        Package Name (NTLM only): -
        Key Length:             0
```

Some information in this event is the same as in the 4648 event discussed previously, so those fields are not covered again here.

The Logon Type field contains a logon type number. For interactive logons it is 2. See Table 4-1 for information about all logon types.

Virtual Account identifies whether the logged-in account is a managed service account (MSA) or a group managed service account (GMSA).

Managed service accounts are special local accounts, designed to be used as accounts for local services. Passwords for these accounts are automatically managed by the operating system and, by default, are changed every month. Group managed service accounts have the same purpose as managed service accounts, but they are domain accounts.

The `Elevated Token` field indicates whether a full token (elevated) or a filtered token is used for a new logon session. Accounts with an elevated token are usually a part of a privileged security group (local administrators, backup operators, server operators, and so on) or have one or more special user privileges assigned (see Table 11.2 for more details).

The `Impersonation Level` field indicates which impersonation level the logon used. It may have one of the following values:

- **Identification (%%1832):** The process knows the client's identity information (such as group membership, account name, and so on) and can perform access validation checks, but it cannot impersonate the client (act on behalf of a client). This type of impersonation is useful for access validation attempts, when there is no need to act as a client.

- **Impersonation (%%1833):** The process can completely impersonate the client on the local machine and act on behalf of the client. This type of impersonation does not allow the process to impersonate a client outside of the system, as such connecting to other hosts on behalf of the client.

- **Delegation (%%1840):** The process can completely impersonate the client on the local and remote machine. This type of impersonation is usually set up in Active Directory environments by using the Delegation tab for the computer or user object.

The `Logon ID` field contains a unique local logon identifier (LUID) in hexadecimal format for a newly created session.

The `Linked Logon ID` field contains the Logon ID for a user session with a filtered/restricted token, if User Account Control is enabled in the system. The 4624 logon event for linked logon with a filtered/restricted token usually appears right after the logon event for an elevated token. You can use the free LogonSessions tool from Microsoft to list all current logon sessions. (This tool is available at `https://docs.microsoft.com/en-us/sysinternals/downloads/logonsessions`.) Figure 4-3 shows an output example of the LogonSessions tool.

As you can see from the LogonSessions output, user account Andrei has two logon sessions; one of them has an elevated token, and the other has a filtered/restricted token.

The `Network Information` section contains information about a host from which a logon request was received. Information in these fields depends on information received from authentication package (or SSP), which was used during authentication. The Kerberos authentication package, for example, does not usually report `Workstation Name`.

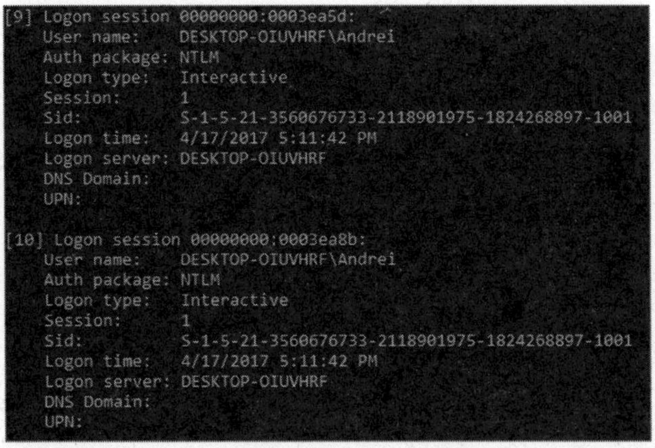

Figure 4-3: LogonSessions tool output example

The `Detailed Authentication Information` field contains detailed authentication-related information. Only those fields present in the current example are discussed here.

The `Logon Process` field shows the name of a Windows component that was invoked to perform a logon. Here are some logon process examples:

- The `User32` (`user32.dll`) logon process is common for type 2 (interactive) and type 11 (cached credentials) logon types.

- The `Advapi` (Advanced API - `advapi32.dll`) logon process is common for logon type 5 (service), because `advapi32.dll` contains service-related functions and is used to run/start system services.

The `Authentication Package` field contains information about which AP, SSP, or SSP/AP was invoked to perform authentication. Table 4-4 has more information about authentication packages.

The `Transited Services`, `Package Name (NTLM only)`, and `Key Length` fields are discussed in more detail in Chapter 9.

After every 4624 successful logon event, the 4627 event (see Listing 4-13) is invoked. It contains SIDs for all groups of which the user is a member.

Listing 4-13: Event ID 4627: Group membership information.

```
Task Category: Group Membership
Keywords: Audit Success
Subject:
      Security ID:          S-1-5-18 (SYSTEM)
      Account Name:         DESKTOP-OIUVHRF$
      Account Domain:       WORKGROUP
      Logon ID:             0x3E7
Logon Type:                 2
```

```
New Logon:
        Security ID:            S-1-5-21-3560676733-2118901975-1824268897-
                                1001 (DESKTOP-OIUVHRF\Andrei)
        Account Name:           Andrei
        Account Domain:         DESKTOP-OIUVHRF
        Logon ID:               0x3EA5D
Event in sequence:              1 of 1
Group Membership:
                                List of group SIDs
```

If a user's elevated token has one of the special privileges (see Chapter 11) in it, a 4672 event is generated containing all detected special privileges (see Listing 4-14).

Listing 4-14: Event ID 4672: Special privileges assigned to new logon.

```
Task Category: Special Logon
Keywords: Audit Success
Subject:
        Security ID:            S-1-5-21-3560676733-2118901975-1824268897-1001
                                (DESKTOP-OIUVHRF\Andrei)
        Account Name:           Andrei
        Account Domain:         DESKTOP-OIUVHRF
        Logon ID:               0x3EA5D
Privileges:         SeSecurityPrivilege
                    SeTakeOwnershipPrivilege
                    SeLoadDriverPrivilege
                    SeBackupPrivilege
                    SeRestorePrivilege
                    SeDebugPrivilege
                    SeSystemEnvironmentPrivilege
                    SeImpersonatePrivilege
                    SeDelegateSessionUserImpersonatePrivilege
```

Step 10: User Logon Rights Verification

LSASS verifies that the account logon type requested/performed by the user account is allowed for this user account.

All user logon rights policies are stored in the following local group policy section: `Local Computer Policy\Computer Configuration\Windows Settings\Security Settings\Local Policies\User Right Assignments`. Chapter 11 provides more information about user rights and privileges.

If, for example, a user performs an interactive logon and the local group policy setting allows this logon type for this specific user account, the user account passes the validation. If not, the logon process will fail.

Step 11: Security Token Generation

LSASS constructs the security token for a user's session. The security token contains the following main information:

- User's account security identifier (SID)
- SIDs of the local security groups of which the user is a member
- SIDs of the extra security principals, such as Authenticated Users or Everyone.
- List of the user's privileges, such as SeSecurityPrivilege or SeTcbPrivilege.

Step 12: SSPI Call

After a user token is created, LSASS notifies all available SSPs. At this point each SSP can perform additional actions with the user's authentication data, such as copy the NTLM hash into an SSP's memory or even copy a cleartext password if needed. All this behavior depends on the operating system version.

Step 13: LSASS Replies to Winlogon

A user's security token along with information about a successful authentication is sent to the Winlogon process.

Step 14: Userinit and Explorer.exe

At the end of the local interactive logon authentication process, Winlogon sends information to the userinit.exe process, which loads the user's profile. After the user's profile is loaded, userinit.exe creates a local shell, invoking the explorer.exe process.

The events shown in Listing 4-15 are related to this phase.

Listing 4-15: Event ID 4688: A new process has been created.

```
Task Category: Process Creation
Keywords: Audit Success
```

You should see two 4688 events: one for userinit.exe and another one for explorer.exe.

Winlogon.exe creates userinit.exe and then userinit.exe creates explorer.exe.

Unsuccessful Local User Account Interactive Logon

The most common reason for an unsuccessful local logon attempt is an invalid username and/or password. The events in Listing 4-16 occur in the Windows security event log if a local interactive logon attempt for a local account was unsuccessful.

NOTE The event logs described in this section are available in this chapter's downloads, in the Unsuccessful Local User Account Interactive Logon.evtx file.

Listing 4-16: Event ID 4776: The computer attempted to validate the credentials for an account.

```
Task Category: Credential Validation
Keywords: Audit Failure
Authentication Package:    MICROSOFT_AUTHENTICATION_PACKAGE_V1_0
Logon Account:             Andrei
Source Workstation:        DESKTOP-OIUVHRF
Error Code:                0xC000006A
```

This is an audit failure 4776 event, which was discussed in Step 9 of the "Successful Local User Account Interactive Logon" section. In this example it shows that credential validation failed.

The reason it failed is shown in the Error Code field. In this particular example, the error code is 0xC000006A, which means that a misspelled or bad password was entered for the Andrei account.

You can find all error codes for the 4776 event in Table 9.1.

Many fields in event 4625 shown in Listing 4-17 were already discussed when we spoke about event 4624 in Step 9 of the "Successful Local User Account Interactive Logon" section.

Listing 4-17: Event ID 4625: An account failed to log on.

```
Task Category: Logon
Keywords: Audit Failure
Subject:
      Security ID:         S-1-5-18 (SYSTEM)
      Account Name:        DESKTOP-OIUVHRF$
      Account Domain:      WORKGROUP
      Logon ID:            0x3E7
Logon Type:                2
Account For Which Logon Failed:
      Security ID:         S-1-0-0 (NULL SID)
      Account Name:        Andrei
      Account Domain:      DESKTOP-OIUVHRF
Failure Information:
      Failure Reason:      %%2313 (Unknown user name or bad password.)
      Status:              0xC000006D
      Sub Status:          0xC000006A
```

```
Process Information:
      Caller Process ID:      0x214
      Caller Process Name: C:\Windows\System32\svchost.exe
Network Information:
      Workstation Name:      DESKTOP-OIUVHRF
      Source Network Address: 127.0.0.1
      Source Port:            0
Detailed Authentication Information:
      Logon Process:          User32
      Authentication Package: Negotiate
      Transited Services:     -
      Package Name (NTLM only):-
      Key Length:             0
```

The `Account For Which Logon Failed` section contains information about the account for which a logon attempt failed.

The `Account For Which Logon Failed\Security ID` field is `S-1-0-0` (NULL SID) for all failed logon attempts. The reason for this is that information is not yet available at the moment the 4625 event is generated, because the account is not yet authenticated.

The `Failure Information` section contains information why the logon attempt failed.

`Failure Reason` contains a human-readable representation of the `Status` field or `Sub Status` field if it exists.

The `Status` field contains a status code that explains why the attempt failed.

The `Sub Status` field may contain some additional information for specific status codes, such as `0xC000006D` (bad username or password). This field will contain an additional code that shows whether it was the username or the password that was not correct. It also may contain the same value as the `Status` field or `0x0`, which means there is no additional information in the `Sub Status` field.

Table 4-5 contains information about possible values for the `Failure Reason`, `Status`, and `Sub Status` fields.

Table 4-5: Failure Reason, Status, and Sub Status Fields Values for the 4625 Event

STATUS CODE	FAILURE REASON CODE	FAILURE REASON TEXT	DESCRIPTION
0xC000005E	%%2304	An Error occured during Logon.	There are currently no logon servers available to service the logon request.
0xC000006D	%%2313	Unknown user name or bad password.	Unknown username or bad password. See Sub Status for more details.

Start of Sub Statuses for 0xC000006D

Continues

Table 4-5 (*continued*)

STATUS CODE	FAILURE REASON CODE	FAILURE REASON TEXT	DESCRIPTION
0xC0000064	%%2313	Unknown user name or bad password.	User logon with misspelled or bad user account.
0xC000006A	%%2313	Unknown user name or bad password.	User logon with misspelled or bad password.
0xc000019b	%%2314	Domain sid inconsistent.	Duplicate or incorrect SID was detected.
0xC0000133	%%2304	An Error occured during Logon.	Clocks between DC and other computer too far out of sync.
End Of Sub Statuses for 0xC000006D			
0xC000006E	%%2312	User not allowed to logon at this computer.	User not allowed to logon at this computer. See Sub Status for more details.
Start of Sub Statuses for 0xC000006E			
0xC000006F	%%2311	Account logon time restriction violation.	User logon outside authorized hours. Sub Status for 0xC000006E.
0xC0000070	%%2312	User not allowed to logon at this computer.	User logon from unauthorized workstation. Sub Status for 0xC000006E.
0xC0000071	%%2309	The specified account's password has expired.	User logon with expired password. Sub Status for 0xC000006E.
0xC0000072	%%2310	Account currently disabled.	User logon to account disabled by administrator. Sub Status for 0xC000006E.
End of Sub Statuses for 0xC000006E			

STATUS CODE	FAILURE REASON CODE	FAILURE REASON TEXT	DESCRIPTION
0xC00000DC	%%2304	An Error occured during Logon.	Indicates the Sam Server was in the wrong state to perform the desired operation.
0xC000015B	%%2308	The user has not been granted the requested logon type at this machine.	The user has not been granted the requested logon type (logon right) at this machine.
0xC000018C	%%2304	An Error occured during Logon.	The logon request failed because the trust relationship between the primary domain and the trusted domain failed.
0xC0000192	%%2306	The NetLogon component is not active.	An attempt was made to logon, but the Netlogon service was not active.
0xC0000193	%%2305	The specified user account has expired.	User logon with expired account.
0xC0000224	%%2309	The specified account's password has expired.	User is required to change password at next logon.
0xC0000225	%%2304	An Error occured during Logon.	Unknown error occurred during logon.
0xC0000234	%%2307	Account locked out.	User logon with account locked.
0xC00002EE	%%2304	An Error occured during Logon.	Unknown error occurred during logon.
0xC0000413	%%2304	An Error occured during Logon.	The machine you are logging onto is protected by an authentication firewall. The specified account is not allowed to authenticate to the machine.
0x0	–	0x0	No Sub Status.

All other fields were already discussed in the "Successful Local User Account Interactive Logon" section.

Successful Domain User Account Interactive Logon

The domain user interactive logon process is similar to the local user logon process, but with a few differences. The flow for interactive domain user logons is shown in Figure 4-4.

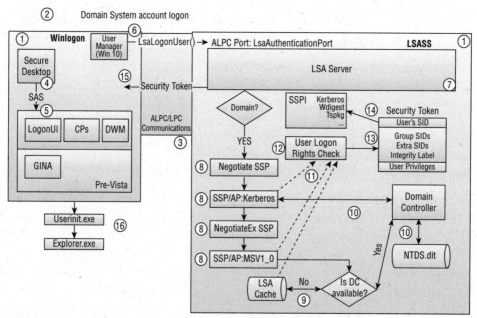

Figure 4-4: Windows interactive logon flow for domain user accounts

> **NOTE** The event logs described in this section are available in this chapter's downloads, in the `Successful Domain User Account Interactive Logon.evtx` file.

Steps 1–7: User Logon Process

Steps 1–7 are the same steps as for local user account interactive logons.

Step 8: Authentication Package Negotiation

Negotiate SSP selects an appropriate authentication package to handle the authentication request. It will always try Kerberos AP first. If Kerberos AP is able to proceed with the request, the data is sent to the domain controller for validation.

If Kerberos AP is not able to validate the credentials, Negotiate SSP sends a request to NegotiateEx SSP, which was discussed earlier in the "Successful Local User Account Interactive Logon" section.

If NegotiateEx SSP is not able to proceed with the request, information is sent to the MSV1_0 AP.

MSV1_0 AP sends the data to the domain controller for validation.

Step 9: LSA Cache

If the domain controller is unavailable, MSV1_0 queries the LSA cache to find any cached credentials for the account.

The LSA cache is storage location in the Windows registry, at HKLM\Security\ Cache. By default, the LSA cache stores credentials for the last 10 domain user accounts logged in Interactively or RemoteInteractively to the host. The account's password hash is stored in form of the Password-Based Key Derivation Function 2 (PBKDF2) hashing function value.

The 4624 event shown in Listing 4-18 is recorded in the Windows security event log after a successful interactive logon using cached credentials.

NOTE This event log is available in this chapter's downloads, in the Successful Interactive Logon With Cached Credentials.evtx file.

Listing 4-18: Event ID 4624: An account was successfully logged on.

```
Task Category: Logon
Keywords: Audit Success
Subject:
        Security ID:              S-1-5-18
        Account Name:             WIN10-1703$
        Account Domain:           HQCORP
        Logon ID:                 0x3E7
Logon Information:
        Logon Type:               11
        Restricted Admin Mode:    -
        Virtual Account:          No
        Elevated Token:           Yes
Impersonation Level:              Impersonation
New Logon:
        Security ID:              S-1-5-21-1913345275-1711810662-261465553-
                                  500
        Account Name:             Administrator
        Account Domain:           HQCORP
        Logon ID:                 0x3ACC4
        Linked Logon ID:          0x0
        Network Account Name:     -
        Network Account Domain:   -
        Logon GUID:               {00000000-0000-0000-0000-000000000000}
Process Information:
        Process ID:               0x214
        Process Name:             C:\Windows\System32\svchost.exe
Network Information:
        Workstation Name:         WIN10-1703
        Source Network Address:   127.0.0.1
        Source Port:              0
```

```
Detailed Authentication Information:
      Logon Process:           User32
      Authentication Package:  Negotiate
      Transited Services:      -
      Package Name (NTLM only):  -
      Key Length:              0
```

The logon shown in this listing is a type 11 event, which is a logon type for interactive logon using cached credentials.

If the LSA cache does not contain cached credentials for the specific domain user and a domain controller is not available, the authentication fails.

Step 10: Credentials Validation on the Domain Controller

If the Kerberos or MSV1_0 packages were able to reach the domain controller, then the domain controller validates the credentials.

Steps 11–16: Logon Process

Steps 11–16 are the same as Steps 9–14 for local user account interactive logons.

Unsuccessful Domain User Account Interactive Logon

For an unsuccessful domain user account interactive logon, the same events are generated as for unsuccessful local user account interactive logons.

RemoteInteractive Logon

The RemoteInteractive logon type is usually associated with Remote Desktop and Terminal Services connections. In this section you will find information about how RemoteInteractive logon works and which events are recorded in the Windows security event log for successful and unsuccessful RemoteInteractive logons.

This section does not differentiate local users and domain users, because the information for these user types is almost the same in the events.

Successful User Account RemoteInteractive Logon

After RemoteInteractive logon succeeds, the events in Listing 4-19 are recorded in the Windows security event log.

NOTE The event logs described in this section are available in this chapter's downloads, in the Successful User Account RemoteInteractive Logon.evtx **file.**

Listing 4-19: Event ID 4624: An account was successfully logged on.

```
Task Category: Logon
Keywords: Audit Success
Subject:
        Security ID:            S-1-5-18
        Account Name:           WIN10-1703$
        Account Domain:         HQCORP
        Logon ID:               0x3E7
Logon Information:
        Logon Type:             10
        Restricted Admin Mode: %%1843 (No)
        Virtual Account:        %%1843 (No)
        Elevated Token:         %%1842 (Yes)
Impersonation Level:            %%1833 (Impersonation)
New Logon:
        Security ID:            S-1-5-21-1913345275-1711810662-261465553-
                                500
        Account Name:           administrator
        Account Domain:         HQCORP
        Logon ID:               0x319975
        Linked Logon ID:        0x0
        Network Account Name:   -
        Network Account Domain:-
        Logon GUID:             {7325c0ac-0b1d-0c8f-8aae-7fad6d69d4d8}
Process Information:
        Process ID:             0x214
        Process Name:           C:\Windows\System32\svchost.exe
Network Information:
        Workstation Name:       WIN10-1703
        Source Network Address: 10.0.0.15
        Source Port:            0
Detailed Authentication Information:
        Logon Process:          User32
        Authentication Package: Negotiate
        Transited Services:     -
        Package Name (NTLM only): -
        Key Length:             0
```

Logon is initiated by the SYSTEM account (`Subject`), the account under which `svchost.exe` is running.

`Logon Type` 10 means RemoteInteractive logon.

You also can see that it is an elevated token session.

There is no `Linked Logon ID` for RemoteInteractive logon, because only one logon session is initiated for RemoteInteractive logons. It is either elevated or non-elevated.

The `Network Information` section contains information about the host from which the logon request was received. Information in these fields depends on information received from the authentication package (or SSP) that was used during authentication.

`Workstation Name` contains the hostname. If Kerberos SSP/AP was used for authentication (can be hidden behind Negotiate SSP), then this field will contain the name of the target machine to which terminal services logon was performed. If NTLM SSP was used, then this field will contain the name of the source host, from which terminal services logon was initiated. As a general rule, you should not rely on the `Workstation Name` field in events 4624 and 4625. This field does not always contains the name of the host from which logon was initiated.

`Source Network Address` contains an IPv4 or IPv6 address of the host from which the logon session was initiated.

`Restricted Admin Mode` shows whether the connection was performed with `/restrictedAdmin` flag enabled in the terminal client. The Restricted Admin Mode option prevents the user's credentials from being transferred and stored in the target host's memory.

`Logon GUID` can be correlated to the 4769 Kerberos Distribution Center (KDC) event on the domain controller. The correlated event on the domain controller for this example is shown in Listing 4-20.

Listing 4-20: Event ID 4624: An account was successfully logged on.

```
Task Category: Logon
Keywords: Audit Success
Account Information:
        Account Name:           Administrator@HQCORP.LOCAL
        Account Domain:         HQCORP.LOCAL
        Logon GUID:             {7325c0ac-0b1d-0c8f-8aae-7fad6d69d4d8}
Service Information:
        Service Name:           WIN10-1703$
        Service ID:             S-1-5-21-1913345275-1711810662-261465553-
                                1123
...
```

You can find more detailed information about Kerberos events on domain controllers in Chapter 9.

Successful User Account RemoteInteractive Logon Using Cached Credentials

If a domain controller is unavailable and the domain user account's credentials cannot be validated, RemoteInteractive logon will attempt to authenticate the user using cached credentials on the destination host. If this authentication succeeds, you will get the Logon Type 12 event shown in Listing 4-21 in the Windows security event log on the destination host.

> **NOTE** The event logs described in this section are available in this chapter's down-
> loads, in the `Successful User Account RemoteInteractive Logon -`
> `Cached Credentials.evtx` file.

Listing 4-21: Event ID 4624: An account was successfully logged on.

```
Task Category: Logon
Keywords: Audit Success
Subject:
        Security ID:              S-1-5-18
        Account Name:             WIN10-1703$
        Account Domain:           HQCORP
        Logon ID:                 0x3E7
Logon Information:
        Logon Type:               12
        Restricted Admin Mode:    -
        Virtual Account:          %%1843 (No)
        Elevated Token:           %%1842 (Yes)
Impersonation Level:              %%1833 (Impersonation)
New Logon:
        Security ID:              S-1-5-21-1913345275-1711810662-
                                  261465553-500
        Account Name:             Administrator
        Account Domain:           HQCORP
        Logon ID:                 0x18E7445
        Linked Logon ID:          0x0
        Network Account Name:     -
        Network Account Domain:   -
        Logon GUID:               {00000000-0000-0000-0000-000000000000}
Process Information:
        Process ID:               0x414
        Process Name:             C:\Windows\System32\svchost.exe
Network Information:
        Workstation Name:         WIN10-1703
        Source Network Address:   10.0.0.130
        Source Port:              0
Detailed Authentication Information:
        Logon Process:            User32
        Authentication Package:   Negotiate
        Transited Services:       -
        Package Name (NTLM only): -
        Key Length:               0
```

The fields are the same as you saw for successful RemoteInteractive logon in
the previous section; just the `Logon Type` field value is different.

Unsuccessful User Account RemoteInteractive Logon - NLA Enabled

When Network Level Authentication (NLA) is used during terminal services
logon, authentication occurs before a remote desktop (RDP) session is established.
If authentication fails, no RDP session is established.

On a source host, NLA first authenticates the user account for the username and password that were entered on the terminal client in the active directory domain. This request is sent to domain controller from a source host. If authentication is successful, an RDP session will be established with a target host. If not, no events are recorded in the Windows security event log on a target host. Listing 4-22 is an example of the event generated in a domain controller security event log, when NLA authentication for a user account failed on a source host.

Listing 4-22: Event ID 4771: Kerberos pre-authentication failed.

```
Task Category: Kerberos Authentication Service
Keywords: Audit Failure
Account Information:
        Security ID:            S-1-5-21-1913345275-1711810662-
                                261465553-500
        Account Name:           Administrator
Service Information:
        Service Name:           krbtgt/hqcorp
Network Information:
        Client Address:         ::ffff:10.0.0.15
        Client Port:            57605
Additional Information:
        Ticket Options:         0x40810010
        Failure Code:           0x18
        Pre-Authentication Type: 2
```

This event informs you that a Kerberos AS_REQ (TGT request) was sent for user Administrator from a host at IP 10.0.0.15. The TGT ticket was not issued (Audit Failure), because pre-authentication (read authentication) for the user account failed due to a wrong password provided (Failure Code: 0x18). You can find more detailed information about Kerberos events on domain controllers in Chapter 9.

Listings 4-23 and 4-24 show the events on a target host that may be a signal of an unsuccessful RDP connection with failed NLA authentication. These events are a Microsoft-Windows-RemoteDesktopServices-RdpCoreTS/Operational event ID 131 followed by a 226 event. You can find these events in the Applications and Services Logs\Microsoft\Windows\RemoteDesktopServices-RdpCoreTS\ Operational path using the Windows Event Viewer.

The first event indicates that terminal services received TCP connection from IP address 10.0.0.15 (57600 is the source port).

Listing 4-23: Event ID 131: The server accepted a new TCP connection from client

```
Task Category: RemoteFX module
Level: Information
The server accepted a new TCP connection from client 10.0.0.15:57600.
```

The next event occurs at the same time. Together they inform you that terminal services received a new connection from IP address 10.0.0.15 and the connection was not successfully established.

Listing 4-24: Event ID 226: RDP_TCP: An error was encountered.

```
Task Category: RemoteFX module
Level: Information
RDP_TCP: An error was encountered when transitioning from StateUnknown
in response to Event_Disconnect (error code 0x80070040).
```

Unsuccessful User Account RemoteInteractive Logon - NLA Disabled

When Network Level Authentication (NLA) is not used during a terminal logon session, the event shown in Listing 4-25 is recorded on the destination host, when the logon attempt fails.

> **NOTE**   This event log is available in this chapter's downloads, in the Unsuccessful User Account RemoteInteractive Logon - NLA Disabled.evtx file.

Listing 4-25: Event ID 4625: An account failed to log on.

```
Task Category: Logon
Keywords: Audit Failure
Subject:
        Security ID:            S-1-5-18 (SYSTEM)
        Account Name:           WIN10-1703$
        Account Domain:         HQCORP
        Logon ID:               0x3E7
Logon Type:                     10
Account For Which Logon Failed:
        Security ID:            S-1-0-0 (NULL SID)
        Account Name:           administrator
        Account Domain:         hqcorp
Failure Information:
        Failure Reason:         %%2313 (Unknown user name or bad
                                 password.)
        Status:                 0xC000006D
        Sub Status:             0xC000006A
Process Information:
        Caller Process ID:      0x214
        Caller Process Name:    C:\Windows\System32\svchost.exe
Network Information:
        Workstation Name:       WIN10-1703
        Source Network Address: 10.0.0.120
        Source Port:            0
Detailed Authentication Information:
        Logon Process:          User32
        Authentication Package: Negotiate
        Transited Services:     -
        Package Name (NTLM only): -
        Key Length:             0
```

This event is very similar to the 4625 event for Interactive logon type. You can read more information about this event in the "Unsuccessful Local User Account Interactive Logon" section earlier in this chapter.

`Logon Type` 10 means RemoteInteractive logon.

The `Network Information` section contains information about the host from which this logon request was received. Information in these fields depends on information received from the authentication package (or SSP) that was used during authentication. This was discussed earlier in the "Successful User Account RemoteInteractive Logon" section.

Network Logon

The Network logon type is one of the most common logon types in the Windows environment. The most common examples of Network logon type events are:

- Network file share access attempts
- Remote PowerShell commands without using CredSSP
- WMI queries

Successful User Account Network Logon

This section contains an example of successful Network logon to the network file share located on a host.

The events in Listing 4-26 and Listing 4-27 are generated on a destination host in the Windows security event log after a successful network share access attempt.

NOTE The event logs described in this section are available in this chapter's downloads, in the `Successful User Account Network Logon.evtx` file.

Listing 4-26: Event ID 4672: Special privileges assigned to new logon.

```
Task Category: Special Logon
Keywords: Audit Success
Subject:
        Security ID:              S-1-5-21-1913345275-1711810662-261465553-
                                  500
        Account Name:             Administrator
        Account Domain:           HQCORP
        Logon ID:                 0x147B91
Privileges:                       SeSecurityPrivilege
...
```

This event shows the list of special privileges assigned to a new logon. This was discussed previously in the "Successful Local User Account Interactive Logon" section.

Listing 4-27: Event ID 4624: An account was successfully logged on.

```
Task Category: Logon
Keywords: Audit Success
Subject:
       Security ID:            S-1-0-0 (NULL SID)
       Account Name:           -
       Account Domain:         -
       Logon ID:               0x0
Logon Information:
       Logon Type:             3
       Restricted Admin Mode:  -
       Virtual Account:        %%1843 (No)
       Elevated Token:         %%1842 (Yes)
Impersonation Level:           %%1833 (Impersonation)
New Logon:
       Security ID:            S-1-5-21-1913345275-1711810662-261465553-
                               500
       Account Name:           Administrator
       Account Domain:         HQCORP.LOCAL
       Logon ID:               0x147B91
       Linked Logon ID:        0x0
       Network Account Name:   -
       Network Account Domain: -
       Logon GUID:             {bcd31843-45de-e276-57e1-0942a74381e4}
Process Information:
       Process ID:             0x0
       Process Name:           -
Network Information:
       Workstation Name:       -
       Source Network Address: fe80::6d6b:8141:e4ff:6a50
       Source Port:            49208
Detailed Authentication Information:
       Logon Process:          Kerberos
       Authentication Package: Kerberos
       Transited Services:     -
       Package Name (NTLM only): -
       Key Length:             0
```

The process that invoked the authentication is the process with `Process ID` `0x0`, which is a system process, or the system itself. The System process runs under the SYSTEM account, but very often the `Subject` fields show `S-1-0-0` `(NULL SID)` for the system process.

`Logon Type` is 3, which is the Network logon type.

You also may see it is not a Managed Service Account or Group Managed Service Account (`Virtual Account`), but this account has special privileges or membership in the privileged local groups, because it has an elevated token (`Elevated Token = Yes`).

The `Restricted Admin Mode` field is not applicable to the Network logon type.

There is no `Linked Logon ID` for Network logon, because only one logon session is initiated for the Network logon type. This session is elevated or non-elevated.

`Network Account Name` and `Network Account Domain` are applicable only to the NewCredentials logon type and are discussed in "NewCredentials Logon" section.

The `Network Information` section contains information about the host from which the logon request was received. Information in these fields depends on information received from the authentication package (or SSP) that was used during authentication.

`Workstation Name` contains a hostname. If Kerberos SSP/AP was used for authentication (can be hidden behind Negotiate SSP), this field will be empty (will have a - value). If NTLM SSP was used, this field will contain the name of the source host from which this logon was initiated. As a general rule, you should not rely on the `Workstation Name` field in events 4624 and 4625. This field does not always contains the name of the host from which logon was initiated.

`Source Network Address` contains an IPv4 or IPv6 address for the host from which this logon session was initiated.

See the "Successful Local User Account Interactive Logon" section for more details about the other fields in this event.

The `Transited Services`, `Package Name (NTLM only)`, and `Key Length` fields are discussed in more detail in Chapter 9.

The event in Listing 4-28 contains group membership information for the logged-in account. This event was discussed earlier in the "Successful Local User Account Interactive Logon" section.

Listing 4-28: Event ID 4627: Group membership information.

```
Task Category: Group Membership
Keywords: Audit Success
```

Unsuccessful User Account Network Logon

An account logon might be unsuccessful for multiple reasons. The most common are an invalid username and/or password.

The authentication protocol used determines the events that are generated on a target host. In this section you will find information about how to monitor unsuccessful Network logons for NTLM and Kerberos authentication.

Do not forget that each time Kerberos authentication fails (when KDC service on the domain controller is not responding, for example) the system will try to authenticate an account using NTLM. By default, if the host's IP address is used when specifying a target for authentication, NTLM is used, because domain controllers do not register SPNs for host IP addresses.

Unsuccessful User Account Network Logon - NTLM

The event in Listing 4-29 will occur in the Windows security event log if Network logon was not successful and NTLM was used as an authentication protocol (this example is also applicable to domain accounts).

> **NOTE** This event log is available in this chapter's downloads, in the `Unsuccessful User Account Network Logon - NTLM.evtx` file.

Listing 4-29: Event ID 4625: An account failed to log on.

```
Task Category: Logon
Keywords: Audit Failure
Subject:
        Security ID:            S-1-0-0 (NULL SID)
        Account Name:           -
        Account Domain:         -
        Logon ID:               0x0
Logon Type:                     3
Account For Which Logon Failed:
        Security ID:            S-1-0-0 (NULL SID)
        Account Name:           akljdflskfjdlka
        Account Domain:         WIN7
Failure Information:
        Failure Reason:         %%2313 (Unknown user name or bad
                                 password.)
        Status:                 0xC000006D
        Sub Status:             0xC0000064
Process Information:
        Caller Process ID:      0x0
        Caller Process Name:    -
Network Information:
        Workstation Name:       WIN7
        Source Network Address: fe80::6d6b:8141:e4ff:6a50
        Source Port:            49279
Detailed Authentication Information:
        Logon Process:          NtLmSsp
        Authentication Package: NTLM
        Transited Services:     -
        Package Name (NTLM only): -
        Key Length:             0
```

The main difference between NTLM and Kerberos authentication for the Network logon type if the username or password is incorrect, is that, when NTLM is used, a 4625 event is generated on the target host, and when Kerberos is used, it is not generated at all.

`Account For Which Logon Failed\Security ID` is `NULL SID`, because in this particular example, the username used for authentication does not exist on the WIN7 (target) machine. For all such accounts you will see `NULL SID` as the SID value.

Event 4625, as was already discussed in the "Unsuccessful Local User Account Interactive Logon" section, does not contain an SID for the account for which logon failed, because this information is available only after the account is authenticated.

Sub Status 0xC0000064 means "User logon with misspelled or bad user account." See Table 4-4 for more details.

Authentication was received by the NtLmSsp (Logon Process) logon process and the NTLM Authentication Package was used to handle the request. Unsuccessful NTLM authentication attempts have less information in the Detailed Authentication Information section. You can read more about this in Chapter 9.

Unsuccessful User Account Network Logon - Kerberos

Kerberos authentication requests are handled by Active Directory domain controllers. Keep in mind that if a username is valid but the password is not correct for the specific domain account, NTLM authentication will not be performed after Kerberos authentication. If the username was not found on the domain controller, NTLM fall back will occur.

If user authentication fails, the event in Listing 4-30 is generated in the Windows security event log on a domain controller.

> **NOTE** This event log is available in this chapter's downloads, in the Unsuccessful User Account Network Logon - Kerberos.evtx file.

Listing 4-30: Event ID 4771: Kerberos pre-authentication failed.

```
Task Category: Kerberos Authentication Service
Keywords: Audit Failure
Account Information:
        Security ID:                S-1-5-21-1913345275-1711810662-261465553-
                                    500
        Account Name:               Administrator
Service Information:
        Service Name:               krbtgt/HQCORP
Network Information:
        Client Address:             ::ffff:10.0.0.15
        Client Port:                50241
Additional Information:
        Ticket Options:             0x40810010
        Failure Code:               0x18
        Pre-Authentication Type:    2
```

A Kerberos AS_REQ (krbtgt/HQCORP) authentication request was sent to the domain controller from IP 10.0.0.15 for user Administrator but failed (Audit Failure) with code 0x18 (the wrong password was provided).

No events are generated on the destination host in scenarios where Kerberos authentication failed and no NTLM fall back occurred (such as wrong user's password).

Batch and Service Logon

Scheduled tasks and Windows services run under some security principal context to perform their duties. The account, under which a service/task will run, can be configured - for example, in the service or scheduled task properties using the Windows Task Scheduler tool. In this section you will find information about which events are generated in the Windows security event log for successful and unsuccessful Batch and Service account logon types.

Successful Service / Batch Logon

Not many differences exist between Service and Batch logon type events.The 4648 and 4624 event examples in Listings 4-31 and 4-32 explain both the Service and Batch logon types.

The first event for service or scheduled task logon to appear in the Windows security event log is the 4648 event.

> **NOTE** The event logs described in this section are available in this chapter's downloads, in the `Successful Batch User Logon.evtx` **and** `Successful Service User Logon.evtx` **files.**

Listing 4-31: Event ID 4648: A logon was attempted using explicit credentials.

```
Task Category: Logon
Keywords: Audit Success
Subject:
        Security ID:            S-1-5-18 (SYSTEM)
        Account Name:           WIN10-1703$
        Account Domain:         HQCORP
        Logon ID:               0x3E7
        Logon GUID:             {00000000-0000-0000-0000-000000000000}
Account Whose Credentials Were Used:
        Account Name:           Administrator
        Account Domain:         HQCORP
        Logon GUID:             {f68ce018-f8da-cdda-70d1-808a4278aea6}
Target Server:
        Target Server Name:     localhost
        Additional Information:localhost
Process Information:
        Process ID:             0x328
        Process Name:           Batch - C:\Windows\System32\svchost.exe
                                Service - C:\Windows\System32\services.exe
Network Information:
        Network Address:        -
        Port:                   -
```

Event 4648 informs you that the account and password for account authentication were explicitly specified, which is the case for almost all local logon types.

The `Target Server` section shows `localhost` as the value for both the `Target Server Name` and `Additional Information` fields, because both services and scheduled tasks run locally. The `Network Information` section is empty, again, because this event is for local authentication.

You will find more information about `Process Name` field differences in the 4624 event explanation following Listing 4-31.

Listing 4-32 is an example of the 4624 event, which appears in the Windows security event log after a 4648 event when a service or scheduled task switches to running mode.

Listing 4-32: Event ID 4624: An account was successfully logged on.

```
Task Category: Logon
Keywords: Audit Success
Subject:
        Security ID:              S-1-5-18 (SYSTEM)
        Account Name:             WIN10-1703$
        Account Domain:           HQCORP
        Logon ID:                 0x3E7
Logon Information:
        Logon Type:               Service - 5
                                  Batch - 4
        Restricted Admin Mode:    -
        Virtual Account:          %%1843 (No)
        Elevated Token:           %%1842 (Yes)
Impersonation Level:              %%1833 (Impersonation)
New Logon:
        Security ID:              S-1-5-21-1913345275-1711810662-261465553-
                                  500
        Account Name:             Administrator
        Account Domain:           HQCORP
        Logon ID:                 0x14647CE
        Linked Logon ID:          0x0
        Network Account Name:     -
        Network Account Domain:   -
        Logon GUID:               {ee0409ee-b09e-5ad7-8f7a-5c4a30b03ff2}
Process Information:
        Process ID:               0x414
        Process Name:             Batch - C:\Windows\System32\svchost.exe
                                  Service - C:\Windows\System32\
                                  services.exe
Network Information:
        Workstation Name:         WIN10-1703
        Source Network Address:   -
        Source Port:              -
Detailed Authentication Information:
        Logon Process:            Advapi
        Authentication Package:   Negotiate
        Transited Services:       -
        Package Name (NTLM only): -
        Key Length:               0
```

Scheduled tasks are run by the Task Scheduler system service, which runs under one of the `svchost.exe` (`Process Name`) instances in `netsvcs.dll`. All authentication attempts for scheduled tasks are sent from this service (read `svchost.exe` process).

Services are controlled by the Service Control Manager (`services.exe`), which is responsible for many service-related operations, such as service start, stop, install, uninstall, and so on. One of Service Control Manager's responsibilities is to validate a user's credentials during service startup.

The `Logon Type` code for service logon is 5; for batch logon it's 4.

`Subject` is a SYSTEM account, because both the Task Scheduler service and the Service Control Manager run under the SYSTEM account.

The `New Logon` section shows information about the account under which the scheduled task or service runs. There is no `Linked Logon ID` for the batch and service logons, because there is only one session created for these logon types.

Both services and scheduled tasks use the `Advapi` (Advanced API - advapi32.dll) `Logon Process` for authentication, because Advapi32.dll contains functions related to authentication for scheduled tasks and services.

The Negotiate `Authentication Package` is used to select between the Kerberos, NegotiateEx, and MSV1_0 authentication packages.

The `Network Information` section always points to the local machine, on which the task or service was started.

`Logon GUID` can be correlated to the 4769 Kerberos Distribution Center (KDC) event on the domain controller. It is explained in more detail in Chapter 9.

After a successful 4624 event, the events in Listings 4-33 and 4-34 might also appear in the event log.

Listing 4-33: Event ID 4627: Group membership information.

```
Task Category: Group Membership
Keywords: Audit Success
```

Listing 4-34: Event ID 4672: Special privileges assigned to new logon.

```
Task Category: Special Logon
Keywords: Audit Success
```

Unsuccessful Service / Batch Logon

Multiple reasons exist for why a scheduled task or service won't start successfully. Not all of them are related to the user account logon step. There might be an application or configuration error, for example.

NOTE The event logs described in this section are available in this chapter's downloads, in the `Unsuccessful Batch User Logon.evtx` **and** `Unsuccessful Service User Logon.evtx` **files.**

The most common problems related to the account logon stage for scheduled tasks and system services are the following:

- Incorrect or expired credentials
- Account restrictions
- Insufficient user privileges (discussed in Chapter 11)

This section covers the first two items. Both generate the same 4625 event shown in Listing 4-35, but have different failure reasons.

Listing 4-35: Event ID 4625: An account failed to log on.

```
Task Category: Logon
Keywords: Audit Failure
Subject:
        Security ID:            S-1-5-18 (SYSTEM)
        Account Name:           WIN10-1703$
        Account Domain:         HQCORP
        Logon ID:               0x3E7
        Logon Type:             Service - 5
                                Batch - 4
Account For Which Logon Failed:
        Security ID:            S-1-0-0 (NULL SID)
        Account Name:           Administrator
        Account Domain:         HQCORP
Failure Information:
        Failure Reason:         %%2313 (Unknown user name or bad
                                 password.)
        Status:                 0xC000006D
        Sub Status:             0xC000006A
Process Information:
        Caller Process ID:      0x328
        Caller Process Name:    Batch - C:\Windows\System32\svchost.exe
                                Service - C:\Windows\System32\
                                services.exe
Network Information:
        Workstation Name:       WIN10-1703
        Source Network Address: -
        Source Port:            -
Detailed Authentication Information:
        Logon Process:          Advapi
        Authentication Package: Negotiate
        Transited Services:     -
        Package Name (NTLM only):-
        Key Length:             0
```

All fields for this event were discussed earlier in the "Unsuccessful Local User Account Interactive Logon" section.

NetworkCleartext Logon

The NetworkCleartext logon type (Type 8) is the same as the Network logon type (Type 3) except that credentials are passed in cleartext format (Base64 encoded) via the network. It is considered to be a safer option to encrypt cleartext credentials during transfer (for example, SSL/TLS or IPsec tunnel) rather than sending them unencrypted. This logon type is most commonly used in Internet Informational Services (IIS) basic authentication.

This section covers this scenario in detail.

Successful User Account NetworkCleartext Logon - IIS Basic Authentication

You can enable basic authentication on IIS. Figure 4-5 shows an example of the credentials prompt on a client when it connects to an IIS site that supports basic authentication using Internet Explorer.

Figure 4-5: Internet Explorer basic authentication logon dialog window

If basic authentication is successful, the event shown in Listing 4-36 is generated on the IIS host in the security event log:

NOTE   This event log is available in this chapter's downloads, in the `Successful User Account NetworkCleartext Logon - IIS Basic Authentication.evtx` **file.**

Listing 4-36: Event ID 4624: An account was successfully logged on.

```
Task Category: Logon
Keywords: Audit Success
Subject:
```

```
              Security ID:            S-1-5-18
              Account Name:           2016DC$
              Account Domain:         HQCORP
              Logon ID:               0x3E7
Logon Information:
              Logon Type:             8
              Restricted Admin Mode:  -
              Virtual Account:        %%1842 (No)
              Elevated Token:         %%1843 (Yes)
Impersonation Level:                  %%1833 (Impersonation)
New Logon:
              Security ID:            S-1-5-21-1913345275-1711810662-261465553-
                                      500
              Account Name:           administrator
              Account Domain:         HQCORP
              Logon ID:               0x26FCEC
              Linked Logon ID:        0x0
              Network Account Name:   -
              Network Account Domain: -
              Logon GUID:             {f1d06c00-14f1-d336-14cd-198ea41ead50}
Process Information:
              Process ID:             0xe30
              Process Name:           C:\Windows\System32\inetsrv\w3wp.exe
Network Information:
              Workstation Name:       2016DC
              Source Network Address: 10.0.0.130
              Source Port:            49703
Detailed Authentication Information:
              Logon Process:          Advapi
              Authentication Package: Negotiate
              Transited Services:     -
              Package Name (NTLM only):-
              Key Length:             0
```

Most of the fields are similar to the Network logon (Type 3) type discussed earlier in this chapter, but there are some differences, which are explained here.

The Subject section contains information about the account that handles the authentication request. This is the account under which an application pool (under which IIS site/application is running), is configured to run.

The Process Information section contains information about the process which handles the authentication. For IIS this is usually w3wp.exe.

Workstation Name contains the name of the destination (IIS) machine for Kerberos authentication and the name of source machine for NTLM-family authentication.

Source Network Address contains an IPv4 or IPv6 address of the host from which the logon session was initiated.

The Logon Process field for basic authentication is always Advapi, because ADVAPI is used to handle basic authentication requests.

Figure 4-6 shows how basic authentication traffic looks in the network packet analyzer.

```
22 5.144719      10.0.0.130      10.0.0.10      HTTP      480 GET / HTTP/1.1
∨ Hypertext Transfer Protocol
  > GET / HTTP/1.1\r\n
    Accept: image/gif, image/jpeg, image/pjpeg, application/x-ms-application, application/xaml+xml, application/x-ms-xbap, */*\r\n
    Accept-Language: en-US\r\n
    User-Agent: Mozilla/4.0 (compatible; MSIE 7.0; Windows NT 10.0; WOW64; Trident/7.0; Touch; .NET4.0C; .NET4.0E; Tablet PC 2.0)\r\n
    Accept-Encoding: gzip, deflate\r\n
    Host: 2016dc\r\n
    Connection: Keep-Alive\r\n
    DNT: 1\r\n
  ∨ Authorization: Basic QWRtaW5pc3RyYXRvcjoxcTJ3I0UkUg==\r\n
      Credentials: Administrator:1q2w#E$R
    \r\n
    [Full request URI: http://2016dc/]
```

Figure 4-6: IIS basic authentication request traffic capture example

Unsuccessful User Account NetworkCleartext Logon - IIS Basic Authentication

For unsuccessful Type 8 logons, event 4625 will be generated in the security event log. It is similar to the 4625 event for Type 3 logon.

> **NOTE** This event log is available in this chapter's downloads, in the `Unsuccessful User Account NetworkCleartext Logon - IIS Basic Authentication. evtx` file.

NewCredentials Logon

The NewCredentials logon type is specifically designed to be used in combination with the Secondary Logon Windows service to run local applications using the logged-in user's credentials, but perform network activity using another account's credentials.

The easiest way to create a new logon session with the NewCredentials logon type is to use `runas /netonly /user:user_name application_name`, where `user_name` is the name of the account for which a new session is established and `application_name` is the name of the application being run using new logon session. After the command is executed, a prompt appears that asks the user to type a password for `user_name` account. The events in Listings 4-37 and 4-38 should be generated in the Windows security event log after this action.

> **NOTE** The event logs described in this section are available in this chapter's downloads, in the `NewCredentials Logon Type.evtx` files.

Listing 4-37: Event ID 4611: A trusted logon process has been registered with the Local Security Authority. This logon process will be trusted to submit logon requests.

```
Task Category: Security System Extension
Keywords: Audit Success
Subject:
        Security ID:          S-1-5-18 (SYSTEM)
        Account Name:         2016SRV$
        Account Domain:       HQCORP
        Logon ID:             0x3E7
Logon Process Name:           Secondary Logon Service
```

As a result of a successful `LsaRegisterLogonProcess()` function call, a 4611 event is generated.

This event contains the name of a logon process (`Logon Process Name`) that was successfully registered using the `LsaRegisterLogonProcess()` function. Logon processes are authorized to perform credential validation requests (call APIs) to `lsass.exe`.

The `Secondary Logon Service` logon process is associated with the `Secondary Logon Windows` system service and is required to perform NewCredentials logon type logons.

Listing 4-38: Event ID 4624: An account was successfully logged on.

```
Task Category: Logon
Keywords: Audit Success
Subject:
        Security ID:              S-1-5-21-1913345275-1711810662-261465553-
                                 500
        Account Name:            Administrator
        Account Domain:          HQCORP
        Logon ID:                0x6B61D8
Logon Information:
        Logon Type:              9
        Restricted Admin Mode:   -
        Virtual Account:         %%1843 (No)
        Elevated Token:          %%1842 (Yes)
Impersonation Level:             %%1833 (Impersonation)
New Logon:
        Security ID:             S-1-5-21-1913345275-1711810662-261465553-
                                 500
        Account Name:            Administrator
        Account Domain:          HQCORP
        Logon ID:                0x94FECB
        Linked Logon ID:         0x0
        Network Account Name:    andrei
        Network Account Domain:  hqcorp
        Logon GUID:              {00000000-0000-0000-0000-000000000000}
Process Information:
        Process ID:              0x4f4
        Process Name:            C:\Windows\System32\svchost.exe
Network Information:
        Workstation Name:
        Source Network Address:  ::1
        Source Port:             0
Detailed Authentication Information:
        Logon Process:           seclogo
        Authentication Package:  Negotiate
        Transited Services:      -
        Package Name (NTLM only):-
        Key Length:              0
```

The `Subject` section contains information about the account that invoked the new logon session.

The `Logon Type` is 9 (NewCredentials). The `Restricted Admin Mode` field is not applicable to the NewCredentials logon type.

The `Elevated Token` field shows the token type for the newly created local session. This token elevation type does not apply to network activities, only to local sessions, for which the `Subject` account will still be used.

The `New Logon` section contains information about the new logon session created for the account specified in the `Subject` section, which will be used for local activities and it also contains information about an account which will be used for network activities. If you use `runas /netonly`, the local session for new applications will be associated with the account in the `New Logon` section, but all network communications will be done using the `Network Account Name` account.

`Network Account Name` contains the name of the account for network activities.

`Network Account Domain` contains a domain name for the account specified in the `Network Account Name` field.

The `Logon GUID` field does not have a value in it, because when the 4624 logon event occurs, the system does not authenticate the new user (`Network Account Name`). Authentication is performed after a newly started application performs network activities.

`Process Information` will contain a reference to the `svchost.exe` process, under which the Secondary Logon Windows service is running.

The `Logon Process` is `seclogo`, which is a Secondary Logon Windows service. The `seclogo` logon process gets information about new credentials and performs authentication when it is required.

Listing 4-39 shows group membership information for a new logon.

Listing 4-39: Event ID 4627: Group membership information.

```
Task Category: Group Membership
Keywords: Audit Success
Subject:
        Security ID:            S-1-5-21-1913345275-1711810662-261465553-
                                500
        Account Name:           Administrator
        Account Domain:         HQCORP
        Logon ID:               0x6B61D8
Logon Type:                     9
New Logon:
        Security ID:            S-1-5-21-1913345275-1711810662-261465553-
                                500
        Account Name:           Administrator
        Account Domain:         HQCORP
        Logon ID:               0x94FECB
Event in sequence:              1 of 1
Group Membership:

                                Groups Omitted In This Example
```

These events are related to a new session for the account that invoked logon with the NewCredentials type. New credentials will be used only for network connections; no local authentication occurs using these new credentials.

Interactive and RemoteInteractive Session Lock Operations and Unlock Logon Type

Each time a user unlocks the machine, event 4624 with Logon Type 7 is generated in the Windows security event log.

> **NOTE** This event log is available in this chapter's downloads, in the `Unlock Logon.evtx` file.

Unlock logon type sessions are temporary and they disappear after the user successfully unlocks the machine, which is done to unlock the initial Interactive or RemoteInteractive session. You will find the 4634 event right after the 4624 Logon Type 7 security event. Listing 4-40 is an example of such a 4634 event.

> **NOTE** The event logs described next are available in this chapter's downloads, in the `Machine Lockout and Unlock Events.evtx` file.

Listing 4-40: Event ID 4634: An account was logged off.

```
Task Category: Logoff
Keywords: Audit Success
Subject:
        Security ID:           S-1-5-21-1913345275-1711810662-261465553-500
        Account Name:          Administrator
        Account Domain:        HQCORP
        Logon ID:              0x248D666
Logon Type:                    7
```

An additional event you will find after a machine is locked out is shown in Listing 4-41.

Listing 4-41: Event ID 4800: The workstation was locked.

```
Task Category: Other Logon/Logoff Events
Keywords: Audit Success
Subject:
        Security ID:           S-1-5-21-1913345275-1711810662-261465553-500
        Account Name:          Administrator
        Account Domain:        HQCORP
        Logon ID:              0x24A3F2
        Session ID:            2
```

The event in Listing 4-42 occurs after the machine is unlocked.

Listing 4-42: Event ID 4801: The workstation was unlocked.

```
Task Category: Other Logon/Logoff Events
Keywords: Audit Success
Subject:
        Security ID:          S-1-5-21-1913345275-1711810662-261465553-500
        Account Name:         Administrator
        Account Domain:       HQCORP
        Logon ID:             0x24A3F2
        Session ID:           2
```

Account Logoff and Session Disconnect

Windows has two different events that inform you about an account logoff operation. Only one of these events is generated when a user's session is logged off:

■ **4647: User initiated logoff:** Occurs when the ExitWindowsEx() function is called for the current user's Interactive or RemoteInteractive session. This function is invoked, for example, when a user uses the standard Start Menu "Sign out" option to sign out while logged in Interactively or RemoteInteractively.

■ **4634: An account was logged off:** This event generates when an account's session is logged off, by any means other than that in the previous item.

Basically speaking, you will see ether a 4647 event for standard Interactive and RemoteInteractive sessions sign out operations, or 4634 for all other logoff ("session end") system events.

No event is generated, if, for example, the machine is unplugged from the power supply or a battery is removed from a laptop when it is not plugged in to the power socket. So there is no guarantee that a logoff event will be generated. Also, for some logon types, such as Network logon, the logoff event may occur automatically after the session is not active for some period of time.

Listing 4-43 is an example of a 4647 event.

NOTE This event log is available in this chapter's downloads, in the User Initiated Logoff.evtx **file.**

Listing 4-43: Event ID 4647: User initiated logoff.

```
Task Category: Logoff
Keywords: Audit Success
Subject:
        Security ID:          S-1-5-21-1913345275-1711810662-261465553-500
        Account Name:         Administrator
        Account Domain:       HQCORP
        Logon ID:             0x1C6A9CB
```

Logon ID in this event shows you the ID of the Interactive session for which the sign out process was initiated.

Listing 4-44 is an example of an account log off (4634) event.

NOTE This event log is available in this chapter's downloads, in the An Account Was Logged Off.evtx file.

Listing 4-44: Event ID 4634: An account was logged off.

```
Task Category: Logoff
Keywords: Audit Success
Subject:
        Security ID:            S-1-5-21-1913345275-1711810662-261465553-500
        Account Name:           Administrator
        Account Domain:         HQCORP
        Logon ID:               0x1D8EBA3
Logon Type:                     7
```

Logon ID in this event shows you the ID of the logged-off session.

Logon Type shows the type of the logged-off session.

Terminal Session Disconnect

There is a specific event for a terminal session disconnect action. When an account disconnects its terminal (RemoteInteractive) session without logging off from the session, a 4778 event like that shown in Listing 4-45 is generated.

NOTE This event log is available in this chapter's downloads, in the Terminal Session Disconnect.evtx file.

Listing 4-45: Event ID 4779: A session was disconnected from a Window Station.

```
Task Category: Other Logon/Logoff Events
Keywords: Audit Success
Subject:
        Account Name:           Administrator
        Account Domain:         HQCORP
        Logon ID:               0x1D8EB74
Session:
        Session Name:           RDP-Tcp#22
Additional Information:
        Client Name:            2016DC
        Client Address:         10.0.0.10
```

The Subject section contains information about the account for which the session was disconnected.

The Session Name field contains the name of disconnected terminal session. You can see the list of current sessions on a destination host using the query session command.

The Client Name and Client Address fields are a computer name and IP address, from which the session was established initially.

Special Groups

Special Groups is a feature that was first introduced in Windows Vista and Windows Server 2008.

This feature allows administrators to configure a list of security identifiers (SIDs). When a new logged-in account has one of the listed SIDs in a group membership part of the security token, a special security event is triggered in the system's security event log. This event generates for all logon types. Keep in mind that the event triggers only if a user has specific predefined SID/SIDs in the group membership part of its security access token. If you specify user account's SID itself, there will be no event generated, because this SID is not in a Group Membership section in the token.

In order to configure Special Groups you need to create new registry key value in the HKEY_LOCAL_MACHINE\System\CurrentControlSet\Control\ Lsa\Audit registry key. The value name is SpecialGroups, and the type is string. Then you need to add SIDs to this value, separated by semicolon (;) character, like this: S-1-5-21-1913345275-1711810662-261465553- 512;S-1-5-21-1913345275-1711810662-261465553-518.

If the list of SIDs in the SpecialGroups registry key value was modified, the event in Listing 4-46 will be generated in the Windows security event log.

> **NOTE** The event logs described in this section are available in this chapter's downloads, in the Special Groups.evtx files.

Listing 4-46: Event ID 4908: Special Groups Logon table modified.

```
Task Category: Audit Policy Change
Keywords: Audit Success
Special Groups:
            %{S-1-5-21-1913345275-1711810662-261465553-512}
            %{S-1-5-21}
```

This event lists all current SIDs in the SpecialGroups registry key value. This event does not show you which SIDs were removed or added to the Special Groups logon table.

The %{S-1-5-21} value is always present at the end of the SIDs configured for Special Groups. When an account that is a member of any security group listed in the SpecialGroups registry key value logs in to the machine using any logon type, the event in Listing 4-47 is generated in the Windows security event log.

Listing 4-47: Event ID 4964: Special groups have been assigned to a new logon.

```
Task Category: Special Logon
Keywords: Audit Success
```

```
Subject:
        Security ID:          S-1-5-18
        Account Name:         WIN10-1703$
        Account Domain:       HQCORP
        Logon ID:             0x3E7
        Logon GUID:           {00000000-0000-0000-0000-000000000000}
New Logon:
        Security ID:          S-1-5-21-1913345275-1711810662-261465553-500
        Account Name:         Administrator
        Account Domain:       HQCORP
        Logon ID:             0x2020668
        Logon GUID:           {00000000-0000-0000-0000-000000000000}
        Special Groups Assigned:
                              S-1-5-21-1913345275-1711810662-261465553-512
```

For each logon you will get one 4964 event that contains all special groups detected for the specific account.

The `Subject` section contains information about the account that requested the logon.

The `New Logon` section contains information for the logged-in account, for which special groups were detected in the list of groups that account is a member of.

The `Logon GUID` field does not always contain a correct GUID value. It's better to find the correlated 4624 logon event with the same `Logon ID` and check the value of the `Logon GUID` there if you need it.

Anonymous Logon

ANONYMOUS LOGON (S-1-5-7) basically means someone or something without associated credentials (no username, no password).

The important thing to notice is that anonymous logon, by default, is supported only by NTLM authentication, because Kerberos does not have Service Principal Name registered for the NT Authority\ANONYMOUS LOGON built-in security principal.

Multiple scenarios exist in the Windows world when an anonymous user might appear. In this section you will find information about the most common scenarios where an ANONYMOUS LOGON account is used.

Default ANONYMOUS LOGON Logon Session

By default, when a Windows operating system starts, the local ANONYMOUS LOGON session is automatically created. The LOCAL SYSTEM, LOCAL SERVICE, NETWORK SERVICE, and ANONYMOUS LOGON built-in accounts create their logon sessions at system startup. These sessions are then used to run processes under these accounts.

You can verify the list of current active logon sessions using the `logonsessions.exe` tool from Microsoft, which was discussed in the "Successful Local User Account Interactive Logon" section. Figure 4-7 shows an example of `logonsessions.exe` output showing the default ANONYMOUS LOGON logon session.

```
[10] Logon session 00000000:000292b7:
    User name:    NT AUTHORITY\ANONYMOUS LOGON
    Auth package: NTLM
    Logon type:   Network
    Session:      0
    Sid:          S-1-5-7
    Logon time:   4/25/2017 4:46:23 PM
    Logon server:
    DNS Domain:
    UPN:
```

Figure 4-7: Default ANONYMOUS LOGON logon session

Listing 4-48 is an example of the security event generated at startup for the session in Figure 4-7.

> **NOTE** This event log is available in this chapter's downloads, in the `Default`
> `ANONYMOUS LOGON Logon Session.evtx` file.

Listing 4-48: Event ID 4624: An account was successfully logged on.

```
Task Category: Logon
Keywords: Audit Success
Subject:
        Security ID:            S-1-0-0 (NULL SID)
        Account Name:           -
        Account Domain:         -
        Logon ID:               0x0
Logon Information:
        Logon Type:             3
        Restricted Admin Mode:  -
        Virtual Account:        %%1843 (No)
        Elevated Token:         %%1843 (No)
Impersonation Level:            %%1833 (Impersonation)
New Logon:
        Security ID:            S-1-5-7 (ANONYMOUS LOGON)
        Account Name:           ANONYMOUS LOGON
        Account Domain:         NT AUTHORITY
        Logon ID:               0x292B7
        Linked Logon ID:        0x0
        Network Account Name:   -
        Network Account Domain:-
        Logon GUID:             {00000000-0000-0000-0000-000000000000}
Process Information:
        Process ID:             0x0
        Process Name:           -
```

```
Network Information:
      Workstation Name:       -
      Source Network Address:-
      Source Port:            -
Detailed Authentication Information:
      Logon Process:          NtLmSsp
      Authentication Package: NTLM
      Transited Services:     -
      Package Name (NTLM only): NTLM V1
      Key Length:             0
```

Explicit Use of Anonymous Credentials

Some applications might be hardcoded to use anonymous credentials. This will generate logon attempts with an ANONYMOUS LOGON account.

You can test this behavior using the net use built-in Windows command-line application. Use the following command in order to try anonymous access to the remote machine:

```
net use \\host\IPC$ /user:"" ""
```

This command requests anonymous access to the target's Inter-process Communications (IPC$) share. You can find more information about the IPC$ share in Chapter 15.

The result of the net use command with anonymous access might be, if successful, as shown in Listing 4-49.

> **NOTE** This event log is available in this chapter's downloads, in the Explicit Use of Anonymous Credentials.evtx file.

Listing 4-49: Event ID 4624: An account was successfully logged on.

```
Task Category: Logon
Keywords: Audit Success
Subject:
      Security ID:            S-1-0-0 (NULL SID)
      Account Name:           -
      Account Domain:         -
      Logon ID:               0x0
Logon Information:
      Logon Type:             3
      Restricted Admin Mode:  -
      Virtual Account:        %%1843 (No)
      Elevated Token:         %%1843 (No)
Impersonation Level:          %%1833 (Impersonation)
New Logon:
      Security ID:            S-1-5-7 (ANONYMOUS LOGON)
      Account Name:           ANONYMOUS LOGON
      Account Domain:         NT AUTHORITY
      Logon ID:               0x281BA25
```

```
        Linked Logon ID:        0x0
        Network Account Name:   -
        Network Account Domain: -
        Logon GUID:             {00000000-0000-0000-0000-000000000000}
Process Information:
        Process ID:             0x0
        Process Name:           -
Network Information:
        Workstation Name:       2016SRV
        Source Network Address: 10.0.0.15
        Source Port:            50577
Detailed Authentication Information:
        Logon Process:          NtLmSsp
        Authentication Package: NTLM
        Transited Services:     -
        Package Name (NTLM only): NTLM V1
        Key Length:             128
```

In this event you might see the hostname (`Workstation Name`) and IP address (`Source Network Address`) from which the logon was initiated. The Workstation Name field contains the name of a source machine only if NTLM-family protocol is used, which is the case for anonymous logons, because only Kerberos does not support anonymous authentication.

The `Detailed Authentication Information` section contains additional details about the authentication protocol, logon process, and authentication package. The `Logon Process` and `Authentication Package` fields were discussed in the "Step 9: Local User Logon: MSV1_0 Answer" section earlier this chapter. For more information about the `Transited Services`, `Package Name (NTLM only)`, and `Key Length` fields, see Chapter 9.

Use of Account That Has No Network Credentials

Some of the accounts, such as the LOCAL SERVICE account, exist only within a host and when these accounts are used for network communications the system uses ANONYMOUS LOGON. It is easy to reproduce this by creating a scheduled task that runs under the LOCAL SERVICE account, as an Action set something like `explorer \\`*`remote_host_name`*`\c$`. When you run this scheduled task you will receive an ANONYMOUS LOGON logon event on the target host.

Computer Account Activity from Non–Domain-Joined Machine

When computer account identities (LOCAL SYSTEM, NETWORK SERVICE) are used to access any network resource from a non–domain-joined machine, the system tries anonymous access. You can reproduce such activity using the method described in the previous section. Create a scheduled task on non–domain-joined machine, which runs under a LOCAL SYSTEM or NETWORK SERVICE account, as an Action set something like `explorer \\remote_host_name\c$`. When you run this scheduled task you will receive an ANONYMOUS LOGON logon event on the target host.

Allow Local System to Use Computer Identity for NTLM

There is legacy compatibility behavior in which processes running as a LOCAL SYSTEM account would become anonymous if they fell back to NTLM authentication. Back in Windows NT4, computers were not first-class principals and could not perform user authentication. As a result, processes that ran as the system were anonymous in network authentication. Prior to Windows 7 and Windows Server 2008 R2, this remained the default behavior in order to preserve compatibility with Windows NT4. In Windows 7 and Windows Server 2008 R2, the default behavior was changed and the "Network security: Allow Local System to use computer identity for NTLM" policy setting was added to control this behavior. The policy setting is located under Computer Policy\Windows Settings\Security Settings\Local Policies\Security Options. The policy setting can be applied to Windows Vista or Windows Server 2008 hosts. Figure 4-8 shows an example of this group policy setting.

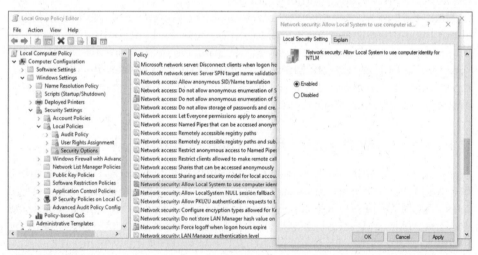

Figure 4-8: "Network security: Allow Local System to use computer identity for NTLM" group policy setting

Considering this information, computers running Windows versions prior to Windows 7 and Windows Server 2008 R2 will use ANONYMOUS LOGON for NTLM authentication when a LOCAL SYSTEM account is used. Also, the same behavior will occur if the "Network security: Allow Local System to use computer identity for NTLM" policy setting is disabled on a host.

CHAPTER 5

Local User Accounts

All Microsoft Windows operating system versions have number of pre-defined built-in local user accounts. These accounts have different purposes depending on which operating system version is in use or which OS features, software, and roles are installed/enabled. All these accounts have different default property values that depend on many variables, which we discuss further in this chapter.

Some of these local user accounts, such as the built-in "Guest" account, are disabled by default and, in most companies, should remain disabled. Some other accounts, such as the built-in local "Administrator" account on the Microsoft Windows server family operating systems, are enabled by default and usually remain enabled in most companies.

Highly privileged local accounts, such as the built-in local Administrator account, should also be monitored for each modification and action performed by such accounts.

This chapter provides information about different built-in local user accounts on Microsoft Windows operating systems and specific monitoring scenarios for the most important operations/changes done to these accounts.

Built-in Local User Accounts

As a first step in the process of learning about possible anomalous behavior related to built-in local user accounts you should, first of all, know which built-in local user accounts exist on different Microsoft Windows operating system versions. You should know their default settings, purpose, group membership information, and so on. This section covers the information you need to know about default Windows local accounts.

Administrator

This account considered the most privileged default user account on Windows operating systems.

THE BUILT-IN LOCALSYSTEM ACCOUNT

Strictly speaking, the most privileged account in the Windows operating system is the LocalSystem account (also appears as System or Local System account). This account, basically, represents the operating system itself. It has no password and there is no ability to see and change its properties using default tools, such as the Computer Management snap-in. The LocalSystem account always has the same Security Identifier (SID): S-1-5-19. But this account does not represent any real user and it is not considered to be a *user account* in this book. Nevertheless, this account is mentioned in many chapters of this book, so I've added this brief description.

The built-in local Administrator user account is intended for OS administration, and should be used for administrative tasks only, such as software installation, making changes to operating system settings, changing system registry key values, and so on. This account is usually the first account attackers try to compromise, but many companies still use this account to run, among other things, system services, scheduled tasks, and daily operations.

By default, the built-in local Administrator account has no user privileges and logon rights associated directly to it, but it has privileges and logon rights inherited from membership in the local Administrators security group. The local Administrators security group has the following user privileges (applicable to all modern Microsoft Windows operating system versions):

- Adjust memory quotas for a process
- Back up files and directories
- Bypass traverse checking
- Change the system time

- Change the time zone
- Create a pagefile
- Create global objects
- Create symbolic links
- Debug programs
- Force shutdown from a remote system
- Impersonate a client after authentication
- Increase scheduling priority
- Load and unload device drivers
- Manage auditing and security logs
- Modify firmware environment values
- Obtain an impersonation token for another user in the same session (Windows Server 2016 only)
- Perform volume maintenance tasks
- Profile single process
- Profile system performance
- Remove computer from docking station
- Restore files and directories
- Shut down the system
- Take ownership of files or other objects

The local Administrators security group has the following user logon rights (applicable to all modern Microsoft Windows OS versions):

- Access this computer from the network (Network logon type)
- Allow log on locally (Interactive logon type)
- Allow log on through Remote Desktop Services (RemoteInteractive logon type)
- Log on as a batch job (Batch logon type)

The built-in local Administrator account has the following default characteristics and parameters, no matter which version of operating system, considering only modern versions, it belongs to:

- It is a member of the local Administrators security group. It cannot be removed from this group.
- It has the "Password never expires" parameter enabled, which means that its password will never expire.

- It cannot be easily locked out or deleted, and doing so may cause significant operational difficulties.

- It has default Relative Identifier (RID) in its SID: 500.

In Microsoft Windows 7, 8, 8.1, and 10 this account is disabled by default. For server operating system versions it is enabled.

If the Microsoft "Homegroup" feature is enabled and the computer is a member of any homegroup, the built-in local Administrator account will also be a member of the HomeUsers local group. The Homegroup feature is available only on Microsoft Windows client operating system versions.

The built-in local Administrator account is automatically enabled when the computer is booted using safe mode. In client operating system versions, the built-in local Administrator account is usually treated as an "emergency account" that should be used in case a user forgets the password for the normal local user account, which typically is created during the operating system installation. In server operating systems this account is also used as an "emergency account" or "break glass" account.

Guest

The Guest account is considered to be the least privileged default user account in the Windows operating system. It is designed to be used when you need to provide limited access to your computer to someone for Internet browsing or access to some default applications like Calculator or WordPad.

By default, the Guest account is not a member of any User Rights group policy settings on Windows *server* operating systems. But on *client* operating systems (Windows 7, 8, 8.1, and 10) it is a member of the following User Rights and Logon Rights group policy settings:

- Allow log on locally (Interactive logon type)

- Deny access to this computer from the network

- Deny log on locally

- Bypass traverse checking (inherited from the Everyone security principal)

Because the Guest account is included in the "Deny log on locally" policy setting on client systems, you will not be able to log on locally using the Guest account right after you enable it. To log on locally, you must first remove it from the "Deny log on locally" local policy setting.

The Guest account has the following default characteristics and parameters no matter which version of operating system it belongs to:

- It is a member of the local Guests security group.

- It has the "Password never expires" parameter enabled, which means that its password will never expire even if it is empty.

- It has the "User cannot change password" parameter enabled, which prevents anyone using the Guest account from changing or setting the Guest account's password.
- It is disabled.
- It cannot be easily deleted, and doing so may cause significant operational difficulties.
- It has the default Relative Identifier (RID) in its SID: 501.

In general, this account should not be enabled in most companies, because it has only a limited number of scenarios in which it is useful. Also, this account allows for logging on to the system without a password, which is a big security issue.

Custom User Account

During installation, all modern Microsoft Windows client operating systems ask you to create a new local account with local administrative permissions, which should be used instead of the built-in local Administrator account.

By default, a manually created custom user account has no user privileges and logon rights associated directly to it, but it has privileges and logon rights inherited from a membership in the local Administrators security group. See the "Administrator" section earlier in this chapter for more information.

A custom user account has the following default characteristics and parameters no matter which version of operating system it belongs to:

- It is a member of the local Administrators security group.
- It has the "Password never expires" parameter enabled, which means that its password will never expire.

If the Microsoft Homegroup feature is enabled and the computer is a member of any homegroup, the custom user account will also be a member of the HomeUsers local group. The Homegroup feature is available only on Microsoft Windows client operating systems.

In general, this account is used as a regular daily account on non–domain-joined machines.

HomeGroupUser$

The HomeGroupUser$ account is an optional account. It exists only if the Windows Homegroup feature is enabled. This account allows your computer to share files with other computers on your network, if they also have the Homegroup feature enabled and they are members of the same homegroup as your computer. The HomeGroupUser$ account's password acts as a shared secret for communications between computers within the same homegroup.

The Homegroup feature is available only on Microsoft Windows client operating systems.

On client operating systems (Windows 7, 8, 8.1, and 10), if a computer is a member of any homegroup, HomeGroupUser$ is included in the following User Rights local policy settings:

- Deny log on locally
- Deny log on as a batch job

The HomeGroupUser$ account has the following default characteristics and parameters no matter which version of client operating system it belongs to:

- It is a member of local HomeUsers security group.
- It has the "Password never expires" parameter enabled, which means that its password will never expire.

DefaultAccount

The DefaultAccount is a new local account that first appeared in the Windows 10 and Windows Server 2016 operating systems. This account is undocumented and managed by the operating system itself.

By default, the DefaultAccount user account has no user privileges and logon rights associated directly to it or inherited.

The DefaultAccount has the following default characteristics and parameters:

- It is a member of the local System Managed Accounts Group security group.
- It has the "Password never expires" parameter enabled, which means that its password will never expire.
- It is disabled.

If the Microsoft Homegroup feature is enabled and the computer is a member of any homegroup, the DefaultAccount will also be a member of the HomeUsers local group. The Homegroup feature is available only on Microsoft Windows client operating systems.

Built-in Local User Accounts Monitoring Scenarios

In this section you learn about monitoring operations related to user accounts, such as account creation, deletion, change, and so on.

New Local User Account Creation

New local user accounts can be created using multiple ways: manual creation by another user, created as part of installation process of the new software or feature, automatic creation by script or application, and so on. At the end, the result is always the same: a new user account.

The most important questions to answer about monitoring user creation activity are: should someone ever create local user accounts on this machine and if yes, should you be informed about it? Typically, after initial system setup, software installation, creation of system services, and so on, no new local accounts should be created. Because of that, it's recommended that you track all local account creation events and perform root cause analysis, especially on high-priority/critical systems.

Two types of user creation security events exist:

- A user was successfully created.
- An attempt was made to create a user account, but failed for some reason.

In both cases the information you probably want to know is:

- Who created the user account?
- When was the user account created?
- What is the name of newly created account?
- How was this account created?

This information is useful in investigations and is important for monitoring systems.

For unsuccessful account creation events, it is also important to know why an account creation action failed.

Successful Local User Account Creation

The sequence of security events that appears in the security event log when new user account is created using the standard Computer Management snap-in is discussed in this section. The standard user Computer Management snap-in user creation window is shown in Figure 5-1.

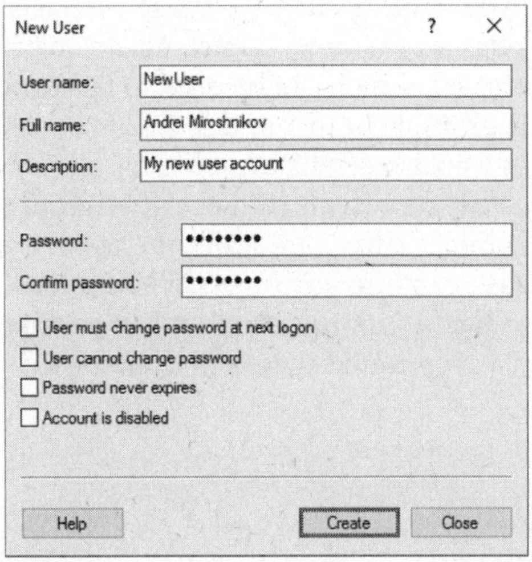

Figure 5-1: User account creation using the Computer Management snap-in

NOTE The event logs described in this section are available in this chapter's downloads, in the `Successful Local User Account Creation.evtx` file.

The events shown in Listing 5-1 appear in the Windows security event log when a new local user account is successfully created:

Listing 5-1: Event ID 4656: A handle to an object was requested.

```
Task Category: SAM
Keywords: Audit Success
Subject:
        Security ID:           S-1-5-21-1913345275-1711810662-261465553-500
        Account Name:          Administrator
        Account Domain:        2016DC
        Logon ID:              0x293F6B
Object:
        Object Server:         Security Account Manager
        Object Type:           SAM_DOMAIN
        Object Name:           2016DC
        Handle ID:             0x184580fcf70
        Resource Attributes:   -
Process Information:
        Process ID:            0x30c
        Process Name:          C:\Windows\System32\lsass.exe
Access Request Information:
        Transaction ID:        {00000000-0000-0000-0000-000000000000}
        Accesses:              %%5392 (ReadPasswordParameters)
                               %%5396 (CreateUser)
                               %%5401 (LookupIDs)

        Access Reasons:        -
        Access Mask:           0x211
        Privileges Used for Access Check: -
        Restricted SID Count: 0
```

The first step in local user account creation is that `CreateUser` access (along with other access types) is requested for the local Security Account Manager (SAM) database, where all local account objects are stored. As a result, an object handle for the SAM database will be returned, which can be used to perform the required operation. The event in this example is an `Audit Success` event, which means that requested access types were successfully granted.

`Object Server:Security Account Manager` represents the Security Account Manager system module, which is responsible for managing the Security Account Manager database. This database contains information about local user accounts, their passwords (stored as hashes), parameters, and so on. You can find more information about Security Account Manager in Chapter 4.

`Object Type:SAM_DOMAIN` represents a type of SAM object for which a handle was requested. The SAM_DOMAIN object type represents an entity of the SAM database domain, usually the machine itself.

This event shows you that the account with the name `Administrator` originated from domain `2016DC` (it's a machine name in this case) and requested the `%%5392` (`ReadPasswordParameters`), `%%5396` (`CreateUser`), and `%%5401` (`LookupIDs`) access permissions for the Security Account Manager's `SAM_DOMAIN` object named `2016DC` (machine name). The request was sent by the process named `C:\Windows\System32\lsass.exe` and `Process ID 0x30c`.

The Windows Event Viewer automatically resolves all access type constants into values. For example, the `%%5392` constant will be shown in the Windows Event Viewer as `ReadPasswordParameters`.

The `Access Mask` field contains a hexadecimal value for the sum of requested access rights. Table 5-1 contains a list of constants and access mask values that are defined for `SAM_DOMAIN` object type in Windows operating systems.

Table 5-1: SAM_DOMAIN Object Access Rights

ACCESS MASK	CONSTANT	VALUE
0x01	%%5392	ReadPasswordParameters
0x02	%%5393	WritePasswordParameters
0x04	%%5394	ReadOtherParameters
0x08	%%5395	WriteOtherParameters
0x10	%%5396	CreateUser
0x20	%%5397	CreateGlobalGroup
0x40	%%5398	CreateLocalGroup
0x80	%%5399	GetLocalGroupMembership
0x100	%%5400	ListAccounts
0x200	%%5401	LookupIDs
0x400	%%5402	AdministerServer

`Access Mask` in the current event has a value of `0x2110`, which is a sum of the following hexadecimal access right constants: `0x200` (`LookupIDs`) + `0x10` (`CreateUser`) + `0x01` (`ReadPasswordParameters`).

The `Subject:Security ID` field contains the Security Identifier (SID) of the security principal that performed this access request. The Windows Event Viewer automatically resolves SIDs whenever possible.

Listing 5-2 is the main event, which shows you that the new account was successfully created.

Listing 5-2: Event ID 4720: A user account was created.

```
Task Category: User Account Management
Keywords: Audit Success
Subject:
        Security ID:          S-1-5-21-1913345275-1711810662-261465553-500
        Account Name:         Administrator
        Account Domain:       2016DC
        Logon ID:             0x293F6B
New Account:
        Security ID:          S-1-5-21-1913345275-1711810662-261465553-1002
        Account Name:         NewUser
        Account Domain:       2016DC
Attributes:
        SAM Account Name:     NewUser
        Display Name:         %%1793 (<value not set>)
        Other fields...
        Password Last Set:    %%1794 (<never>)
        Other fields...
        Primary Group ID:     513
        AllowedToDelegateTo:  -
        Old UAC Value:        0x0
        New UAC Value:        0x15
User Account Control:
                %%2080 (Account Disabled)
                %%2082 ('Password Not Required' - Enabled)
                %%2084 ('Normal Account' - Enabled)
Other fields...
```

This event contains answers for some of our initial questions:

- Who created the user account?

    Answer: `Subject: Account Domain` + `Subject: Account Name`.

- When was the user account created?

    Answer: the event creation time.

The important information here is the `New Account: Account Name` field, because it contains the name of the newly created account.

Note that any local user account created using the Computer Management snap-in, by default, is created in a disabled state and has the `Password Not Required` flag set. Both these attributes/flags will be changed after the account is created, as you see later in this chapter. Also, the default global primary group for all newly created local accounts is the built-in local None security group. You can see it in the `Primary Group ID` attribute value `513`, which is a Relative Identifier (RID) of the built-in local None security group. It means that account has no global primary group. It is interesting to know that in an Active Directory environment, an RID of 513 corresponds to the default Domain Users group, instead of None for non–domain-joined machines. You see more information about the "None" local security group in the next section.

By default, if you use the Computer Management snap-in, local user accounts are created with a blank/empty password and then the password reset operation is performed. That is why the `Password Last Set` attribute for newly created accounts has a value of `%%1794` (`<never>`).

The `Display Name` attribute, by default, is `%%1793` (`<value not set>`).

New user accounts, by default, are created with the following account properties:

■ `%%2080` (`Account Disabled`)

■ `%%2082` (`'Password Not Required' - Enabled`)

■ `%%2084` (`'Normal Account' - Enabled`)

Table 5-2 contains a complete list of user account UAC setting constants and access mask values defined in Windows operating systems.

Table 5-2: User Account UAC Flags

CONSTANT	ACCESS MASK	VALUE
%%2048		Account Enabled
%%2049		'Home Directory Required' - Disabled
%%2050		'Password Not Required' - Disabled
%%2051		'Temp Duplicate Account' - Disabled
%%2052		'Normal Account' - Disabled
%%2053		'MNS Logon Account' - Disabled
%%2054		'Interdomain Trust Account' - Disabled
%%2055		'Workstation Trust Account' - Disabled
%%2056		'Server Trust Account' - Disabled
%%2057		'Don't Expire Password' - Disabled
%%2058		Account Unlocked
%%2059		'Encrypted Text Password Allowed' - Disabled
%%2060		'Smartcard Required' - Disabled
%%2061		'Trusted For Delegation' - Disabled
%%2062		'Not Delegated' - Disabled
%%2063		'Use DES Key Only' - Disabled
%%2064		'Don't Require Preauth' - Disabled

Continues

Table 5-2 (*continued*)

CONSTANT	ACCESS MASK	VALUE
%%2065		'Password Expired' - Disabled
%%2066		'Trusted To Authenticate For Delegation' - Disabled
%%2067		'Exclude Authorization Information' - Disabled
%%2068		'Undefined UserAccountControl Bit 20' - Disabled
%%2069		'Protect Kerberos Service Tickets with AES Keys' - Disabled
%%2080	0x01	Account Disabled
%%2081	0x02	'Home Directory Required' - Enabled
%%2082	0x04	'Password Not Required' - Enabled
%%2083	0x08	'Temp Duplicate Account' - Enabled
%%2084	0x10	'Normal Account' - Enabled
%%2085	0x20	'MNS Logon Account' - Enabled
%%2086	0x40	'Interdomain Trust Account' - Enabled
%%2087	0x80	'Workstation Trust Account' - Enabled
%%2088	0x100	'Server Trust Account' - Enabled
%%2089	0x200	'Don't Expire Password' - Enabled
%%2090	0x400	Account Locked
%%2091	0x800	'Encrypted Text Password Allowed' - Enabled
%%2092	0x1000	'Smartcard Required' - Enabled
%%2093	0x2000	'Trusted For Delegation' - Enabled
%%2094	0x4000	'Not Delegated' - Enabled
%%2095	0x8000	'Use DES Key Only' - Enabled
%%2096	0x10000	'Don't Require Preauth' - Enabled
%%2097	0x20000	'Password Expired' - Enabled
%%2098	0x40000	'Trusted To Authenticate For Delegation' - Enabled
%%2099	0x80000	'Exclude Authorization Information' - Enabled
%%2100	0x100000	'Undefined UserAccountControl Bit 20' - Enabled
%%2101	0x200000	'Protect Kerberos Service Tickets with AES Keys' - Enabled

You can also see these flags in a hexadecimal mask in the New UAC Value field. It's equal to 0x15 in our example. Table 5-2 contains all hexadecimal values for all possible UAC flags for user account objects. All flags are disabled by default. You will see more information about Old UAC Value and New UAC Value fields in the "Local User Account Change" section later in this chapter.

This event also contains many other attributes, but they are not as important as those discussed in this section.

As shown in Listing 5-3, immediately after creation, the new user account (Member: Security ID) becomes a member of the built-in *global* None security group, which, basically means this account is not a member of any global group. This built-in group is not displayed by the whoami /groups command or the Computer Management snap-in, but it is a valid local security principal and has an RID of 513.

Listing 5-3: Event ID 4728: A member was added to a security-enabled global group.

```
Task Category: Security Group Management
Keywords: Audit Success
Subject:
        Security ID:         S-1-5-21-1913345275-1711810662-261465553-500
        Account Name:        Administrator
        Account Domain:      2016DC
        Logon ID:            0x293F6B
Member:
        Security ID:         S-1-5-21-1913345275-1711810662-261465553-1002
        Account Name:        -
Group:
        Security ID:         S-1-5-21-1913345275-1711810662-261465553-513
        Group Name:          None
        Group Domain:        2016DC
Other fields...
```

NOTE   It's important to note that this event contains information related to a *global* security group, not local.

The term *global security group* is applicable to the Microsoft Active Directory environment. Local accounts are not members of any global security groups, but local accounts still have the Global Group property, which can be shown using the net user command as shown in Figure 5-2.

The Global Group property might be used by some non-Microsoft systems for specific purposes.

Listing 5-4 shows the account being enabled, because by default all local user accounts that are created using the Computer Management snap-in are created in the disabled state.

Figure 5-2: Local user account properties

Listing 5-4: Event ID 4722: A user account was enabled.

```
Task Category: User Account Management
Keywords: Audit Success
Subject:
        Security ID:            S-1-5-21-1913345275-1711810662-261465553-500
        Account Name:           Administrator
        Account Domain:         2016DC
        Logon ID:               0x293F6B
Target Account:
        Security ID:            S-1-5-21-1913345275-1711810662-261465553-1002
        Account Name:           NewUser
        Account Domain:         2016DC
```

Listing 5-5 shows a password reset event, which informs you about a password set operation performed on a newly created account. The password, which you typed during account creation, is set at this step.

Listing 5-5: Event ID 4724: An attempt was made to reset an account's password.

```
Task Category: User Account Management
Keywords: Audit Success
Subject:
        Security ID:            S-1-5-21-1913345275-1711810662-261465553-500
        Account Name:           Administrator
        Account Domain:         2016DC
        Logon ID:               0x293F6B
```

```
Target Account:
        Security ID:          S-1-5-21-1913345275-1711810662-261465553-1002
        Account Name:         NewUser
        Account Domain:       2016DC
```

The 4738 event shown in Listing 5-6 informs you that the `Password Not Required` UAC flag was set to `Disabled`. Unfortunately, the 4738 event doesn't really show you which attribute was changed; it just shows you a value, which can be a newly set value or an unchanged current value. For example, in this case it's not clear whether `Password Last Set` changed or still shows its previous/current value. The `User Account Control` section shows only information about changes; if no changes were made, this section will be empty.

Listing 5-6: Event ID 4738: A user account was changed.

```
Task Category: User Account Management
Keywords: Audit Success
Other fields...
Changed Attributes:
        SAM Account Name:     NewUser
        Display Name:         NewUser
        Password Last Set:    12/21/2016 11:29:46 AM
        User Account Control:
                %%2048 (Account Enabled)
                %%2050 ('Password Not Required' - Disabled)
        Other fields...
```

This event also shows that the `Display Name` user account property got the same value as the `SAM Account Name` field.

The 4738 event will be covered in more detail later in this book.

The event in Listing 5-7 informs you that the previously opened handle with ID `0x184580fcf70` was closed. This handle was opened for the `CreateUser` operation for the Security Account Manager `SAM_DOMAIN 2016DC` object.

Listing 5-7: Event ID 4658: The handle to an object was closed.

```
Task Category: Other Object Access Events
Keywords: Audit Success
Other fields...
Object:
        Object Server:        Security Account Manager
        Handle ID:            0x184580fcf70
Other fields...
```

The event in Listing 5-8 exists only on Windows Server 2016 and Windows 10 operating systems. Multiple 4798 events are shown in the security event log during new local user account creation.

Listing 5-8: Event ID 4798: A user's local group membership was enumerated.

```
Task Category: User Account Management
Keywords: Audit Success
Subject:
        Security ID:          S-1-5-21-1913345275-1711810662-261465553-500
        Account Name:         Administrator
        Account Domain:       2016DC
        Logon ID:             0x293F6B
User:
        Security ID:          S-1-5-21-1913345275-1711810662-261465553-1002
        Account Name:         NewUser
        Account Domain:       2016DC
Process Information:
        Process ID:           0xe54
        Process Name:         C:\Windows\System32\mmc.exe
```

Event 4798 informs you that the `Administrator` account (`Subject`) enumerated the local group membership of the `NewUser` account (`User`) using `C:\Windows\System32\mmc.exe`. This means that one of the Microsoft Management Console (MMC) tools were used—in this case it was `usermgmt.msc`.

This event is informational only in the case of new user creation.

Listing 5-9 shows that at this time some access types (`Accesses`) are requested for the Security Account Manager's `SAM_USER` object with the name `DOMAINS\Account\Users\000003EA`.

Listing 5-9: Event ID 4656: A handle to an object was requested.

```
Task Category: SAM
Keywords: Audit Success
Subject:
        Security ID:          S-1-5-21-1913345275-1711810662-261465553-500
        Account Name:         Administrator
        Account Domain:       2016DC
        Logon ID:             0x293F6B
Object:
        Object Server:        Security Account Manager
        Object Type:          SAM_USER
        Object Name:          DOMAINS\Account\Users\000003EA
        Handle ID:            0x184580fc100
        Resource Attributes: -
Process Information:
        Process ID:           0x30c
        Process Name:         C:\Windows\System32\lsass.exe
Access Request Information:
        Transaction ID:       {00000000-0000-0000-0000-000000000000}
        Accesses:             %%1538 (READ_CONTROL)
                              %%1539 (WRITE_DAC)
                              %%5442 (WritePreferences)
                              %%5444 (ReadAccount)
```

```
                                    %%5445 (WriteAccount)
                                    %%5447 (SetPassword (without knowledge of old
                                                password))
                                    %%5448 (ListGroups)
Access Mask:                        0x601B4
Other fields...
```

The `SAM_USER` object type represents a local user account entity.
`DOMAINS\Account\Users\000003EA` is a path in the Security Account Manager database to the object to which access was requested.

SECURITY ACCOUNT MANAGER DATABASE

One method to see what the SAM database looks like is to use the built-in Windows Registry Editor application. Perform the following steps to see the SAM database content:

1. Run the `regedit` command with administrative privileges.

2. Navigate to the `\HKEY_LOCAL_MACHINE\SAM\SAM` registry key.

3. Assign "Read" permissions to your account for this registry key.

Now you can see what is inside the SAM database (Figure 5-3).

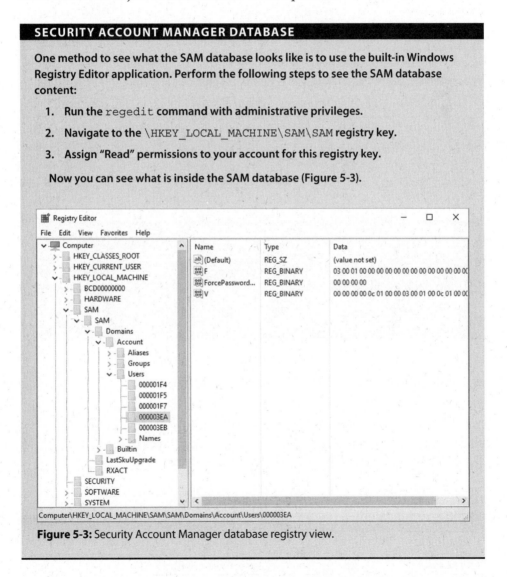

Figure 5-3: Security Account Manager database registry view.

`000003EA` represents the account's RID in hexadecimal format, which is 1002 in decimal. It is the RID of our newly created account.

You can use the following PowerShell code to get the SID of a specific local user account:

```
$objUser = New-Object System.Security.Principal.NTAccount
                                ("ACCOUNT_NAME")
$strSID = $objUser.Translate([System.Security.Principal.
                                SecurityIdentifier])
$strSID.Value
```

Figure 5-4 shows an example of an output of this script for the "newuser" local account.

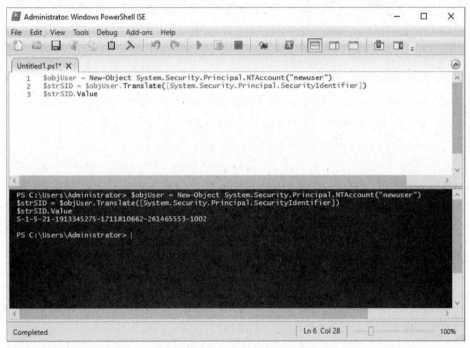

Figure 5-4: Local user account SID extraction using PowerShell

The `Accesses` field contains a list of access rights requested for the `SAM_USER` object. Table 5-3 contains a list of access right constants that are defined for `SAM_USER` object types in Windows operating systems.

Table 5-3: SAM_USER Object Access Right Constants

CONSTANT	ACCESS MASK	TEXT
%%5440	0x01	ReadGeneralInformation
%%5441	0x02	ReadPreferences
%%5442	0x04	WritePreferences

CONSTANT	ACCESS MASK	TEXT
%%5443	0x08	ReadLogon
%%5444	0x10	ReadAccount
%%5445	0x20	WriteAccount
%%5446	0x40	ChangePassword (with knowledge of old password)
%%5447	0x80	SetPassword (without knowledge of old password)
%%5448	0x100	ListGroups
%%5449	0x200	ReadGroupMembership
%%5450	0x400	ChangeGroupMembership

The Access Mask field contains the hexadecimal value for the sum of requested access rights.

The Access Mask in the current event is 0x601B4, which is a sum of the following SAM_USER object access rights: 0x04 (WritePreferences) + 0x10 (ReadAccount) + 0x20 (WriteAccount) + 0x80 (SetPassword (without knowledge of old password)) + 0x100 (ListGroups) and the standard access rights 0x20000 (READ_CONTROL) + 0x40000 (WRITE_DAC). The following sidebar contains information about standard access rights.

STANDARD ACCESS RIGHTS

Many objects in the Windows operating system have specific access rights, applicable only to a specific object type. For example, the SAM_USER Security Account Manager object has the SetPassword (without knowledge of old password) access right, which is a unique access right applicable only to this object type.

At the same time there are access rights that are applicable to almost all securable object types. These access rights are called *standard access rights*.

Table 5-4 contains the list of standard access rights.

Table 5-4: Standard Access Rights

HEX VALUE	CONSTANT	VALUE
0x10000	%%1537	DELETE
0x20000	%%1538	READ_CONTROL
0x40000	%%1539	WRITE_DAC
0x80000	%%1540	WRITE_OWNER
0x100000	%%1541	SYNCHRONIZE
0x200000	%%1542	ACCESS_SYS_SEC
0x400000	%%1543	MAX_ALLOWED

Returning to the event in Listing 5-9, basically speaking, it shows you that some access types were successfully requested for our newly created user account SAM object.

The event in Listing 5-10 shows us that the user account's Display Name property was changed to Andrei Miroshnikov. But, as I already mentioned, for some properties (Display Name is one of them) this event always shows a value, whether was it changed or not, and in this case you can only guess whether this property changed or not. In this example we know that it was changed only because we made the change. In practice, you wouldn't know by looking at this.

Listing 5-10: Event ID 4738: A user account was changed.

```
Task Category: User Account Management
Keywords: Audit Success
Subject:
        Security ID:           S-1-5-21-1913345275-1711810662-261465553-500
        Account Name:          Administrator
        Account Domain:        2016DC
        Logon ID:              0x293F6B
Target Account:
        Security ID:           S-1-5-21-1913345275-1711810662-261465553-1002
        Account Name:          NewUser
        Account Domain:        2016DC
Changed Attributes:
        SAM Account Name:      NewUser
        Display Name:          Andrei Miroshnikov
Other fields...
```

Then, as Listing 5-11 shows, the handle with ID 0x184580fc100 was closed.

Listing 5-11: Event ID 4658: The handle to an object was closed.

```
Task Category: SAM
Keywords: Audit Success
```

Next, a handle request event is issued for the Security Account Manager's SAM_USER object with the name DOMAINS\Account\Users\000003EA. Refer to Listing 5-9; this request is identical.

The event in Listing 5-12 is absolutely the same as the previous 4738 event in Listing 5-10. One of the problems related to the "4738: A user account was changed" event is that for some actions it triggers but doesn't show the real change that causes it. For example, when the user account description (Description property) changes it triggers a 4738 event, but doesn't show the Description property change in the event itself. Because there is no information about this change in the event, you can only guess what really was changed.

Listing 5-12: Event ID 4738: A user account was changed.

```
Task Category: User Account Management
Keywords: Audit Success
Subject:
        Security ID:          S-1-5-21-1913345275-1711810662-261465553-500
        Account Name:         Administrator
        Account Domain:       2016DC
        Logon ID:             0x293F6B
Target Account:
        Security ID:          S-1-5-21-1913345275-1711810662-261465553-1002
        Account Name:         NewUser
        Account Domain:       2016DC
Changed Attributes:
        SAM Account Name:     NewUser
        Display Name:         Andrei Miroshnikov
Other fields...
```

So, this event shows us that something was changed in the user account `NewUser` but it does not tell us what exactly was changed.

Listing 5-13 shows that the handle, which was opened for the previous account change operation, was closed.

Listing 5-13: Event ID 4658: The handle to an object was closed.

```
Task Category: SAM
Keywords: Audit Success
```

The event in Listing 5-14 shows that some access permissions (`Accesses`) are requested for the Security Account Manager's `SAM_ALIAS` object with the name "`DOMAINS\Builtin\Aliases\00000221`".

Listing 5-14: Event ID 4656: A handle to an object was requested.

```
Task Category: SAM
Keywords: Audit Success
Subject:
        Security ID:          S-1-5-21-1913345275-1711810662-261465553-500
        Account Name:         Administrator
        Account Domain:       2016DC
        Logon ID:             0x293F6B
Object:
        Object Server:        Security Account Manager
        Object Type:          SAM_ALIAS
        Object Name:          DOMAINS\Builtin\Aliases\00000221
        Handle ID:            0x184580fb290
        Resource Attributes:
Process Information:
        Process ID:           0x30c
        Process Name:         C:\Windows\System32\lsass.exe
```

```
Access Request Information:
        Transaction ID:        {00000000-0000-0000-0000-000000000000}
        Accesses:              %%5424 (AddMember)
                               %%5425 (RemoveMember)
                               %%5426 (ListMembers)
                               %%5427 (ReadInformation)
Access Mask:        0xF
Other fields...
```

The `SAM_ALIAS` object type represents the local security group entity.

`DOMAINS\Builtin\Aliases\00000221` is a path in the Security Account Manager database to the object to which access was requested. You already know how you can view the real object in the SAM database using `regedit.exe` application. The hexadecimal value `0x221` converts into decimal `545` and belongs to the built-in local Users security group.

This event shows you that the handle for the local Users security group was requested, which allows the following: operations: `AddMember`, `RemoveMember`, `ListMembers`, and `ReadInformation`.

The `Access Mask` field contains a hexadecimal value for the sum of the requested access permissions. Possible access permissions for the `SAM_ALIAS` object are listed in Table 5-5.

Table 5-5: SAM_ALIAS Object Access Permissions

ACCESS MASK	CONSTANT	PERMISSION
0x01	%%5424	AddMember
0x02	%%5425	RemoveMember
0x04	%%5426	ListMembers
0x08	%%5427	ReadInformation
0x10	%%5428	WriteAccount

The `Access Mask` in the current event is `0xF`, which is a sum of the following `SAM_ALIAS` object access rights: `0x01` (AddMember) + `0x02` (RemoveMember) + `0x04` (ListMembers) + `0x08` (ReadInformation).

Listing 5-15 shows the next event which, as expected, tells you that the account with SID `S-1-5-21-3815211123-123488468-2019406087-1002` (NewUser) was added to the security group with SID `S-1-5-32-545` (Users) by the `Administrator` account. Unfortunately, the `Member: Account Name` field is designed to show information only about domain accounts, not local accounts. For domain accounts it shows the account's distinguished name (DN).

Listing 5-15: Event ID 4732: A member was added to a security-enabled local group.

```
Task Category: Security Group Management
Keywords: Audit Success
Subject:
       Security ID:         S-1-5-21-1913345275-1711810662-261465553-500
       Account Name:        Administrator
       Account Domain:      2016DC
       Logon ID:            0x293F6B
Member:
       Security ID:         S-1-5-21-1913345275-1711810662-261465553-1002
       Account Name:        -
Group:
       Security ID:         S-1-5-32-545
       Group Name:          Users
       Group Domain:        Builtin
```

Listing 5-16 shows that the handle, which was opened for the previous group membership change operation, was closed.

Listing 5-16: Event ID 4658: The handle to an object was closed.

```
Task Category: SAM
Keywords: Audit Success
```

Now you know the sequence of events that shows in the Security event log each time a new local user account is created using the Computer Management snap-in. And now you know the answers for the following questions (see Listing 5-2: Event ID 4720: A user account was created.):

- Who created the user account?

  The answer is in the event Subject section.

- When was the user account created?

  Event 4720 provides the event creation time.

- The name of newly created account?

  The account name is shown in the event New Account section.

- How was this account created?

  There is no easy way to detect how exactly the account was created, using which tools, scripts, applications, or other methods. A general recommendation here is to inspect all events prior to the account creation event and try to find any information about methods being used to create the account. For example, you may search for the "4688: A new process has been created" event to find the name of the application that was run right before the account was created.

  Sometimes you may find some useful events in the "Application" event log that were generated at the same time the user account was created.

Unsuccessful Local User Account Creation: Access Denied

The unsuccessful local user account creation events sequence, where the `Subject` account had no required permissions to create new local account, has only one event in it, shown in Listing 5-17.

Listing 5-17: Event ID 4656: A handle to an object was requested.

```
Task Category: SAM
Keywords: Audit Failure
Subject:
        Security ID:           S-1-5-21-1913345275-1711810662-261465553-1003
        Account Name:          amirosh
        Account Domain:        2016DC
        Logon ID:              0x34EC46
Object:
        Object Server:         Security Account Manager
        Object Type:           SAM_DOMAIN
        Object Name:           2016DC
        Handle ID:             0x0
        Resource Attributes:   -
Process Information:
        Process ID:            0x30c
        Process Name:          C:\Windows\System32\lsass.exe
Access Request Information:
        Transaction ID:        {00000000-0000-0000-0000-000000000000}
        Accesses:              %%5392 (ReadPasswordParameters)
                               %%5396 (CreateUser)
                               %%5401 (LookupIDs)
        Access Mask:           0x211
```

NOTE The event logs described in this section are available in this chapter's downloads, in the `Unsuccessful Local User Account Creation - Access Denied. evtx` file.

This is a failed handle request event. It is almost the same as the 4656 handle request event that you saw for the successful local user account creation operation in the Listing 5-1, but in this case it has an `Audit Failure` event type.

This event shows you that account `amirosh` (`Subject`) requested `ReadPasswordParameters`, `CreateUser`, and `LookupIDs` access types for the `SAM_DOMAIN` `2016DC` Security Account Manager object and the request failed.

Here are the answers for the most important questions you might have about a failed local account creation event, where the reason for the failure is "access denied" (see Listing 5-17: Event ID 4656: A handle to an object was requested):

- Who tried to create new user account?

  The answer is in the Subject section.

- When did this happen?

  4656 is the Audit Failure event creation time.

- How did it happen?

  In an Audit Failure event you can see information about the process that was used for the handle request operation (Process Information section).

- Where can I find more details about the account that is supposed to be created?

  There is no event in the security event log that provides this information You might try to find this information in the application-specific logs.

Unsuccessful Local User Account Creation: Other

If the Subject account has all required permissions to create a new local user account but the creation operation failed for some other reason (for example, a user account with the same name already exists), you will find the event shown in Listing 5-18 in the security event log.

Listing 5-18: Event ID 4656: A handle to an object was requested.

```
Task Category: SAM
Keywords: Audit Success
Subject:
        Security ID:          S-1-5-21-1913345275-1711810662-261465553-500
        Account Name:         Administrator
        Account Domain:       2016DC
        Logon ID:             0xA603F9
Object:
        Object Server:        Security Account Manager
        Object Type:          SAM_DOMAIN
        Object Name:          2016DC
        Handle ID:            0x184580fadc0
        Resource Attributes:  -
Process Information:
        Process ID:           0x30c
        Process Name:         C:\Windows\System32\lsass.exe
Access Request Information:
        Transaction ID:       {00000000-0000-0000-0000-000000000000}
        Accesses:             %%5392 (ReadPasswordParameters)
                              %%5396 (CreateUser)
                              %%5401 (LookupIDs)
```

NOTE   The event logs described in this section are available in this chapter's downloads, in the Unsuccessful Local User Account Creation - other.evtx file.

Because the Subject account has all required permissions to create new local user accounts, it will not have any problems getting a handle to the SAM_DOMAIN COMPUTER_NAME Security Account Manager object with the CreateUser access permission.

However, after the handle is received by Subject, the account creation operation may fail at the application level and no more events will be recorded in the security event log. In this situation only the "ID 4658: The handle to an object was closed" Audit Success event will be recorded after a successful "ID 4656: A handle to an object was requested" event.

But this event still must be considered a new local user account creation attempt by an account with sufficient permissions, which failed for some other reason.

Monitoring Scenarios: Local User Account Creation

Useful events to monitor for successful and unsuccessful local user account creation are shown in Table 5-6.

Table 5-6: Events to Monitor for Local User Account Creation

SUCCESSFUL LOCAL ACCOUNT CREATION		
SECURITY EVENT	SUBCATEGORY	EVENT TYPE
4720: A user account was created	User Account Management	Audit Success
UNSUCCESSFUL LOCAL ACCOUNT CREATION		
SECURITY EVENT	SUBCATEGORY	EVENT TYPE
4656: A handle to an object was requested	SAM	Audit Failure
4656: A handle to an object was requested	SAM	Audit Success

Any successful local user account creation events should be monitored on high-value and critical hosts. Usually, after initial system setup, no local user accounts are created. Each local account creation event must be investigated and the root cause of this operation must be found.

Some scenarios in which a new local user account needs to be created include:

- By malware, as persistence method for the malware to remain in the system
- By software, server role, or feature installation
- Manually, as a dedicated account for system service or scheduled tasks

You should monitor for any "4720: A user account was created" Audit Success events.

On high-value and critical hosts, monitor for any unsuccessful local user account creation event that fails due to insufficient access permissions. Each such attempt is important because someone or something tried to create a local user account without having required permissions.

In this case you should monitor for "4656. A handle to an object was requested" Audit Failure events with an Access Mask field equal to "0x211" and the Object Type field equal to SAM_DOMAIN.

The XPath filter for this is shown in the following code:

```
*[System[band(Keywords,4503599627370496) and (EventID=4656)]] and
*[EventData[Data[@Name='ObjectType'] and (Data='SAM_DOMAIN')]] and
*[EventData[Data[@Name='AccessMask'] ='0x211']]
```

It is recommended that you have a list of accounts (domain and local) that are allowed to create local user accounts. If you have such a list, you should compare every "4720: A user account was created" event Subject field with this list.

For example, you know that only Domain Admins should be used to create local user accounts on domain-joined machines. You should compare the Security ID field with the SIDs of all Domain Admins accounts in order to verify that. In this case you should set an event importance level to "High" if any other account was used to create a local user account.

For non–domain-joined machines, for example, only the built-in local Administrator account should be used to create new local user accounts by default. In this case you could check the Account Name field in the 4720 event—it should have an "Administrator" value. Or, you can check that the Security ID value has an RID of 500.

Monitor these events:

- Monitor for "4720: A user account was created" Audit Success events.

- Monitor for "4656: A handle to an object was requested" Audit Failure events with an Access Mask field value equal to "0x211" and the Object Type field value equal to SAM_DOMAIN.

- Monitor for "4656: A handle to an object was requested" Audit Success events where the Access Mask field value equals "0x211" and the Object Type equals SAM_DOMAIN. Unfortunately, in this case, there is no information in the event about whether the account creation operation completed successfully or not. You need to also verify whether there are any "4720: A user account was created" events in the event log after the "4656: A handle to an object was requested" event. If not, the account creation attempt was not successful.

All local user accounts created using built-in Windows operating system tools (such as the Computer Management snap-in, the `net user` command, and so on) have the following default property values in the "4720: A user account was created" event:

- Primary Group ID: 513
- New Uac Value: 0x15, which means:
  - Account Disabled
  - 'Password Not Required' - Enabled
  - 'Normal Account' - Enabled

Check that all "4720: A user account was created" events have these properties set to their default values using the following snippets. This method might help you to detect local user account creation actions that were performed using nondefault system tools/applications.

The XPath filter for `Primary Group ID != 513` is:

```
*[System[band(Keywords,9007199254740992) and (EventID=4720)]] and
*[EventData[Data[@Name='PrimaryGroupID'] !='513']]
```

The XPath filter for `NewUacValue != 0x15` is:

```
*[System[band(Keywords,9007199254740992) and (EventID=4720)]] and
*[EventData[Data[@Name='NewUacValue'] !='0x15']]
```

You can verify that all newly created local user accounts follow a specific naming convention. Check the `New Account: Account Name` field value in the "4720: A user account was created" event for naming convention rules.

Local User Account Deletion

Local user accounts are usually deleted manually or as one of the steps during an application or feature removal/uninstall operation. These events are not routine or common for hosts, which is why I recommend monitoring for any such event, especially on high-value and critical hosts. This section presents information about detection methods for both successful and unsuccessful local user account deletion attempts.

When there is a successful local account deletion operation it is good to know the answers to the following questions:

- Who deleted the user account?
- When was the user account deleted?
- Which account was deleted?
- How was this account deleted?

For unsuccessful account deletion attempts you also should know why the deletion attempt was unsuccessful.

Successful Local User Account Deletion

To better understand the local user account deletion process, look at the events that appear in the Windows security event log when a local account is deleted using the standard Computer Management snap-in.

> **NOTE** The event logs described in this section are available in this chapter's downloads, in the `Successful Local User Account Deletion.evtx` file.

The event shown in Listing 5-19 exists only on Windows Server 2016 and Windows 10.

Listing 5-19: Event ID 4798: A user's local group membership was enumerated.

```
Task Category: User Account Management
Keywords: Audit Success
Subject:
        Security ID:            S-1-5-21-1913345275-1711810662-261465553-500
        Account Name:           Administrator
        Account Domain:         2016DC
        Logon ID:               0x471386
User:
        Security ID:            S-1-5-21-1913345275-1711810662-261465553-1002
        Account Name:           NewUser
        Account Domain:         2016DC
Process Information:
        Process ID:             0x1244
        Process Name:           C:\Windows\System32\mmc.exe
```

It is mostly for informational purposes and informs you that account `Administrator` (`Subject`) enumerated the group membership of the `NewUser` account (`User`) using `C:\Windows\System32\mmc.exe`.

Listing 5-20 shows an important access request event for the `DOMAINS\Builtin\Aliases\00000221 SAM_ALIAS` SAM object (you already know that it is the built-in local `Users` group) for the `RemoveMember` access permission.

Listing 5-20: Event ID 4656: A handle to an object was requested.

```
Task Category: SAM
Keywords: Audit Success
Subject:
        Security ID:            S-1-5-21-1913345275-1711810662-261465553-500
        Account Name:           Administrator
        Account Domain:         2016DC
        Logon ID:               0x471386
```

```
Object:
        Object Server:          Security Account Manager
        Object Type:            SAM_ALIAS
        Object Name:            DOMAINS\Builtin\Aliases\00000221
        Handle ID:              0x184580fd910
        Resource Attributes:    -
Process Information:
        Process ID:             0x30c
        Process Name:           C:\Windows\System32\lsass.exe
Access Request Information:
        Transaction ID:         {00000000-0000-0000-0000-000000000000}
        Accesses:               %%5425 (RemoveMember)
        Access Mask:            0x2
Other fields...
```

This user account should be removed from all groups when it's deleted. This handle request action for one of the groups the deleted user belongs to is a first step in the user deletion process. In this example the deleted user is a member of only one local security group: Users.

The event shown in Listing 5-21 informs you that the account with SID S-1-5-21-1913345275-1711810662-261465553-1002 was successfully removed from the Builtin\Users local group.

Listing 5-21: Event ID 4733: A member was removed from a security-enabled local group.

```
Task Category: SAM
Keywords: Audit Success
Subject:
        Security ID:            S-1-5-21-1913345275-1711810662-261465553-500
        Account Name:           Administrator
        Account Domain:         2016DC
        Logon ID:               0x471386
Member:
        Security ID:            S-1-5-21-1913345275-1711810662-261465553-1002
        Account Name:           -
Group:
        Security ID:            S-1-5-32-545
        Group Name:             Users
        Group Domain:           Builtin
Other fields...
```

The handle 0x184580fd910, which was previously opened to remove the deleted user from the "Users" local security group, was closed (Listing 5-22).

Listing 5-22: Event ID 4658: The handle to an object was closed.

```
Task Category: SAM
Keywords: Audit Success
```

As you saw in the "Successful Local User Creation" section earlier in this chapter, during account creation, the account is added to the None global security group. When an account is deleted, it also needs to be removed from this None global security group (Listing 5-23).

Listing 5-23: Event ID 4729: A member was removed from a security-enabled global group.

```
Task Category: Security Group Management
Keywords: Audit Success
Subject:
        Security ID:           S-1-5-21-1913345275-1711810662-261465553-500
        Account Name:          Administrator
        Account Domain:        2016DC
        Logon ID:              0x471386
Member:
        Security ID:           S-1-5-21-1913345275-1711810662-261465553-1002
        Account Name:          -
Group:
        Security ID:           S-1-5-21-1913345275-1711810662-261465553-513
        Group Name:            None
        Group Domain:          2016DC
Other fields...
```

Listing 5-24 is a handle request for DELETE access for the local SAM_USER account DOMAINS\Account\Users\000003EA object (NewUser) in the SAM database. This handle will be used later for an account deletion operation.

Listing 5-24: Event ID 4656: A handle to an object was requested.

```
Task Category: SAM
Keywords: Audit Success
Subject:
        Security ID:           S-1-5-21-1913345275-1711810662-261465553-500
        Account Name:          Administrator
        Account Domain:        2016DC
        Logon ID:              0x471386
Object:
        Object Server:         Security Account Manager
        Object Type:           SAM_USER
        Object Name:           DOMAINS\Account\Users\000003EA
        Handle ID:             0x184580fc5d0
        Resource Attributes:   -
Process Information:
        Process ID:            0x30c
        Process Name:          C:\Windows\System32\lsass.exe
Access Request Information:
        Transaction ID:        {00000000-0000-0000-0000-000000000000}
        Accesses:              %%1537 (DELETE)
        Access Mask:           0x10000
Other fields...
```

Listing 5-25 is the main security event, which informs you about successful user account deletion. In this event you can see who (Subject) deleted which (Target Account) account. There is no information about how or using which tool the account was deleted in this event.

Listing 5-25: Event ID 4726: A user account was deleted.

```
Task Category: User Account Management
Keywords: Audit Success
Subject:
        Security ID:            S-1-5-21-1913345275-1711810662-261465553-500
        Account Name:           Administrator
        Account Domain:         2016DC
        Logon ID:               0x471386
Target Account:
        Security ID:            S-1-5-21-1913345275-1711810662-261465553-1002
        Account Name:           NewUser
        Account Domain:         2016DC
```

Event 4726 is the most important event for account deletion, which shows you the fact that account was successfully deleted.

Because a user account object in the SAM database was deleted, there is also a separate 4660 event (Listing 5-26) that informs you about changes in the SAM database.

Listing 5-26: Event ID 4660: An object was deleted.

```
Task Category: Other Object Access Events
Keywords: Audit Success
Subject:
        Security ID:            S-1-5-21-1913345275-1711810662-261465553-500
        Account Name:           Administrator
        Account Domain:         2016DC
        Logon ID:               0x471386
Object:
        Object Server:          Security Account Manager
        Handle ID:              0x184580fc5d0
Process Information:
        Process ID:             0x30c
        Process Name:           C:\Windows\System32\lsass.exe
        Transaction ID:         {00000000-0000-0000-0000-000000000000}
```

There is no detailed information about the object that was deleted, but it is possible to find a "4656: A handle to an object was requested" event with the same handle ID (0x184580fc5d0) and get the details. You already saw the corresponding 4656 event in Listing 5-24.

Listing 5-27 shows that the handle 0x184580fc5d0, which was previously opened to delete the NewUser account, was closed.

Listing 5-27: Event ID 4658: The handle to an object was closed.

```
Task Category: SAM
Keywords: Audit Success
```

Here are the answers to the questions posed at the beginning of this section about a successful account deletion operation (see Listing 5-25: Event ID 4726: A user account was deleted):

- Who deleted the user account?

  The answer is in the `Subject` section.

- When was the user account deleted?

  Event "4726: A user account was deleted" provides the event creation time.

- Which account was deleted?

  The answer is in the `Target Account` section.

- How was this account deleted?

  There is no easy way to detect how exactly the account was deleted, using which tools, scripts, applications, or other methods. A general recommendation here is to inspect all events prior to the account deletion event and try to find any information about methods being used to delete the account. For example, you may search for the "4688: A new process has been created" event to find the name of application that was run right before the account was deleted.

  Sometimes you may find some useful events in the "Application" event log at the same time when the user account was deleted.

Unsuccessful Local User Account Deletion - Access Denied

This section provides information about an event that is triggered when the `NewUser` account tries to delete the `amirosh` user account, but fails due to insufficient access rights.

> **NOTE** The event logs described in this section are available in this chapter's downloads, in the `Unsuccessful Local User Account Deletion - Access Denied.evtx` file.

An unsuccessful local user account deletion operation using the standard Computer Management snap-in leaves only the two events shown in Listings 5-28 and 5-29 in the Windows security event log.

Listing 5-28: Event ID 4798: A user's local group membership was enumerated.

```
Task Category: User Account Management
Keywords: Audit Success
Subject:
        Security ID:            S-1-5-21-1913345275-1711810662-261465553-1004
        Account Name:           NewUser
        Account Domain:         2016DC
        Logon ID:               0x9DA480
User:
        Security ID:            S-1-5-21-1913345275-1711810662-261465553-1003
        Account Name:           amirosh
        Account Domain:         2016DC
Process Information:
        Process ID:             0x890
        Process Name:           C:\Windows\System32\mmc.exe
```

The event in Listing 5-28 is triggered no matter which method is used to delete the account. It informs you that amirosh's account group membership was enumerated.

Listing 5-29: Event ID 4656: A handle to an object was requested.

```
Task Category: SAM
Keywords: Audit Failure
Subject:
        Security ID:            S-1-5-21-1913345275-1711810662-261465553-1004
        Account Name:           amirosh
        Account Domain:         2016DC
        Logon ID:               0xAE8066
Object:
        Object Server:          Security Account Manager
        Object Type:            SAM_USER
        Object Name:            DOMAINS\Account\Users\000003EC
        Handle ID:              0x0
        Resource Attributes:    -
Process Information:
        Process ID:             0x30c
        Process Name:           C:\Windows\System32\lsass.exe
Access Request Information:
        Transaction ID:         {00000000-0000-0000-0000-000000000000}
        Accesses:               %%1537 (DELETE)
        Access Mask:            0x10000
Other fields...
```

Listing 5-29 shows an unsuccessful attempt to open a handle to the DOMAINS\ Account\Users\000003EC SAM_USER SAM database object for DELETE access. In this event you can see an access to the object (Object) that was requested and by which account (Subject).

The answers to initial questions about this account deletion operation are (see Listing 5-29: Event ID 4656: A handle to an object was requested):

- Who tried to delete the user account?

  The answer is in the Subject section.

- When was the attempt made?

  Event "4656: A handle to an object was requested" provides the event creation time.

- The name of the target account?

  The answer is in the Object section.

- How was this account deleted?

  There is no information about this in event 4656. You should use the methods described in the "Successful Local User Account Deletion" section earlier in this chapter to find this information.

Unsuccessful Local User Account Deletion - Other

Sometimes, a user account has all required permissions to delete another local user account, but fails for some other reasons.

NOTE The event logs described in this section are available in this chapter's downloads, in the Unsuccessful Local User Account Deletion - other.evtx file.

One example of such a scenario is when an account with sufficient permissions tries to delete a built-in system account, such as the built-in local Administrator account, and gets a delete operation error, because system accounts cannot be deleted using standard Windows account management tools.

In this case the events in Listings 5-30 and 5-31 will be displayed in the Windows security event log.

Listing 5-30: Event ID 4656: A handle to an object was requested.

```
Task Category: SAM
Keywords: Audit Success
Subject:
      Security ID:          S-1-5-21-1913345275-1711810662-261465553-500
      Account Name:         Administrator
      Account Domain:       2016DC
      Logon ID:             0xA603F9
Object:
      Object Server:        Security Account Manager
      Object Type:          SAM_USER
      Object Name:          DOMAINS\Account\Users\000001F4
      Handle ID:            0x184580fadc0
      Resource Attributes: -
```

```
Process Information:
      Process ID:           0x30c
      Process Name:         C:\Windows\System32\lsass.exe
Access Request Information:
      Transaction ID:       {00000000-0000-0000-0000-000000000000}
      Accesses:             %%1537 (DELETE)
      Access Mask:          0x10000
```

The `Administrator` (`Subject`) account successfully obtained a handle with DELETE access to the `DOMAINS\Account\Users\000001F4 SAM_USER` SAM object, which is a built-in local Administrator account SAM object (0x1F4 = 500).

Listing 5-31: Event ID 4658: The handle to an object was closed.

```
Task Category: SAM
Keywords: Audit Success
```

Right after the "4656: A handle to an object was requested" event you will see "4658: The handle to an object was closed" in which the just-opened handle to the `DOMAINS\Account\Users\000001F4 SAM_USER` SAM object was closed.

Account deletion failure occurs at the application level and is not recorded in the Windows security event log. Unfortunately, built-in Windows applications, such as the `net user` command or the Computer Management snap-in, have no dedicated event logs to verify why an account deletion operation failed.

There is no information in the security event log explaining why a target account was not deleted, and you will not find a "4726: A user account was deleted" event in the security event log if the target account was not successfully deleted when error occurs on the application level.

Monitoring Scenarios: Local User Account Deletion

Useful events to monitor for successful and unsuccessful local user account deletion are shown in Table 5-7.

Table 5-7: Events to Monitor for Local User Account Deletion

SUCCESSFUL LOCAL ACCOUNT DELETION		
SECURITY EVENT	SUBCATEGORY	EVENT TYPE
4726: A user account was deleted	User Account Management	Audit Success
UNSUCCESSFUL LOCAL ACCOUNT DELETION		
SECURITY EVENT	SUBCATEGORY	EVENT TYPE
4656: A handle to an object was requested	SAM	Audit Failure
4656: A handle to an object was requested	SAM	Audit Success

All successful local user account deletion operations should be monitored, especially on high-value and critical hosts. The main reason why these operations are important is that there are not many local user account delete operations performed during a machine's lifecycle. Such operations might be an indicator of someone trying to:

- Remove all signs of compromise after the machine is compromised
- Delete some important accounts to facilitate performing denial of service attacks
- Hide or correct configuration errors or mistakes

This is not an exhaustive list. There can be other reasons for account deletion operations that are dependent on a variety of circumstances.

You should monitor for "4726: A user account was deleted" Audit Success events.

All unsuccessful local user account "access denied" deletion attempts must be monitored on all categories of hosts. All attempts to delete a local user account without having required permissions might be an indicator of malware activity or other suspicious activity. There is also a chance that someone forgets to run an application using administrative privileges, that is, with a nonelevated token, and the operation fails. This should be considered a false positive alert.

You should monitor for "4656: A handle to an object was requested" Audit Failure events where the Accesses field has a %%1537 (DELETE) access type and the Object Type field equals SAM_USER.

Monitor for this using the following XPath filter:

```
*[System[band(Keywords,4503599627370496) and (EventID=4656)]] and
*[EventData[Data[@Name='ObjectType'] and (Data='SAM_USER')]] and
*[EventData[Data[@Name='AccessList']
='%%1537&#xD;&#xA;&#x09;&#x09;&#x09;&#x09;']]
```

It is recommended that you have a list of accounts (domain and local) that are allowed to delete local user accounts. If you have such a list, you should compare every "4726: A user account was deleted" event's Subject fields with this list.

Refer to the examples for this monitoring recommendation in the "Monitoring Scenarios: Local User Account Creation" section earlier in this chapter.

It is recommended that you have a list of critical local user accounts that should never be deleted—for example, service accounts or accounts for scheduled tasks. Monitor all "4726: A user account was deleted" events where the Target Account section fields contain any of your critical local account names or SIDs.

Local User Account Password Modification

You are able to detect two main operations with local user account passwords using the Windows security event log:

- **Password reset:** This operation is usually performed by another account. For a password reset operation you don't need to know the current account's password. If you have appropriate permissions, you can reset another account's password using built-in tools, such as the Computer Management snap-in.

- **Password change:** This operation allows you to change the password for the account. It requires entering the account's current password. The most common way to invoke the password change dialog is to press Alt+Ctrl+Del and click the "Change a password" menu item.

Successful Local User Account Password Reset

Listings 5-32 through 5-35 are the events that show in the Windows security event log when an account's password is reset.

NOTE   The event logs described in this section are available in this chapter's downloads, in the Successful Local User Account Password Reset.evtx **file..**

The event in Listing 5-32 shows you that someone (Subject) requested a handle for SAM account "DOMAINS\Account\Users\000003EC" (the account for which the password will be reset) with multiple access permissions, and one of these access permissions is %%5447 (SetPassword (without knowledge of old password)).

Listing 5-32: Event ID 4656: A handle to an object was requested.

```
Task Category: SAM
Keywords: Audit Success
```

You will find the event in Listing 5-33 with the Password Last Set: field value equal to the time when the account's password was reset.

Listing 5-33: Event ID 4738: A user account was changed.

```
Task Category: User Account Management
Keywords: Audit Success
```

Listing 5-34 is the most important event, which informs you that the Subject account successfully reset the password for the Target Account.

Listing 5-34: Event ID 4724: An attempt was made to reset an account's password.

```
Task Category: User Account Management
Keywords: Audit Success
Subject:
        Security ID:        S-1-5-21-1913345275-1711810662-261465553-500
        Account Name:       Administrator
```

```
        Account Domain:        2016DC
        Logon ID:              0x3051D
Target Account:
        Security ID:           S-1-5-21-1913345275-1711810662-261465553-1004
        Account Name:          NewUser
        Account Domain:        2016DC
```

After the password was reset, there is no need to keep the handle to SAM account "DOMAINS\Account\Users\000003EC" open, so the event in Listing 5-35 reports that it is closed.

Listing 5-35: Event ID 4658: The handle to an object was closed.

```
Task Category: SAM
Keywords: Audit Success
```

Unsuccessful Local User Account Password Reset - Access Denied

When an account tries to reset the password for another user account without having the required permissions to perform that action, it will get an "Access Denied" response at the handle request phase. The event related to the "Access Denied" response is shown in Listing 5-36.

NOTE The event logs described in this section are available in this chapter's downloads, in the Unsuccessful Local User Account Password Reset - Access Denied.evtx file.

Listing 5-36: Event ID 4656: A handle to an object was requested.

```
Task Category: SAM
Keywords: Audit Failure
Subject:
        Security ID:           S-1-5-21-1913345275-1711810662-261465553-1004
        Account Name:          NewUser
        Account Domain:        2016DC
        Logon ID:              0x49ED2B
Object:
        Object Server:         Security Account Manager
        Object Type:           SAM_USER
        Object Name:           DOMAINS\Account\Users\000001F4
        Handle ID:             0x0
        Resource Attributes:   -
Process Information:
        Process ID:            0x310
        Process Name:          C:\Windows\System32\lsass.exe
```

```
Access Request Information:
        Transaction ID:        {00000000-0000-0000-0000-000000000000}
        Accesses:              %%1538 (READ_CONTROL)
                               %%1539 (WRITE_DAC)
                               %%5442 (WritePreferences)
                               %%5444 (ReadAccount)
                               %%5445 (WriteAccount)
                               %%5447 (SetPassword (without knowledge of old
                                      password))
                               %%5448 (ListGroups)
        Access Mask:           0x601B4
```

The NewUser account was not able to grant one or multiple permissions from the requested READ_CONTROL, WRITE_DAC, WritePreferences, ReadAccount, WriteAccount, SetPassword (without knowledge of old password), or ListGroups access permissions to the SAM account DOMAINS\Account\Users\000001F4. Event 4656 does not show you which access permissions, from the Accesses field, were not granted: it might be one of these permissions, it might be all of them.

Unsuccessful Local User Account Password Reset - Other

One example of when a password reset failure event is generated is when a new account's password does not meet the local password group policy.

> **NOTE**   The event logs described in this section are available in this chapter's downloads, in the Unsuccessful Local User Account Password Reset - other.evtx file..

The events in Listings 5-37 through 5-39 are generated in the Windows security event log when a new account's password length is less than minimum password length defined in the local password group policy.

Listing 5-37: Event ID 4656: A handle to an object was requested.

```
Task Category: SAM
Keywords: Audit Success
```

The event in Listing 5-38 informs you that Subject tried to reset Target Account's password, but the operation failed for some reason. Also, for some reason, this event does not have an Account Name field value when the password reset operation is performed for local user accounts, but does have a Security ID field value present.

Listing 5-38: Event ID 4724: An attempt was made to reset an account's password.

```
Task Category: User Account Management
Keywords: Audit Failure
Subject:
        Security ID:           S-1-5-21-1913345275-1711810662-261465553-500
        Account Name:          Administrator
```

```
        Account Domain:      2016DC
        Logon ID:            0x3051D

Target Account:
        Security ID:         S-1-5-21-1913345275-1711810662-261465553-1004
        Account Name:
        Account Domain:      2016DC
```

Listing 5-39: Event ID 4658: The handle to an object was closed.

```
Task Category: SAM
Keywords: Audit Success
```

Monitoring Scenarios: Password Reset

Useful events to monitor for successful and unsuccessful local user account password resets are shown in Table 5-8.

Table 5-8: Events to Monitor for Local User Account Password Resets

SUCCESSFUL LOCAL ACCOUNT PASSWORD RESETS		
SECURITY EVENT	**SUBCATEGORY**	**EVENT TYPE**
4724: An attempt was made to reset an account's password	User Account Management	Audit Success
UNSUCCESSFUL LOCAL ACCOUNT PASSWORD RESETS		
SECURITY EVENT	**SUBCATEGORY**	**EVENT TYPE**
4656: A handle to an object was requested	SAM	Audit Failure
4724: An attempt was made to reset an account's password	User Account Management	Audit Failure

If you know, for example, that the only local account on the host is the built-in local Administrator account and a password reset operation is not performed for this account at all or performed once a month at the same time/day for all hosts in the company, you should monitor for all password reset events for local user accounts.

All successful and unsuccessful password reset events for critical local accounts, such as built-in local Administrator or local service accounts, must be monitored. To make this task easier it is recommended that you have a list of such important local accounts. Here are some account examples that might be included in such a list:

- Built-in local Administrator account (or renamed local Administrator account)
- Fake (honeypot account) local Administrator account

- Any other accounts that have local administrative rights
- Local accounts for system services
- Local accounts for scheduled tasks
- Local accounts for Internet Informational Services (IIS) application pools

Monitor for these events:

- "4724: An attempt was made to reset an account's password" `Audit Success` and `Audit Failure` events. Check the `Target Account` section fields.
- "4656: A handle to an object was requested" `Audit Failure` events. Verify that the Accesses field has %%5447 (SetPassword without knowledge of old password) access permission in the list.

All unsuccessful password reset attempts due to insufficient permissions should be monitored. These attempts might indicate some suspicious activity or, also, might be a result of using an application without elevated privileges (such as not using "Run as administrator" option in Windows Explorer).

Because the password reset operation for local accounts is not a regular system or maintenance operation, it's recommended that you monitor for any successful and unsuccessful password reset attempts on all hosts, especially on critical and high business impact hosts.

Successful Local User Account Password Change

Now let's switch to password change operations. Multiple events in the Windows security event log appear when a user changes its password. Most of these events are related to the logon process right after the password change.

> **NOTE** The event logs described in this section are available in this chapter's downloads, in the `Successful Local User Account Password Change.evtx` file.

The most important event directly related to password change is shown in Listing 5-40.

Listing 5-40: Event ID 4723: An attempt was made to change an account's password.

```
Task Category: User Account Management
Keywords: Audit Success
Subject:
        Security ID:        S-1-5-21-1913345275-1711810662-261465553-500
        Account Name:       Administrator
```

```
        Account Domain:        2016DC
        Logon ID:              0x70ADAD

Target Account:
        Security ID:           S-1-5-21-1913345275-1711810662-261465553-500
        Account Name:          Administrator
        Account Domain:        2016DC
```

This event informs you that the Administrator account successfully changed its password.

Unsuccessful Local User Account Password Change

In all cases other than a successful local user account change, such as:

- User typed incorrect current account's password.
- User account has "User cannot change password" setting enabled and tries to change its password.
- New password does not match local password policy settings.

The message shown in Listing 5-41 is generated in the Windows security event log.

NOTE The event logs described in this section are available in this chapter's downloads, in the Unsuccessful Local User Account Password Change.evtx file.

Listing 5-41: Event ID 4723: An attempt was made to change an account's password.

```
Task Category: User Account Management
Keywords: Audit Failure
Subject:
        Security ID:           2016DC\Administrator
        Account Name:          Administrator
        Account Domain:        2016DC
        Logon ID:              0x70ADAD

Target Account:
        Security ID:           2016DC\Administrator
        Account Name:          Administrator
        Account Domain:        2016DC
```

You will not find any details in the Windows security event log about why the password change operation failed.

Monitoring Scenarios: Password Change

Useful events to monitor for successful and unsuccessful local user account password changes are shown in Table 5-9.

Table 5-9: Events to Monitor for Local User Account Password Change

SUCCESSFUL LOCAL ACCOUNT PASSWORD CHANGE		
SECURITY EVENT	**SUBCATEGORY**	**EVENT TYPE**
4723: An attempt was made to change an account's password	User Account Management	Audit Success
UNSUCCESSFUL LOCAL ACCOUNT PASSWORD CHANGE		
SECURITY EVENT	**SUBCATEGORY**	**EVENT TYPE**
4723: An attempt was made to change an account's password	User Account Management	Audit Failure

If you know that no *local* accounts should change their own password (all password reset operations are made using a script, application, scheduled task, or some other method), you should monitor for all successful and unsuccessful password change events.

Successful and unsuccessful password change events are important to monitor for high-privileged or critical accounts, such as local accounts with administrative rights, local service accounts, accounts for scheduled tasks, and so on.

Monitor for "4723: An attempt was made to change an account's password" `Audit Success` and `Audit Failure` events. Check the `Target Account` or `Subject` section fields.

Local User Account Enabled/Disabled

Some local user accounts are disabled by default after operating system installation, such as the `Guest` account, and some of them are enabled, such as the local built-in `Administrator` account on Windows server family operating systems. This section covers how to track whether an account was enabled or disabled and which scenarios are more important to monitor.

Local User Account Was Enabled

After a local user account is enabled using the standard Computer Management snap-in or other methods, the events in Listings 5-42 through 5-45 will appear in the Windows security event log.

NOTE The event logs described in this section are available in this chapter's downloads, in the `Local User Account Enabled.evtx` file.

The event in Listing 5-42 shows you that someone (`Subject`) requested a handle for the SAM account `DOMAINS\Account\Users\000001F5` (local `Guest` account) with multiple access rights, and one of the access rights requested is `WriteAccount`.

Listing 5-42: Event ID 4656: A handle to an object was requested.

```
Task Category: SAM
Keywords: Audit Success
```

Listing 5-43 is the main event, which informs you that `Subject` enabled the `Target Account` account.

Listing 5-43: Event ID 4722: A user account was enabled.

```
Task Category: User Account Management
Keywords: Audit Success
Subject:
        Security ID:          S-1-5-21-1913345275-1711810662-261465553-500
        Account Name:         Administrator
        Account Domain:       2016DC
        Logon ID:             0x70ADAD
Target Account:
        Security ID:          S-1-5-21-1913345275-1711810662-261465553-501
        Account Name:         Guest
        Account Domain:       2016DC
```

Listing 5-44 shows an "A user account was changed" event, which contains the same information as the previous "A user account was enabled" event, because "`Account enabled`" is a change to the user's User Account Control (UAC) property. Local user accounts change monitoring is covered in more detail in the "Local User Account Change Events" section later in this chapter.

Listing 5-44: Event ID 4738: A user account was changed.

```
Task Category: User Account Management
Keywords: Audit Success
```

Listing 5-45 shows that "the handle, opened for account enable operation, was closed."

Listing 5-45: Event ID 4658: The handle to an object was closed.

```
Task Category: SAM
Keywords: Audit Success
```

Local User Account Was Disabled

All events for a "disable account" operation are the same as for "enable account," except that the "4722: A user account was enabled" event will be replaced by the event in Listing 5-46.

Listing 5-46: Event ID 4725: A user account was disabled.

```
Task Category: User Account Management
Keywords: Audit Success
Subject:
        Security ID:          S-1-5-21-1913345275-1711810662-261465553-500
        Account Name:         Administrator
        Account Domain:       2016DC
        Logon ID:             0x70ADAD

Target Account:
        Security ID:          S-1-5-21-1913345275-1711810662-261465553-501
        Account Name:         Guest
        Account Domain:       2016DC
```

In this example the Administrator account disabled the built-in local Guest account.

Monitoring Scenarios: Account Enabled/Disabled

Useful events to monitor for account disable/enable status changes are listed in Table 5-10.

Table 5-10: Events to Monitor for Account Status Changes

SECURITY EVENT	SUBCATEGORY	EVENT TYPE
4722: A user account was enabled	User Account Management	Audit Success
4725: A user account was disabled	User Account Management	Audit Success

Monitor for "Account Enabled" events for local accounts that should never be enabled, such as:

- Guest
- Administrator (for Windows clients operating system family)
- DefaultAccount
- Any other accounts that must remain disabled

Monitor for "4722: A user account was enabled" `Audit Success` events. Check the `Target Account` section fields.

Monitor for "Account Disabled" events for critical local accounts that should always remain enabled, such as:

- Administrator (for Windows server operating system family)
- Service accounts
- Accounts for scheduled tasks
- Accounts for IIS application pools
- Depending on your situation, any other accounts that might also need to be always enabled

Monitor for "4725: A user account was disabled" `Audit Success` events. Check the `Target Account` section fields.

It's recommended that you have a list of accounts that have permissions to enable/disable other local accounts. For example, this list may contain only the local `Administrator` account and all members of the Domain Admins domain security group. Monitor for "4725: A user account was disabled" and "4722: A user account was enabled" `Audit Success` events. Check the `Subject` section fields.

Local User Account Lockout Events

Local user lockout events appear in the Windows security event log if the number of account logon attempts using invalid password reached the "Account lockout threshold" local policy setting value.

The account lockout policy settings path is `Computer Configuration\Windows Settings\Security Settings\Account Policies\Account Lockout Policy`.

Figure 5-5 shows an example of account lockout policy settings in Windows 10.

By default, all non–domain-joined machines have the following account lockout policy settings:

- **Account lockout duration:** Not Applicable
- **Account lockout threshold:** 0
- **Reset account lockout counter after:** Not Applicable

Account lockout is usually not enabled on non–domain-joined machines and local accounts will never be locked out on such hosts.

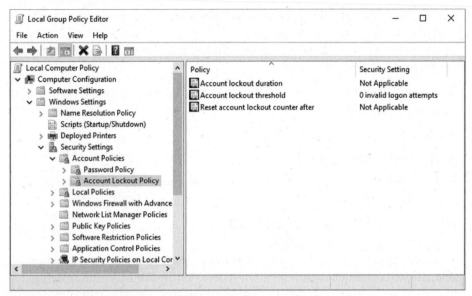

Figure 5-5: Account lockout group policy settings

Additionally, no matter which local account lockout policy settings are applied to the operating system, the built-in local Administrator account will never be locked out.

Local account lockout policy settings can be changed locally or applied from domain group policy, if the computer is joined to the domain.

Local User Account Lockout

No matter which logon type is used (Interactive, RemoteInteractive, Network, Service, Batch job, and so on) the events shown in Listings 5-47, 5-48, and 5-49 will be recorded in the Windows security event log.

> **NOTE** The event examples discussed in this section are available in this chapter's downloads. The names for the logon types follow this format (where *logon_type* is replaced with the specific logon type name): Local User Account Lockout - logon_type.evtx.

The Logon Type field will have different values depending on the logon type used, and the Failure Reason field for all logon types will have a value of Unknown user name or bad password.

Event 4625 (shown in Listing 5-47) is the only source of the following information for account lockout operation:

- Logon type
- Name of the process that invoked authentication request

- IP address of remote workstation (for "remote" logon types, such as Network or RemoteInteractive logon types)
- Source port of the authentication connection request
- Logon Process name
- Authentication Package name

Listing 5-47: Event ID 4625: An account failed to log on.

```
Task Category: Logon
Keywords: Audit Failure
```

You can get more information about account logon events in Chapter 4.

The `Subject` field in the event shown in Listing 5-48 is always the Local System account, which represents the local machine.

Listing 5-48: Event ID 4740: A user account was locked out.

```
Task Category: User Account Management
Keywords: Audit Success
Subject:
        Security ID:        S-1-5-18
        Account Name:       2016DC$
        Account Domain:     WORKGROUP
        Logon ID:           0x3E7
Account That Was Locked Out:
        Security ID:        S-1-5-21-1913345275-1711810662-261465553-1004
        Account Name:       NewUser
Additional Information:
Caller Computer Name:       2016DC
```

For "remote" logon types such as Network or RemoteInteractive, the `Caller Computer Name` field will contain either the NetBIOS name or the IP address of a computer from which the authentication request was received.

The event in Listing 5-49 informs you that the credential validation for `Logon Account` failed with error code `0xC000006A` (Account logon with misspelled or bad password).

Listing 5-49: Event ID 4776: The computer attempted to validate the credentials for an account.

```
Task Category: Credential Validation
Keywords: Audit Failure
Authentication Package:    MICROSOFT_AUTHENTICATION_PACKAGE_V1_0
Logon Account:             NewUser
Source Workstation:        2016DC
Error Code:                0xC000006A
```

All logon types for local accounts will use NTLM-family protocol, because the Kerberos authentication protocol is available only in Active Directory environments for domain accounts.

`Source Workstation` is an important field that shows the machine name from which the authentication request was received. This field is more important for "remote" logon types. The `Source Workstation` field contains the same information as the `Caller Computer Name` field from the "4740: A user account was locked out" event.

Local User Account Unlock

Following are two typical scenarios for user account unlock operations:

- Manual unlock
- Automatic unlock after the number of minutes, defined in the "Account lockout duration" local policy setting, passed

NOTE The event logs described in this section are available in this chapter's downloads, in the `Local User Account Manual Unlock.evtx` file.

A manual local user account unlock operation will trigger the events shown in Listings 5-50 through 5-53 in the Windows security event log.

The event in Listing 5-50 shows you that someone (`Subject`) requested a handle for the SAM account `DOMAINS\Account\Users\000003EC` (local `NewUser` account) object with multiple access rights, and one of the access rights requested is `WriteAccount`.

Listing 5-50: Event ID 4656: A handle to an object was requested.

```
Task Category: SAM
Keywords: Audit Success
```

Listing 5-51 shows that `Subject` account unlocked `Target Account`.

Listing 5-51: Event ID 4767: A user account was unlocked.

```
Task Category: User Account Management
Keywords: Audit Success
Subject:
        Security ID:         S-1-5-21-1913345275-1711810662-261465553-500
        Account Name:        Administrator
        Account Domain:      2016DC
        Logon ID:            0xBD72CB

Target Account:
        Security ID:         S-1-5-21-1913345275-1711810662-261465553-1004
        Account Name:        NewUser
        Account Domain:      2016DC
```

The "A user account was changed" event shown in Listing 5-52 is generated because the account has changed (become unlocked), but, unfortunately, there is no information about this change in the event itself.

Listing 5-52: Event ID 4738: A user account was changed.

```
Task Category: User Account Management
Keywords: Audit Success
```

Listing 5-53: Event ID 4658: The handle to an object was closed.

```
Task Category: SAM
Keywords: Audit Success
```

No events are generated in Windows security event log for automatic local user account unlocks.

Monitoring Scenarios: Account Enabled/Disabled

Useful events to monitor for account lockout/unlock operations are shown in Table 5-11.

Table 5-11: Events to Monitor for Account Lockout and Unlock Operations

SECURITY EVENT	EVENT SUBCATEGORY	EVENT TYPE
4767: A user account was unlocked	User Account Management	Audit Success
4740: A user account was locked out	User Account Management	Audit Success

It's recommended that you monitor for all "4740: A user account was locked out" events for local user accounts, especially on high business impact and critical hosts. The main reason why these events are important is that local accounts are not often in use in comparison with domain user accounts, so any local account lockout event can be a sign of a password brute force or password guess attack.

If you do not expect anyone to manually unlock local user accounts, you should also track all "4767: A user account was unlocked" events.

Local User Account Change Events

Almost every change to a local user account will generate events in the Windows security event log, but it is not always possible to find what exactly was changed.

A local account change event contains detailed information about the following local user account properties:

- User Account Flags:
  - User must change password at next logon

- User cannot change password
- Password never expires
- Account is disabled
- Account is locked out
- Account Name
- Full Name (Display Name)
- Profile tab:
  - User Profile Path
  - User Profile Logon Script
  - User Profile Home Directory
  - User Profile Home Drive

A change to the Description field value on the General user account properties tab (Computer Management snap-in) generates a local user account change event, but no information about the Description field change exists in the event.

Changes in the Member Of local user account tab (Computer Management snap-in) do not invoke a local account change event.

For Windows server operating systems, changes in the following local user account tabs will invoke local account change event, but this event will not have any details about the change:

- Environment
- Sessions
- Remote Control
- Remote Desktop Services Profile
- Dial-in

For all changes to the fields in these tabs, the above User Parameters field will have the following value: %%1792 (<value changed, but not displayed>).

Local User Account Change Event

The events shown in Listings 5-54, 5-55, and 5-56 will appear in the Windows security event log after the account's "Password never expires" property has been enabled:

NOTE The event logs described in this section are available in this chapter's downloads, in the Local User Account Change.evtx file.

Listing 5-54 shows you that someone (Subject) requested a handle for the SAM account DOMAINS\Account\Users\000003EC (a local NewUser account) with multiple access rights, and one of the access rights requested is WriteAccount.

Listing 5-54: Event ID 4656: A handle to an object was requested.

```
Task Category: SAM
Keywords: Audit Success
```

Listing 5-55 shows who (Subject) made changes to which (Target Account) account.

Listing 5-55: Event ID 4738: A user account was changed.

```
Task Category: User Account Management
Keywords: Audit Success
Subject:
        Security ID:            S-1-5-21-1913345275-1711810662-261465553-500
        Account Name:           Administrator
        Account Domain:         2016DC
        Logon ID:               0xBD72CB
Target Account:
        Security ID:            S-1-5-21-1913345275-1711810662-261465553-1004
        Account Name:           NewUser
        Account Domain:         2016DC
Changed Attributes:
        SAM Account Name:       NewUser
        Display Name:           Andrei Miroshnikov
        User Principal Name:    -
        Home Directory:         \\localhost\c$
        Home Drive:             Z:
        Script Path:            temp\Startup.bat
        Profile Path:           %%1793 (<value not set>)
        User Workstations:      %%1793 (<value not set>)
        Password Last Set:      12/24/2016 3:10:45 PM
        Account Expires:        %%1794 (<never>)
        Primary Group ID:       513
        AllowedToDelegateTo:    -
        Old UAC Value:          0x10
        New UAC Value:          0x210
        User Account Control:
                %%2089 ('Don't Expire Password' - Enabled)
        User Parameters:        %%1792 (<value changed, but not displayed>)
        SID History:            -
        Logon Hours:            %%1797 (All)
```

The biggest problem with the "4738: A user account was changed" event is that the only fields that guarantee that their values have been changed are New

UAC Value and User Account Control. For all other fields there is no way to determine whether they changed. They will always contain the current value, whether it was changed or not.

In the current example, the User Parameters field has the value %%1792 <value changed, but not displayed>, but no properties from the Environment, Sessions, Remote Control, Remote Desktop Services Profile, or Dial-in tabs were changed. It has that value because some of the fields from these mentioned tabs were changed before and now it's treated as current value for the User Parameters field. This is applicable to only Windows server operating systems.

The only way to verify which field value was changed (except for the New UAC Value and User Account Control fields) is to compare them with the default values shown in Table 5-12.

Table 5-12: Event Field Default Values

EVENT FIELD	CONSTANT	VALUE
Home Directory	%%1793	<value not set>
Home Drive	%%1793	<value not set>
Script Path	%%1793	<value not set>
Profile Path	%%1793	<value not set>
User Parameters	%%1793	
Display Name	<value not set>	Same as SAM Account Name

After the default value is changed, the only way to track which property was changed (again, except for the New UAC Value and User Account Control fields) is to maintain a database with current settings for all local user accounts, which is not possible in most environments.

Basically speaking, the only event fields that show that something was really changed—and it's easy to verify—are New UAC Value and User Account Control.

The Old UAC Value field contains the previous User Account Control attribute value. The New UAC Value field contains the new User Account Control attribute value or will have the same value as the Old UAC Value field, if the UAC attribute was not changed. The User Account Control field contains changes to the UAC attribute in human-readable format.

Table 5-13 contains information that will help you in New UAC Value and Old UAC Value fields analysis.

Table 5-13: UAC Property Hexadecimal Values

HEX VALUE	UNSET	SET
0x01	Account Enabled	Account Disabled
0x02	'Home Directory Required' - Disabled	'Home Directory Required' - Enabled
0x04	'Password Not Required' - Disabled	'Password Not Required' - Enabled
0x08	'Temp Duplicate Account' - Disabled	'Temp Duplicate Account' - Enabled
0x10	'Normal Account' - Disabled	'Normal Account' - Enabled
0x20	'MNS Logon Account' - Disabled	'MNS Logon Account' - Enabled
0x40	'Interdomain Trust Account' - Disabled	'Interdomain Trust Account' - Enabled
0x80	'Workstation Trust Account' - Disabled	'Workstation Trust Account' - Enabled
0x100	'Server Trust Account' - Disabled	'Server Trust Account' - Enabled
0x200	'Don't Expire Password' - Disabled	'Don't Expire Password' - Enabled
0x400	Account Unlocked	Account Locked
0x800	'Encrypted Text Password Allowed' - Disabled	'Encrypted Text Password Allowed' - Enabled
0x1000	'Smartcard Required' - Disabled	'Smartcard Required' - Enabled
0x2000	'Trusted For Delegation' - Disabled	'Trusted For Delegation' - Enabled
0x4000	'Not Delegated' - Disabled	'Not Delegated' - Enabled
0x8000	'Use DES Key Only' - Disabled	'Use DES Key Only' - Enabled
0x10000	'Don't Require Preauth' - Disabled	'Don't Require Preauth' - Enabled
0x20000	'Password Expired' - Disabled	'Password Expired' - Enabled
0x40000	'Trusted To Authenticate For Delegation' - Disabled	'Trusted To Authenticate For Delegation' - Enabled
0x80000	'Exclude Authorization Information' - Disabled	'Exclude Authorization Information' - Enabled
0x100000	'Undefined UserAccountControl Bit 20' - Disabled	'Undefined UserAccountControl Bit 20' - Enabled
0x200000	'Protect Kerberos Service Tickets with AES Keys' - Disabled	'Protect Kerberos Service Tickets with AES Keys' - Enabled

Basically speaking, the UAC attribute is a bitmask and UAC fields in the "4738: A user account was changed" event just show you its previous and current hexadecimal values.

In the current example, the Old UAC Value equals "0x10", which means the 'Normal Account' - Enabled bit is set in the user's account UAC attribute. The New UAC Value equals "0x210", which means 0x10 + 0x200 = " 'Normal Account' - Enabled" + " 'Don't Expire Password' - Enabled". The User Account Control field shows information only about changes in the UAC attribute.

The following "4738: A user account was changed" event fields are not applicable to local user accounts and always should have default values set:

```
User Principal Name:          -
User Workstations:            %%1793 (<value not set>)
Account Expires:              %%1794 (<never>)
AllowedToDelegateTo:          -
SID History:                  -
Logon Hours:                  %%1797 (All)
```

For some changes, for example changes in a user's account Profile tab, two identical "4738: A user account was changed" events will be generated.

For changes in the Environment, Sessions, Remote Control, Remote Desktop Services Profile, or Dial-in user account tabs, an additional "empty" "4738: A user account was changed" event will be generated as shown in Figure 5-6. This is applicable only to Windows servers operating systems.

Listing 5-56: Event ID 4658: The handle to an object was closed.

```
Task Category: SAM
Keywords: Audit Success
```

Local User Account Name Change Event

A dedicated event is generated in the Windows security event log for local account name change operations.

NOTE The event logs described in this section are available in this chapter's downloads, in the Local User Account Name Change.evtx file.

After a local account name has been changed, the events in this section will appear in Windows security event log.

The event in Listing 5-57 shows who (Subject) changed which (Target Account) name. It also shows old and new account name values.

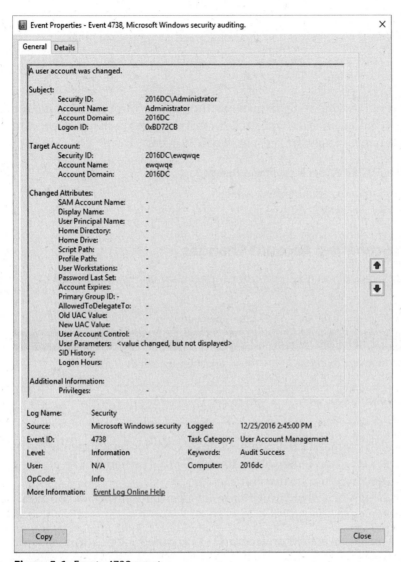

Figure 5-6: Empty 4738 event

Listing 5-57: Event ID 4782: The name of an account was changed.

```
Task Category: User Account Management
Keywords: Audit Success
Subject:
        Security ID:          S-1-5-21-1913345275-1711810662-261465553-500
        Account Name:         Administrator
        Account Domain:       2016DC
        Logon ID:             0xBD72CB
```

```
Target Account:
     Security ID:          S-1-5-21-1913345275-1711810662-261465553-1004
     Account Domain:       2016DC
     Old Account Name:     NewUser
     New Account Name:     OldUser
```

The 4738 event (Listing 5-58) also shows the new account name value for account `NewUser`, but, again, it's not possible to verify whether it changed, because the old account name value isn't present in a 4738 event.

Listing 5-58: Event ID 4738: A user account was changed.

```
Task Category: User Account Management
Keywords: Audit Success
```

Monitoring Scenarios: Account Changes

Table 5-14 shows useful events to monitor for account change operations.

Table 5-14: Events to Monitor for Account Change Operations

SECURITY EVENT	SUBCATEGORY	EVENT TYPE
4738: A user account was changed	User Account Management	Audit Success
4782: The name of an account was changed	User Account Management	Audit Success

It's not typical to change local account names, except for renaming the built-in local `Administrator` and Guest accounts. All "4782: The name of an account was changed" events should be monitored.

Any change to high-privileged and important local accounts should be monitored. Examples of such accounts are:

- Built-in local Administrator account (or renamed local Administrator account)
- Fake (honeypot account) local Administrator account
- Any other accounts that have local administrative rights
- Guest account
- Local accounts for system services
- Local accounts for scheduled tasks
- Local accounts for Internet Informational Services (IIS) application pools

Monitor for "4738: A user account was changed" `Audit Success` events. Check the `Target Account` section fields.

On critical and high-value hosts, monitor for any "4738: A user account was changed" event.

It's recommended that you have a list of accounts that have permissions to change other local accounts. For example, only members of the local Administrators security group can make such changes.

Monitor for "4738: A user account was changed" Audit Success events. Check the Subject section fields.

Monitor for all events showing that the "Password never expires" setting was enabled, but it should not have been, or when that setting was disabled, but must be enabled.

Monitor for "4738: A user account was changed" Audit Success events. Check the New UAC Value field to determine whether the "Password never expires" bit is set or not.

Monitor for all events showing that the "User cannot change password" setting was enabled, but should not have been, or when that setting was disabled, but must be enabled.

Monitor for "4738: A user account was changed" Audit Success events. Check the New UAC Value field to determine whether the "User cannot change password" bit is set or not.

The following XPath filter will filter all "4738: A user account was changed" events where the New UAC Value is not set to the default "0x10" - " 'Normal Account' - Enabled" or not equal "-" value:

```
*[System[(EventID=4738)]] and *[EventData[Data[@Name='NewUacValue']
!='0x10']] and *[EventData[Data[@Name='NewUacValue'] !='-']]
```

Blank Password Existence Validation

An internal API function, SamQueryInformationUser, queries the Security Account Manager (SAM) database for information about a user. This function takes three parameters, one of which is an enumeration of the information about the user you want—for example, the user's name, the user's logon hours, and so on. One option in this enumeration is UserLogonUIInformation, which includes a Boolean value to indicate whether the user has a blank password.

If the following requirements are met, a 4797 event is generated in the security event log:

- The SamQueryInformationUser function is called.
    - UserLogonUIInformation is specified as one of the things you're interested in.
    - You are querying a user who is not you.
    - You are neither a local administrator nor running with SeTcbPrivilege.

Listing 4.50 is an example of a 4797 event.

NOTE This event log is available in this chapter's downloads, in the `Blank Password Existence Validation.evtx` file.

Listing 4.50: ID 4797: An attempt was made to query the existence of a blank password for an account.

```
Task Category: User Account Management
Keywords: Audit Success
Subject:
        Security ID:              S-1-5-19
        Account Name:             LOCAL SERVICE
        Account Domain:           NT AUTHORITY
        Logon ID:                 0x3E5
Additional Information:
        Caller Workstation:       WIN10-CLIENT
        Target Account Name:      Administrator
        Target Account Domain:    WIN10-CLIENT
```

The `Subject` section contains information about the account that called the `SamQueryInformationUser` function.

The `Caller Workstation` field contains name of the workstation making the request.

The `Target Account Name` field contains the name of the account for which the information was requested.

The `Target Account Domain` field contains the domain or machine name to which the target account belongs.

If you want to know what's causing this, you need to figure out what is calling `SamQueryInformationUser`; however, at the end of the day, this seems manifestly uninteresting. It's likely that somebody has written something that calls `SamQueryInformationUser` for some reasonable purpose and they request all the information types available for the user. Even if this was something malicious, though, the event itself doesn't seem to indicate anything valuable unless you actually had users with blank passwords.

Local Security Groups

Security groups are a primary mechanism for assigning permissions or roles to security principals in Microsoft Windows operating systems. Each modern Windows operating system has a set of default built-in local security groups. Each such group has its own set of access permissions defined for operating system objects, and has specific user privileges, logon rights, and so on, because each group has its own purpose. Built-in local security groups cannot be deleted and each has a hardcoded relative identifier (RID), which is the last part of a unique security identifier (SID), assigned to it.

Windows allows you to easily create, delete, and add members to a security group and perform other operations with security groups. Because security groups are used to assign permissions to specific accounts or groups, which are members of these groups, it's important to have good monitoring mechanisms for all actions performed with local security groups, especially with high privileged groups, like the local Administrators group.

Non–domain-joined machines have only two types of security groups that can be used within a machine:

- Local security groups
- Global security groups

NOTE   You might be surprised to learn that global security groups exist on local systems. You will find more information about global groups later in this chapter.

All non–built-in local security groups are stored in the Security Account Manager database at the following registry path: `HKLM\SAM\SAM\Domains\Account\Aliases`. The path for built-in local security groups is `HKLM\SAM\SAM\Domains\Builtin\Aliases`. Viewing the Security Account Manager database using Windows Registry Editor is explained in Chapter 5. Figure 6-1 shows an example of the Security Account Manager database with one manually created local security group named `NewGroup`.

Figure 6-1: Local security groups in Security Account Manager database

As you can see, security group properties are stored in the registry key as a hexadecimal value, which is the group's relative identifier (RID). In Figure 6-1, 000003E9, which is the RID of a newly created group named `NewGroup`. The registry value `C`, located inside the `000003E9` registry key, contains the group's properties. If you open this `C` value, you can even find a description of the security group.

The `Members` registry key contains all members of a specific security group. In the example in Figure 6-1, `NewGroup` has only one member in it.

The `Names` registry key contains group names. There is only one name in the example "NewGroup", which is the name of the group related to 000003E9 registry key. Group names ordered the same way as group registry keys, so they have the same sequence.

In this chapter you learn about different scenarios related to local security groups, such as security group creation, deletion, and modification. You see which events appear in the Windows security event log for most common scenarios related to security groups.

Built-in Local Security Groups

Each modern Microsoft Windows version has a specific set of built-in local security groups, but these groups vary depending on operating system type (server or client) and version. Table 6-1 contains information about built-in security groups present in each modern Microsoft Windows operating system version.

Table 6-1: Built-in Local Security Groups by Microsoft Windows OS Version

GROUP NAME	2008R2	2012/2012R2	2016	WIN 7	WIN 8/8.1	WIN 10
Access Control Assistance Operators		+	+		+	+
Administrators	+	+	+	+	+	+
Backup Operators	+	+	+	+	+	+
Certificate Service DCOM Access	+	+	+			
Cryptographic Operators	+	+	+	+	+	+
Distributed COM Users	+	+	+	+	+	+
Event Log Readers	+	+	+	+	+	+
Guests	+	+	+	+	+	+
Hyper-V Administrators					+	+
IIS_IUSRS	+	+	+	+	+	+
Network Configuration Operators	+	+	+	+	+	+
Performance Log Users	+	+	+	+	+	+
Performance Monitor Users	+	+	+	+	+	+
Power Users	+	+	+	+	+	+
Print Operators	+	+	+			
RDS Endpoint Servers		+	+			
RDS Management Servers		+	+			
RDS Remote Access Servers		+	+			
Remote Desktop Users	+	+	+	+	+	+
Remote Management Users		+	+		+	+

Continues

Table 6-1 (*continued*)

GROUP NAME	2008R2	2012/2012R2	2016	WIN 7	WIN 8/8.1	WIN 10
Replicator	+	+	+	+	+	+
Storage Replica Administrators			+			
System Managed Accounts Group			+			+
Users	+	+		+	+	+
WinRMRemoteWMIUsers__		+	+		+	

As shown in Table 6-1 some operating system versions have specific built-in local security groups. For example, only Windows Server 2016 has a "Storage Replica Administrators" local security group.

One way to view the list of local security groups that exist on the system is to use the built-in "Computer Management" snap-in (compmgmt.msc). Figure 6-2 shows an example of the Computer Management snap-in's output with the local security groups for the newly installed Windows 10 operating system.

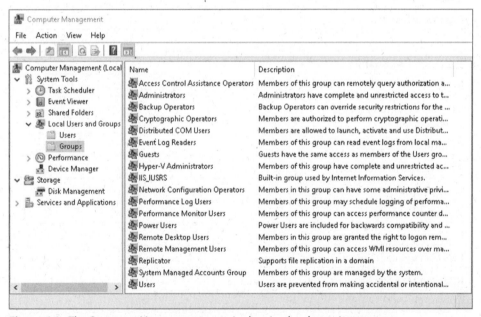

Figure 6-2: The Computer Management snap-in showing local security groups

The following sections describe each of local security groups listed in Table 6.1 and discuss which of these groups are critical to monitor and why.

Access Control Assistance Operators

Members of this group can remotely query authorization attributes and permissions for resources on the local computer. There is not much information available about access permissions this group has. It has no members in it by default. It is recommended to monitor any account added or removed from this group, because it is, usually, remains empty.

Administrators

The built-in local Administrators security group is considered the most privileged built-in security group. Members of this group can perform any action on the local machine. It has one default member: the built-in Administrator account. It might also have other members created during installation, which is typical for client operating systems, or it might have members previously added to this group if the system was upgraded. This group should be considered as critical and any changes to it must be monitored. This group cannot be deleted, but can be renamed.

Backup Operators

Members of this group can back up and restore files and folders on the system, shut down the system, log on as a batch job, and log on locally. Because of backup and restore privileges this group should be considered critical. These privileges allow users to take a copy of any file in the system, including the Security Account Manager database, and then perform any action with these files offline. This group cannot be deleted, but can be renamed. It is empty by default. You can find more information about user privileges in Chapter 11.

Certificate Service DCOM Access

This group only applies to servers with the Certification Authority role installed. All security principals that need to enroll certificates from the Certification Authority must be a member of this security group on Certification Authority servers. Membership in this security group doesn't give accounts any critical privileges. This group should be considered as a low-privileged group. This group cannot be deleted, but can be renamed. It is empty by default.

Cryptographic Operators

The Federal Information Processing Standards Publication 140-2 (FIPS 140-2) defines a "Crypto Officer" role, which is represented by the Cryptographic Operators group in Windows.

When the "System cryptography: Use FIPS compliant algorithms for encryption, hashing, and signing" security policy setting is configured in local or group policy objects, only members of the Cryptographic Operators group or the local Administrators group can configure Cryptography Next Generation (CNG) settings. Specifically, Cryptographic Operators can edit the cryptographic settings in the IPsec policy of Windows Firewall with Advanced Security (WFAS).

This security group is very rarely in use and doesn't have any critical permissions associated with it. This group should be considered a low-privileged group. This group cannot be deleted, but can be renamed. It is empty by default.

Distributed COM Users

The Distributed COM Users group by default has the "Local Access" and "Remote Access" access permissions security limits set for all COM objects on the system. It also has the "Local Launch," "Remote Launch," "Local Activation," and "Remote Activation" launch and activation permission security limits set for all COM objects on the system. These permissions can be set using the "Component Services" management console (`comexp.msc`) as illustrated in Figure 6-3.

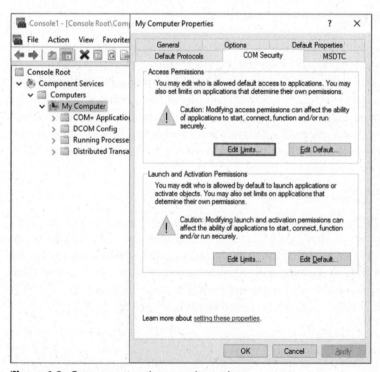

Figure 6-3: Component services security settings

It is important to understand that by default Distributed COM Users group is included only in "Security Limits" and doesn't have any DCOM permissions by default. "Security Limits" defines the permissions limit for any COM object in the system. Basically, if COM application permissions will somehow get beyond the "Security Limits," only permissions defined in the "Security Limits" will work. The Distributed COM Users group, theoretically, can have unlimited local and remote access for any COM application, if these permissions are set for that application manually. The criticality level of this group depends on individual settings for each COM application in the system. Members of this group, by default, cannot log on the system locally. This group has no members by default. I recommend considering this security group to be of medium importance and monitoring any change to it.

Event Log Readers

Members of this group can read any event log on the local system, but cannot log on into the system locally. This group has only read access to event logs. Membership in this group often includes other computers that monitor or query local log events, but this group is empty by default. It is recommended that this group is considered to be of medium criticality.

Guests

The Guests group is designed to provide guest access to the system if it's required. This group has similar permissions as the built-in Users group, but is more restricted. The only default member of this group is the Guest account. Members of this group, because of default local security policy settings, cannot log on to the system locally. If guest access is not needed, it is recommended to remove the Guest account from this group and performing monitoring of this group for any change, because no changes to this group should occur.

Hyper-V Administrators

This group is designed for Hyper-V administrators. All members of this group have unrestricted access to all Hyper-V features on the local machine. Members of this group, by default, cannot log on in to the system locally. The importance level of this group depends on the importance of Hyper-V virtual machines, installed on the system. I recommend considering this group to be of low criticality, because this group exists only on Windows client operating systems, which don't typically have any critical virtual machines installed.

IIS_IUSRS

The IIS_IUSRS group is designed to be used by the Internet Information Services (IIS) component. IIS_IUSRS is the group for IIS Worker Process Accounts, which means the identity that the IIS application pool itself runs under. By default, if the Internet Information Services component is not installed, this group has no user privileges associated to it and has no members. After you install the IIS, this group gets the following privileges:

- Log on as a batch job
- Impersonate a client after authentication

If the IIS component is not installed on the system this group has a low importance level. After the IIS component is installed, the IIS_IUSRS group gains the "Impersonate a client after authentication" privilege, which may be used to impersonate more privileged user accounts logged in to the machine using RPC, COM, or named pipes. The probability of such attacks is quite low, but still, I recommend treating this group as of high importance, because of "Impersonate a client after authentication" privileges, and monitoring any change to this group.

Network Configuration Operators

Network Configuration Operators group members can perform the following actions:

- Modify the Transmission Control Protocol/Internet Protocol (TCP/IP) properties for a local area network (LAN) connection, which includes the IP address, the subnet mask, the default gateway, and the name servers
- Rename the LAN connections or remote access connections that are available to all the users
- Enable or disable a LAN connection
- Modify the properties of all of remote access connections of the user
- Delete all the remote access connections of the user
- Rename all the remote access connections of the user
- Issue `ipconfig/release` or `ipconfig/renew` commands
- Enter the PIN Unblock Key (PUK) for Mobile Broadband devices that support a SIM card

Because members of this group have the ability to change TCP/IP settings, this group should be considered as of high importance. By default this group is empty. I recommend that you monitor any change to this security group, because it is uncommon for this group to be in use.

Performance Log Users

This group is designed to provide access to measure system performance using performance counters, trace providers, and so on. The main difference between Performance Log Users and Performance Monitor Users is that Performance Log Users has Write access (can modify the logging schedule, for example), whereas Performance Monitor Users has only Read access. This group has the "Log on as a batch job" user privilege by default. I recommend considering this security group to be of low importance, because setting performance counters may affect overall system performance, but it is hard to use this functionality to compromise the system.

Performance Monitor Users

Members of this group can view real-time performance data in Windows Performance Monitor (`Perfmon.msc`), and can change the Performance Monitor display properties while viewing real-time data. This group has only Read access permission to performance counter data. I recommend considering this group to be of low importance.

Power Users

This group initially was designed to provide users limited administrative access to the system, such as installing software that does not modify operating system files or installing system services, running legacy applications, and so on. Starting from Windows Vista, Power Users permissions were reduced, mostly to provide access to some system configuration tasks, such as changing the system time zone. Usually, there is no need to use the Power Users group, but, because this group still has the ability to change some system settings, I would recommend considering this group to be of medium importance and monitoring any change to it.

Print Operators

This group is essentially designed for Active Directory Domain Controllers and on local servers it does not have any logon rights or user privileges assigned to it. Members of this group can modify, create, share, and delete printers connected to domain controllers in the domain. On standalone servers this group should remain empty. There is no need to use it, because it does not have any permissions and user rights associated to it on member servers.

Remote Desktop Users

Members of this group have "Allow log on through Remote Desktop Services" user privileges and are able to remotely log on to the local machine using a Remote Desktop connection. I recommend treating this group as a high importance group, because it provides remote access to the machine, and monitoring any change to this group.

Remote Management Users

This group is designed mainly to provide remote management access to the local machine using the WS-Management protocol (for example, remote connections using Server Management console use this protocol). This group also allows connection to the host using Windows Remote Management (WinRM) protocol, which is used, for example, by remote PowerShell connections. By default this group has no user rights assigned to it. Because this group provides remote access to the local machine, it should be considered as a high importance group and any change to this group should be monitored.

Replicator

The Replicator group is designed to support Active Directory replication operations. This group should remain empty on member servers. It has no object permissions, logon rights, or user privileges associated to it on member servers. I recommend considering this group to be of low criticality on member servers.

Storage Replica Administrators

The Storage Replica Administrators group is dedicated for Storage Replica feature administrators. Members of this group have full access to all Storage Replica features. By default this group is empty. If the Storage Replica feature is not in use, it has no object permissions, logon rights, or user privileges associated to it. I recommend considering this group as of low criticality on member servers.

System Managed Accounts Group

This built-in security group is not well documented yet. It contains accounts managed by the operating system. This group provides full access for local machine account (Local System) to all members of this group. By default, this group has only one member in it, the DefaultAccount account. (See Chapter 5 for more information about the DefaultAccount account.) I recommend considering this group as of low criticality.

Users

Any new local user account becomes a member of this security group by default right after it is created. The main purpose of this security group is to provide users with all the non-administrative functions needed to use the computer.

Membership in this group does not provide any type of administrative access to the machine, but allows members to, for example, run applications which don't require elevation of privileges, use local and network printers, and lock the computer.

Windows server operating system versions have the following logon right and user privileges assigned to the Users security group:

- Allow Log on locally
- Access this computer from the network
- Bypass traverse checking
- Increase a process working set

Windows client versions additionally have the following user privileges assigned to the Users security group:

- Remove computer from docking station
- Shut down the system
- Change the Time Zone

Basically speaking, the Users security group has more privileges on Windows client system versions than on server versions.

This group should be considered as of medium criticality; changes in this group might indicate local user account deletion or creation operation. Any change to this group should be monitored, especially on critical servers and workstations.

WinRMRemoteWMIUsers__

The WinRMRemoteWMIUsers__ group initially was designed to allow its members to run Windows PowerShell commands remotely. Starting from Windows 2016 and Windows 10 this group was completely replaced by the "Remote Management Users" security group. By default this group has no members and permissions assigned to it. Because this group provides remote access to the local machine, it should be considered as of high importance and any change to this group should be monitored.

Built-in Local Security Groups Monitoring Scenarios

Different actions can be performed with security groups: groups can be created, deleted, modified, and so on. All these scenarios generate different events in the Windows security event log. It's important to know which events are generated in the security event log for all typical operations and which useful information is available for monitoring in these events.

In this section of the chapter you will find information about security events generated during typical operations with local security groups.

Local Security Group Creation

You can use several methods to create a local security group, including the Computer Management console (compmgmt.msc), Microsoft PowerShell commands, the net group command, and so on. All these methods generate the same set of events in the Windows security event log.

During creation of new local security group using the Computer Management console you can specify the following group parameters:

- Group name
- Description
- Group members

That is all that is available to change for local security groups.

For each local security group creation event it's important to know the following information:

- Who created the group?
- When the group was created?
- How this group was created? Which tools were used?
- What is the name of new group?

In this section you will find information about how to find answers to all of these questions.

Successful Local Security Group Creation

The events shown in Listings 6-1 through 6-7 will appear in the Windows security event log when a new local security group is successfully created.

> **NOTE** You can find an example of events from this section in the Successful Local Security Group Creation.evtx file in this book's downloads.

Listing 6-1: Event ID 4656: A handle to an object was requested.

```
Task Category: SAM
Keywords: Audit Success
Subject:
        Security ID:        S-1-5-21-3212943211-794299840-588279583-500
        Account Name:       Administrator
        Account Domain:     2016SRV
        Logon ID:           0x3B09A
Object:
        Object Server:      Security Account Manager
```

```
      Object Type:          SAM_DOMAIN
      Object Name:          2016SRV
      Handle ID:            0x267040d8460
      Resource Attributes:  -
Process Information:
      Process ID:           0x300
      Process Name:         C:\Windows\System32\lsass.exe
Access Request Information:
      Transaction ID:       {00000000-0000-0000-0000-000000000000}
      Accesses:             %%5398 (CreateLocalGroup)
                            %%5401 (LookupIDs)
      Access Reasons:       -
      Access Mask:          0x240
      Privileges Used for Access Check: -
      Restricted SID Count:    0
```

This event represents a handle request invoked by the Subject.

To create a new local security group a request to create a new local group (CreateLocalGroup access type) should be sent to the Security Account Manager SAM_DOMAIN instance.

The Object Server:Security Account Manager represents the Security Account Manager system module, which is responsible for managing the Security Account Manager database. This database contains information about local security groups, local user accounts, user account passwords (stored as hashes), user account parameters, the group's parameters, and so on.

Object Type:SAM_DOMAIN represents a Security Account Manager domain in which a new local security group is created. The Object Name field contains the name of the SAM_DOMAIN object. It can be an Active Directory domain name if it is a domain group created on a domain controller, or a machine name for local security groups.

The access types (Accesses field) requested for the Security Account Manager SAM_DOMAIN are:

- %%5398: CreateLocalGroup

- %%5401: LookupIDs

(See Table 5.1 for the full list of SAM_DOMAIN object access rights.)

The CreateLocalGroup access type is required to create a new local group. The list of requested access permissions in this event might be different, but it must contain CreateLocalGroup access type.

The Access Mask field contains the hexadecimal mask of requested accesses. More information about SAM_DOMAIN access type hexadecimal values is shown in Table 5.1.

This event also shows a Process Information section, which usually contains lsass.exe (Local Security Authority Subsystem Service) as the process that was used to perform a handle request. lsass.exe is a default process that is authorized to manage Security Account Manager objects. This event is not supposed to tell you which process was initially used to request specific accesses. It shows you the process which invoked Security Account Manager functions (lsass.exe). It does not show you which process initially requested a new handle using lsass.exe functions.

There is no information about how a new local security group was created or which tools were used. You can try to track 4688 process creation events, which occur prior to new local group creation events, to find which applications were run before a new local security group was created.

The event in Listing 6-2 informs you about new local security group creation.

Listing 6-2: Event ID 4731: A security-enabled local group was created.

```
Task Category: Security Group Management
Keywords: Audit Success
Subject:
        Security ID:            S-1-5-21-3212943211-794299840-588279583-500
        Account Name:           Administrator
        Account Domain:         2016SRV
        Logon ID:               0x3B09A
New Group:
        Security ID:            S-1-5-21-3212943211-794299840-588279583-1002
        Group Name:             NewGroup
        Group Domain:           2016SRV
Attributes:
        SAM Account Name:       NewGroup
        SID History:            -
```

There are two types of local groups that you might see in Windows security events:

- **Security-enabled:** Standard security groups
- **Security-disabled:** Active Directory distribution groups

In this event you also can find who created a new group (Subject) and some information about the newly created group. For local security groups the Group Name always has the same value as the SAM Account Name.

The SID History attribute is not applicable to nondomain security groups.

This 4731 event contains all important information about successful local group creation:

- **Who created a new group:** Subject
- **The name of newly created group:** Group Name
- **When new group was created:** Event generation time

Listing 6-3 shows a local security group change event. The biggest problem with this event is that it shows changes to only a limited set of attributes: SAM Account Name and SID History. Basically, it shows only changes to SAM Account

`Name` attribute, which is a name of the security group, because SID History field is not applicable to local security groups.

Listing 6-3: Event ID 4735: A security-enabled local group was changed.

```
Task Category: Security Group Management
Keywords: Audit Success
Subject:
        Security ID:            S-1-5-21-3212943211-794299840-588279583-500
        Account Name:           Administrator
        Account Domain:         2016SRV
        Logon ID:               0x3B09A
Group:
        Security ID:            S-1-5-21-3212943211-794299840-588279583-1002
        Group Name:             NewGroup
        Group Domain:           2016SRV
Changed Attributes:
        SAM Account Name:       -
        SID History:            -
```

In this event you see that a change was made to the `NewGroup` local security group, but, unfortunately, there is no information in this event about what exactly was changed. This happens when some attribute of the group was changed, for example Description field or group access permissions (DACL), which is not included in the 4735 event schema.

Listing 6-4 shows that the handle, which was opened to the `SAM_DOMAIN` entity for a group creation operation, was closed, because all required actions were completed.

Listing 6-4: Event ID 4658: The handle to an object was closed.

```
Task Category: Other Object Access Events
Keywords: Audit Success
Subject :
        Security ID:            S-1-5-21-3212943211-794299840-588279583-500
        Account Name:           Administrator
        Account Domain:         2016SRV
        Logon ID:               0x3B09A
Object:
        Object Server:          Security Account Manager
        Handle ID:              0x267040d8460
Process Information:
        Process ID:             0x300
        Process Name:           C:\Windows\System32\lsass.exe
```

The `Handle ID` field in this event will have the same value as the `Handle ID` field in the initial handle request 4656 event.

Listing 6-5 is another handle request, but this time it is for the `SAM_ALIAS Security Account Manager` object. The `SAM_ALIAS` object type represents the local security group entity.

Listing 6-5: Event ID 4656: A handle to an object was requested.

```
Task Category: SAM
Keywords: Audit Success
Subject:
        Security ID:            S-1-5-21-3212943211-794299840-588279583-500
        Account Name:           Administrator
        Account Domain:         2016SRV
        Logon ID:               0x3B09A
Object:
        Object Server:          Security Account Manager
        Object Type:            SAM_ALIAS
        Object Name:            DOMAINS\Account\Aliases\000003EA
        Handle ID:              0x267040d8920
        Resource Attributes:    -
Process Information:
        Process ID:             0x300
        Process Name:           C:\Windows\System32\lsass.exe
Access Request Information:
        Transaction ID:         {00000000-0000-0000-0000-000000000000}
        Accesses:               %%5428 (WriteAccount)
        Access Reasons:         -
        Access Mask:            0x10
        Privileges Used for Access Check: -
        Restricted SID Count:        0
```

The `Object Name` field contains a path to the requested local security group object in the `Security Account Manager` database. The last part, `000003EA`, represents relative identifier (RID) of the group for which the handle was requested in hexadecimal format. Hexadecimal `000003EA` is decimal `1002`.

You also can see that the `WriteAccount` access type was requested (`Accesses` field). The `Access Mask` field contains the hexadecimal mask value for requested accesses. More information about `SAM_ALIAS` access type hexadecimal values you can find in Table 5.5.

This event means that the `Subject` requested `WriteAccount` access to the local security group with RID = `1002`. WriteAccount access means a Write operation to the Security Account Manager object. It can be interpreted as an object modification request.

Listing 6-6 shows local security group change event without any information about what exactly was changed. This change was initiated using the handle requested in the previous 4656 event.

Listing 6-6: Event ID 4735: A security-enabled local group was changed.

```
Task Category: Security Group Management
Keywords: Audit Success
Subject:
        Security ID:            S-1-5-21-3212943211-794299840-588279583-500
        Account Name:           Administrator
        Account Domain:         2016SRV
        Logon ID:               0x3B09A
```

```
Group:
      Security ID:          S-1-5-21-3212943211-794299840-588279583-1002
      Group Name:           NewGroup
      Group Domain:         2016SRV
Changed Attributes:
      SAM Account Name:     -
      SID History:          -
```

Listing 6-7 shows that the handle, which was opened to the SAM_ALIAS DOMAINS\ Account\Aliases\000003EA object, was closed, because all required actions were completed.

Listing 6-7: Event ID 4658: The handle to an object was closed.

```
Task Category: Other Object Access Events
Keywords: Audit Success
```

Unsuccessful Local Security Group Creation - Access Denied

When an account doesn't have required permissions to create a local security group, the event in Listing 6-8 is recorded in the Windows security event log.

Listing 6-8: Event ID 4656: A handle to an object was requested.

```
Task Category: SAM
Keywords: Audit Failure
Subject:
      Security ID:          S-1-5-21-3212943211-794299840-588279583-1000
      Account Name:         Andrei
      Account Domain:       2016SRV
      Logon ID:             0x2E8F13
Object:
      Object Server:        Security Account Manager
      Object Type:          SAM_DOMAIN
      Object Name:          2016SRV
      Handle ID:            0x0
      Resource Attributes:  -
Process Information:
      Process ID:           0x300
      Process Name:         C:\Windows\System32\lsass.exe
Access Request Information:
      Transaction ID:       {00000000-0000-0000-0000-000000000000}
      Accesses:             %%5398 (CreateLocalGroup)
                            %%5401 (LookupIDs)
      Access Reasons:       -
      Access Mask:          0x240
      Privileges Used for Access Check: -
      Restricted SID Count:      0
```

NOTE The event log described in this section is in the Unsuccessful Local Security Group Creation - Access Denied.evtx file in the download materials on this book's website on Wiley.com.

This event is an `Audit Failure` event that informs you that the `Subject` failed to get `CreateLocalGroup` and/or `LookupIDs` access types for the `SAM_DOMAIN Security Account Manager` entity. Event 4656 does not show you which access or accesses from the list of requested access types were not granted.

No other events will be recorded for an `Access Denied` local group creation scenario. After the `Subject` fails to get the required accesses/access to create a new local security group, no other operations are possible.

Monitoring Scenarios: Local Security Group Creation

A useful event to monitor for successful local security group creation is:

SECURITY EVENT	SUBCATEGORY	EVENT TYPE
4731: A security-enabled local group was created	Security Group Management	`Audit Success`

A useful event to monitor for unsuccessful local security group creation is:

SECURITY EVENT	SUBCATEGORY	EVENT TYPE
4656: A handle to an object was requested	SAM	`Audit Failure`

In general, all successful and, especially, unsuccessful local security group creation events should be monitored. Highest priority should be given to monitor any security group creation operation on high-importance/critical hosts, such as critical servers, administrative workstations, and so on.

Creation of a new local security group is not a common action performed after initial system setup. After a new system is provisioned and all required roles, components, features, and software are installed, it's not typical for additional local security groups to be created.

Monitor these events:

- Monitor for any "4731: A security-enabled local group was created" event.

- Monitor for "4656: A handle to an object was requested" `Audit Failure` events with the `Access Mask` field equal to `0x240` and the `Object Type` field equal to `SAM_DOMAIN`.

  Here is the XPath filter for this monitoring:

```
*[System[band(Keywords,4503599627370496) and (EventID=4656)]] and
*[EventData[Data[@Name='ObjectType'] and (Data='SAM_DOMAIN')]] and
*[EventData[Data[@Name='AccessMask'] ='0x244']]
```

Local Security Group Deletion

A local security group deletion operation is not something you will usually see in Windows security event logs. This operation cannot be performed against built-in local security groups, such as the built-in local Administrators group, and it's not common to see any local security groups deleted, especially after initial system setup.

In this section you will see examples of events that are generated after successful and unsuccessful local security group deletion operations.

Successful Local Security Group Deletion

The events in Listings 6-9 through 6-12 appear in the Windows security event log when a local security group is successfully deleted.

> **NOTE** Examples of the events in this section are in the Successful Local Security Group Deletion.evtx file in the download materials on this book's website on Wiley.com. The order of events in the file is different from that shown in this section.

Listing 6-9: Event ID 4656: A handle to an object was requested.

```
Task Category: SAM
Keywords: Audit Success
Subject:
        Security ID:            S-1-5-21-3212943211-794299840-588279583-500
        Account Name:           Administrator
        Account Domain:         2016SRV
        Logon ID:               0x3670BF
Object:
        Object Server:          Security Account Manager
        Object Type:            SAM_ALIAS
        Object Name:            DOMAINS\Account\Aliases\000003EA
        Handle ID:              0x26fddeb73e0
        Resource Attributes:    -
Process Information:
        Process ID:             0x300
        Process Name:           C:\Windows\System32\lsass.exe
Access Request Information:
        Transaction ID:         {00000000-0000-0000-0000-000000000000}
        Accesses:               %%1537 (DELETE)
        Access Reasons:         -
        Access Mask:            0x10000
        Privileges Used for Access Check: -
        Restricted SID Count:        0
```

This is the initial handle request for this security group operation.

A handle with DELETE access must be requested for the specific SAM_ALIAS Security Account Manager object that represents the group to be deleted. In this example, the local security group SAM object for deletion is DOMAINS\Account\

Aliases\000003EA. The last part of the Object Name field value represents the RID of a local security group.

Event 4734 (Listing 6-10) indicates a successful local security group deletion operation.

Listing 6-10: Event ID 4734: A security-enabled local group was deleted.

```
Task Category: Security Group Management
Keywords: Audit Success
Subject:
        Security ID:            S-1-5-21-3212943211-794299840-588279583-500
        Account Name:           Administrator
        Account Domain:         2016SRV
        Logon ID:               0x3670BF
Group:
        Security ID:            S-1-5-21-3212943211-794299840-588279583-1002
        Group Name:             NewGroup
        Group Domain:           2016SRV
```

This event has answers for the following questions:

- **Who deleted the security group:** Subject
- **Which local security group was deleted:** Group

A local security group is an object in the Security Account Manager database. Because an object for specific local security group was deleted, you will see the event in Listing 6-11, which informs you about this.

Listing 6-11: Event ID 4660: An object was deleted.

```
Task Category: Other Object Access Events
Keywords: Audit Success
Subject:
        Security ID:            S-1-5-21-3212943211-794299840-588279583-500
        Account Name:           Administrator
        Account Domain:         2016SRV
        Logon ID:               0x3670BF
Object:
        Object Server:          Security Account Manager
        Handle ID:              0x26fddeb73e0
Process Information:
        Process ID:             0x300
        Process Name:           C:\Windows\System32\lsass.exe
        Transaction ID:         {00000000-0000-0000-0000-000000000000}
```

The only way to get information about which object was deleted is to find the corresponding "4656: A handle to an object was requested" event with DELETE access requested and with the same Handle ID (0x26fddeb73e0) field value.

Listing 6-12 shows that the handle that was opened to the SAM_ALIAS DOMAINS\ Account\Aliases\000003EA object for this deletion operation, was closed, because all required actions were completed.

Listing 6-12: Event ID 4658: The handle to an object was closed.

```
Task Category: Other Object Access Events
Keywords: Audit Success
```

Unsuccessful Local Security Group Deletion - Access Denied

When a user doesn't have DELETE permissions for a specific local security group, a handle request will fail and the event shown in Listing 6-13 will be generated in the Windows security event log.

Listing 6-13: Event ID 4656: A handle to an object was requested.

```
Task Category: SAM
Keywords: Audit Failure
Subject:
        Security ID:            S-1-5-21-3212943211-794299840-588279583-1000
        Account Name:           Andrei
        Account Domain:         2016SRV
        Logon ID:               0x27C339
Object:
        Object Server:          Security Account Manager
        Object Type:            SAM_ALIAS
        Object Name:            DOMAINS\Account\Aliases\000003EC
        Handle ID:              0x0
        Resource Attributes:    -
Process Information:
        Process ID:             0x300
        Process Name:           C:\Windows\System32\lsass.exe
Access Request Information:
        Transaction ID:         {00000000-0000-0000-0000-000000000000}
        Accesses:               %%1537 (DELETE)
        Access Reasons:         -
        Access Mask:            0x10000
        Privileges Used for Access Check: -
        Restricted SID Count:       0
```

> **NOTE** The event log described in this section are in the Unsuccessful Local Security Group Deletion - Access Denied.evtx file in the download materials on this book's website on Wiley.com.

The Andrei account was not able to get a handle with DELETE permissions for the DOMAINS\Account\Aliases\000003EC SAM_ALIAS object.

The `Audit Failure` 4656 event is the only event generated when a user account has no required permissions to delete a specific security group SAM object.

Unsuccessful Local Security Group Deletion - Other

When a local security group is not deleted for another reason—for example, if someone tried to delete a built-in local security group such as the local Guests group—the event shown in Listing 6-14 is generated in the Windows security event log.

Listing 6-14: Event ID 4656: A handle to an object was requested.

```
Task Category: SAM
Keywords: Audit Success
Subject:
        Security ID:            S-1-5-21-3212943211-794299840-588279583-500
        Account Name:           Administrator
        Account Domain:         2016SRV
        Logon ID:               0x2A0002
Object:
        Object Server:          Security Account Manager
        Object Type:            SAM_ALIAS
        Object Name:            DOMAINS\Builtin\Aliases\00000222
        Handle ID:              0x2c8d7f147a0
        Resource Attributes:    -
Process Information:
        Process ID:             0x300
        Process Name:           C:\Windows\System32\lsass.exe
Access Request Information:
        Transaction ID:         {00000000-0000-0000-0000-000000000000}
        Accesses:               %%1537 (DELETE)
        Access Reasons:         -
        Access Mask:            0x10000
```

NOTE The event log described in this section are in the `Unsuccessful Local Security Group Deletion - other.evtx` file in the download materials on this book's website on Wiley.com.

The "4656: A handle to an object was requested" `Audit Success` event is the only event generated if a local security group is not successfully deleted and the reason is not insufficient permissions.

From the system's perspective, access to the specific local security group was successfully granted, but then it was denied at the application level, which the system does not monitor. You should verify whether a "4734: A security-enabled local group was deleted" event occurs after a handle request event. If yes, the security group was successfully deleted; if no, it was not deleted, but someone tried to do it.

Monitoring Scenarios: Local Security Group Deletion

A useful event to monitor for successful local security group deletion is:

SECURITY EVENT	SUBCATEGORY	EVENT TYPE
4734: A security-enabled local group was deleted	Security Group Management	Audit Success

Useful events to monitor for unsuccessful local security group deletion are:

SECURITY EVENT	SUBCATEGORY	EVENT TYPE
4656: A handle to an object was requested	SAM	Audit Failure
	SAM	Audit Success
4656: A handle to an object was requested		

Any successful and unsuccessful access denied local security group deletion events should be monitored on all hosts. As is true for local security group creation actions, a local security deletion operation is not a common action performed during a system's lifetime. Even at initial system setup, local security group deletion is not usually performed. It's more likely that a group creation operation will be performed.

Monitor these events:

- Monitor for any "4734: A security-enabled local group was deleted" event.
- Monitor for "4656: A handle to an object was requested" Audit Failure events with Access Mask field equals to "0x10000" and Object Type field equals SAM_ALIAS.

The XPath filter for this monitoring is:

```
*[System[band(Keywords,4503599627370496) and (EventID=4656)]] and
*[EventData[Data[@Name='ObjectType'] and (Data='SAM_ALIAS')]] and
*[EventData[Data[@Name='AccessMask'] ='0x10000']]
```

Local Security Group Change

Not many parameters can be changed for local security groups using built-in Windows tools. The available changes are:

- Group name change
- Group description change
- Group members removed/added

In this section you will find information about how to monitor the first two changes from the preceding list.

Successful Local Security Group Change

Any change to the local security group, except changes in group membership, will generate the events shown in Listings 6-16 through 6-18

To make changes to the local security group object, an account must have `WriteAccount` permission for this group. The event in Listing 6-15 occurs for any change and shows an access request for a specific `SAM_ALIAS` Security Account Manager object.

Listing 6-15: Event ID 4656: A handle to an object was requested.

```
Task Category: SAM
Keywords: Audit Success
Other fields...
Object:
        Object Server:       Security Account Manager
        Object Type:         SAM_ALIAS
        Object Name:         DOMAINS\Account\Aliases\000003EC
        Handle ID:           0x2c8d7f172f0
Other fields...
Access Request Information:
        Transaction ID:      {00000000-0000-0000-0000-000000000000}
        Accesses:            %%5428 (WriteAccount)
        Access Reasons:      -
        Access Mask:         0x10
```

NOTE The event logs described in this section are in the `Successful Local Security Group Change.evtx` file in the download materials on this book's website on Wiley.com.

The local security group change event shown in Listing 6-16 provides the following important information:

- **Which group was changed:** `Group`
- **Who made a change:** `Subject`

Listing 6-16: Event ID 4735: A security-enabled local group was changed.

```
Task Category: Security Group Management
Keywords: Audit Success
Subject:
        Security ID:         S-1-5-21-3212943211-794299840-588279583-500
        Account Name:        Administrator
        Account Domain:      2016SRV
        Logon ID:            0x2A0002
```

```
Group:
      Security ID:          S-1-5-21-3212943211-794299840-588279583-1004
      Group Name:           NewGroup
      Group Domain:         2016SRV
Changed Attributes:
      SAM Account Name:     -
      SID History:          -
```

Unfortunately, changes to a security group's description field are not shown in the 4735 event. The only included changed attributes are:

- **SAM Account Name:** Group's name

- **SID History:** Not applicable to local security groups

Changes in the `Description` attribute of a local security group will invoke a 4735 event, but this event will not have any information about what exactly was changed.

Group membership delete/add operations do not generate a 4735 event.

If the group's name was changed, both the `Group` and `Changed Attributes` sections will show the new group name, but you will not be able to get the group's previous name:

```
Group:
      Security ID:          S-1-5-21-3212943211-794299840-588279583-1004
      Group Name:           NewGroupName
      Group Domain:         2016SRV

Changed Attributes:
      SAM Account Name:     NewGroupName
      SID History:          -
```

If the security group name was changed, then in addition to a 4735 event, the 4781 event shown in Listing 6-17 is generated.

Listing 6-17: Event ID 4781: The name of an account was changed:

```
Task Category: User Account Management
Keywords: Audit Success
Subject:
      Security ID:          S-1-5-21-3212943211-794299840-588279583-500
      Account Name:         Administrator
      Account Domain:       2016SRV
      Logon ID:             0x298C3

Target Account:
      Security ID:          S-1-5-21-3212943211-794299840-588279583-1004
      Account Domain:       2016SRV
      Old Account Name:     OldGroup
      New Account Name:     NewGroup
```

> **NOTE** The event logs described in Listings 6-17 and 6-18 are in the `Successful Local Security Group Change - group name.evtx` file in the download materials on this book's website on Wiley.com.

The event in Listing 6-18 has an `Old Account Name` field, which shows you group's previous name. After the group name change is done, the handle, which was requested for this operation, is released (Listing 6-18).

Listing 6-18: Event ID 4658: The handle to an object was closed.

```
Task Category: Other Object Access Events
Keywords: Audit Success
```

Unsuccessful Local Security Group Change - Access Denied

By default, only local administrators and the Local System account can change a local group's name. If any nonadministrative account tries to change the settings for any local security group, it will get an access denied message and the event shown in Listing 6-19 will be generated in the Windows security event log.

Listing 6-19: Event ID 4656: A handle to an object was requested.

```
Task Category: SAM
Keywords: Audit Failure
Subject:
        Security ID:            S-1-5-21-3212943211-794299840-588279583-1000
        Account Name:           Andrei
        Account Domain:         2016SRV
        Logon ID:               0x275FFC
Object:
        Object Server:          Security Account Manager
        Object Type:            SAM_ALIAS
        Object Name:            DOMAINS\Account\Aliases\000003EC
        Handle ID:              0x0
        Resource Attributes:    -
Process Information:
        Process ID:             0x300
        Process Name:           C:\Windows\System32\lsass.exe
Access Request Information:
        Transaction ID:         {00000000-0000-0000-0000-000000000000}
        Accesses:               %%5428 (WriteAccount)
        Access Reasons:         -
        Access Mask:            0x10
        Privileges Used for Access Check: -
        Restricted SID Count:       0
```

> **NOTE** The event described in Listing 6-19 is available on the book's website, in the `Unsuccessful Local Security Group Change - Access Denied .evtx` file.

In an "Access Denied" scenario you will see an `Audit Failure` event, with a `WriteAccount` access request to a specific Security Account Manager security group object. No other events will be generated.

Monitoring Scenarios: Local Security Group Change

Useful events to monitor for successful local security group change are:

SECURITY EVENT	SUBCATEGORY	EVENT TYPE
4735: A security-enabled local group was changed	Security Group Management	`Audit Success`
4781: The name of an account was changed	User Account Management	`Audit Success`

A useful event to monitor for unsuccessful local security group change is:

SECURITY EVENT	SUBCATEGORY	EVENT TYPE
4656: A handle to an object was requested	SAM	`Audit Failure`

Security group name modification is a very uncommon operation. Usually it's not critical to monitor security group name changes, but in some scenarios it might be needed. For example, you should track any changes on critical hosts and any changes to specific high-importance local security groups, such as the built-in local Administrators group. In general, security group changes (except operations with group membership) are not important to monitor.

Local Security Group Membership Operations

It is important to monitor changes to local security group membership.

The most privileged built-in local security groups are:

- Administrators
- Backup Operators
- Network Configuration Operators
- Remote Desktop Users
- Remote Management Users
- WinRMRemoteWMIUsers__

You should also verify all manually created local groups and determine which of them should be considered critical or high privileged. All changes related to critical/high-privileged groups should be monitored.

There are different ways to add/remove users from specific groups, including the Computer Management console (`compmgmt.msc`), PowerShell scripts, and so on. These methods all generate the same set of events in the Windows security event log.

In this section you will find information about auditing group member addition and removal operations.

Successful New Local Group Member Add Operation

When a new member is added to a local security group, the messages shown in Listings 6-20 through 6-23 occur in the Windows security event log.

As shown in Listing 6-20 the following access rights are requested by default when a new member is added to the security group using the Computer Management console:

- `%%5424 (AddMember)`

- `%%5425 (RemoveMember)`

- `%%5426 (ListMembers)`

- `%%5427 (ReadInformation)`

Listing 6-20: Event ID 4656: A handle to an object was requested.

```
Task Category: SAM
Keywords: Audit Success
Other fields...
Object:
        Object Server:          Security Account Manager
        Object Type:            SAM_ALIAS
        Object Name:            DOMAINS\Builtin\Aliases\00000220
        Handle ID:              0x2a87f397c60
Other fields...
Access Request Information:
        Transaction ID:         {00000000-0000-0000-0000-000000000000}
        Accesses:               %%5424 (AddMember)
                                %%5425 (RemoveMember)
                                %%5426 (ListMembers)
                                %%5427 (ReadInformation)
        Access Reasons:         -
        Access Mask:            0xF
    Other fields...
```

NOTE The event logs described in this section are in the `Successful Local Security Group Add Member.evtx` file in the download materials on this book's website on Wiley.com.

Whether an account is added or removed from the security group, all four access types will be requested by the Computer Management console. The only access permission that must be requested to add a new member is AddMember. It is up to an application which permissions to request for a specific operation.

Listing 6-21 informs you about the addition of a new member to a local security group.

Listing 6-21: Event ID 4732: A member was added to a security-enabled local group.

```
Task Category: Security Group Management
Keywords: Audit Success
Subject:
        Security ID:          S-1-5-21-3212943211-794299840-588279583-500
        Account Name:         Administrator
        Account Domain:       2016SRV
        Logon ID:             0x298B1F
Member:
        Security ID:          S-1-5-7
        Account Name:         -
Group:
        Security ID:          S-1-5-32-544
        Group Name:           Administrators
        Group Domain:         Builtin
```

This event has the following information in it:

- **Who added the new member to the local security group:** Subject
- **What new member was added to the group:** Member
- **To which group was the new member added:** Group

The Member: Account Name field is always empty for local security groups, because it's designed to show the distinguished name for Active Directory groups and users. See more information in Chapter 7.

For all built-in local security groups, which were listed at the beginning of this chapter, the Group Domain field is always Builtin. For all manually created local security groups this field has a value equal to the local machine name:

```
Group:
        Security ID:          S-1-5-21-3212943211-794299840-
588279583-1004
        Group Name:           NewGroup
        Group Domain:         2016SRV
```

Event 4658 in Listing 6-22 shows that a handle opened for a previous operation has been closed.

Listing 6-22: Event ID 4658: The handle to an object was closed.

```
Task Category: Other Object Access Events
Keywords: Audit Success
```

The event in Listing 6-23 generates each time group membership for a local security group is enumerated.

Listing 6-23: Event ID 4799: A security-enabled local group membership was enumerated.

```
Task Category: Security Group Management
Keywords: Audit Success
Subject:
        Security ID:            S-1-5-21-3212943211-794299840-588279583-500
        Account Name:           Administrator
        Account Domain:         2016SRV
        Logon ID:               0x298B1F
Group:
        Security ID:            S-1-5-32-544
        Group Name:             Administrators
        Group Domain:           Builtin
Process Information:
        Process ID:             0xf48
        Process Name:           C:\Windows\System32\mmc.exe
```

This event happens, for example, when the Computer Manager (compmgmt
.msc) console application gathers information about group members for a specific security group. It happens when you open any group details, as illustrated
in Figure 6-4.

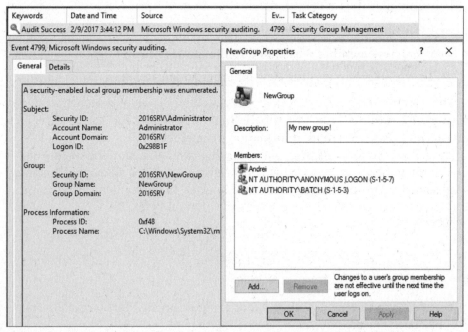

Figure 6-4: Group membership enumeration event and group properties window in the
Computer Manager console.

If you use other methods to add a member to a local security group, which do not perform group membership enumeration, such as the following PowerShell script:

```
$group = [ADSI]"WinNT://2016srv/newgroup,group"
$group.Add("WinNT://2016srv/andrei,user")
```

then a "4799: A security-enabled local group membership was enumerated" event will *not* be generated.

Useful information in this event is the `Process Name` field, which shows the name of the process used to perform the action.

Successful Local Group Member Remove Operation

A group member removal operation, performed using the Computer Management console, has exactly the same events recorded in the Windows security event log as a successful new local group member add operation, except the "4732: A member was added to a security-enabled local group" event is replaced by the event shown in Listing 6-24.

Listing 6-24: Event ID 4733: A member was removed from a security-enabled local group.

```
Task Category: Security Group Management
Keywords: Audit Success
Subject:
        Security ID:        S-1-5-21-3212943211-794299840-588279583-500
        Account Name:       Administrator
        Account Domain:     2016SRV
        Logon ID:           0x298B1F
Member:
        Security ID:        S-1-5-21-3212943211-794299840-588279583-1000
        Account Name:       -
Group:
        Security ID:        S-1-5-32-544
        Group Name:         Administrators
        Group Domain:       Builtin
```

> **NOTE** The event logs described in this section are in the `Successful Local Security Group Remove Member.evtx` file in the download materials on this book's website on Wiley.com.

This event has the same fields as the "4732: A member was added to a security-enabled local group" event, and shows you which security principal was removed from the specific local security group.

Unsuccessful Local Group Member Remove/Add Operation - Access Denied

If a user account doesn't have sufficient permissions to add/remove members from a security group it will get an "Access Denied" message. Both add and remove operations generate the event in Listing 6-25 in the Windows security event log.

Listing 6-25: Event ID 4656: A handle to an object was requested.

```
Task Category: SAM
Keywords: Audit Failure
Subject:
        Security ID:            S-1-5-21-3212943211-794299840-588279583-1000
        Account Name:           Andrei
        Account Domain:         2016SRV
        Logon ID:               0x5A07AB
Object:
        Object Server:          Security Account Manager
        Object Type:            SAM_ALIAS
        Object Name:            DOMAINS\Builtin\Aliases\00000220
        Handle ID:              0x0
        Resource Attributes:    -
Process Information:
        Process ID:             0x300
        Process Name:           C:\Windows\System32\lsass.exe
Access Request Information:
        Transaction ID:         {00000000-0000-0000-0000-000000000000}
        Accesses:               %%5424 (AddMember)
                                %%5425 (RemoveMember)
                                %%5426 (ListMembers)
                                %%5427 (ReadInformation)
        Access Reasons:         -
        Access Mask:            0xF
```

> **NOTE** The event logs described in this section are in the `Unsuccessful Local Security Group Members Operations - Access Denied.evtx` file in the download materials on this book's website on Wiley.com.

Both "add member" and "remove member" events have `AddMember`, `RemoveMember`, `ListMembers`, and `ReadInformation` access types in a handle request when operation is performed using the Computer Management console. There is no ability to differentiate which exact operation was requested: remove member or add member. Member add operations require AddMember permission and member remove operations require RemoveMember permissions.

Monitoring Scenarios: Local Security Group Members Changes

Useful events to monitor for successful local security group members changes are:

SECURITY EVENT	SUBCATEGORY	EVENT TYPE
4733: A member was removed from a security-enabled local group	Security Group Management	Audit Success
	Security Group Management	Audit Success
4732: A member was added to a security-enabled local group		

A useful event to monitor for unsuccessful local security group members changes is:

SECURITY EVENT	SUBCATEGORY	EVENT TYPE
4656: A handle to an object was requested	SAM	Audit Failure

It is critically important to perform monitoring of any successful and unsuccessful change to critical and high-privileged built-in and manually created security groups. The following built-in local security groups are considered high privileged:

- Administrators
- Backup Operators
- Network Configuration Operators
- Remote Desktop Users
- Remote Management Users
- WinRMRemoteWMIUsers__

Also, it's unusual to remove or add members to local security groups too often. Usually it happens when a machine joins the Active Directory domain or during role, feature, or application installation or removal. Any successful and unsuccessful member add and remove operations should be monitored.

Monitor these events:

- Monitor any "4733: A member was removed from a security-enabled local group" event.
- Monitor any "4732: A member was added to a security-enabled local group" event.
- Monitor for "4656: A handle to an object was requested" Audit Failure events with Access Mask field equals to "0xF" and Object Type field equals SAM_ALIAS.

The XPath filter for this monitoring is:

```
*[System[band(Keywords,4503599627370496) and (EventID=4656)]] and
*[EventData[Data[@Name='ObjectType'] and (Data='SAM_ALIAS')]] and
*[EventData[Data[@Name='AccessMask'] ='0xF']]
```

Local Security Group Membership Enumeration

The last scenario for monitoring using the Windows security event log is group membership enumeration. This event triggers when someone queries a list of members for a specific local security group. For example, it will be triggered when someone opens a local security group's properties, which automatically shows you a list of the current group's members.

The event in listing 6-26 is generated in the Windows security event log when a local security group membership is enumerated.

Listing 6-26: Event ID 4799: A security-enabled local group membership was enumerated.

```
Task Category: Security Group Management
Keywords: Audit Success
Subject:
        Security ID:            S-1-5-21-3212943211-794299840-588279583-500
        Account Name:           Administrator
        Account Domain:         2016SRV
        Logon ID:               0x23133
Group:
        Security ID:            S-1-5-32-544
        Group Name:             Administrators
        Group Domain:           Builtin
Process Information:
        Process ID:             0x77c
        Process Name:           C:\Windows\System32\mmc.exe
```

> **NOTE** The event logs described in this section are in the `Successful Local Security Group Membership Enumeration.evtx` file in the download materials on this book's website on Wiley.com.

A 4799 event contains the following information:

- **Who performed the action:** `Subject`
- **Membership of which group was enumerated:** `Group`
- **Which process requested this operation:** `Process Information`

By default, all members of a built-in local Users group can enumerate membership for any local security group.

Monitoring Scenarios: Local Security Group Membership Enumeration

A useful event to monitor for successful local security group membership enumeration is:

SECURITY EVENT	SUBCATEGORY	EVENT TYPE
4799: A security-enabled local group membership was enumerated	Security Group Management	Audit Success

A local security group membership enumeration event is mostly informational and could be monitored if needed.

Microsoft Active Directory

Microsoft Active Directory provides the ability to centrally manage assets in your network environment. It also acts as a foundation for many other technologies, such as Active Directory Federation Services, Public Key Infrastructure service, RADIUS servers, and many other services and components.

In this chapter you will find information about the most common monitoring scenarios for Active Directory, such as user or computer account creation, operations with groups, operations with trusts, and so on. Chapter 8 builds on this chapter with detailed information about monitoring Active Directory changes and operations with objects, such as group policy creation and organization unit modification, as well as others.

Active Directory Built-in Security Groups

In addition to the standard security groups included in any Windows server operating system, which were discussed in Chapter 6, a number of special security groups are available after a server is promoted to an Active Directory domain controller. In this section you will find information about the additional security groups that exist in an Active Directory domain environment.

Administrators

Administrators is a built-in domain local security group. Members of this group have administrative access to all Active Directory domain controllers in the domain this group is located in, which makes this group critical to monitor. By default, this group has the following members:

- Administrator account
- Domain Admins group
- Enterprise Admins group

Via membership in the Administrators group, these members receive administrative permissions on all domain controllers in the domain.

Account Operators

Members of the Account Operators group can create and modify domain accounts. They can reset passwords for nonprivileged accounts, create computer objects, and so on. Members of this security group have local logon rights to any domain controller in the domain. This group should be considered as privileged and monitored for any modification and group membership changes.

By default this group has no members.

Incoming Forest Trust Builders

Members of this group can create incoming one-way forest trusts. This group does not have any specific logon rights or user privileges assigned to it. Consider this group as low priority for monitoring, but, because it is rarely in use, it is a good practice to monitor changes to this group anyway.

Pre-Windows 2000 Compatible Access

This group was designed to provide backward compatibility for Windows NT 4.0 and earlier systems. Members of this group can read the properties of all user and computer objects in the domain. The most important thing to monitor is that this group does not have an ANONYMOUS LOGON security principal as a member. Anonymous binds to Active Directory are not allowed since Windows Server 2003, but monitoring is still recommended for the "Pre-Windows 2000 Compatible Access" group, especially for environments where anonymous binds are allowed. Also, it is a good practice to monitor for any change in this group.

Server Operators

The Server Operators group is a high-privileged group. Its members have the following logon rights and user privileges on domain controllers:

- Allow log on locally
- Back up files and directories
- Change the system time
- Change the time zone
- Force shutdown from a remote system
- Restore files and directories
- Shut down the system

The "Back up files and directories" privilege (SeBackupPrivilege) allows members of this group to create a backup of the NTDS.dit file, as well as any other file, and have access to all information (including account password hashes) offline. It is critical to monitor any changes to this group and, also, it is recommended to not use this group due to extensive permissions.

By default this group has no members.

Terminal Server License Servers

This group is designed to provide the ability to change terminal service license information for Active Directory user accounts. This group has no logon rights or user privileges by default. Consider this group low priority for monitoring, but, because this group is rarely in use, it is a good practice to monitor changes to this group anyway.

Windows Authorization Access

Members of this group have Read access to the token-groups-global-and-universal (TGGAU) attribute of all user and computer accounts in the domain. The TGGAU attribute is dynamically generated and contains information about user or computer universal and global group membership. Basically speaking, this attribute contains group membership information for global and universal groups for specific user or computer accounts.

This group has no logon rights or user privileges by default. Consider this group low priority for monitoring, but, because it is rarely in use, it is a good practice to monitor changes to this group anyway.

Allowed RODC Password Replication Group

Members of this group are allowed to replicate their password hashes to Read Only Domain Controllers (RODCs). By default, this group is empty. Perform monitoring of this group if you use RODCs in your environment.

Denied RODC Password Replication Group

Members of this group are denied to replicate their password hashes to Read Only Domain Controllers (RODCs). Membership in this group overrides membership in the Allowed RODC Password Replication Group. By default, the group has the following members:

- Cert Publishers
- Domain Admins
- Domain Controllers
- Enterprise Admins
- Group Policy Creator Owners
- krbtgt
- Read-Only Domain Controllers
- Schema Admins

Perform monitoring of this group if you use RODCs in your environment.

Cert Publishers

Members of this group can publish certificates for users or computer objects in an Active Directory domain. Usually it contains the computer accounts of online enterprise Certification Authority (CA) servers related to Active Directory Certificate Services. This group has no logon rights or user privileges by default. Consider this group medium priority for monitoring, but, because it is rarely in use, it is a good practice to monitor changes to this group anyway. This group becomes critical to monitor if you use user or computer certificates for authentication, such as smart cards or 802.1x authentication.

DnsAdmins

Members of this group have Read, Write, Create All Child objects, Delete Child objects, and Special Permissions access permissions on the Active Directory DomainDNSZones partition in the domain. Membership in this group should be considered as high privileged and should be monitored.

RAS and IAS Servers

Members of this group have some special permissions for Active Directory user objects, such as Read Account Restrictions, Read Logon Information, and Read Remote Access Information. This group is designed mainly for Internet Authentication Services servers and Network Policy Servers, which need to have access to the Active Directory user objects just mentioned.

This group has no logon rights or user privileges by default. Consider this group low priority for monitoring, but, because it is rarely in use, it is a good practice to monitor changes to this group anyway.

Cloneable Domain Controllers

This group contains domain controller computer account objects that can be cloned. This is required for virtual domain controllers that can be deployed by cloning existing domain controllers starting with Windows Server 2012. Usually this group doesn't need to be monitored.

DnsUpdateProxy

Members of this group can perform dynamic DNS updates on behalf of other clients on a DNS server. The most common member of this group is an account used by DHCP servers to dynamically register A, AAAA, and PTR records for hosts. Membership in this group should be considered as sensitive, because group members can change any DNS record. Any change to this group should be monitored.

Domain Admins

The Domain Admins group should be considered one of the most privileged group in the domain. This group is a member of the local Administrators group on all domain-joined computers and domain controllers. Members of this security group are, by default, owners of many Active Directory objects. It is critical to monitor any change to this group.

Domain Computers

This group contains computer objects for all domain-joined machines, except domain controllers. This group does not contain computer objects that were manually created. Usually this group doesn't need to be monitored.

Domain Controllers

This group contains computer objects for all domain controllers in the domain. It is a good practice to monitor changes in this group to track creation and removal of domain controller objects.

Domain Users

This group contains all domain user accounts. Domain Users is a member of the Users group on all domain-joined machines (see Chapter 6 for more detail). By default it has two members: the Administrator and krbtgt accounts. Usually this group doesn't need to be monitored.

Group Policy Creator Owners

Members of this group can manage Active Directory group policy objects in the domain: create, modify, delete, link, etc. By default the only member of this group is the built-in Administrator account. This group has no logon rights or user privileges by default. But still, the ability to manage domain group policies is a high privilege, and it is recommended to monitor this group for any modification.

Protected Users

Members of this group have the following authentication restrictions applied:

- These Security Support Providers are disabled: NTLM, Digest, CredSSP.
- DES and RC4 encryption is disabled for Kerberos.
- Kerberos delegation for accounts is not allowed.
- Kerberos ticket-granting ticket (TGT) lifetime is set to 4 hours.

If the protected users group is in use in your environment it is important to monitor it for modifications, especially for user accounts removed from the group.

Read-Only Domain Controllers

This group contains all Read Only Domain Controllers (RODCs) computer objects in the domain. Usually this group doesn't need to be monitored.

Enterprise Read-Only Domain Controllers

This group contains all read-only domain controllers (RODCs) computer objects in the forest. Usually this group doesn't need to be monitored.

Enterprise Admins

Members of the Enterprise Admins group have permissions to perform forest-wide operations, such as installation of a new Certification Authority server. This group is added to the Administrators domain group in each domain in the forest. This group exists only in the root domain of an Active Directory forest. The only default member of this group is the built-in Administrator account.

It is critical to monitor any change to this group. This group should remain empty except that it has members only temporarily when forest-wide operation need to be performed.

Schema Admins

Members of this group can modify Active Directory schema. This group exists only in the root domain of an Active Directory forest. The only default member of this group is the built-in Administrator account.

Schema modification operations cannot be reversed, so it is critical to control membership in the Schema Admins group and even add accounts to this group only for a short period of time, when schema modification is required.

It is critical to monitor any change to this group.

Built-in Active Directory Accounts

If you've read Chapter 5, you learned about some built-in local accounts that exist on regular Windows client and server operating system versions. In this section you will find information about built-in accounts that exist in every Active Directory environment. However, this section does not provide information about Guest and DefaultAccount accounts, which also exist in the domain. You can read about these accounts in Chapter 5.

Administrator

The Administrator account is usually considered an emergency account and is a member of the following domain groups:

- Administrators
- Domain Admins
- Domain Users
- Group Policy Creator Owners
- Schema Admins (for root domain only)
- Enterprise Admins (for root domain only)

The Administrator account has a default RID of 500. It is considered a high-privileged account and any use or modification of this account must be monitored.

Krbtgt

The krbtgt account is a built-in domain account. Its password's hash is used as a Kerberos Distribution Center (KDC) key (see Chapter 9 for more detail). This account is disabled by default and should not be enabled. It is recommended to monitor it for any modification or attempted use. This account is a member of the following domain groups by default:

- Denied RODC Password Replication Group
- Domain Users

Directory Services Restore Mode (DSRM) Account

Every domain controller has a Directory Services Restore Mode (DSRM) account, which is an emergency local account to be used when the Domain Controller service is not operational. A domain controller can be run in DSRM mode and the DSRM account's password can be used to perform local logon. Any change to the DSRM's account password should be monitored. The event in Listing 7-1 will appear in the Windows security event log on the domain controller if the DSRM password was successfully modified.

NOTE The event logs described in this section are available on the book's website, in the Successful DSRM Password Change.evtx file.

Listing 7-1: Event ID 4794: An attempt was made to set the Directory Services Restore Mode administrator password.

```
Task Category: User Account Management
Keywords: Audit Success
Subject:
     Security ID:          S-1-5-21-1913345275-1711810662-261465553-500
     Account Name:         administrator
     Account Domain:       HQCORP
     Logon ID:             0x2F336F
Additional Information:
     Caller Workstation:   2016DC
     Status Code:          0x0
```

The Subject section contains information about the account that requested the DSRM account's password reset operation.

The `Caller Workstation` field contains the name of the computer account from which the password reset command was received.

`Status Code` contains the status code for `Audit Failure` events, if the DSRM account's password reset operation was not successful.

Monitor this account for both `Audit Success` and `Audit Failure` 4794 events.

Active Directory Accounts Operations

There are two main types of Active Directory accounts: user and computer. In this section you will find information about common scenarios related to user and computer accounts and which events are generated for each scenario.

Active Directory User Accounts Operations

Most of the events related to operations with Active Directory user accounts are the same as for local user accounts discussed in Chapter 5. In this part we will discuss only information related to Active Directory for each scenario. If you do not find a description for some fields in the event, please see Chapter 5 for details.

Successful Active Directory User Creation

Depending on the method used to create a new Active Directory account, a different set of events is generated. Listing 7-2 shows an example of the event generated when an account is created using the following PowerShell command:

```
New-ADUser -Name "Andrei Miroshnikov" -SamAccountName amiroshnikov
```

Listing 7-2: Event ID 4720: A user account was created.

```
Task Category: User Account Management
Keywords: Audit Success
Subject:
    Security ID:           S-1-5-21-1913345275-1711810662-261465553-500
    Account Name:          administrator
    Account Domain:        HQCORP
    Logon ID:              0x2F336F
New Account:
    Security ID:           S-1-5-21-1913345275-1711810662-261465553-1126
    Account Name:          amiroshnikov
    Account Domain:        HQCORP
Attributes:
    SAM Account Name:      amiroshnikov
    Display Name:          -
```

```
    User Principal Name:    -
    Home Directory:         -
    Home Drive:             -
    Script Path:            -
    Profile Path:           -
    User Workstations:      -
    Password Last Set:      %%1794 (<never>)
    Account Expires:        %%1794 (<never>)
    Primary Group ID:       513
    Allowed To Delegate To: -
    Old UAC Value:          0x0
    New UAC Value:          0x11
    User Account Control:
                %%2080 (Account Disabled)
                %%2084 ('Normal Account' - Enabled)
    User Parameters:        -
    SID History:            -
    Logon Hours:            %%1793 (<value not set>)
Additional Information:
    Privileges              -
```

NOTE The event described above is available on the book's website, in the `Successful Active Directory User Creation - PowerShell.evtx` file.

The `Subject` section contains information about the account that created the new user account.

The `New Account` section contains information about the newly created user account.

The `SAM Account Name` field contains the value of the new account's `samAccountName` attribute. The `samAccountName` attribute was used by pre-Windows 2000 systems for authentication, but it is still exists in recent operating system versions.

Table 7-1 contains information about 4720 event fields and mapped user account properties.

Table 7-1: Mappings between 4720 Event Fields and User Account Properties

FIELD NAME	PROPERTY NAME
SAM Account Name	sAMAccountName
Display Name	displayName
User Principal Name	userPrincipalName
Home Directory	homeDirectory
Home Drive	homeDrive
Script Path	scriptPath

FIELD NAME	PROPERTY NAME
Profile Path	profilePath
User Workstations	userWorkstations
Password Last Set	pwdLastSet
Account Expires	accountExpires
Primary Group ID	primaryGroupID
Allowed To Delegate To	AllowedToDelegateTo
SID History	sIDHistory
Logon Hours	logonHours

The Old UAC Value field contains the hexadecimal mask of the flags that were previously set in the account's userAccountControl attribute. You can see more information about hexadecimal values for each UAC flag in Table 5.2. In this example, no flags were previously set (0x0) because it is a brand-new user account.

The New UAC Value field contains the new hexadecimal mask for the user-AccountControl attribute. In this example the following flags were set:

- **0x10:** 'Normal Account' - Enabled

- **0x1:** Account Disabled

- **0x10 + 0x1 = 0x11:** The New UAC Value field's value.

The Primary Group ID field contains the Relative Identifier (RID) of the user object's primary group SID. It is usually set to 513 (Domain Users) by default for all new domain user accounts.

You can find more information about the 4720 event in Chapter 5.

As mentioned previously, different account creation methods generate different 4720 events and may also invoke some additional events. For example, the events in Listings 7-3 through 7-8 are generated in the Windows security event log on the domain controller when a user is created using the Active Directory Users and Computers (ADUC) management snap-in.

Listing 7-3: Event ID 4720: A user account was created.

```
Task Category: User Account Management
Keywords: Audit Success
Subject:
    Security ID:        S-1-5-21-1913345275-1711810662-261465553-500
    Account Name:       administrator
    Account Domain:     HQCORP
    Logon ID:           0x2F336F
New Account:
    Security ID:        S-1-5-21-1913345275-1711810662-261465553-1125
    Account Name:       Sergey
    Account Domain:     HQCORP
```

```
Attributes:
     SAM Account Name:        Sergey
     Display Name:            Sergey
     User Principal Name:     Sergey@hqcorp.local
     Home Directory:          -
     Home Drive:              -
     Script Path:             -
     Profile Path:            -
     User Workstations:       -
     Password Last Set:       %%1794 (<never>)
     Account Expires:         %%1794 (<never>)
     Primary Group ID:        513
     Allowed To Delegate To: -
     Old UAC Value:           0x0
     New UAC Value:           0x15
     User Account Control:
                 %%2080 (Account Disabled)
                 %%2082 ('Password Not Required' - Enabled)
                 %%2084 ('Normal Account' - Enabled)
     User Parameters:         -
     SID History:             -
     Logon Hours:             %%1793 (<value not set>)
Additional Information:
     Privileges               -
```

NOTE The events from Listing 7-3 through 7-8 are available on the book's website, in the Successful Active Directory User Creation - ADUC.evtx file.

As you can see in this example, the User Principal Name field is automatically set using ADUC. Also, the 'Password Not Required' - Enabled flag is set by ADUC at creation time, even if it was not initially set during account creation.

Listing 7-4 shows that the new account's password was set. It is recorded as a separate event during user account creation using ADUC.

Listing 7-4: Event ID 4738: A user account was changed.

```
Task Category: User Account Management
Keywords: Audit Success
Other fields...
          Password Last Set:     6/9/2017 4:30:05 PM
Other fields...
```

Listing 7-5 shows an additional event informing you about a successful password reset for the newly created account.

Listing 7-5: Event ID 4724: An attempt was made to reset an account's password.

```
Task Category: User Account Management
Keywords: Audit Success
Subject:
    Security ID:            S-1-5-21-1913345275-1711810662-261465553-500
    Account Name:           Administrator
    Account Domain:         HQCORP
    Logon ID:               0xC2A414
Target Account:
    Security ID:            S-1-5-21-1913345275-1711810662-261465553-1125
    Account Name:           Sergey
    Account Domain:         HQCORP
```

Initially, when ADUC is used for a new user creation operation, the 'Password Not Required' flag is enabled. The event in Listing 7-6 informs you that it was disabled, which means that this user account requires a password to log on.

Listing 7-6: Event ID 4738: A user account was changed.

```
Task Category: User Account Management
Keywords: Audit Success
Other fields...
    Old UAC Value:          0x15
    New UAC Value:          0x11
    User Account Control:
            %%2050 ('Password Not Required' - Disabled)
Other fields...
```

Initially the account is created in a disabled state. The event in Listing 7-7 informs you that the account was enabled.

Listing 7-7: Event ID 4738: A user account was changed.

```
Task Category: User Account Management
Keywords: Audit Success
Other fields...
    Old UAC Value:          0x11
    New UAC Value:          0x10
    User Account Control:
            %%2048 (Account Enabled)
Other fields...
```

Listing 7-8 shows a dedicated event, in addition to previous 4738 event, which informs you that the account was enabled.

Listing 7-8: Event ID 4722: A user account was enabled.

```
Task Category: User Account Management
Keywords: Audit Success
Subject:
      Security ID:            S-1-5-21-1913345275-1711810662-261465553-500
      Account Name:           administrator
      Account Domain:         HQCORP
      Logon ID:               0x2F336F
Target Account:
      Security ID:            S-1-5-21-1913345275-1711810662-261465553-1125
      Account Name:           Sergey
      Account Domain:         HQCORP
```

As you can see, a PowerShell script invokes only one event in the event log, but the ADUC user creation process invokes six events.

Unsuccessful Active Directory User Creation

Events generated for unsuccessful user creation in Active Directory depend on the method used to create a new account.

If, for example, a user account does not have required permissions and uses the New-ADUser PowerShell command to create a new user account, no events are recorded in the Windows security event log on a domain controller.

> **NOTE** The event logs described in this section are available on the book's website, in the Unsuccessful Active Directory User Creation.evtx file.

But if the net user /add command is used to create a new user account, the event in Listings 7-9 is generated in the Windows security event log on a domain controller.

Listing 7-9: Event ID 4661: A handle to an object was requested.

```
Task Category: SAM
Keywords: Audit Success
Subject :
      Security ID:            S-1-5-21-1913345275-1711810662-261465553-1120
      Account Name:           Andrei
      Account Domain:         HQCORP
      Logon ID:               0x33395C
Object:
      Object Server:          Security Account Manager
      Object Type:            SAM_DOMAIN
      Object Name:            DC=hqcorp,DC=local
      Handle ID:              0x1a916ce9640
Process Information:
      Process ID:             0x31c
      Process Name:           C:\Windows\System32\lsass.exe
```

```
Access Request Information:
      Transaction ID:        {00000000-0000-0000-0000-000000000000}
      Accesses:              %%1538 (READ_CONTROL)
                             %%5394 (ReadOtherParameters)
                             %%5396 (CreateUser)
                             %%5399 (GetLocalGroupMembership)
                             See more information about these values in
                               chapter 8
      Access Reasons:        -
      Access Mask:           0x20094
```

This event shows a successful request for READ_CONTROL, ReadOtherParameters, CreateUser, and GetLocalGroupMembershipaccess permissions for the DC=hqcorp,DC=local SAM_DOMAIN object. But the operation was not successful, so unfortunately this information is not reported in the Windows security event log by default.

This scenario can be monitored using the Audit Failure handle request events discussed in Chapter 8, if the appropriate SACL is configured to audit failed creation of User objects.

Successful Active Directory User Deletion

With successful domain user account deletion, the event shown in Listing 7-10 is generated in the domain controller's security event log.

Listing 7-10: Event ID 4726: A user account was deleted.

```
Task Category: User Account Management
Keywords: Audit Success
Subject:
      Security ID:           S-1-5-21-1913345275-1711810662-261465553-1120
      Account Name:          andrei
      Account Domain:        HQCORP
      Logon ID:              0x35D03E
Target Account:
      Security ID:           S-1-5-21-1913345275-1711810662-261465553-1126
      Account Name:          amiroshnikov
      Account Domain:        HQCORP
Additional Information:
      Privileges       -
```

NOTE The event logs described in this section are available on the book's website, in the Successful Active Directory User Deletion.evtx file.

This event shows that the Subject account deleted the Target Account.

Unsuccessful Active Directory User Deletion

Different event logs will appear in the domain controller's security event log depending on the method being used for domain user account removal.

If standard ADUC was used to delete an account and the operation failed due to lack of permissions (access denied), no events will be generated in the security event log on the domain controller.

If the `net user /delete` command is used, multiple events will be generated in the security event log on the domain controller, but none of them signals anything about an access denied result or unsuccessful deletion.

You can see an example of events generated for unsuccessful Active Directory user account deletion using the `net user /delete` command in the `Unsuccessful Active Directory User Deletion.evtx` file in downloads for this chapter.

This scenario can be monitored using the `Audit Failure` handle request events discussed in Chapter 8, if the appropriate SACL is configured to audit failed User object deletions.

Other Active Directory User Account Operations

The following operations report the same events as operations discussed in Chapter 5:

- User account password reset
- User account password modification
- User account enable or disable operations
- Account lockout
- Account modifications

Refer to Chapter 5 for more information about these operations.

Successful Active Directory User SID History Addition

All Active Directory user accounts have an attribute called `sIDHistory`. The `sIDHistory` attribute is designed for accounts that are migrated from one domain to another. It contains a list of security group SIDs from the account's previous domain. `sIDHistory` SIDs are added to the user logon session token like normal group membership information.

It is critical to control the use of the `sIDHistory` attribute when no account migrations are taking place.

If an SID was successfully added to the `sIDHistory` attribute for a domain user account, the event in Listing 7-11 will appear in the domain controller's security event log.

Listing 7-11: Event ID 4765: SID History was added to an account.

```
Task Category: User Account Management
Keywords: Audit Success
Subject:
     Security ID:          S-1-5-21-2634088540-571122920-1382659128-500
     Account Name:         Administrator
     Account Domain:       MAINCORP
     Logon ID:             0x432C8
Target Account:
     Security ID:          S-1-5-21-2634088540-571122920-1382659128-1104
     Account Name:         Andrei
     Account Domain:       MAINCORP
Source Account:
     Security ID:          S-1-5-21-2634088540-571122920-1382659128-512
     Account Name:         maincorp.local\Domain Admins
```

> **NOTE** The event logs described in this section are available on the book's website, in the `Successful SID History Add.evtx` file.

The `Subject` section contains information about the account that performed the operation.

The `Target Account` section contains information about which account's `sIDHistory` attribute was changed.

The `Source Account` field contains information about the SID being added to the `Target Account` SID history.

All 4765 events should be monitored when no account migrations are taking place.

Active Directory Computer Account Operations

Active Directory computer accounts can be created automatically when a new machine joins an Active Directory domain. They can also be created manually using the Active Directory Users and Computers management console, a PowerShell script, or any other method. In this section you will find information about the ways to monitor automated and manual operations with computer accounts.

Successful Computer Account Creation - Joining a Domain

During a normal domain join procedure, a new computer account is created in Active Directory for the host that joins the domain. Listing 7-12 shows how the event for computer account creation looks on a domain controller, when an account is created during standard domain join operation.

Listing 7-12: Event ID 4741: A computer account was created.

```
Task Category: Computer Account Management
Keywords: Audit Success
Subject:
      Security ID:            S-1-5-21-1913345275-1711810662-261465553-500
      Account Name:           Administrator
      Account Domain:         HQCORP
      Logon ID:               0x50E982
New Computer Account:
      Security ID:            S-1-5-21-1913345275-1711810662-261465553-1127
      Account Name:           2012R2SRV$
      Account Domain:         HQCORP
Attributes:
      SAM Account Name:       2012R2SRV$
Other fields...
      Password Last Set:      6/12/2017 6:10:23 PM
      Account Expires:        %%1794 (<never>)
      Primary Group ID:       515
      AllowedToDelegateTo:    -
      Old UAC Value:          0x0
      New UAC Value:          0x80
      User Account Control:
              %%2087 ('Workstation Trust Account' - Enabled)
      User Parameters:        -
      SID History:            -
      Logon Hours:            %%1793 (<value not set>)
      DNS Host Name:          2012r2srv.hqcorp.local
      Service Principal Names:
          HOST/2012r2srv.hqcorp.local
          RestrictedKrbHost/2012r2srv.hqcorp.local
          HOST/2012R2SRV
          RestrictedKrbHost/2012R2SRV
Other fields...
```

NOTE The event logs described in this section are available on the book's website, in the `Successful Computer Account Creation - joining a domain .evtx` file.

The following fields in the event are not normally applicable to computer accounts:

- `Display Name`
- `User Principal Name`
- `Home Directory`
- `Home Drive`

- Script Path
- Profile Path
- User Workstations
- Logon Hours

For normal domain join operations all accounts are created by the domain account that was specified during the domain join procedure (Subject).

Password Last Set is set at the moment an account is created.

The Primary Group ID field contains the Relative Identifier (RID) of a computer object's primary group SID. It usually has one of the following values:

- **515 (Domain Computers):** For member servers and workstations.
- **516 (Domain Controllers):** For domain controllers.
- **521 (Read-only Domain Controllers):** For Read-Only Domain Controllers (RODC).

All new computer objects, which are not domain controllers, have the 'Workstation Trust Account' flag enabled in UAC.

Computer account creation event uses the same schema as user account creation, but adds some extra fields. That is why some fields in the event are not applicable to computer accounts. There are two new fields added in the 4741 event:

- **DNS Host Name:** The value of the dNSHostName attribute of the new computer object. Contains the name of computer account as registered in DNS.
- **Service Principal Names:** The value of the servicePrincipalName attribute of new computer object. Contains a list of Service Principal Names (SPNs), registered for the computer account.

Successful Computer Account Creation - Manual Creation

As shown in Listing 7-13, when a computer account is created manually using the Active Directory Users and Computers (ADUC) management console, the event in the security event log will look a little bit different from the event generated when an account is automatically generated.

Listing 7-13: Event ID 4741: A computer account was created.

```
Task Category: Computer Account Management
Keywords: Audit Success
Subject:
     Security ID:         S-1-5-21-1913345275-1711810662-261465553-500
     Account Name:        Administrator
     Account Domain:      HQCORP
     Logon ID:            0x241D46
```

```
New Computer Account:
      Security ID:           S-1-5-21-1913345275-1711810662-261465553-1128
      Account Name:          NEWCLIENT$
      Account Domain:        HQCORP
Attributes:
      SAM Account Name:      NEWCLIENT$
Other fields...
      Password Last Set:     %%1794 (<never>)
      Account Expires:       %%1794 (<never>)
      Primary Group ID:      515
      AllowedToDelegateTo:   -
      Old UAC Value:         0x0
      New UAC Value:         0x85
      User Account Control:
                  %%2080 (Account Disabled)
                  %%2082 ('Password Not Required' - Enabled)
                  %%2087 ('Workstation Trust Account' - Enabled)
      User Parameters:           -
      SID History:               -
      Logon Hours:           %%1793 (<value not set>)
      DNS Host Name:             -
      Service Principal Names: -
```

NOTE The event logs described in this section are available on the book's website,
in the `Successful Computer Account Creation - manual creation`
`.evtx` **file.**

The `Subject` section contains information about the account being used for
new computer account creation.

Differences between a manually created computer account using ADUC and
an automatically created account are:

- The `Account Disabled` flag is set, which means the account is disabled
  by default.

- The `Password Not Required` flag is set by default.

- `Password Last Set` has a value of `never`, which means there is no password set for the account by default.

- No `DNS Host Name` and `Service Principal Names` field values are set.

Unsuccessful Computer Account Creation

There is no dedicated event for unsuccessful computer account creation operation.

Failed computer account creation due to insufficient access rights can be monitored using the `Audit Failure` handle request events discussed in Chapter 8, if
the appropriate SACL is configured to audit failed Computer objects creation.

Successful Computer Account Deletion

There are many ways an Active Directory computer account can be deleted: using the Active Directory Users and Computers management console, command-line tools, PowerShell commands, and so on. All these methods will trigger the event in Listing 7-14 in the Windows security event log on a domain controller.

Listing 7-14: Event ID 4743: A computer account was deleted.

```
Task Category: Computer Account Management
Keywords: Audit Success
Subject:
      Security ID:            S-1-5-21-1913345275-1711810662-261465553-500
      Account Name:           Administrator
      Account Domain:         HQCORP
      Logon ID:               0x241D46
Target Computer:
      Security ID:            S-1-5-21-1913345275-1711810662-261465553-1128
      Account Name:           NEWCLIENT$
      Account Domain:         HQCORP
```

NOTE The event logs described in this section are available on the book's website, in the Successful Computer Account Deletion.evtx **file.**

The Subject section contains information about the account used to delete a computer account.

The Target Computer section contains information about the computer being deleted.

Unsuccessful Computer Account Deletion

There is no dedicated event for unsuccessful computer account deletion operations.

Failed computer account deletion due to insufficient access permissions can be monitored using the Audit Failure handle request events discussed in Chapter 8, if the appropriate SACL is configured to audit failed Computer object deletions.

Successful Computer Account Modification

If any attribute of the Active Directory computer account is modified, the computer account modification event shown in Listing 7-15 is generated in the security event log on a domain controller.

Listing 7-15: Event ID 4742: A computer account was changed.

```
Task Category: Computer Account Management
Keywords: Audit Success
```

```
Subject:
     Security ID:             S-1-5-21-1913345275-1711810662-261465553-500
     Account Name:            Administrator
     Account Domain:          HQCORP
     Logon ID:                0x1D9153
Computer Account That Was Changed:
     Security ID:             S-1-5-21-1913345275-1711810662-261465553-1131
     Account Name:            WINDOWS-CLIENT$
     Account Domain:          HQCORP
Changed Attributes:
Other fields...
     AllowedToDelegateTo:     -
     Old UAC Value:           0x84
     New UAC Value:           0x2084
     User Account Control:
               %%2093 ('Trusted For Delegation' - Enabled)
     User Parameters:         -
     SID History:             -
     Logon Hours:             -
     DNS Host Name:           -
     Service Principal Names: -
Additional Information:
     Privileges:              -
```

NOTE   The event logs described in this section are available on the book's website, in the `Successful Computer Account Modification.evtx` file.

Computer account modification events use the same schema as computer creation 4741 events. If any of the parameters listed in the event were modified, you will see a new value in the appropriate field.

There is no information about a previous value for a modified attribute except the `Old UAC Value` field.

If, for example, some attribute was modified but it does not exist in the event's schema, a 4742 event will be generated with all fields having a value of "-". It's impossible to find out which attribute was modified; the only thing you can be sure of is that it was not one of the attributes included in the event.

In this example, the `Old UAC Value` is `0x84`, which is:

- **0x80:** `'Workstation Trust Account' - Enabled`

- **0x4:** `'Password Not Required' - Enabled`

The UAC was changed to `0x2084`. `0x2000` was added, which is `'Trusted For Delegation' - Enabled`.

The `User Parameters` field is a cumulative field for dial-in attributes and, if changed, is usually shown as `<value changed, but not displayed>` (`%%1792`) without showing any details about a change.

Unsuccessful Computer Account Modification

There is no dedicated event for unsuccessful computer account modification operation.

Failed computer account modification due to insufficient access permissions can be monitored using the `Audit Failure` handle request events discussed in Chapter 8, if the appropriate SACL is configured to audit failed Computer object modifications.

Active Directory Group Operations

There are two main types of Active Directory groups:

- **Security groups:** used to assign security access permissions and act as a valid Active Directory security principal.

- **Distribution groups:** Cannot be used to assign security access permissions, mainly used as e-mail distribution groups.

Security and distribution groups are also divided into the group types that define a group scope. Table 7-2 contains the group scope types available in Active Directory.

Table 7-2: Active Directory Group Scope Types

SCOPE TYPE	CAN INCLUDE	PERMISSIONS SCOPE	CONVERT
Domain local	Accounts from any domain Global groups from any domain Universal groups from any domain Domain local groups from the same domain	Same domain as domain local group's domain	Can be converted to Universal group
Global	Accounts from the same domain Global groups from the same domain	Any domain within a forest	Can be converted to Universal group
Universal	Accounts from any domain within the forest Global groups from any domain within the forest Universal groups from any domain within the forest	Any domain or forest	Can be converted to domain local or global group

Security group events belong to the `Security Group Management` auditing subcategory, while distribution group events belong to the `Distribution Group Management` subcategory.

In this section you will find information about how to monitor the most common operations with security and distribution groups.

Active Directory Group Creation

As mentioned previously in this chapter, a different number and combination of events may appear in the security event log when different group creation methods are used. But the events discussed in this section will always occur in the security event log on a domain controller, no matter which method is used for its creation.

Table 7-3 contains information about event IDs and event names associated with different group creation events.

Table 7-3: Active Directory Group Creation Events

GROUP TYPE	GROUP SCOPE	EVENT ID	EVENT NAME
Security	Domain local	4731	A security-enabled local group was created
	Global	4727	A security-enabled global group was created
	Universal	4754	A security-enabled universal group was created
Distribution	Domain local	4744	A security-disabled local group was created
	Global	4749	A security-disabled global group was created
	Universal	4759	A security-disabled universal group was created

All events listed in Table 7-3 have the same schema.

NOTE The event logs described in this section are available on the book's website, in the `Active Directory Group Creation Events.evtx` file.

Listing 7-16 is an example of a 4731 event.

Listing 7-16: Event ID 4731: A security-enabled local group was created.

```
Task Category: Security Group Management
Keywords: Audit Success
Subject:
     Security ID:          S-1-5-21-1913345275-1711810662-261465553-500
     Account Name:         Administrator
```

```
     Account Domain:          HQCORP
     Logon ID:                0x1D9153
New Group:
     Security ID:             S-1-5-21-1913345275-1711810662-261465553-1133
     Group Name:              Security Domain local
     Group Domain:            HQCORP
Attributes:
     SAM Account Name:        Security Domain local
     SID History:             -
```

The Subject section contains information about the account used to create the new group.

The New Group section contains information about the newly created group.

The SAM Account Name field contains the value of the sAMAccountName attribute of the created group.

The SID History field contains the value of the sIDHistory attribute of the created group. The sIDHistory attribute might have some values associated to it if the group was migrated from another domain.

All events listed in Table 7-3 have the same schema as the 4731 event.

Active Directory Group Deletion

As is the case with Active Directory group creation, there are different events for different group types and group scopes.

Table 7-4 contains information about event IDs and event names associated with different group deletion operations.

Table 7-4: Active Directory Group Deletion Events

GROUP TYPE	GROUP SCOPE	EVENT ID	EVENT NAME
Distribution	Domain local	4748	A security-disabled local group was deleted
	Global	4753	A security-disabled global group was deleted
	Universal	4763	A security-disabled universal group was deleted
Security	Domain local	4734	A security-enabled local group was deleted
	Global	4730	A security-enabled global group was deleted
	Universal	4758	A security-enabled universal group was deleted

> **NOTE** The event logs described in this section are available on the book's website, in the `Active Directory Group Deletion Events.evtx` file.

Listing 7-17 is an example of a 4758 event.

Listing 7-17: Event ID 4758: A security-enabled universal group was deleted.

```
Task Category: Security Group Management
Keywords: Audit Success
Subject:
     Security ID:          S-1-5-21-1913345275-1711810662-261465553-500
     Account Name:         Administrator
     Account Domain:       HQCORP
     Logon ID:             0x1D9153
Group:
     Security ID:          S-1-5-21-1913345275-1711810662-261465553-1135
     Group Name:           Security Universal
     Group Domain:         HQCORP
```

The `Subject` section contains information about the account that was used to delete the group.

The `Group` section contains information about a deleted group.

Active Directory Group Modification

Not much information is provided in Active Directory group modification events. As is true for group creation, there are different events for different group types and group scopes.

Table 7-5 contains information about event IDs and event names associated with different group modification operations.

Table 7-5: Active Directory Group Modification Events

GROUP TYPE	GROUP SCOPE	EVENT ID	EVENT NAME
Distribution	Domain local	4745	A security-disabled local group was changed
	Global	4750	A security-disabled global group was changed
	Universal	4760	A security-disabled universal group was changed
Security	Domain local	4735	A security-enabled local group was changed
	Global	4737	A security-enabled global group was changed
	Universal	4755	A security-enabled universal group was changed

The primary problem related to Active Directory group modification events is that they don't show details about most modification actions. The only information you get about what was modified is about sAMAccountName and sID-History attribute modification. If another attribute was modified, for example description, a modification event will be generated, but it will not have any details about what exactly was modified. Also, some attributes, like the info attribute, do not invoke any event at all.

NOTE   The event logs described in this section are available on the book's website, in the Active Directory Group Modification Events.evtx file.

Listing 7-18 is an example or 4755 event.

Listing 7-18: Event ID 4755: A security-enabled universal group was changed.

```
Task Category: Security Group Management
Keywords: Audit Success
Subject:
      Security ID:              S-1-5-21-1913345275-1711810662-261465553-500
      Account Name:            Administrator
      Account Domain:          HQCORP
      Logon ID:                0x1D9153
Group:
      Security ID:              S-1-5-21-1913345275-1711810662-261465553-1141
      Group Name:              Security Universal Group New
      Group Domain:            HQCORP
Changed Attributes:
      SAM Account Name:        Security Universal Group New
      SID History:             -
```

The Subject section contains information about the account used to modify the group.

The Group section contains information about the modified group.

The SAM Account Name field contains the new value of the sAMAccountName attribute of the group, if it was modified.

The SID History field contains the new value of the sIDHistory attribute of the group, if it was modified.

Active Directory Group New Member Added

When a new member is added to an Active Directory group, one of the events listed in Table 7-6 is generated, depending on group type and group scope.

Table 7-6: Active Directory Group New Member Added Events

GROUP TYPE	GROUP SCOPE	EVENT ID	EVENT NAME
Distribution	Domain local	4746	A member was added to a security-disabled local group
	Global	4751	A member was added to a security-disabled global group
	Universal	4761	A member was added to a security-disabled universal group
Security	Domain local	4732	A member was added to a security-enabled local group
	Global	4728	A member was added to a security-enabled global group
	Universal	4756	A member was added to a security-enabled universal group

NOTE The event logs described in this section are available on the book's website, in the `Active Directory Group Member Add Events.evtx` file.

Listing 7-19 is an example of a 4756 event.

Listing 7-19: Event ID 4756: A member was added to a security-enabled universal group.

```
Task Category: Security Group Management
Keywords: Audit Success
Subject:
      Security ID:          S-1-5-21-1913345275-1711810662-261465553-500
      Account Name:         Administrator
      Account Domain:       HQCORP
      Logon ID:             0x1D9153
Member:
      Security ID:          S-1-5-21-1913345275-1711810662-261465553-1120
      Account Name:         CN=Andrei,CN=Users,DC=hqcorp,DC=local
Group:
      Security ID:          S-1-5-21-1913345275-1711810662-261465553-1141
      Account Name:         Security Universal Group New
      Account Domain:       HQCORP
```

The `Subject` section contains information about the account used to add the new member to the group.

The `Member` section contains information about the new member added to the group.

The `Member\Account Name` field contains information about the added member's distinguished name (DN). This value is stored in the `distinguishedName` attribute of the added account or group.

The `Group` section contains information about the group to which a new member was added.

Active Directory Group Member Removed

When a member is removed from an Active Directory group, one of the events listed in Table 7-7 is generated, depending on group type and group scope.

Table 7-7: Active Directory Group Member Removed Events

GROUP TYPE	GROUP SCOPE	EVENT ID	EVENT NAME
Distribution	Domain local	4747	A member was removed from a security-disabled local group
	Global	4752	A member was removed from a security-disabled global group
	Universal	4762	A member was removed from a security-disabled universal group
Security	Domain local	4733	A member was removed from a security-enabled local group
	Global	4729	A member was removed from a security-enabled global group
	Universal	4757	A member was removed from a security-enabled universal group

NOTE The event logs described in this section are available on the book's website, in the `Active Directory Group Member Remove Events.evtx` file.

Listing 7-20 is an example of a 4757 event.

Listing 7-20: Event ID 4757: A member was removed from a security-enabled universal group.

```
Task Category: Security Group Management
Keywords: Audit Success
Subject:
      Security ID:          S-1-5-21-1913345275-1711810662-261465553-500
      Account Name:         Administrator
      Account Domain:       HQCORP
      Logon ID:             0x1D9153
Member:
      Security ID:          S-1-5-21-1913345275-1711810662-261465553-1120
      Account Name:         CN=Andrei,CN=Users,DC=hqcorp,DC=local
```

```
Group:
      Security ID:          S-1-5-21-1913345275-1711810662-261465553-1141
      Group Name:          Security Universal Group New
      Group Domain:        HQCORP
```

The Subject section contains information about the account used to remove a member from the group.

The Member section contains information about the removed member.

The Member\Account Name field contains information about the removed member's distinguished name (DN). This value is stored in the distinguished-Name attribute of the removed member's Active Directory object.

The Group section contains information about a group from which the member was removed.

A separate 4757 event is generated for each removed member.

Group Type and Scope Type Changes

It is possible to change a group's general type from security to distribution and vice versa. It is also possible to change a group's scope. When group type or scope is changed the event in Listing 7-21 is generated in the domain controller's security event log.

Listing 7-21: Event ID 4764: A group's type was changed.

```
Task Category: Security Group Management
Keywords: Audit Success
Subject:
      Security ID:          S-1-5-21-1913345275-1711810662-261465553-500
      Account Name:        Administrator
      Account Domain:      HQCORP
      Logon ID:            0x1D9153
Change Type:       Security Disabled Global Group Changed to Security
                     Enabled Universal Group.
Group:
      Security ID:          S-1-5-21-1913345275-1711810662-261465553-1143
      Group Name:          Distribution Global Group New
      Group Domain:        HQCORP
```

NOTE The event logs described in this section are available on the book's website, in the Active Directory Group Type or Scope Modification.evtx file.

The `Subject` section contains information about the account used to change a group type.

The `Change Type` field shows the group's previous type and its new type. This field has the format `%%1 Changed To %%2`, where `%%1` and `%%2` may have one of the following values:

- `Security Disabled Local Group`
- `Security Disabled Universal Group`
- `Security Disabled Global Group`
- `Security Enabled Local Group`
- `Security Enabled Universal Group`
- `Security Enabled Global Group`

In this example the group type was changed from `Security Disabled Global Group` (Distribution Global) to `Security Enabled Universal Group` (Security Universal).

The `Group` section contains information about the group whose type was changed.

Active Directory Trust Operations

Active Directory trusts provide the ability to implement trust relationships between Active Directory domains and forests. If there is a trust between Active Directory domains or forests, accounts from the trusted domain or forest are allowed to authenticate on trusting domain or forest hosts.

Active Directory trusts support Kerberos and NTLM authentication protocols.

Trust relationship settings for domains are stored in trusted domain objects (TDOs). Each domain trust has a unique TDO associated to it. TDOs are stored in the `System` container in a domain and named as the name of trusted/trusting domain. TDOs belong to the `trustedDomain` class. Figure 7-1 shows an example of a TDO object in Active Directory.

Active Directory Trust Creation Operations

Each time new trust is created the event in Listing 7-22 is generated in the Windows security event log on a domain controller.

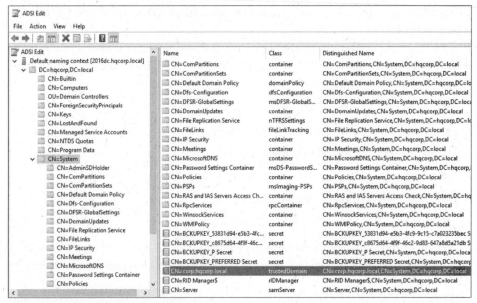

Figure 7-1: Active Directory TDOs location

Listing 7-22: Event ID 4706: A new trust was created to a domain.

```
Task Category: Authentication Policy Change
Keywords: Audit Success
Subject:
        Security ID:           S-1-5-18
        Account Name:          2016SRV$
        Account Domain:        HQCORP
        Logon ID:              0x3E7
Trusted Domain:
        Domain Name:           hqcorp.local
        Domain ID:             S-1-5-21-1913345275-1711810662-261465553
Trust Information:
        Trust Type:            2
        Trust Direction:       3
        Trust Attributes:      32
        SID Filtering:         %%1796 (Disabled)
```

NOTE   The event logs described in this section are available on the book's website, in the `Active Directory Trust Creation Operation.evtx` **file.**

4706 events basically inform you about new TDO object creation in a domain.

The `Subject` section contains information about the account that created a new TDO for a new trust. That account is usually the `S-1-5-18` (`SYSTEM`) account.

The `Trusted Domain` section contains information about a domain for which a TDO was created:

- **Domain Name:** Name of the domain for the newly created TDO. This is the `trustPartner` attribute of the TDO object.

- **Domain ID:** Unique identifier of the domain for which the TDO was created. It has the following structure: `S-1-5-21-DOMAIN_GUID`. This is the `securityIdentifier` attribute of the TDO object. For non-Windows domain trusts, such as `TRUST_TYPE_MIT` (MIT Kerberos) trusts, the `Domain ID` field usually has a value of `S-1-0-0` (NULL SID).

The `Trust Information` section contains detailed information about TDO object's settings.

The `Trust Type` field contains the decimal value of the `trustType` attribute for the new TDO. It shows the type of the newly created Active Directory trust. Table 7-8 contains a list of possible values for this field.

Table 7-8: Active Directory Trust Types

HEX CODE	TYPE	DESCRIPTION
0x1	TTD (TRUST_ TYPE_ DOWNLEVEL)	The domain controller of the trusted domain is running an operating system earlier than Windows 2000.
0x2	TTU (TRUST_ TYPE_ UPLEVEL)	The domain controller of the trusted domain is running Windows 2000 or later.
0x3	TTM (TRUST_ TYPE_MIT)	The trusted domain is a Massachusetts Institute of Technology (MIT) Kerberos realm.
0x4	TTDCE (TRUST_ TYPE_DCE)	Obsolete version of Kerberos realm used in Distributed Computing Environment (DCE) systems.
0x5 - 0x000FFFFF	-	Reserved for future use.
0x00100000 - 0xFFF00000	-	Reserved for provider-specific types.

The `Trust Direction` field contains the decimal value of the `trustDirection` attribute for the new TDO. It shows the direction of the newly created Active Directory trust. Figure 7-2 illustrates trust direction types that can be used in Microsoft Active Directory.

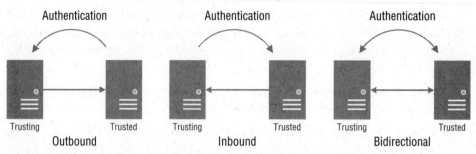

Figure 7-2: Active Directory trust directions

Active Directory trusts may have one of the following directions:

- **Outbound:** In the outbound direction the trusting domain trusts authentication requests from a trusted domain.

- **Inbound:** In the inbound direction the trusting domain's authentication requests are trusted by a trusted domain.

- **Bidirectional:** This is a combination of both outbound and inbound trust types.

Table 7-9 contains a list of possible values for the `Trust Direction` field.

Table 7-9: Active Directory Trust Direction Types

HEX CODE	TYPE	DESCRIPTION
0x0	TRUST_DIRECTION_DISABLED	This type is shown when a trust is in a disabled state.
0x1	TRUST_DIRECTION_INBOUND	Inbound trust.
0x2	TRUST_DIRECTION_OUTBOUND	Outbound trust.
0x3	TRUST_DIRECTION_ BIDIRECTIONAL	Bidirectional trust.

The `Trust Attributes` field contains the decimal value of the `trustAttributes` attribute for the new TDO. The `trustAttributes` attribute contains a hexadecimal mask for multiple trust attributes. Table 7-10 contains a list of values for trust attribute flags.

Table 7-10: Active Directory Trust Attributes

HEX CODE	ATTRIBUTE NAME	DESCRIPTION
0x1	TRUST_ATTRIBUTE_NON_TRANSITIVE	Nontransitive trust.
0x2	TRUST_ATTRIBUTE_UPLEVEL_ONLY	Trust can be used only by Windows 2000 and newer operating system clients.
0x4	TRUST_ATTRIBUTE_QUARANTINED_DOMAIN	The trusted domain is a quarantined domain.
0x8	TRUST_ATTRIBUTE_FOREST_TRANSITIVE	Cross-forest trust type. Active Directory trust between the root domains of two forests.
0x10	TRUST_ATTRIBUTE_CROSS_ORGANIZATION	Trust to domain or forest that is not part of the Active Directory organization.
0x20	TRUST_ATTRIBUTE_WITHIN_FOREST	Trust to the domain within the same Active Directory forest.
0x40	TRUST_ATTRIBUTE_TREAT_AS_EXTERNAL	Trust should be treated as an external trust by the SID Filtering mechanism. This applies least strict SID Filtering policies to the trust.
0x80	TRUST_ATTRIBUTE_USES_RC4_ENCRYPTION	Trust is capable of using RC4 encryption. Can be set only for TRUST_TYPE_MIT trusts.
0x200	TRUST_ATTRIBUTE_CROSS_ORGANIZATION_NO_TGT_DELEGATION	Tickets granted under this trust must not be trusted for delegation.
0x400	TRUST_ATTRIBUTE_PIM_TRUST	Trust should be treated as Privileged Identity Management trust by SID Filtering mechanism.

Keep in mind that values in Table 7-10 are hexadecimal. You will need to convert the `Trust Attributes` field value from decimal format to hexadecimal to "deconstruct" it.

The SID Filtering field shows whether the SID Filtering feature is enabled for a new trust. It can have one of the following values:

- %%1795: Enabled
- %%1796: Disabled

If the SID Filtering feature is enabled for a trust, accounts from trusted domains with SIDs that do not belong to a trusted domain will have those SIDs ignored/filtered and not included in any session token during authentication in the trusting domain.

Active Directory Trust Modification Operations

When the TDO for a trust is changed, the event in Listing 7-23 is generated in the Windows security event log.

Listing 7-23: Event ID 4716: Trusted domain information was modified.

```
Task Category: Authentication Policy Change
Keywords: Audit Success
Subject:
      Security ID:            S-1-5-21-1913345275-1711810662-261465553-500
      Account Name:           Administrator
      Account Domain:         HQCORP
      Logon ID:               0x3FA80
Trusted Domain:
      Domain Name:            -
      Domain ID:              S-1-5-21-3212943211-794299840-588279583
New Trust Information:
      Trust Type:             2
      Trust Direction:        3
      Trust Attributes:       36
      SID Filtering:          %%1795 (Enabled)
```

> **NOTE** The event logs described in this section are available on the book's website, in the Active Directory Trust Modification Operation.evtx file.

Fields in the 4716 event are the same as fields in the 4706 event.

This event does not show which field from the New Trust Information section was modified. It shows only current values of the domain trust TDO. It is not possible to verify from this event whether, for example, SID Filtering was enabled or the Trust Type changed.

The Domain Name field for the 4716 event is not captured and has a value of "not set" (-). You can verify which domain trust object was modified only using the Domain ID field.

In some cases `SID Filtering` is also captured as not set (-). For such cases it is not possible to determine the current status of the SID Filtering mechanism from this event.

Some changes, such as changes to the Kerberos AES encryption supportability option (Figure 7-3), trigger a 4716 event, but the event will not have any information about what exactly was changed in the TDO object, because Kerberos AES encryption-related support settings are not included in the event's schema.

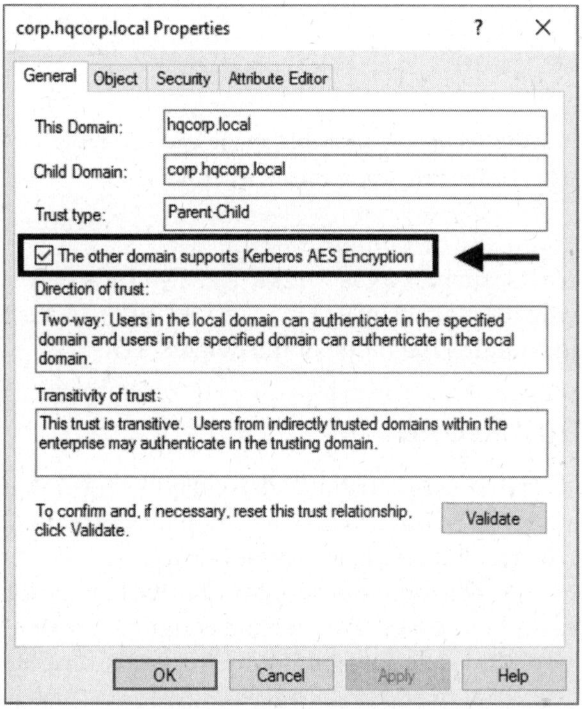

Figure 7-3: Active Directory TDO Kerberos AES encryption supportability option

For non-Windows domain trusts, such as `TRUST_TYPE_MIT` (MIT Kerberos) trusts, the `Domain ID` field usually has a value of `S-1-0-0` (NULL SID), which makes it hard to identify which TDO object was modified.

Active Directory Trust Deletion Operations

After a trust TDO is deleted, either manually as an Active Directory object (using the `adsiedit.msc` or `LDP.exe` tools, as an example) or using the Active Directory Domains and Trusts management console, the event in Listing 7-24 is generated in the security event log on the domain controller from which the deletion operation was initiated.

Listing 7-24: Event ID 4707: A trust to a domain was removed.

```
Task Category: Authentication Policy Change
Keywords: Audit Success
Subject:
     Security ID:          S-1-5-21-1913345275-1711810662-261465553-500
     Account Name:         Administrator
     Account Domain:       HQCORP
     Logon ID:             0x3FA80
Domain Information:
     Domain Name:          HQMAIN
     Domain ID:            S-1-0-0
```

> **NOTE** The event logs described in this section are available on the book's website,
> in the `Active Directory Trust Deletion Operation.evtx` file.

All fields in this event should already be familiar to you.

For non-Windows domain trusts, such as `TRUST_TYPE_MIT` (MIT Kerberos) trusts, the `Domain ID` field usually has a value of `S-1-0-0` (NULL SID). In such cases the `Domain Name` field still contains the name of the deleted TDO.

Operations with Forest Trust Records

TDOs have an `msDS-TrustForestTrustInfo` attribute (also called `FtInfo`) that has no associated value for domain trusts, but contains additional information, such as a list of all domains in the trusted forest, for forest trust.

The `msDS-TrustForestTrustInfo` attribute may contain multiple records, which may have different types and purposes. This section contains information about creation, modification, and deletion operations for `msDS-TrustForestTrustInfo` records.

Active Directory Forest Trust Record Creation Operations

If a new inbound, outbound, or bidirectional forest trust is created in the root domain, the events in Listing 7-25 are generated in the security event log on a domain controller, where the forest trust was added.

Listing 7-25: Event ID 4706: A new trust was created to a domain.

```
Task Category: Authentication Policy Change
Keywords: Audit Success
Other fields...
Trust Information:
     Trust Type:          2
     Trust Direction:     1
     Trust Attributes:    8
     SID Filtering:       %%1796 (Disabled)
```

NOTE The event logs described in this section are available on the book's website, in the `Active Directory Forest Trust Record Creation Operation .evtx` file.

From the `Trust Information` section you may learn the following information about a new trust:

- **Trust Type: 2:** `TRUST_TYPE_UPLEVEL`. The domain controller of the trusted domain is running Windows 2000 or later.

- **Trust Direction: 1:** It is an inbound trust.

- **Trust Attributes: 8:** `TRUST_ATTRIBUTE_FOREST_TRANSITIVE`. It is an Active Directory trust between the root domains of two forests.

By default, multiple 4865 events are generated during new forest trust creation, because new records are added to the `msDS-TrustForestTrustInfo` attribute in a new forest trust TDO. These 4865 events are for different record types. In Listing 7-26 you can see an example of one such event.

Listing 7-26: Event ID 4865: A trusted forest information entry was added.

```
Task Category: Authentication Policy Change
Keywords: Audit Success
Subject:
        Security ID:            S-1-5-21-3212943211-794299840-588279583-500
        Account Name:           Administrator
        Account Domain:         PARTNER
        Logon ID:               0x9B378
Trust Information:
        Forest Root:            hqcorp.local
        Forest Root SID:        S-1-5-21-1913345275-1711810662-261465553
        Operation ID:           0x59FE5A
        Entry Type:             0
        Flags:                  0
        Top Level Name:         hqcorp.local
        DNS Name:               -
        NetBIOS Name:           -
        Domain SID:             S-1-0-0
```

The `Subject` section contains information about an account that was used to add a new record.

The `Forest Root` field contains information about a forest trust TDO to which the record was added. It is the `trustPartner` attribute of the TDO object.

The `Forest Root SID` contains information about the SID of a forest to which the record was added. It is the `securityIdentifier` attribute of the TDO object.

The `Operation ID` field contains a unique transaction ID for events 4865, 4866, and 4867. These events may have the same `Operation ID` if they belong to the same transaction. For example, this can happen when a transaction is a new forest trust creation operation and two records are added as part of this operation. Both 4865 events for this operation will have the same `Operation ID`.

The `Entry Type` field contains the type of the new record. TDO records are the `LSA_FOREST_TRUST_RECORD_TYPE` structure objects. Table 7-11 contains a list of possible `msDS-TrustForestTrustInfo` record types.

Table 7-11: msDS-TrustForestTrustInfo Record Types

CODE	NAME	DESCRIPTION
0	ForestTrustTopLevelName	Record for routing included name suffix.
1	ForestTrustTopLevelNameEx	Record for routing excluded name suffix.
2	ForestTrustDomainInfo	Contains information about domain in the trusted forest. Has LSA_FOREST_TRUST_ DOMAIN_INFO structure type.

The `Flags` field contains additional information about the added record. It's a hexadecimal mask that may contain multiple flags enabled. Table 7-12 contains information about possible `msDS-TrustForestTrustInfo` record flags, depending on record type.

Table 7-12: msDS-TrustForestTrustInfo Record Flags

FLAG	RECORD TYPE	FLAG NAME	DESCRIPTION
0x1	0,1	LSA_TLN_DISABLED_ NEW	Disabled record.
	2	LSA_SID_DISABLED_ ADMIN	Entry is disabled for SID, NetBIOS, and DNS name–based matches by the administrator.
0x2	0,1	LSA_TLN_DISABLED_ ADMIN	Record disabled by administrator.
	2	LSA_SID_DISABLED_ CONFLICT	Entry is disabled for SID, NetBIOS, and DNS name–based matches due to a SID or DNS name–based conflict with another trusted domain.
0x4	0,1	LSA_TLN_DISABLED_ CONFLICT	Record is disabled due to a conflict with another trusted domain.
	2	LSA_NB_DISABLED_ ADMIN	Entry is disabled for NetBIOS name– based matches by the administrator.
0x8	0,1	–	
	2	LSA_NB_DISABLED_ CONFLICT	Entry is disabled for NetBIOS name– based matches due to a NetBIOS domain name conflict with another trusted domain.

The `Top Level Name` field is applicable to record types 0 and 1. It shows the DNS name of the trusted forest.

The `DNS Name`, `NetBIOS Name`, and `Domain SID` fields are not applicable to type 0 and 1 records. They are applicable only to type 2 records, as shown in Listing 7-27 and are discussed later in this chapter.

Listing 7-27: Event ID 4865: A trusted forest information entry was added.

```
Task Category: Authentication Policy Change
Keywords: Audit Success
Other fields...
Trust Information:
        Forest Root:              hqcorp.local
        Forest Root SID:          S-1-5-21-1913345275-1711810662-261465553
        Operation ID:             0x59FE5A
        Entry Type:               2
        Flags:                    0
        Top Level Name:           -
        DNS Name:                 hqcorp.local
        NetBIOS Name:             HQCORP
        Domain SID:               S-1-5-21-1913345275-1711810662-261465553
```

Active Directory Forest Trust Record Modification Operations

If a forest trust record was modified, the event in Listing 7-28 is generated in the security event log of a domain controller, on which the record was modified.

Listing 7-28: Event ID 4867: A trusted forest information entry was modified.

```
Task Category: Authentication Policy Change
Keywords: Audit Success
Subject:
        Security ID:              S-1-5-21-3212943211-794299840-588279583-500
        Account Name:             Administrator
        Account Domain:           PARTNER
        Logon ID:                 0x9B378
Trust Information:
        Forest Root:              hqcorp.local
        Forest Root SID:          S-1-5-21-1913345275-1711810662-261465553
        Operation ID:             0x8FB930
        Entry Type:               0
        Flags:                    2
        Top Level Name:           -
        DNS Name:                 -
        NetBIOS Name:             -
        Domain SID:               S-1-0-0
```

NOTE The event logs described in this section are available on the book's website, in the `Active Directory Forest Trust Record Modification Operation.evtx` file.

All fields in the 4867 events were discussed earlier in this chapter.

This event does not show which field from the `Trust Information` section was modified. It shows only the current values of the forest trust record. It is not possible to verify from this event whether, for example, `Flags` or `Entry Type` was changed.

Active Directory Forest Trust Record Remove Operations

When a forest trust record is removed, the event in Listing 7-29 is generated in the security event log of a domain controller, on which the record was removed.

Listing 7-29: Event ID 4866: A trusted forest information entry was removed.

```
Task Category: Authentication Policy Change
Keywords: Audit Success
Subject:
        Security ID:            S-1-5-21-3212943211-794299840-588279583-500
        Account Name:           Administrator
        Account Domain:         PARTNER
        Logon ID:               0x9B378
Trust Information:
        Forest Root:            hqcorp.local
        Forest Root SID:        S-1-5-21-1913345275-1711810662-261465553
        Operation ID:           0x8F9382
        Entry Type:             1
        Flags:                  0
        Top Level Name:         corp.hqcorp.local
        DNS Name:               -
        NetBIOS Name:           -
        Domain SID:             S-1-0-0
```

NOTE The event logs described in this section are available on the book's website, in the `Active Directory Forest Trust Record Remove Operation.evtx` file.

This event contains detailed information about the forest trust record being removed. This event has the same schema as 4867 and 4865 events.

Domain Policy Changes

Active Directory infrastructure provides the ability to centrally manage user and computer policies for domain hosts using group policies. In this section you will find information about domain policies and domain options that can be monitored using built-in security events without modifying any SACLs on Active Directory objects.

Password and Account Lockout Policies

Windows operating systems contain group policy settings that allow you to set password and account lockout policies.

Password policy can be configured using group policy settings located in `Computer Configurations\Policies\Windows Settings\Security Settings\ Account Policy\Password Policy`. The following group policy settings are available for configuration:

- Enforce password history
- Maximum password age
- Minimum password age
- Minimum password length
- Password must meet complexity requirements
- Store passwords using reversible encryption

Also, account lockout policy settings are located in `Computer Configurations\ Policies\Windows Settings\Security Settings\Account Policy\Account Lockout Policy`. The following group policy settings are available for configuration:

- Account lockout duration
- Account lockout threshold
- Reset account lockout counter after

Security event 4739 is designed to show changes to these local group policy security settings. This event generates on the host where the local policy was modified or to which new domain group policy settings were applied. That host can be a client, server, or domain controller. Listing 7-30 shows this event.

Listing 7-30: Event ID 4739: Domain Policy was changed.

```
Task Category: Authentication Policy Change
Keywords: Audit Success
Change Type:                    Lockout Policy modified
Subject:
        Security ID:            SYSTEM
        Account Name:           2016DC$
        Account Domain:         HQCORP
        Logon ID:               0x3E7
Domain:
        Domain Name:            HQCORP
        Domain ID:              HQCORP\
Changed Attributes:
        Min. Password Age:      -
        Max. Password Age:      -
        Force Logoff:           -
        Lockout Threshold:      10
        Lockout Observation Window:
        Lockout Duration:
        Password Properties:
        Min. Password Length:
        Password History Length:
        Machine Account Quota:
        Mixed Domain Mode:
        Domain Behavior Version:
        OEM Information:        -
```

> **NOTE** The event logs described in this section are available on the book's website, in the `Password and Account Lockout Policies.evtx` file.

The problem with the 4739 event is that it is not always recorded correctly on all supported Windows operating systems. It often contains corrupted data or does not contain any information about what exactly was modified.

This event, unfortunately, does not provide any reliable information; it can even show changes which were not performed.

Kerberos Policy

Kerberos protocol policy settings can be defined on the domain level and are applicable to domain controllers (KDC role holders). They are located at the following group policy path: `Computer Configurations\Policies\Windows Settings\Security Settings\Account Policy\Kerberos Policy`.

The following Kerberos policies are available for configuration:

- **Enforce user logon restrictions:** Enforces validation of user account restrictions, such as logon hours and machine restrictions for each Kerberos Ticket-Granting Service (TGS) ticket request.

- **Maximum lifetime for service ticket:** Specifies lifetime of Ticket-Granting Service (TGS) ticket in seconds.

- **Maximum lifetime for user ticket:** Specifies maximum number of hours after which Ticket-Granting Ticket (TGT) ticket must be renewed.

- **Maximum lifetime for user ticket renewal:** Specifies maximum number of days after which Ticket-Granting Ticket (TGT) ticket must be re-issued.

- **Maximum tolerance for computer clock synchronization:** Specifies maximum allowed difference in minutes between Key Distribution Center (domain controller) and Kerberos client.

If any of these Kerberos policy settings on a domain controller were changed, the event in Listing 7-31 is generated in the security event log on a domain controller.

Listing 7-31: Event ID 4713: Kerberos policy was changed.

```
Task Category: Authentication Policy Change
Keywords: Audit Success
Subject:
        Security ID:            S-1-5-18
        Account Name:           2016DC$
        Account Domain:         HQCORP
        Logon ID:               0x3E7
Changes Made:
('--' means no changes, otherwise each change is shown as:
(Parameter Name):       (new value) (old value))
KerOpts: 0x0 (0x80);  KerMinT: 0x45d964b800 (0x53d1ac1000);
  KerMaxT: 0x649534e000 (0x53d1ac1000);  KerMaxR:
 0x649534e0000 (0x58028e44000);  KerProxy: 0x165a0bc00 (0xb2d05e00);
```

> **NOTE** The event logs described in this section are available on the book's website, in the `Kerberos Policy.evtx` file.

If changes to multiple Kerberos policies were made at the same time, they all will be included in one 4713 event.

The `Subject` section contains information about the account that performed a Kerberos policy change. It is usually the `S-1-5-18` (`SYSTEM`) account, because group policies are applied by `Winlogon.exe`, which runs under the `SYSTEM` account.

The `Changes Made` section contains changes made to the Kerberos policy in the following format: (`Parameter Name`): (`new value`) (`old value`). New and old values are recorded in hexadecimal format. Here is the list of possible parameter names and ways to interpret values for these parameters:

- **KerProxy:** Maximum tolerance for computer clock synchronization. To get number of minutes you need to convert value to decimal format and divide it by 600,000,000. In this example the policy was changed from 5 to 10 minutes.

- **KerMaxR:** Maximum lifetime for user ticket renewal. To get number of days you need to convert the value to decimal format and divide it by 864,000,000,000. In this example the policy was changed from 7 to 8 days.

- **KerMaxT:** Maximum lifetime for user ticket. To get number of hours you need to convert the value to decimal format and divide it by 36,000,000,000. In this example the policy was changed from 10 to 12 hours.

- **KerMaxT:** Maximum lifetime for user ticket. To get number of hours you need to convert the value to decimal format and divide it by 36,000,000,000. In this example the policy was changed from 10 to 12 hours.

- **KerMinT:** Maximum lifetime for service ticket. To get number of minutes you need to convert the value to decimal format and divide it by 600,000,000. In this example the policy was changed from 600 to 500 minutes.

- **KerOpts:** Enforce user logon restrictions. May have one of the following values:
  - **0x0:** Disabled
  - **0x80:** Enabled

Account Password Migration

Active Directory provides the ability to migrate security principals, such as computer or user accounts, from one domain to another. Such migration might be required because of a company acquisition or domain consolidation procedures.

Account migration, if using Microsoft tools, is usually performed by using the Active Directory Migration Toolkit (ADMT). ADMT contains multiple wizards, which walk you through all steps required to migrate accounts to another domain.

One option during account migration is to maintain the account's current password. If this option is used, the account's password hash is exported and transferred to the target domain. Figure 7-4 shows the ADMT wizard page with the password migration option.

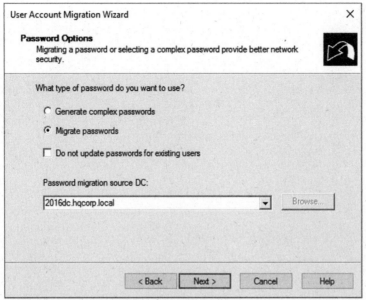

Figure 7-4: Password migration option in ADMT

During password migration, on a destination domain controller to which an account is migrated, the event in Listing 7-32 is generated in the Windows security event log.

Listing 7-32: Event ID 4782: The password hash an account was accessed.

```
Task Category: Other Account Management Events
Keywords: Audit Success
Subject:
        Security ID:           S-1-5-18
        Account Name:          2016DC$
        Account Domain:        HQCORP
        Logon ID:              0x3E7
Target Account:
        Account Name:          Andrei
        Account Domain:        HQCORP
```

The subject section contains information about the account that imported the target's account hash. It is usually the S-1-5-18 (SYSTEM) account, because the Password Migration Server (PES)—the component that is installed on the destination domain controller and performs password migration—usually runs under the SYSTEM account.

The Target Account section contains information about the account that was migrated.

Active Directory Objects

The Microsoft Active Directory database contains a variety of predefined object classes, such as user, computer, contact, and so on. It also contains attribute objects, which can be used in classes.

An Active Directory class, defined as a `classSchema` type object, defines attributes for specific class, default values for those attributes, and security settings. For example, the `user` class is defined as a `classSchema` object type.

An Active Directory attribute, defined as an `attributeSchema` type object, defines settings for a specific attribute that then can be used in multiple classes. For example, the `cn` attribute is defined as an `attributeSchema` object type.

All `classSchema` and `attributeSchema` objects are stored in the special Active Directory partition, called the schema partition. You can view all schema partition objects using, for example, the `adsiedit.msc` tool. Figure 8-1 shows an example of the schema partition view in `adsiedit.msc`.

All `classSchema` and `attributeSchema` objects have a unique Globally Unique Identifier (GUID) attribute named `schemaIDGUID`. Many Windows mechanisms, including the Windows auditing subsystem, use these GUIDs to refer to a specific class or attribute. Schema GUIDs for default Active Directory classes and attributes have predefined values and are the same for any Active Directory instance.

In this chapter you will find information about common operations with Active Directory objects, such as object creation, deletion, modification, and so on.

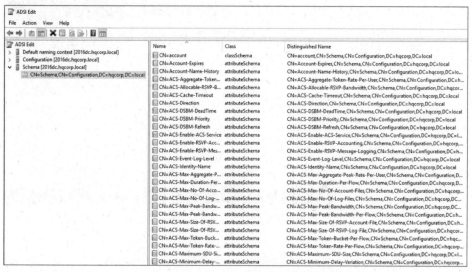

Figure 8-1: Active Directory schema partition view in adsiedit.msc

Active Directory Object SACL

You learned some basic information about system access control lists (SACLs) in previous chapters, but in this section you will find specifics related to Active Directory object SACLs.

Each Active Directory class instance, such as an instance of a `user` or `group` class, has its own SACL. You can view the content of an object's SACL using built-in tools, such as Active Directory Users and Computers (`dsa.msc`) or ADSI Edit (`adsiedit.msc`). To view an Active Directory object's SACL using `adsiedit.msc`, perform the following actions:

1. Right-click an object and select `Properties`.

2. Switch to the `Security` tab.

3. Click the `Advanced` button.

4. Switch to the `Auditing` tab.

Figure 8-2 shows an example of a SACL for a user account object.

Most of the specifics related to SACLs were discussed in Chapter 13, and the same principles are applicable to Active Directory object SACLs. But some specific settings related to Active Directory objects only are discussed in this section.

An Active Directory object SACL has a "Restore defaults" button in the `adsiedit.msc` tool interface that restores the SACL of the object, depending on the object's class, to a default SACL. A default security descriptor is defined in the `classSchema` object related to a specific class. The attribute for a default SACL object is `defaultSecurityDescriptor` and it contains an SDDL string that defines the default SACL. After you click the "Restore defaults" button, the SACL is changed to one defined in the `defaultSecurityDescriptor` attribute of the corresponding `classSchema` object. Usually, the default SACL is empty. A default SACL does not disable inheritance; inherited ACEs will still remain in the SACL. You can find more information about SDDL syntax in Chapter 10.

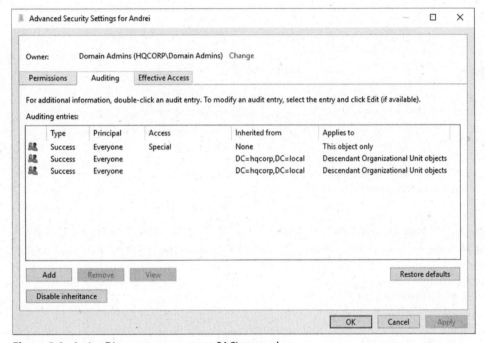

Figure 8-2: Active Directory user account SACL example

Inherited ACEs can only be viewed, not edited. It is not possible to modify them or remove them from the object that inherited the ACEs (the child object) unless you first disable inheritance on the child object. You can also modify or remove a specific ACE from the object from which it was initially inherited.

Figure 8-3 shows an example of a user account SACL ACE configuration interface.

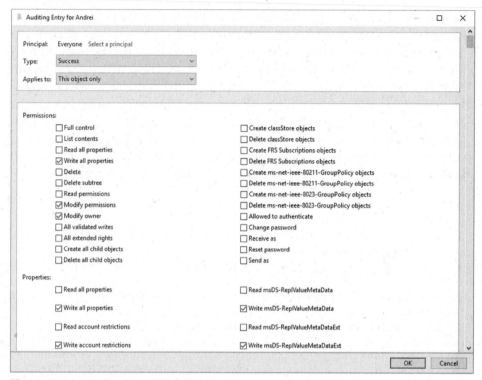

Figure 8-3: Active Directory SACL ACE example

The `Principal` section contains the security principal to which the specific ACE applies. It can be assigned to one of the following security principal types:

- Built-in security principal
- Service account
- Computer
- Group
- User

Only one security principal can be defined per ACE.

The `Type` parameter defines an ACE type that can be set to one of the following options:

- **Success:** Audit only `Audit Success` events
- **Fail:** Audit only `Audit Failure` events
- **All:** Audit both `Audit Success` and `Audit Failure` events

The "Applies to" section defines the scope of the ACE. It may have one of the following settings:

- **This object only:** Applies to the object itself only.

- **This object and all descendant objects:** Applies to the object itself and all possible **descendant** objects. This ACE will be inherited by all descendant objects.

- **All descendant objects:** Applies to all possible **descendant** objects, but does not apply to the object itself. This ACE will be inherited by all descendant objects.

- **Descendant `classSchema_object_name` objects:** The list of all `classSchema` object names defined in the Active Directory forest schema in the specific organization. Even if a parent object cannot have a child object with a specific class, like a `user` class object cannot have child `group` class objects, you still can define the ACE for that class. Such an ACE will just not generate any events.

Some classes cannot have any child objects—the `infrastructureUpdate` class is one example. The "Applies to" section is not shown for objects that belong to such classes.

Depending on what option is selected in the "Applies to" section, the `Permissions` section will show a list of permissions whose usage you can monitor. For "This object only," "This object and all descendant objects," and "All descendant objects" options, the `Permissions` section will have the list of permissions that apply only to the object for which you are configuring the SACL itself. For the "Descendant `classSchema_object_name` objects" option, the Permissions section will show permissions applicable to the selected `classSchema` object.

There is a default set of Active Directory permissions available for configuration in the SACL editor for most of the Active Directory class objects, but not all of these permissions will generate audit records if enabled for auditing. This will be clarified later in this chapter. The list of default Active Directory class object permissions, available for configuration using the built-in SACL editor, is shown in Table 8-1. It also contains associated access permissions for SACL editor permission.

Table 8-1: Active Directory Class SACL Editor Permissions with Associated Access Permissions

OBJECT PERMISSION	DESCRIPTION	ASSOCIATED ACCESS PERMISSION
List contents	View the name of all the immediate child objects of this object.	List Contents
List object	View the name of this object.	No audit events generated
Read all properties	Read all attributes of this object, except the owner and DACL.	Read Property
Write all properties	Write to all attributes of this object, except the owner and DACL.	Write Property

Continues

Table 8-1 (*continued*)

OBJECT PERMISSION	DESCRIPTION	ASSOCIATED ACCESS PERMISSION
Delete	Delete this object.	DELETE
Delete subtree	Delete everything under this object, including all nested objects.	Delete Tree
Read permissions	Read the owner and DACL of this object.	READ_CONTROL
Modify permissions	Change the DACL of this object; does not include SACL modifications.	WRITE_DAC
Modify owner	Modify an owner of this object.	WRITE_OWNER
All validated writes	Perform any validated write to the object. Validate writes are explained later in the book.	Write Self
All extended rights	Contains all extended rights for an object. Explained later in the book.	Control Access
Create all child objects	Create any child object under this object.	Create Child
Delete all child objects	Delete immediate child objects of this object.	Delete Child

Basically speaking, when the "Read all properties" permission is enabled for auditing in the object's SACL, a "Read Property" audit event will be reported in the security event log.

`List object` permission is not shown in the built-in Windows DACL/SACL editor interface by default. To enable this permission you must modify `CN=Directory Service,CN=Windows NT,CN=Services,CN=Configuration,DC=DomainName` object. The `dSHeuristics` attribute of the *Directory Service* object should have a value of `001` to enable this permission. This permission works in DACL but does not have any effect in SACL. To be able to see the new permission in the Active Directory Users and Computers or ADSI Edit applications, you will need to restart them if they were already running.

The permissions in Table 8-1, when enabled for auditing, aren't the same as the permissions reported in the Windows security event log. Table 8-2 contains a list of permissions that can be reported for Active Directory objects along with generic permissions listed in Table 5-4.

Table 8-2: Active Directory Object Auditing Permissions

PERMISSION	CODE	HEX	DESCRIPTION
Create Child	%%7680	0x1	Create any child object under this object
Delete Child	%%7681	0x2	Delete any child object under this object
List Contents	%%7682	0x4	View the name of all the immediate child objects of this object
Write Self	%%7683	0x8	
Read Property	%%7684	0x10	Read an attribute of this object, except the owner and DACL
Write Property	%%7685	0x20	Write an attribute of this object, except the owner and DACL
Delete Tree	%%7686	0x40	Delete everything under this object, including all nested objects
List Object	%%7687	0x80	View the name of this object
Control Access	%%7688	0x100	The right to perform an operation controlled by an extended access right

Child Object Creation and Deletion Permissions

The `Permissions` section in Figure 8-3 may have additional Create `classSchema_object_name` and Delete `classSchema_object_name` permissions listed if the object's class name, for which the SACL ACE is configured, is included in any `classSchema` object's `systemPossSuperiors` attribute. For example, the `user` class is listed in the `systemPossSuperiors` attribute of the following `classSchema` objects:

- `ms-net-ieee-80211-GroupPolicy`
- `ms-net-ieee-8023-GroupPolicy`
- `classStore`
- `NTFRS-Subscriptions`

These classes will be added to `Permissions` section of any object that belongs to the `user` class.

Child object creation and deletion permissions are usually displayed, if available, after the list of standard Active Directory access permissions, as shown in Figure 8-4. Check boxes for these permissions are checked in Figure 8-4.

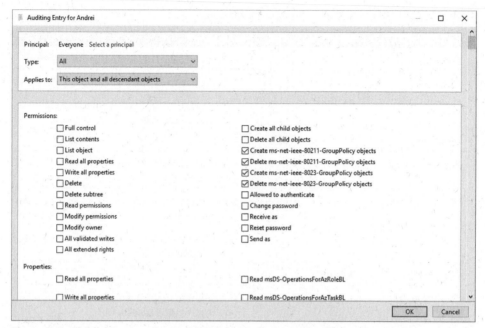

Figure 8-4: Child object creation and deletion permissions example for a user account

The following access permissions are linked to the Active Directory permissions:

OBJECT PERMISSION	ACCESS PERMISSION
Create `classSchema_object_name`	Create Child
Delete `classSchema_object_name`	Delete Child

If an object has at least one pair of child object `Create` and `Delete` permissions, the following two new options will appear in the ACE editor's Permissions section:

- **Create all child objects:** Selects all "Create `classSchema_object_name`" permissions which are available for all child objects.

- **Delete all child objects:** Selects all "Delete `classSchema_object_name`" permissions which are available for all child objects.

Extended Rights

Some Active Directory object classes, such as `user`, have extended access permissions in addition to generic (Table 5.4) and standard Active Directory object permissions (Table 8-1). Those permissions are called extended rights. The `user` class, for example, has the following extended rights:

EXTENDED RIGHT	SCHEMA GUID
Allowed to authenticate	{68b1d179-0d15-4d4f-ab71-46152e79a7bc}
Change Password	{ab721a53-1e2f-11d0-9819-00aa0040529b}
Reset Password	{00299570-246d-11d0-a768-00aa006e0529}
Receive As	{ab721a56-1e2f-11d0-9819-00aa0040529b}
Send As	{ab721a54-1e2f-11d0-9819-00aa0040529b}

Extended rights for all Active Directory objects are stored in the Active Directory forest's Configuration partition as controlAccessRight class objects. They are stored in the CN=Extended-Rights,CN=Configuration,DC=domain, DC=domain container. An example of Extended-Rights container content is shown in Figure 8-5.

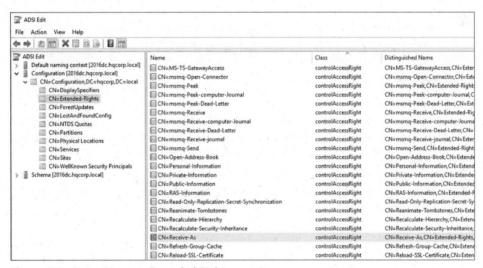

Figure 8-5: Active Directory Extended-Rights container

If you open the properties of any controlAccessRight class object in the Extended-Rights container you will find the appliesTo attribute, which contains a list of the Active Directory class object's schema GUIDs (schemaIDGUID) to which the right is applicable. For example, the Send-To access right applies only to the bf967a9c-0de6-11d0-a285-00aa003049e2 schema GUID, which belongs to the group class. How to easily it is to find which class is associated with a specific GUID is discussed later in this chapter.

Extended rights are usually listed after child object Create and Delete rights. If child object Create and Delete rights don't exist, existing rights are displayed right after standard Active Directory object rights. Figure 8-6 shows an example of the extended rights section for a user account. Extended rights check boxes are checked in Figure 8-6.

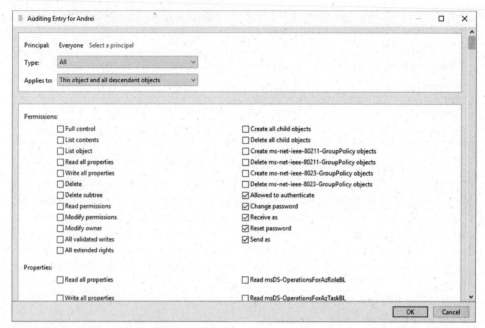

Figure 8-6: User's account extended rights

If an object has at least one extended right, the new "All extended rights" option will appear in the ACE editor's `Permissions` section, which allows you to select all extended rights for the current object.

The use of any extended right is reported as a `Control Access (%%7688)` access permission. You will find more examples of extended rights monitoring events later in this chapter.

Validated Writes

Active Directory has a built-in mechanism to validate changes made by an object itself to some of its own attributes. This mechanism uses predefined validation logic to validate a new value for an attribute. For example, a new DNS hostname attribute (`dNSHostName`) value for a computer account should have the format *computerName.fullDomainDnsName*, where:

■ *computerName* is the current `sAMAccountName` of the object (without the final `$` character)

■ `fullDomainDnsName` is the DNS name of the domain or one of the values of `msDS-AllowedDNSSuffixes` on the domain (if any) where the object that is being modified is located.

A new value for the DNSHostName attribute can be validated by the Active Directory domain controller for the rules in the preceding list if a new value for this attribute is specified.

Such attributes, like dNSHostName, require additional rights to perform any validated changes made by the object itself. These rights are called validated writes rights.

Table 8-3 contains a list of validated writes access rights available in Active Directory and corresponding attributes for each right.

Table 8-3: Validated Writes Access Rights and Corresponding Attributes

RIGHT NAME	ATTRIBUTE	SCHEMA GUID
Validated write to computer attributes	-	-
Validated write to DNS Host Name	dNSHostName	{72e39547-7b18-11d1-adef-00c04fd8d5cd}
Validated write to MS DS Additional DNS Host Name	msDS-Addition-alDnsHostName	{80863791-dbe9-4eb8-837e-7f0ab55d9ac7}
Validated write to MS DS Behavior Version	msDS-Behavior-Version	{d31a8757-2447-4545-8081-3bb610cacbf2}
Validated write to service principal name	servicePrinci-palName	{f3a64788-5306-11d1-a9c5-0000f80367c1}

Any Active Directory object has the "All validated writes" option in the ACE editor's Permissions section, which allows you to select all validated writes access rights for the current object. If no validated writes access rights are available for the object, this option does not perform any action.

The use of any validated writes access right is reported as Write Self (%%7683) access permission.

Properties

Each Active Directory class has a number of attributes associated with it. Attributes are stored in the schema partition as attributeSchema class objects. Read and Write operations with an object's attributes can be audited using the Windows auditing subsystem.

The Properties section, shown in Figure 8-3, allows you to configure Read and Write operations auditing for a specific object's attributes. Not all properties are displayed by default in built-in Windows SACL or DACL ACE editors, because the list of all properties available for a specific Active Directory class can be very long. The `%WINDIR%\system32\dssec.dat` file on a domain control-ler contains DACL and SACL editor user interface display settings for multiple Active Directory `classSchema` objects attributes. Figure 8-7 shows an example of the `dssec.dat` file configuration items for the user class.

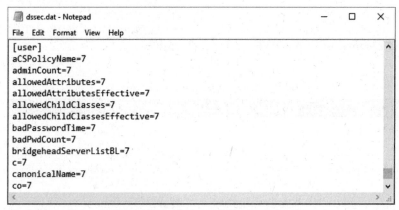

Figure 8-7: Dssec.dat file configuration items for the `user` class

The `classSchema` object name is displayed in square brackets (for example, `[user]`). After the `classSchema` object name you may see the list of visibility settings for class parameters. The following values can be set to class attributes:

- **0:** Enable Read and Write DACL and SACL entries
- **5:** Enable only Write DACL and SACL entries
- **6:** Enable only Read DACL and SACL entries
- **7:** Attribute is not shown in the DACL and SACL ACE editors

For example, the `adminCount` attribute for user class objects is not shown in the built-in DACL and SACL editors by default. You can enable it by changing settings in the `dssec.dat` file for the `[user]` class `adminCount` attribute from 7 to 0.

The `Read all properties` and `Write all properties` items, located in both the `Properties` and `Permissions` sections, allow you to select Read or Write operations for all attributes listed in the Properties section.

Every Read operation performed with an attribute generates a `Read Property` access permission audit record. Every Write operation performed with an attri-bute generates a `Write Property` access permission audit record.

Default SACLs

Many Active Directory objects have a default SACL set right out of the box. In this section you will find information about default SACLs for some Active Directory objects and classes.

Schema Partition

The only object that has a default SACL in the schema partition is the partition container itself. Table 8-4 contains information for default SACL for the CN=Schema, CN=Configuration, DC=ForestRootDomain object.

Table 8-4: CN=Schema,CN=Configuration,DC=ForestRootDomain Object SACL

TYPE	PRINCIPAL	APPLIES TO	PERMISSIONS
Success	Everyone	This object only	Write all properties
			Delete
			Delete subtree
			Modify permissions
			Modify owner
			All validated writes
			Create all child objects
			Delete all child objects
Success	Everyone	This object and all descendant objects	Write all properties
Success	Domain Users	This object only	All extended rights
Success	Administrators	This object only	All extended rights
Success	Everyone	This object only	Change schema master
Success	Everyone	This object only	Reanimate tombstones

All modifications performed to the schema partition object itself are monitored. Also, each new child object creation and deletion, such as a new classSchema or attributeSchema class object, will generate an audit record.

Each property modification for all objects in the schema partition container is monitored.

A number of extended rights are related to the schema partition, and any use of these rights by the Domain Users and the Administrators groups is monitored.

Change schema master and Reanimate tombstones extended rights are monitored for all accounts. The Change schema master permission allows for changing the schema master Flexible Single Master Operation (FSMO) role owner. By default only the Schema Admins security group has this permission. The Reanimate tombstones permission is required to reanimate the Active Directory tombstone object. The tombstone object is a representation of a deleted Active Directory object; reanimating it restores it back to a normal object.

Configuration Partition

The configuration partition contains a number of important containers for which default SACLs are set. These are discussed in the following sections.

CN=Configuration,DC=ForestRootDomain

Table 8-5 contains information for the default SACL for the `CN=Configuration, DC=ForestRootDomain` object.

Table 8-5: CN=Configuration,DC=ForestRootDomain Object SACL

TYPE	PRINCIPAL	APPLIES TO	PERMISSIONS
Success	Everyone	This object only	Write all properties
			Modify permissions
			Modify owner
Success	Domain Users	This object only	All extended rights
Success	Administrators	This object only	All extended rights
Success	Everyone	This object only	Reanimate tombstones

All SACLs for the configuration partition object are applicable only to the object itself. Properties, owner, and permissions modifications are monitored for all users as well as the `Reanimate tombstones` extended right, which was discussed earlier in this chapter.

All extended rights usage is also monitored for the Domain Users and the Administrators groups' members.

CN=Sites,CN=Configuration,DC=ForestRootDomain

The `Sites` object contains information about existing Active Directory sites. Table 8-6 contains information for the default SACL for the `CN=Sites,CN= Configuration,DC=ForestRootDomain` object.

Table 8-6: CN=Sites,CN=Configuration,DC=ForestRootDomain Object SACL

TYPE	PRINCIPAL	APPLIES TO	PERMISSIONS
Success	Everyone	This object only	Delete
			Delete subtree
			Create all child objects
			Delete all child objects
Success	Everyone	Descendant Domain Controller Settings objects	All extended rights

TYPE	PRINCIPAL	APPLIES TO	PERMISSIONS
Success	Everyone	Descendant Site objects	Write gPLink property
			Write gPOptions property
Success	Everyone	Descendant Subnet objects	Write siteObject property

The Sites object itself is monitored for any deletion operation and for creation or deletion of any child object.

All successful group policy link operations (gPLink property) to descendant Active Directory site objects are also audited. Changes to the gPOptions property, which is a property that contains group policy inheritance settings, are also audited for all Site objects.

Any write operation to the siteObject property for all Subnet class objects is audited. The siteObject property contains the name of a site to which a subnet is linked.

CN=Partitions,CN=Configuration,DC=ForestRootDomain

The Partitions object contains information about existing Active Directory partitions. Table 8-7 contains information for the default SACL for the CN=Partitions,CN=Configuration,DC=ForestRootDomain object.

Table 8-7: CN=Partitions,CN=Configuration,DC=ForestRootDomain Object SACL

TYPE	PRINCIPAL	APPLIES TO	PERMISSIONS
Success	Everyone	This object and all descendant objects	Write all properties
			Delete
			Delete subtree
			Modify permissions
			Modify owner
			All extended rights
			Create all child objects
			Delete all child objects

Any modification to the Partitions object and all descendant objects are audited as well as creation of new child objects.

dSHeuristics Property

The dSHeuristics attribute of the CN=Directory Service,CN=Windows NT, CN=Services,CN=Configuration,DC=ForestRootDomain object contains global settings for the entire Active Directory forest. This property was mentioned earlier in this chapter. It should be modified, for example, to enable List Object access permission. The default SACL to monitor any change to the dSHeuristics attribute is shown in Table 8-8.

Table 8-8: CN=Directory Service,CN=Windows NT,CN=Services,CN=Configuration,DC=Forest-RootDomain Object SACL

TYPE	PRINCIPAL	APPLIES TO	PERMISSIONS
Success	Everyone	This object only	Write dSHeuristics property

Domain Partition

Domain partitions contain a number of important domain-related containers for which default SACLs are set.

DC=domain,DC=ForestRootDomain

Each Active Directory domain in the forest has its own domain partition object. Table 8-9 contains information for the default SACL for each domain partition object.

Table 8-9: DC=domain,DC=ForestRootDomain object SACL

TYPE	PRINCIPAL	APPLIES TO	PERMISSIONS
Success	Everyone	This object only	Write all properties
			Modify permissions
			Modify owner
Success	Domain Users	This object only	All extended rights
Success	Administrators	This object only	All extended rights
Success	Everyone	Descendant Organizational Unit objects	Write gPLink property
			Write gPOptions property

Every property modification of the domain object itself is monitored as well as access permissions and owner modifications.

The use of any extended right is audited for members of the Domain Users and the Administrators groups.

For all organizational unit objects in the domain, group policy link operations are monitored via a change to the gPLink attribute. Group policy inheritance settings are also monitored using the gPOptions attribute.

OU=Domain Controllers,DC=domain,DC=ForestRootDomain

The Domain Controllers organizational unit (OU) contains computer objects for all domain controllers in the domain. This OU also has the default SACL shown in Table 8-10.

Table 8-10: OU=Domain Controllers,DC=domain,DC=ForestRootDomain object SACL

TYPE	PRINCIPAL	APPLIES TO	PERMISSIONS
Success	Everyone	This object only	Delete
			Delete subtree
			Modify permissions
			Modify owner
			Create all child objects
			Delete all child objects
Success	Everyone	This object and all descendant objects	Write all properties

Any permission, property, and owner modifications are monitored for the OU itself as well as deletion operations to the OU.

Creation and deletion of any child object, usually the domain controller's computer object, is also audited.

For all descendant objects, which, again, usually are computer objects, modification for all properties is monitored, which means that any change to the domain controller computer object will be captured in the security event log.

CN=Infrastructure,DC=domain,DC=ForestRootDomain

Each Active Directory domain has a specific Flexible Single Master Operation (FSMO) role called the infrastructure master. The infrastructure master is responsible for an unattended process that fixes stale object references, known as *phantoms*, within the Active Directory database. The current owner of the infrastructure role is written in the CN=Infrastructure,DC=domain,DC=Forest-RootDomain object. Table 8-11 contains a default SACL for the CN=Infrastructure object.

Table 8-11: CN=Infrastructure,DC=domain,DC=ForestRootDomain object SACL

TYPE	PRINCIPAL	APPLIES TO	PERMISSIONS
Success	Everyone	This object only	Write all properties
			All extended rights

Changes to all attributes of the CN=Infrastructure object are monitored.

The CN=Infrastructure object has only one extended right: Change infrastructure master. This right is required to change the current holder of the infrastructure master FSMO role in the domain.

CN=Policies,CN=System,DC=domain,DC=ForestRootDomain

All Active Directory domain policies are stored in the CN=Policies,CN=System,DC=domain,DC=ForestRootDomain object as groupPolicyContainer class objects. The CN=Policies container also has a default SACL, which is shown in Table 8-12.

Table 8-12: CN=Policies,CN=System,DC=domain,DC=ForestRootDomain Object SACL

TYPE	PRINCIPAL	APPLIES TO	PERMISSIONS
Success	Everyone	This object only	Create groupPolicyContainer objects
			Delete groupPolicyContainer objects
Success	Everyone	Descendant groupPolicy-Container objects	Write all properties
			Modify permissions

By default, each time a new group policy object is created or an existing group policy is deleted, the audit record will be created.

All group policy objects in the domain are audited for any change in attributes and any permissions modifications.

CN=AdminSDHolder,CN=System,DC=domain, DC=ForestRootDomain

The AdminSDHolder container plays a very important role within an Active Directory domain environment. Without going into detail, the DACL and SACL from AdminSDHolder container is replicated to the set of accounts—individual accounts and members of specific protected groups—every 60 minutes by the Security Descriptor Propagator (SDPROP) mechanism. Table 8-13 contains a list of user accounts and security groups to which the SDPROP mechanism is applicable depending on the domain controller's operating system version.

Table 8-13: User Accounts and Security Groups to Which the SDPROP Mechanism Is Applicable

GROUP\USER	WINDOWS 2000 <SP4	WINDOWS 2000 SP4 - WINDOWS SERVER 2003 RTM	WINDOWS SERVER 2003 SP1	WINDOWS SERVER 2008, 2008 R2, 2012, 2012 R2
Account Operators		+	+	+
Administrator		+	+	+
Administrators	+	+	+	+
Backup Operators		+	+	+
Cert Publishers		+		
Domain Admins	+	+	+	+
Domain Controllers		+	+	+
Enterprise Admins	+	+	+	+
Krbtgt		+	+	+
Print Operators		+	+	+
Read-only Domain Controllers				+
Replicator		+	+	+
Schema Admins	+	+	+	+
Server Operators		+	+	+

You may notice that, because of the SDPROP mechanism, members of the groups listed in Table 8-13 have an additional SACL ACE in addition to the standard user account ACEs. Table 8-14 contains the default SACL for the AdminSDHolder object.

Table 8-14: CN=AdminSDHolder,CN=System,DC=domain, DC=ForestRootDomain Object SACL

TYPE	PRINCIPAL	APPLIES TO	PERMISSIONS
Success	Everyone	This object only	Write all properties
			Modify permissions
			Modify owner

Attributes, permissions, and owner changes will be audited for all objects for which the SDPROP mechanism is enabled.

CN=RID Manager$, CN=System,DC=domain,DC=ForestRootDomain

The RID Manager$ object is similar to the Infrastructure object discussed earlier. It contains information about the current owner of the RID Master FSMO role and settings for the RID Manager component, such as the available RID pool.

Table 8-15 contains the default SACL for the RID Manager$ object.

Table 8-15: CN=RID Manager$,CN=System,DC=domain,DC=ForestRootDomain Object SACL

TYPE	PRINCIPAL	APPLIES TO	PERMISSIONS
Success	Everyone	This object only	Write all properties
			All extended rights

Changes to all attributes of the CN=RID Manager$ object are monitored.

The CN=RID Manager$ object has only one extended right: Change RID master. This right is required to change the current holder of the RID Master FSMO role in the domain.

Active Directory Object Change Auditing

A number of changes to Active Directory objects can be monitored using the built-in Windows auditing subsystem:

- Object creation
- Object deletion
- Object undeletion
- Object movement
- Object modification

Only successful changes can be monitored. To monitor for unsuccessful change attempts use access rights handle request auditing, which is discussed later in this chapter.

In this section you will find detailed information about each of the preceding change types.

Active Directory Object Creation

Active Directory object creation auditing can be enabled at the parent level to monitor for all child object creation operations or to monitor for only creations of objects with specific classes.

For example, to monitor for new user object creations within a specific organizational unit only, which were performed by any account, you should enable the following audit settings on the organizational unit object:

- **Principal:** Everyone
- **Type:** Success or All
- **Applies to:** This object only
- **Permissions:** Create User objects

The event in Listing 8-1 is recorded in the Windows security event log when a new user account is created under the object with the preceding SACL settings.

Listing 8-1: Event ID 5137: A directory service object was created.

```
Task Category: Directory Service Changes
Keywords: Audit Success
Subject:
        Security ID:        S-1-5-21-1913345275-1711810662-261465553-500
        Account Name:       Administrator
        Account Domain:     HQCORP
        Logon ID:           0x7005A
Directory Service:
        Name:               hqcorp.local
        Type:               %%14676 (Active Directory Domain Services)
Object:
        DN:                 cn=Anton,OU=IT Labs,DC=hqcorp,DC=local
        GUID:               {BF1EC9A2-742D-4E6A-A9CD-9196DD913701}
        Class:              user
Operation:
        Correlation ID:     {EA9C7AA0-E06F-4C08-8F5F-50E64159F2A1}
        Application Correlation ID:    -
```

NOTE The event described in this section is available on the book's website, in the `Active Directory Object Creation.evtx` **file.**

A 5137 event informs you that a new Active Directory object was successfully created.

The `Subject` section contains information about the account that created the new object.

The `Directory Service` section contains information about the domain in which the new object was created:

- **Name:** The name of domain in which the new object was created.

- **Type:** Active Directory services type. May have one of the following two values:

  - **%%14676:** Active Directory Domain Services
  - **%%14677:** Active Directory Lightweight Directory Services

The `Object` section contains detailed information about the newly created object.

The `Object\DN` field contains the value of the `distinguishedName` attribute of the newly created object.

The `Object\GUID` field contains the value of the `objectGUID` attribute of the newly created object.

The `Object\Class` field contains the name of the class (`classSchema` object) of the newly created object.

The `Correlation ID` field contains the GUID of the transaction that uniquely identifies one or multiple Active Directory operations performed together. You may find the same `Correlation ID` field value in multiple Active Directory change events, such as 5136, 5137, 5138, 5139, and 5141. If multiple events have the same `Correlation ID` field value, they are parts of the same transaction.

Active Directory Object Deletion

Active Directory object deletion operations auditing SACL ACE should be configured on the object itself, or be inherited from the object's parent.

The two types of LDAP delete operations are:

- **Delete:** Delete an object that does not have any child objects.

- **Delete subtree:** Delete an object that has child objects. As result of this operation all child objects also will be deleted.

If, for example, you want to monitor for user account deletion operations performed by any account within a specific OU and all descendant OUs, you need to set the following SACL ACE at the OU level:

- **Principal:** Everyone
- **Type:** Success or All
- **Applies to:** Descendant user objects
- **Permissions:** Delete; Delete subtree

The event in Listing 8-2 is recorded in the Windows security event log if a user account is deleted under the object with the preceding SACL settings.

Listing 8-2: Event ID 5141: A directory service object was created.

```
Task Category: Directory Service Changes
Keywords: Audit Success
Subject:
        Security ID:         S-1-5-21-1913345275-1711810662-261465553-500
        Account Name:        Administrator
        Account Domain:      HQCORP
        Logon ID:            0x7005A
Directory Service:
        Name:                hqcorp.local
        Type:                %%14676 (Active Directory Domain Services)
Object:
        DN:                  CN=Sergey,CN=Users,DC=hqcorp,DC=local
        GUID:                {7F2E1A54-2827-43FF-AB57-46C3E059B212}
        Class:               user
Operation:
        Tree Delete:         %%14679 (No)
        Correlation ID:      {FC10A26B-78D7-4308-AFA1-84504E5F7E02}
        Application Correlation ID:      -
```

NOTE The event described in this section is available on the book's website, in the `Active Directory Object Deletion.evtx` file.

This event is similar to event 5137 discussed earlier, but it has one new field: `Tree Delete`. The `Tree Delete` field shows whether or not the `Delete subtree` permission was used to delete the object, including all child objects. This field may have one of the following two values:

- **%%14678:** Yes
- **%%14679:** No

Active Directory Object Undeletion

Active Directory has two main options to undelete/restore deleted objects:

- **Tombstone reanimation:** When an Active Directory object is deleted, a special `tombstone` object is created for this object in the `CN=Deleted Objects,DC=domain,DC=ForestRootDomain` container. A `tombstone` object contains a stripped set of attributes and can be undeleted/recovered using, for example, the `ldp.exe` tool.

- **Active Directory recycle bin restoration:** A feature that was introduced in Windows Server 2008 R2 and allows enhanced object restoration options, such as restore object with all attributes. It also has new PowerShell commands for Active Directory object restoration.

All deleted Active Directory objects are stored in the `CN=Deleted Objects,DC =domain,DC=ForestRootDomain` container. An example of `CN=Deleted Objects` content using the `ldp.exe` tool is shown in Figure 8-8.

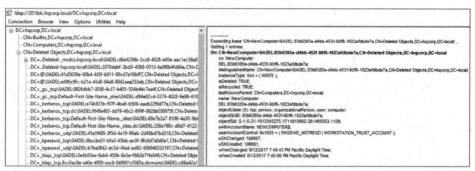

Figure 8-8: CN=Deleted Objects content view using ldp.exe tool

Both tombstone reanimation and recycle bin restoration methods generate an event in the Windows security event log if the container to which the object is restored has `Success` auditing enabled for object creation operations. For example, if you need to monitor for all restored user objects within a specific organizational unit, you need to set the following SACL ACE on that organizational unit:

- **Principal:** Everyone
- **Type:** Success or All
- **Applies to:** This object only
- **Permissions:** Create User objects

The event in Listing 8-3 is recorded in the Windows security event log if a user account is undeleted/recovered under the object with the preceding SACL settings.

Listing 8-3: Event ID 5138: A directory service object was undeleted.

```
Task Category: Directory Service Changes
Keywords: Audit Success
Subject:
      Security ID:      S-1-5-21-1913345275-1711810662-261465553-500
      Account Name:     Administrator
      Account Domain:   HQCORP
      Logon ID:         0x27A336
Directory Service:
      Name:             hqcorp.local
      Type:             %%14676 (Active Directory Domain Services)
```

```
Object:
      Old DN:                CN=Anton\0ADEL:9cca13a1-7960-4c12-9885
                                -83a7606c41a6,CN=Deleted Objects,
                                DC=hqcorp,DC=local
      New DN:                CN=Anton,OU=IT Labs,DC=hqcorp,DC=local
      GUID:                  {9CCA13A1-7960-4C12-9885-83A7606C41A6}
      Class:                 user
Operation:
      Correlation ID:    {8FD5D6AF-C520-4355-801F-B393F9FBC49B}
      Application Correlation ID:        -
```

NOTE The event described in this section is available on the book's website, in the `Active Directory Object Undeletion.evtx` file.

This event is similar to events 5141 and 5137; the only difference is the Old DN and New DN fields.

The Old DN field contains the old distinguished name for the undeleted object. Usually it is an object within the CN=Deleted Objects,DC=domain,DC=Forest RootDomain container.

The New DN field contains the new distinguished name for the object. It shows to which container the object was restored.

Active Directory Object Movement

An Active Directory object can be moved from one location to another. For example, a computer account can be moved from one organizational unit to another. Object movement actions generate an event in the Windows security event log if the container to which the object is moved has Success auditing enabled for object creation operations. For example, if you need to monitor when any user object is moved to a specific organizational unit, you need to set the following SACL ACE on the destination container level:

- **Principal:** Everyone
- **Type:** Success or All
- **Applies to:** This object only
- **Permissions:** Create User objects

The event in Listing 8-4 is recorded in the Windows security event log if a user account is moved to the container with the preceding SACL settings.

Listing 8-4: Event ID 5139: A directory service object was moved.

```
Task Category: Directory Service Changes
Keywords: Audit Success
Subject:
      Security ID:         S-1-5-21-1913345275-1711810662-261465553-500
      Account Name:        Administrator
```

```
           Account Domain:       HQCORP
           Logon ID:             0x27A336
Directory Service:
           Name:                 hqcorp.local
           Type:                 %%14676 (Active Directory Domain Services)
Object:
           Old DN:               CN=Sergey,CN=Users,DC=hqcorp,DC=local
           New DN:               CN=Sergey,OU=IT Labs,DC=hqcorp,DC=local
           GUID:                 {7F2E1A54-2827-43FF-AB57-46C3E059B212}
           Class:                user
Operation:
           Correlation ID:       {8F5DBCF8-5F32-42FD-863E-DE9BB4DB2F65}
           Application Correlation ID:      -
```

NOTE The event described in this section is available on the book's website, in the `Active Directory Object Movement.evtx` **file.**

This event is exactly the same as the 5138 event in Listing 8-3.

Active Directory Object Modification

If an Active Directory object is modified, that means that some of its attributes were changed. The two types of modification operations available to be performed for an attribute are:

▪ **Add value:** Adds a new value to the attribute for which no value is set. Note that the value can be added only if there is no current value set for the attribute.

▪ **Delete value:** Removes an attribute's value.

All object modification operations are implemented using these two operations. Examples of common modification operations with Active Directory objects and the way they translate into the Add value and Delete value operations are:

▪ **Clear/Remove attribute's value:** Delete value

▪ **Set value for attribute, if current value is empty:** Add value

▪ **Change value:** Delete value and then Add value

Add value operations are shown in the security event log as %%14674 (Value Added). Delete value operations are shown as %%14675 (Value Deleted)

Add Value Operation

Listing 8-5 is an example of an event in the Windows security event log if an Add value operation is performed on an object's attribute.

Listing 8-5: Event ID 5136: A directory service object was modified.

```
Task Category: Directory Service Changes
Keywords: Audit Success
Subject:
        Security ID:            S-1-5-21-1913345275-1711810662-261465553-500
        Account Name:           Administrator
        Account Domain:         HQCORP
        Logon ID:               0x27A336
Directory Service:
        Name:                   hqcorp.local
        Type:                   %%14676 (Active Directory Domain Services)
Object:
        DN:                     CN=Andrei,CN=Users,DC=hqcorp,DC=local
        GUID:                   {AB7B24D8-A4AF-4D09-8541-F4A37D3F8BC0}
        Class:                  user
Attribute:
        LDAP Display Name:      description
        Syntax (OID):           2.5.5.12
        Value:                  Engineer
Operation:
        Type:                   %%14674 (Value Added)
        Correlation ID:         {3837CFF2-937E-4885-9912-BA1BECA14F78}
        Application Correlation ID:     -
```

NOTE The event described in this section is available on the book's website, in the `Active Directory Object Modification.evtx` **file.**

The `Subject` section contains information about the account that made a change.

The `Directory Service` and `Object` sections were discussed earlier in this chapter.

The `Attribute` section contains detailed information about an attribute that was changed.

The `LDAP Display Name` field contains the value of the `lDAPDisplayName` attribute of the `attributeSchema` class object associated with the attribute being modified.

The `Syntax (OID)` field contains the object identifier (OID) of the value type (syntax) for the modified attribute. Table 8-16 contains information about the value type OIDs available in Active Directory.

Table 8-16: Active Directory Value Syntax OIDs

OID	NAME	DESCRIPTION
2.5.5.1	Object(DS-DN)	String that contains a distinguished name (DN).
2.5.5.2	String(Object-Identifier)	An OID string, which is a string that contains digits (0–9) and decimal points (.).

Continues

Table 8-16 (continued)

OID	NAME	DESCRIPTION
2.5.5.3	String(Case Sensitive)	A case-sensitive string.
2.5.5.4	String(Teletex)	A case-insensitive string that contains characters from the teletex character set.
2.5.5.5	String(IA5) or String(Printable)	A case-sensitive string that contains characters from the IA5 character set. Or a case-sensitive string that contains characters from the printable character set.
2.5.5.6	String(Numeric)	A string that contains digits.
2.5.5.7	Object(DN-Binary)	An octet string that contains a binary value and a distinguished name (DN). A value with this syntax has the following format: B:\<char count\>:\<binary value\>:\<object DN\>
2.5.5.8	Boolean	Can have TRUE or FALSE value.
2.5.5.9	Integer	32-bit signed integer value.
2.5.5.10	Object(Replica-Link) or String(Octet)	Syntax used by Active Directory itself for internal operations or a string that represents an array of bytes.
2.5.5.11	String(Generalized-Time) or String(UTC-Time)	A time string format defined by ASN.1 standards.
2.5.5.12	String(Unicode)	A case-insensitive Unicode string.
2.5.5.13	Object(Presentation-Address)	A string that contains Open Systems Interconnection (OSI) presentation addresses.
2.5.5.14	Object(DN-String)	An octet string that contains a string value and a DN. A value with this syntax has the following format: S:\<char count\>:\<string value\>:\<object DN\>
2.5.5.15	String(NT-Sec-Desc)	An octet string that contains a Windows NT or Windows 2000 security descriptor.
2.5.5.16	LargeInteger or Interval	Time interval value or 64-bit signed integer value.
2.5.5.17	String(Sid)	An octet string that contains a security identifier (SID).

The Operation\Type field might have one of the following values:

- **Value Added (%%14674):** Add value operation
- **Value Deleted (%%14675):** Delete value operation

The Correlation ID field was discussed earlier in this chapter.

Delete Value Operation

A Delete value operation event is the same as an Add value operation event, with the following differences:

- The Value field shows the value that was deleted.
- The Type field has a value of %%14675 (Value Deleted).

Active Directory Object Operation Attempts

In addition to Active Directory change auditing events, Windows provides the ability to monitor successful and unsuccessful Active Directory object operation attempts. Operation attempts align to the list of access rights in Table 8-1 and generate security events with the access right shown in the Associated Access Permission column.

Active Directory change auditing does not show unsuccessful operation attempts; it shows only successful changes. Operation attempts auditing shows both successful and unsuccessful attempts, but does not provide as much detail as change auditing provides.

Successful Active Directory Object Operation Attempts

Active Directory change auditing covers many operations with objects and provides more detailed information about the change. But some operations are not covered by change auditing, such as Read Property operations. Table 8-17 shows information about which successful operations are covered by Active Directory change auditing and which you need to monitor using operation attempts auditing.

Table 8-17: Active Directory Successful Operations Auditing Methods

OPERATION	AUDIT METHOD	EVENT IDS
List contents	Operation attempts	4662
List object	Operation attempts	4662

Continues

Table 8-17 (*continued*)

OPERATION	AUDIT METHOD	EVENT IDS
Read all properties	Operation attempts	4662
Write all properties	Change auditing	5136
Delete	Change auditing	5141
Delete subtree	Change auditing	5141
Read permissions	Operation attempts	4662
Modify permissions	Change auditing Operation attempts	5136 (nTSecurityDescriptor attribute) 4662
Modify owner	Change auditing Operation attempts	5136 (nTSecurityDescriptor attribute) 4662
All validated writes	Change auditing	5136
All extended rights	Operation attempts	4662
Create all child objects	Change auditing	5137, 5138
Delete all child objects	Change auditing	5141

Listing 8-6 is an example of the event that occurs when a `Read Property` operation is successfully performed on the object's attribute/property.

Listing 8-6: Event ID 4662: An operation was performed on an object.

```
Task Category: Directory Service Access
Keywords: Audit Success
Subject :
      Security ID:          S-1-5-21-1913345275-1711810662-261465553-500
      Account Name:         Administrator
      Account Domain:       HQCORP
      Logon ID:             0x67C23
Object:
      Object Server:        DS
      Object Type:          %{bf967aba-0de6-11d0-a285-00aa003049e2} (user)
      Object Name:          %{9cca13a1-7960-4c12-9885-83a7606c41a6}
                               (CN=Anton,OU=IT Labs,DC=hqcorp,DC=local)
      Handle ID:            0x0
Operation:
      Operation Type:       Object Access
      Accesses:             %%7684 (Read Property)
      Access Mask:          0x10
      Properties:           %%7684 (Read Property)
            {59ba2f42-79a2-11d0-9020-00c04fc2d3cf}
                  {c3dbafa6-33df-11d2-98b2-0000f87a57d4}
```

```
{bf967aba-0de6-11d0-a285-00aa003049e2}
Additional Information:
    Parameter 1:              -
    Parameter 2:
```

NOTE The event described in this section is available on the book's website, in the `Successful Active Directory Object Operation Attempts - Read Property.evtx` **file.**

The `Subject` section contains information about the account that made a change.

The `Object Server` field contains information about the type of Active Directory instance where the target object is located. It can have one of the following two values:

- **DS:** Directory Services

- **LDS:** Lightweight Directory Services

The `Object Type` field contains the GUID (`schemaIDGUID` attribute) of the class (`classSchema` object) of the target object in the following format: `%{GUID}`.

The `Object Name` field contains the value of the `objectGUID` attribute of the target object with which operation has been performed in the following format: `%{GUID}`.

The `Operation Type` field for object operation attempts auditing has a value of `Object Access`.

The `Accesses` field contains the access right requested. Table 8-2 contains a list of Active Directory access rights. Table 5.4 contains a list of generic access rights.

The `Access Mask` field contains a hexadecimal representation of access rights requested. See Table 8-2 and Table 5.4 for more details.

The `Properties` field contains a property tree that shows you the complete path to the property or properties with which an operation was performed. There is a problem with the order of elements—often the root element is displayed at the end of the sequence. Each property is displayed as its `schemaIDGUID` attribute value. Let's resolve all GUIDs to real objects for the current example:

- **bf967aba-0de6-11d0-a285-00aa003049e2:** user class (`classSchema`)

  - **59ba2f42-79a2-11d0-9020-00c04fc2d3cf:** General Information property set

    - **c3dbafa6-33df-11d2-98b2-0000f87a57d4:** sDRightsEffective property (`attributeSchema`)

Here is the PowerShell command you can use to find Active Directory `attributeSchema` and `classSchema` objects by GUID (`schemaIDGUID` attribute value):

```
Get-ADObject -LDAPFilter "(&(objectClass=*)(schemaIDGUID=\a6\af\db\c3\
                    df\33\d2\11\98\b2\00\00\f8\7a\57\d4))"
-pr DistinguishedName -SearchBase (Get-ADRootDSE).schemanamingcontext
```

To use the GUID from a 4662 event in this script, the following transformations need to be done:

STEP #	STEP DESCRIPTION	RESULT
1	Initial GUID	`c3dbafa6-33df-11d2-98b2-0000f87a57d4`
2	Take first three parts of the GUID	`c3dbafa6-33df-11d2`
3	Flip bytes in the last two parts	`c3dbafa6-df33-d211`
4	Flip bytes in the first part as shown in the example	`a6afdbc3-df33-d211`
5	Add the last two parts	`a6afdbc3-df33-d211-98b2-0000f87a57d4`
6	Remove "-" characters	`a6afdbc3df33d21198b20000f87a57d4`
7	Add "\" character after each byte	`\a6\af\db\c3\df\33\d2\11\98\b2\00\00\f8\7a\57\d4`

Figure 8-9 shows an example of the output of the preceding script.

Figure 8-9: Search for Active Directory object by schemaIDGUID attribute value

As you can see in Figure 8-9 the `c3dbafa6-33df-11d2-98b2-0000f87a57d4` GUID belongs to the SD-Rights-Effective `attributeSchema` object.

You probably noticed that `59ba2f42-79a2-11d0-9020-00c04fc2d3cf` does not belong to the `attributeSchema` or `classSchema` classes. It belongs to one of the *property sets*. A property set consists of a set of related attributes. An attribute whose `attributeSchema` object has a value for the `attributeSecurityGUID` attribute belongs to that property set; the property set is identified by the property set GUID, which is the `attributeSecurityGUID` value.

Table 8-18 contains a list of built-in Active Directory property sets.

Table 8-18: Active Directory Property Sets

PROPERTY SET NAME	GUID
Domain Password and Lockout Policies	`C7407360-20BF-11D0-A768-00AA006E0529`
General Information	`59BA2F42-79A2-11D0-9020-00C04FC2D3CF`

PROPERTY SET NAME	GUID
Account Restrictions	4C164200-20C0-11D0-A768-00AA006E0529
Logon Information	5F202010-79A5-11D0-9020-00C04FC2D4CF
Group Membership	BC0AC240-79A9-11D0-9020-00C04FC2D4CF
Phone and Mail Options	E45795B2-9455-11D1-AEBD-0000F80367C1
Personal Information	77B5B886-944A-11D1-AEBD-0000F80367C1
Web Information	E45795B3-9455-11D1-AEBD-0000F80367C1
Public Information	E48D0154-BCF8-11D1-8702-00C04FB96050
Remote Access Information	037088F8-0AE1-11D2-B422-00A0C968F939
Other Domain Parameters	B8119FD0-04F6-4762-AB7A-4986C76B3F9A
DNS Host Name Attributes	72E39547-7B18-11D1-ADEF-00C04FD8D5CD
MS-TS-GatewayAccess	FFA6F046-CA4B-4FEB-B40D-04DFEE722543
Private Information	91E647DE-D96F-4B70-9557-D63FF4F3CCD8
Terminal Server License Server	5805BC62-BDC9-4428-A5E2-856A0F4C185E

As you can see in Table 8-18, the `59ba2f42-79a2-11d0-9020-00c04fc2d3cf` GUID belongs to the `General Information` property set. To find out which properties belong to a specific property set you can use the following PowerShell command:

```
Get-ADObject -LDAPFilter "(&(objectClass=*)(attributeSecurityGUID=\42\
    2f\ba\59\a2\79\d0\11\90\20\00\c0\4f\c2\d3\cf))" -pr DistinguishedName
    -SearchBase (Get-ADRootDSE).schemanamingcontext
```

This command searches for all objects for which the `attributeSecurityGUID` attribute contains a GUID of specific property set. The GUID needs to be converted using the steps explained earlier in this chapter. Figure 8-10 shows an example of the output of this script.

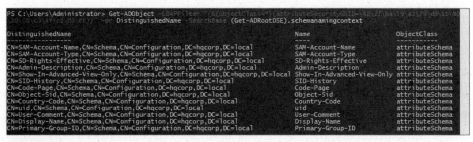

Figure 8-10: Search for Active Directory property set associated properties

The Parameter 1 and Parameter 2 fields in Listing 8-6 are used to show the object's previous distinguishedName and new distinguishedName attribute values for object move operations:

- **Parameter 1:** Object's previous distinguishedName, before object was moved

- **Parameter 2:** Object's new distinguishedName, after object was moved

To summarize, the 4662 event in Listing 8-6 informs you that the Administrator account reads the sDRightsEffective property of the CN=Anton,OU=IT Labs,DC=hqcorp,DC=local user object.

All other object operation attempts generate the same 4662 event with the following differences (see Tables 8-1 and 8-2 for additional details):

- List contents (List Contents)
  - The Properties field contains the class's GUID of the object on which the List Contents operation was performed. It is usually the same GUID specified in the Object Type property.
- List object
  - No audit events are generated for this operation type.
- Read all properties (Read Property)
  - Discussed in this chapter, see the 4662 event example in Listing 8-6.
- Modify permissions (WRITE_DAC)
  - The Properties field contains the class's GUID of the object on which the "Modify permissions" operation was performed. It is usually the same GUID specified in the Object Type property.
- Modify owner (WRITE_OWNER)
  - The Properties field contains the class's GUID of the object on which the "Modify owner" operation was performed. It is usually the same GUID specified in the Object Type property.
- All extended rights (Control Access)
  - The Properties field contains a list of properties on which the extended right was used.

Unsuccessful Active Directory Object Operation Attempts

The Active Directory object change events discussed earlier in this chapter do not audit unsuccessful/failed access attempts. That can only be done using operation attempts auditing.

Active Directory objects can be monitored for unsuccessful access attempts for the access permissions listed in Table 8-1.

For the auditing subsystem to record unsuccessful operation attempts, the correct SACL must be configured on the object. For example, if you need to monitor for an unsuccessful attribute modification attempt for all user objects within a specific organizational unit, the following SACL must be set for the organizational unit object:

- **Principal:** Everyone
- **Type:** Fail or All
- **Applies to:** Descendant User objects
- **Permissions:** Write all properties, Modify permissions, Modify owner

Listing 8-7 is an example of the event recorded in the Windows security event log on a domain controller after an unsuccessful object's attribute modification attempt.

Listing 8-7: Event ID 4662: An operation was performed on an object.

```
Task Category: Directory Service Access
Keywords: Audit Failure
Subject :
        Security ID:          S-1-5-21-1913345275-1711810662-261465553-1120
        Account Name:         andrei
        Account Domain:       HQCORP
        Logon ID:             0x14501BE
Object:
        Object Server:        DS
        Object Type:          %{bf967aba-0de6-11d0-a285-00aa003049e2}
        Object Name:          %{7f2e1a54-2827-43ff-ab57-46c3e059b212}
        Handle ID:            0x0
Operation:
        Operation Type:       Object Access
        Accesses:             %%7685 (Write Property)
        Access Mask:          0x20
        Properties:           ---
              {e48d0154-bcf8-11d1-8702-00c04fb96050}
                    {bf967950-0de6-11d0-a285-00aa003049e2}
        {bf967aba-0de6-11d0-a285-00aa003049e2}
```

NOTE The event described in this section is available on the book's website, in the Unsuccessful Active Directory Object Operation Attempts - Write Property.evtx file.

This Audit Failure 4662 event is the same as the Audit Success 4662 event. It shows you that an access attempt failed due to lack of permissions.

Active Directory Objects Auditing Examples

In this section you will find some examples of how to configure SACLs for Active Directory objects for some common monitoring scenarios.

Organizational Unit Creation/Deletion

To monitor for all successful and unsuccessful organizational unit creation/deletion events in the domain, add the following ACE to the domain object SACL:

- **Principal:** Everyone
- **Type:** All
- **Applies to:** This object and all descendant objects
- **Permissions:** Create Organizational Unit objects/Delete Organizational Unit objects

Organizational Unit Child Object Creation/Deletion

To monitor for all successful and unsuccessful new object creations/deletions, such as computer, group, or user objects, within any organizational unit in the domain, add the following ACE to the domain object SACL:

- **Principal:** Everyone
- **Type:** All
- **Applies to:** Descendant Organizational Unit objects
- **Permissions:** Create all child objects/Delete all child objects

adminCount Attribute Modification for User Accounts

By default, the adminCount attribute is not shown in the built-in DACL and SACL ACE editors. Follow the process explained in the "Properties" section earlier in this chapter to make the adminCount attribute visible in the SACL editor.

   To monitor for all successful and unsuccessful adminCount attribute modifications for any user object in the domain, add the following ACE to the domain object SACL:

- **Principal:** Everyone
- **Type:** All
- **Applies to:** Descendant User objects
- **Permissions:** Write adminCount

Group Policy Link/Unlink Operations

To monitor for all successful and unsuccessful group policy link/unlink operations for all organizational units in the domain, add the following ACE to the domain object SACL:

- **Principal:** Everyone
- **Type:** All
- **Applies to:** Descendant Organizational Unit objects
- **Permissions:** Write gPLink

Authentication Protocols

Microsoft Windows supports the following authentication protocols: LAN Manager (LM), NT LAN Manager (NTLM) Version 1 and 2, and Kerberos.

In this chapter you will find information about how LM, NTLM, NTLMv2, and Kerberos protocols work and how to monitor most common scenarios involving these protocols.

NTLM-family Protocols

The NTLM-family protocols include LAN Manager (LM), NT LAN Manager (NTLM), and NT LAN Manager V2 (NTLMv2). This section explains how these protocols work and also which events are generated on different hosts during authentication using these protocols.

This section also contains information about the NTLM Security Support Provider (NTLMSSP), NTLMv1 Session Security, and NTLMv2 Session Security mechanisms.

Challenge-Response Basics

LAN Manager (LM), NT LAN Manager (NTLM), and NT LAN Manager V2 (NTLMv2) use a challenge-response mechanism for network authentication.

The NTLM-family challenge-response mechanism is just a method of credential validation via a network, without sending cleartext credentials or an original password hash over the network. NTLM-family protocols do not have any default transport protocol to carry them over a network. That is why no default ports are associated with the LM, NTLM, and NTLMv2 protocols. The most common transports for NTLM-family protocols are SMB, HTTP, and SMTP.

A basic challenge-response process flow is illustrated in Figure 9-1. It will help you to understand more detailed topics introduced later in this book. Figure 9-1 is an example of challenge-response mechanism for authentication using a local account located on a destination host. Later in this chapter, you will find more detailed information about each protocol challenge-response mechanism and authentication scenario.

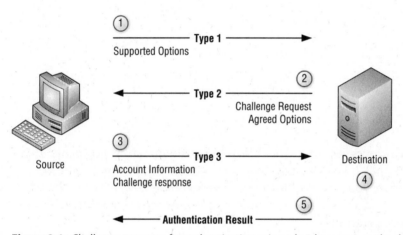

Figure 9-1: Challenge-response for authentication using a local account on the destination host

The numbers in the following list correspond to the numbers in Figure 9-1:

1. As a first step, the source host sends an authentication request to the destination host. It is called an NTLM Type 1 message.

2. The destination host generates a challenge string and sends it to the source host. It is called an NTLM Type 2 message. Also, protocol version and settings selection occur at this stage.

3. The client receives the challenge string and constructs a challenge-response message based on specific operations with the user account's password hash and the initial challenge message received from the destination host. It is called an NTLM Type 3 message. These operations depend on the authentication protocol being used. Information about different

challenge-response message-generation algorithms and password hashes is given in the next sections of this chapter. After a response is generated, the source host sends it to the destination host.

4. The destination host receives the response from the source host, extracts all additional fields if required, and performs the same operations with the user's password hash stored locally on it. If its own generated string and received challenge response string are the same, the destination host considers the password to be legitimate/valid, or not valid if the results are not the same.

5. The destination host sends the response back to the source host with authentication results.

The next sections show you different implementations of hash-generation functions and challenge-response mechanisms based on the authentication protocol being used (LM, NTLM, NTLMv2).

LAN Manager

The LAN Manager (LM) authentication protocol was a default authentication protocol in the late 1980s as part of the LAN Manager operating system developed by Microsoft and 3COM Corporation.

LM contains of two main parts: a locally stored LM hash and a challenge-response authentication mechanism.

LM Hash

Every time a new user is created, an LM hash of the user account's password is generated and stored in the local credentials database. You can change this behavior and disable LM hash generation using the "Computer Configuration\Windows Settings\Security Settings\Local Policies\Security Options\Network security: Do not store LAN Manager hash value on next password change" group policy setting. This is enabled by default starting from Windows Vista and Windows Server 2008.

For local users, the LM hash is stored in the local Security Account Manager (SAM) database along with other user-related information. The SAM database is a registry hive, located in the HKLM\SAM\SAM registry path. The file for this registry hive is %systemroot%\System32\config\SAM.

Local user accounts are stored in the following registry path: HKEY_LOCAL_MACHINE\SAM\SAM\Domains\Account\Users. Each user account has its own registry key assigned with the hexadecimal value of the user's relative identifier (RID). Each user account key has at least two values assigned: V and F. Figure 9-2 shows an example of the SAM registry key for a user account.

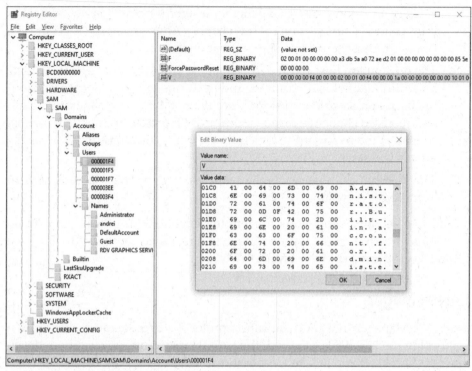

Figure 9-2: SAM registry key for user accounts

Figure 9-2 shows the SAM registry key for a user account with RID 500 (1F4), which is a default RID for the built-in Administrator account. The V registry key value contains an offset for the LM (and NTLM) hash in the SAM database.

For domain accounts, the LM hash is stored in the NTDS.dit file, which is replicated between Active Directory domain controllers within the same domain.

Figure 9-3 shows the process of LM hash generation from the password.

The numbers in the following list correspond to the numbers in Figure 9-3:

1. The maximum password length allowed for an LM hash to be generated is 14 characters. At the time LM was developed, 14 characters seemed far more than needed for strong passwords. If the password length is less than 14 characters, "0" characters are used to bring the length up to 14 characters. If over 14 characters, it is filled in with the built-in default LM "null" hash, skipping all characters after the 14th.

2. The LAN Manager operating system was not case sensitive and it is still applicable to current Windows systems. LM authentication developers decided that the password on which an LM hash is generated should also be case insensitive, as is the operating system.

3. To prepare a password for use by the Data Encryption Standard (DES) block cipher, it is split into two pieces, each of which is 7 characters long.

4. A NULL bit is inserted after each 7 bits of each block, resulting in blocks that are 8 bytes long.

5. Both pieces are used separately as a key to encrypt the "KGS!@#$%" constant string. Each piece produces cipher text output that's 8 bytes long.

6. The 8-byte cipher text outputs from both initial password parts are concatenated together. This is the final LM hash.

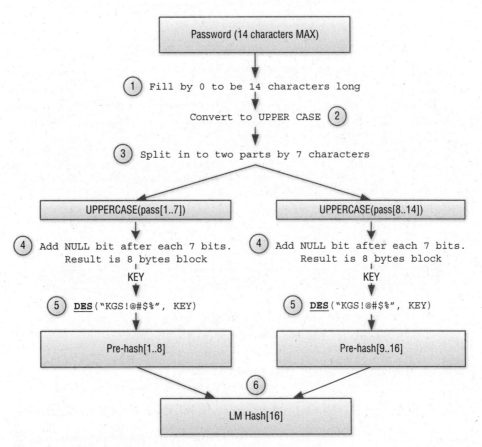

Figure 9-3: LM hash generation process

LM Challenge-Response Mechanism

As shown in Figure 9-1, the destination host sends a challenge request message to the source host as part of the NTLM Type 2 message in the authentication process. After the source host receives the challenge string from the destination host, it starts generating the LM challenge-response string using the algorithm shown in Figure 9-4.

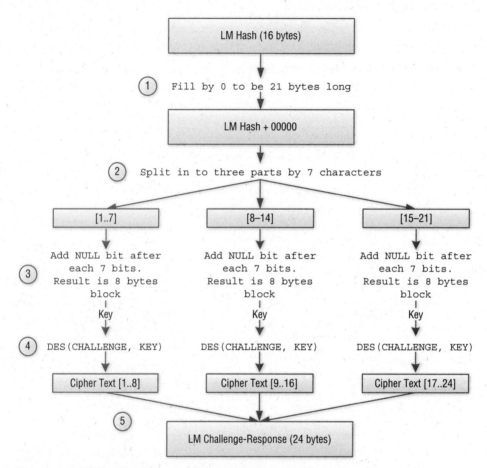

Figure 9-4: LM challenge-response string generation process

The numbers in the following list correspond to the numbers in Figure 9-4:

1. The LM hash is taken as a basis for challenge-response generation. The LM challenge-response algorithm utilizes DES encryption, which is the primary reason, as was explained in previous section, the initial LM hash is filled by zeros to be 21 bytes long.

2. The result from the previous stage is split into three blocks of 7 bytes each, in order to be used by the DES block cipher.

3. A NULL bit is inserted after each 7 bits of each block, resulting in blocks that are 8 bytes long.

4. All pieces are used separately as a key to encrypt the 8-byte challenge string received from the destination host. Each piece produces cipher text output that's 8 bytes long.

5. The 8-byte cipher text outputs are concatenated together. This is the final LM challenge-response string.

After the LM challenge-response string is generated, it is sent to the destination host for validation as part of an NTLM Type 3 message. The destination host performs the steps just described using the hash stored in its local SAM database (regular hosts) or the NTDS.dit file (domain controllers). The final stage compares the challenge-response string received from the source host with the locally generated challenge-response string on the destination host.

NT LAN Manager

The NT LAN Manager (NTLM) authentication protocol was first introduced in Windows NT 3.1. NTLM is an enhanced version of the LM protocol and has a completely new local hash-generation algorithm. This change makes the local hash-generation algorithm more secure in comparison with the DES-based algorithm used in the LM protocol.

Similar to LM, NTLM consists of two main parts: a locally stored NTLM hash and a challenge-response authentication mechanism.

NTLM Hash

Every time a new user is created, an NTLM hash of the user account's password is generated and stored in the local database. An NTLM hash is independent from the LM hash and may coexist with it. There is no group policy setting to disable NTLM hash generation for new user accounts. Methods exist to remove an NTLM hash after it is generated (Active Directory Protected Users), but these methods are not within the scope of the book.

Figure 9-5 shows the process of NTLM hash generation from the password.

The entire complicated DES-based algorithm, used in the LM local hash-generation process, was replaced by the more secure (at the time the protocol was created) and faster Message-Digest 4 (MD4) one-way hash function. This removes the 14-character limitation for the user's password. The password length limitation with NTLM is 127 characters.

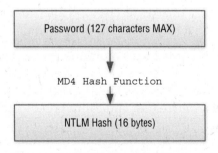

Figure 9-5: NTLM hash-generation process

NTLM Challenge-Response Mechanism

The NTLM challenge-response string generation algorithm is exactly the same as for the LM protocol (Figure 9-4), discussed earlier in this chapter. The only difference is that the NTLM hash is used for the first step instead of an LM hash.

NT LAN Manager V2

NT LAN Manager V2 (NTLMv2) is a major improvement for challenge-response mechanism security. It does not change local hash generation and still uses NTLM hashes. NTLMv2 was first introduced in Windows NT 4.0 SP4.

NTLMv2 improves both LM and NTLM challenge-response algorithms.

NTLMv2 uses an NTLM hash for all operations. There is no NTLMv2 hash.

NTLMv2 Challenge-Response Mechanism

NTLMv2 replaces both NTLM and LM challenge-response mechanisms. Basically, when a source host receives a challenge from a destination host it will generate two responses: NTv2 and LMv2. You will find more details about why an LMv2 response is generated later in this section.

NTLMv2 has a built-in security feature that helps protocols resist a pre-compute hash table attack using a fake destination host. NTLM and LM are vulnerable to the following attack:

1. Attacker sets up a fake destination host.

2. Attacker generates a hash table based on a specific challenge string. Because the attacker owns the destination server, he/she can send a pre-defined challenge string to the source host in the challenge request message. Prior to doing this, the attacker generates a database of pre-computed challenge-response messages using a known challenge string and different passwords.

3. Attacker convinces the source host to connect to the fake server.

4. Attacker sends a pre-defined challenge string to the source host.

5. Attacker receives a challenge-response from the source host and performs a hash table attack against it.

NTLMv2 uses a unique client challenge string that is used in challenge-response generation on a source host side. This attack will not work in such a scenario, because the attacker, who owns the target server, does not have control of a source host and cannot predict the client challenge string value.

NTLMv2 OWF

In the first step in NTLMv2 challenge-response creation, the so-called NTLMv2 One Way Function (OWF) is generated on the source host side using the algorithm shown in Figure 9-6.

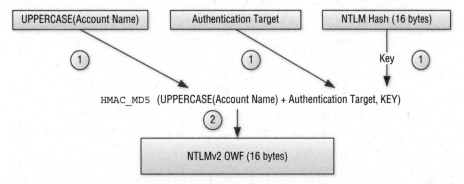

Figure 9-6: NTLMv2 OWF generation process

The numbers in the following list correspond to the numbers in Figure 9-6: NTLMv2 OWF is 16 bytes long and will be used for NTv2 and LMv2 response generation.

1. The source host prepares the following information to be used in the NTLMv2 OWF generation algorithm:

   ■ Uppercase name of account for which authentication is performed.

   ■ Authentication Target, which is the server name (for local accounts) or domain name (for domain accounts) to which the account belongs.

   ■ NTLM hash of the user's account password.

2. The HMAC_MD5 function is taken from the concatenated values of UPPERCASE (User Name) and Authentication Target, using the NTLM hash as a key. The result is a 16-byte HMAC_MD5 hash, which is the NTLMv2 OWF.

NTv2 Response

In the second step of NTLMv2 response creation, the NTv2 Response is generated on the source host. An NTv2 Response replaces the NTLM response. Figure 9-7 shows the algorithm for NTv2 Response string creation.

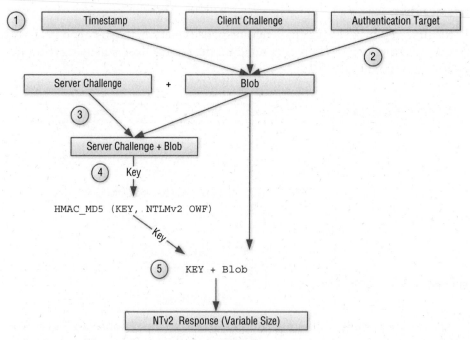

Figure 9-7: NTv2 Response string generation process

The following steps are performed to generate an NTv2 Response string. The numbers in the list correspond to the numbers in Figure 9-7:

1. The source host prepares the following information to be used in the so-called Blob object:

   ■ **Timestamp:** Number of tenths of a microsecond since 1 January 1601.

   ■ **Client Challenge:** 8 bytes of random data generated by source host.

   ■ **Authentication Target:** A server name (for local accounts) or domain name (for domain accounts) to which the account belongs.

2. The Timestamp, Client Challenge, and Authentication Target become a part of a Blob object. More detailed information about the structure of the Blob object is beyond the scope of this book.

3. The Server Challenge string, which was received from the destination host, and a Blob are concatenated together.

4. The HMAC_MD5 function is taken from the concatenated values of the Server Challenge and Blob, using NTLMv2 OWF as a key.

5. The result of the HMAC_MD5 function is concatenated with a Blob, forming the final NTv2 Response object, which has variable length.

LMv2 Response

In the third step of NTLMv2 response creation, the LMv2 Response is generated on the source host. The LMv2 response replaces the LM response. Figure 9-8 shows the algorithm for LMv2 Response string creation.

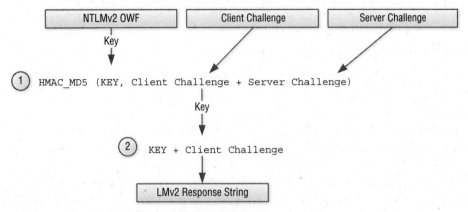

Figure 9-8: LMv2 response string generation process

The following steps are performed to generate the LMv2 Response. The numbers in the list correspond to the numbers in Figure 9-8.

1. The HMAC_MD5 function is generated from the concatenated values of the Client Challenge and Server Challenge, using NTLMv2 OWF as a key.

2. The result of the HMAC_MD5 function is concatenated with a Client Challenge, forming the final 24-byte long LMv2 Response string.

NTLMSSP and Anonymous Authentication

NTLM Security Support Provider (NTLMSSP) is a part of MSV1_0 SSP/AP and implemented based on SSPI model specifications. See Chapter 4 for more information about SSPI and SSP.

NTLMSSP implements the LM, NTLM, and NTLMv2 authentication protocols and also contains NTLMv1 Session Security and NTLMv2 Session Security mechanisms, which we will discuss later in this section.

NTLMSSP also provides standard signing and sealing SSP features for applications to use.

NTLMv1 Session Security and NTLMv2 Session Security

NTLMSSP provides, along with authentication function, signing and sealing capabilities for applications. Two components of NTLMSSP are responsible for signing and sealing: NTLMv1 Session Security and NTLMv2 Session Security.

NTLMv2 Session Security is the newest/enhanced version of NTLMv1 Session Security. The main differences between them are algorithms for signing and sealing key negotiation/generation and the length of a signing and sealing key:

- NTLMv1 Session Security supports 40-bit and 56-bit long keys.
- NTLMv2 Session Security supports 40-bit, 56-bit, and 128-bit long keys.

NTLMv2 Session Response

As discussed earlier in this chapter, NTLMv2 has a built-in security feature that helps it resist pre-computed hash table attacks using a fake destination host. NTLM and LM are vulnerable to this type of attack.

NTLMSSP has the ability to protect NTLM and LM against pre-computed hash table attacks. This feature is called NTLMv2 Session Response and it is a part of NTLMv2 Session Security.

NTLMv2 Session Response can be negotiated between the source and destination host by NTLMSSP to bring additional protection to NTLM and LM authentication, if any of those is selected for authentication. NTLMv2 Session Response replaces the regular NTLM response. Figure 9-9 shows the algorithm for NTLMv2 Session Response creation.

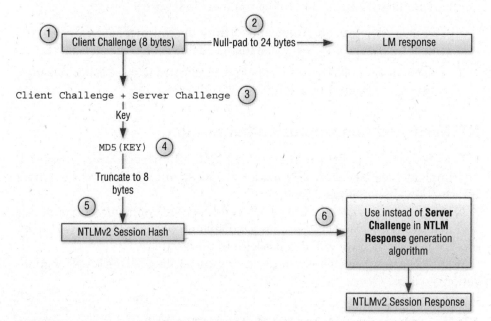

Figure 9-9: NTLMv2 Session Response generation process

The following steps are performed to generate an NTLMv2 Session Response. The numbers in the list correspond to the numbers in Figure 9-9:

1. The source host generates a random 8-byte long client challenge.

2. The `Client Challenge` is null-padded to 24 bytes and inserted into the LM Response field. This is how the `Client Challenge` gets to the destination host.

3. The `Client Challenge` is concatenated with the initial `Server Challenge`.

4. The MD5 hashing function is applied to the result of the concatenation. The result is a 16-byte long MD5 hash.

5. The MD5 hash is truncated to 8 bytes. This is called the NTLMv2 Session Hash.

6. The NTLMv2 Session Hash replaces the `Server Challenge` in NTLM Response generation. The result is the NTLMv2 Session Response.

Anonymous Authentication

The LM, NTLM, and NTLMv2 protocols support anonymous authentication. This type of authentication is used in scenarios where no authentication is required and a connection should be made anonymously. One example of such a scenario is remote anonymous connection to an IPC$ network file share for available file shares enumeration. Anonymous authentication can be negotiated as part of a standard authentication handshake. Chapter 4 has more information about anonymous logons.

NTLM-family Protocols Monitoring

This section explains the steps performed during the most common NTLM-family authentication scenarios and shows the security events that are generated.

Network Security: Restrict NTLM Security Group Policy Settings

In addition to standard Windows security event log events, a new set of NTLM-family protocol monitoring capabilities were introduced with "Network Security:Restrict NTLM" security group policy settings. These policy settings were first introduced in Windows 7 and Windows Server 2008 R2 operating systems. They are located under the `Computer Configuration\Windows Settings\ Security Settings\Local Policies\Security Options` group policy path.

These policy settings allow you to restrict and/or monitor usage of NTLM-family protocols in Windows environments.

Detailed explanation of these policy settings is out of scope of this book; you can find more information about them on official Microsoft sites.

Local Account Authentication

Figure 9-10 illustrates the challenge-response mechanism for authentication using a local account located on a target host.

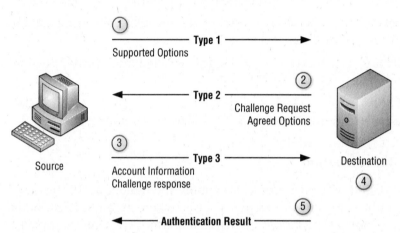

Figure 9-10: Challenge-response for authentication using a local account on the destination host

Step 1: NTLM Type 1 Message

In the first step, a NTLM Type 1 message is sent by the client to initiate authentication and to send a list of NTLM-family protocols supported by the source host. When this happens and "Network Security: Restrict NTLM" policy settings are set for auditing mode, there is always an 8001 event in the `Applications and Services Logs\Microsoft\Windows\NTLM` event log on the source host, as shown in Listing 9-1.

Listing 9-1: Event ID 8001: NTLM client blocked audit: Audit outgoing NTLM authentication traffic that would be blocked.

```
Task Category: Auditing NTLM
Level: Information
Target server:              cifs/10.0.0.110
Supplied user:              Andrei
Supplied domain:            10.0.0.110
PID of client process:      4
Name of client process:
LUID of client process:     0x2BB5E3
User identity of client process:                Administrator
Domain name of user identity of client process: 2016SRV
Mechanism OID:              (NULL)
```

NOTE The event described in Listing 9-1 is available on the book's website, in the `NTLM Successful Local User Account Logon - source host NTLM log.evtx` file.

NOTE Restrict NTLM events in the "Applications and Services Logs\Microsoft\ Windows\NTLM" event log are only generated if the corresponding policy settings are enabled. The policy settings are out of the scope of this book.

The `Target server` field contains the Service Principal Name (SPN) of the requested service on the destination host. The SPN has the following format: *service_name/destination_host*. In this example, the authentication request was sent to the Common Internet File System (CIFS) subsystem/service on the destination host.

The `Supplied user` field contains the name of the user, supplied for authentication. It has a `(NULL)` value if the username was not initially specified.

The `Supplied domain` field contains the target host's name or the domain name of the user account specified in the `Supplied user` field. It has a `(NULL)` value if the supplied user domain was not initially specified. For example, if a user does not explicitly specify a hostname for the new remote desktop connection using the default Microsoft Terminal Services (`mstsc.exe`) client, the `Supplied domain` field value will be `(NULL)`.

One scenario for which you may see a `(NULL)` value for the `Supplied user` and `Supplied domain` fields is CIFS/SMB single sign on, when, for example, a user connects to the remote C$ share without specifying additional credentials, but rather using the currently logged-in user's credentials.

The `PID of client process` field contains the process identifier (PID) of the process that performed/requested authentication, in decimal format.

The `Name of client process` field contains the name of the process that performed/requested authentication. For the system process (PID 4) this field will be empty.

The `LUID of client process` field contains the logon session ID of the user account specified in the `User identity of client process` field.

The `User identity of client process` field contains the name of the account that initially invoked/requested authentication.

The `Domain name of user identity of client process` field contains the hostname or domain name of the user account specified in the `User identity of client process` field.

The `Mechanism OID` field contains object identifier (OID) of the SSPI mechanism being used for authentication. For example, an OID of 1.3.6.1.4.1.311.2.2.10 is related to NTLM-family protocols (MS-NLMP specification). This field is not always populated.

There is no difference on the source host regardless of whether authentication was successful. The 8001 event will still be the same.

Step 2: NTLM Type 2 Message

In step 2, the destination host selects the strongest protocol it supports and sends an NTLM Type 2 message, which is also called a *challenge request message*, to the client. A challenge request message contains a challenge—an 8-byte string of randomly generated characters—which then will be used by the client to construct an NTLM Type 3 (challenge response) message.

The client receives the challenge request message and constructs a challenge response message (NTLM Type 3). This message contains a response string generated by a specific algorithm, based on the version of the NTLM-family protocol used. This algorithm is created by performing multiple hashing and/or encryption operations with the received challenge request string and the user's password hash.

Successful Authentication

Multiple events appear in the Windows security and NTLM event logs on a destination host when NTLM-family authentication for a local account is successful. You can review Chapter 4 to see which events are generated for different logon types.

A 4624 security event contains a section with more details about authentication data for the logged in account:

```
Detailed Authentication Information:
      Logon Process:                NtLmSsp
      Authentication Package:       NTLM
      Transited Services:           -
      Package Name (NTLM only):     NTLM V1
      Key Length:                   128
```

The `Authentication Package` field may have a value of `NTLM` or `Negotiate`. If Negotiate SSP/AP was used for authentication, there will be no additional NTLM-related data in the `Package Name (NTLM only)` and `Key Length` fields.

If an NTLM authentication package was used, then:

- **`Package Name (NTLM only)`:** Contains the name of NTLM-family authentication protocol. This field may have one of the following values:

  - LM

  - NTLM V1

  - NTLM V2

  - - (for non-NTLM authentication or Negotiate SSP/AP)

- **Key Length:** Contains the length of the signing and sealing key negotiated by NTLMv1 Session Security or NTLMv2 Session Security. This field may have one of the following values:

  - 128

  - 56

  - 40

  - 0 (for non-NTLM authentication or Negotiate SSP/AP)

For each successful NTLM authentication using a local user account, in addition to a 4624 event, the event in Listing 9-2 is triggered in the Windows security event log on the destination host where the account's credentials are stored.

Listing 9-2: Event ID 4776: The computer attempted to validate the credentials for an account.

```
Task Category: Credential Validation
Keywords: Audit Success
Authentication Package:      MICROSOFT_AUTHENTICATION_PACKAGE_V1_0
Logon Account:               Administrator
Source Workstation:          2016SRV
Error Code:                  0x0
```

NOTE The event described in Listing 9-2 is available on the book's website, in the NTLM Successful Local User Account Logon - destination host Security log.evtx file.

A 4776 event generates on the host where account credentials are stored and when this host receives a credential validation request for that account. The Authentication Package field contains the name of the authentication package that handled NTLM authentication. The only default package name you should see in a Windows environment is MICROSOFT_AUTHENTICATION_PACKAGE_V1_0.

The Logon Account field contains the name of the account for which credentials were validated.

The Source Workstation field contains the name of the host from which the credentials validation request was received.

The Error Code field contains the error code for unsuccessful credential validations, which will be discussed later in this chapter. For successful credentials validation this field always has a value of 0x0.

In addition to these security events, for each successful NTLM authentication using a local user account, the event in Listing 9-3 is triggered in the Windows NTLM event log.

Listing 9-3: Event ID 8002: NTLM server blocked audit: Audit Incoming NTLM Traffic that would be blocked.

```
Task Category: Auditing NTLM
Level: Information
Calling process PID:           4
Calling process name:
Calling process LUID:          0x3E7
Calling process user identity:  WIN10-1703$
Calling process domain identity: WORKGROUP
Mechanism OID:                 (NULL)
```

NOTE The event described in Listing 9-3 is available on the book's website, in the `NTLM Successful Local User Account Logon - destination host NTLM log - non domain-joined.evtx` **file.**

The `Calling process PID` field contains the process identifier (PID) of the local process on the destination host that handled the authentication request, in decimal format. It does not contain information about the process that invoked authentication from the source host.

The `Calling process name` field contains the process name of the local process on the destination host that handled the authentication request. It does not contain information about the process name from the source host. For system process (PID 4) this field will be empty.

The `Calling process LUID` field contains the logon ID of the user account logon session for the account specified in the `Calling process user identity` field.

The `Calling process user identity` field for local account authentication contains the name of the account, under which the process that handled the authentication on the destination host runs. Keep in mind that the LOCAL SYSTEM or LOCAL SERVICE account may "hide" behind the computer account name. They will have different `Calling process LUID` field values:

- **0x3E4:** LOCAL SYSTEM

- **0x3E5:** LOCAL SERVICE

The `Calling process domain identity` field contains the domain or workgroup name (if the destination host is not domain-joined) to which the `Calling process user identity` account belongs.

The `Mechanism OID` field contains the object identifier (OID) of the SSPI mechanism being used for authentication. For example, the OID 1.3.6.1.4.1.311.2.2.10 is related to NTLM-family protocols (MS-NLMP specification). This field is not always populated.

Generally speaking, the 8002 event for local accounts does not provide information about from where the NTLM-family protocol request originated. It shows you only that an NTLM-family protocol request was received.

If a destination host is *joined to an Active Directory domain*, an 8003 event will be generated in the Windows NTLM event log on the destination host, in addition to an 8002 event. The 8003 event is shown in Listing 9-4.

Listing 9-4: Event ID 8003: NTLM server blocked in the domain audit: Audit NTLM authentication in this domain

```
Task Category: Auditing NTLM
Level:         Information
User:          administrator
Domain:        10.0.0.110
Workstation:   2016SRV
PID:           4
Process:
Logon type:    3
InProc:        true
Mechanism:     (NULL)
```

NOTE The event described in Listing 9-4 is available on the book's website, in the `NTLM Successful Local User Account Logon - destination host NTLM log - domain-joined.evtx` **file.**

The `User` field contains the account name for which the authentication attempt was performed.

The `Domain` field contains the IP-address of a host to which the user account, specified in the `User` field, belongs.

The `Workstation` field contains the hostname from which the authentication request was received.

The `PID` field contains the process identifier (PID) of the local process on the destination host that handled the authentication request, in decimal format. It does not contain information about the process that initiated authentication from the source host.

The `Process` field contains process name of the local process on the destination host that handled the authentication request. It does not contain information about the process from the source host. For system process (PID 4) this field will be empty.

The `Logon type` field contains the type of logon that was initiated from the source host. Table 4.1 contains the available logon type codes.

The `Mechanism` field contains the object identifier (OID) of the SSPI mechanism being used for authentication. For example, the OID 1.3.6.1.4.1.311.2.2.10 is related to NTLM-family protocols (MS-NLMP specification). This field is not always populated.

Step 3: NTLM Type 3 Message

After a response is generated (Step 2), the source host sends it to the destination host in an NTLM Type 3 message. The destination host receives the Type 3 message, extracts all additional fields if required, and performs the same operations with the user's locally stored password hash. If the destination host gets the same results as the source host, the destination host considers the password to be legitimate/valid. If the results are not the same, the password is not valid.

The destination host sends the response back to the source host with authentication results.

Unsuccessful Local Account Authentication

On a source host, the same 8001 NTLM event will be generated, whether or not the authentication is successful.

Only an 8002 NTLM event will be generated on the destination host for unsuccessful authentication. An 8003 event is generated only for successful NTLM authentications and only on the domain-joined hosts. There is no difference between successful and unsuccessful authentication 8002 events.

A 4625 security event will be generated instead of a 4624 event and will usually contain the following information in the `Detailed Authentication Information` section:

```
Detailed Authentication Information:
     Logon Process:               NtLmSsp
     Authentication Package:      NTLM
     Transited Services:          -
     Package Name (NTLM only):    -
     Key Length:                  0
```

A 4625 event does not usually provide information about the NTLM-family protocol name (`Package Name (NTLM only)`) and NTLMv1/v2 Session Security key length (`Key Length`).

For each unsuccessful NTLM authentication using a local user account, event in Listing 9-5 is generated in the Windows security event log on the destination host where the account's credentials are stored.

Listing 9-5: Event ID 4776: The computer attempted to validate the credentials for an account.

```
Task Category: Credential Validation
Keywords: Audit Failure
Authentication Package:      MICROSOFT_AUTHENTICATION_PACKAGE_V1_0
Logon Account:               Administrator
Source Workstation:          2016SRV
Error Code:                  0xC000006A
```

NOTE The event described in Listing 9-5 is available on the book's website, in the `NTLM Unsuccessful Local User Account Logon - destination host Security log.evtx` **file.**

4776 events were discussed with Listing 9-2. This is an Audit Failure event, which informs you that credentials validation failed.

The Error Code field contains a hexadecimal failure code. The most common error codes for 4776 events are presented in Table 9-1.

Table 9-1: 4776 Event Error Codes

ERROR CODE	DESCRIPTION
0xC000005E	There are currently no logon servers available to service the logon request.
0xC000006D	Unknown user name or bad password.
	Issue with NTLM-family protocol version negotiation.
0xC0000064	User logon with misspelled or bad user account.
0xC000006A	User logon with misspelled or bad password.
0xc000019b	Duplicate or incorrect SID was detected.
0xC000006F	User logon outside authorized hours.
0xC0000070	User logon from unauthorized workstation.
0xC0000071	User logon with expired password.
0xC0000072	User logon to account disabled by administrator.
0xC00000DC	Indicates the Sam Server was in the wrong state to perform the desired operation.
0xC000015B	The user has not been granted the requested logon type (logon right) at this machine.
0xC000018C	The logon request failed because the trust relationship between the primary domain and the trusted domain failed.
0xC0000192	An attempt was made to logon, but the Netlogon service was not active.
0xC0000193	User logon with expired account.
0xC0000224	User is required to change password at next logon.
0xC0000225	Unknown error occurred during logon.
0xC0000234	User logon with account locked.
0xC00002EE	Unknown error occurred during logon.
0xC0000413	The machine you are logging onto is protected by an authentication firewall. The specified account is not allowed to authenticate to the machine.

Domain Account Authentication

Figure 9-11 illustrates the NTLM-family challenge-response mechanism for authentication using a domain account to the domain-joined destination host, if the destination host is not a domain controller. If a host is a domain controller, the challenge-response mechanism is similar to that described for a local account in the "Local Account Authentication" section earlier in this chapter.

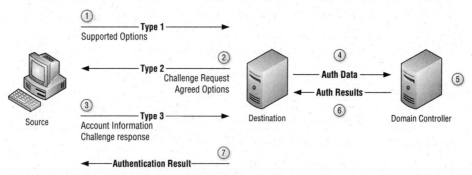

Figure 9-11: Challenge-response for domain accounts

The numbers in the following list correspond to the numbers in Figure 9-11:

1–3. These are the same as they are for a local account as described previously in this chapter.

4. Because the destination host does not have access to domain user credentials, it cannot perform credentials validation. The destination host sends all data that is required for validation, such as username, initial challenge string, and challenge response, to one of the domain controllers for validation.

5. The domain controller performs credentials validation using the method described in the "Local Account Authentication" section.

6. After credentials validation is finished, the domain controller sends the authentication results back to the destination server.

7. The destination server sends the results back to the source host.

Successful Domain Account Authentication

From an auditing perspective, some differences exist between successful local and domain accounts authentication.

An 8001 event on the source host is the same as the 8001 event discussed in the "Local Account Authentication" section.

On a destination host you will find all events that you saw in the "Local Account Authentication" section, except the 4776 event, because the destination server cannot validate credentials for a domain account. Credentials for domain accounts are stored on domain controllers.

On an Active Directory domain controller the event in Listing 9-6 occurs in the Windows security event log after successful NTLM-family protocol authentication for domain accounts.

Listing 9-6: Event ID 4776: The computer attempted to validate the credentials for an account.

```
Task Category: Credential Validation
Keywords: Audit Success
Authentication Package:  MICROSOFT_AUTHENTICATION_PACKAGE_V1_0
Logon Account:           Administrator
Source Workstation:      WIN10-1703
Error Code:              0x0
```

NOTE The event described in Listing 9-6 is available on the book's website, in the `NTLM Successful Domain User Account Logon - Domain Controller - security log.evtx` file.

This event was discussed after Listing 9-2. Some parts of this event are specific to domain controllers.

The Logon Account field shows the name of the domain account for which credentials were validated.

Source Workstation shows the name of the host from which a validation request was received by the destination host.

There is no information about the authentication target host (destination) in this event.

In addition to a 4776 event, the 8004 event in Listing 9-7 is generated in the NTLM event log on the domain controller.

Listing 9-7: Event ID 8004: Domain Controller Blocked Audit: Audit NTLM authentication to this domain controller.

```
Task Category: Auditing NTLM
Level:               Information
Secure Channel name: 2016SRV
User name:           Administrator
Domain name:         HQCORP
Workstation name:    WIN10-1703
Secure Channel type: 2
```

> **NOTE** The event described in Listing 9-7 is available on the book's website, in the
> `NTLM Successful Domain User Account Logon - Domain Controller - NTLM log.evtx` **file.**

8004 is a dedicated event for NTLM-family protocol credentials validation requests. It generates for both successful and unsuccessful authentication requests.

The `Secure Channel name` field contains information about the authentication target/destination host name.

The `User Name` field shows the name of the domain account for which credentials were validated.

The `Domain Name` field contains information about the domain name to which the `User name` account belongs.

The `Workstation name` field contains information about the source host from which an authentication request was received by the destination host.

The `Secure Channel type` field contains the type of secure channel through which the authentication request was received by domain controller. Table 9-2 contains a list of possible values for the `Secure Channel` field.

Table 9-2: Secure Channel Types

TYPE CODE	NAME	DESCRIPTION
0	NullSecureChannel	Unauthenticated secure channel.
1	MsvApSecureChannel	Local secure channel between MSV1_0 SSP/AP and NetLogon service.
2	WorkstationSecureChannel	Secure channel between domain host and domain controller.
3	TrustedDnsDomainSecureChannel	Secure channel between domain controllers from different Active Directory domains.
4	TrustedDomainSecureChannel	Secure channel between domain controllers from the same Active Directory domain.
5	UasServerSecureChannel	Obsolete.
6	ServerSecureChannel	Secure channel from a backup domain controller to a primary domain controller.
7	CdcServerSecureChannel	Secure channel from a read-only domain controller (RODC) to a writable domain controller.

Unsuccessful Domain Account Authentication

The messages for unsuccessful domain account authentication are the same as for successful authentication, with only one difference: there will be an `Audit`

`Failure` 4776 event on the domain controller instead of `Audit Success`, as shown in Listing 9-8.

Listing 9-8: Event ID 4776: The computer attempted to validate the credentials for an account.

```
Task Category: Credential Validation
Keywords: Audit Failure
Authentication Package:  MICROSOFT_AUTHENTICATION_PACKAGE_V1_0
Logon Account:           sdasd
Source Workstation:      WIN7
Error Code:              0xC0000064
```

NOTE The event described in Listing 9-8 is available on the book's website, in the `NTLM Unsuccessful Domain User Account Logon - Domain Controller - security log.evtx` file.

This event was discussed following Listing 9-2.

Cross-Domain Challenge-Response

Figure 9-12 illustrates the NTLM-family challenge-response mechanism for authentication using a domain account to the domain-joined destination host, where the user account is an account from one of the trusted domains.

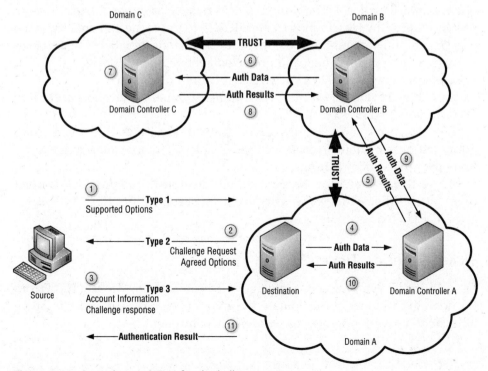

Figure 9-12: Cross-domain NTLM-family challenge-response

Figure 9-12 illustrates an example of authentication using the Domain C user account on the Domain A joined host. Domain A trusts Domain B, Domain B trusts Domain C, so Domain A trusts (indirectly) Domain C. This is an example of a transitive trust relationship.

The numbers in the following list correspond to the numbers in Figure 9-12:

1–4. These are the same as the domain account scenario (refer to Figure 9-11).

5. Domain Controller A sends credentials to Domain Controller B using the only direct trust Domain A has. Domain Controller A is aware of Domain C because of the trust with Domain B, but cannot send credentials directly to Domain C, because there is no direct trust between them.

6. Domain Controller B redirects authentication data to Domain Controller C.

7. Domain Controller C performs credentials validation.

8–11. The response from Domain Controller C goes back to the destination host, which then answers to the source host with the authentication results.

Kerberos

Kerberos was first introduced as a default Microsoft Windows authentication protocol for Active Directory domain environment in Windows 2000. It is an open standard protocol. The Kerberos uses tickets issued by a trusted host/ party (called a Key Distribution Center [KDC]) to prove the authenticity of the user or computer account. It provides secure authentication because Kerberos tickets are encrypted, signed, and protected against replay attacks.

Kerberos uses ports UDP 88 or TCP 88 for communications.

In a Microsoft Active Directory environment, domain controllers act as Key Distribution Centers (KDCs).

The Kerberos protocol settings can be chained domain wide, using a group policy settings on a domain controller. See Chapter 7 for more information about Kerberos group policy settings.

This section explains how Kerberos tickets are issued, and provides detailed information about Windows security event log events for AS_REQ, TGS_REQ, and AP_REQ request monitoring.

Ticket-Granting Ticket (TGT)

Each Active Directory account must get a Ticket-Granting Ticket (TGT) from the domain controller of the domain the account belongs to, in order to prove its credentials were validated by the domain controller.

A TGT, which is also called an authentication ticket, is valid for 10 hours by default. After 10 hours the TGT ticket must be renewed. It can be renewed multiple times before it reaches the lifetime limit of 7 days. After 7 days a TGT ticket expires and a new TGT ticket must be requested.

Figure 9-13 shows the TGT issuing process for authentication using a password. The numbers in the following list correspond to the numbers in Figure 9-13:

1. The client sends the authentication request (AS_REQ) to get a TGT for a user or computer account from the domain controller (KDC). Each client host has access to the authenticating account's Client Key, which is a key generated based on the account's password.

   The client sends information to the KDC, which includes the following main items:

   - **User Principal Name (UPN):** The UPN of the user or computer account for which an AS_REQ is sent. By default, the UPN has the following format: `account_name@domain_name`. For example, `amirosh@company.com`.

   - **Domain Name (Realm):** The name of domain for the account for which authentication is performed. In the Kerberos world, Active Directory domains are called *realms*.

   - **Service Principal Name (SPN):** The SPN for a service requested from a domain controller. The SPN is a unique identifier of a service instance and has the following format: `service_name/target_name`. For AS_REQ (TGT) it always has the following format: `krbtgt/realm_name`.

   - **Supported Cipher Suites:** The list of cryptographic algorithms supported by the client. The KDC and a client negotiate the strongest cryptographic algorithms supported by both sides. You will find more information about Kerberos cryptographic algorithms later in this chapter.

   - **Pre-Authentication Timestamp:** This is an optional field, but it is sent by default in a Microsoft Active Directory environment. This field is used to authenticate the user or computer account before it asks for a TGT. The pre-authentication timestamp is the number of seconds since Jan 1, 1970, also called epoch time. It is encrypted by the Client Key, so the domain controller, which also has access to the Client Key for the domain account, will be able to validate the timestamp. You can enable or disable pre-authentication timestamp generation using the "Do not require Kerberos preauthentication" checkbox of the user's Active Directory account properties in the Active Directory Users and Computers snap-in.

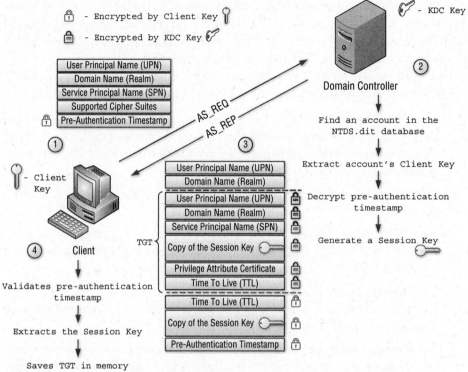

Figure 9-13: Kerberos TGT issuing process

2. After the domain controller receives the AS_REQ from the client, it performs the following actions:

   ▪ Finds the account, for which the authentication request is performed, in the domain controller's configuration database (NTDS.dit).

   ▪ Extracts the account's Client Key.

   ▪ Decrypts the pre-authentication timestamp using the extracted Client Key. If the Client Key is the same as the Client Key that was used to initially encrypt the timestamp, the domain controller will be able to successfully decrypt and validate it. The timestamp is successfully validated if it has a valid timestamp format and the difference between decrypted timestamp and timestamp generated on the domain controller is not greater that 5 minutes (default setting, but can be changed).

   ▪ Generates a Session Key, which will be used for further communications between the client and domain controller instead of a Client Key.

3. The domain controller sends the following unencrypted information back to the client in the AS_REP message :

   ▪ User Principal Name (UPN): The UPN of the user for which the TGT was issued.

- Domain Name (Realm): The name of realm/domain for the account for which the TGT was issued.

Items of the TGT-related fields are encrypted by a KDC Key. A KDC Key is based on the built-in domain local krbtgt account's password (stored as a hash). This account exists by default in every Active Directory domain and its default RID is 502. TGT fields are encrypted with a KDC Key, so only domain controllers from the same domain can decrypt this TGT. The following items form the TGT and are encrypted by the KDC Key:

- **User Principal Name (UPN):** The UPN of the user for which a TGT was issued.

- **Domain Name (Realm):** The name of the realm/domain for the account for which a TGT was issued.

- **Service Principal Name (SPN):** The SPN for a service for which a TGT was issued. For TGTs it always has the following format: krbtgt/ realm_name.

- **Copy of the Session Key:** A copy of the Session Key for future use by domain controllers in the Ticket Granting Service (TGS) tickets issuing process for the user account.

- **Privilege Attribute Certificate (PAC):** This is Microsoft's extension of the Kerberos protocol, which may contain additional information. For example, a PAC field is used to store authorization information, such as domain group membership information for an account for which a TGT was issued.

- **Time To Live (TTL):** Contains the time when a TGT must be renewed and the time when it must be reissued.

Some fields in the AS_REP are encrypted using a Client Key, so only the owner of the Client Key will be able to decrypt them. Here are the fields:

- **Time To Live (TTL):** This field contains time when a TGT must be renewed and the time when it must be reissued.

- **Copy of the Session Key:** A copy of the Session Key for future use by the client in TGS ticket requests to domain controllers.

- **Pre-Authentication Timestamp:** This provides mutual authentication, so the client also validates the timestamp, encrypted by domain controller using the Client Key, to make sure the domain controller has access to its Client Key.

4. The client receives an AS_REP message from the domain controller and performs the following steps:

- Validates the pre-authentication timestamp, as described earlier in this section.

- Extracts the Session Key that will be used by the client in TGS ticket requests (TGS_REQ) to domain controllers in the future.
- Saves the TGT in the Kerberos SSP/AP memory, so it can be used when it is needed.

Successful AS_REQ Message

If authentication is successful (the TGT is successfully issued) the event in Listing 9-9 is generated in the domain controller's security event log.

Listing 9-9: Event ID 4768: A Kerberos authentication ticket (TGT) was requested.

```
Task Category: Kerberos Authentication Service
Keywords: Audit Success
Account Information:
        Account Name:           Administrator
        Supplied Realm Name:    HQCORP.LOCAL
        User ID:                S-1-5-21-1913345275-1711810662-261465553
                                   -500
Service Information:
        Service Name:           krbtgt
        Service ID:             S-1-5-21-1913345275-1711810662-261465553
                                   -502
Network Information:
        Client Address:         ::ffff:10.0.0.110
        Client Port:            56814
Additional Information:
        Ticket Options:         0x40810010
        Result Code:            0x0
        Ticket Encryption Type: 0x12
        Pre-Authentication Type: 2
Certificate Information:
        Certificate Issuer Name:
        Certificate Serial Number:
        Certificate Thumbprint:
```

NOTE The event described in Listing 9-9 is available on the book's website, in the `Successful AS_REQ Message.evtx` **file.**

It's important to note that a 4768 event is related to an AS_REQ, not to a TGT ticket. It is an AS_REQ monitoring event.

The `Account Name` field contains the name of the account for which an AS_REQ was sent. The computer account name is followed by a $ character; for example, `WIN10$`.

The `Supplied Realm Name` field contains the value of the domain name (realm) specified in the AS_REQ. For TGT requests for interactive authentication, this field usually contains a full domain name, such as `HQCORP.LOCAL`. For other types of logons it is usually just a NETBIOS domain name such as HQCORP, but this really depends on the username format the client specifies for the TGT request.

The User ID field contains the SID of the user for which the AS_REQ was sent.

The Service Name field contains the requested service name. For TGT requests it is always krbtgt or krbtgt/*DOMAIN_NETBIOS_NAME*.

The Service ID field contains the SID of the krbtgt account on the domain controller to which the AS_REQ request was addressed.

The Client Address field contains the IP-address from which the AS_REQ was received. It may contain an IPv6 address or IPv4. An IPv4 address has the following format: ::ffff:*ipv4_address*.

The Client Port field contains the original TCP or UDP port number on the client side, from which the AS_REQ request was received.

The Ticket Options field contains a bitmask in hexadecimal format of AS_REQ ticket options requested by the client. See Appendix A for more information about AS_REQ, TGS_REQ, and AP_REQ message ticket options.

The Result Code field contains the hexadecimal result code of the AS_REQ validation on the domain controller. For successful AS_REQ requests, when the TGT was issued, it will have a value of 0x0. See Appendix B for more information about possible values for this field.

The Ticket Encryption Type field contains the hexadecimal cipher suite code that was negotiated during the AS_REQ. Table 9-3 contains a list of encryption type hexadecimal values you may see in this field.

Table 9-3: Kerberos TGT and TGS Tickets Encryption Types

VALUE	NAME	DESCRIPTION
0x1	DES-CBC-CRC	DES with Cipher Block Chaining mode. Cyclic Redundancy Check (CRC) integrity control algorithm.
0x3	DES-CBC-MD5	DES with Cipher Block Chaining mode. Message Digest 5 (MD5) integrity control algorithm.
0x11	AES128-CTS-HMAC-SHA1-96	Advanced Encryption Standard with 128-bit key length with ciphertext stealing mode. HMAC-SHA1-96 integrity control algorithm.
0x12	AES256-CTS-HMAC-SHA1-96	Advanced Encryption Standard with 256-bit key length with ciphertext stealing mode. HMAC-SHA1-96 integrity control algorithm.
0x17	RC4-HMAC	Rivest Cipher 4 encryption algorithm. HMAC integrity control algorithm.
0x18	RC4-HMAC-EXP	Rivest Cipher 4 encryption algorithm. HMAC Express integrity control algorithm.
0xFFFFFFFF or 0xffffffff	-	Shown in 4768 Audit Failure event for AP_REQ message.

The `Pre-Authentication Type` field contains the decimal pre-authentication type code that was received in the AS_REQ request by the domain controller. Table 9-4 contains a list of pre-authentication type decimal values you may see in this field.

Table 9-4: Kerberos TGT Tickets Pre-Authentication Types

VALUE	NAME	DESCRIPTION
0	Not defined	Pre-authentication was not used in the AS_REQ.
2	PA-ENC-TIMESTAMP	Pre-authentication with encrypted timestamp.
15	PA-PK-AS-REP_OLD	PKINIT (Smart Cards) pre-authentication.
20	PA-SVR-REFERRAL-INFO	KDC Referral ticket pre-authentication.
138	PA-ENCRYPTED-CHALLENGE	FAST (Kerberos Armoring) pre-authentication.
No value	-	Shown in 4768 and 4771 `Audit Failure` events.

The `Certificate Information` section contains information about the user or computer certificate used for smart card authentication.

The `Certificate Issuer Name` field contains the name of the Certification Authority that issued the user's or computer's certificate.

The `Certificate Serial Number` field contains the serial number of the smart card authentication certificate used for authentication.

The `Certificate Thumbprint` field contains the thumbprint of the smart card authentication certificate used for authentication.

After a TGT ticket is successfully issued, it is saved in the memory of the Kerberos SSP/AP on the client machine. To view the TGT issued for the current user logon session you can use the `klist tgt` command. An example of the `klist tgt` command output is illustrated in Figure 9-14.

Unsuccessful AS_REQ Message - Password Expired, Wrong Password, Smart Card Logon Issues

There is a dedicated 4771 event for AS_REQ requests that fail because a wrong password was provided, the password is expired, or some specific smart card authentication–related issues. All these scenarios are related to pre-authentication. If a 4771 event is generated, no 4768 `Audit Failure` event is generated.

Listing 9-10 is an example of a 4771 event, which generates when a user specifies the wrong password for Kerberos authentication. This event is generated in the domain controller's security event log.

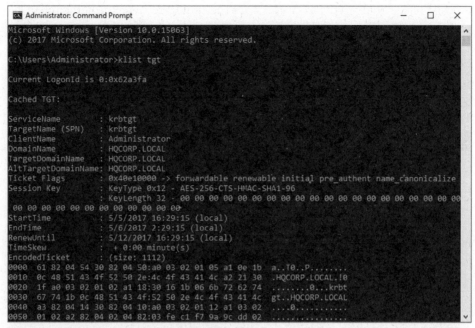

Figure 9-14: Klist tgt command output example

Listing 9-10: Event ID 4771: Kerberos pre-authentication failed.

```
Task Category: Kerberos Authentication Service
Keywords: Audit Failure
Account Information:
        Security ID:                S-1-5-21-1913345275-1711810662-261465553
                                      -500
        Account Name:               Administrator
Service Information:
        Service Name:               krbtgt/HQCORP
Network Information:
        Client Address:             ::ffff:10.0.0.110
        Client Port:                56905
Additional Information:
        Ticket Options:             0x40810010
        Failure Code:               0x18
        Pre-Authentication Type: 2
Certificate Information:
        Certificate Issuer Name:
        Certificate Serial Number:
        Certificate Thumbprint:
```

NOTE The event described in Listing 9-10 is available on the book's website, in the `Unsuccessful AS_REQ Message - password expired, wrong password, smart card logon issues.evtx` file.

Most of the fields in the 4771 event are the same and have the same meaning as fields of the 4768 event.

The only difference is the possible values for the Failure Code field. Table 9-5 contains a list of failure code hexadecimal values you may see in this field for a 4771 event.

Table 9-5: Event 4771 Failure Codes

VALUE	NAME	DESCRIPTION
0x10	KDC_ERR_PADATA_TYPE_NOSUPP	This code is usually triggered for certificate-related problems on domain controller, such as no valid certificate found on domain controller to be used for domain controller authentication.
0x17	KDC_ERR_KEY_EXPIRED	Account's password has expired.
0x18	KDC_ERR_PREAUTH_FAILED	Account's password is wrong.

Unsuccessful AS_REQ Message - Other Scenarios

For scenarios not covered in the previous section, a 4768 Audit Failure event is generated in the domain controller's security event log. Listing 9-11 is an example of Kerberos authentication attempt for a disabled user account.

Listing 9-11: Event ID 4768: A Kerberos authentication ticket (TGT) was requested.

```
Task Category: Kerberos Authentication Service
Keywords: Audit Failure
Account Information:
        Account Name:              Administrator
        Supplied Realm Name:       HQCORP
        User ID:                   S-1-0-0 (NULL SID)
Service Information:
        Service Name:              krbtgt/HQCORP
        Service ID:                S-1-0-0 (NULL SID)
Network Information:
        Client Address:            ::ffff:10.0.0.110
        Client Port:               56927
Additional Information:
        Ticket Options:            0x40810010
        Result Code:               0x12
        Ticket Encryption Type:    0xFFFFFFFF
        Pre-Authentication Type:   -
Certificate Information:
        Certificate Issuer Name:
        Certificate Serial Number:
        Certificate Thumbprint:
```

NOTE The event described in Listing 9-11 is available on the book's website, in the `Unsuccessful AS_REQ Message - other scenarios.evtx` **file**.

The 4768 event's fields were discussed following Listing 9-9. But some differences still exist between a 4768 `Audit Failure` event and a 4758 `Audit Success` event.

The `User ID` field in a 4768 `Audit Failure` event always has a value of `S-1-0-0`.

The `Service ID` field in a 4768 `Audit Failure` event always has a value of `S-1-0-0`.

The `Ticket Encryption Type` field in a 4768 `Audit Failure` event always has a value of `0xFFFFFFFF` or `0xffffffff`.

The `Pre-Authentication Type` field in a 4768 `Audit Failure` event always has a value of `-`.

This event has a `Result Code` value of `0x12`, which means authentication using a disabled account. See Appendix B for more information about possible values for the `Result Code` field.

TGT Renewal

Every 10 hours a TGT can be renewed automatically by Kerberos SSP/AP. Every time a TGT is renewed the event in Listing 9-12 is generated in the domain controller's security event log.

Listing 9-12: Event ID 4770: A Kerberos service ticket was renewed.

```
Task Category: Kerberos Service Ticket Operations
Keywords: Audit Success
Account Information:
        Account Name:          WIN10-1703$@HQCORP.LOCAL
        Account Domain:        HQCORP.LOCAL
Service Information:
        Service Name:          krbtgt
        Service ID:            S-1-5-21-1913345275-1711810662-261465553
                               -502
Network Information:
        Client Address:        ::ffff:10.0.0.110
        Client Port:           57041
Additional Information:
        Ticket Options:        0x10002
        Ticket Encryption Type: 0x12
```

NOTE The event described in Listing 9-12 is available on the book's website, in the `TGT Renewal.evtx` **file**.

Event 4770 is in the "Kerberos Service Ticket Operations" auditing subcategory, because TGT renewal is done by a TGS_REQ message.

The `Account Information` section contains information about the account for which a TGT was renewed.

The `Service Name` field always has a value of `krbtgt` or `krbtgt/ DOMAIN_NETBIOS_NAME`.

The `Service ID` field contains the SID of the `krbtgt` account in the domain.

The `Network Information` section contains information about the source host from which a TGT renewal request was received. The format for values in these fields was discussed in the "Successful AS_REQ Message" section.

The `Ticket Options` field contains a bitmask in hexadecimal format of the TGT ticket options requested by the client. See Appendix A for more information about AS_REQ, TGS_REQ, and AP_REQ message options.

The `Ticket Encryption Type` field contains hexadecimal cipher suite code that was used in the renewed TGT ticket. Refer to Table 9-3 for more information.

Ticket-Granting Service (TGS) Ticket

After a client gets a TGT, it is able to request Ticket-Granting Service (TGS) tickets, which allow access to a specific service on a specific host. A TGT acts as proof of credential validity. With a TGT, a client can request TGS tickets from a domain controller to access other resources.

A TGS ticket, which is also called a *service ticket*, is valid for 10 hours by default. After 10 hours a TGS ticket expires and a new TGS ticket should be requested. In Microsoft Active Directory TGS tickets cannot be renewed.

Figure 9-15 shows the TGS ticket issuing process.

The numbers in the following list correspond to the numbers in Figure 9-15:

1. The client initiates a TGS_REQ request to a domain controller. A TGS request is a special type of Kerberos message used to request TGS tickets from a KDC (domain controller). The client sends information to the KDC in the TGS_REQ, which includes the following main items:

   - **User Principal Name (UPN):** The UPN of the user or computer account for which a TGS_REQ is sent.

   - **Domain Name (Realm):** The name of the domain for the account for which the TGS_REQ is sent. In the Kerberos world, Active Directory domains are called realms.

   - **Service Principal Name (SPN):** The SPN for which the TGS ticket is requested. The SPN is a unique identifier of a service instance and has the following format: *service_name/target_name*. A TGS_REQ usually has a destination hostname as a *target_name*. For example, `cifs/2016srv` is an SPN for requesting CIFS/SMB service on a hostname's `2016srv`.

   - **Ticket-Granting Ticket (TGT):** A TGT, previously issued by KDC. It is encrypted by a KDC Key.

- **Pre-Authentication Timestamp:** This field has the same purpose as discussed in the "Ticket-Granting Ticket (TGT)" section, with the difference that a Session Key is used to encrypt the timestamp instead of a Client Key. A Session Key was given to the client in the AS_REP message from the KDC.

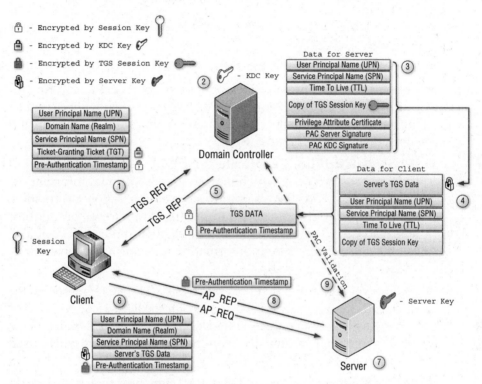

Figure 9-15: Kerberos TGS ticket issuing process

2. After the KDC receives a TGS_REQ it performs the following actions:

   - Decrypts the TGT using the KDC Key.

   - Extracts the Session Key from TGT.

   - Validates the pre-authentication timestamp using the extracted Session Key.

   - Generates a TGS Session Key, which will be used for further communications between client and destination server, on which the requested service runs. They will use a new key (TGS Session Key) to mutually authenticate each other.

   The Session Key used on the client side to encrypt the timestamp must be the same as the Session Key saved in the TGT. If validation of the timestamp was successful, the KDC starts the process of TGS_REP message creation.

3. In the first step of TGS_REP generation, the KDC creates a TGS_REP message section (we will call it the Server's TGS Data) that is forwarded to the destination host (Server) by the client. The following information is included in this Server's TGS Data:

    ▪ **User Principal Name (UPN):** The UPN of the user for which the TGS was issued.

    ▪ **Service Principal Name (SPN):** The SPN for the service for which the TGS was issued.

    ▪ **Time To Live (TTL):** The time during which the TGS is valid.

    ▪ **Copy of the TGS Session Key:** A copy of the TGS Session Key for future use by the destination host (server). This key will be used by the server to validate the client's pre-authentication timestamp and sign a timestamp for an AP_REP.

    ▪ **Privilege Attribute Certificate (PAC):** Microsoft's extension of the Kerberos protocol, which may contain additional information. For example, a PAC field is used to store authorization information, such as domain group membership information for an account for which a TGS ticket was issued. The destination server will be able to use this group membership information to create a session security token for the logon session.

    ▪ **PAC Server Signature:** A keyed/salted hash (HMAC) signature of the PAC field. A Server Key is used as a key for the HMAC algorithm. The Server Key is known only by the KDC and a server. It is based on the server's computer account password hash. This signature will be used by the server to validate the integrity of the PAC field.

    ▪ **PAC KDC Signature:** An additional PAC signature, which is a keyed/salted hash (HMAC) signature of the PAC Server Signature field. The KDC Key is used as a key for the HMAC algorithm. This field is used by the KDC for PAC validation procedure, which is discussed in Step 9.

    These fields are encrypted by a Server Key and are shown in Figure 9-15 as the Server's TGS Data item. The Server Key is known only by the KDC and a server specified in the SPN. The Server Key is based on the server's computer account password hash. These fields are embedded into the TGS_REP as part of data sent back to the client.

4. In addition to the Server's TGS Data field, the following information is sent to the client:

    ▪ **User Principal Name (UPN):** The UPN of the user or computer account for which a TGS was issued.

    ▪ **Service Principal Name (SPN):** The SPN for a service for which a TGS ticket was issued.

- **Time To Live (TTL):** The time during which the TGS ticket is valid.
- **Copy of the TGS Session Key:** A copy of the TGS Session Key for future use by the client. This key will be used by the client to sign a timestamp for the AP_REQ and validate the server's pre-authentication timestamp.

These fields are encrypted by a Session Key and are shown in Figure 9-15 as the TGS DATA item. The Session Key is known only by the KDC and a client.

5. In the final step of TGS_REP generation, the Pre-Authentication Timestamp field with a timestamp encrypted by the Session Key is added to the TGS_REP by the KDC. It provides mutual authentication, so the client also validates the timestamp, encrypted by the domain controller using the Session Key, to make sure the domain controller has access to the Session Key stored in TGT.

6. After the client receives the TGS_REP it performs the following actions:

   - Validates the pre-authentication timestamp in the TGS_REP message using a Session Key.
   - Extracts the TGS Session Key.

   The client is unable to decrypt the Server's TGS Data field, because it does not know a Server Key.

   The client then sends the following information to the server in the AP_REQ in order to authenticate on the server:

   - All standard fields such as User Principal Name, Domain Name (Realm), Service Principal Name.
   - The Server's TGS Data field from TGS_REP.
   - The Pre-Authentication Timestamp encrypted by TGS Session Key, which was extracted from the TGS_REP message received from KDC.

7. The server receives the AP_REQ message and performs the following actions:

   - Decrypts the Server's TGS Data using a Server Key.
   - Extracts a copy of the TGS Session Key.
   - Validates the Pre-Authentication Timestamp in the AP_REQ message using a TGS Session Key.

   If the AP_REQ timestamp was successfully validated, the server successfully authenticates the account. This happens because only the KDC that knows the Server Key is able to encrypt the Server's TGS Data. The server was able to decrypt the data, which means the data comes from a trusted KDC. The client also was able to extract the TGS Session Key, which means that the KDC authenticated the client.

8. In the last step of the TGS ticket issuing process, the server sends the AP_REP message back to the client. The AP_REP message, in addition to other fields, contains a Pre-Authentication Timestamp field encrypted by the TGS Session Key. The client validates this field to verify the authenticity of the server. If the server was able to encrypt a timestamp in the AP_REP message using the TGS Session Key extracted from the Server's TGS Data field (AP_REQ message), then the Pre-Authentication Timestamp will be successfully decrypted and validated by the client using the same TGS Session Key. Which also means that the server is authenticated, because it was able to decrypt the Server's TGS Data field.

9. (optional) In theory, if the client has access to the Server Key, it can modify data in the PAC field, for example, change group membership information. The mechanism called PAC Validation is designed specifically to address this security issue. The server can send a KERB_VERIFY_PAC_REQUEST message to the KDC and ask the KDC to additionally validate the PAC signature. The following actions briefly explain the PAC Validation process:

   ▪ The server sends a KERB_VERIFY_PAC_REQUEST message to the KDC, which includes a salted hash (HMAC) signature of the PAC field received by server in the AP_REQ message—let's call it the Server PAC Signature. The Server Key is used as a key for the HMAC algorithm. The KERB_VERIFY_PAC_REQUEST message also includes the PAC KDC Signature field data received in the AP_REQ from the client.

   ▪ The KDC receives the message and generates a keyed/salted hash (HMAC) signature of the Server PAC Signature field received from the server. The result is compared with the PAC KDC Signature field value. If the values are the same, it means that the PAC field was not modified.

Successful TGS_REQ Message

TGS_REQ requests always come to a domain controller first. Listing 9-13 is an example of a 4769 event, which generates on domain controller each time a TGS ticket is issued by a domain controller based on a successful TGS_REQ.

Listing 9-13: Event ID 4769: A Kerberos service ticket was requested.

```
Task Category: Kerberos Service Ticket Operations
Keywords: Audit Success
Account Information:
        Account Name:           Administrator@HQCORP.LOCAL
        Account Domain:         HQCORP.LOCAL
        Logon GUID:             {2F3E02E3-BD72-248B-FDFE-31DEC9C9FE4F}
```

```
Service Information:
      Service Name:            WIN10-1703$
      Service ID:              S-1-5-21-1913345275-1711810662-261465553
                                 -1123
Network Information:
      Client Address:          ::ffff:10.0.0.110
      Client Port:             57011
Additional Information:
      Ticket Options:          0x40810000
      Ticket Encryption Type:  0x12
      Failure Code:            0x0
      Transited Services:      -
```

NOTE The event described in Listing 9-13 is available on the book's website, in the `Successful TGS_REQ Message.evtx` **file.**

It is important to note that the 4769 event is related to TGS_REQ, not to TGS tickets. It is a TGS_REQ monitoring event.

The `Account Name` field contains the name of the account that requested the ticket. It has the following format: *account_name@domain_name*.

The `Account Domain` field contains the domain name to which the `Account Name` account belongs.

The `Logon GUID` field value can be correlated with the `Logon GUID` field in the 4624, 4648, and 4964 events on the destination/target host (server). The `Logon GUID` fields are not always the same on the domain controller and the destination server for some reason, so sometimes they do not match.

The `Service Name` field contains the domain computer account name on which a service was requested. A 4769 event does not show which exact service was requested.

The `Service ID` field contains the SID for the `Service Name` computer account.

The `Network Information` section contains information about the source host from which the TGS request was received. The format of values for these fields was already discussed in the "Successful AS_REQ Message" section.

The `Ticket Options` field contains a bitmask in hexadecimal format of TGS ticket options requested by the client. See Appendix A for more information about AS_REQ, TGS_REQ, and AP_REQ messages options.

The `Ticket Encryption Type` field contains hexadecimal cipher suite code that was used for the TGS ticket. See Table 9-3 for more information.

The `Failure Code` for `Audit Success` events always has a value of `0x0`.

The `Transited Services` field contains a list of SPNs requested by the client for delegation. Applicable only to Kerberos delegation requests.

You may find some 4769 events with a `Service Name` field of `krbtgt` and a `Service ID` field of the SID of the `krbtgt` account in the domain.

These messages are related to Kerberos delegation with a forwarded TGT. See https://msdn.microsoft.com/en-us/library/cc246080.aspx for more information about Kerberos delegation with a forwarded TGT.

Unsuccessful TGS_REQ and AP_REQ Messages

TGS_REQ or AP_REQ requests received by a domain controller might fail for multiple reasons. The most common failure reason for AP_REQ requests is an expired TGS ticket in the access request to the domain controller itself—for example, the SYSVOL or NETLOGON network shares access requests. Listing 9-14 is an example of the event that is generated in the Windows security event log on a domain controller when it receives an AP_REQ with an expired TGS ticket. When someone tries to access a service on the domain controller itself.

Listing 9-14: Event ID 4769: A Kerberos service ticket was requested.

```
Task Category: Kerberos Service Ticket Operations
Keywords: Audit Failure
Account Information:
      Account Name:
      Account Domain:
      Logon GUID:              {00000000-0000-0000-0000-000000000000}
Service Information:
      Service Name:
      Service ID:              S-1-0-0
Network Information:
      Client Address:         ::ffff:10.0.0.15
      Client Port:            50322
Additional Information:
      Ticket Options:         0x10002
      Ticket Encryption Type: 0xFFFFFFFF
      Failure Code:           0x20
      Transited Services:     -
```

NOTE   The event described in Listing 9-14 is available on the book's website, in the Unsuccessful TGS_REQ and AP_REQ Messages.evtx file.

It is important to note that a 4769 Audit Failure event is related to a TGS_REQ or AP_REQ sent to a domain controller, not to TGS tickets. It is a failed TGS_REQ and AP_REQ monitoring event.

If a 4769 event is generated for an AP_REQ failed request, it will not have any details in the Account Information and Service Information sections.

The Network Information section contains information about the source host from which a TGS_REQ or AP_REQ request was received. The format of values for these fields was already discussed in the "Successful AS_REQ Message" section.

The `Ticket Options` field contains a bitmask in hexadecimal format of TGS_REQ or AP_REQ request options set by the client. See Appendix A for more information about AS_REQ, TGS_REQ, and AP_REQ message options.

The `Ticket Encryption Type` field contains hexadecimal cipher suite code that was used for a TGS ticket if the domain controller received a TGS_REQ. If a 4769 event is generated for an AP_REQ failed request, it will have a value of `0xFFFFFFFF` or `0xffffffff` for this field. See Table 9-3 for more information.

The `Failure Code` field contains in hexadecimal code the reason the TGS_REQ or AP_REQ failed. The `0x20` failure code in Listing 9-14 is related to expired tickets received in the AP_REQ. It is common to see such error codes when the KDC receives an expired TGS ticket in AP_REQ. Based on such responses a client might ask for a new TGS ticket. See Appendix B for more information about possible values for this field.

The `Transited Services` field contains a list of SPNs requested by the client for delegation. Applicable only to Kerberos delegation requests.

Operating System Events

Operating system events are events that show system parameter modifications and important operations within Windows. Multiple important events that should be monitored may occur on the system. The list of such events is quite long, so here are examples of some of them:

- System startup/shutdown
- System setting changes, such as system time
- New scheduled task or service installation
- Changes in the local audit group policy settings

These and many other events might indicate anomalous activity. Some examples of such activities might be:

- Installation of a new service on a critical host
- Unexpected system restart
- Security event log erasure

Many system events, which are available for monitoring using the Windows security event log, are important and should be investigated if they occur.

This chapter contains information about different system events that might indicate anomalous activity performed on the system.

System Startup/Shutdown

System shutdown may be invoked using different methods:

- Normal shutdown by using internal APIs that require the `SeShutdownPrivilege` user privilege. `SeShutdownPrivilege` can be granted by the "Computer Configuration\Windows Settings\Security Settings\ Local Policies\User Rights Assignment\Shut down the system" group policy setting.

- Emergency shutdown by disabling the power supply

Normal shutdown can be successful, or it can be unsuccessful if someone tried to use `SeShutdownPrivilege` privilege without having it.

Unfortunately, emergency system shutdown is, in most cases, impossible to detect.

Successful Normal System Shutdown

A successful normal system shutdown operation generates the event in Listing 10-1 in the Windows security event log.

Listing 10-1: Event ID 4674: An operation was attempted on a privileged object.

```
Task Category: Sensitive Privilege Use
Keywords: Audit Success
Subject:
        Security ID:        S-1-5-21-1913345275-1711810662-261465553-500
        Account Name:       Administrator
        Account Domain:     HQCORP
        Logon ID:           0x3995D
Object:
        Object Server:      Win32 SystemShutdown module
        Object Type:        -
        Object Name:        -
        Object Handle:      0x0
Process Information:
        Process ID:         0x2a4
        Process Name:       C:\Windows\System32\wininit.exe
Requested Operation:
        Desired Access:     0
        Privileges:         SeShutdownPrivilege
```

> **NOTE** The event described in Listing 10-1 is available on the book's website, in the `Successful Normal System Shutdown.evtx` file.

This event shows that the `Subject` successfully (`Audit Success`) invoked/ used the `SeShutdownPrivilege` privilege for the `Win32 SystemShutdown` module.

The `Win32 SystemShutdown module` is a system module that performs system shutdown operations.

This event also generates when a shutdown command is invoked from a remote machine.

Listing 10-2 is another event that indicates normal system shutdown and will be generated in the System event log.

Listing 10-2: Event System Event Log ID 1074.

```
Task Category: None
Source: User32

The process C:\Windows\Explorer.EXE (2016DC) has initiated the power off
of computer 2016DC on behalf of user HQCORP\Administrator for the
following reason: Other (Unplanned)
Reason Code: 0x5000000
Shutdown Type: power off
Comment:
```

> **NOTE** The event described above is available on the book's website, in the `Successful System Shutdown - System Log.evtx` file.

This event has the parameters shown in Table 10-1.

Table 10-1. Event 1074 **Parameters.**

PARAMETER	DESCRIPTION	VALUE
param1	Process Name	`C:\Windows\Explorer.EXE (2016DC)`
param2	Local Host Name	`2016DC`
param3	Shutdown Reason	`Other (Unplanned)`
param4	Reason Code	`0x5000000`
param5	Shutdown Type	`power off`
param6	Comment	
param7	User Name	`HQCORP\Administrator`

A 1074 event has more information than a 4674 event from the Windows security event log. It has the name of the process that invoked system shutdown/restart, the reason for the shutdown, a reason code, and the shutdown type.

The `param2` field contains the hostname or IP address of the host from which system shutdown/restart was initiated. For a local shutdown/restart it contains the local hostname, and for a remote shutdown/restart, it shows the IP address of the remote machine from which an operation was initiated.

The most common reason codes are:

- `0x5000000`: Other (Unplanned)
- `0x0`: Other (Unplanned)
- `0x80070000`: Legacy API shutdown
- `0x84020004`: Operating System: Reconfiguration (Planned)
- `0x80020003`: Operating System: Upgrade (Planned)
- `0x85000000`: Other (Planned)

Possible values for `Shutdown Type` fields are:

- `power off`
- `shutdown`
- `restart`

Very often you will see two 1074 events generated at the same time in a user-invoked system shutdown procedure. One of them will have a `Shutdown Type` of `power off` and the other `shutdown`. The event with a `Shutdown Type` of `power off` has a full directory path for the executable filename that initiated the shutdown.

Unsuccessful Normal System Shutdown - Access Denied

Any unsuccessful system shutdown attempt that failed because of insufficient user privileges will generate the event in Listing 10-3 in the Windows security event log.

Listing 10-3: Event ID 4674: An operation was attempted on a privileged object.

```
Task Category: Sensitive Privilege Use
Keywords: Audit Failure
Subject:
        Security ID:            S-1-5-21-1913345275-1711810662-261465553-1003
        Account Name:           amirosh
        Account Domain:         HQCORP
        Logon ID:               0x168E85
Object:
        Object Server:          Win32 SystemShutdown module
        Object Type:            -
        Object Name:            -
        Object Handle:          0x0
Process Information:
        Process ID:             0x2a0
        Process Name:           C:\Windows\System32\wininit.exe
Requested Operation:
        Desired Access:         0
        Privileges:             SeRemoteShutdownPrivilege
```

NOTE The event described above is available on the book's website, in the `Unsuccessful Service Shutdown Operation - Access Denied.evtx` **file.**

An `Audit Failure` 4674 event shows that some specific operation failed. This event looks exactly like a 4674 `Audit Success` event shown in Listing 10-1, except the event type will be `Audit Failure`.

Successful System Startup

Successful system startup operations generate the event in Listing 10-4 in the Windows security event log.

Listing 10-4: Event ID 4608: Windows is starting up.

```
Task Category: Security State Change
Keywords: Audit Success

This event is logged when LSASS.EXE starts and the auditing subsystem
is initialized.
```

NOTE The event described above is available on the book's website, in the `Successful System Startup.evtx` **file.**

There are no custom fields in the 4608 event. It informs you only that the system is starting up.

Monitoring Scenarios: System Startup/Shutdown

Useful events to monitor for successful and unsuccessful system startup/shutdown are shown in Table 10-2.

Table 10-2: Events to Monitor for System Startup/Shutdown

SUCCESSFUL SYSTEM STARTUP/SHUTDOWN		
Security Event	**Subcategory**	**Event Type**
4608: Windows is starting up.	Security State Change	Audit Success
4674: An operation was attempted on a privileged object.	Non Sensitive Privilege Use	Audit Success
UNSUCCESSFUL SYSTEM STARTUP/ SHUTDOWN		
Security Event	**Subcategory**	**Event Type**
4674: An operation was attempted on a privileged object.	Non Sensitive Privilege Use	Audit Failure

All successful and unsuccessful system startup and shutdown operations should be monitored, especially on highly important or critical hosts.

It is important to monitor system startup events for specific systems that should remain shut down. All startup events for such systems must generate an alert. An example of such a system could be some type of terminal that should be turned on only to perform specific operations that have been approved beforehand.

Unsuccessful system shutdown attempts are always important to monitor, because, usually, accounts that don't have SeShutdownPrivilege should not try to shut down the system.

- Monitor these events: Any "4674: An operation was attempted on a privileged object" Audit Failure events with an Object Server field of Win32 SystemShutdown module and a Privileges field of SeRemoteShutdownPrivilege.

  Monitor for this using the following XPath filter:

  ```
  *[System[band(Keywords,4503599627370496) and (EventID=4674)]] and
  *[EventData[Data[@Name='PrivilegeList'] and
  (Data='SeRemoteShutdownPrivilege')]] and *[EventData[Data[@Name=
  'ObjectServer'] ='Win32 SystemShutdown module']]
  ```

- Any "4608: Windows is starting up" and "4674: An operation was attempted on a privileged object" Audit Success events with an Object Server field of Win32 SystemShutdown module and a Privileges field of SeRemoteShutdownPrivilege on all high privilege and critical hosts.

- Any "4608: Windows is starting up" events on hosts that should remain turned off or should be turned on only under specific circumstances.

System Time Changes

In this section you will find information about monitoring the following two actions:

- System time zone change
- System clock change

These changes can be performed manually or automatically by the operating system, if the "Set time automatically" and/or "Set time zone automatically" system settings are turned on. When the machine is domain joined, the system clock settings will be, sometimes, automatically adjusted to be synchronized with the domain controller clocks.

The "Change the time zone" (SeTimeZonePrivilege) privilege is required to change the local time zone. By default, the security principals in Table 10-3 have the SeTimeZonePrivilege user right.

Table 10-3: Security Principals with the SeTimeZonePrivilege User Right

SECURITY PRINCIPAL NAME	WINDOWS SERVER OS	WINDOWS CLIENT OS
Administrators	Yes	Yes
LOCAL SERVICE	Yes	Yes
Users	No	Yes

The "Change the system zone" (SeSystemtimePrivilege) privilege is required to change the local system clock. By default, the following security principals have the SeSystemtimePrivilege user privilege on all Windows operating system versions:

- Administrators
- LOCAL SERVICE

Successful System Time Zone Change

The system time zone can be changed from the Control Panel using the graphical user interface. It also can be changed, for example, using a PowerShell command or the tzutil console application.

The event in Listing 10-5 will appear in the Windows security event log if the local time zone was successfully modified.

Listing 10-5: Event ID 4673: A privileged service was called.

```
Task Category: Sensitive Privilege Use
Keywords: Audit Success
Subject:
      Security ID:        S-1-5-21-3212943211-794299840-588279583-500
      Account Name:       Administrator
      Account Domain:     2016SRV
      Logon ID:           0x296D6
Service:
      Server:             Security
      Service Name:       -
Process:
      Process ID:         0x1268
      Process Name:       C:\Windows\ImmersiveControlPanel\
                             SystemSettings.exe
Service Request Information:
      Privileges:         SeTimeZonePrivilege
```

NOTE The event described above is available on the book's website, in the
`Successful System Time Zone Change.evtx` file.

The `SeTimeZonePrivilege` privilege is required to change the local time zone.
This event informs you that `Subject` successfully used the `SeTimeZonePrivilege`
user privilege. The `Process Name` field contains the full path to the application
that was used to change system time zone.

The `Server` field shows the name of the local subsystem to which the specified privileges were called.

Unfortunately, there is no information in the Windows security log about the
previous and new local time zone settings.

Unsuccessful System Time Zone Change

Unfortunately, no events are generated for an unsuccessful system time zone
change event in the Windows security, system, application, and setup logs.
Specific logs dedicated for some applications allow you to change the local system
time zone settings, for example - `tzutil`. You can find the `tzutil` event log in
the Windows Event Viewer on the following path: `Windows Logs\Applications
and Services Logs\Microsoft\Windows\TZUtil\Operational`.

Successful System Clock Settings Change

The events in Listings 10-6 and 10-7 appear in the Windows security event log
if local clock settings were successfully modified.

Listing 10-6: Event ID 4673: A privileged service was called.

```
Task Category: Sensitive Privilege Use
Keywords: Audit Success
Subject:
        Security ID:          S-1-5-21-3212943211-794299840-588279583-500
        Account Name:         Administrator
        Account Domain:       2016SRV
        Logon ID:             0x3C8AE6
Service:
        Server:               Security
        Service Name:         -
Process:
        Process ID:           0xfc0
        Process Name:         C:\Windows\System32\rundll32.exe
Service Request Information:
        Privileges:           SeSystemtimePrivilege
```

NOTE   The event logs described in this section are in the download files for this chapter, in the `Successful System Clock Change.evtx` file.

The `Subject` used `C:\Windows\System32\rundll32.exe` to change local system time. To change local system time the `SeSystemtimePrivilege` privilege is required.

Event 4616 is designed to show changes to the local system time. It does not generate if the local time zone settings were changed.

Listing 10-7: Event ID 4616: The system time was changed.

```
Task Category: Security State Change
Keywords: Audit Success
Subject:
        Security ID:            S-1-5-21-3212943211-794299840-588279583-500
        Account Name:           Administrator
        Account Domain:         2016SRV
        Logon ID:               0x3C8AE6
Process Information:
        Process ID:             0xfc0
        Name:                   C:\Windows\System32\rundll32.exe
Previous Time:                  2017-02-15T21:11:03.176993700Z
New Time:                       2017-02-15T22:11:02.000000000Z
```

`Process Information: Name:` shows you information about which process was used to change system time settings. If, for example, the `time` command line application is used to set system time, this field will have a value of `C:\Windows\System32\cmd.exe`.

Both the `Previous Time` and `New Time` fields have the format *YYYY-MM-DDThh:mm:ss.nnnnnnnZ*, where:

- **YYYY:** Years
- **MM:** Months
- **DD:** Days
- **T:** The beginning of the time element, as specified in ISO 8601
- **hh:** Hours
- **mm:** Minutes
- **ss:** Seconds
- **nnnnnnn:** Fractional seconds
- **Z:** The zone designator for the zero UTC offset, also called "Zulu" time. `09:30` UTC is therefore represented as `09:30Z`.

In this example the system time was increased by one hour.

You may get many 4616 events with `Account Name` equals `LOCAL SERVICE`. These events are usually generated by the "Windows Time" service and, usually, represent automatic time adjustment activities.

Unsuccessful System Clock Settings Change

There are no events in the Windows security log indicating unsuccessful local system clock settings changes.

Monitoring Scenarios: System Time Changes

Useful events to monitor for successful system time change are shown in Table 10-4.

Table 10-4: Events to Monitor to Detect System Time Changes

SECURITY EVENT	SUBCATEGORY	EVENT TYPE
4673: A privileged service was called.	Sensitive Privilege Use	Audit Success
4616: The system time was changed.	Security State Change	Audit Success

On regular workstations, system time changes are not usually important and are usually unmonitored. It is more important to monitor system time changes on critical hosts, especially on hosts where the correct time is critical for local applications or services.

Monitor these events:

- Any "4673: A privileged service was called" `Audit Success` events with an `Object Server` field of `Security` and a `Privileges` field of `SeTimeZonePrivilege`.

  Monitor for this using the following XPath filter:

  ```
  *[System[band(Keywords,4503599627370496) and (EventID=4656)]] and
  *[EventData[Data[@Name='PrivilegeList'] and
  (Data='SeTimeZonePrivilege')]] and
  *[EventData[Data[@Name='ObjectServer'] ='Security']]
  ```

- Any "4616: The system time was changed" event on critical hosts that does not have a LOCAL SERVICE account specified in the Subject section, especially on hosts where the correct time is critical for local applications or services.

System Services Operations

System services are among the most popular methods that malicious software and viruses use to perform malicious actions and remain in the system.

It's critical to monitor all system service installations on servers and critical hosts. It's also important to be notified when a critical service is stopped, or any particular service is started.

Windows stores passwords for accounts under which the system service is running, locally (in the system registry key called LSA Secrets). These passwords are stored in an encoded form, which allows any account with administrative privileges to extract this password. Because of that it's important to monitor any change to the system service any time a user account under which the service is running is changed, especially if the account was changed to local or domain user account.

Other scenarios are also important to monitor, but let's first discuss the events that are generated in Windows event log files by the most common operations with services.

Successful Service Installation - Prior to Windows 10/2016

System services are usually installed by software installers or setup packages. It is also possible to install a system service using the sc create command.

Prior to Windows 10 and Windows Server 2016, the main source of information about system services was the System event log.

The event in Listing 10-8 will be generated in the Windows system event log if a new service is installed in the system.

Listing 10-8: Event System Event ID 7045: A service was installed in the system.

```
Source: Service Control Manager
Task Category: None


Service Name:       Open TFTP Server, MultiThreaded
Service File Name:  C:\OpenTFTPServer\OpenTFTPServerMT.exe
Service Type:       user mode service
Service Start Type: auto start
Service Account:    LocalSystem
```

NOTE The event logs described in this section are in the download files for this chapter, in the Successful Service Installation - pre-Win10-2016 .evtx file.

The built-in User field (not shown in Listing 10-8) shows information about an account (SID) that performed a service installation.

The Service Account field contains the name of the account under which the service will be running. This field contains the name, not the SID, of the account. Here are some examples of the Service Account field value for some accounts:

- **LOCAL SYSTEM:** LocalSystem
- **LOCAL SERVICE:** NT AUTHORITY\LocalService

- **Local account:** *ComputerName**AccountName*. Example: win81\Administrator

- **Domain account:** *DomainName**AccountName*. Example: hqcorp\Andrei

This field can be empty for some specific service types; for example, for the "kernel mode driver" type.

The Service Name field contains the full name of the service. This is the name as it's shown in the Display Name property of the service in the Windows services management console (see Figure 10-1).

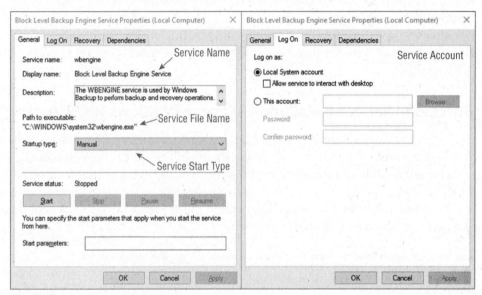

Figure 10-1: System service properties.

The Service File Name field contains the full path and filename for the newly installed service's executable image.

The Service Type field may have one of the following values:

- user mode service

- kernel mode driver

user mode service represents one of the following two service types:

- **Shared:** A service that shares its process with other services. The most common example is the svchost.exe process, under which many services are running.

- **Own:** A service that has its own dedicated process.

The `Shared` and `Own` process types can also be interactive or Win32 (noninteractive). An interactive service can interact with the user's session, receive commands or input from the user, and so on. Win32 services are not able to do that.

The `kernel mode service` represents one of the following service types:

- **Kernel:** System driver
- **Filesys:** Filesystem driver
- **Rec:** Specific filesystem driver responsible for detecting the filesystem version on the system at the early system startup stage

A 7045 event does not contain any detailed information about the service type; it just shows the main category: `user mode service` or `kernel mode service`. `Service Start Type` field can have one of the following values:

- **auto start:** Service starts automatically with the system.
- **demand start:** Service should be started manually.
- **system start:** Specific for system drivers that will be started during the kernel initialization stage.
- **boot start:** Specific for system drivers that will be loaded by the system boot loader.
- **disabled:** Service is disabled.

Successful Service Installation - Windows 10/2016

Windows 10 and Windows Server 2016 have a new event in the Windows security event log that logs every time a new service is installed in the system. Listing 10-9 shows this event.

Listing 10-9: Event ID 4697: A service was installed in the system.

```
Task Category: Security System Extension
Keywords: Audit Success
Subject:
      Security ID:         S-1-5-21-3212943211-794299840-588279583-500
      Account Name:        Administrator
      Account Domain:      2016SRV
      Logon ID:            0x43B34
Service Information:
      Service Name:        Cleint Service Demon
      Service File Name:   c:\windows\system32\ClientService.exe
      Service Type:        0x10
      Service Start Type:  2
      Service Account:     LocalSystem
```

NOTE The event described above is available on the book's website, in the `Successful Service Installation - Win10-2016.evtx` **file.**

This event has the same fields but also has some differences in comparison with the 7045 event shown in Listing 10-8.

`Service Start Type` has an integer value instead of a string. Here is a list of possible values:

- **0:** Boot start
- **1:** System start
- **2:** Auto start
- **3:** Demand start
- **4:** Disabled

The `Service Type` field has more detailed information about the service type. Possible hexadecimal values for this field are (see section "Successful Service Installation - Prior to Windows 10/2016" for more details):

- **0x1:** System driver.
- **0x2:** Filesystem driver.
- **0x8:** Recognizer driver. Specific filesystem driver that is responsible for detection of the filesystem version on the system at the early system startup stage.
- **0x10:** Win32 Own.
- **0x20:** Win32 Shared.
- **0x110:** Interactive Own.
- **0x120:** Interactive Shared.

Basically speaking, the 4697 event contains more information than the 7045 event.

Unsuccessful Service Installation - Access Denied

If someone tries to install a new system service, but gets an "Access Denied" result due to insufficient access rights, the event in Listing 10-10 is generated in the Windows security event log.

Listing 10-10: Event ID 4656: A handle to an object was requested.

```
Task Category: Other Object Access Events
Keywords: Audit Failure
Subject:
      Security ID:        S-1-5-21-3212943211-794299840-588279583-1000
      Account Name:       Andrei
```

```
        Account Domain:        2016SRV
        Logon ID:              0xA2C0A4
Object:
        Object Server:         SC Manager
        Object Type:           SC_MANAGER OBJECT
        Object Name:           ServicesActive
        Handle ID:             0x0
        Resource Attributes:   -
Process Information:
        Process ID:            0x2f4
        Process Name:          C:\Windows\System32\services.exe
Access Request Information:
        Transaction ID:        {00000000-0000-0000-0000-000000000000}
        Accesses:              %%7168 (Connect to service controller)
                               %%7169 (Create a new service)
                               See table 10.2 for more details
        Access Reasons:        -
        Access Mask:           0x3 (See table 10.2 for more details)
        Privileges Used for Access Check: -
        Restricted SID Count: 0
```

NOTE The event logs described in this section are in the download files for this chapter, in the Unsuccessful Service Installation - Access Denied .evtx file.

This event shows a typical failed object handle request, but it's related to system service operations.

Object Server contains information about a subsystem to which a handle request was addressed. In this case it's SC Manager, which is a Service Control Manager system component. Service Control Manager is responsible for all operations with system services. It has its own service database that stores information about the currently installed system services, and it can stop/start/pause services, change their settings, and so on.

The Object Type field has a value of SC_MANAGER OBJECT, which represents all Service Control Manager objects in general.

The Object Name field contains the name of the Service Control Manager database to which the handle request was sent. For all service installation requests the value will always be ServicesActive. Other possible values are NULL or ServicesFailed:

■ The ServicesActive database contains all system services.

■ ServicesFailed seems to be obsolete.

Process Name usually has a value of C:\Windows\System32\services.exe, which is an executable file for the System Control Manager.

The `Accesses` field contains a list of access permissions requested from the `ServicesActive` database. Table 10-5 contains information about possible access permissions for the Service Control Manager's `ServicesActive` database.

Table 10-5: Service Control Manager Access Permissions.

ACCESS MASK	CONSTANT	VALUE
0x01	%%7168	Connect to service controller
0x02	%%7169	Create a new service
0x04	%%7170	Enumerate services
0x08	%%7171	Lock service database for exclusive access
0x10	%%7172	Query service database lock state
0x20	%%7173	Set last-known-good state of service database
0x40	%%7174	Query service configuration information
0x80	%%7185	Set service configuration information
0x100	%%7186	Query status of service
0x200	%%7187	Enumerate dependencies of service
0x400	%%7188	Start the service
0x800	%%7189	Stop the service
0x1000	%%7190	Pause or continue the service
0x2000	%%7191	Query information from service
0x4000	%%7192	Issue service-specific control commands

The `Access Mask` field contains a hexadecimal sum of all requested access permissions. See Table 10-5 for more details.

System Service State Changes

The event in Listing 10-11 will be recorded in the Windows system event log after system service was successfully stopped.

Listing 10-11: Event System Event ID 7036.

```
Source: Service Control Manager
Task Category: None

The Windows Event Log service entered the stopped state..
```

NOTE The event logs described in this section are in the download files for this chapter, in the `System Service State Changes.evtx` and "Successful Service Stop Operation" files.

This event has the parameters listed in Table 10-6.

Table 10-6: Parameters for the 7036 Event

PARAMETER	DESCRIPTION	VALUE
param1	Service full name	`Windows Event Log`
param2	Service status	`Stopped`

`param1` contains the full service name.
`param2` can have one of the following values:

- `running`
- `stopped`
- `paused`

Unfortunately, 7036 events don't record the `User` property value. It has value of `N/A`, which makes it difficult to detect who performed this operation.

Unsuccessful Service Stop Operation - Access Denied

The last event we will discuss in this section is generated by unsuccessful service stop operations. This event indicates that someone/something tried to stop a specific system service, but was not able to do it due to insufficient permissions. The event in Listing 10-12 is generated in the Windows security event log in this case.

Listing 10-12: Event ID 4656: A handle to an object was requested.

```
Task Category: Other Object Access Events
Keywords: Audit Failure
Subject:
        Security ID:            S-1-5-21-3212943211-794299840-588279583-1000
        Account Name:           Andrei
        Account Domain:         2016SRV
        Logon ID:               0x12BC9E
Object:
        Object Server:          SC Manager
        Object Type:            SERVICE OBJECT
        Object Name:            netprofm
```

```
        Handle ID:              0x0
        Resource Attributes: -
Process Information:
        Process ID:             0x300
        Process Name:           C:\Windows\System32\services.exe
Access Request Information:
        Transaction ID:         {00000000-0000-0000-0000-000000000000}
        Accesses:               %%7189 (Stop the service)
                                See table 10.2 for more details
        Access Reasons:         -
        Access Mask:            0x20 (See table 10.2 for more details)
        Privileges Used for Access Check: -
        Restricted SID Count: 0
```

NOTE The event logs described in this section are in the download files for this chapter, in the Unsuccessful Service Stop Operation - Access Denied.evtx file.

Subject requested Stop the service access to stop the SC Manager SERVICE_ OBJECT with the name netprofm, but this access request failed, because Subject had no required permissions.

One of the problems associated with this event is that, for example, the built-in Windows Services.msc management console verifies all user account permissions for a specific service when this user opens the properties of the service, or right-clicks it to open a context menu. In this case the user might not even try to stop a specific service, but a 4656 Audit Failure event will be generated whether or not the user tried to stop the service.

Monitoring Scenarios: System Services Operations

Useful events to monitor related to system services operations are shown in Table 10-7.

Table 10-7: System Services Operations Events

SECURITY EVENT	SUBCATEGORY	EVENT TYPE
System Event ID 7045	N/A	Information
4697: A service was installed in the system.	Security System Extension	Audit Success
4656: A handle to an object was requested.	Other Object Access Events	Audit Failure
System Event ID 7036	N/A	Information

The most important Windows system services events to monitor are successful and unsuccessful service installation events.

As mentioned at the beginning of this section, services are one of the most popular methods used by malicious software, malware, and viruses to maintain persistence and perform malicious actions. Every new service installation, especially on highly important and critical hosts, such as Active Directory domain controllers or database servers, is important to monitor.

You also should be notified if an account, under which a service is running, was changed to a real local or domain user account, instead of built-in accounts, such as Local System or Local Service. When service runs under a local or domain user account, its password might be easily compromised using an account with administrative privileges.

Monitor these events:

■ **Windows 10/2016 only:** Any "4697: A service was installed in the system" on all highly important and critical hosts.

■ **Windows 10/2016 only:** Any "4697: A service was installed in the system" where the Service Account field is not LocalSystem, NT AUTHORITY\ LocalService, or NT AUTHORITY\NetworkService.

Monitor for this using the following XPath filter:

```
*[System[band(Keywords,4503599627370496) and (EventID=4656)]] and
*[EventData[Data[@Name='ServiceAccount'] != 'LocalSystem']] and
*[EventData[Data[@Name='ServiceAccount'] != 'NT AUTHORITY\
LocalService']]
and *[EventData[Data[@Name='ServiceAccount'] !=
 'NT AUTHORITY\NetworkService']]
```

■ Any 7045 event in the Windows system event log on all highly important and critical hosts.

■ Any 7045 event in the Windows system event log where the AccountName field is not LocalSystem, NT AUTHORITY\LocalService, or NT AUTHORITY\ NetworkService.

Monitor for this using the following XPath filter:

```
*[System[(EventID=7045)]] and *[EventData[Data[@Name='AccountName'] !=
'LocalSystem']] and *[EventData[Data[@Name='AccountName'] !=
'NT AUTHORITY\LocalService']] and *[EventData[Data[@Name=
'AccountName']
 != 'NT AUTHORITY\NetworkService']]
```

This XPath filter also shows you all "kernel mode driver" installations, because they don't have an AccountName field value.

- Any "4656: A handle to an object was requested" Audit Failure events with an Object Server field of SC manager and an AccessMask field of 0x3 for unsuccessful service installation.

Monitor for this using this XPath filter:

```
*[System[band(Keywords,4503599627370496) and (EventID=4656)]] and
*[EventData[Data[@Name='AccessMask'] and (Data='0x3')]] and
*[EventData[Data[@Name='ObjectServer'] ='SC Manager']]
```

- Service start/stop operations are optional to monitor. If, for example, you need to monitor for Windows Defender or other antivirus service stop operations, you should monitor for System Event ID 7036 with param1 = Windows Defender Service and param2 = stopped.

Monitor for this with the following XPath filter:

```
*[System[(EventID=7036)]] and *[EventData[Data[@Name='param1'] =
'Windows Defender Service']] and
*[EventData[Data[@Name='param2'] = 'stopped']]
```

- Monitoring for unsuccessful system service stop operations is optional due to, as was explained earlier in this chapter, the high probability of false positive events.

Security Event Log Operations

The most important operations related to the Windows security event log are:

- Security event log clear operation
- Security event log service shutdown

These two operations are discussed in this section.

Successful Security Event Log Erase Operation

Usually, on regular production servers and workstations the security event log should never be erased. The only reason to do that is to free some space on a hard drive when it's full, but this is a temporary solution because the log will fill again. And initially the system should be set up to maintain the security event log with its maximum size defined in its properties. An unexpected clearing of logs should be considered a high priority event.

More often, security event logs are erased on machines within a lab environment or for testing/research purposes. Such hosts might be excluded from monitoring for security event log erase operations if they generate much noise.

The event in Listing 10-13 will be recorded in the Windows security event log when a local security event log is erased.

Listing 10-13: Event ID 1102: The audit log was cleared.

```
Task Category: Log clear
Keywords: Audit Success
Subject:
       Security ID:       S-1-5-21-3212943211-794299840-588279583-500
       Account Name:      Administrator
       Domain Name:       2016SRV
       Logon ID:          0x536D1
```

NOTE The event logs described in this section are in the download files for this chapter, in the `Successful Security Event Log Erase.evtx` file.

Basically, the only information this event provides is about the `Subject`, who requested a security event log erase operation.

Unsuccessful Security Event Log Erase Operation

The only information available in the event logs about unsuccessful security event log erase operations are process creation (ID 4688) and termination (ID 4689) events for an application that was used to erase the event log. Using only this information it's almost impossible to detect unsuccessful security event log erase operations.

Successful Security Event Log Service Shutdown

In addition to the standard System Event ID 7036 event, the Windows security event log will contain the event in Listing 10-14 when the Windows Event Log service is stopped.

Listing 10-14: Event ID 1100: The event logging service has shut down.

```
Task Category: Service shutdown
Keywords: Audit Success

The event logging service has shut down.
```

NOTE The event logs described in this section are in the download files for this chapter, in the `Successful Security Event Log Service Shutdown.evtx` file.

Event 1100 does not contain information about which account stopped the event logging service.

This event also generates each time the system is shut down.

Unsuccessful Security Event Log Service Shutdown

This activity will generate the same event explained in the "Unsuccessful Service Shutdown Operation - Access Denied" section earlier in this chapter.

Monitoring Scenarios: Security Event Log Operations

Useful events to monitor related to security event log operations are shown in Table 10-8.

Table 10-8: Security Event Log Operations Events

SECURITY EVENT	SUBCATEGORY	EVENT TYPE
System Event ID 1100	Service shutdown	Audit Success
System Event ID 1102	Log clear	Audit Success

System Event ID 1100 generates during a normal system shutdown process. Monitoring for this event ID is optional, because the Windows Event Log service is automatically turned back on if it's stopped manually. In this case it is useful to monitor for two events that occur at almost the same time: System Event ID 1100 and System Event ID 7036 with `param2 = running`.

It is recommended to monitor the "Log clear" event on hosts, which should not have their local security event log cleared. It's recommended to exclude lab machines and other machines where users will manually erase logs as part of their job-related activities.

Changes in Auditing Subsystem Settings

It's important to control changes in auditing group policy settings applied to a host. All hosts should have auditing group policy settings and auditing subsystem parameters applied based on their host type, and you should be notified of any unplanned change in these settings.

Changes in auditing settings may disable the ability to audit activities on a specific host and the attacker/malicious person may avoid being detected.

This section provides information about the most important operations/changes made to local auditing subsystem settings.

Successful Auditing Subsystem Security Descriptor Change

Every Windows operating system has a security descriptor applied to the local auditing subsystem. This security descriptor defines access rights to the auditing subsystem and the ability to change local auditing settings. By default each Windows system has a default auditing subsystem security descriptor applied.

All Windows operating systems starting from Windows 7 and Windows Server 2008 R2 have the following default security descriptor set for the auditing subsystem:

```
D:(A;;DCSWRPDTRC;;;BA)(A;;DCSWRPDTRC;;;SY)
```

The security descriptor uses Security Descriptor Definition Language (SDDL). SDDL is a language used for the security descriptor string definition. SDDL string has the following format:

```
[O:owner][G:primary group][D: (ACE_1)(ACE_2)..(ACE_N)][S: (ACE_1)
(ACE_2)..(ACE_N)]
```

[O:owner] defines the owner of the object. This part is optional and if it's not defined, as you see in the preceding example, it means that the object owner parameter is not applicable to that object. The owner parameter can have one of the pre-defined values listed in Table 10-9, or can contain the SID of an account that is the owner of the object. Here are some examples of [O:owner] values:

- O:EA

- O:S-1-5-21-3212943211-794299840-588279583-500

Table 10-9: Pre-defined Values for [O:owner] SDDL Parameter.

VALUE	TRANSLATION	VALUE	TRANSLATION
AO	Account operators	"PA"	Group Policy administrators
RU	Pre-Windows 2000 compatible access	"IU"	Interactively logged-on user
AN	Anonymous logon	"LA"	Local administrator
AU	Authenticated users	"LG"	Local guest
BA	Built-in administrators	"LS"	Local service account
BG	Built-in guests	"SY"	Local system
BO	Backup operators	"NU"	Network logon user
BU	Built-in users	"NO"	Network configuration operators
CA	Certificate server administrators	"NS"	Network service account
CG	Creator group	"PO"	Printer operators
CO	Creator owner	"PS"	Personal self
DA	Domain administrators	"PU"	Power users

Continues

Table 10-9 (*continued*)

VALUE	TRANSLATION	VALUE	TRANSLATION
DC	Domain computers	"RS"	RAS servers group
DD	Domain controllers	"RD"	Terminal server users
DG	Domain guests	"RE"	Replicator
DU	Domain users	"RC"	Restricted code
EA	Enterprise administrators	"SA"	Schema administrators
ED	Enterprise domain controllers	"SO"	Server operators

[G:primary group] defines the SID of the primary group to which the object belongs. This parameter is optional and is designed to be used for compatibility with Macintosh and POSIX-based systems. It has the same format as the [O:owner] parameter. See Chapters 5 and 6 for more information about primary groups.

[D:inheritance(ACE_1)(ACE_2)..(ACE_N)] contains a list of discretionary access control list (DACL) access control entries (ACEs). ACEs define access permissions for the object. The inheritance parameter can be set to one of the following three values:

- **P:** Inheritance from containers that are higher in the folder hierarchy are blocked.

- **AI:** Inheritance is allowed, assuming that P is not also set.

- **AR:** Child objects inherit permissions from this object.

[S: inheritance(ACE_1)(ACE_2)..(ACE_N)] contains a list of system access control list (SACL) access control entries (ACEs). These ACEs define auditing rules for the object. The inheritance parameter can be set to the same values as discussed for discretionary access control lists.

Access control entry (ACE) has the following format:

(*type;flags;permissions;object GUID;inherit object GUID;security principal*)

- **type:** ACE type. Can have one of the following values:

VALUE	MEANING	VALUE	MEANING
A	ACCESS ALLOWED	AU	SYSTEM AUDIT
D	ACCESS DENIED	A	SYSTEM ALARM
OA	OBJECT ACCESS ALLOWED	OU	OBJECT SYSTEM AUDIT
OD	OBJECT ACCESS DENIED	OL	OBJECT SYSTEM ALARM

▪ `flags:` ACE flags. Can have one or a combination of the following values:

VALUE	MEANING	VALUE	MEANING
CI	CONTAINER INHERIT	ID	ACE IS INHERITED
OI	OBJECT INHERIT	SA	SUCCESSFUL ACCESS AUDIT
NP	NO PROPAGATE	FA	FAILED ACCESS AUDIT
IO	INHERITANCE ONLY		

▪ **permissions:** Access or auditing permissions. All permissions present as two-letter constants or hexadecimal values. You can find more information about possible values for the `permissions` section in Appendix C.

▪ **security principal:** Security principal to which the current ACE applies. It can have an SID of the security principal, or any value from Table 10-9.

Going back to the default security descriptor for a local auditing system:
`D:(A;;DCSWRPDTRC;;;BA)(A;;DCSWRPDTRC;;;SY)`

▪ **D:** This is DACL.
`(A;;DCSWRPDTRC;;;BA)`

▪ **type - A:** ACCESS ALLOWED. This ACE allows access.

▪ **flags:** no flags set.

▪ **rights:** DCSWRPDTRC

   ▪ **DC:** Delete All Child Objects

   ▪ **SW:** All Validated Writes

   ▪ **RP:** Read All Properties

   ▪ **DT:** Delete Subtree

   ▪ **RC:** Read Permissions

▪ **object GUID:** no object GUID set.

▪ **inherit object GUID:** no inherit object GUID set.

▪ **security principal:** BA (Built-in Administrators)
`(A;;DCSWRPDTRC;;;SY)`

▪ **type - A:** ACCESS ALLOWED. This ACE allows access.

▪ **flags:** no flags set.

▪ **rights:** DCSWRPDTRC, same as previous ACE.

▪ **object GUID:** no object GUID set.

▪ **inherit object GUID:** no inherit object GUID set.

▪ **security principal:** SY (Local System).

Basically speaking this DACL allows full access to the local auditing subsystem for the security principals Built-in Administrators group and a Local System account.

The security descriptor is stored as the AuditPolicySD registry value in the following registry key: HKEY_LOCAL_MACHINE\SYSTEM\CurrentControlSet\ Control\Lsa\Audit\AuditPolicy\.

When a security event log's ACL is changed, the events in Listings 10-14, 10-15, and 10-16 are generated in the local security event log.

> **NOTE** The event logs described in this section are in the download files for this chapter, in the Successful Auditing Subsystem Security Descriptor Change.evtx file.

A 4703 event (Listing 10-15) informs you that some privileges were enabled or disabled in the user's session token. See Chapter 11 for more information about user privileges and logon rights events.

Listing 10-15: Event ID 4703: A token right was adjusted.

```
Task Category: Token Right Adjusted Events
Keywords: Audit Success
Subject:
        Security ID:            S-1-5-21-3212943211-794299840-588279583-500
        Account Name:           Administrator
        Account Domain:         2016SRV
        Logon ID:               0x29594
Target Account:
        Security ID:            S-1-0-0
        Account Name:           Administrator
        Account Domain:         2016SRV
        Logon ID:               0x29594
Process Information:
        Process ID:             0xfb8
        Process Name:           C:\Windows\System32\auditpol.exe
Enabled Privileges:

                                SeSecurityPrivilege
Disabled Privileges:

                                -
```

By default all privileges in the session token are disabled. If an account needs to use any of these privileges, the privilege must be enabled first. This event shows that Subject enabled SeSecurityPrivilege in the Target Account session token.

To change auditing subsystem settings, the account making the change must have the SeSecurityPrivilege privilege enabled in its session token. This privilege is granted to an account if it's listed in the "Computer Configuration\

Windows Settings\Security Settings\Local Policies\User Rights Assignment\
Manage auditing and security log" local security policy setting.

In this example the built-in local Administrator account enabled some privileges
for itself, but the `Target Account\Security ID` field shows an SID of `S-1-0-0`,
which is `Nobody` or `No Security Principal`. When `Target Account\Security`
`ID` equals `S-1-0-0` it means that target account equals subject.

The `Process Name` field shows information about the process that requested
`SeSecurityPrivilege` to be enabled.

After the required privileges are enabled in the session token, these privileges
can be used. Event 4674 (Listing 10-16) informs you that the `SeSecurityPrivilege`
privilege was successfully used to perform operations on the Local Security
Authority (`LSA`) object server, which means on the local auditing system.

Listing 10-16: Event ID 4674: An operation was attempted on a privileged object.

```
Task Category: Sensitive Privilege Use
Keywords: Audit Success
Subject:
        Security ID:            S-1-5-21-3212943211-794299840-588279583-500
        Account Name:           Administrator
        Account Domain:         2016SRV
        Logon ID:               0x29594
Object:
        Object Server:          LSA
        Object Type:            -
        Object Name:            -
        Object Handle:          0x0
Process Information:
        Process ID:             0x308
        Process Name:           C:\Windows\System32\lsass.exe
Requested Operation:
        Desired Access:         16777216
        Privileges:             SeSecurityPrivilege
```

The `Desired Access` field contains the decimal access mask for requested
accesses. The value should be converted from decimal to hexadecimal format
first and then, depending on object type, found in the appropriate table.

`16777216` is 0x1000000 in hexadecimal format. That translates to ACCESS_
SYS_SEC, which is the right to get or set a system access control list (SACL) for
an object's security descriptor. (See Table 5.4 for information about this access
right.) This operation shows you that the LSA's SACL (security event log SACL)
was modified. Based on my research, every time `SeSecurityPrivilege` is in
use the desired access mask requested is always the same.

The process that invoked this operation is `C:\Windows\System32\lsass.exe`.

The event in Listing 10-17 informs you that that auditing subsystem security
descriptor was modified. The event name says that the SACL was changed, but

it generates every time any part of the security descriptor for the local auditing subsystem is changed, not only its SACL part.

Listing 10-17: Event ID 4715: The audit policy (SACL) on an object was changed.

```
Task Category: Audit Policy Change
Keywords: Audit Success
Subject:
        Security ID:            S-1-5-21-3212943211-794299840-588279583-500
        Account Name:           Administrator
        Account Domain:         2016SRV
        Logon ID:               0x29594
Audit Policy Change:
        Original Security Descriptor: D:(A;;DCSWRPDTRC;;;BA)
            (A;;DCSWRPDTRC;;;SY)
        New Security Descriptor: D:(A;;DCSWRPDTRC;;;BA)(A;;DCSWRPDTRC;;;
            SY)(A;;DCSWRPDTRC;;;LA)S:NO_ACCESS_CONTROL
```

A 4715 event shows you who changed the descriptor (`Subject`) and also shows you the new and previous values for the security descriptor.

In this example a new DACL ACE was added to the security descriptor: `(A;;DCSWRPDTRC;;;LA)`, which provides full access to the local security event log for the local administrator (LA) account.

In the `New Security Descriptor` field's value you also can see that an `S:NO_ACCESS_CONTROL` string was added to the security descriptor. By default there is no SACL set for local auditing system. When someone uses the `auditpol /set /sd` command to set the security descriptor, the system automatically adds `NO_ACCESS_CONTROL` to indicate that no SACL is currently set.

Unsuccessful Auditing Subsystem Security Descriptor Change

When someone tries to get or set the local auditing system's security descriptor (using `auditpol /get /sd` or `auditpol /set /sd` commands, for example), but does not have the SeSecurityPrivilege privilege to perform the operation, the event in Listing 10-18 is generated in the Windows security event log.

Listing 10-18: Event ID 4674: An operation was attempted on a privileged object.

```
Task Category: Sensitive Privilege Use
Keywords: Audit Failure
Subject:
        Security ID:            S-1-5-21-3212943211-794299840-588279583-1000
        Account Name:           Andrei
        Account Domain:         2016SRV
        Logon ID:               0x713BE9
Object:
        Object Server:          LSA
        Object Type:            -
```

```
        Object Name:            -
        Object Handle:          0x0
Process Information:
        Process ID:             0x308
        Process Name:           C:\Windows\System32\lsass.exe
Requested Operation:
        Desired Access:         16777216
        Privileges:             SeSecurityPrivilege
```

NOTE The event logs described in this section are in the download files for this chapter, in the Unsuccessful Auditing Subsystem Log Security Descriptor Change.evtx file.

SeSecurityPrivilege was requested for the LSA object, but the request failed. This event is the same as the 4674 event you saw in Listing 10-16, but it has an Audit Failure type.

Successful System Audit Policy Changes

Multiple methods can be used to change local audit policy settings. Examples are:

- Gpedit.msc, a built-in management console
- Auditpol, a built-in local console application
- PowerShell commands
- Active Directory group policies

Advanced audit policies can be modified using the auditpol tool available in all Windows versions starting from Windows Server 2008 and Windows Vista. Starting from Windows 7 and Windows Server 2008 R2, advanced audit policy settings can be modified using the Group Policy Editor management console. The advanced audit policy settings are located in the Computer Configuration\ Windows Settings\Security Settings\Advanced Audit Policy Configuration folder. See Chapter 3 for more information about legacy and advanced audit policy settings.

If any of the audit policy subcategory settings are changed, the event in Listing 10-19 is generated in the Windows security event log.

Listing 10-19: Event ID 4719: System audit policy was changed.

```
Task Category: Audit Policy Change
Keywords: Audit Success
Subject:
        Security ID:            S-1-5-18
        Account Name:           2016SRV$
        Account Domain:         WORKGROUP
        Logon ID:               0x3E7
```

```
Audit Policy Change:
     Category:              %%8273   (Logon/Logoff)
     Subcategory:           %%12547  (IPsec Main Mode)
     Subcategory GUID:      {0cce9218-69ae-11d9-bed3-505054503030}
     Changes:               %%8449   (Success Added)
See table 10.4 for more details
```

NOTE   The event logs described in this section are in the download files for this chapter, in the `Successful System Audit Policy Changes.evtx` file.

Changes made by the Group Policy Editor for Advanced Audit Policy Configuration section settings will always be recorded in the Windows security event log, as done in this example, by the SYSTEM account (`S-1-5-18`).

See Table 10-10 for a list of all constants for audit categories and subcategories.

Each subcategory has its own Global Unique Identifier (GUID), which can be found in Table 10-10.

When a legacy audit category is changed, you will see the same number of 4719 events as the number of audit subcategories in the category that was changed, one for each subcategory.

Table 10-10: Auditing Categories and Subcategories IDs and GUIDs.

CATEGORY	SUBCATEGORY	ID	GUID
Account Logon		%%8280	
	Credential Validation	%%14336	{0CCE923F-69AE-11D9-BED3-505054503030}
	Kerberos Authentication Service	%%14339	{0CCE9242-69AE-11D9-BED3-505054503030}
	Kerberos Service Ticket Operations	%%14337	{0CCE9240-69AE-11D9-BED3-505054503030}
	Other Account Logon Events	%%14338	{0CCE9241-69AE-11D9-BED3-505054503030}
Account Management		%%8278	
	Application Group Management	%%13828	{0CCE9239-69AE-11D9-BED3-505054503030}
	Computer Account Management	%%13825	{0CCE9236-69AE-11D9-BED3-505054503030}
	Distribution Group Management	%%13827	{0CCE9238-69AE-11D9-BED3-505054503030}
	Other Account Management Events	%%13829	{0CCE923A-69AE-11D9-BED3-505054503030}

CATEGORY	SUBCATEGORY	ID	GUID
	Security Group Management	%%13826	{0CCE9237-69AE-11D9-BED3-505054503030}
	User Account Management	%%13824	{0CCE9235-69AE-11D9-BED3-505054503030}
Detailed Tracking		%%8276	
	DPAPI Activity	%%13314	{0CCE922D-69AE-11D9-BED3-505054503030}
	Plug and Play Events	%%13316	{0CCE9248-69AE-11D9-BED3-505054503030}
	Process Creation	%%13312	{0CCE922B-69AE-11D9-BED3-505054503030}
	Process Termination	%%13313	{0CCE922C-69AE-11D9-BED3-505054503030}
	RPC Events	%%13315	{0CCE922E-69AE-11D9-BED3-505054503030}
	Token Right Adjusted Events	%%13317	{0CCE924A-69AE-11D9-BED3-505054503030}
DS Access		%%8279	
	Detailed Directory Service Replication	%%14083	{0CCE923E-69AE-11D9-BED3-505054503030}
	Directory Service Access	%%14080	{0CCE923B-69AE-11D9-BED3-505054503030}
	Directory Service Changes	%%14081	{0CCE923C-69AE-11D9-BED3-505054503030}
	Directory Service Replication	%%14082	{0CCE923D-69AE-11D9-BED3-505054503030}
Logon/Logoff		%%8273	
	Account Lockout	%%12546	{0CCE9217-69AE-11D9-BED3-505054503030}
	User/Device Claims	%%12553	{0CCE9247-69AE-11D9-BED3-505054503030}
	Group Membership	%%12554	{0CCE9249-69AE-11D9-BED3-505054503030}
	IPsec Extended Mode	%%12550	{0CCE921A-69AE-11D9-BED3-505054503030}
	IPsec Main Mode	%%12547	{0CCE9218-69AE-11D9-BED3-505054503030}

Continues

Table 10-10 (continued)

CATEGORY	SUBCATEGORY	ID	GUID
	IPsec Quick Mode	%%12549	{0CCE9219-69AE-11D9-BED3-505054503030}
	Logoff	%%12545	{0CCE9216-69AE-11D9-BED3-505054503030}
	Logon	%%12544	{0CCE9215-69AE-11D9-BED3-505054503030}
	Network Policy Server	%%12552	{0CCE9243-69AE-11D9-BED3-505054503030}
	Other Logon/Logoff Events	%%12551	{0CCE921C-69AE-11D9-BED3-505054503030}
	Special Logon	%%12548	{0CCE921B-69AE-11D9-BED3-505054503030}
Object Access		%%8274	
	Application Generated	%%12806	{0CCE9222-69AE-11D9-BED3-505054503030}
	Certification Services	%%12805	{0CCE9221-69AE-11D9-BED3-505054503030}
	Detailed File Share	%%12811	{0CCE9244-69AE-11D9-BED3-505054503030}
	File Share	%%12808	{0CCE9224-69AE-11D9-BED3-505054503030}
	File System	%%12800	{0CCE921D-69AE-11D9-BED3-505054503030}
	Filtering Platform Connection	%%12810	{0CCE9226-69AE-11D9-BED3-505054503030}
	Filtering Platform Packet Drop	%%12809	{0CCE9225-69AE-11D9-BED3-505054503030}
	Handle Manipulation	%%12807	{0CCE9223-69AE-11D9-BED3-505054503030}
	Kernel Object	%%12802	{0CCE921F-69AE-11D9-BED3-505054503030}
	Other Object Access Events	%%12804	{0CCE9227-69AE-11D9-BED3-505054503030}
	Registry	%%12801	{0CCE921E-69AE-11D9-BED3-505054503030}
	Removable Storage	%%12812	{0CCE9245-69AE-11D9-BED3-505054503030}

CATEGORY	SUBCATEGORY	ID	GUID
	SAM	%%12803	{0CCE9220-69AE-11D9-BED3-505054503030}
	Central Policy Staging	%%12813	{0CCE9246-69AE-11D9-BED3-505054503030}
Policy Change		%%8277	
	Audit Policy Change	%%13568	{0CCE922F-69AE-11D9-BED3-505054503030}
	Authentication Policy Change	%%13569	{0CCE9230-69AE-11D9-BED3-505054503030}
	Authorization Policy Change	%%13570	{0CCE9231-69AE-11D9-BED3-505054503030}
	Filtering Platform Policy Change	%%13572	{0CCE9233-69AE-11D9-BED3-505054503030}
	MPSSVC Rule-Level Policy Change	%%13571	{0CCE9232-69AE-11D9-BED3-505054503030}
	Other Policy Change Events	%%13573	{0CCE9234-69AE-11D9-BED3-505054503030}
Privilege Use		%%8275	
	Non Sensitive Privilege Use	%%13057	{0CCE9229-69AE-11D9-BED3-505054503030}
	Other Privilege Use Events	%%13058	{0CCE922A-69AE-11D9-BED3-505054503030}
	Sensitive Privilege Use	%%13056	{0CCE9228-69AE-11D9-BED3-505054503030}
System		%%8272	
	IPsec Driver	%%12291	{0CCE9213-69AE-11D9-BED3-505054503030}
	Other System Events	%%12292	{0CCE9214-69AE-11D9-BED3-505054503030}
	Security State Change	%%12288	{0CCE9210-69AE-11D9-BED3-505054503030}
	Security System Extension	%%12289	{0CCE9211-69AE-11D9-BED3-505054503030}
	System Integrity	%%12290	{0CCE9212-69AE-11D9-BED3-505054503030}

The Changes field may contain one of the following values:

- **%%8449:** Success Added
- **%%8451:** Failure added
- **%%8448:** Success removed
- **%%8450:** Failure removed

The Changes field can also contain a combination of these values. For example:

```
Changes: %%8448, %%8450
```

Unsuccessful System Audit Policy Changes

When someone tries to view or change local audit category/subcategory settings (auditpol /get or auditpol /set command), but does not have the required privileges to perform the operation, the same 4674 event as shown in Listing 10-18 appears in the Windows security event log.

> **NOTE** The event logs described in this section are in the download files for this chapter, in the Unsuccessful System Audit Policy Changes.evtx file.

Monitoring Scenarios: Changes in Auditing Subsystem Settings

Useful events to monitor related to changes in auditing subsystem settings are shown in Table 10-11.

Table 10-11: Security Events for Changes in Auditing Subsystem Settings

SECURITY EVENT	SUBCATEGORY	EVENT TYPE
4715: The audit policy (SACL) on an object was changed.	Audit Policy Change	Audit Success
4719: System audit policy was changed.	Audit Policy Change	Audit Success
4674: An operation was attempted on a privileged object.	Sensitive Privilege Use	Audit Failure

All changes to the Windows local auditing subsystem security descriptor should be monitored and, if not done by an authorized account, investigated. My experience shows that security descriptors for local auditing subsystems almost never change. The "Manage auditing and security log" user right is given to a required group or account instead. My research showed that even if you grant permission to modify local auditing policy to an account in the security descriptor it still needs to have the SeSecurityPrivilege privilege to perform modification. And if you grant SeSecurityPrivilege to an account but include a Deny rule in the security descriptor, the account will still be able to modify local auditing policy settings.

Any change to system audit policy settings should be monitored. Changes to audit policy settings are usually made once a policy is defined and applied centrally. After a policy is applied no changes are usually made to the systems.

You should monitor for failed attempts to use SeSecurityPrivilege, but it's also recommended to exclude events with LOCAL SERVICE, NETWORK SERVICE, and Local System Subjects, because they are normally generated during normal operating system operations and can, in most cases, be ignored. A "4674: An operation was attempted on a privileged object" event, unfortunately, can be interpreted not only as a local auditing policies change, but also, for example, as a per-user auditing database change, as you will see in the following section.

Monitor for these events:

- Any event ID "4715: The audit policy (SACL) on an object was changed."
- Any event ID "4719: System audit policy was changed."
- Any event ID 4674 in the Windows security event log where the SubjectUserSid field is not S-1-5-18 (LocalSystem), S-1-5-19 (NT AUTHORITY\LocalService), or S-1-5-20 (NT AUTHORITY\NetworkService). You also should filter for events where ObjectSertver is LSA and PrivilegeList is SeSecurityPrivilege.

Monitor for these conditions with this XPath filter:

```
*[System[band(Keywords,4503599627370496) and (EventID=4674)]] and
*[EventData[Data[@Name='SubjectUserSid'] != 'S-1-5-18']] and
*[EventData[Data[@Name='SubjectUserSid'] != 'S-1-5-19']] and
*[EventData[Data[@Name='SubjectUserSid'] != 'S-1-5-20']] and
*[EventData[Data[@Name='ObjectServer'] = 'LSA']] and
*[EventData[Data[@Name='PrivilegeList'] = 'SeSecurityPrivilege']]
```

Per-User Auditing Operations

Per-user audit policies were first introduced in Windows XP SP2 and Windows Server 2003 SP1. This feature allows for defining different auditing subcategory settings per user account. These settings are applied individually locally for each host; there are no group policy settings to configure per-user auditing. Security groups are not supported to be used in per-user auditing settings.

Per-user auditing settings are stored in the following registry path: HKEY_LOCAL_MACHINE\SYSTEM\CurrentControlSet\Control\Lsa\Audit\PerUserAuditing\. For each account the system will create a dedicated registry key with audit policy settings.

Changes to the local per-user auditing database can be made with the `auditpol.exe` tool.

The following per-user auditing actions are available for monitoring using the Windows security event log:

- Changes in the per-user auditing database
- Per-user auditing database initialization

In this section you will find information about monitoring of these per-user auditing scenarios.

Successful Per-User Auditing Policy Changes

The following changes are available to perform against per-user auditing policies:

- Include success auditing
- Include failure auditing
- Exclude success auditing
- Exclude failure auditing
- Remove all policies from a user account

Exclude and include operations can be done using the `auditpol /set /user` command. Removing all policies for a specific user or all users can be done using the `auditpol /remove` command.

Any of these changes generate the events in Listings 10-19, 10-20, and 10-21 in the Windows security log.

NOTE   The event logs described in this section are in the download files for this chapter, in the `Successful Per-User Auditing Policy Changes.evtx` file.

As shown in Listing 10-20, to perform changes on per-user auditing policies configurations the `SeSecurityPrivilege` privilege must be used.

Listing 10-20: Event ID 4703: A token right was adjusted.

```
Task Category: Token Right Adjusted Events
Keywords: Audit Success
Subject:
        Security ID:            S-1-5-21-3212943211-794299840-588279583-500
        Account Name:           Administrator
        Account Domain:         2016SRV
        Logon ID:               0x2714BD
Target Account:
        Security ID:            S-1-0-0
        Account Name:           Administrator
```

```
      Account Domain:       2016SRV
      Logon ID:             0x2714BD
Process Information:
      Process ID:           0xa98
      Process Name:         C:\Windows\System32\auditpol.exe
Enabled Privileges:

                            SeSecurityPrivilege
```

Then SeSecurityPrivilege is applied on the LSA object server. The event in Listing 10-21 is the same as you can see in Listing 10-15.

Listing 10-21: Event ID 4674: An operation was attempted on a privileged object.

```
Task Category: Sensitive Privilege Use
Keywords: Audit Success
```

Event 4912 (Listing 10-22) notifies you about any change in the per-user auditing policy associated to the Policy For Account\Security ID account.

Listing 10-22: Event ID 4912: Per User Audit Policy was changed.

```
Task Category: Audit Policy Change
Keywords: Audit Success
Subject:
      Security ID:          S-1-5-21-3212943211-794299840-588279583-500
      Account Name:         Administrator
      Account Domain:       2016SRV
      Logon ID:             0x2714BD
Policy For Account:
      Security ID:          S-1-5-21-3212943211-794299840-588279583-1000
Policy Change Details:
      Category:             %%8274 (Object Access)
      Subcategory:          %%12800 (File System)
      Subcategory GUID:     {0cce921d-69ae-11d9-bed3-505054503030}
      Changes:              %%8455 (Success exclude added)
See table 10.4 for more details
```

See Table 10-10 for possible values for the Category, Subcategory, and Subcategory GUID fields.

This event might be interpreted in the following manner: Subject made changes to the S-1-5-21-3212943211-794299840-588279583-1000 (Policy For Account) account, and the Audit Success setting (Success excluded added) was excluded for the File System (Subcategory) subcategory, which is under the Object Access (Category) category.

Here is the list of possible values for Changes field:

- %%8452: Success include removed
- %%8453: Success include added

- **%%8454:** Success exclude removed
- **%%8455:** Success exclude added
- **%%8456:** Failure include removed
- **%%8457:** Failure include added
- **%%8458:** Failure exclude removed
- **%%8459:** Failure exclude added

For every subcategory change a dedicated 4912 event is generated.

Unsuccessful Per-User Auditing Policy Changes

Unsuccessful per-user auditing policy change operations will produce the same event as shown in Listing 10-18.

Per-User Auditing Database Initialization

Every time the system starts and there are any per-user auditing policies configured on the machine, the event in Listing 10-23 is generated in the Windows security event log.

Listing 10-23: Event ID 4902: The per-user audit policy table was created.

```
Task Category: Audit Policy Change
Keywords: Audit Success

Number of Elements: 2
Policy ID:          0x98D4
```

NOTE The event logs described in this section are in the download files for this chapter, in the `Per-user Auditing Database Initialization.evtx` file.

The `Number of Elements` field represents the number of unique user accounts with assigned policies in the per-user auditing database.

The `Policy ID` field contains the unique identifier of the local per-user auditing policy database.

Monitoring Scenarios: Per-User Auditing Operations

Useful events to monitor related to changes in the local per-user auditing database are shown in Table 10-12.

Table 10-12: Security Events for Per-User Auditing Operations

SECURITY EVENT	SUBCATEGORY	EVENT TYPE
4912: Per User Audit Policy was changed.	Audit Policy Change	Audit Success
4902: The Per-user audit policy table was created.	Audit Policy Change	Audit Success
4674: An operation was attempted on a privileged object.	Sensitive Privilege Use	Audit Failure

Companies very rarely use per-user auditing policies. If you do not expect per-user auditing policies in your environment, you should monitor for 4912 and 4902 events, which will inform you that, for some reason, these policies were enabled on the machine.

If you already have per-user auditing policies applied, all of the changes to them should be monitored. Basically the same rules apply as for normal auditing policies. Also, when per-user auditing policies are in use, database initialization events have a mostly informational purpose.

A "4674: An operation was attempted on a privileged object" event, unfortunately, can be interpreted not only as a per-user auditing database change, but also as a local auditing policies change.

If per-user auditing polices are in use, monitor for changes to local per-user auditing policies using event "4912: Per User Audit Policy was changed."

If per-user auditing polices are *not* in use monitor for any event ID "4912: Per User Audit Policy was changed" and "4902: The Per-user audit policy table was created." These events will inform you that per-user auditing policies were enabled on the host.

Scheduled Tasks

Microsoft Task Scheduler is a Windows feature that was first introduced in Windows 2000 and called Task Scheduler 1.0. Windows Task Scheduler 2.0 was introduced in Windows Vista and Windows Server 2008 and includes more features and settings.

Task Scheduler 2.0 stores all scheduled tasks in XML format in the `%systemroot%\System32\Tasks` directory.

Task Scheduler 1.0 (legacy version) stores all tasks in the `%systemroot%\Tasks` folder.

Tasks are stored as files, but at the same time they have their own records in the Windows Registry:

- HKEY_LOCAL_MACHINE\SOFTWARE\Microsoft\Windows NT\CurrentVersion\ Schedule\TaskCache\Tasks

  This registry key contains a list of subkeys, and each of them represents a scheduled task. Each scheduled task container has the task's GUID as the name of the registry key, for example {0017043B-B863-4092-B894-6330CAA84DE9}, which is a unique identifier for a specific scheduled task.

  Each scheduled task registry key contains a set of values that represent settings of the specific scheduled task. For example, you can find a path to the XML file related to a specific scheduled task in the Path value.

- HKEY_LOCAL_MACHINE\SOFTWARE\Microsoft\Windows NT\CurrentVersion\ Schedule\TaskCache\Tree

  This registry key represents the structure of the Windows Task Scheduler, which is organized as a tree. Also, registry keys associated with scheduled tasks have an Id value, which contains the GUID of the task associated to the key. Using this GUID you can find an object for a specific scheduled task in the HKEY_LOCAL_MACHINE\SOFTWARE\Microsoft\Windows NT\ CurrentVersion\Schedule\TaskCache\Task registry key. This object contains all of the settings for the specific task.

Overall, scheduled tasks are a powerful mechanism that allows users to schedule actions for a specific time or perform actions when a specific event is triggered in the system.

Malicious software and attackers may use this feature to maintain persistence in the system or to perform some actions based on a schedule or triggers.

In this section you will find information about monitoring for the most common actions related to scheduled tasks.

Successful Scheduled Task Creation

Multiple methods can be used to create a scheduled task. Here are some of those methods/tools:

- Task Scheduler management console
- Schtasks command-line tool
- PowerShell scripts

No matter which method is used for new scheduled task creation, the event in Listing 10-24 is generated in the Windows security event log.

Listing 10-24: Event ID 4698: A scheduled task was created.

```
Task Category: Other Object Access Events
Keywords: Audit Success
Subject:
        Security ID:          S-1-5-21-3212943211-794299840-588279583-500
        Account Name:         Administrator
        Account Domain:       2016SRV
        Logon ID:             0x2DEB1
Task Information:
        Task Name:            \Microsoft\Windows\Personal\NewTask
        Task Content:         <?xml version="1.0" encoding="UTF-16"?>
<Task version="1.2" xmlns="http://schemas.microsoft.com/windows/2004/02/
                                                               mit/task">
Task XML is not present in this book - see detailed information in the
                                                               .evtx file.
</Task>
```

This event shows you the account used to create the scheduled task and all parameters, in XML format, for the newly created task.

> **NOTE** The complete text of the `Task Content` field is in the `Successful Scheduled Task Creation.evtx` file in the downloads for this chapter.

The `Task Name` field holds the name of the newly created task and the path in the Task Scheduler folders tree to this new object. This path can also be considered as a path under the following registry key: HKEY_LOCAL_MACHINE\ SOFTWARE\Microsoft\Windows NT\CurrentVersion\Schedule\TaskCache\Tree.

The most interesting fields in the task's XML, from information security perspective, are the following:

- `<UserId> </UserId>`: Contains an account name, under which the task is running. This parameter contains the name of the account in form *domain\ account*. It does not contain the account's SID. Built-in system accounts will have the following values:

ACCOUNT NAME	XML VALUE
Local System	NT AUTHORITY\SYSTEM
Local Service	NT AUTHORITY\LOCAL SERVICE
Network Service	NT AUTHORITY\NETWORK SERVICE

- `<LogonType> </LogonType>`: Contains a logon type for an account that is used to run the task. May have one of the following values:
  - `InteractiveToken`: "Run only when user is logged on."

- **Password:** "Run whether user is logged on or not."
- **s4U:** "Do not store password. The task will only have access to local computer resources."

- **<RunLevel> </RunLevel>:** Contains information about a token type that will be used for the scheduled task account logon session:
  - **HighestAvailable:** Elevated token. Represents "Run with highest privileges" checkbox in the Task Scheduler user interface window for the task properties.
  - **LeastPrivilege:** Non-elevated token.

- **<Hidden> </Hidden>:** This parameter specifies whether the new task should be hidden in the Task Scheduler interface. To see hidden tasks, the View ⇨ Show Hidden Tasks main menu checkbox needs to be set in the Task Scheduler. The value of this parameter can be true or false.

- **<Command> </Command>:** The command that will be executed when the task starts.

- **<Arguments> </Arguments>:** Arguments that will pass to the <Command> when the task starts.

Scheduled task creations occur periodically as part of a system's normal operations and are usually performed by the SYSTEM account or the logged-in user's account.

Unsuccessful Scheduled Task Creation - Access Denied

There is no specific event that can inform you that a scheduled task was not created because the account that tried to create it does not have the required permissions to perform the operation. But it is possible to, for example, track process creation and termination events for some tools, such as schtasks.exe. When an "Access Denied" message appears while using schtasks.exe, the events in Listings 10-25 and 10-26 appear in the Windows security event log.

Listing 10-25: Event ID 4688: A new process has been created.

```
Task Category: Process Creation
Keywords: Audit Success
Creator Subject:
        Security ID:        S-1-5-21-3212943211-794299840-588279583-1000
        Account Name:       Andrei
        Account Domain:     2016SRV
        Logon ID:           0x59C0B5
```

```
Target Subject:
      Security ID:          S-1-0-0
      Account Name:         -
      Account Domain:       -
      Logon ID:            0x0
Process Information:
      New Process ID:       0x88c
      New Process Name:     C:\Windows\System32\schtasks.exe
      Token Elevation Type: %%1936
      Mandatory Label:      S-1-16-8192
      Creator Process ID:   0x3fc
      Creator Process Name: C:\Windows\System32\cmd.exe
      Process Command Line: SchTasks  /Create /SC DAILY /TN "My Task"
         /TR "C:RunMe.bat" /ST 09:00 /RL HIGHEST
```

NOTE The event logs described in this section are in the download files for
this chapter, in the `Unsuccessful Scheduled Task Creation - Access`
`Denied.evtx` file.

The most interesting part in this process creation event is the `Process Command`
`Line` field. Here you can find the command that was executed using `cmd.exe`.
The `SchTasks /Create` command allows a user to create a new scheduled task.

There is no information about an "Access Denied" error or that the command
failed in the 4688 event, as you can see. That is why you need to monitor for the
event in Listing 10-26, which will appear right after 4688 event.

Listing 10-26: Event ID 4689: A process has exited.

```
Task Category: Process Termination
Keywords: Audit Success
Subject:
      Security ID:          S-1-5-21-3212943211-794299840-588279583-1000
      Account Name:         Andrei
      Account Domain:       2016SRV
      Logon ID:            0x59C0B5
Process Information:
      Process ID:           0x88c
      Process Name:         C:\Windows\System32\schtasks.exe
      Exit Status:          0x1
```

You see that the process with ID 0x88c (the same as you saw in event 4688)
has exited. But also, what is important is that there is the `Exit Status` field with
the value 0x1, which for `schtasks.exe` means "Failure."

It's important to mention that you should first detect the 4688 event where
the `Process Command Line` field contains the `schtasks /create` command and
then find the 4689 event with `Exit Status` = 0x1.

See Chapter 12 for more information about 4688 and 4689 events.

Successful Scheduled Task Deletion

If a scheduled task is deleted, the event in Listing 10-27 appears in the Windows security event log.

Listing 10-27: Event ID 4699: A scheduled task was deleted.

```
Task Category: Other Object Access Events
Keywords: Audit Success
Subject:
        Security ID:          S-1-5-21-3212943211-794299840-588279583-500
        Account Name:         Administrator
        Account Domain:       2016SRV
        Logon ID:             0x315BC
Task Information:
        Task Name:            \Microsoft\Windows\Personal\NewTask
        Task Content:
```

> **NOTE**   The event logs described in this section are in the download files for this chapter, in the `Successful Scheduled Task Deletion.evtx` file.

The only information this event contains is:

- **Who deleted the task:** `Subject`
- **Which task was deleted:** `Task Name`

There are no details about the deleted task in the 4699 event and the `Task Content` field is always empty. More information about deleted scheduled tasks can be collected using registry auditing for scheduled tasks registry keys. See Chapter 14 for more information.

Scheduled task deletions occur periodically as part of normal system operations and usually are performed by the SYSTEM account or the logged-in user's account.

Unsuccessful Scheduled Task Deletion

There are no specific events or event sequences that inform you about unsuccessful scheduled task deletion.

Successful Scheduled Task Change

There are two main types of a scheduled task change operations:

- **Intentional:** Occurs when an account intentionally modifies the parameters of some scheduled task using Task Scheduler, for example.
- **Unintentional:** Occurs when you open a scheduled task's properties using Task Scheduler and click the OK button without doing any modifications.

In that case you will see an event in the Windows security event log that informs you that the task was modified, even if it was not. Unintentional changes are also performed regularly for built-in tasks by SYSTEM, NETWORK SERVICE, and current user accounts.

Whether or not the modification was intentional, the event in Listing 10-28 appears in the Windows security event log.

Listing 10-28: Event ID 4702: A scheduled task was updated.

```
Task Category: Other Object Access Events
Keywords: Audit Success
Subject:
        Security ID:            S-1-5-21-3212943211-794299840-588279583-500
        Account Name:           Administrator
        Account Domain:         2016SRV
        Logon ID:               0x315BC
Task Information:
        Task Name:              \Microsoft\Windows\Personal\New Task
        Task New Content:       <?xml version="1.0" encoding="UTF-16"?>
<Task version="1.2" xmlns="http://schemas.microsoft.com/windows/2004/02
                                                               /mit/task">
Task XML is not present in this book - see detailed information in the
                                                           .evtx file.
</Task>
```

NOTE The event logs described in this section are in the download files for this chapter, in the `Successful Scheduled Task Modification.evtx` file.

A 4702 event contains only new XML content for the scheduled task. It doesn't highlight or specify changes and always shows a full listing of the task's new XML.

It's hard to detect what exactly was changed from a 4702 event or whether this change was made intentionally or unintentionally.

Unsuccessful Scheduled Task Change

There are no specific events or event sequences that inform you about an unsuccessful scheduled task change/update operation.

Successful Scheduled Task Enable/Disable Operations

When a task is disabled, the event in Listing 10-29 occurs in the Windows security event log.

Listing 10-29: Event ID 4701: A scheduled task was disabled.

```
Task Category: Other Object Access Events
Keywords: Audit Success
Subject:
        Security ID:            S-1-5-21-3212943211-794299840-588279583-500
        Account Name:           Administrator
        Account Domain:         2016SRV
        Logon ID:               0x315BC
Task Information:
        Task Name:              \Microsoft\Windows\Personal\New Task
        Task Content:           <?xml version="1.0" encoding="UTF-16"?>
<Task version="1.2" xmlns="http://schemas.microsoft.com/windows/2004/02
                                                                /mit/task">
Task XML is not present in this book - see detailed information in the
                                                             .evtx file.

</Task>
```

NOTE The event logs described in this section are in the download files for this chapter, in the `Successful Scheduled Task Enable-Disable Operations.evtx` file.

When a task is enabled, the event in Listing 10-30 occurs in the Windows security event log.

Listing 10-30: Event ID 4700: A scheduled task was enabled.

```
Task Category: Other Object Access Events
Keywords: Audit Success
Subject:
        Security ID:            S-1-5-21-3212943211-794299840-588279583-500
        Account Name:           Administrator
        Account Domain:         2016SRV
        Logon ID:               0x315BC
Task Information:
        Task Name:              \Microsoft\Windows\Personal\New Task
        Task Content:           <?xml version="1.0" encoding="UTF-16"?>
<Task version="1.2" xmlns="http://schemas.microsoft.com/windows/2004/02
                                                                /mit/task">
Task XML is not present in this book - see detailed information in the
                                                             .evtx file.

</Task>
```

Both these events contain the same information you saw in events 4702 (Listing 10-28) and 4698 (Listing10-24).

These events also occur periodically as part of normal system operations and these enable/disable actions are usually performed by the SYSTEM account.

Monitoring Scenarios: Scheduled Tasks

A useful event to monitor related to scheduled tasks is shown in Table 10-13.

Table 10-13: Security Events for Scheduled Tasks

SECURITY EVENT	SUBCATEGORY	EVENT TYPE
4698: A scheduled task was created.	Other Object Access Events	Audit Success

Because all events related to scheduled tasks occur on a daily basis as part of normal operating system routines, it's hard to recognize potentially malicious changes to scheduled tasks or the creation of a potentially malicious task.

Built-in XPath filtering does not have functionality to correctly parse a task's XML from security events, but this filtering is required in order to detect suspicious activities.

Some of the problems related to scheduled task monitoring include:

- Many built-in scheduled tasks have the `<Hidden>` parameter set to `true`.
- Many built-in scheduled tasks run with an elevated token ("Run with highest privileges").
- A big number of built-in scheduled tasks have the "Run whether user is logged on or not" flag set.

The following filtering rules will help you to detect suspicious actions:

- If a scheduled task was created, deleted, modified, enabled, or disabled by a `Subject` that should not perform any actions on the host.
- If a newly created task is hidden (`<Hidden> </Hidden>`), it is a good idea to verify why it's hidden.
- If possible, perform filtering for `<Command> </Command>` and `<Arguments> </Arguments>` fields to detect potentially malicious programs (such as Mimikatz or pwdump) or scripts (such as suspicious PowerShell or command-line scripts).
- Very often suspicious scheduled tasks are created in the root of the task scheduler tree or inside the `\Microsoft` folder. You should verify the path for new scheduled tasks in the `Task Name` field.

Boot Configuration Data Changes

Boot configuration data (BCD) is a mechanism that allows operating systems to communicate with the Windows Boot Manager to specify parameters that will be used during the operating system boot process.

BCD replaces the legacy `Boot.ini` configuration file, which was used prior to Windows Vista and Windows Server 2008, as a communication method between the operating system and the Windows Boot Manager. BCD is stored in the boot configuration data store on BIOS and UEFI systems.

Every time you install a new version of Microsoft Windows (Vista and newer) an additional logical partition is created on the primary hard disk. For example, Windows Server 2016 creates a 500 MB NTFS partition at the beginning of the hard disk for this purpose. This partition contains boot information for the Windows Boot Manager. BCD is located in `\Boot\BCD`.

After the Windows Boot Manager gets BCD settings it passes them to the Windows operating system loader, which uses them to change boot settings for the operating system.

The most common tool used to modify BCD settings is the built-in `bcdedit.exe` tool, which is included by default in all Windows versions starting from Windows 7 and Windows Server 2008.

Starting from Windows 8 and Windows Server 2012, every time the system starts the event in Listing 10-31 appears in the Windows security event log, which contains current BCD settings.

Listing 10-31: Event ID 4826: Boot Configuration Data loaded.

```
Task Category: Other Policy Change Events
Keywords: Audit Success
Subject:
        Security ID:            S-1-5-18
        Account Name:           -
        Account Domain:         -
        Logon ID:               0x3E7
General Settings:
        Load Options:                   HELLO_WORLD
        Advanced Options:               %%1843 (No)
        Configuration Access Policy:    %%1846 (Default)
        System Event Logging:           %%1843 (No)
        Kernel Debugging:               %%1843 (No)
        VSM Launch Type:                %%1848 (Off)
Signature Settings:
        Test Signing:           %%1843 (No)
        Flight Signing:         %%1843 (No)
        Disable Integrity Checks: %%1843 (No)
HyperVisor Settings:
        HyperVisor Load Options: -
        HyperVisor Launch Type:  %%1848 (Off)
        HyperVisor Debugging:    %%1843 (No)
```

NOTE   The event logs described in this section are in the download files for this chapter, in the `Boot Configuration Data Changes.evtx` file.

Each time the operating system starts, BCD options are loaded during the system boot process.

The `Subject` for this event is always `S-1-5-18` (SYSTEM).

The `Load Options` parameter contains additional parameters that were set to the Windows system boot loader in the BCD. Load options can be set using the `bcdedit.exe /set loadoptions` command. In this example the `HELLO_WORLD` load option was specified. It's possible to specify any load option; it just needs to be understandable by the operating system. In this case, the `HELLO_WORLD` option is simply ignored during system boot. It's empty by default, so it has a value of `" "`.

`Advanced Options` controls the behavior of the legacy menu (F8) during system startup. If the `Advanced Options` field has a `Yes` (`%%1842`) value, it means that BCD settings for last boot were set to display the legacy menu (F8). A `Yes` value also means that the F8 button was pressed during the boot process. Advanced options can be set using the `bcdedit /set onetimeadvancedoptions` command. The default for this field is `No`.

The `Configuration Access Policy` parameter controls whether the system uses memory-mapped I/O to access the PCI manufacturer's configuration space or falls back to using the HAL's I/O port access routines. This parameter can be configured using the following command: `bcdedit /set configaccesspolicy`. Possible values are:

- `%%1846:` Default

- `%%1847:` DisallowMmConfig

The `System Event Logging` field shows whether remote event logging is enabled or disabled in the system. This field can have `%%1842` (`Yes`) or `%%1843` (`No`) values. The default value for this field is `No`. It can be configured using the following command: `bcdedit /event`.

The `Kernel Debugging` field shows whether Windows kernel debugging is enabled or disabled. This field can have `%%1842` (`Yes`) or `%%1843` (`No`) values. The default for this field is `No`. It can be configured using the `bcdedit /debug` command.

The `VSM Launch Type` field displays the setting for the Virtual Secure Mode (VSM) feature. VSM isolates `lsass.exe` into a Hyper-V virtual machine/container, which gives it more protection against malicious software or hacking tools. It can have one of the following values (the default is `Off`):

- `%%1848:` Off

- `%%1849:` Auto

The Virtual Secure Mode (VSM) launch type can be configured using the following command: `bcdedit /set vsmlaunchtype`.

The `Test Signing` field specifies whether test-signed kernel-mode code is allowed to be loaded by the operating system. Basically this option allows loading drivers and modules signed by any certificate, not only by trusted certificates. It can have one of the following values (the default is No):

- **%%1843:** No

- **%%1842:** Yes

Test signing can be enabled or disabled using the following command: bcdedit.exe -set testsigning.

The Flight Signing field shows settings for flight-signed executables and drivers. Flight signing certificates are not trusted by default by Windows operating systems and are used internally to sign Insider Preview builds. Enabling this functionality allows your system to trust Windows Insider Preview builds. This field can have one of the following values (the default is No):

- **%%1843:** No

- **%%1842:** Yes

Flight signing can be enabled or disabled using the following command: bcdedit.exe -set flightsigning.

The Disable Integrity Checks field shows whether unsigned drivers are allowed to be loaded during the system boot process. Enabling this feature allows you to install drivers that are not signed by a code signing certificate. It can have one of the following values (the default is No):

- **%%1843:** No

- **%%1842:** Yes

Integrity check enforcement can be enabled or disabled using the bcdedit .exe -set nointegritychecks command.

The HyperVisor Load Options field contains the hypervisor (Hyper-V) load-options, if any of these options are set. It can be configured using the bcdedit /set hypervisorloadoptions command. The default value is -.

The HyperVisor Launch Type field controls the hypervisor (Hyper-V) start mode. The hypervisor can be disabled or enabled with one of the following values (the default is Off):

- **%%1848:** Off

- **%%1849:** Auto

The hypervisor start type can be changed using the following command: bcdedit.exe -set hypervisorlaunchtype.

The HyperVisor Debugging parameter shows hypervisor (Hyper-V) debugging settings. Debugging may be allowed (Yes) or not allowed (No). This functionality can be configured using the following command: bcdedit.exe -set hypervisordebug.

Monitoring Scenarios: Boot Configuration Data

A useful event to monitor related to BCD is shown in Table 10-14.

Table 10-14: Security Events for Boot Configuration Data

SECURITY EVENT	SUBCATEGORY	EVENT TYPE
4826: Boot Configuration Data loaded.	Other Policy Change Events	Audit Success

Any change to BCD settings requires administrative privileges. All BCD settings should be considered as highly sensitive security-related settings. They aren't usually changed during a system's lifetime, with the exceptions of `HyperVisor Launch Type` and `Advanced Options`. These may change in some common scenarios such as when the F8 key is pressed during system startup or a Hyper-V role is installed or uninstalled, but even these changes should be considered highly sensitive.

The changes listed in Table 10-15 should be monitored with highest priority.

Table 10-15: Changes to BCD Settings That Should Be Monitored

FIELD	CONDITION	NOTES
Load Options	Not -	
Advanced Options	%%1842	Yes. Set on critical and high-priority hosts.
Configuration Access Policy	%%1847	DisallowMmConfig
System Event Logging	%%1842	Yes
Kernel Debugging	%%1842	Yes
VSM Launch Type	%%1848 or %%1849	Off or Auto, depends on whether VSM should be enabled on the host.
Test Signing	%%1842	Yes
Flight Signing	%%1842	Yes
Disable Integrity Checks	%%1842	Yes
HyperVisor Load Options	Not -	
HyperVisor Launch Type	%%1848 or %%1849	Off or Auto, depends on whether Hyper-V should be enabled on the host.
HyperVisor Debugging	%%1842	Yes

Logon Rights and User Privileges

Logon rights and user privileges are essential security mechanisms embedded in Microsoft Windows operating systems. Logon rights are designed to allow or limit the ability of accounts to use specific logon methods, such as Interactive logon or Network logon. User privileges control access to the most sensitive system operations, such as shutting down the system or managing the security event log.

In this chapter you will find detailed information about monitoring logon rights and user privileges policy changes, user privileges use, and use of backup and restore privileges.

Logon Rights

As you read in Chapter 4, multiple logon types exist in the Microsoft Windows world. If you review Figure 4-1, you will see that at Step 10 `lsass.exe` verifies user logon rights. Logon rights verification is also performed for other logon types, such as the RemoteInteractive and Network logon types. To allow or deny a specific logon type for an account, there's a set of security group policy settings available on Windows systems for configuration. These settings are located in the `Local Computer Policy\Computer Configuration\Windows Settings\Security Settings\Local Policies\User Right Assignments` group policy path. Table 11-1 contains a list of group policy settings related to user rights and the corresponding logon types for each group policy setting.

Table 11-1: Logon Rights and Related Logon Types

GROUP POLICY SETTING NAME	LOGON RIGHT NAME	LOGON TYPES
Allow log on locally	`SeInteractiveLogonRight`	Interactive
Deny log on locally	`SeDenyInteractiveLogonRight`	Interactive
Access this computer from the network	`SeNetworkLogonRight`	Network
Deny access to this computer from the network	`SeDenyNetworkLogonRight`	Network
Allow log on through Remote Desktop Services	`SeRemoteInteractiveLogonRight`	RemoteInteractive
Deny log on through Remote Desktop Services	`SeDenyRemoteInteractiveLogonRight`	RemoteInteractive
Log on as a batch job	`SeBatchLogonRight`	Batch
Deny log on as a batch job	`SeDenyBatchLogonRight`	Batch
Log on as a service	`SeServiceLogonRight`	Service
Deny log on as a service	`SeDenyServiceLogonRight`	Service

There are two types of logon rights policies:

- **Allow policies:** Allow a specific logon type
- **Deny policies:** Deny a specific logon type

By default, if an account is not listed in the allow policy, it is automatically denied.

Logon Rights Policy Modification

Logon rights group policy settings can be modified manually in the local machine security policy or centrally applied using Active Directory group policy.

Logon Rights Policy Settings - Member Added

Each time a new member is added to one of the group policy settings listed in Table 11-1, the event in Listing 11-1 is generated in the Windows security event log on the machine where policy setting was modified.

Listing 11-1: Event ID 4717: System security access was granted to an account.

```
Task Category: Authentication Policy Change
Keywords: Audit Success
Subject:
     Security ID:          S-1-5-21-1913345275-1711810662-261465553-500
     Account Name:         administrator
     Account Domain:       HQCORP
     Logon ID:             0x381C3
Account Modified:
     Account Name:         S-1-5-21-1913345275-1711810662-261465553-1120
Access Granted:
     Access Right:         SeDenyBatchLogonRight
```

NOTE The event described in Listing 11-1 is available on the book's website, in the `Logon Rights Policy Settings - Member Added.evtx` file.

This event generates for both allow and deny logon group policies. A separate event is generated for each group policy change.

The `Subject` section contains information about the account that added a new member for a logon rights policy.

The `Account Modified` section includes an `Account Name` field that contains the SID of the account or group that was added to the group policy setting.

The `Access Right` field contains the name of the access right group policy setting is related to. See Table 11-1 for a complete list of all logon rights names.

Logon Rights Policy Settings - Member Removed

As is true for logon right granting, the event in Listing 11-2 is triggered in the Windows security event log each time a member is removed from one of the group policy settings listed in Table 11-1.

Listing 11-2: Event ID 4718: System security access was removed from an account.

```
Task Category: Authentication Policy Change
Keywords: Audit Success
Subject:
     Security ID:          S-1-5-21-3212943211-794299840-588279583-500
     Account Name:         Administrator
     Account Domain:       2016SRV
     Logon ID:             0x49CDA
```

```
Account Modified:
      Account Name:           S-1-5-32-555
Access Removed:
      Access Right:           SeRemoteInteractiveLogonRight
```

NOTE The event described in Listing 11-2 is available on the book's website, in the `Logon Rights Policy Settings - Member Removed.evtx` file.

This event generates for both allow and deny logon group policy settings. A separate event is generated for each group policy setting change.

The `Subject` section contains information about the account that removed a member from a logon right policy setting.

The `Account Modified` section includes the `Account Name` field that contains the SID of the member that was removed from the group policy setting. Both groups and accounts can be members.

The `Access Right` field contains the name of the logon right that was removed from the account or group. See Table 11.1 for a complete list of all logon rights names.

Unsuccessful Logons Due to Lack of Logon Rights

Every time a user is not able to log on due to lack of specific logon rights, when a specific logon right is denied to the user, a 4625 logon failure event is generated on the host with a failure status of `0xC000015B`. See Chapter 4 for more details about this type of unsuccessful logon attempt.

User Privileges

The list in this section presents the user privileges, also called user rights, that can be assigned to an account's logon session. These rights are required to perform specific operations, such as shutting down the machine or changing the operating system's time zone. User rights were implemented to bring additional control for most sensitive operations accounts may perform. They can be controlled using local group policy settings located at the `Local Computer Policy\Computer Configuration\Windows Settings\Security Settings\Local Policies\User Right Assignments` group policy path. By default, if an account or group is not listed under a specific policy setting, it does not have a specific user privilege.

- **Replace a process-level token (SeAssignPrimaryTokenPrivilege)**

  `SeAssignPrimaryTokenPrivilege` is required to assign the primary token of a process.

  With this privilege, the user can initiate a process to replace the default token associated with a started sub-process.

▪ **Generate security audits (SeAuditPrivilege)**

With this privilege, the user can register event providers and add entries to the security event log.

▪ **Back up files and directories (SeBackupPrivilege)**

`SeBackupPrivilege` is required to perform backup operations.

With this privilege, the user can bypass file and directory, registry keys, and other persistent securable object permissions for the purpose of backing up the system.

This privilege causes the system to grant Read access to any persistent securable object, regardless of the access control list (ACL) specified for the object. Any access request other than Read is still evaluated with the DACL. The following access rights are granted if this privilege is held:

▪ `READ_CONTROL`

▪ `ACCESS_SYSTEM_SECURITY`

▪ `FILE_GENERIC_READ`

▪ `FILE_TRAVERSE`

▪ **Bypass traverse checking (SeChangeNotifyPrivilege)**

`SeChangeNotifyPrivilege` is required to receive notifications of changes to files or directories. This privilege also causes the system to skip all traversal access checks.

With this privilege, the user can traverse directory trees even though the user may not have permissions on the traversed directory. This privilege does not allow the user to list the contents of a directory, only to traverse directories. The `Everyone` security principal is a member of this policy setting by default.

▪ **Create global objects (SeCreateGlobalPrivilege)**

`SeCreateGlobalPrivilege` is required to create named file mapping objects in the global namespace during a Terminal Services sessions.

▪ **Create a pagefile (SeCreatePagefilePrivilege)**

With this privilege, the user can create and change the size of a system pagefile.

▪ **Create permanent shared objects (SeCreatePermanentPrivilege)**

`SeCreatePermanentPrivilege` is required to create a permanent object.

This privilege is useful to kernel-mode components that extend the object namespace. Components that are running in kernel mode already have this privilege inherently; it is not necessary to assign them the privilege.

- **Create symbolic links (SeCreateSymbolicLinkPrivilege)**

  SeCreateSymbolicLinkPrivilege is required to create symbolic links.

- **Create a token object (SeCreateTokenPrivilege)**

  SeCreateTokenPrivilege allows a process to create a token that it can then use to get access to any local resources when the process uses NtCreateToken() or other token-creation APIs.

- **Debug programs (SeDebugPrivilege)**

  SeDebugPrivilege is required to debug and adjust the memory of a process owned by another account.

  With this privilege, the user can attach a debugger to any process or to the kernel. This user right provides complete access to sensitive and critical operating system components.

- **Enable computer and user accounts to be trusted for delegation (SeEnableDelegationPrivilege)**

  SeEnableDelegationPrivilege is required to mark user and computer accounts as trusted for delegation.

  With this privilege, the user can set the "Trusted for Delegation" setting on a user or computer object in Active Directory.

  This privilege is valid only on domain controllers.

- **Impersonate a client after authentication (SeImpersonatePrivilege)**

  With this privilege, the user can impersonate other accounts.

- **Increase scheduling priority (SeIncreaseBasePriorityPrivilege)**

  This privilege is required to increase the base (execution) priority of a process.

  A user with this privilege can, for example, change the scheduling priority of a process through the Task Manager user interface.

- **Adjust memory quotas for a process (SeIncreaseQuotaPrivilege)**

  This privilege is required to increase the quota assigned to a process.

  With this privilege, the user can change the maximum memory that can be consumed by a process.

- **Increase a process working set (SeIncreaseWorkingSetPrivilege)**

  SeIncreaseWorkingSetPrivilege is required to allocate more memory for applications that run in the context of users.

- **Load and unload device drivers (SeLoadDriverPrivilege)**

  SeLoadDriverPrivilege is required to load or unload a device driver.

With this privilege, the user can dynamically load and unload device drivers or other code in to kernel mode. This user right does not apply to Plug and Play device drivers.

▪ **Lock pages in memory (SeLockMemoryPrivilege)**

This privilege is required to lock physical pages in memory.

With this privilege, the user can use a process to keep data in physical memory, which prevents the system from paging the data to virtual memory on disk.

▪ **Add workstations to domain (SeMachineAccountPrivilege)**

With this privilege, the user can create a computer account.

This privilege is valid only on domain controllers.

▪ **Perform volume maintenance tasks (SeManageVolumePrivilege)**

This privilege is required to run maintenance tasks on a volume, such as defragmentation.

▪ **Profile single process (SeProfileSingleProcessPrivilege)**

`SeProfileSingleProcessPrivilege` is required to gather profiling information for a single process.

With this privilege, the user can use performance monitoring tools to monitor the performance of non-system processes.

▪ **Modify an object label (SeRelabelPrivilege)**

This privilege is required to modify the mandatory integrity level of an object.

▪ **Force shutdown from a remote system (SeRemoteShutdownPrivilege)**

`SeRemoteShutdownPrivilege` is required to shut down a system from remote machine.

▪ **Restore files and directories (SeRestorePrivilege)**

This privilege is required to perform restore operations. It causes the system to grant Write access permissions to any persistent securable object, such as file or registry key, regardless of the DACL specified for the object. Any access request other than Write is still evaluated with the DACL. Additionally, this privilege enables account to change an object's owner. The following access permissions are granted if this privilege is held:

▪ `WRITE_DAC`

▪ `WRITE_OWNER`

▪ `ACCESS_SYSTEM_SECURITY`

▪ `FILE_GENERIC_WRITE`

- `FILE_ADD_FILE`
- `FILE_ADD_SUBDIRECTORY`
- `DELETE`

■ **Manage auditing and security log (SeSecurityPrivilege)**

`SeSecurityPrivilege` is required to perform a number of security-related functions related to security event log, such as changing event log's settings and clearing it.

With this privilege, the user can view and modify object access auditing options (SACL) for individual securable objects, such as files, Active Directory objects, and registry keys.

■ **Shut down the system (SeShutdownPrivilege)**

This privilege is required to shut down a system locally.

■ **Synchronize directory service data (SeSyncAgentPrivilege)**

With this privilege, the user can synchronize Active Directory service data. This is also known as Active Directory replication.

This privilege is valid only on domain controllers.

■ **Modify firmware environment values (SeSystemEnvironmentPrivilege)**

This right is needed to modify the environmental/memory variables in Windows.

■ **Profile system performance (SeSystemProfilePrivilege)**

`SeSystemProfilePrivilege` is required to gather profiling information for the entire system.

With this privilege, the user can use performance monitoring tools, such as Performance Monitor, to monitor the performance of system processes.

■ **Change the system time (SeSystemtimePrivilege)**

`SeSystemtimePrivilege` is required to modify the system time.

With this privilege, the user can change the time and date on the internal clock of the computer.

■ **Take ownership of files or other objects (SeTakeOwnershipPrivilege)**

This privilege is required to take ownership of an object without being granted "Take ownership" access.

With this privilege, the user can take ownership of any securable object in the system, including Active Directory objects, files and folders, printers, registry keys, processes, and threads.

- **Act as part of the operating system (SeTcbPrivilege)**

  This privilege identifies its holder as part of the trusted computer base.

  This user right allows a process to impersonate any user without authentication.

- **Change the time zone (SeTimeZonePrivilege)**

  `SeTimeZonePrivilege` is required to adjust the time zone associated with the computer's internal clock.

- **Access Credential Manager as a trusted caller (SeTrustedCredMan-AccessPrivilege)**

  `SeTrustedCredManAccessPrivilege` is required to perform backup and restore operations for Windows Credential Manager.

- **Remove computer from docking station (SeUndockPrivilege)**

  This privilege is required to undock a laptop.

  It is needed to allow a laptop to change from the Docked to the Undocked hardware profile.

- **No user right policy setting associated with this privilege (SeUnsolicitedInputPrivilege)**

  `SeUnsolicitedInputPrivilege` is required to read unsolicited input from a terminal device.

User Privileges Policy Modification

User privileges group policy settings can be modified manually in the local machine security policy or centrally applied using Active Directory group policy.

User Privileges Policy Settings - Member Added

If a new member was added to one of the user privilege group policy settings, the event in Listing 11-3 is generated in the Windows security event log on the machine on which the policy was modified.

Listing 11-3: Event ID 4704: A user right was assigned.

```
Task Category: Authorization Policy Change
Keywords: Audit Success
Subject:
      Security ID:        S-1-5-21-3212943211-794299840-588279583-500
      Account Name:       Administrator
      Account Domain:     2016SRV
      Logon ID:           0x49CDA
```

```
Target Account:
        Account Name:       S-1-5-21-3212943211-794299840-588279583-1002
New Right:
        User Right:         SeTimeZonePrivilege
```

NOTE The event described in Listing 11-3 is available on the book's website, in the `User Privileges Policy Settings - Member Added.evtx` **file.**

A separate event is generated for each group policy setting change.

This event shows which account modified the policy (`Subject`), which policy (`User Right`) was changed, and which member was added to the policy (`Target Account`).

User Privileges Policy Settings - Member Removed

When a member is removed from one of the user privilege group policy settings, the event Listing 11-4 is generated in the Windows security event log on the machine on which the policy was modified.

Listing 11-4: Event ID 4705: A user right was removed.

```
Task Category: Authorization Policy Change
Keywords: Audit Success
Subject:
        Security ID:        S-1-5-21-3212943211-794299840-588279583-500
        Account Name:       Administrator
        Account Domain:     2016SRV
        Logon ID:           0x49CDA
Target Account:
        Account Name:       S-1-5-21-3212943211-794299840-588279583-1002
New Right:
        User Right:         SeTimeZonePrivilege
```

NOTE The event described in Listing 11-4 is available on the book's website, in the `User Privileges Policy Settings - Member Removed.evtx` **file.**

A separate event is generated for each group policy setting change.

This event shows which account modified the policy setting (`Subject`), which setting (`User Right`) was changed and which member was removed from the policy (`Target Account`).

Special User Privileges Assigned at Logon Time

As was discussed in Chapter 4, during account logon an account's user privileges are added to the logon session's token. There is a list of so-called special privileges, which are considered the most important and critical to monitor. This list is built into the Windows operating system. Table 11-2 contains a list of special privileges.

Table 11-2: Special User Privileges

PRIVILEGE NAME	GROUP POLICY SETTING NAME
SeTcbPrivilege	Act as part of the operating system
SeBackupPrivilege	Back up files and directories
SeCreateTokenPrivilege	Create a token object
SeDebugPrivilege	Debug programs
SeEnableDelegationPrivilege	Enable computer and user accounts to be trusted for delegation
SeAuditPrivilege	Generate security audits
SeImpersonatePrivilege	Impersonate a client after authentication
SeLoadDriverPrivilege	Load and unload device drivers
SeSecurityPrivilege	Manage auditing and security log
SeSystemEnvironmentPrivilege	Modify firmware environment values
SeAssignPrimaryTokenPrivilege	Replace a process-level token
SeRestorePrivilege	Restore files and directories
SeTakeOwnershipPrivilege	Take ownership of files or other objects

Each time one or more of the special privileges are assigned to an account's logon session, the event in Listing 11-5 is generated in the Windows security event log.

Listing 11-5: Event ID 4672: Special privileges assigned to new logon.

```
Task Category: Special Logon
Keywords: Audit Success
Subject:
        Security ID:            S-1-5-21-3212943211-794299840-588279583-500
        Account Name:           Administrator
        Account Domain:         2016SRV
        Logon ID:               0x660898
```

```
Privileges:        SeSecurityPrivilege
                   SeTakeOwnershipPrivilege
                   SeLoadDriverPrivilege
                   SeBackupPrivilege
                   SeRestorePrivilege
                   SeDebugPrivilege
                   SeSystemEnvironmentPrivilege
                   SeEnableDelegationPrivilege
                   SeImpersonatePrivilege
                   SeDelegateSessionUserImpersonatePrivilege
```

NOTE The event described Listing 11-5 is available on the book's website, in the `Special User Privileges Assigned at Logon Time.evtx` **file.**

The `Subject` section contains information about the account being logged in. The `Privileges` section contains a list of special privileges assigned to the logon session.

Logon Session User Privileges Operations

All logon session privileges in the session's token are disabled by default after the session is created. In order to use any user privilege, it should be first enabled using the `AdjustPrivilegesToken` function. If a privilege or number of privileges were enabled for a specific logon session, the event in Listing 11-6 is generated in the Windows security event log.

Listing 11-6: Event ID 4703: A token right was adjusted.

```
Task Category: Token Right Adjusted Events
Keywords: Audit Success
Subject:
        Security ID:            S-1-5-21-3212943211-794299840-588279583-500
        Account Name:           Administrator
        Account Domain:         2016SRV
        Logon ID:               0x49CDA
Target Account:
        Security ID:            S-1-0-0
        Account Name:           Administrator
        Account Domain:         2016SRV
        Logon ID:               0x49CDA
Process Information:
        Process ID:             0x10f4
        Process Name:           C:\Windows\System32\cleanmgr.exe
Enabled Privileges:

                                SeBackupPrivilege
Disabled Privileges:

                                -
```

NOTE The event described Listing 11-6 is available on the book's website, in the `A Token Right Was Adjusted.evtx` file.

The `Subject` section contains information about the account that invoked `AdjustPrivilegesToken` function.

The `Target Account` section contains information about the account for which session token privileges were enabled. The `Security ID` field contains the SID of that account. If the target account is the same as `Subject`, then this field will have a value of `S-1-0-0` (NULL SID).

The `Process Information` section contains information about the `Process Name` and `Process ID` for the process that invoked the `AdjustPrivilegesToken` function.

The `Enabled Privileges` section contains a list of enabled privileges.

After a privilege or privileges are enabled, it is up to the application to disable them after they're used. In this case the same 4703 event will be generated, but the `Enabled Privileges` section will be empty and the `Disabled Privileges` section will contain a list of disabled user privileges.

Privilege Use

When a privilege is enabled in the session token it does not mean it will be used. Depending on the operation performed, privilege use actions are divided into two categories:

- Privileged service called
- Operation performed on a privileged object

Successful Call of a Privileged Service

This category contains calls to functions and services that require user privileges to be invoked. One of the common examples is the `LsaRegisterLogonProcess` function, which was discussed in Chapter 4. To call this function, an account must have the `SeTcbPrivilege` user privilege.

For all successful privileged function and service calls, a 4673 event is generated in the Windows security event log. When a user privilege that is required to call a service or function is a special privilege (see Table 11-2), a 4673 event from the "Audit sensitive privilege use" subcategory is generated. For all non-special privileges, a 4673 event from the "Audit non sensitive privilege use" subcategory is generated.

Listing 11-7 shows an example of an `LsaRegisterLogonProcess` function call that requires the `SeTcbPrivilege` privilege.

Listing 11-7: Event ID 4673: A privileged service was called.

```
Task Category: Sensitive Privilege Use
Keywords: Audit Success
Subject:
        Security ID:            S-1-5-18
        Account Name:           2016SRV$
        Account Domain:         HQCORP
        Logon ID:               0x3E7
Service:
        Server:                 NT Local Security Authority /
                                    Authentication Service
        Service Name:           LsaRegisterLogonProcess()
Process:
        Process ID:             0x30c
        Process Name:           C:\Windows\System32\lsass.exe
Service Request Information:
        Privileges:             SeTcbPrivilege
```

NOTE The event described Listing 11-7 is available on the book's website, in the `Successful Call of a Privileged Service.evtx` **file.**

The `Subject` section contains information about the account that invoked a function or service.

The `Server` field contains the general category the called function or service belongs to.

The `Service Name` field contains the name of the function or service being called. This field might be empty or it might contain the same value as the `Server` field. It is not always clear which exact function or service was called.

The `Process` section contains information about the process that called the function or service.

The `Privileges` field contains the privilege or list of privileges used to call the function or service.

Unsuccessful Call of a Privileged Service

For unsuccessful service or function calls, the same 4673 event is generated, but it will be an `Audit Failure` event. There is no information in the event regarding why the call failed. You can see an example of an unsuccessful service call event in the `Unsuccessful Call of a Privileged Service.evtx` file in the download material for this chapter.

Successful Operation with a Privileged Object

When an operation is performed on an object that requires specific user rights, such as a change of owner for a file or registry key that requires the `SeTakeOwnershipPrivilege` privilege, a 4674 event is generated in the Windows security event log.

When a user privilege required for operation is a special privilege (see Table 11-2), a 4674 event from the "Audit sensitive privilege use" subcategory is generated. For all non-special privileges, a 4674 event from the "Audit non sensitive privilege use" subcategory is generated.

Listing 11-8 is an example of a 4674 event generated when a file properties are opened using Windows File Explorer.

Listing 11-8: Event ID 4674: An operation was attempted on a privileged object.

```
Task Category: Sensitive Privilege Use
Keywords: Audit Success
Subject:
        Security ID:            S-1-5-21-3212943211-794299840-588279583-500
        Account Name:           Administrator
        Account Domain:         2016SRV
        Logon ID:               0x49CDA
Object:
        Object Server:          Security
        Object Type:            File
        Object Name:            C:\icacls\WindowsServer2003.
                                   WindowsXP-KB943043-x64-ENU.exe
        Object Handle:          0x3e8
Process Information:
        Process ID:             0xd1c
        Process Name:           C:\Windows\System32\dllhost.exe
Requested Operation:
        Desired Access:         %%1538 (READ_CONTROL)
                                %%1539 (WRITE_DAC)
                                %%1540 (WRITE_OWNER)
                                %%1542 (ACCESS_SYS_SEC)
        Privileges:             SeSecurityPrivilege
                                SeTakeOwnershipPrivilege
```

NOTE The event described Listing 11-8 is available on the book's website, in the `Successful Operation With Privileged Object.evtx` **file.**

This event does not mean that all requested accesses were really used. This event shows you only that privileges were used to request specific access.

Usually two 4674 events are generated for each operation: one is the same as this 4674 event, and the other is a 4674 event with an access mask in decimal format instead of a list of accesses.

The Subject section contains information about the account that performed an operation on an object.

The Object section contains information about the object on which an operation was performed. The Object Type, Object Name, and Object Handle fields are optional. In this example, you can see that the target object is C:\icacls\ WindowsServer2003.WindowsXP-KB943043-x64-ENU.exe with an open handle ID 0x3e8.

The Object Server field may have, but is not limited to, one of the following values:

- Security
- Security Account Manager
- NT Local Security Authority / Authentication Service
- SC Manager
- Win32 SystemShutdown module
- LSA

The Object Type field may have, but is not limited to, one of the following values:

FilterCommunicationPort	Controller	Profile
Key	Job	ALPC Port
Event	Type	Section
EventPair	SymbolicLink	Desktop
WaitablePort	Port	Semaphore
Timer	File	WindowStation
Driver	WmiGuid	KeyedEvent
Callback	FilterConnectionPort	Adapter
Device	Token	DebugObject
IoCompletion	Process	SC_MANAGER OBJECT.

The Process Information section contains information about a process that was used to perform an operation on an object.

The Desired Access field contains a list of accesses requested during an operation. See Chapter 13 for more information about file access types. This field also can contain a decimal access mask instead of a list of accesses.

The `Privileges` field contains the privilege or list of privileges that were used during the operation.

Unsuccessful Operation with a Privileged Object

For an unsuccessful operation with a privileged object, the same 4674 event is generated as shown in the previous section, but it will be an `Audit Failure` event. There is no information in the event regarding why the operation failed.

Backup and Restore Privilege Use Auditing

The backup (`SeBackupPrivilege`) and restore (`SeRestorePrivilege`) privilege audit has a dedicated group policy setting to configure in case you want to track use of these privileges. The full path and the name of the group policy setting is `Local Computer Policy\Computer Configuration\Windows Settings\ Security Settings\Local Policies\Security Options\Audit: Audit the use of Backup and Restore privilege`. It is disabled by default.

The `FullPrivilegeAuditing` registry key value located under the `HKLM\ System\CurrentControlSet\Control\Lsa` registry key is associated with backup and restore privilege use auditing group policy setting discussed previously.

The reason backup and restore privilege auditing is controlled separately is that during system backup or restore procedures these activities generate thousands of events and may overwrite all events in the security event log. Even when there is no backup process running, you will see many routine uses of the backup privilege.

Another problem with backup and restore privilege auditing is that 4674 events related to these operations do not always contain information about which object was backed up or restored.

To enable backup and restore privilege auditing, the group policy just mentioned should be enabled and, also, the "Audit Sensitive Privilege Use" auditing subcategory should be enabled for success, failure, or both.

Listing 11-9 is an example of a 4674 event related to `SeBackupPrivilege` use.

Listing 11-9: Event ID 4674: An operation was attempted on a privileged object.

```
Task Category: Sensitive Privilege Use
Keywords: Audit Success
Subject:
        Security ID:        S-1-5-21-3212943211-794299840-588279583-500
        Account Name:       Administrator
        Account Domain:     2016SRV
        Logon ID:           0x49CDA
```

```
Object:
      Object Server:          Security
      Object Type:            -
      Object Name:            -
      Object Handle:          0xd18
Process Information:
      Process ID:             0xe0c
      Process Name:           C:\Windows\System32\mmc.exe
Requested Operation:
      Desired Access:         1048577
      Privileges:             SeBackupPrivilege
```

NOTE The event described Listing 11-8 is available on the book's website, in the `Backup and Restore Privilege Use Auditing.evtx` **file.**

As you can see, the `Object Type` and `Object Name` fields are empty. This information is not always present in the 4674 event.

Windows Applications

There are multiple types of Windows applications: console, desktop, service, and so on. Applications can be portable, which don't require installation, or installable, which need to be installed and registered in the local Windows application registry. Applications are almost always involved in cybersecurity incidents—for example, malware is often executable, malicious macros run in Microsoft Word, and phishing e-mail can be received by Microsoft Outlook.

It is important to monitor use of applications on the host. You should monitor activities such as application installation, removal, execution, application crashes, and application blocking events by AppLocker. In this chapter you will find detailed information about monitoring these scenarios and more.

New Application Installation

Depending on how software installation is designed, it may register an application in the Windows software manager database. The software manager is designed to provide users an easy-to-use interface to remove, modify, and repair installed applications, components, and updates.

In Windows Server 2016 and Windows 10, the software manager can be invoked using Programs and Features item in Control Panel or using the command `rundll32.exe shell32.dll,Control_RunDLL appwiz.cpl`. Figure 12-1 shows the Windows Server 2016 software manager.

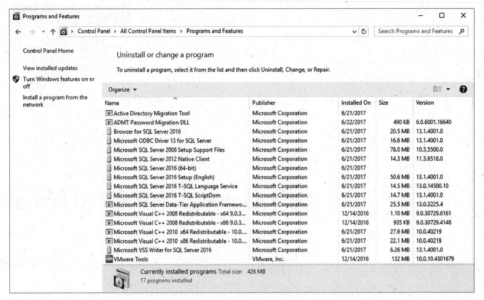

Figure 12-1: Windows Server 2016 software manager

The software manager records are stored in the following registry keys:

- x86 applications: `HKEY_LOCAL_MACHINE\SOFTWARE\Microsoft\Windows\CurrentVersion\Uninstall`

- x64 applications: `HKEY_LOCAL_MACHINE\SOFTWARE\Wow6432Node\Microsoft\Windows\CurrentVersion\Uninstall`

These registry keys contain nested keys for each application. Depending on the method used to install an application, these keys are usually named using one of the following methods:

- **Application product code (GUID) in figure brackets:** A 128-bit integer number, converted to hexadecimal format, which uniquely identifies an application. A GUID is globally unique, not only within a specific host. GUIDs are usually assigned to programs installed using Windows Installer from `.msi` packages. Other installers, such as InstallShield, may also use GUIDs. An example of a GUID is `{976C3D92-0DEC-37A6-A870-FF4FC18CD029}`.

- **Application name or identification string:** An application item can also have any name that developers put into an application installation program.

Figure 12-2 shows an example of an application uninstall item from one of the software manager's registry keys:

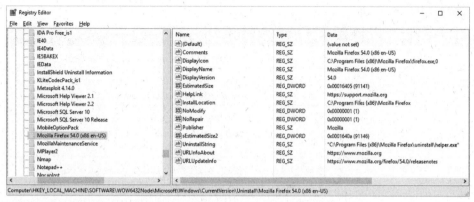

Figure 12-2: Windows software manager application uninstall item

The most common fields of an application uninstall item are listed in Table 12-1.

Table 12-1: Most Common Application Uninstall Items

REGISTRY VALUE	TYPE	DESCRIPTION
Comments	REG_SZ	Text displayed in the `Comments` section of the application item in the software manager.
DisplayIcon	REG_SZ	Path to the icon that is displayed for an uninstall item in the software manager.
DisplayName	REG_SZ	Name of the item; how it will be displayed in the software manager.
DisplayVersion	REG_SZ	Text displayed in the `Product version` section of the application item in the software manager.
EstimatedSize	REG_DWORD	The size of the installed application in kilobytes. This information is displayed in the `Size` section of the application item in the software manager.
HelpLink	REG_SZ	URL displayed in the `Help link` of the application item in the software manager.
InstallLocation	REG_SZ	Contains a path where an application's files are located.
NoElevateOnModify	REG_DWORD	Allow (0) or deny (1) use of elevated token for modification action.
NoModify	REG_DWORD	Allow (0) or deny (1) modification action.
NoRepair	REG_DWORD	Allow (0) or deny (1) repair action.

Continues

Table 12-1 (*continued*)

REGISTRY VALUE	TYPE	DESCRIPTION
NoRemove	REG_DWORD	Allow (0) or deny (1) uninstall action.
Publisher	REG_SZ	Value displayed in the `Publisher` column of the application item in the software manager.
UninstallString	REG_SZ	Path to a command that is executed if the `Uninstall` option is selected for an application item.
ModifyPath	REG_SZ	Path to a command that is executed if the `Change` option is selected for an application item.
URLInfoAbout	REG_SZ	URL displayed in the `Support link` section of the application item in the software manager.
URLUpdateInfo	REG_SZ	URL displayed in the `Update information` section of the application item in the software manager.
WindowsInstaller	REG_DWORD	Set to 1 if an application was installed using Windows Installer.

Some applications might not set all the items listed in Table 12-1, but `DisplayName` and `UninstallString` values must be present.

Application Installation Using Windows Installer

Windows Installer application installations are easier to monitor than custombuilt installers, because they leave more logs in the Windows event log.

Listing 12-1 is an example of an event that is recorded in Windows security event log if an application was installed using Windows Installer.

Listing 12-1: Event ID 4688: A new process has been created.

```
Event Log: Security
Task Category: Process Creation
Keywords: Audit Success
Creator Subject:
    Security ID:           S-1-5-21-1913345275-1711810662-261465553-500
    Account Name:          Administrator
    Account Domain:        HQCORP
    Logon ID:              0x4A7B4
Target Subject:
    Security ID:           S-1-0-0
    Account Name:          -
    Account Domain:        -
    Logon ID:              0x0
```

```
Process Information:
    New Process ID:        0xb2c
    New Process Name:      C:\Windows\System32\msiexec.exe
    Token Elevation Type:  %%1936 (TokenElevationTypeDefault)
    Mandatory Label:       S-1-16-12288 (Mandatory Label\
                               High Mandatory Level)
    Creator Process ID:    0x1054
    Creator Process Name:  C:\Windows\explorer.exe
    Process Command Line:  "C:\Windows\System32\msiexec.exe" /i
                               "C:\Users\Administrator\Desktop\
                                           LogParser.msi"
```

NOTE The event described in Listing 12-1 is available on the book's website, in the `Application Installation Using Windows Installer - Security Log.evtx` **file.**

You will find more information about process creation events later in this chapter, but from this event you should note that the `"C:\Windows\System32\msiexec.exe" /i "C:\Users\Administrator\Desktop\LogParser.msi"` command was executed by the `Administrator` account (`Account Name`) using `C:\Windows\explorer.exe` as the initiating process.

`Token Elevation Type %%1936 (TokenElevationTypeDefault)` informs you that the full token, instead of a limited or elevated token, was used without using the User Account Control (UAC) mechanism. That is correct, because UAC is usually disabled by default for the built-in Administrator account (RID 500). You will find more information about token types in the "Successful Process Creation" section of this chapter.

Event 1040 (Listing 12-2) in the Application event log shows the beginning of a Windows Installer transaction. A transaction can be any action, such as package installation, modification, or removal. It only informs you that a transaction is started. This event is generated right after Windows Installer executes an MSI package.

Listing 12-2: Event ID 1040: Beginning a Windows Installer transaction

```
Event Log: Application
Source: MsiInstaller
Beginning a Windows Installer transaction: C:\Users\Administrator\
    Desktop\LogParser.msi. Client Process Id: 2860.

Param 1: C:\Users\Administrator\Desktop\LogParser.msi
Param 2: 2860
```

NOTE The events described in Listings 12-2, 12-3, and 12-4 are available on the book's website, in the `Application Installation Using Windows Installer - Application Log.evtx` **file.**

`Param 1` contains a value that was passed to the transaction. This example shows information about an installation transaction based on a 4688 event in the security event log. You can see that `Param 1` shows a parameter that was passed to `msiexec.exe /i`.

`Param 2` contains the process ID value for the new installation process.

Event 11707 (Listing 12-3) informs you that a specific application (`Param 1`) was successfully installed.

Listing 12-3: Event ID 11707: Installation completed successfully.

```
Event Log: Application
Source: MsiInstaller
Product: Log Parser 2.2 -- Installation completed successfully

Param 1: Product: Log Parser 2.2 -- Installation completed successfully.
Param 7: 7B34414332333137382D454542432D344241462D384343302D4142313543383
   839374143397D
```

`Param 7` contains the hexadecimal representation of a product GUID. You need to convert the hexadecimal value to ASCII text. In this example the value `7B34414332333137382D454542432D344241462D384343302D41423135433838393` `74143397D` represents a GUID of `{4AC23178-EEBC-4BAF-8CC0-AB15C8897AC9}`, which is a GUID of Log Parser 2.2 application.

The event in Listing 12-4 is usually the final event after a new product is installed by Windows Installer.

Listing 12-4: Event ID 1033: Windows Installer installed the product.

```
Event Log: Application
Source: MsiInstaller
Windows Installer installed the product. Product Name: Log Parser 2.2.
Product Version: 2.2.10. Product Language: 1033. Manufacturer: Microsoft
 Corporation. Installation success or error status: 0.

Param 1: Log Parser 2.2
Param 2: 2.2.10
Param 3: 1033
Param 4: 0
Param 5: Microsoft Corporation
Param 7: 7B34414332333137382D454542432D344241462D384343302D414231354338
3839374143397D30303030306133335383565343961613032303435626461363231636533
3864306164376364303030303030393034
```

It contains the following parameters:

- `Param 1`: Application name.
- `Param 2`: Application version.
- `Param 3`: Application locale ID. You can find locale ID value numbers on the official Microsoft sites.

- Param 4: Installation status. You can find Windows Installer status codes value numbers on the official Microsoft sites.

- Param 5: Publisher name.

- Param 6: Does not exist.

- Param 7: The first 61 characters of the value are the hexadecimal representation of a product GUID. You need to convert hexadecimal values to ASCII text to get a GUID value.

Application Removal Using Windows Installer

Windows Installer has /x and /I options, which are usually used to invoke the application uninstall procedure. These options should be followed by the product GUID, for example: MsiExec.exe /X{976C3D92-0DEC-37A6-A870-FF4FC18CD029}.

All items in the software manager installed by Windows Installer usually have the MsiExec.exe /X{GUID} command as the UninstallString registry value.

Listings 12-5, 12-6, and 12-7 are examples of events recorded in the Application event log when an application is uninstalled using Windows Installer.

NOTE The events described in Listings 12-5, 12-6 and 12-7 are available on the book's website, in the Application Removal Using Windows Installer - Application Log.evtx file.

The first event (Listing 12-5) shows the beginning of a Windows Installer transaction.

Listing 12-5: Event ID 1040: Beginning a Windows Installer transaction.

```
Event Log: Application
Source: MsiInstaller
Beginning a Windows Installer transaction: {4AC23178-EEBC-4BAF-8CC0-
   AB15C8897AC9}. Client Process Id: 4180.

Param 1: {4AC23178-EEBC-4BAF-8CC0-AB15C8897AC9}
Param 2: 4180
```

As discussed for application installation in the previous section, there is no information in this event about which transaction, such as installation, removal, or repair, was started, only about the product GUID passed to the transaction.

Listing 12-6 shows the same event as the 11707 event discussed in Listing 12-3, except that it shows you that the product was removed instead of installed.

Listing 12-6: Event ID 11724: Removal completed successfully.

```
Event Log: Application
Source: MsiInstaller
Product: Log Parser 2.2 -- Removal completed successfully.
```

```
Param 1: Product: Log Parser 2.2 -- Removal completed successfully.
Param 7: 7B34414332333137382D454542432D344241462D384343302D4142313543383
   839374143397D
```

The last event (Listing 12-7) shows more information about the uninstalled product and has the same schema as the 1033 event discussed in Listing 12-4.

Listing 12-7: Event ID 1034: Windows Installer removed the product.

```
Event Log: Application
Source: MsiInstaller
Windows Installer removed the product. Product Name: Log Parser 2.2.
   Product Version: 2.2.10. Product Language: 1033. Manufacturer:
   Microsoft Corporation. Removal success or error status: 0.
Param 1: Log Parser 2.2
Param 2: 2.2.10
Param 3: 1033
Param 4: 0
Param 5: Microsoft Corporation
Param 7: 7B34414332333137382D454542432D344241462D384343302D4142313543383
   839374143397D30303030306133353835653439616130323034356264613631636533
   386430616437636430303030303030393034
```

Application Installation Using Other Methods

Unfortunately, it can be very hard to detect when a new application is installed in the system, because of the different ways an installation can be performed. There might be a lot of noise generated by application installation, such as when a new service is installed in the system, a new registry key is added to the software manager registry, a named pipe is created, and so on. On the other hand, software might just copy some files to a folder and this is almost impossible to detect.

In this section you will learn about some methods you can use to detect when a new application is installed that doesn't use Windows Installer.

Application Installation - Process Creation

Each software installation should be invoked deliberately and with appropriate authorization. Usually software installation is a process, executed by a user account. Listing 12-8 is an example of a process creation event for a software installation package.

Listing 12-8: Event ID 4688: A new process has been created.

```
Task Category: Process Creation
Keywords: Audit Success
Creator Subject:
      Security ID:            S-1-5-21-1913345275-1711810662-261465553-500
      Account Name:           Administrator
      Account Domain:         HQCORP
      Logon ID:               0x4A7B4
Target Subject:
      Security ID:            S-1-0-0
      Account Name:           -
      Account Domain:         -
      Logon ID:               0x0
Process Information:
      New Process ID:         0xdc4
      New Process Name:       C:\Users\Administrator\Desktop\TMACv6.0.7
                                                           _Setup.exe

      Token Elevation Type:   %%1936 (TokenElevationTypeDefault (1))
      Mandatory Label:        S-1-16-12288 (Mandatory Label\High
                                                 Mandatory Level)
      Creator Process ID:     0x1054
      Creator Process Name:   C:\Windows\explorer.exe
      Process Command Line:   "C:\Users\Administrator\Desktop\TMACv6.0.7
                                                           _Setup.exe"
```

NOTE The event described in Listing 12-8 is available on the book's website, in the `Application Installation - Process Creation.evtx` file.

This event doesn't provide many indicators to tell you that this specific process creation event is a software installation process.

One indication is that software installation processes usually have a `High Mandatory Level` `Mandatory Label`. But that is not always the case. Software installed in the user's own security context (a Google Chrome browser install, for example) will have a `Medium Mandatory Level`. Later in this chapter you will find more information about integrity level labels.

Another indicator of software installation in a 4688 event might be specific substrings such as `setup`, `installer`, or version numbers (`6.0.7` in this case) in the `New Process Name` field.

Also, as mentioned previously, most legitimate software installations are invoked by user accounts. It is a good idea to additionally verify all installations run by built-in security principals, such as SYSTEM, or run by service accounts to find nonlegitimate or potentially malicious software installations.

Application Installation - Software Registry Keys

An application installer may add information into the `Software` registry hive. This may be used to monitor new application installations.

Auditing settings (SACL) should be configured for both 64-bit and 32-bit application registry keys:

- `HKEY_LOCAL_MACHINE\SOFTWARE\Microsoft\Windows\CurrentVersion\Uninstall`

- `HKEY_LOCAL_MACHINE\SOFTWARE\Wow6432Node\Microsoft\Windows\CurrentVersion\Uninstall`

Figure 12-3 shows the access list entry (ACE) that should be added to both of these registry key SACLs in order to monitor new registry key creation operations.

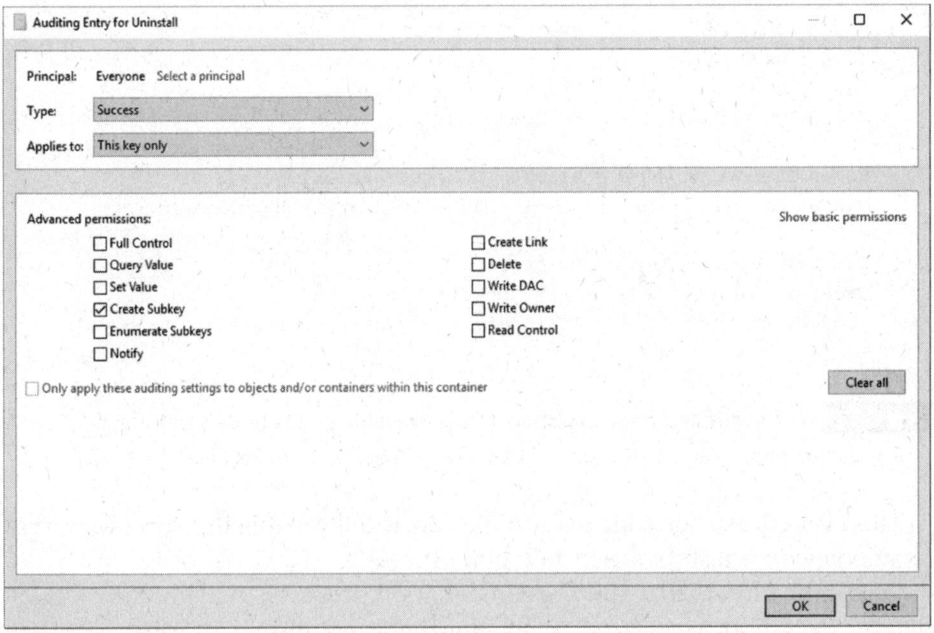

Figure 12-3: Registry auditing settings for new program installation monitoring

In Chapter 14 you will learn more about how to monitor operations with registry keys and registry key values.

Listing 12-9 is an example of an event that is recorded in the security event log when registry key auditing is configured, as explained in this section.

Listing 12-9: Event ID 4656: A handle to an object was requested.

```
Task Category: Registry
Keywords: Audit Success
Subject:
        Security ID:            S-1-5-18
        Account Name:           2016DC$
        Account Domain:         HQCORP
        Logon ID:               0x3E7
```

```
Object:
      Object Server:          Security
      Object Type:            Key
      Object Name: \REGISTRY\MACHINE\SOFTWARE\WOW6432Node\Microsoft\
         Windows\CurrentVersion\Uninstall
      Handle ID:              0x1e4
      Resource Attributes:    -
Process Information:
      Process ID:             0x9f4
      Process Name:           C:\Windows\System32\CompatTelRunner.exe
Access Request Information:
      Transaction ID:         {00000000-0000-0000-0000-000000000000}
      Accesses:               %%1537 (DELETE)
                              %%1538 (READ_CONTROL)
                              %%1539 (WRITE_DAC)
                              %%1540 (WRITE_OWNER)
                              %%4432 (Query key value)
                              %%4433 (Set key value)
                              %%4434 (Create sub-key)
                              %%4435 (Enumerate sub-keys)
                              %%4436 (Notify about changes to keys)
                              %%4437 (Create Link)
Some fields omitted...
```

NOTE The event described in Listing 12-9 is available on the book's website, in the `Application Installation - Software Registry Keys.evtx` **file.**

This event shows that `CompatTelRunner.exe` requested the `Create sub-key` access right. This event is recorded because `Create sub-key` auditing is enabled for `\REGISTRY\MACHINE\SOFTWARE\WOW6432Node\Microsoft\Windows\CurrentVersion\Uninstall` key.

Unfortunately, this event does not have the name of the newly created registry key and no other events are generated that will indicate the specific registry key that was just created. You can try to find a 4663 event, which *may* follow the 4656 event with an `Accesses` field value of `Query key value`, but there is no guarantee that 4663 event will be generated, because after a handle is requested it can be just closed without performing any action.

Recent Windows systems have a so-called Microsoft Compatibility Telemetry mechanism, which, in case of software installation, handles changes to the `\REGISTRY\MACHINE\SOFTWARE\WOW6432Node\Microsoft\Windows\CurrentVersion\Uninstall` and `\REGISTRY\MACHINE\SOFTWARE\Microsoft\Windows\CurrentVersion\Uninstall` registry keys, and you will see `CompatTelRunner.exe` as the process that made a change, instead of the real process name.

You can disable the scheduled task associated with the Microsoft Compatibility Telemetry mechanism, but doing so will completely disable handling of `Uninstall` registry keys auditing. No events will be generated. If you do want to disable the Microsoft Compatibility Telemetry scheduled task, in Windows Server 2016 and Windows 10 it is located in `\Task Scheduler Library\Microsoft\Windows\ Application Experience`. The name of the task is Microsoft Compatibility Appraiser.

To summarize, this event will inform you that a new application was installed, but you will not be able to easily find the name of newly installed application or the process that was used to install (installer/setup) the application.

Application Installation - New Folders in Program Files and Program Files (x86) Folders

As you will learn in Chapter 13, it is not really possible to monitor for folder creation operations.

Application Removal Using Other Methods

Methods discussed in the "Application Installation Using Other Methods" section might also be used to detect application removal operations.

Application Removal - Process Creation

The same as for application installation (Listing 12-8), a 4688 event will also be generated when an uninstaller is executed. Listing 12-10 is an example of such an event.

Listing 12-10: Event ID 4688: A new process has been created.

```
Task Category: Process Creation
Keywords: Audit Success
Creator Subject:
    Security ID:            S-1-5-21-1913345275-1711810662-261465553-500
    Account Name:           Administrator
    Account Domain:         HQCORP
    Logon ID:               0x42F59
Target Subject:
    Security ID:            S-1-0-0
    Account Name:           -
    Account Domain:         -
    Logon ID:               0x0
```

```
Process Information:
    New Process ID:         0x1154
    New Process Name:       C:\Users\ADMINI~1\AppData\Local\Temp\9061700701.
                                                    71356\Installer.exe
    Token Elevation Type:   %%1936 (TokenElevationTypeDefault)
    Mandatory Label:        S-1-16-12288 (Mandatory Label\High
                                                    Mandatory Level)
    Creator Process ID:     0x4a8
    Creator Process Name:   C:\Program Files (x86)\Technitium\TMACv6.0\
                                                    Installer.exe
    Process Command Line:
"C:\Users\ADMINI~1\AppData\Local\Temp\9061700701.71356\Installer.exe" /u
```

> **NOTE** The event described in Listing 12-10 is available on the book's website, in the `Application Removal - Process Creation.evtx` file.

4688 event, generated by software removal, might have specific substrings such as `uninstall`, `installer`, or `unins` in the `New Process Name` field.

Uninstallers are usually executed from temporary locations. This allows the uninstaller to completely remove the application folder. Search for a `\Temp\` substring in the `New Process Name` field to detect such operations.

Most legitimate software removal operations are invoked by user accounts. It is a good idea to additionally verify all application removal operations run by built-in security principals, such as SYSTEM, and those run by service accounts.

Application Removal - Software Registry Keys

Fortunately, registry key removal operations in `Uninstall` sections are not handled by the Microsoft Compatibility Telemetry mechanism, so it is possible to detect which application deleted a key.

To handle registry key removal operations, auditing settings (SACL) should be configured for both registry keys:

- HKEY_LOCAL_MACHINE\SOFTWARE\Microsoft\Windows\CurrentVersion\Uninstall
- HKEY_LOCAL_MACHINE\SOFTWARE\Wow6432Node\Microsoft\Windows\CurrentVersion\Uninstall

Figure 12-4 shows an access list entry (ACE) that should be added to both of these registry key SACLs in order to monitor for registry key Delete operations.

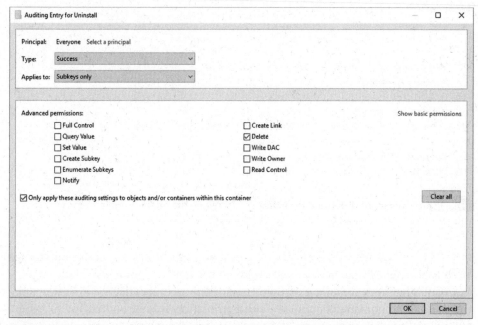

Figure 12-4: Registry auditing settings for application removal monitoring

Multiple events might be triggered in the Windows security event log for application registry key deletion operations, but the most informative is shown in Listing 12-11.

Listing 12-11: Event ID 4663: An attempt was made to access an object.

```
Task Category: Registry
Keywords: Audit Success
Subject:
        Security ID:            S-1-5-21-1913345275-1711810662-261465553-500
        Account Name:           Administrator
        Account Domain:         HQCORP
        Logon ID:               0x42F59
Object:
        Object Server:          Security
        Object Type:            Key
        Object Name: \REGISTRY\MACHINE\SOFTWARE\WOW6432Node\Microsoft\
                Windows\CurrentVersion\Uninstall\FileZilla Client
        Handle ID:              0x34c
        Resource Attributes:    -
Process Information:
        Process ID:             0x150
        Process Name:           C:\Users\ADMINI~1\AppData\Local\Temp\
                                        ~nsuA.tmp\Un_A.exe
Access Request Information:
        Accesses:               %%1537 (DELETE)
        Access Mask:            0x10000
```

NOTE The event described in Listing 12-11 is available on the book's website, in the `Application Removal - Software Registry Keys.evtx` file.

In this event you can find who (`Subject`) deleted the registry key (`Object Name`) and which process performed this operation (`Process Name`).

In Chapter 14 you will learn more about how to perform monitoring of operations with registry keys and registry key values.

Application Removal - Folder Removal in the Program Files and Program Files (x86) Folders

One of the ways to detect an application removal action is to monitor for folder deletion in the Program Files and Program Files (x86) folders. This method will not work for all possible application removal procedures, because some applications may be installed in folders other than Program Files, or may not delete its folder after removal. But this method will work for most standard application removal operations.

To handle folder removal operations, auditing settings (SACL) should be configured for both folders:

- `%systemdrive%\Program Files`
- `%systemdrive%\Program Files (x86)`

In addition to these two folders, the AppData folder, located under the user profile folder, for each user account might also be in the list in order to monitor applications installed in the user's context, such as Google Chrome.

Figure 12-5 shows an access list entry (ACE) that should be added to both these folders' SACLs in order to monitor for folder removal operations.

Multiple events might be triggered in the Windows security event log for folder deletion operations, but the most informative is in Listing 12-12.

Listing 12-12: Event ID 4663: An attempt was made to access an object.

```
Task Category: Removable Storage
Keywords: Audit Success
Subject:
     Security ID:          S-1-5-21-1913345275-1711810662-261465553-500
     Account Name:         Administrator
     Account Domain:       HQCORP
     Logon ID:             0x42F59
Object:
     Object Server:        Security
     Object Type:          File
     Object Name:          C:\Program Files\FileZilla FTP Client
     Handle ID:            0x350
     Resource Attributes:  S:AI
```

```
Process Information:
        Process ID:           0xaa0
        Process Name:         C:\Users\ADMINI~1\AppData\Local\Temp\
                                            ~nsuA.tmp\Un_A.exe
Access Request Information:
        Accesses:             %%1537 (DELETE)
        Access Mask:          0x10000
```

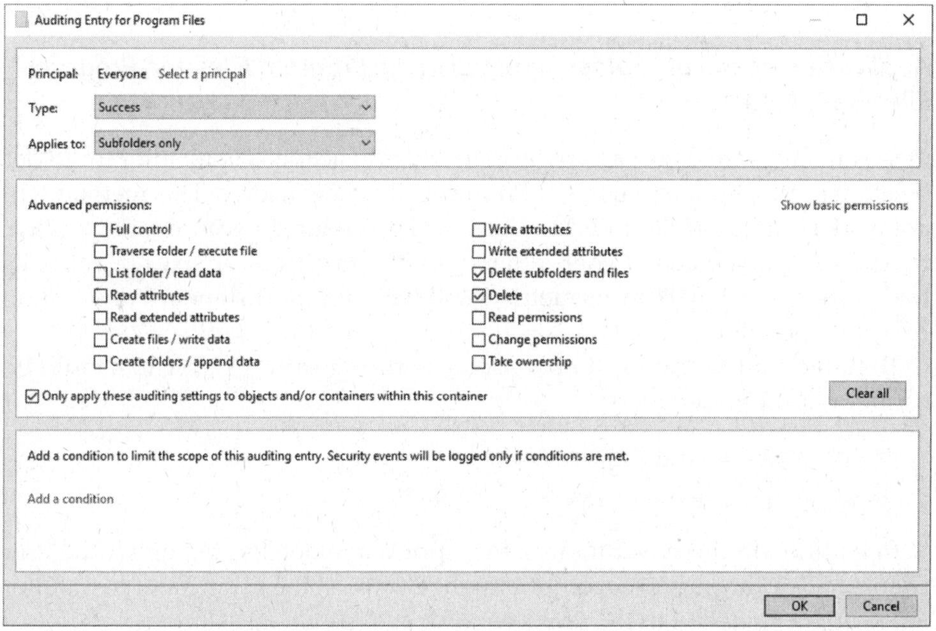

Figure 12-5: NTFS auditing settings for application removal monitoring in Program Files folders

> **NOTE** The event described in Listing 12-12 is available on the book's website, in the `Application Removal - Folder Removal in Program Files and Program Files (x86) Folders.evtx` file.

The `Object Name` field contains the name of a deleted folder from which you may be able to determine what application was deleted.

The `Subject` section contains information about the account that invoked the operation.

`Process Name` contains the name of the process that performed the `DELETE` operation.

In Chapter 13 you will learn more about how to perform monitoring of operations with file system files and folders.

Application Execution and Termination

When executed, all Windows applications, both console and Graphical User Interface (GUI) applications, create a new executable process.

Table 12-2 contains a list of standard processes for Windows 10 and Windows Server 2016.

Table 12-2: Standard Windows 10 and Windows Server 2016 Processes

PROCESS NAME	IMAGE DIRECTORY	USER NAME
smss.exe	%WINDIR%\System32\	SYSTEM
csrss.exe	%WINDIR%\System32\	SYSTEM
wininit.exe	%WINDIR%\System32\	SYSTEM
services.exe	%WINDIR%\System32\	SYSTEM
svchost.exe	%WINDIR%\System32\	Various accounts
WmiPrvSE.exe	%WINDIR%\System32\wbem\	NETWORK SERVICE
RuntimeBroker.exe	%WINDIR%\System32\	Current user account
ShellExperienceHost.exe	%WINDIR%\SystemApps\ShellExperienceHost_cw5n1h2txyewy\	Current user account
SearchUI.exe	%WINDIR%\SystemApps\Microsoft.Windows.Cortana_cw5n1h2txyewy\	Current user account
sihost.exe	%WINDIR%\System32\	Current user account
taskhostw.exe	%WINDIR%\System32\	SYSTEM
spoolsv.exe	%WINDIR%\System32\	SYSTEM
MsMpEng.exe	%SystemDrive%\Program Files\Windows Defender\	SYSTEM
lsass.exe	%WINDIR%\System32\	SYSTEM
winlogon.exe	%WINDIR%\System32\	SYSTEM
dwm.exe	%WINDIR%\System32\	One of DWM accounts
explorer.exe	%WINDIR%\	Current user account

Here are the descriptions for processes listed in Table 12-2:

- **smss.exe (Session Manager):** smss.exe is responsible for session management and initialization. Some examples of the actions performed for session initialization by smss.exe are:

  - SAM, Security and Software hives initialization

  - Paging file initialization

  - Systemwide environment variables creation

- **csrss.exe (Client/Server Run-time Subsystem):** This implements some user-mode system functions, such as operations with Windows console applications.

- **wininit.exe (Windows Initialization Process):** wininit.exe performs systemwide initialization functions, such as:

  - Services.exe process creation

  - Lsass.exe process initialization

  - Creation of the %windir%\temp folder

- **services.exe (Service Control Manager):** services.exe is responsible for starting, stopping, and interacting with Windows services.

- **svchost.exe (Service Host Process):** The svchost.exe system process is designed to host multiple system services. Usually, system services with similar functions are grouped together under one svchost.exe process, such as services related to the networking subsystem. See Chapter 10 for more information about svchost.exe.

- **WmiPrvSE.exe (WMI Provider Services):** This is the host process for WMI provider services.

- **RuntimeBroker.exe:** This process is responsible for permissions control and management for Windows universal (metro style) applications.

- **ShellExperienceHost.exe (Windows Shell Experience Host):** ShellExperienceHost.exe is responsible for rendering universal (metro style) applications. For example, it handles Windows 10 "start menu" operations and rendering.

- **SearchUI.exe (Search and Cortana Application):** This supports Microsoft Cortana and unified search features.

- **sihost.exe (Shell Infrastructure Host):** This process is responsible for functions related to universal applications, such as the new Start menu or Cortana interface.

- **`taskhostw.exe` (Host Process for Windows Tasks):** This process is responsible for running Windows scheduled tasks.

- **`spoolsv.exe` (Spooler Service):** `spoolsv.exe` is responsible for managing spooled print/fax jobs.

- **`MsMpEng.exe` (Microsoft Malware Protection Engine):** `MsMpEng.exe` is a malware detection and quarantining engine used by multiple Microsoft products, such as Windows Defender and Microsoft Security Essentials.

- **`lsass.exe` (Local Security Authority Subsystem Service):** This implements Windows security subsystem components. See Chapter 4 for more information about `lsass.exe`.

- **`winlogon.exe`:** This handles interactive logons and logoffs. You can find more information about the `Winlogon.exe` process in Chapter 4.

- **`dwm.exe` (Desktop Window Manager):** This process is responsible for graphical user interface rendering and hardware acceleration management.

- **`explorer.exe` (Windows Explorer):** This process represents a Windows graphical shell for a user session, which contains such components as a desktop, taskbar, and other interface components.

Successful Process Creation

Each time a new process successfully starts, the event in Listing 12-13 is generated in the Windows security event log.

Listing 12-13: Event ID 4688: A new process has been created.

```
Task Category: Process Creation
Keywords: Audit Success
Creator Subject:
      Security ID:           S-1-5-21-1913345275-1711810662-261465553-500
      Account Name:          Administrator
      Account Domain:        HQCORP
      Logon ID:              0x4471A
Target Subject:
      Security ID:           S-1-0-0 (NULL SID)
      Account Name:          -
      Account Domain:        -
      Logon ID:              0x0
Process Information:
      New Process ID:        0x119c
      New Process Name:      C:\Windows\System32\auditpol.exe
      Token Elevation Type:  %%1936 (TokenElevationTypeDefault (1))
      Mandatory Label:       S-1-16-12288 (Mandatory Label\High
                                          Mandatory Level)
```

```
Creator Process ID:     0x8a8
Creator Process Name:   C:\Windows\System32\cmd.exe
Process Command Line:   auditpol /get /category:*
```

NOTE The event described in Listing 12-13 is available on the book's website, in the `Successful Process Creation.evtx` **file.**

The `Creator Subject` section contains information about an account under which its parent process (`Creator Process ID`) runs. It is important to understand that the new process does not always use the same credentials as it's parent (creator).

The `Target Subject` section contains information about an account in which context (using which token) the new process is created. If the target account is the same as the creator account, the `Target Subject` section will have the following values for its fields:

```
Security ID:        S-1-0-0 (NULL SID)
Account Name:       -
Account Domain:     -
Logon ID:           0x0
```

The `New Process ID` field contains information about the Process ID (PID) assigned to the new process. All Windows processes are assigned PIDs. PIDs are unique within a host. When the system starts, it starts some base processes, such as `smss.exe` and `csrss.exe`, which get PIDs with low numbers, such as 512 or 600. The higher the PID, the later the process was created. Two processes always have the same PIDs in any Windows machine:

- **System Idle Process (PID 0):** This is a built-in process that does not have any executable file/image associated with it. It shows a percentage of time the processor is idle.

- **System (PID 4):** This is a special process for kernel-mode threads.

Usually, user-initiated processes have higher PID numbers, because they are started after all Windows system processes have started.

The `New Process Name` field contains the full directory path and name of the executable image for the newly created process.

The `Mandatory Label` field contains information about the integrity label assigned to the new process. Each process and securable object, such as a file or registry key, has an integrity label associated with it. Integrity labels are part of the mandatory integrity control (MIC) mechanism implemented in Windows systems. MIC works in conjunction with the standard discretionary access control mechanism (access control lists), which gives more flexibility in defining access control rules for operating system objects. A process integrity label is included in the process token (described later in this section) as a SID. Table 12-3 contains a list of process integrity labels that can be used in Windows operating systems.

Table 12-3: Windows Process Integrity Labels

SID	NAME	USE EXAMPLE
S-1-16-0	SECURITY_MANDATORY_ UNTRUSTED_RID (Mandatory Label\Untrusted Mandatory Level)	Processes started by Anonymous account
S-1-16-4096	SECURITY_MANDATORY_LOW_RID (Mandatory Label\Low Mandatory Level)	Internet Explorer Protected Mode process or AppContainer process
S-1-16-8192	SECURITY_MANDATORY_MEDIUM_ RID (Mandatory Label\Medium Mandatory Level)	Process for regular applications with enabled UAC
S-1-16-8448	SECURITY_MANDATORY_MEDIUM_ PLUS_RID	Can be used as a priority between medium and high
S-1-16-12288	SECURITY_MANDATORY_HIGH_RID (Mandatory Label\High Mandatory Level)	Applications executed with UAC elevation
S-1-16-16384	SECURITY_MANDATORY_SYSTEM_ RID (Mandatory Label\System Mandatory Level)	Services or system applications, such as Winlogon and Wininit
S-1-16-20480	SECURITY_MANDATORY_ PROTECTED_PROCESS_RID	Included in a token for protected processes
S-1-16-28672	SECURITY_MANDATORY_SECURE_ PROCESS_RID	Included in a token for protected processes, new for Windows 10

Usually a process inherits its integrity level from its parent process, but it is also possible to lower the integrity level of a child process if a parent process explicitly specifies it while invoking a child process.

In addition to integrity levels, mandatory policies may be applied to different object types. Mandatory policies control how the MIC mechanism works for specific objects. Here is the list of available policies:

- **NO_WRITE_UP:** Restricts write access if an object with lower priority tries to modify/write an object with higher priority. This policy is enabled by default for all Windows objects.

- **NO_READ_UP:** Restricts read access if an object with lower priority tries to read an object with higher priority. This policy is enabled by default for all process objects.

- **NO_EXECUTE_UP:** Restricts execute access if an object with lower priority tries to execute an object with higher priority. This policy is enabled by default for all COM classes to prevent execution of a COM class by lower integrity objects.

The `Token Elevation Type` field contains information about the account's security token type with which a new process was created. Windows uses a process token to perform security access checks on objects and verify user privileges. Each process has a token of the user account under which this process runs. A process security token contains the following main information sections:

- Information about an account under which the process runs

- Group membership information for the account under which the process runs

- User privileges information for the account under which the process runs

If User Account Control (UAC) is enabled for a specific account, during account logon the system performs a review of group membership and user privileges information for the account. It verifies the following conditions:

- User is a member of one or more of the following security groups:
  - Built-In Administrators
  - Certificate Administrators
  - Domain Administrators
  - Enterprise Administrators
  - Policy Administrators
  - Schema Administrators
  - Domain Controllers
  - Enterprise Read-Only Domain Controllers
  - Read-Only Domain Controllers
  - Account Operators
  - Backup Operators
  - Cryptographic Operators
  - Network Configuration Operators
  - Print Operators
  - System Operators

- RAS Servers
- Power Users
- Pre–Windows 2000 Compatible Access
- User has one or more of the user privileges listed in Table 12-4.

Table 12-4: Sensitive Privileges Verified by UAC

PRIVILEGE NAME	DESCRIPTION
SeBackupPrivilege	Back up files and directories
SeCreateTokenPrivilege	Create a token object
SeDebugPrivilege	Debug programs
SeImpersonatePrivilege	Impersonate a client after authentication
SeLabelPrivilege	Create system labels
SeLoadDriverPrivilege	Load and unload device drivers
SeRestorePrivilege	Restore files and directories
SeTakeOwnershipPrivilege	Take ownership of files or other objects
SeTcbPrivilege	Act as part of the operating system

If any of these conditions is true, UAC creates two user sessions:

- **Elevated session:** Contains user's full security token (`Token-ElevationTypeFull`) with all user privileges and groups.

- **Restricted session:** Has filtered token type (`TokenElevationTypeLimited`) to which the following restrictions are applied:

  - All processes created using filtered token have maximum of Medium integrity level.

  - All privileges are removed from the token, except the following:

PRIVILEGE NAME	DESCRIPTION
SeChangeNotifyPrivilege	Bypass traverse checking
SeShutdownPrivilege	Shut down the system
SeUndockPrivilege	Remove computer from docking station
SeIncreaseWorkingSetPrivilege	Increase a process working set
SeTimeZonePrivilege	Change the time zone

  - User groups mentioned earlier in this section, marked as deny-only. Deny-only groups are denied access by any deny ACE entry in the object's DACL. They cannot be overridden by an access granting ACE.

Otherwise, if both restrictions mentioned in the preceding list are not true and UAC mechanism is disabled, one user session is created with a default user token (`TokenElevationTypeDefault`), which is not modified by the system. You can find more information about security tokens in Chapter 4 and more details about user privileges in Chapter 11.

Table 12-5 contains a list of process token types available in Windows systems.

Table 12-5: Windows Process Token Types

VALUE	TYPE	DESCRIPTION
%%1936	TokenElevationTypeDefault (1)	Full token for user session with disabled UAC
%%1937	TokenElevationTypeFull (2)	Elevated/full token with enabled UAC
%%1938	TokenElevationTypeLimited (3)	Restricted token with enabled UAC

The `Creator Process ID` field contains information about the parent's process ID.

The `Creator Process Name` field contains the full directory path and name of the executable image for a parent (creator) process.

The `Process Command Line` field contains the executed command string with parameters. If no parameters were passed to an executable, only the executable name will be present in this field.

By default, command-line auditing is disabled and the `Process Command Line` field will be empty. To enable command-line auditing, enable the `Computer Configuration\Policies\Administrative Templates\System\Audit Process Creation\Include command line in process creation events` group policy setting.

Successful Process Creation - CreateProcessWithLogonW initiated

New processes, by default, are assigned their parent's security token. But it is possible to run a new process using a different token by invoking the `CreateProcessWithLogonW` function. This function performs user logon for a specified account and creates a new process using that account's token. The most common application that uses `CreateProcessWithLogonW` is `RunAs.exe`.

Listing 12-14 is an example of an event that appears in the Windows security event log when a process is created using a token different than the parent's process token.

Listing 12-14: Event ID 4688: A new process has been created.

```
Task Category: Process Creation
Keywords: Audit Success
Creator Subject:
        Security ID:          S-1-5-18 (SYSTEM)
        Account Name:         2016DC$
        Account Domain:       HQCORP
        Logon ID:             0x3E7
Target Subject:
        Security ID:          S-1-5-21-1913345275-1711810662-261465553-
                                                                    1120

        Account Name:         Andrei
        Account Domain:       HQCORP
        Logon ID:             0x6ABE88
Process Information:
        New Process ID:       0xdf0
        New Process Name:     C:\Windows\System32\auditpol.exe
        Token Elevation Type: %%1938 (TokenElevationTypeLimited (3))
        Mandatory Label:      S-1-16-8192 (Mandatory Label\Medium
                                              Mandatory Level)

        Creator Process ID:   0x194
        Creator Process Name: C:\Windows\System32\runas.exe
        Process Command Line: auditpol /get /category:*
```

NOTE The event described in Listing 12-14 is available on the book's website, in the
`Successful Process Creation - CreateProcessWithLogonW initiated`
`.evtx` file.

As you can see, the `Target Subject` section contains information about the
account that is different than the account in the `Creator Subject` section.

Unsuccessful Process Creation

A process might not successfully start for multiple reasons: an application error,
insufficient permissions, application execution policy restrictions, and so on.

There is no universal way to monitor for all possible unsuccessful process
creation events. But it is possible to monitor unsuccessful `Execute` access attempts
for executable files.

Figure 12-6 shows an access list entry (ACE) that should be added to the
executable file's SACL in order to monitor unsuccessful execution attempts.

Multiple events might be triggered in the Windows security event log for
unsuccessful `Traverse folder / Execute` access attempt operations, but the
most informative is shown in Listing 12-15.

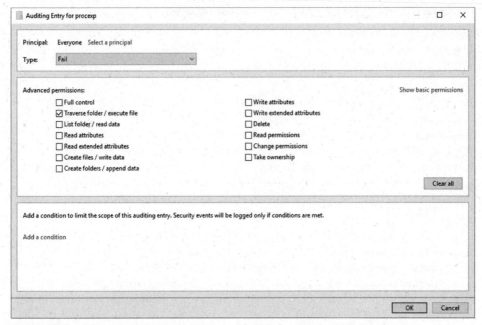

Figure 12-6: NTFS auditing settings for unsuccessful `Execute` access attempts

Listing 12-15: Event ID 4656: A handle to an object was requested.

```
Task Category: File System
Keywords: Audit Failure
Subject:
        Security ID:            S-1-5-21-1913345275-1711810662-261465553-
                                                                    1120
        Account Name:           Andrei
        Account Domain:         HQCORP
        Logon ID:               0x6F6F9D
Object:
        Object Server:          Security
        Object Type:            File
        Object Name:            C:\temp\procexp.exe
        Handle ID:              0x0
        Resource Attributes:    -
Process Information:
        Process ID:             0x57c
        Process Name:           C:\Windows\System32\svchost.exe
Access Request Information:
        Transaction ID:         {00000000-0000-0000-0000-000000000000}
        Accesses:               %%1541 (SYNCHRONIZE)
                                %%4421 (Execute/Traverse)
        Access Reasons:         %%1541 (SYNCHRONIZE): %%1805 (Not granted)
                                %%4421 (Execute/Traverse): %%1805 (Not
                                                              granted)
        Access Mask:            0x100020
```

NOTE The event described in Listing 12-15 is available on the book's website, in the Unsuccessful Process Creation.evtx file.

In this event you can see that an Execute/Traverse access attempt failed for account Andrei when it tried to execute C:\temp\procexp.exe.

The drawback of this detection method is that Failure audit for Traverse folder / Execute access attempts should be set in SACL for all executable objects or for specific files.

You can find more information about filesystem monitoring in Chapter 13.

Process Termination

Process termination events are generated when a process exits or is terminated. Listing 12-16 is an example of a process termination event recorded in the Windows security event log.

Listing 12-16: Event ID 4689: A process has exited.

```
Task Category: Process Termination
Keywords: Audit Success
Subject:
        Security ID:          S-1-5-21-1913345275-1711810662-261465553-500
        Account Name:         Administrator
        Account Domain:       HQCORP
        Logon ID:             0x4471A
Process Information:
        Process ID:           0xb50
        Process Name:         C:\Windows\System32\cmd.exe
        Exit Status:          0xC000013A
```

NOTE The event described in Listing 12-16 is available on the book's website, in the Process Termination.evtx file.

The Subject section contains information about an account under which the terminated process was running.

The Process ID field contains information about the process ID that was assigned to the terminated/exited process.

The Process Name field contains the full directory path and name of the exited/terminated process.

The Exit Status field contains the hexadecimal status code of the reason the process exited. This status code might be generated by an application or it might be one of the standard Windows error codes or NTSTATUS values. Table 12-6 contains a list of the most common Exit Status field values.

Table 12-6: The Most Common Exit Status Field Values for the 4689 Event

CODE	CODE NAME	DESCRIPTION
0x0	ERROR_SUCCESS	The operation completed successfully
0x1	ERROR_INVALID_FUNCTION	Incorrect function
0x2	ERROR_FILE_NOT_FOUND	The system cannot find the file specified
0x3	ERROR_PATH_NOT_FOUND	The system cannot find the path specified
0x4	ERROR_TOO_MANY_OPEN_FILES	The system cannot open the file
0x5	ERROR_ACCESS_DENIED	Access is denied
0x131	ERROR_SHORT_NAMES_NOT_ENABLED_ON_VOLUME	Short names are not enabled on this volume
0x522	ERROR_PRIVILEGE_NOT_HELD	A required privilege is not held by the client
0xC000013A	STATUS_CONTROL_C_EXIT	The application terminated as a result of a CTRL+C

You can find more information about Windows system error codes and NTSTATUS codes on the official Microsoft MSDN site.

Application Crash Monitoring

When an application encounters an error and cannot function properly, it hangs or crashes. If an application crashes, it exits, and its process or processes are also terminated.

An application crash may be a sign of malicious activity. A vulnerability or bug, when exploited, can lead to potential malicious code execution after application crash. Applications can also crash due to an unhandled error that is not related to any malicious activity.

An application may crash due to:

- Buffer overflow errors
- Unhandled exceptions
- Memory read or write operations to an area of memory that is not allowed to be modified or read by the application
- Attempt to access system resources that an application has no permissions to access
- Access invalid memory addresses

One method to detect malicious activity in the network is to monitor for multiple application crashes involving the same application on multiple machines. You can also monitor for unique application crash events that were not previously discovered in the infrastructure.

If an application crash occurs, the event in Listing 12-17 is recorded in the Windows application event log.

Listing 12-17: Event ID 1000

```
Event Log: Application
Source: Application Error
Level: Error
Faulting application name: pythonw.exe, version: 0.0.0.0, time stamp:
                                                           0x527fcf5d
Faulting module name: QtGui4.dll, version: 4.8.5.0, time stamp:
                                                           0x51cbf4e8
Exception code: 0xc0000005
Fault offset: 0x0017e6ee
Faulting process id: 0x2f20
Faulting application start time: 0x01d2e893c117c504
Faulting application path: C:\Users\amirosh\Downloads\reader\Visual
                Novel Reader\Library\Frameworks\Python\pythonw.exe
Faulting module path: C:\Users\amirosh\Downloads\reader\Visual Novel
                Reader\Library\Frameworks\Qt\PySide\QtGui4.dll
Report Id: e64738ab-25ab-451c-b24b-4f5c30d2fa40
Faulting package full name:
Faulting package-relative application ID:

Param 1: pythonw.exe
Param 2: 0.0.0.0
Param 3: 527fcf5d
Param 4: QtGui4.dll
Param 5: 4.8.5.0
Param 6: 51cbf4e8
Param 7: c0000005
Param 8: 0017e6ee
Param 9: 2f20
Param 10: 01d2e893c117c504
Param 11: C:\Users\amirosh\Downloads\reader\Visual Novel Reader\Library\
                              Frameworks\Python\pythonw.exe
Param 12: C:\Users\amirosh\Downloads\reader\Visual Novel Reader\Library\
                              Frameworks\Qt\PySide\QtGui4.dll
Param 13: e64738ab-25ab-451c-b24b-4f5c30d2fa40
Param 14:
Param 15:
```

NOTE The event described in Listing 12-17 is available on the book's website, in the Application Crash.evtx file.

Event 1000 in the Application event log that originated from an `Application Error` event source informs you that a critical error occurred in the application. This event usually means that the application stopped working.

The `Param 1` field contains the name of an executable file where the error occurred. It does not contain a full path for an application image, just the name of an executable file.

The `Param 2` field contains an application version. If an executable does not contain a version number, this field will have a value of `0.0.0.0`.

The `Param 3` field contains a hexadecimal representation of the number of seconds since Jan 1, 1970, also called epoch time. This field shows the last modification time for the executable file, which is stored in the `Date modified` file property. You need to convert this value to decimal format to get an actual number of seconds. For example, `527fcf5d` represents 10 November 2013 06:24:29 PM (GMT+0).

The `Param 4` field contains the name of the module in which failure occurred. It can be the name of a loaded DLL, an executable image itself, or even an `unknown` value if the system was not able to determine which module failed.

The `Param 5` field contains the version number of the faulting module. If the module does not have a version number, this field will have a value of `0.0.0.0`.

The `Param 6` field contains the hexadecimal representation of the number of seconds since Jan 1, 1970, also called epoch time. This field shows the last time the faulting module was modified, which is stored in the `Date modified` file property.

The `Param 7` field contains the exception code of the error. The exception code might be generated by the application or it might be one of the standard Windows error codes or `NTSTATUS` values. In this example `0xc0000005` is an `NTSTATUS` code, which translates as `STATUS_ACCESS_VIOLATION`. That means that an application tried to access a memory offset without having permissions to perform the attempt. See Table 12-6 for the most common exception codes.

The `Param 8` field contains a memory offset at which an error occurs. It can be an offset accessed by an application that causes an Access Violation to occur. For example, Access Violation error offset 0x00000000 means that an application accessed a `null` pointer.

The `Param 9` field contains the hexadecimal process ID value of the faulting application process.

The `Param 10` field contains the time when an application was initially started as a Win32 FileTime structure. You can convert a FileTime structure to a human-readable format using the `[datetime]::FromFileTime()` PowerShell function. Figure 12-7 shows an example of the `FromFileTime()` function usage.

The `Param 11` field contains the full directory path and name of the faulting application image.

The `Param 12` field contains the full directory path and name of the faulting application module.

Figure 12-7: Win32 FileTime object conversion using the FromFileTime() function

The `Param 13` field contains the unique GUID for a generated crash report. The crash report is explained later in this chapter.

The `Param 14` and `Param 15` fields are not used in application crash events.

Windows Error Reporting

Windows Error Reporting (WER) is a mechanism designed to provide extended information about software crashes and errors to software developers and vendors. Each time an application crash occurs, a detailed report is created for the crash and a WER authorization dialog appears asking if you want to send this report to Microsoft. All WER operations are done by Windows Event Reporting Service (WerSvc). WerSvc sends a crash report to Microsoft servers if the user authorized it to do so. Software and hardware vendors can access WER reports related to their products in the Microsoft Hardware Dev Center portal.

Information about local Windows 10 and Windows Server 2016 event reports is located in the `Problem Reports` section, which can be accessed via the `Control Panel\All Control Panel Items\Security and Maintenance\Problem Reports` item. Figure 12-8 contains an example of the `Problem Reports` page.

Each time an application crash occurs, a WER report is automatically generated and the event in Listing 12-18 is recorded in the Windows application event log on the host where the crash occurred.

Listing 12-18: Event ID 1001

```
Event Log: Application
Source: Windows Error Reporting
Level: Information
Fault bucket (PARAM 1) 73123247202, type (PARAM 2) 1
Event Name: (PARAM 3) APPCRASH
Response: (PARAM 4) Not available
Cab Id: (PARAM 5) 0
Problem signature:
P1: (PARAM 6) pythonw.exe
P2: (PARAM 7) 0.0.0.0
P3: (PARAM 8) 527fcf5d
P4: (PARAM 9) QtGui4.dll
P5: (PARAM 10)  4.8.5.0
P6: (PARAM 11) 51cbf4e8
```

```
P7:  (PARAM 12) c0000005
P8:  (PARAM 13) 0017e6ee
P9:  (PARAM 14)
P10: (PARAM 15)
Attached files: (PARAM 16)
\\?\C:\ProgramData\Microsoft\Windows\WER\Temp\
        WER53FA.tmp.WERInternalMetadata.xml
\\?\C:\Users\amirosh\AppData\Local\Temp\WER5B7D.tmp.appcompat.txt
These files may be available here: (PARAM 17)
C:\ProgramData\Microsoft\Windows\WER\ReportArchive\AppCrash_pythonw.exe_
        71d8c3825e78ff1b423bd038baa9605f553435_bb008de6_09415dae
Analysis symbol: (PARAM 18)
Rechecking for solution: (PARAM 19) 0
Report Id: (PARAM 20) e64738ab-25ab-451c-b24b-4f5c30d2fa40
Report Status: (PARAM 21) 1
Hashed bucket: (PARAM 22) e76d998cdbf1e26b4380e7b7d933b9be
```

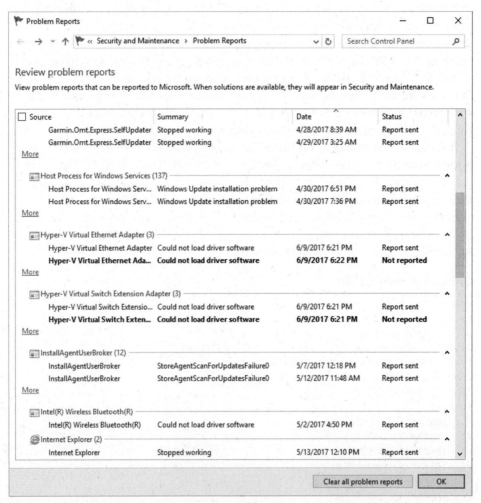

Figure 12-8: Problem Reports page in the Control Panel

NOTE   The event described in Listing 12-18 is available on the book's website, in the `Application Crash.evtx` file.

The PARAM 1 field contains an application crash fault bucket number. A fault bucket identification number is a number assigned by the system to identify specific types of errors. Usually this correlates to problems showing in the Windows Event Viewer. Also, this identification number is what is used by Microsoft to identify a particular program error when you send a WER error report.

The PARAM 2 field contains a fault bucket type. It can be assigned to one of the following types:

- 0: Fault bucket was not assigned/determined
- 1: Crash32 buckets
- 2: Setup buckets
- 3: Crash64 buckets
- 4: Generic reports
- 5: Phony error bucket

The PARAM 3 field contains a human-readable event name. This field may contain various event names. The following names are the most commonly reported in the 1001 event:

- **WindowsUpdateFailure3:** Errors associated with Windows Update service.
- **CLR20r3:** Errors related to Microsoft .NET Framework Common Language Runtime (CLR) v2.0.
- **APPCRASH:** Application crash event.
- **RADAR_PRE_LEAK_WOW64:** Error triggered by memory leak detection logic.
- **BEX:** Buffer Overflow Exception error.
- **LiveKernelEvent:** OS kernel-level error. Usually this indicates hardware compatibility problems.
- **PnPDeviceProblemCode:** Indicates a problem with a PnP device.

The PARAM 4 field contains a response string from the Windows Error Reporting server or the string Not available if no response was received.

The PARAM 5 field contains the unique iCab identifier returned in the Windows Error Reporting server response. The iCab identifier uniquely identifies the .cab archive that was sent to the Windows Event Reporting server, on the server side.

Params 6 - 15 depend on a fault bucket type and name. For example, for APPCRASH events these parameters are the same as parameters 1–10 in the event ID 1000 discussed in the previous section.

The PARAM 16 field contains a list of files that were included in the WER report. At the time the error is generated, these files are placed in the temporary folders. After an error occurs, they are copied to the folder specified in the PARAM 17 field for long-term storage.

The PARAM 19 field contains an indicator that shows whether the report was resubmitted by a user to check for a response or solution for the error. It may have the following values:

- ▪ 0: The report *was not* resubmitted to find a solution.

- ▪ 1: The report *was* resubmitted to find a solution.

The PARAM 20 field contains the unique GUID for a generated crash report. The crash report is explained later in this chapter.

The PARAM 21 field contains a decimal mask for report status. Table 12-7 contains a list of the most common status codes for WER reports.

Table 12-7: Status Codes for WEF Reports

CODE	NAME	DESCRIPTION
1	REPORT_CANCELLED	Report submission was cancelled by the user
2	REPORT_NO_NETWORK	No network connection was available to send a report
4	REPORT_QUEUED	The report was queued for whatever reason
8	REPORT_SERVER_REQUEST	Server requested additional data to be collected
16	REPORT_IN_RAC_SAMPLE	Set whenever the computer is in the rights account certificate (RAC) sample for data collection
32	REPORT_STAGE1_FAILED	Stage 1 of a WER error report submission failed
64	REPORT_STAGE2_FAILED	Stage 2 of a WER error report submission failed
128	REPORT_STAGE3_FAILED	Stage 3 of a WER error report submission failed
256	REPORT_STAGE4_FAILED	Stage 4 of a WER error report submission failed
512	REPORT_STAGE5_FAILED	Stage 5 of a WER error report submission failed
1024	REPORT_CABBING_FAILED	Set if a creation of a .CAB file for WER report failed
2048	INITIAL_CONSENT_DECLINED	Set whenever an initial consent dialog is shown and cancelled

An event's status code value can be a combination of values. For example, if the status code value is 96, it is a combination of 64 (REPORT_STAGE2_FAILED) and 32 (REPORT_STAGE1_FAILED).

The PARAM 22 field contains a hashed version of a fault bucket number (PARAM 1).

WER Report

WER reports are stored in the C:\ProgramData\Microsoft\Windows\WER\ ReportArchive\ folder. Each WER report has its own folder and is saved in .wer format. These reports contain more detailed information about the error, such as the list of modules loaded at the moment an error occurred.

Windows AppLocker Auditing

AppLocker is a technology that was designed to provide the ability to create execution restriction or permit rules for applications and dynamic link libraries (DLL) on a host. It does not require any additional software to be installed and is easily configured using standard Active Directory group policies. AppLocker was first introduced in Windows 7 and Windows 2008 R2 operating systems as a replacement for the Software Restriction Policies technology, giving more agility, better auditing capabilities, and better performance. In this section you will find information about how to use AppLocker's auditing capabilities for application execution monitoring.

AppLocker Policy

Without an AppLocker policy applied, the Application Identity service (AppIDSvc), which implements AppLocker functionality on the host, is not enabled/running. AppLocker policies are located under the following group policy path: Computer Configuration\Policies\Windows Settings\Security Settings\ Application Control Policies\AppLocker.

The following categories of files can be controlled using AppLocker rules:

- **Executables:** Refers to .exe and .com files that are executed from the local computer, removable media, or from a network location.

- **Windows Installers:** Refers to traditional application packages that are installed by the Windows Installer service (msiserver). It includes the installer packages themselves (.msi), application patches (.msp), and application transforms (.mst).

- **Scripts:** Refers to PowerShell (.ps1), Windows command interpreter (.cmd and .bat), VB script (.vbs), and JavaScript (.js) files.

- **Packaged Apps:** Packaged apps (.appx) are the new application delivery model introduced in Windows 8/Server 2012.
- **Dynamic Link Libraries and controls:** Refers to .dll and .ocx files that are shared between applications and loaded by the applications that require them.

For each category of files just listed (except .dll and .ocx files), AppLocker can be configured to operate in one of the following two modes:

- **Enforce rules:** Enable all rules in the specified category and allow AppLocker to block applications from being executed based on configured rules.
- **Audit only:** AppLocker does not prevent applications from execution, but this mode allows you to test configured rules using extended event log records for potentially blocked applications.

Figure 12-9 shows an example of a group policy interface for AppLocker enforcement mode configuration.

AppLocker Monitoring

Some of the use cases for application execution monitoring using AppLocker are:

- Monitoring of all application executions that were performed from outside of the %SystemDrive%\Program Files, %SystemDrive%\Program Files (x86), and %WINDIR% folders.
- Monitoring of all application executables that are not signed by Microsoft-issued code-signing certificates.
- Audit everything that was not in the approved/allowed software baseline when the computer was first given to the end-user, so that there is a history of everything installed and executed after that point.

AppLocker events are stored in the Application and Services Logs\ Microsoft\Windows\AppLocker folder in the Windows Event Viewer event log tree and have the following event log journals based on rule type:

- EXE and DLL
- MSI and Script
- Packaged app-Deployment
- Packaged app-Execution

AppLocker event logs may contain the following events (see Table 12-8) depending on the rule type that triggered the event.

Figure 12-9: AppLocker enforcement mode configuration interface

Table 12-8: AppLocker Events Generated by Different Rule Types

RULE TYPE	EVENT LOG	LEVEL	EVENT ID	EVENT NAME
Executable and DLL	EXE and DLL	Information	8002	*FILE_NAME* was allowed to run.
		Warning	8003	*FILE_NAME* was allowed to run but would have been prevented from running if the AppLocker policy were enforced.
		Error	8004	*FILE_NAME* was prevented from running.

Continues

Table 12-8 (*continued*)

RULE TYPE	EVENT LOG	LEVEL	EVENT ID	EVENT NAME
Windows Installer and Script	MSI and Script	Information	8005	*SCRIPT_OR_INSTALLER_NAME* was allowed to run.
		Warning	8006	*SCRIPT_OR_INSTALLER_NAME* was allowed to run but would have been prevented from running if the AppLocker policy were enforced.
		Error	8007	*SCRIPT_OR_INSTALLER_NAME* was prevented from running.
Packaged app Rules	Packaged app-Execution	Information	8020	*APP_NAME* was allowed to run.
		Warning	8021	*APP_NAME* was allowed to run but would have been prevented from running if the AppLocker policy were enforced.
		Error	8022	*APP_NAME* was prevented from running.
Packaged app Rules	Packaged app-Deployment	Information	8023	*APP_NAME* was allowed to be installed.
		Warning	8024	*APP_NAME* was allowed to run but would have been prevented from running if the AppLocker policy were enforced.
		Error	8025	*APP_NAME* was prevented from running.

EXE and DLL

The EXE and DLL event log contains events for `Executable` and `DLL` rules. Three events are associated with `.exe`, `.com`, `.dll`, and `.ocx` files:

- `Event ID 8002:` *FILE_NAME* was allowed to run.

- `Event ID 8003`: *FILE_NAME* was allowed to run but would have been prevented from running if the AppLocker policy were enforced.

- `Event ID 8004`: *FILE_NAME* was prevented from running.

They all have the same schema, but not all fields have values in all three events.

Listing 12-19 is an example of the event that is generated in the AppLocker event log when an application is allowed to run and the AppLocker policy for executable files is set to "Audit only."

Listing 12-19: Event ID 8002

```
Event Log: Microsoft-Windows-AppLocker/EXE and DLL
Source: AppLocker
Level: Information
%PROGRAMFILES%\INTERNET EXPLORER\IEXPLORE.EXE was allowed to run.

PolicyName        EXE
RuleId            {921CC481-6E17-4653-8F75-050B80ACCA20}
RuleName          (Default Rule) All files located in the Program Files
                                                              folder
RuleSddl          D:(XA;;FX;;;S-1-1-0;(APPID://PATH Contains
                                 "%PROGRAMFILES%\*"))
TargetUser        S-1-5-21-1913345275-1711810662-261465553-1120
TargetProcessId   3292
FilePath          %PROGRAMFILES%\INTERNET EXPLORER\IEXPLORE.EXE
FileHash          0A70CF0A6D691825F0A5F3899B0A3B3978D0F2F0B66CE1B9023CC1C
                                                              950E6777A
Fqbn              O=MICROSOFT CORPORATION, L=REDMOND, S=WASHINGTON,
                  C=US\INTERNET EXPLORER\IEXPLORE.EXE\11.0.15063.00
TargetLogonId     0x138d2f
```

NOTE The events described in this section are available on the book's website, in the `AppLocker EXE and DLL - Audit Mode.evtx` **and** `AppLocker EXE and DLL - Enforcement Mode.evtx` **files.**

The `PolicyName` field contains a type of AppLocker policy to which the generated event belongs. This field may have one of the following values:

- `EXE`: Executable rules
- `DLL`: DLL rules
- `SCRIPT`: Script rules
- `MSI`: Windows Installer rules
- `APPX`: Packaged application rules

The `RuleId` field contains a GUID, which is a hexadecimal number that uniquely identifies each rule. The GUID is not shown in the AppLocker group policy interface.

HOW TO VIEW APPLOCKER RULE GUIDS

You can view rule GUIDs using the `Get-AppLockerPolicy` **PowerShell command. For example, to get detailed information about effective AppLocker rules applied to the local machine, use the following command:**

```
Get-AppLockerPolicy -Effective -XML > c:\AppLocker.xml
```

It is up to you which path you want to specify for an output `.xml` **file. Here is an example of how the output may look:**

```
<AppLockerPolicy Version="1">
<RuleCollection Type="Appx" EnforcementMode="Enabled">
      <FilePublisherRule Id="a9e18c21-ff8f-43cf-b9fc-db40eed693ba"
Name=
   "(Default Rule) All signed packaged apps" Description="Allows
members
         of the Everyone group to run packaged apps that are
signed."
      UserOrGroupSid="S-1-1-0" Action="Allow">
         <Conditions>
               <FilePublisherCondition PublisherName="*"
ProductName=
                                       "*" BinaryName="*">
               <BinaryVersionRange LowSection="0.0.0.0"
                                       HighSection="*" />
            </FilePublisherCondition>
         </Conditions>
      </FilePublisherRule>
</RuleCollection>
<RuleCollection Type="Dll" EnforcementMode="AuditOnly" />
<RuleCollection Type="Exe" EnforcementMode="AuditOnly" />
<RuleCollection Type="Msi" EnforcementMode="AuditOnly" />
<RuleCollection Type="Script" EnforcementMode="AuditOnly" />
</AppLockerPolicy>
```

The rule GUID is located in the `Id` **parameter for each AppLocker rule.**

The `RuleName` field contains the name of the rule that allowed the application to run.

The `RuleSddl` field contains a Security Descriptor Definition Language (SDDL) string that defines rule actions. It has a specific SDDL ACE type called a *conditional ACE*. A conditional ACE may have one of the following four types:

- **XA:** Access Allowed Callback. Used in AppLocker allow rules.
- **XD:** Access Denied Callback. Used in AppLocker deny rules.
- **ZA:** Access Allowed Object Callback.
- **ZU:** Audit Callback.

An SDDL string can be interpreted in the following manner:

`D:(XA;;FX;;;S-1-1-0;(APPID://PATH Contains "%PROGRAMFILES%\*"))`

- **D::** DACL entry.
- **XA:** AppLocker Allow rule.
- **FX:** `FILE_GENERIC_EXECUTE` rule. This rule is applicable to file execute actions.
- **S-1-1-0:** This rule is applicable to Everyone (`S-1-1-0`).
- **APPID://PATH Contains "%PROGRAMFILES%*":** Rule scope.

You can find more information about SDDL syntax in Chapter 10.

The `TargetUser` field contains the SID of the account under which the application was executed.

The `TargetProcessId` field contains the process ID (PID) that was assigned to the new process.

The `FilePath` field contains the full directory and filename of the executed process. This field usually contains the AppLocker system path variables listed in Table 12-9.

Table 12-9: AppLocker System Path Variables

VARIABLE	WINDOWS VARIABLE	PATH
`%WINDIR%`	`%SystemRoot%`	Windows directory
`%SYSTEM32%`	`%SystemDirectory%`	`%WINDIR%\System32`
`%OSDRIVE%`	`%SystemDrive%`	Drive on which Windows files are installed
`%PROGRAMFILES%`	`%ProgramFiles%` and `%ProgramFiles(x86)%`	Program Files and Program Files (x86) folders
`%REMOVABLE%`	–	Removable media, such as CD, DVD, Blu-Ray, and so on
`%HOT%`	–	Removable storage, such as USB sticks or USB drives

The `FileHash` field contains the Authenticode hash of the executed file. AppLocker computes the hash value itself. Internally it uses the SHA2 Authenticode hash for Portable Executables (EXE and DLL) and Windows Installers and a SHA2 flat-file hash for the rest. If the policy was applied in `Enforce mode`, this field is always empty.

The `Fqbn` field contains the composed value in the following format:

```
Publisher/Product name/Original filename/File version
```

The `Fqbn` field will have a value of - if:

- Executable is not signed

- AppLocker policy was applied in `Enforce mode`

- Executable was not properly signed, signing certificate is invalid, or the file was modified

The `TargetLogonId` field contains the logon ID of a session for an account under which the application was executed.

Listing 12-20 is an example of the event generated in the AppLocker event log if an application was allowed to run but would have been prevented from running if the AppLocker policy was enforced and the AppLocker policy for executable files is set to "Audit only."

Listing 12-20: Event ID 8003

```
Event Log: Microsoft-Windows-AppLocker/EXE and DLL
Source: AppLocker
Level: Warning
%SYSTEM32%\NOTEPAD.EXE was allowed to run but would have been prevented
                 from running if the AppLocker policy were enforced.

PolicyName       EXE
RuleId           {00000000-0000-0000-0000-000000000000}
RuleName         -
RuleSddl         -
TargetUser       S-1-5-21-1913345275-1711810662-261465553-1120
TargetProcessId  1484
FilePath         %SYSTEM32%\NOTEPAD.EXE
FileHash         0C67E3923EDA8154A89ADCA8A6BF47DF7C07D40BB41963DEB16ACBC
                                                              F2E54803E
Fqbn             O=MICROSOFT CORPORATION, L=REDMOND, S=WASHINGTON,
     C=US\MICROSOFT® WINDOWS® OPERATING SYSTEM\NOTEPAD.EXE\10.0.15063.00
TargetLogonId    0x138d2f
```

The 8003 event has the same schema as the 8002 event discussed earlier.

The only difference is that the 8003 event does not capture information for the following fields:

- **RuleID:** Always equals {00000000-0000-0000-0000-000000000000}

- **RuleName:** Always equals "-"
- **RuleSddl:** Always equals "-"

Listing 12-21 is an example of the event generated in the AppLocker event log if an application was not allowed to run.

Listing 12-21: Event ID 8004

```
Event Log: Microsoft-Windows-AppLocker/EXE and DLL
Source: AppLocker
Level: Error
%SYSTEM32%\NOTEPAD.EXE was prevented from running.

PolicyName       EXE
RuleId           {00000000-0000-0000-0000-000000000000}
RuleName         -
RuleSddl         -
TargetUser       S-1-5-21-1913345275-1711810662-261465553-1120
TargetProcessId  4860
FilePath         %SYSTEM32%\NOTEPAD.EXE
FileHash
Fqbn             -
TargetLogonId    0x138d2f
```

The 8004 event has the same schema as the 8002 event discussed earlier.

The only difference is that 8004 event does not capture information for the following fields:

- **RuleID:** Always equals {00000000-0000-0000-0000-000000000000}
- **RuleName:** Always equals "-"
- **RuleSddl:** Always equals "-"
- **FileHash:** Always empty
- **Fqbn:** Always equals "-"

MSI and Script

The MSI and Script event log contains events for Windows Installer and Script rules. Three events are associated with Windows Installer and Script rules:

- **Event ID 8005:** *SCRIPT_OR_INSTALLER_NAME* was allowed to run.
- **Event ID 8006:** *SCRIPT_OR_INSTALLER_NAME* was allowed to run but would have been prevented from running if the AppLocker policy were enforced.
- **Event ID 8007:** *SCRIPT_OR_INSTALLER_NAME* was prevented from running.

NOTE See this chapter's download materials for an example of MSI and Script event log events (.evtx files).

Events 8005 and 8006

Events 8005 and 8006 have the same fields and specifics as events 8002 and 8003, which were discussed earlier, with the following difference:

- **Fqbn field:** Most installers do not contain the File version property so the File version will be shown as 0.0.0.00. Also, the installation file may not have the Product name and Original filename properties, and those will not be captured in the event if they are not present. An Fqbn field in an 8005/8006 event for Windows Installer rule might look like this:

  O=MICROSOFT CORPORATION, L=REDMOND, S=WASHINGTON, C=US\\\0.0.0.00.

Event 8007

Event 8007 has the same fields and specifics as event 8004, which was discussed earlier.

Packaged app-Execution and Packaged app-Deployment

The difference between the previously discussed events and the 8020, 8021, 8022, 8023, 8024, and 8025 events is that they don't have the FilePath, FileHash, and TargetLogonId fields.

Also all packaged application AppLocker events have an additional field: Package. It contains a packaged application name, for example, MICROSOFT .WINDOWS.CORTANA.

Event 8024 is triggered when you look at an application installation page without installing the application.

> **NOTE** See this chapter's download materials for an example of Packaged app-Execution and Packaged app-Deployment event logs events (.evtx files).

Process Permissions and LSASS.exe Access Auditing

Each process and thread in Windows has its own DACL, SACL, and owner assigned to it. For most processes the SACL is not defined, but it can be defined at the moment the process is created.

One of the tools you can use to view or set a process's SACL, DACL and an owner is Microsoft Process Explorer (formerly Sysinternals). Another free Microsoft command line tool you can use for the same purpose is SubInAcl.exe.

Figure 12-10 shows an example of the DACL modification dialog in the Process Explorer.

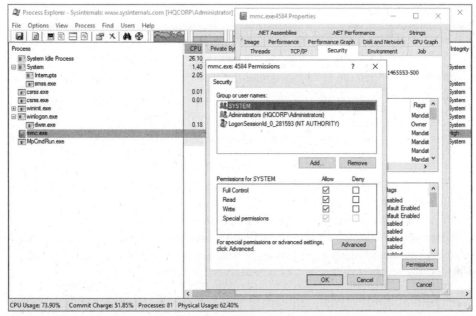

Figure 12.10: Process Explorer DACL modification interface

Processes have their own set of access rights, which are listed in Table 12.10.

Table 12.10: Process Access Rights

CONSTANT	HEX	PERMISSION	EVENT LOG DISPLAY TEXT
%%4480	0x0001	Terminate	Force process termination
%%4481	0x0002	Create Thread	Create new thread in process
%%4482	0x0004	Set Session ID	Set process session ID
%%4483	0x0008	Memory Operations	Perform virtual memory operation
%%4484	0x0010	Read Memory	Read from process memory
%%4485	0x0020	Write Memory	Write to process memory
%%4486	0x0040	Duplicate Handle	Duplicate handle into or out of process
%%4487	0x0080	Create Process	Create a subprocess of process
%%4488	0x0100	Set Quota	Set process quotas
%%4489	0x0200	Set Information	Set process information

Continues

Table 12-10 (*continued*)

CONSTANT	HEX	PERMISSION	EVENT LOG DISPLAY TEXT
%%4490	0x0400	Query Information	Query process information
%%4491	0x0800	Suspend/Resume	Set process termination port
%%4492	0x1000	Query Limited Information	Undefined Access (no effect) Bit 12
%%4493	0x2000	Set Limited Information	Undefined Access (no effect) Bit 13

DELETE, READ_CONTROL, WRITE_DAC, WRITE_OWNER and SYNCHRONIZE standard access rights are also applicable to processes. You can find more information about standard access rights in Chapter 5.

If you set a SACL for a process or thread, you might get one of the following two events in the security event log if the access attempt matches the SACL, depending on the other settings enabled in the system:

- **4656 (A handle to an object was requested):** This event is generated if the "Object Access\Audit Kernel Objects" and "Object Access\Audit Handle Manipulation" subcategories are enabled.

- **4663 (An attempt was made to access an object):** This event is generated if the "Object Access\Audit Kernel Objects" subcategory is enabled.

You will find more information about 4656 and 4663 events in the next chapters.

LSASS's Process Default SACL

Windows 10 and Windows Server 2016 have a default SACL set for the lsass .exe process: S:(AU;SAFA;0x0010;;;WD). Here is what this SACL means:

S:(AU;SAFA;0x0010;;;WD)

- **S:** SACL section
- **AU:** SYSTEM AUDIT ACE type
- **SAFA:** ACE flags:
  - **SA:** Successful Access audit
  - **FA:** Failed Access audit
- **0x0010:** Read Memory (PROCESS_VM_READ) access permission. See Appendix C for more details.
- **WD:** applied to Everyone (WD)

This ACE reports any successful or failed memory read access attempts performed against lsass.exe. The "Object Access\Audit Kernel Objects" sub-category should be enabled, as mentioned previously, in order to get events for access attempts to processes or threads. It might be very noisy, for example, every time you run Task Manager, the Read Memory operation is performed against lsass.exe.

Failed access attempts are reported by the 4656 event.

Listing 12.22 is an example of the 4663 event that appears in the Windows security event log when a successful Read Memory access attempt is performed against lsass.exe.

Listin 12.22: ID 4663: An attempt was made to access an object.

```
Task Category: Kernel Object
Keywords: Audit Success
Subject:
        Security ID:            S-1-5-21-1913345275-1711810662-261465553-500
        Account Name:           Administrator
        Account Domain:         HQCORP
        Logon ID:               0x438DE
Object:
        Object Server:          Security
        Object Type:            Process
        Object Name:            \Device\HarddiskVolume2\Windows\System32\
                                                            lsass.exe
        Handle ID:              0x3d0
        Resource Attributes:-
Process Information:
        Process ID:             0x618
        Process Name:           C:\Windows\System32\Taskmgr.exe
Access Request Information:
        Accesses:               %%4484 (Read from process memory)
        Access Mask:            0x10
```

NOTE The event described in Listing 12.22 is available on the book's website, in the LSASS's Process Default SACL.evtx file.

The Subject section contains information about the account that performed the access attempt.

The Object section contains information about the object being accessed. The Object Type for processes is always Process.

Object Name contains the path to the process being accessed. All removable storage devices have a unique \Device\ identifier assigned to them, which is a symbolic link for this object. For hard drives this symbolic link will have a format of `HarddiskVolume#`. Chapter 13 contains information about how you can translate HarddiskVolume symbolic links to a logical drive letter.

The `Process Information` section contains information about the process that performed access attempt.

The `Accesses` section shows the access rights that were requested. See Table 12.10 for more details.

The `Access Mask` section shows in hexadecimal format the access rights that were requested. See Table 12.10 for more details.

CHAPTER 13

Filesystem and Removable Storage

This chapter is probably one of the most interesting chapters in the book, because it answers some of the most common questions asked during incident investigation procedures:

- Who deleted the file?
- Who created the file?
- How was this file accessed—using which tool or application?
- When was this file deleted?
- Who changed this file?
- and so on

Some of these questions are easy to answer, but some of them are not. In this chapter you will find information about monitoring recommendations for most common scenarios related to the local drive and removable storage filesystem objects.

Windows Filesystem

Currently the most common Windows filesystem is the New Technology File System (NTFS). You can still find the File Allocation Table 32 (FAT32) filesystem, most likely on some USB drives or legacy operating systems, like Windows 98, for example.

The FAT32 filesystem was developed as an extension and replacement of the older FAT16 filesystem to overcome some FAT16 filesystem limitations, such as maximum file size limitations, and to improve other characteristics.

FAT16 was first introduced in November 1987, with FAT32 coming in 1996. Table 13-1 compares some of the characteristics of these two filesystems.

Table 13-1: FAT16 Compared to FAT32

LIMIT	FAT16	FAT32
Max. volume size	4 GB (64KB clusters)	16 TB (4KB sectors)
Max. file size	4 GB	4 GB
Max. number of files	65,460 (32KB clusters)	268,173,300 (32KB clusters)
Max. filename length	8.3 format (8 characters)	8.3 format (8 characters)

Some disadvantages of FAT filesystems are:

- FAT systems don't perform boot sector backups, so if the boot sector becomes corrupt, there is no backup copy to restore it.
- They have no built-in filesystem security, encryption, or compression features.
- They have no quota or limiting mechanisms for user accounts or groups.
- They have slower filesystem access speed compared to NTFS.
- They have no self-recovery mechanisms.

Considering these disadvantages, the first version of the new NTFS filesystem was introduced in 1993 for the Microsoft Windows NT 3.1 operating system. It didn't address all the issues just listed, but it was a first step on the road to fixing them.

Here are some features of NTFS v3.0, which was first introduced in Windows 2000:

- **Security:** Security descriptors are assigned to each file and folder on NTFS. An access control list, called the *discretionary access control list* (DACL), is available for configuring access permissions for filesystem objects. A *system access control list* (SACL) provides the possibility to specify auditing rules for specific permissions defined for security principals.

- **Sparse files:** NTFS provides support for files with empty segments inside.

- **Scalability:** NTFS supports bigger maximum volume size, maximum files size, and maximum number of files that can be maintained.

- **Encryption:** Encryption for files and folders is supported by the embedded Encrypting File System (EFS).

- **Quotas:** This feature allows setting disk quotas for user accounts.

- **Volume shadow copy:** This feature allows keeping previous file versions, so users can revert to the previous file version if needed.

- **Transactions:** Allows grouping filesystem operations in transactions. Transactions guarantee that all operations within a transaction will be performed or all of them will be cancelled, and allows rolling back the entire transaction.

- **File compression:** Allows compressing files and folders.

- **Journaling:** Allows tracking changes to the disk volumes, which gives the ability to roll back some changes if, for example, a system crash or other system error occurred.

- **Alternate data streams:** Allows one file to have multiple data streams associated with it.

This book concentrates on the NTFS filesystem, because filesystem auditing is available only in NTFS on Windows operating systems.

You will find more detailed information about NTFS in the scenarios discussed further in the book.

NTFS Security Descriptors

The first step in learning the NTFS auditing mechanism is to understand what discretionary access control lists (DACLs), system access control lists (SACLs), and object owners are and how they can be assigned.

Every file and folder on NTFS has a security descriptor applied to it, which contains the following main sections:

- **Object owner:** Has full control on the object.
- **DACL:** Defines object access permissions.
- **SACL:** Defines object auditing settings.

The object's owner has full access permissions for the object. Also, by default, members of the built-in local Administrators group can take ownership of any file and folder object on the system, because they are members of the "Take ownership of files or other object" user right group policy setting. Any account that has been assigned the "Take ownership of files or other object" (SeTakeOwnershipPrivilege) user right can take ownership of any file or directory in the system.

Also, any account that has the "Restore files and directories" (SeRestorePrivilege) user right can take ownership of any filesystem object.

Another way to give an account permission to take ownership of files or folders is to give this account "Take ownership" permission in the object's DACL as discussed later in this section.

You can change the filesystem object's owner, DACL, and SACL using the built-in filesystem object security descriptor editor. Open the properties of the object using Windows Explorer, switch to the Security tab, and click the Advanced button. Figure 13-1 shows the Windows Server 2016 security descriptor editor for the filesystem object.

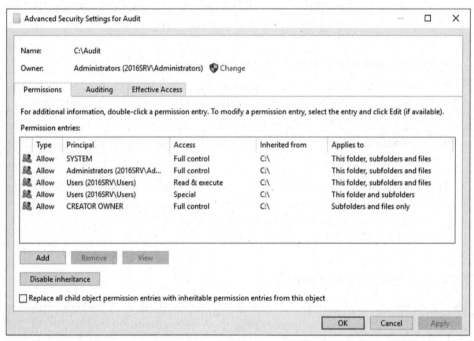

Figure 13-1: Windows filesystem object security descriptor editor

To change the filesystem object's owner, click the Change button located near the Owner section. The object's owner can be a security group, user/computer account, or a built-in security principal.

The Permissions tab illustrated in Figure 13-1 contains access control entries (ACEs) of the object's DACL. They control access to the filesystem object. Figure 13-2 shows the property editor for an ACE in the DACL.

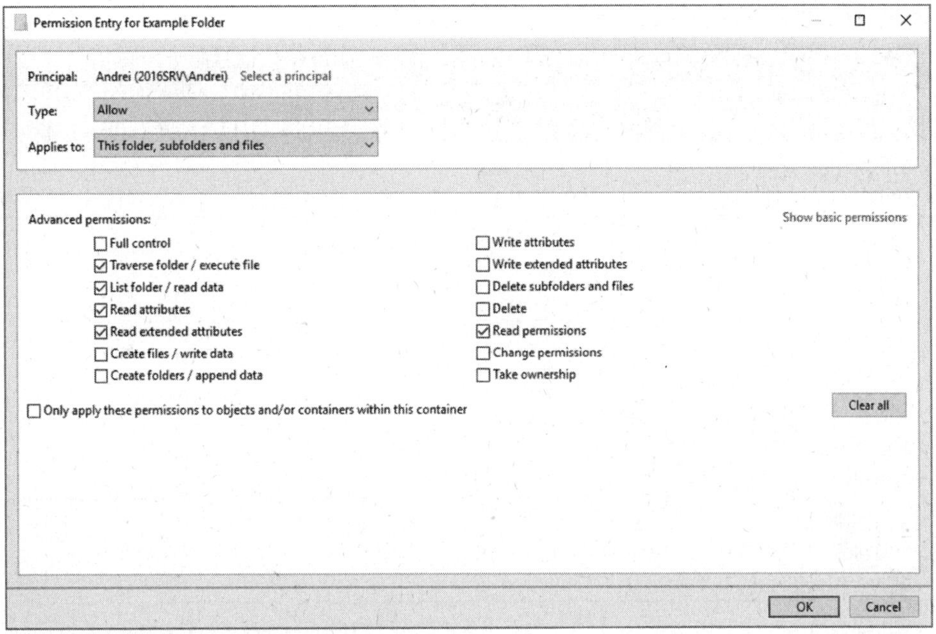

Figure 13-2: Filesystem object's DACL ACE

The `Principal` section contains the security principal (account or security group) to which the ACE applies.

The `Type` section has the following values:

- **Allow:** ACE that allows access.

- **Deny:** ACE that denies access.

At the bottom of Figure 13-2 you can see the "Only apply these permissions to objects and/or containers within this container" checkbox. This checkbox is displayed only for folders; it's not displayed for files. Its main purpose is to limit the scope of the current ACE to only files and folders within current folder. Access permissions will not be inherited by any object within current folder's subfolders; they will be applied only to direct members (child folders and files).

The "Applies to" section is displayed only for folders and allows you to define the scope of the current ACE. Table 13-2 contains information about possible values of this field and information about objects to which the ACE will be applied.

Table 13-2: DACL ACE Scope

VALUE	CURRENT FOLDER	SUBFOLDERS IN CURRENT FOLDER	FILES IN CURRENT FOLDER	ALL SUBSEQUENT SUBFOLDERS	ALL FILES IN SUBSEQUENT SUBFOLDERS
This folder only	+				
This folder, subfolders, and files	+	+	+	+	+
This folder and subfolders	+	+		+	
This folder and files	+		+		+
Subfolders and files only		+	+	+	+
Subfolders only		+	+		
Files only			+		+

If the "Only apply these permissions to objects and/or containers within this container" checkbox is enabled, the "All subsequent subfolders" and "All files in subsequent subfolders" columns in Table 13-2 are not applicable and permissions will not be inherited by objects within subfolders.

The "Advanced permissions" section contains information about permissions that are allowed or denied by the ACE. Table 13-3 contains the list of permissions that may be defined for folders and/or files.

Table 13-3: File/Folder Permissions

PERMISSION	FILE	FOLDER
Full control	All possible permissions.	All possible permissions.
Traverse folder/ execute file	File execution. Applicable to executable files only.	Permission to navigate through the folder tree. It does not include the "List folder" permission. This permission is ignored for accounts that have "Bypass traverse checking" user right assigned in the local group policy.

PERMISSION	FILE	FOLDER
List folder/read data	Read the content of the file. In order to read the file's content account it must also have "Read permissions" and "Read extended attributes" permissions assigned.	List the names of files and folders within the folder.
Read attributes	Read standard attributes of the file: ■ read-only ■ hidden ■ system ■ archive	Read standard attributes of the folder: ■ read-only ■ hidden ■ system ■ archive
Read extended attributes	Read extended attributes of the file, such as Alternate Data Streams (ADS).	Read extended attributes of the folder.

Use the `fsutil usn readdata` command to get a list of all attributes for a specific file or folder. Search for the `File Attributes` field in the `fsutil` command output. Here is the list of all attributes with corresponding hexadecimal values:

■ 0x1: FILE_ATTRIBUTE_READONLY

■ 0x2: FILE_ATTRIBUTE_HIDDEN

■ 0x4: FILE_ATTRIBUTE_SYSTEM

■ 0x10: FILE_ATTRIBUTE_DIRECTORY

■ 0x20: FILE_ATTRIBUTE_ARCHIVE

■ 0x80: FILE_ATTRIBUTE_NORMAL

■ 0x100: FILE_ATTRIBUTE_TEMPORARY

■ 0x200: FILE_ATTRIBUTE_SPARSE_FILE

■ 0x400: FILE_ATTRIBUTE_REPARSE_POINT

■ 0x800: FILE_ATTRIBUTE_COMPRESSED

■ 0x1000: FILE_ATTRIBUTE_OFFLINE

■ 0x2000: FILE_ATTRIBUTE_NOT_CONTENT_INDEXED

■ 0x4000: FILE_ATTRIBUTE_ENCRYPTED

■ 0x8000: FILE_ATTRIBUTE_INTEGRITY_STREAM

■ 0x10000: FILE_ATTRIBUTE_VIRTUAL

■ 0x20000: FILE_ATTRIBUTE_NO_SCRUB_DATA

In order to read the extended attributes the account must also have "Read permissions" and "List folder/read data" permissions assigned.

Continues

Table 13-3 (*continued*)

PERMISSION	FILE	FOLDER
Create files/ write data	Allows making changes to the file and rewrite the content.	Create files within the folder.
Create Folders/ append Data	Allows appending data to the file without modifying its previous content.	Create folders within the folder.
Write attributes	Allows changing standard file attributes, such as the Read-Only property.	Allows changing standard folder attributes, such as the Read-Only property.
Write extended attributes	Allows changing extended file attributes, such as Alternate Data Streams (ADS).	Allows changing extended folder attributes, such as Alternate Data Streams (ADS).
Delete subfolders and files	Not applicable.	Allows deleting all subfolders and files even if the account does not have Delete permissions for nested objects.
Delete	Delete file. "Read permissions" permission also required to delete a file.	Delete folder. You have to make sure that you also have Delete access to all objects inside of the folder you are trying to delete. "Read permissions" permission also required to delete a folder.
Read permissions	Permission to read information about an owner and DACL from file's security descriptor. Associated with READ_CONTROL access right.	Permission to read information about an owner and DACL from a directory's security descriptor. Associated with READ_CONTROL access right.
Change permissions	Permission to change owner and DACL in the file's security descriptor.	Permission to change owner and DACL in the folder's security descriptor.
Take ownership	Permission to take ownership for a file.	Permission to take ownership for a folder.

Many operations in Windows operating system require more than one permission; for example, if you need to delete the file using Windows Explorer, your account should contain not only the Delete permission, but also the "Read permissions" access permission.

Inheritance

By default, if inheritance is not disabled, every new filesystem object inherits permissions from its parent object (folder or drive) if the new object is in the scope of its parent's DACL ACEs. For example, if you create a new file within a folder that has a DACL ACE applied to "This folder and files," the new file will inherit this ACE and add it to its security descriptor. If you create a new file within a folder that has a DACL ACE applied to "This folder only," then the new file will not inherit this ACE.

Inheritance can be disabled on a file or folder by clicking the "Disable inheritance" button in the Advanced Security Settings window. You can see this button in Figure 13-1. When you click it, the dialog shown in Figure 13-3 appears.

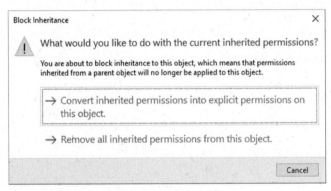

Figure 13-3: Block inheritance dialog window

The "Convert inherited permissions into explicit permissions on this object" option will disable inheritance and convert all DACL ACEs that were inherited into direct ACEs for the object.

The "Remove all inherited permissions from this object" option will remove all inherited ACEs from the object's DACL.

You can also overwrite all permissions for all nested files and folders (including all subsequent objects) using the "Replace all child object permissions entries with inheritable permission entries from this object" checkbox in the Advanced Security Settings window (Figure 13-1). By checking this checkbox all DACL ACEs of nested filesystem objects will be erased and replaced by inherited ACEs from the primary object. Only ACEs that can be inherited from the primary to the destination object (Applies to) will be inherited.

Inherited Deny permissions do not prevent access to an object if the object has an explicit Allow permission entry. Explicit permissions take precedence over inherited permissions, even inherited Deny permissions.

SACL

To view and modify a filesystem object's SACL, a user account must have the SeSecurityPrivilege enabled in its session token. The SeSecurityPrivilege can be assigned by the "Manage auditing and security log" user right group policy setting.

To edit a SACL for a filesystem object, open the Auditing tab in the Advanced Security Settings window as shown in Figure 13-4.

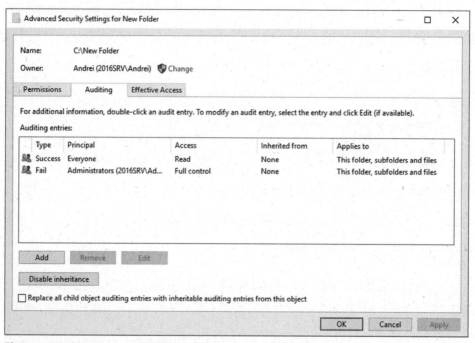

Figure 13-4: Directory's auditing settings (SACL)

The only difference between a DACL ACE and a SACL ACE is the Type field. For SACL it can have one of the following values:

- **All:** Success and failed access attempts.
- **Fail:** Only failed access attempts.
- **Success:** Only success access attempts.

All other settings are identical to DACL settings and works the same way.

File and Folder Operations

In this section you will find information about common operations related to files and folders, such as file/folder creation, modification, deletion, and so on.

File/Folder Creation

File and folder creation operations can be successful or unsuccessful. If an account has no permissions to create new filesystem object, then an attempt will be unsuccessful. In this section you will find more information about file and folder creation monitoring.

Successful File Creation

New files can be created using Windows File Explorer, command-line tools, PowerShell scripts, and other methods. These methods generate different sets of events, but they share some events that are generated for all methods.

To handle successful file creation events, the folder in which a new file will be created must have an ACE in the SACL that should:

- Track activity for specific account (Principal). Set Principal to Everyone to track activities for any account.
- Have a Success type.
- Have the "Create files/write data" advanced permission set.

You also need to set a scope for the ACE using "Applies to" parameter to, for example, "This folder and subfolders." This will exclude all file modification events, which also fall in to the "Create files/write data" permission use category, because the files will not be in the scope of this ACE.

Listing 13-1 is an example of the event usually generated in the Windows security event log when a new file is created in an audited folder using cmd.exe.

Listing 13-1: Event ID 4656: A handle to an object was requested.

```
Task Category: Removable Storage
Keywords: Audit Success
Subject:
        Security ID:            S-1-5-21-3212943211-794299840-588279583-500
        Account Name:           Administrator
        Account Domain:         2016SRV
        Logon ID:               0x153A5E1
Object:
        Object Server:          Security
        Object Type:            File
        Object Name:            C:\New Folder\NewFile.txt
        Handle ID:              0x48
        Resource Attributes:    -
```

```
Process Information:
      Process ID:              0x5fc
      Process Name:            C:\Windows\System32\cmd.exe
Access Request Information:
      Transaction ID:          {00000000-0000-0000-0000-000000000000}
      Accesses:                %%1538 (READ_CONTROL)
                               %%1541 (SYNCHRONIZE)
                               %%4417 (WriteData (or AddFile))
                               %%4418 (AppendData (or AddSubdirectory or
                                                      CreatePipeInstance))
                               %%4420 (WriteEA)
                               %%4423 (ReadAttributes)
                               %%4424 (WriteAttributes)
                               See tables 13-4 and 5-4 for more details
      Access Reasons:          -
      Access Mask:             0x120196 (See tables 13-4 and 5-4 for more
                                                      details)
```

NOTE The events described in this section are available on the book's website, in the Successful File Creation - command line.evtx and Successful File Creation - windows explorer.evtx files.

The application requests a handle for a new file. A handle request does not mean that the permissions were used, as shown in the 4663 event discussed later in this chapter. A handle request event means only that permissions were requested and successfully granted.

The Subject section contains information about the account that requested the handle.

Object Server always has a value of Security and Object Type always has a value of File, regardless of whether a new file or a new folder was created.

Object Name contains the new file's name and the full path to the file.

The Process Information section contains information about the process that was used to request the handle.

Transaction ID is a field designed to show information about NTFS transactions (Transact NTFS), if the action was a part of any transaction. All events, which are part of the same transaction, will have the same Transaction ID value.

The Accesses field contains a list of requested access permissions. You can find information about standard/generic access rights in Table 5-4 (Chapter 5).

Table 13-4 contains information about constant values and hexadecimal values associated with filesystem object access permissions.

Table 13-4: Filesystem Object Access Permissions

CONSTANT	HEXADECIMAL	PERMISSION CONSTANT	PERMISSION NAME
`%%4416`	`0x1`	`ReadData (or ListDirectory)`	List folder/read data
`%%4417`	`0x2`	`WriteData (or AddFile)`	Create files/write data
`%%4418`	`0x4`	`AppendData (or AddSubdirectory or CreatePipeInstance)`	Create folders/ append data
`%%4419`	`0x8`	`ReadEA`	Read extended attributes
`%%4420`	`0x10`	`WriteEA`	Write extended attributes
`%%4421`	`0x20`	`Execute/Traverse`	Traverse folder/ execute file
`%%4422`	`0x40`	`DeleteChild`	Delete subfolders and files
`%%4423`	`0x80`	`ReadAttributes`	Read attributes
`%%4424`	`0x100`	`WriteAttributes`	Write attributes

Each application decides on its own which access permissions to request. That is why in different scenarios (file creation using cmd.exe or Windows File Explorer) a different set of requested access permissions is shown in the 4656 event.

The event in Listing 13-2 specifies which access permissions, from the list of requested permissions in the 4656 event in Listing 13-1, were really used.

Listing 13-2: Event ID 4663: An attempt was made to access an object.

```
Task Category: Removable Storage
Keywords: Audit Success
Subject:
      Security ID:          S-1-5-21-3212943211-794299840-588279583-500
      Account Name:         Administrator
      Account Domain:       2016SRV
      Logon ID:             0x153A5E1
Object:
      Object Server:        Security
      Object Type:          File
      Object Name:          C:\New Folder\New Bitmap Image.bmp
      Handle ID:            0x5a0
```

```
        Resource Attributes:
Process Information:
        Process ID:            0x1148
        Process Name:          C:\Windows\explorer.exe
Access Request Information:
        Accesses:              %%4417 (WriteData (or AddFile)).
                                        See tables 13-4 and 5-4
        Access Mask:           0x2 (See tables 13-4 and 5-4)
```

In this case you see that only the WriteData (or AddFile) permission was used. 4656 and 4663 events can be linked together using the Handle ID field; they both will be reporting the same Handle ID.

The list of Accesses may be different in other file creation events, but it always contains the WriteData (or AddFile)) access permission.

Unfortunately, there is no way to detect using event 4663 whether a new file was created or the existing file was modified. 4663 events for these two actions look exactly the same. But, if you enabled the Create files/write data access permission auditing only on the directory level, then file modification events will not be monitored and you will only see file creation 4663 events in the Windows security event log.

The event in Listing 13-3 informs you that the handle, which was initially requested in event 4656, was closed

Listing 13-3: Event ID 4658: The handle to an object was closed.

```
Task Category: Removable Storage
Keywords: Audit Success
```

Unsuccessful File Creation

To monitor unsuccessful file creation events, the folder in which a new file is going to be created must have an auditing (SACL) ACE applied, which should:

- Track activity for a specific account (Principal). Set Principal to Everyone to track activities for any account.
- Have a Fail type.
- Have "Create files/write data" advanced permissions set.

Listing 13-4 is an example of the event that is recorded in the Windows security event log if the file creation attempt failed due to lack of access permissions.

Listing 13-4: Event ID 4656: A handle to an object was requested.

```
Task Category: File System
Keywords: Audit Failure
Subject:
        Security ID:           S-1-5-21-3212943211-794299840-588279583-500
        Account Name:          Administrator
```

```
        Account Domain:      2016SRV
        Logon ID:            0x153A5E1
Object:
        Object Server:       Security
        Object Type:         File
        Object Name:         C:\New Folder\NewFile.txt
        Handle ID:           0x0
        Resource Attributes: -
Process Information:
        Process ID:          0x5fc
        Process Name:        C:\Windows\System32\cmd.exe
Access Request Information:
        Transaction ID:      {00000000-0000-0000-0000-000000000000}
        Accesses:         %%1538 (READ_CONTROL)
                          %%1541 (SYNCHRONIZE)
                          %%4417 (WriteData (or AddFile))
                          %%4418 (AppendData (or AddSubdirectory or
                                              CreatePipeInstance))
                          %%4420 (WriteEA)
                          %%4423 (ReadAttributes)
                          %%4424 (WriteAttributes)
        Access Reasons: %%1538 (READ_CONTROL):            %%1809
                                         (Unknown or unchecked)
                          %%1541 (SYNCHRONIZE):           %%1809
                                         (Unknown or unchecked)
                          %%4417 (WriteData (or AddFile)):   %%1802
                               (Denied by)    D:(D;OICI;DC;;;
                   S-1-5-21-3212943211-794299840-588279583-500)
                          %%4418 (AppendData (or AddSubdirectory or
          CreatePipeInstance)):      %%1809 (Unknown or unchecked)
                          %%4420 (WriteEA):          %%1809 (Unknown or
                                                            unchecked)
                          %%4423 (ReadAttributes):   %%1809 (Unknown or
                                                            unchecked)
                          %%4424 (WriteAttributes):  %%1809 (Unknown or
                                                            unchecked)
                        See tables 13-4, 13-5 and 5-4 for more details
        Access Mask:    0x120196 (See tables 13-4 and 5-4 for more details)
```

NOTE The event described in this section is available on the book's website, in the Unsuccessful FIle Creation.evtx **file.**

When an access request to the file is denied, a 4656 failure event is generated. The Access Reasons section contains status information about each requested access permission validation result. Table 13-5 contains information about possible Access Reason field values and their descriptions.

Table 13-5: Filesystem Object Access Reasons

CONSTANT	TEXT	DESCRIPTION
%%1801	Granted by	The requested permission was granted by explicit Allow ACE. This type of access reason also contains details about an ACE in the DACL that allowed the requested access permission. This entry contains an ACE in Security Descriptor Definition Language (SDDL) format, which is described in Chapter 10.
%%1802	Denied by	The requested permission was denied by explicit Deny ACE. This type of access reason also contains details about an ACE in the DACL that denied the requested access permission. This entry contains an ACE in Security Descriptor Definition Language (SDDL) format, which is described in Chapter 10.
%%1803	Denied by Integrity Policy check	If the access request was sent by a process with a lower integrity level than the integrity level of the filesystem object, you will get this access reason.
%%1804	Granted by Ownership	Access was granted because the account that performed the operation is an object owner. This usually applies to the READ_CONTROL access permission.
%%1805	Not granted	If there is no ACE entry to deny or allow a specific access type to the file, this status will appear. By default, if there is no ACE to allow or deny access, access is denied.
%%1806	Granted by NULL DACL	If there is no DACL associated with the filesystem object (DACL is completely removed), you will get this access reason.
%%1807	Denied by Empty DACL	If there are no ACEs in the filesystem object's DACL (it's empty, no entries), you will get this access reason.
%%1808	Granted by NULL Security Descriptor	If there is no security descriptor applied to the filesystem object (security descriptor does not exist), you will get this access reason.
%%1809	Unknown or unchecked	This means that the specified permission was not verified yet or verification status is unknown.
%%1810	Not granted due to missing	If the account requested access that requires additional user rights permissions (SeSecurityPrivilege, for example), but the account doesn't have the required permissions, you will get this access reason. The most common example is when a user tries to change a filesystem object's SACL and access is denied, because the user doesn't have the SeSecurityPrivilege user right.

CONSTANT	TEXT	DESCRIPTION
%%1811	Granted by ACE on parent folder	If access permission was granted because of an inherited ACE from a parent object, you will get this access reason. This type of access reason also contains details about the DACL ACE that allowed the requested access permission. This entry contains an ACE in Security Descriptor Definition Language (SDDL) format, which is described in Chapter 10.
%%1812	Denied by ACE on parent folder	If access permission was denied because of an inherited ACE from a parent object, you will get this access reason. This type of access reason also contains details about the DACL ACE that denied the requested access permission. This entry contains an ACE in Security Descriptor Definition Language (SDDL) format, which is described in Chapter 10.

The problem is that each application decides by itself which set of permissions to request for file creation operations. But it must request `WriteData (or AddFile))` permission. One way to verify that the action was an unsuccessful file creation or modification operation is to search for any `WriteData (or AddFile))` access requests with one of the following access reasons:

- **%%1802:** `Denied by`
- **%%1803:** `Denied by Integrity Policy check`
- **%%1805:** `Not granted`
- **%%1806:** `Granted by NULL DACL`
- **%%1807:** `Denied by Empty DACL`
- **%%1810:** `Not granted due to missing`
- **%%1812:** `Denied by ACE on parent folder`

Successful Folder Creation

It's not currently possible to monitor for successful folder creation operations because if the "Create folders/append data" access permission success auditing is enabled on the specific folder, no events are generated in the Windows security event log when a new subfolder is created.

If "Full control" access permission success auditing is enabled on the specific folder, the event in Listing 13-5 is generated.

Listing 13-5: Event ID 4656: A handle to an object was requested.

```
Task Category: Removable Storage
Keywords: Audit Success
Subject:
        Security ID:          S-1-5-21-3212943211-794299840-588279583-500
        Account Name:         Administrator
        Account Domain:       2016SRV
        Logon ID:             0x153A5E1
Object:
        Object Server:        Security
        Object Type:          File
        Object Name:          C:\New Folder\Subfolder
        Handle ID:            0x9c
        Resource Attributes:  -
Process Information:
        Process ID:           0x10ec
        Process Name:         C:\Windows\System32\cmd.exe
Access Request Information:
        Transaction ID:       {00000000-0000-0000-0000-000000000000}
        Accesses:             %%1541 (SYNCHRONIZE)
                              %%4416 (ReadData (or ListDirectory))
                              See tables 13-4 and 5-4 for more details
        Access Reasons:       -
        Access Mask:          0x100001
            (See tables 13-4 and 5-4 for more details)
```

NOTE The event described in this section is available on the book's website, in the `Successful Folder Creation.evtx` **file.**

This event does not have any information about folder creation actions. You see SYNCHRONIZE and ReadData (or ListDirectory) accesses requested, but they do not indicate that a new folder was created.

Unsuccessful Folder Creation

It's not currently possible to monitor for unsuccessful folder creation because if "Create folders/append data" access permission fail auditing is enabled on the specific folder, no events are generated in the Windows security event log when the new subfolder creation attempt failed.

NOTE You can see an example of events generated for unsuccessful folder creation attempt on the book's website, in the `Unsuccessful Folder Creation.evtx` **file.**

File/Folder Deletion

As discussed for file and folder creation in the previous section, deletion operations can also be monitored using the Windows security event log. This section provides additional information about file and folder deletion operations monitoring.

Successful File Deletion

To audit successful file deletion attempts, the Delete permission item should be enabled for the Success auditing type in the object's SACL.

Depending on the method used to delete a file, different sets of events will be recorded in the Windows security event log. But, no matter which method was used to delete a file, a 4663 event as shown in Listing 13-6 will be generated, which will contain the DELETE access permission in the Accesses field.

Listing 13-6: Event ID 4663: An attempt was made to access an object.

```
Task Category: Removable Storage
Keywords: Audit Success
Subject:
        Security ID:          S-1-5-21-3212943211-794299840-588279583-500
        Account Name:         Administrator
        Account Domain:       2016SRV
        Logon ID:             0x24839
Object:
        Object Server:        Security
        Object Type:          File
        Object Name:          C:\New Folder\New Rich Text Document.rtf
        Handle ID:            0x958
        Resource Attributes:  S:AI
Process Information:
        Process ID:           0xc44
        Process Name:         C:\Windows\explorer.exe
Access Request Information:
        Accesses:             %%1537 (DELETE)
                              See tables 13-4 and 5-4 for more details
        Access Mask:          0x10000
                              (See tables 13-4 and 5-4 for more details)
```

NOTE The event described in this section is available on the book's website, in the Successful File Deletion.evtx **file.**

Event 4663 shows you that DELETE access was successfully used to delete the C:\New Folder\New Rich Text Document.rtf file.

The `Resource Attributes` field contains additional information about the file's attributes. This entry contains the attributes string in SDDL format, which is described in Chapter 10. In this example `S:AI` means that inheritance for the object's SACL (`S:`) is allowed. `AI` means `SDDL_AUTO_INHERITED` inheritance is allowed.

All other fields were discussed earlier in this chapter.

Unsuccessful File Deletion

To audit unsuccessful file deletion attempts, the `Delete` permission item should be enabled for the `Fail` auditing type in the object's SACL.

You will get a similar 4656 event as for an unsuccessful file creation operation.

The same recommendations as provided for unsuccessful file creation operations are applicable for unsuccessful file deletion operations. But instead of `WriteData (or AddFile))` access permission, you should look for `DELETE` permission.

> **NOTE** You can see an example of events generated for unsuccessful file deletion attempt on the book's website, in the `Unsuccessful File Deletion.evtx` file.

Successful Folder Deletion

To audit successful folder deletion attempts, the `Delete` permission item should be enabled for the `Success` auditing type in the object's SACL.

Depending on the method used to delete a folder, different sets of events will be recorded in the Windows security event log. But, no matter which method was used to delete a folder, a 4663 event will be generated, which will contain `DELETE` access permission in the `Accesses` field.

> **NOTE** You can see an example of events generated for successful folder deletion attempt on the book's website, in the `Successful Folder Deletion.evtx` file.

The only difference between folder deletion and file deletion is that in a folder deletion event, the `Object Name` field contains the name of the folder instead of a filename. The only way to differentiate files and folders in these events is to verify that the deleted object has a file type (`.txt`, for example), but in this case files without a file type will be treated as folders.

Unsuccessful Folder Deletion

To audit unsuccessful folder deletion attempts, the `Delete` permission item should be enabled for the `Fail` auditing type in the object's SACL.

> **NOTE** You can see an example of events generated for unsuccessful folder deletion attempt on the book's website, in the `Unsuccessful Folder Deletion.evtx` file.

The same recommendations as provided for unsuccessful file creation operations are applicable for unsuccessful folder deletion operations. But instead of `WriteData (or AddFile))` access permission, you should look for `DELETE` permission.

File Content Modification

File content modification operations might be important to monitor in some scenarios. This section provides information about security events generated by these operations.

Successful File Content Modification

To audit successful file content modification attempts, "Create files/write data" and "Create folders/append data" permissions should be enabled for the `Success` auditing type in the object's SACL.

No matter which method is used to modify the data of the file, a 4663 event will be generated, which will contain `WriteData (or AddFile)` or/and `AppendData (or AddSubdirectory or CreatePipeInstance)` access permissions in the `Accesses` field.

> **NOTE** You can see an example of events generated for successful file content modification attempt on the book's website, in the `Successful File Content Modification.evtx` file.

`WriteData (or AddFile)` permission is required to create a new file or rewrite the file.

`AppendData (or AddSubdirectory or CreatePipeInstance)` permission is required to append data to the file without changing its previous content.

Which of these access permissions an application will use to change the file is unknown. In this case you need to monitor for 4663 events that contain one of these access permissions.

Unsuccessful File Content Modification

To audit unsuccessful file content modification attempts, "Create files/write data" and "Create folders/append data" permissions should be enabled for the `Fail` auditing type in the object's SACL.

You will get a similar 4656 event as for unsuccessful file creation operations.

> **NOTE** You can see an example of events generated for unsuccessful file content modification attempt on the book's website, in the `Unsuccessful File Content Modification.evtx` file.

The same recommendations as provided for unsuccessful file creation operations are applicable for unsuccessful file data modification operations. But instead of `WriteData (or AddFile))` access permission, you should look for `WriteData (or AddFile)` or/and `AppendData (or AddSubdirectory or CreatePipeInstance)` permissions.

File Read Data

Every time the content of a file is accessed for viewing, file "Read data" permission is requested. This section contains information about security events generated for file read operations.

Successful File Read Data Operations

To audit successful file read data attempts, the "List folder/read data" permission should be enabled for the `Success` auditing type in the object's SACL.

Depending on the method used to read a file, different sets of events will be recorded in the Windows security event log. But, no matter which method is used to open the file, a 4663 event will be generated, which will contain the `ReadData (or ListDirectory)` access permission in the `Accesses` field.

> **NOTE** You can see an example of events generated for successful file content read attempt on the book's website, in the `Successful File Read Data.evtx` file.

Unsuccessful File Read Data Operations

To audit unsuccessful file read attempts, "List folder/read data" permission should be enabled for the `Fail` auditing type in the object's SACL.

You will get a similar 4656 event as for unsuccessful file creation operations.

The same recommendations as provided for unsuccessful file creation operations are applicable for unsuccessful file read operations. But instead of `WriteData (or AddFile))` access permission, you should look for `ReadData (or ListDirectory)` permission.

> **NOTE** You can see an example of events generated for unsuccessful file content read attempt on the book's website, in the `Successful File Read Data.evtx` file.

File/Folder Attribute Changes

File and folder attributes such as Read-Only or Hidden might be important to monitor for modifications. Unfortunately, there is no detailed information available in the Windows security log about which attribute was changed as a result of the operation, but it is possible to audit the fact that an attribute was changed.

Successful File/Folder Attribute Changes

To audit successful file/folder attribute changes (not including permission changes and extended attributes), "Write attributes" permission should be enabled for the `Success` auditing type in the object's SACL.

Depending on the method used to change an attribute, different sets of events will be recorded in the Windows security event log. But, no matter which method is used to change the attribute, a 4663 event will be generated, which will contain `WriteAttributes` access permission in the `Accesses` field.

> **NOTE** You can see an example of events generated for successful file attribute change operation on the book's website, in the `Successful File Attribute Changes.evtx` file.

For extended attributes modification operations, such as adding an Alternate Data Stream to the file, no 4663 event is generated.

Unsuccessful File/Folder Attribute Changes

To audit unsuccessful file/folder attribute change attempts (not including permission changes and extended attributes), "Write attributes" permission should be enabled for the `Fail` auditing type in the object's SACL. For extended attributes modification attempts, "Write extended attributes" permission should be enabled.

You will get a similar 4656 event as for unsuccessful file creation operations.

> **NOTE** You can see an example of events generated for unsuccessful file attribute change attempt on the book's website, in the `Unsuccessful File Attribute Changes.evtx` file.

The same recommendations as provided for unsuccessful file creation operations are applicable for unsuccessful file/folder attributes change operations. But instead of `WriteData (or AddFile))` access permission, you should look for `WriteAttributes` permission or for the extended attribute `WriteEA` permission.

File/Folder Owner Change

A file or folder owner is not often changed during the lifetime of the object. Ownership change operations might be useful to monitor for critical files and/or folders.

Successful File/Folder Owner Change

To audit successful file/folder ownership changes (not including DACL and SACL changes), "Take ownership" permission should be enabled for the `Success` auditing type in the object's SACL.

`Take ownership` operations are allowed if at least one of the following requirements is met:

- Account has `SeTakeOwnershipPrivilege`.
- Account has `SeRestorePrivilege`.
- Account has "Take ownership" access permission allowed in the target object's security descriptor DACL.

There might be different security events generated for different scenarios, but the event in Listing 13-7 is always recorded in the Windows security event log for successful file/folder ownership change operations.

Listing 13-7: Event ID 4670: Permissions on an object were changed.

```
Task Category: Authorization Policy Change
Keywords: Audit Success
```

```
Subject:
      Security ID:          S-1-5-21-3212943211-794299840-588279583-500
      Account Name:         Administrator
      Account Domain:       2016SRV
      Logon ID:             0x24839
Object:
      Object Server:        Security
      Object Type:          File
      Object Name:          C:\New Folder\File.txt
      Handle ID:            0x39c
Process:
      Process ID:           0x198
      Process Name:         C:\Windows\System32\dllhost.exe
Permissions Change:
      Original Security Descriptor:      O:BA
      New Security Descriptor:           O:S-1-5-21-3212943211-794299840
                                                       -588279583-500
```

NOTE The event described in this section is available on the book's website, in the `Successful Owner Change.evtx` file.

This event is designed to show permission changes, including object owner changes, for different system objects such as files, folders, registry keys, and so on.

The `Permissions Change` section contains original and new values of the object's security descriptor. This event does not show SACL and DACL modifications. Only the ownership section (`O:`) in the applied security descriptor is shown in the event. Both the `Original Security Descriptor` and `New Security Descriptor` fields have SDDL format, which is described in Chapter 10.

In this example you can see that an object's owner was changed from `O:BA` (local built-in Administrators group) to `O:S-1-5-21-3212943211-794299840-588279583-500` (SID of the account or group).

Unsuccessful File/Folder Owner Change

To audit unsuccessful file/folder ownership change attempts (not including DACL and SACL changes), "Take ownership" permission should be enabled for the `Fail` auditing type in the object's SACL.

You will get a similar 4656 event as for unsuccessful file creation operations.

NOTE You can see an example of events generated for unsuccessful file/folder owner change attempt on the book's website, in the `Unsuccessful Owner Change.evtx` file.

The same recommendations as provided for unsuccessful file creation operations are applicable for unsuccessful file/folder owner change operations. But instead of WriteData (or AddFile)) access permission, you should look for WRITE_OWNER permission.

File/Folder Access Permissions Change

In some scenarios it is required to monitor any change to a folder's or file's DACL. This section contains information about security events generated for successful and unsuccessful DACL modifications for files and folders.

Successful Access Permissions Changes

To audit successful file/folder access permissions (DACL) changes, the "Change permissions" permission should be enabled for the Success auditing type in the object's SACL.

Depending on the method used to change access permissions (DACL), different sets of events will be recorded in the Windows security event log. But, no matter which method is used to change the attribute, a 4663 event will be generated, which will contain WRITE_DAC access permission in the Accesses field.

In addition to the 4663 event, the event in Listing 13-8 will be generated in the Windows security event log.

Listing 13-8: Event ID 4670: Permissions on an object were changed.

```
Task Category: Authorization Policy Change
Keywords: Audit Success
Subject:
        Security ID:            S-1-5-21-3212943211-794299840-588279583-500
        Account Name:           Administrator
        Account Domain:         2016SRV
        Logon ID:               0x24839
Object:
        Object Server:          Security
        Object Type:            File
        Object Name:            C:\New Folder
        Handle ID:              0x654
Process:
        Process ID:             0x670
        Process Name:           C:\Windows\System32\dllhost.exe
Permissions Change:
        Original Security Descriptor: D:AI(A;OICI;0x120000;;;WD)(A;OICIID;
        FA;;;SY)(A;OICIID;FA;;;BA)(A;OICIID;0x1200a9;;;BU)(A;CIID;LC;;;BU)
                              (A;CIID;DC;;;BU)(A;OICIIOID;GA;;;CO)
        New Security Descriptor: D:ARAI(A;OICIID;FA;;;SY)(A;OICIID;FA;;;
                          BA)(A;OICIID;0x1200a9;;;BU)(A;CIID;LC;;;BU)
                              (A;CIID;DC;;;BU)(A;OICIIOID;GA;;;CO)
```

NOTE The event described in this section is available on the book's website, in the `Successful Access Permissions Changes.evtx` file.

A 4670 event contains detailed information about previous and new DACL values in the object's security descriptor. Both the `Original Security Descriptor` and `New Security Descriptor` fields contain information only about DACL ACEs; no owner, primary group, or SACL information is included. Values for these two fields are shown in SDDL format, which is described in Chapter 10.

Unsuccessful Access Permissions Changes

To audit unsuccessful file/folder access permissions (DACL) change attempts (not including SACL or owner changes), the "Change permissions" permission should be enabled for the `Fail` auditing type in the object's SACL.

You will get a similar 4656 event as for unsuccessful file creation operations.

NOTE You can see an example of events generated for unsuccessful file/folder access permissions change attempt on the book's website, in the `Unsuccessful Access Permissions Changes.evtx` file.

The same recommendations as provided for unsuccessful file creation operations are applicable for unsuccessful file/folder access permissions change operations. But instead of `WriteData (or AddFile))` access permission, you should look for `WRITE_DAC` permission.

File/Folder SACL Changes

Monitoring auditing settings (SACL) is important to control any modification to such settings applied to a file or folder. This section contains information about file and folder SACL modification events.

Successful Auditing Settings (SACL) Change

All read and write operations with all auditable objects' SACLs are audited by default by the Windows auditing subsystem and specific events are written in the security event log without any additional setup required.

All changes to a file's or folder's auditing settings (SACL) requires the account that is attempting to change the SACL to have `SeSecurityPrivilege` permission. `SeSecurityPrivilege` permission is assigned to the account if the account (or security group it belongs to) is included in the "Manage auditing and security log" user right group policy setting applied to the operating system.

The events in Listings 13-9–13-11 will appear in the Windows security event log if a file's or folder's SACL was successfully modified.

Listing 13-9: Event ID 4703: A token right was adjusted.

```
Task Category: Token Right Adjusted Events
Keywords: Audit Success
Subject:
        Security ID:            S-1-5-21-3212943211-794299840-588279583-500
        Account Name:           Administrator
        Account Domain:         2016SRV
        Logon ID:               0x24839
Target Account:
        Security ID:            S-1-0-0
        Account Name:           Administrator
        Account Domain:         2016SRV
        Logon ID:               0x24839
Process Information:
        Process ID:             0xc8
        Process Name:           C:\Windows\System32\dllhost.exe
Enabled Privileges:

                                SeSecurityPrivilege
Disabled Privileges:

                                -
```

NOTE The events described in this section are available on the book's website, in the Successful Auditing Settings Change.evtx file.

SeSecurityPrivilege is required to read or modify an object's SACL. To use this privilege, it must first be enabled in the process's session token. The 4703 event informs you that SeSecurityPrivilege was enabled. See Chapter 11 for more information about user privileges and logon rights.

In the event in Listing 13-10 SeSecurityPrivilege was used to get the following access permission:

■ **ACCESS_SYS_SEC:** To get or set the SACL in an object's security descriptor.

ACCESS_SYS_SEC access permission requires the SeSecurityPrivilege privilege.

Listing 13-10: Event ID 4674: An operation was attempted on a privileged object.

```
Task Category: Sensitive Privilege Use
Keywords: Audit Success
Subject:
        Security ID:            S-1-5-21-3212943211-794299840-588279583-500
        Account Name:           Administrator
        Account Domain:         2016SRV
        Logon ID:               0x24839
```

```
Object:
      Object Server:          Security
      Object Type:            File
      Object Name:            C:\New Folder\notepad.exe
      Object Handle:          0x420
Process Information:
      Process ID:             0xc8
      Process Name:           C:\Windows\System32\dllhost.exe
Requested Operation:
      Desired Access:         %%1538 (READ_CONTROL)
                              %%1542 (ACCESS_SYS_SEC)
                              %%4423 (ReadAttributes)
                              See tables 13-4 and 5-4 for more details
      Privileges:             SeSecurityPrivilege
```

Event 4907 in Listing 13-11 is triggered when the SACL for an auditable object, such as a file, folder, registry key, or kernel object, is changed.

Listing 13-11: Event ID 4907: Auditing settings on object were changed.

```
Task Category: Audit Policy Change
Keywords: Audit Success
Subject:
      Security ID:            S-1-5-21-3212943211-794299840-588279583-500
      Account Name:           Administrator
      Account Domain:         2016SRV
      Logon ID:               0x24839
Object:
      Object Server:          Security
      Object Type:            File
      Object Name:            C:\New Folder\notepad.exe
      Handle ID:              0x420
Process Information:
      Process ID:             0xc8
      Process Name:           C:\Windows\System32\dllhost.exe
Auditing Settings:
      Original Security Descriptor:      S:AI(AU;IDSAFA;WD;;;WD)
      New Security Descriptor:           S:ARAI(AU;IDSAFA;WDWO;;;WD)
```

The Subject section contains information about the account that performed the action.

The Object section contains information about the object which has its SACL modified.

The Auditing Settings section contains previous and new SACL values for the object. Both the Original Security Descriptor and New Security Descriptor fields contain SACL values in SDDL format, which is described in Chapter 10. They only contain information about SACL modifications (S:); no information about object owner or DACL is included.

Unsuccessful Auditing Settings Change

As noted in the previous section, SeSecurityPrivilege privilege is required to make changes to a filesystem object's SACL. If a user account tries to modify a file's or folder's SACL without having SeSecurityPrivilege privilege, the event in Listing 13-12 is generated in the Windows security event log.

Listing 13-12: Event ID 4656: A handle to an object was requested.

```
Task Category: File System
Keywords: Audit Failure
Subject:
        Security ID:            S-1-5-21-3212943211-794299840-588279583-1000
        Account Name:           Andrei
        Account Domain:         2016SRV
        Logon ID:               0xF2D962
Object:
        Object Server:          Security
        Object Type:            File
        Object Name:            C:\Windows\System32\cmd.exe
        Handle ID:              0x0
        Resource Attributes:    -
Process Information:
        Process ID:             0xcb4
        Process Name:           C:\Windows\System32\WindowsPowerShell\v1.0\
                                            powershell_ise.exe
Access Request Information:
        Transaction ID:         {00000000-0000-0000-0000-000000000000}
        Accesses:               %%1538 (READ_CONTROL)
                                %%1539 (WRITE_DAC)
                                %%1542 (ACCESS_SYS_SEC)
        Access Reasons:         %%1538 (READ_CONTROL):   %%1809 (Unknown or
                                                            unchecked)
                                %%1539 (WRITE_DAC):      %%1809 (Unknown or
                                                            unchecked)
                                %%1542 (ACCESS_SYS_SEC):%%1810 (Not granted
                                        due to missing) SeSecurityPrivilege
                                See tables 13-4, 13-5 and 5-4
                                            for more details
        Access Mask:            0x1060000 (See tables 13-4 and 5-4
                                            for more details)
```

NOTE The events described in this section are available on the book's website, in the Unsuccessful Auditing Settings Change.evtx file.

As you can see ACCESS_SYS_SEC access, which allows an account to set or get an object's SACL, was not granted due to the missing SeSecurityPrivilege privilege.

The same recommendations as provided for unsuccessful file creation operations are applicable for unsuccessful file/folder audit settings change operations. But instead of `WriteData (or AddFile))` access permission, you should look for `ACCESS_SYS_SEC` permission.

Removable Storage

If the "Audit Removable Storage" advanced audit policy is enabled, the "Full control" auditing ACE in SACL is applied for all filesystem objects on removable media devices, such as USB drives, CD drives, and so on. You can enable the "Audit Removable Storage" advanced group policy setting to audit successful access attempts and/or failed attempts.

In general, removable storage auditing works exactly like normal filesystem auditing, but SACLs for removable storage files and folders are predefined with a "Full control" ACE.

Listing 13-13 is an example of a successful `WriteData` access attempt performed on a file located on a USB drive.

Listing 13-13: Event ID 4663: An attempt was made to access an object.

```
Task Category: Removable Storage
Keywords: Audit Success
Subject:
      Security ID:          S-1-5-21-813149205-2824403588-1569955807-500
      Account Name:         Administrator
      Account Domain:       C3PO
      Logon ID:             0x4E342783
Object:
      Object Server:        Security
      Object Type:          File
      Object Name:          \Device\HarddiskVolume11\Recovery.txt
      Handle ID:            0x44
      Resource Attributes:
Process Information:
      Process ID:           0x92b0
      Process Name:         C:\Windows\System32\cmd.exe
Access Request Information:
      Accesses:             %%4417 (WriteData (or AddFile))
                            %%4418 (AppendData (or AddSubdirectory or
                                              CreatePipeInstance))
                            See tables 13-4 and 5-4 for more details
```

NOTE The events described in this section are available on the book's website, in the `Removable Storage.evtx` file.

The only difference between normal filesystem object auditing 4663 events and removable storage 4663 events is the `Object Name` field. The `Object Name` field for removable storage events contains the path to the mounted removable media. All removable storage devices have unique `\Device\` identifier assigned to them, which is a symbolic link for this object. For USB drives this symbolic link will have a format of `HarddiskVolume#`.

To translate the `HarddiskVolume` number to the disk drive letter you can use the Microsoft WinObj tool (formerly Sysinternals tool). Figure 13-5 illustrates a disk drive letter assigned to HarddiskVolume11, which can be found in the `GLOBAL??` container.

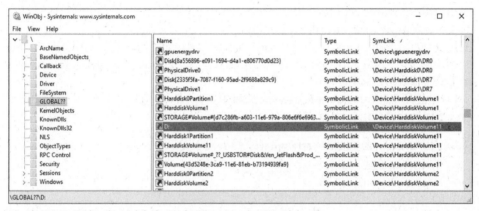

Figure 13-5: Disk volume label translation using the WinObj tool

Also, when a new external device is connected to the system, a 6416 event is generated in the Windows security event log, which also has some additional information about the connected device.

Global Object Access Auditing: Filesystem

Global Object Access Auditing allows you to configure a global SACL for the entire system, which will be applied to all files and folders.

A global SACL for filesystem objects can be defined using the following group policy setting:

```
Local Computer Policy\Computer Configuration\Windows Settings\
Security Settings\Advanced Audit Policy Configuration\System Audit
Policies - Local Group Policy Object\Global Object Access Auditing\
File system.
```

A global SACL works in conjunction with the normal filesystem object SACL. Both of them are applied at the same time.

In addition to standard file system permissions, the following additional permission sets are available to choose for global SACLs:

- **Read:** Includes the following advanced permissions:
    - List folder/read data
    - Read attributes
    - Read extended attributes
    - Read permissions
- **Write:** Includes the following advanced permissions:
    - Create files/write data
    - Create folders/append data
    - Write attributes
    - Write extended attributes
- **Execute:** Includes all permissions listed for Read permission plus "Traverse folder/execute file" permission.

To view the applied global SACL for a local machine, use the following command: `auditpol /resourcesacl /type:File /view`. Figure 13-6 shows an example of the output for this command.

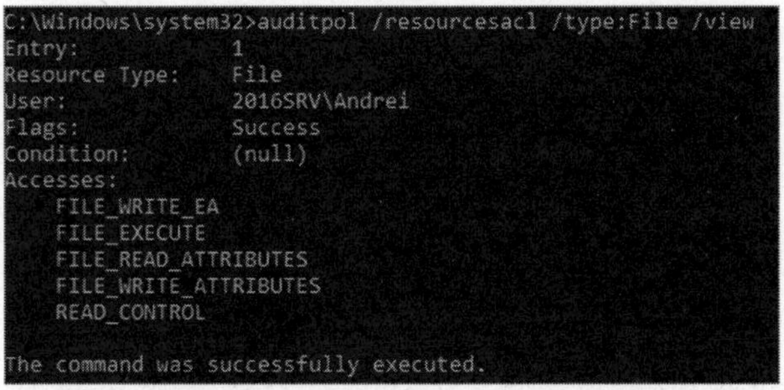

```
C:\Windows\system32>auditpol /resourcesacl /type:File /view
Entry:            1
Resource Type:    File
User:             2016SRV\Andrei
Flags:            Success
Condition:        (null)
Accesses:
    FILE_WRITE_EA
    FILE_EXECUTE
    FILE_READ_ATTRIBUTES
    FILE_WRITE_ATTRIBUTES
    READ_CONTROL

The command was successfully executed.
```

Figure 13-6: View Global Object Access Auditing settings for files and folders using the `auditpol` `.exe` command

File System Object Integrity Levels

Chapter 12 contained information about integrity levels in Microsoft Windows operation systems. Integrity level labels can also be set for file system objects: files and folders.

By default, all unlabeled file system objects have a Medium Mandatory Level integrity level. You can verify the current integrity level for a file or folder using the built-in `icacls` tool. To view the current integrity level label for a file or folder, use the following command: `icacls FILE_OR_FOLDER_NAME`.

Figure 13-7 shows an example of `icacls` tool output when an integrity level label is explicitly set for an object.

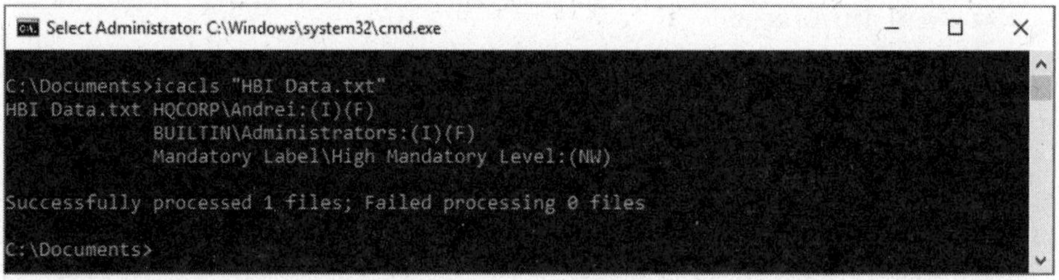

```
C:\Documents>icacls "HBI Data.txt"
HBI Data.txt HQCORP\Andrei:(I)(F)
             BUILTIN\Administrators:(I)(F)
             Mandatory Label\High Mandatory Level:(NW)

Successfully processed 1 files; Failed processing 0 files

C:\Documents>
```

Figure 13-7: Example of `icacls` tool

You can see that the "HBI Data.txt" file has a High Mandatory Level integrity label applied. You can see the list of all integrity level labels in Table 12-3 (Chapter 12).

If there is no integrity level label applied to a file or folder, then it is considered to have a Medium Mandatory Level integrity level.

File System Object Integrity Level Modification

You can use the `icacls` tool to modify an integrity level label for a file or folder. Use the following command to perform this operation: `icacls FILE_OR_FOLDER_NAME /setintegritylevel LEVEL`, where `LEVEL` can be one of the following:

- **Low:** Low Mandatory Level
- **Medium:** Medium Mandatory Level
- **High:** High Mandatory Level

Using this command, it is not possible to set an integrity level for a file or folder to anything except Low, Medium, or High integrity levels. To set an integrity level label to System level you can use publicly available tools such as `CHML` written by Mark Minasi.

To be able to monitor for integrity label modifications, the following requirements need to be met:

- The "Authorization Policy Change" auditing subcategory should be enabled for Success.
- "Take ownership" success auditing should be enabled in the object's SACL.

After an integrity label for a file system object is changed, the event in Listing 13-14 is generated in the security event log.

Listing 13-14: Event ID 4670: Permissions on an object were changed.

```
Task Category: Authorization Policy Change
Keywords: Audit Success
Subject:
        Security ID:              S-1-5-21-1913345275-1711810662-261465553-
                                                                        500
        Account Name:            Administrator
        Account Domain:          HQCORP
        Logon ID:                0x4AE47
Object:
        Object Server:           Security
        Object Type:             File
        Object Name:             C:\Documents\HBI Data.txt
        Handle ID:               0xb8
Process:
        Process ID:              0x12b4
        Process Name:            C:\Windows\System32\icacls.exe
Permissions Change:
        Original Security Descriptor:        S:AI(ML;;NW;;;HI)
        New Security Descriptor:             S:ARAI(ML;;NW;;;LW)
```

NOTE The event described above is available on the book's website, in the `File System Object Integrity Level Modification.evtx` file.

Listings 13-7 and 13-8 discussed the 4670 event. Integrity level labels are located in the object's SACL instead of DACL.

In this event you can see that the SACL for the `HBI Data.txt` file was changed from `S:AI(ML;;NW;;;HI)` to `S:ARAI(ML;;NW;;;LW)`. Here is how you can read the final SACL:

`S:ARAI(ML;;NW;;;LW)`

- **s::** SACL section

- **ARAI**

  - **AR:** child objects inherit permissions from this object

  - **AI:** inheritance is allowed

- **(ML;;NW;;;LW)**

  - **ML:** ACE type is Mandatory Level (**ML**)

  - **NW:** contains the object's integrity policy:

    - **NW:** SDDL_NO_WRITE_UP

    - **NR:** SDDL_NO_READ_UP

- **NX:** SDDL_NO_EXECUTE_UP

    NW is a default integrity policy for all file system objects in Windows. You can read more about integrity policies in Chapter 12.
- **LW:** Low Mandatory Level. Can also be:
    - **ME:** Medium Mandatory Level
    - **HI:** High Mandatory Level
    - **SI:** System Mandatory Level

File System Object Access Attempt - Access Denied by Integrity Policy Check

If, for example, a process with a lower integrity level tries to write to a file with a higher integrity level, an Audit Failure 4656 event with the reason "Denied by Integrity Policy check" is generated. Listing 13-15 is an example of the Access Reasons section of such an event.

Listing 13-15: Event ID 4656: A handle to an object was requested.

```
Task Category: File System
Keywords: Audit Failure

Access Reasons: %%4418 (WriteData (or AddFile)):%%1803 (Denied by
                                    Integrity Policy check)
             %%4420 (WriteEA):%%1803 (Denied by Integrity Policy
                                                check)

        . . .
```

> **NOTE** The event described above is available on the book's website, in the File System Object Access Attempt - Access Denied by Integrity Policy Check.evtx **file.**

You can see that some of the access request was denied by the integrity check policy. This event does not give you any more details about the current integrity policy and label applied to the file system object.

Monitoring Recommendations

Table 13-6 shows useful filesystem events to monitor.

Table 13-6: Recommended File-System Events to Monitor

SECURITY EVENT	SUBCATEGORY	EVENT TYPE
4656: A handle to an object was requested.	File System	`Audit Success`
	Removable Storage	`Audit Failure`
4663: An attempt was made to access an object.	File System	`Audit Success`
	Removable Storage	
4670: Permissions on an object were changed.	Authorization Policy Change	`Audit Success`
4907: Auditing settings on object were changed.	Audit Policy Change	`Audit Success`

Monitoring Scenarios

You may face many scenarios related to filesystem monitoring.

The most difficult and important part is to set appropriate SACLs to filesystem objects. You should select only required permissions for the action you are going to monitor and also limit the scope of the account or group to which new auditing ACEs will be applied.

Monitor for any actions with critical or HBI filesystem objects. In this case most of the events listed in this chapter will be useful to collect and analyze.

CHAPTER

14

Windows Registry

The Windows registry was first introduced in Windows 3.1 as storage for settings related to Component Object Model (COM) objects. In later versions (Windows 95, Windows NT), registry functionality was extended to be used by other Windows components and applications.

The Windows registry is designed as a central hierarchical storage/database to store information and settings for applications, Windows components, user account settings, devices, drivers, and so on. The Windows registry can be used by any application to store application-related information.

In this chapter you will find information about most common registry operations monitoring.

Windows Registry Basics

The registry was designed as a replacement for flat configuration files (.ini, .conf). The most noticeable differences between the registry database and text files are:

- The registry has built-in security and auditing mechanisms to control access to specific keys and audit access attempts.

- The registry has built-in backup and restore mechanisms that help to restore registry files in case of corruption or unnecessary changes.

■ The registry has a mechanism to easily export and import specific settings to/from it.

The most common way to view the Windows registry is to use the built-in Windows Registry Editor (`regedit.exe`), as shown in the Figure 14-1.

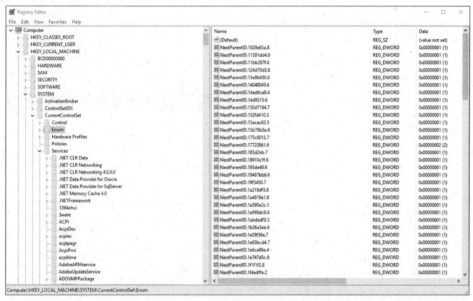

Figure 14-1: Viewing Windows registry using Windows Registry Editor

Windows Registry Editor requires elevated privileges to run it, but there is no requirement to have elevated rights to write data to some registry database areas, and Read access is allowed to many keys (excluding highly secure hives like SAM, for example) in the registry database for all users.

Some of the terms you should know when you are working with Windows registry include:

■ **Key:** A base element in the registry database, its characteristics can be compared to a filesystem directory/folder. A key may contain other registry keys (subkeys) and values. A registry key has its own security descriptor, which contains the registry key owner, discretionary access control list (DACL), and system access control list (SACL).

■ **Subkey:** A registry key that has another registry key as a parent.

■ **Value:** Values can be added to registry keys. They include value name and value data. You can find more information about possible value data types later in this chapter.

- **Hive:** A set of registry keys, subkeys, and values that have separate backup and restore mechanisms. Each registry hive has a set of files associated to it that is used for event logging and backup/recovery procedures. One example of a registry hive is HKEY_LOCAL_MACHINE\Software.

By default, current Windows operating systems store almost all registry hives and associated files in the %SystemRoot%\System32\Config folder. An example of the exception is the HKEY_CURRENT_USER hive; it's stored in the %USERPROFILE% folder.

Table 14-1 contains a default list of registry hives (have files associated with them) and keys, including their purposes.

Table 14-1: Default Registry Keys and Hives

KEY/HIVE	DESCRIPTION	ASSOCIATED FILES
HKEY_LOCAL_MACHINE	Contains local machine configuration items and settings.	-
HKEY_LOCAL_MACHINE\SAM	Contains the Security Account Manager (SAM) database and information used by the SAM Manager.	SAM SAM.LOG1 SAM.LOG2
HKEY_LOCAL_MACHINE\Security	Contains information about the SAM_DOMAIN into which the user is currently logged on, as well as local computer security–related settings. HKEY_LOCAL_MACHINE\SAM is a subkey of HKEY_LOCAL_MACHINE\Security.	SECURITY SECURITY.LOG1 SECURITY.LOG2
HKEY_LOCAL_MACHINE\Software	Contains settings for Windows components and installed software.	SOFTWARE SOFTWARE.LOG1 SOFTWARE.LOG2
HKEY_LOCAL_MACHINE\System	Contains operating system information and settings.	SYSTEM SYSTEM.LOG1 SYSTEM.LOG2
HKEY_LOCAL_MACHINE\Elam	Contains Early Launch Anti-Malware (ELAM) signatures. The ELAM hive is not displayed by default by Windows Registry Editor.	ELAM ELAM.LOG1 ELAM.LOG2
HKEY_LOCAL_MACHINE\Drivers	Contains information about installed drivers.	DRIVERS DRIVERS.LOG1 DRIVERS.LOG2

Continues

Table 14-1 (*continued*)

KEY/HIVE	DESCRIPTION	ASSOCIATED FILES
`HKEY_CURRENT_ CONFIG`	Contains information about hardware devices and the current hardware profile that is used at system startup.	-

`HKEY_USERS\. DEFAULT`	Contains settings for the default system desktop (aka secure desktop).	`DEFAULT`
		
		`DEFAULT.LOG1`
		
		`DEFAULT.LOG2`

`HKEY_CURRENT_USER`	Contains information and configuration settings for the currently logged-in user session.	`NTUSER.DAT`
		
		`NTUSER.DAT.LOG1`
		
		`NTUSER.DAT.LOG2`

`HKEY_USERS`	Contains registry keys data for all currently logged-in users. `HKEY_CURRENT_USER` is a sub-key of `HKEY_USERS`.	-
`HKEY_CLASSES_ROOT`	Contains information about file types and applications associated to these file types. Is a subkey of the `HKEY_ LOCAL_MACHINE\Software` hive.	-

Some registry hive files don't have file extensions.

`.LOG` files contain logs about all registry transactions performed with a hive. For example, they are used to undo or redo pending transactions to registry hives.

You will find more information later in this chapter when we discuss the most common monitoring scenarios for the Windows registry.

Registry Key Permissions

All registry keys have their own security descriptor. See Chapter 13 for more information about security descriptors.

Figure 14-2 shows the DACL ACE editor interface for a registry key.

Most of the core concepts from NTFS system object security descriptors, discussed in Chapter 13, are also applicable to registry keys. But some differences exist between them, which will be discussed in this section.

The "Applies to" field can have one of the following values:

- **This key only:** Applies to only the current key.

- **This key and subkeys:** Applies to the current key and all nested subkeys for the entire subtree.

- **Subkeys only:** Applies to all nested subkeys for the entire subtree.

All standard access rights listed in Table 5-4 are applicable to registry keys. Table 14-2 contains information about permissions specific to registry keys only.

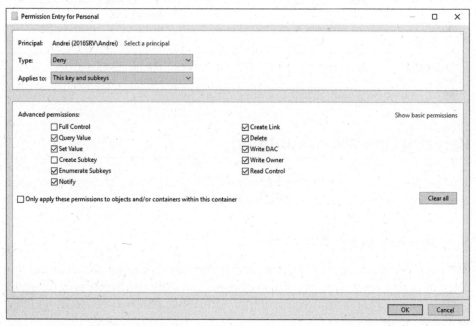

Figure 14-2: Registry key DACL ACE

Table 14-2: Registry Key Permissions

PERMISSION	EVENT TEXT	CONSTANT	HEX	DESCRIPTION
Full Control	-	-	-	All possible access permissions
Query Value	Query key value	%%4432	0x1	Read key values
Set Value	Set key value	%%4433	0x2	Create/modify key values

Continues

Table 14-2 (*continued*)

PERMISSION	EVENT TEXT	CONSTANT	HEX	DESCRIPTION
Create Subkey	Create sub-key	%%4434	0x4	Create subkey
Enumerate Subkeys	Enumerate sub-keys	%%4435	0x8	List all subkeys
Notify	Notify about changes to keys	%%4436	0x10	Allows use of the `RegNotifyChangeKey Value` API function. Basically allows you to receive change notification for attributes or values of the key.
Create Link	Create Link	%%4437	0x20	Create a symbolic link to a subkey

Registry Operations Auditing

This section covers information about the most common registry key and value operations, such as creation, deletion, modification, and so on.

Registry Key Creation

Key creation can be successful, or it can be unsuccessful when, for example, the account that requested the operation does not have the required permissions to create a key. In this section you will find additional information about registry key creation monitoring.

Successful Registry Key Creation

Multiple methods can be used to create a registry key. For example:

- Windows Registry Editor
- `reg add` console command
- `New-Item` PowerShell function
- `RegCreateKeyEx` API function call

No matter which method is used to create a new registry key, the account that performs the action must have the `Create Subkey` advanced permission on the parent registry key.

To monitor successful registry key creation events, the key for which a new subkey will be created must have `Create Subkey` permission auditing enabled for the `Success` type.

When a new registry key is created using Windows Registry Editor, the event in Listing 14-1 will occur in the Windows security event log.

Listing 14-1: Event ID 4656: A handle to an object was requested.

```
Task Category: Registry
Keywords: Audit Success
Subject:
        Security ID:           S-1-5-21-3212943211-794299840-588279583-500
        Account Name:          Administrator
        Account Domain:        2016SRV
        Logon ID:              0x4DC10
Object:
        Object Server:         Security
        Object Type:           Key
        Object Name:           \REGISTRY\MACHINE\SOFTWARE\Personal
        Handle ID:             0x270
        Resource Attributes:   -
Process Information:
        Process ID:            0x1ac
        Process Name:          C:\Windows\regedit.exe
Access Request Information:
        Transaction ID:        {00000000-0000-0000-0000-000000000000}
        Accesses:              %%4434
                 (Create sub-key. See tables 14-2 and 5-4)
        Access Reasons:        -
        Access Mask:           0x4 (See tables 14-2 and 5-4)
```

NOTE The events described in this section are available on the book's website, in the `Successful Registry Key Creation.evtx` file.

This event, as expected, shows you that `Create sub-key` permission was successfully granted (`Audit Success`) to `Subject`. The `Process Information` section contains information about the process used to request specific access permission.

`Transaction ID` is a field designed to show information about registry transactions. For example, the `RegCreateKeyTransacted` and `RegOpenKeyTransacted` functions allow you to use transactions. Transactions guarantee that all operations within a transaction will be performed or all of them will be cancelled, allowing rollback of the entire transaction. All events that are part of the same transaction will have the same `Transaction ID` value.

`Object Server` is always `Security` and `Object Type` is `Key`. See Chapter 5 for more information about the `Object Server` field.

The `Object Name` field contains a registry path to the key for which permissions were requested. This event does not contain the name of the newly created key; it just informs you about an access permission request. This field value has the format `HIVE_VARIABLE\REGISTRY_PATH`, where:

- `HIVE_VARIABLE` is one of the registry values you can find on the local machine in the `HKEY_LOCAL_MACHINE\SYSTEM\CurrentControlSet\Control\hivelist` registry key. The most common examples of `HIVE_VARIABLE` values are:

  - `\REGISTRY\MACHINE\HARDWARE`

  - `\REGISTRY\MACHINE\SAM`

  - `\REGISTRY\MACHINE\SECURITY`

  - `\REGISTRY\MACHINE\SOFTWARE`

  - `\REGISTRY\MACHINE\SYSTEM`

  - `\REGISTRY\USER\SID`, where `SID` is a security identifier of the specific account.

- `REGISTRY_PATH` is the remaining part of the registry path excluding `HIVE_VARIABLE`.

This event does not have the name of the newly created registry key and no other events are generated that will indicate a specific registry key was just created. You can try to find a 4663 event, which *may* follow the 4656 event with `Accesses` of `Query key value`, but there is no guarantee that such a 4663 event will be generated. Also, the `Handle ID` field value in the 4663 event will be different.

Each registry key creation request must contain `Create sub-key` advanced access permission. There might be other access permissions listed in the same event.

Note that for some specific methods—the `reg add` command, for example—no events are generated in the Windows security event log. Also, it's up to the application which permissions to request in order to create a new registry key; some of them may even try to request a handle with full permissions, but `Create sub-key` permission must be in the list.

The event in Listing 14-2 informs you that the handle, which was previously opened in the 4656 event, was closed.

Listing 14-2: Event ID 4658: The handle to an object was closed.

```
Task Category: Registry
Keywords: Audit Success
```

Unsuccessful Registry Key Creation

To monitor unsuccessful registry key creation events, the key for which the new subkey creation attempt is performed must have `Create Subkey` permission auditing enabled for the `Fail` type.

When an unsuccessful registry key creation attempt is performed using Windows Registry Editor, the event in Listing 14-3 occurs in the Windows security event log.

Listing 14-3: Event ID 4656: A handle to an object was requested.

```
Task Category: Registry
Keywords: Audit Failure
Subject:
        Security ID:         S-1-5-21-3212943211-794299840-588279583-1000
        Account Name:        Andrei
        Account Domain:      2016SRV
        Logon ID:            0x519984
Object:
        Object Server:       Security
        Object Type:         Key
        Object Name:         \REGISTRY\MACHINE\SOFTWARE\Personal
        Handle ID:           0x0
        Resource Attributes: -
Process Information:
        Process ID:          0x734
        Process Name:        C:\Windows\regedit.exe
Access Request Information:
        Transaction ID:      {00000000-0000-0000-0000-000000000000}
        Accesses:            %%4434
                 (Create sub-key. See tables 14-2 and 5-4)
        Access Reasons:      -
        Access Mask:         0x4 (See tables 14-2 and 5-4)
```

> **NOTE** The event described in this section is available on the book's website, in the `Unsuccessful Registry Key Creation.evtx` file.

The 4656 `Audit Failure` event with `Accesses: Create sub-key` informs you that `Subject` tried to get specific access using the `Process Information` process, but failed due to insufficient permissions.

Each registry key creation request must contain `Create sub-key` advanced access permission. There might be other access permissions listed in the same event.

Registry Key Deletion

Registry key deletion is a common operation. Some critical registry keys are important to monitor for any deletion attempts. This section will show you security events generated for successful and unsuccessful registry key deletion operations.

Successful Registry Key Deletion

To monitor successful key deletion operations, Success auditing must be enabled for Delete advanced permission.

It is up to the application which accesses to request for the key deletion operation, but Delete access will always be in the list. For example, the reg delete command requires full access to the registry key to perform deletion, whereas regedit requests only the "Query value" "Enumerate subkeys" and "DELETE" permissions.

The event in Listing 14-4 occurs in the Windows security event log when a registry key is successfully deleted, no matter which method is used to perform this action.

Listing 14-4: Event ID 4663: An attempt was made to access an object.

```
Task Category: Registry
Keywords: Audit Success
Subject:
        Security ID:        S-1-5-21-3212943211-794299840-588279583-500
        Account Name:       Administrator
        Account Domain:     2016SRV
        Logon ID:           0x4DC10
Object:
        Object Server:      Security
        Object Type:        Key
        Object Name:        \REGISTRY\MACHINE\SOFTWARE\Personal\Andrei
        Handle ID:          0x21c
        Resource Attributes: -
Process Information:
        Process ID:         0xa94
        Process Name:       C:\Windows\regedit.exe
Access Request Information:
        Accesses:           %%1537 (DELETE. See tables 14-2 and 5-4)
        Access Mask:        0x10000 (See tables 14-2 and 5-4)
```

NOTE   The event described in this section is available on the book's website, in the Successful Registry Key Deletion.evtx **file.**

Event 4663 informs you that an action was made using the "DELETE" permission. Each registry key deletion request must contain the DELETE advanced access permission. There might be other access permissions listed in the same event.

Unsuccessful Registry Key Deletion

The only way to detect unsuccessful key deletion operations is to monitor for `Audit Failure` event 4656, "A handle to an object was requested," where one of the requested permissions will be `DELETE`.

> **NOTE** You can see an example of events generated for unsuccessful registry key deletion attempt on the book's website, in the `Unsuccessful Registry Key Deletion.evtx` file.

The problem with unsuccessful registry key deletion is that it's up to the application which set of permissions to request in order to perform this operation. For example, `regedit` requests only the `DELETE` access permission when you select the "Delete" option in the context menu, whereas the `reg delete` command requests the following permissions:

- DELETE
- READ_CONTROL
- WRITE_DAC
- WRITE_OWNER
- Query key value
- Set key value
- Create sub-key
- Enumerate sub-keys
- Notify about changes to keys
- Create Link

Operations with Registry Key Values

Registry key values can be treated as parameters for registry keys. Registry key values have a type, and they have content/data. Table 14-3 contains a list of the most common registry key value types.

Table 14-3: Registry Key Value Types

CONSTANT	%% VALUE	DESCRIPTION
REG_NONE	%%1872	Undefined type
REG_SZ	%%1873	Null-terminated string
REG_EXPAND_SZ	%%1874	Null-terminated string that contains unexpanded references to environment variables

Continues

Table 14-3 (*continued*)

CONSTANT	%% VALUE	DESCRIPTION
REG_BINARY	%%1875	Binary data
REG_DWORD	%%1876	32-bit number
REG_DWORD_BIG_ENDIAN	%%1877	32-bit number in little-endian format
REG_LINK	%%1878	Registry symbolic link (has the same purpose as file symbolic links, allows registry redirects)
REG_MULTI_SZ (Newlines are replaced with *. A * is replaced with **)	%%1879	Array of REG _SZ
REG_RESOURCE_LIST	%%1880	Device-driver resource list
REG_FULL_RESOURCE_DESCRIPTOR	%%1881	Device resource descriptor
REG_RESOURCE_REQUIREMENTS_LIST	%%1882	Device resource requirements list
REG_QWORD	%%1883	64-bit number

Table 14-4 contains a list of the registry key value operations which can be reported in the security events.

Table 14-4: Registry Key Value Operations

%% VALUE	OPERATION
%%1904	New registry value created
%%1905	Existing registry value modified
%%1906	Registry value deleted

Successful Registry Key Value Creation

To monitor successful registry key value creation operations, Success auditing must be enabled for the Set Value advanced permission on the registry key for which the new value will be created.

The events in Listings 14-5 and 14-6 are recorded in the Windows security event log after the registry value is successfully created.

The first event you will see is the 4663 event in Listing 14-5 with Set key value (%%4433) access requested. There is no such access permission as Create key values; both registry key value modification and creation operations require Set key value permission.

Listing 14-5: Event ID 4663: An attempt was made to access an object.

```
Task Category: Registry
Keywords: Audit Success
```

> **NOTE** The events described in this section are available on the book's website, in
> the `Successful Registry Value Creation.evtx` file.

Event 4657 (Listing 14-6) is a specific event for registry value operations.

Listing 14-6: Event ID 4657: A registry value was modified.

```
Task Category: Registry
Keywords: Audit Success
Subject:
        Security ID:            S-1-5-21-3212943211-794299840-588279583-500
        Account Name:           Administrator
        Account Domain:         2016SRV
        Logon ID:               0x345DB
Object:
        Object Name:            \REGISTRY\MACHINE\SOFTWARE\Personal
        Object Value Name:      RegData
        Handle ID:              0x88
        Operation Type:         %%1904 (New registry value created)
Process Information:
        Process ID:             0x10e4
        Process Name:           C:\Windows\System32\reg.exe
Change Information:
        Old Value Type:         -
        Old Value:              -
        New Value Type:         %%1873 (REG_SZ. See Table 14-3)
        New Value:              This is my data
```

The `Subject` section shows you information about who performed this operation.

The `Object Name` field contains the name of the registry key for which the operation (`Operation Type`) was requested.

The `Object Value Name` field contains the name of the new value.

The `Operation Type` field contains a type of requested operation with the registry key (`Object Name`). For new value creation it has a value of `New registry value created`. See Table 14-4 for more details.

The `Old Value Type` and `Old Value` fields are not applicable for `New registry value created` operation types.

The `New Value Type` field contains the type of the newly created registry key value.

The `New Value` field contains data for the newly created value.

Unsuccessful Registry Key Value Creation

To monitor unsuccessful registry key value creation operations, `Fail` auditing must be enabled for the `Set Value` advanced permission on the registry key for which the new value will be created.

The only way to detect unsuccessful registry key value creation operations is to monitor for `Audit Failure` event 4656, "A handle to an object was requested," where one of the requested permissions will be `Set key value`.

> **NOTE** You can see an example of events generated for unsuccessful registry value creation attempt on the book's website, in the `Unsuccessful Registry Value Creation.evtx` file.

The problem with unsuccessful registry key value creation operations is that it's up to the application which set of permissions to request to perform this operation, but `Set key value` permission will always be in the list. For example, the `reg add` command-line tool requests the following permissions for registry key value add operations:

- `READ_CONTROL`
- `Query key value`
- `Set key value`
- `Create sub-key`
- `Enumerate sub-keys`
- `Notify about changes to keys`

But the `regedit` tool does not generate any events in the Windows security event log for unsuccessful registry key value creation attempts.

Because the `Set key value` permission is used for value creation, deletion, and modification operations, it is not possible to detect which exact operation from these three invoked the 4656 failure event.

Successful Registry Key Value Deletion

To monitor successful registry key value deletion operations, `Success` auditing must be enabled for the `Set Value` advanced permission on the registry key for which a value will be deleted.

Again, it's up to the application which access permissions to request for a specific operation. For registry key value deletion operations, `regedit` requires only `Query Value` and `Set Value` advanced permissions to be enabled for user accounts, whereas the `REG DELETE` command requires the following permissions:

- `DELETE`
- `READ_CONTROL`
- `WRITE_DAC`
- `WRITE_OWNER`
- `Query key value`
- `Set key value`

- Create sub-key

- Enumerate sub-keys

- Notify about changes to keys

- Create Link

The events in Listings 14-7 and 14-8 are recorded in the Windows security event log after a registry key value is successfully deleted.

Listing 14-7 is exactly the same event you saw for a successful registry key value creation operation in Listing 14-5.

Listing 14-7: Event ID 4663: An attempt was made to access an object.

```
Task Category: Registry
Keywords: Audit Success
```

> **NOTE** The events described in this section are available on the book's website, in the `Successful Registry Value Deletion.evtx` **file.**

Listing 14-8: Event ID 4657: A registry value was modified.

```
Task Category: Registry
Keywords: Audit Success
Subject:
        Security ID:            S-1-5-21-3212943211-794299840-588279583-1000
        Account Name:           Andrei
        Account Domain:         2016SRV
        Logon ID:               0x376524
Object:
        Object Name:            \REGISTRY\MACHINE\SOFTWARE\Personal
        Object Value Name:      RegData
        Handle ID:              0x200
        Operation Type:         %%1906 (Registry value deleted)
Process Information:
        Process ID:             0x11ac
        Process Name:           C:\Windows\regedit.exe
Change Information:
        Old Value Type:         %%1873 (REG_SZ. See Table 14-3)
        Old Value:              This is my data
        New Value Type:         -
        New Value:              -
```

`Registry value deleted` is a specific operation type for registry key value deletion operations. Refer to Table 14-4 for more details.

For value deletion operations, the `New Value Type` and `New Value` fields are not applicable.

The `Old Value Type` and `Old Value` fields contain information about the deleted registry key value object.

The `Object Value Name` field contains the name of the deleted registry key value object.

Unsuccessful Registry Key Value Deletion

Recommendations are the same as for an "Unsuccessful registry key value creation" operation, because registry key value creation, deletion, and modification operations require the same access permission: `Set Value`.

Successful Registry Key Value Modification

To monitor successful registry key value modification operations, `Success` auditing must be enabled for the `Set Value` advanced permission on the registry key for which value modification events need to be monitored.

Again, it's up to the application which access permissions to request for a specific operation. For registry key value modification operations, `regedit` requests only the `Query Value` and `Set Value` advanced permissions, whereas the `REG ADD` command requests the following permissions:

- `READ_CONTROL`
- `Query key value`
- `Set key value`
- `Create sub-key`
- `Enumerate sub-keys`
- `Notify about changes to keys`

The events in Listings 14-9 and 14-10 are recorded in the Windows security event log after a registry key value is successfully modified.

Listing 14-9 is exactly the same event you saw for a successful registry key value creation operation in Listing 14-5.

Listing 14-9: Event ID 4663: An attempt was made to access an object.

```
Task Category: Registry
Keywords: Audit Success
```

> **NOTE** The events described in this section are available on the book's website, in the `Successful Registry Value Modification.evtx` file.

Listing 14-10: Event ID 4657: A registry value was modified.

```
Task Category: Registry
Keywords: Audit Success
Subject:
        Security ID:        S-1-5-21-3212943211-794299840-588279583-500
        Account Name:       Administrator
        Account Domain:     2016SRV
        Logon ID:           0x345DB
```

```
Object:
        Object Name:            \REGISTRY\MACHINE\SOFTWARE\Personal
        Object Value Name:      RegData
        Handle ID:              0x200
        Operation Type:         %%1905 (Existing registry value modified)
Process Information:
        Process ID:             0x5e8
        Process Name:           C:\Windows\regedit.exe
Change Information:
        Old Value Type:         %%1873 (REG_SZ. See Table 14-3)
        Old Value:              This is my data
        New Value Type:         %%1873 (REG_SZ. See Table 14-3)
        New Value:              This is my modified data
```

The Existing registry value modified operation type is specific for registry key value modification operations.

The Old Value Type and Old Value fields contain information about the previous value type and data.

The New Value Type and New Value fields contain information about the new value type and data.

Unsuccessful Registry Key Value Modification

Recommendations are the same as for an "Unsuccessful registry key value creation" operation, because registry key value creation, deletion, and modification operations require the same access permission: Set Value.

Registry Key Read and Enumerate Operations

In this section you will find information about the following activities that may be performed with registry keys:

- **Key read/open:** List all values for specific registry key.
- **Enumerate subkeys:** List all subkeys for specific registry key.
- **Access permissions read (DACL):** Read information about access permissions set for the specific registry key.
- **Audit permissions read (SACL):** Read information about audit permissions set for the specific registry key.

Successful Registry Key Read Operation

Multiple methods are available to perform registry key read operations: the regedit application, reg query command, PowerShell commands, and so on. All these methods may request different access rights to perform the same operation. For example, regedit requests only the Query key value advanced access permission to read key values, whereas the `reg query` command requires `READ_CONTROL`, `Query key value`, `Enumerate sub-keys`, and `Notify about changes to keys` permissions. It's always up to the application which access permissions to request, but key read operation requests must always have the `Query key value` advanced access permission.

To audit successful key read operations, `Success` auditing must be enabled for the `Query key value` advanced permission on the specific registry key.

Listing 14-11 is an example of the event that is recorded in the Windows security event log after a successful registry key read operation using `regedit`.

Listing 14-11: Event ID 4663: An attempt was made to access an object.

```
Task Category: Registry
Keywords: Audit Success
Subject:
        Security ID:           S-1-5-21-3212943211-794299840-588279583-1000
        Account Name:          Andrei
        Account Domain:        2016SRV
        Logon ID:              0x33F703
Object:
        Object Server:         Security
        Object Type:           Key
        Object Name:           \REGISTRY\MACHINE\SOFTWARE\Personal
        Handle ID:             0x8c
        Resource Attributes:   -
Process Information:
        Process ID:            0x10a4
        Process Name:          C:\Windows\System32\reg.exe
Access Request Information:
        Accesses:              %%4432 (Query key value.
                               See tables 14-2 and 5-4)
        Access Mask:           0x1 (See tables 14-2 and 5-4)
```

NOTE The event described in this section is available on the book's website, in the `Successful Registry Key Read.evtx` file.

The `Query key value` advanced access permission is the only permission required to perform registry read operations.

Each registry key read request must contain the `Query key value` advanced access permission. There might be other access permissions listed in the same event.

Unsuccessful Registry Key Read Operation

To audit unsuccessful key read operations, `Fail` auditing must be enabled for the `Query key value` advanced permission on the specific registry key.

Any failed access request that has `Query key value` advanced access permission in it may be a registry key read attempt. Each application decides on its own which permissions to request for key read operations, but `Query key value` permission is always in the list.

NOTE You can see an example of events generated for unsuccessful registry key read attempt on the book's website, in the `Unsuccessful Registry Key Read .evtx` file.

Successful Registry Key Subkeys Enumeration

Subkey enumeration operations allow you to list all subkeys for a specific registry key.

Multiple methods are available to perform registry key subkeys enumeration operations: the `regedit` application, `reg query` command, PowerShell commands, and so on. These methods may request different access permissions to perform the same operation. For example, `regedit` requests the `Query key value` and `Enumerate sub-keys` advanced access permissions to enumerate key subkeys, whereas the `reg query` command requires only the `Enumerate sub-keys` permission. It's always up to the application which access permissions to request, but for subkeys enumeration operations, the request must always have the `Enumerate sub-keys` advanced access permission.

To audit successful key subkeys enumeration operations, `Success` auditing must be enabled for the `Enumerate sub-keys` advanced permission on the specific registry key.

Listing 14-12 is an example of a registry key subkeys enumeration request event in the Windows security event log performed using the `reg query` command.

Listing 14-12: Event ID 4663: An attempt was made to access an object.

```
Task Category: Registry
Keywords: Audit Success
Subject:
        Security ID:           S-1-5-21-3212943211-794299840-588279583-1000
        Account Name:          Andrei
        Account Domain:        2016SRV
        Logon ID:              0x33F703
Object:
        Object Server:         Security
        Object Type:           Key
        Object Name:           \REGISTRY\MACHINE\SOFTWARE\Personal
        Handle ID:             0x8c
        Resource Attributes:   -
Process Information:
        Process ID:            0x3e8
        Process Name:          C:\Windows\System32\reg.exe
```

```
Access Request Information:
      Accesses:              %%4435
            (Enumerate sub-keys. See tables 14-2 and 5-4)
      Access Mask:           0x8 (See tables 14-2 and 5-4)
```

NOTE The event described in this section is available on the book's website, in the `Successful Registry Key Subkeys Enumeration.evtx` file.

Unsuccessful Registry Key Subkeys Enumeration

To audit unsuccessful registry key subkeys enumeration operations, `Fail` auditing must be enabled for the `Enumerate sub-keys` advanced permission on the specific registry key.

Any failed access request that has the `Enumerate sub-keys` advanced access permission in it may be a registry key subkeys enumeration attempt. Each application decides on its own which permissions to request for registry key subkeys enumeration operations.

NOTE You can see an example of events generated for unsuccessful registry key subkeys enumeration attempt on the book's website, in the `Unsuccessful Registry Key Subkeys Enumeration.evtx` file.

Successful Registry Key Access Permissions Read

The `Read Control` advanced access permission is required to read ACEs in the registry key DACL.

Multiple methods are available to read registry key access permissions: the `regedit` application, `setacl` command-line tool, PowerShell scripts, and so on.

To audit successful key access permissions read operations, `Success` auditing must be enabled for the `Read Control` advanced permission on the specific registry key.

Listing 14-13 is an example of the event generated in the Windows security event log each time someone uses `regedit` to view a registry key's access permissions.

Listing 14-13: Event ID 4663: An attempt was made to access an object.

```
Task Category: Registry
Keywords: Audit Success
Subject:
      Security ID:         S-1-5-21-3212943211-794299840-588279583-500
      Account Name:        Administrator
```

```
          Account Domain:          2016SRV
          Logon ID:                0x345DB
Object:
          Object Server:           Security
          Object Type:             Key
          Object Name:             \REGISTRY\MACHINE\SOFTWARE\Personal
          Handle ID:               0x284
          Resource Attributes:     -
Process Information:
          Process ID:              0xeac
          Process Name:            C:\Windows\regedit.exe
Access Request Information:
          Accesses:                %%1538
                          (READ_CONTROL. See tables 14-2 and 5-4)
          Access Mask:             0x20000 (See tables 14-2 and 5-4)
```

NOTE The event described in this section is available on the book's website, in the `Successful Registry Key Access Permissions Read.evtx` file.

This is a registry key "read access permissions" operation, because the `Accesses` field contains the `READ_CONTROL` access permission. There might be other access permissions listed in the same event.

Unsuccessful Registry Key Access Permissions Read

To audit an unsuccessful registry key permissions read operation, `Fail` auditing must be enabled for the `Read Control` advanced permission on the specific registry key.

Any failed access request that has the `READ_CONTROL` advanced access permission in it may be a registry key access permissions read attempt. Each application decides on its own which permissions to request for a specific registry key operation.

NOTE You can see an example of events generated for unsuccessful registry key access permissions read attempt on the book's website, in the `Unsuccessful Registry Key Access Permissions Read.evtx` file.

Successful Registry Key Audit Permissions Read

All read and write operations with all auditable objects' SACLs are audited by default by the Windows auditing subsystem, and specific events are written in the security event log without any additional setup required.

Any read or write operations performed with an object's SACL require the requestor to have `SeSecurityPrivilege` enabled in the session token.

SeSecurityPrivilege permission is assigned to the account if the account (or security group it belongs to) is included in the "Manage auditing and security log" user right policy setting on a host.

To use the SeSecurityPrivilege privilege, it must be enabled in the process's session token. The 4703 event in Listing 14-14 informs you that the SeSecurityPrivilege privilege was enabled. See Chapter 11 for more information about user privileges and logon rights.

Listing 14-14: Event ID 4703: A token right was adjusted.

```
Task Category: Token Right Adjusted Events
Keywords: Audit Success
Subject:
        Security ID:             S-1-5-21-3212943211-794299840-588279583-500
        Account Name:            Administrator
        Account Domain:          2016SRV
        Logon ID:                0x345DB
Target Account:
        Security ID:             S-1-0-0
        Account Name:            Administrator
        Account Domain:          2016SRV
        Logon ID:                0x345DB
Process Information:
        Process ID:              0x10f8
        Process Name:            C:\Windows\regedit.exe
Enabled Privileges:
                                 SeSecurityPrivilege
Disabled Privileges:
                                 -
```

> **NOTE** The events described in this section are available on the book's website, in the Successful Registry Key Audit Permissions Read.evtx file.

Notice that in the 4656 event in Listing 14-15, the Privileges Used for Access Check field has a value of SeSecurityPrivilege, which informs you that the SeSecurityPrivilege privilege was used as part of the request.

Listing 14-15: Event ID 4656: A handle to an object was requested.

```
Task Category: Registry
Keywords: Audit Success
Subject:
        Security ID:             S-1-5-21-3212943211-794299840-588279583-500
        Account Name:            Administrator
        Account Domain:          2016SRV
        Logon ID:                0x345DB
Object:
        Object Server:           Security
        Object Type:             Key
```

```
        Object Name:           \REGISTRY\MACHINE\SOFTWARE\Personal
        Handle ID:             0x224
        Resource Attributes:   -
Process Information:
        Process ID:            0x10f8
        Process Name:          C:\Windows\regedit.exe
Access Request Information:
        Transaction ID:        {00000000-0000-0000-0000-000000000000}
        Accesses:              %%1538 (READ_CONTROL)
                               %%1542 (ACCESS_SYS_SEC)
                               %%4432 (Query key value)
                               %%4435 (Enumerate sub-keys)
                               See tables 14-2 and 5-4 for more details
        Access Reasons:        -
        Access Mask:           0x1020009 (See tables 14-2 and 5-4)
        Privileges Used for Access Check: SeSecurityPrivilege
        Restricted SID Count: 0
```

You can see that it's a registry key "read audit permissions" operation, because the `Accesses` field contains the `ACCESS_SYS_SEC` access permission and `SeSecurityPrivilege` is listed in the `Privileges Used for Access Check` field.

Unsuccessful Registry Key Audit Permissions Read

As noted in the previous section, any read or write operations performed with an object's SACL requires the requestor to have `SeSecurityPrivilege`.

Any failed access request that has `ACCESS_SYS_SEC` access permission requested and `SeSecurityPrivilege` used in it should be considered as a registry key "read audit permissions" attempt.

> **NOTE** You can see an example of events generated for unsuccessful registry key audit permissions read attempt on the book's website, in the `Unsuccessful Registry Key Audit Permissions Read.evtx` file.

DACL, SACL, and Ownership Change Operations

In this section you will find information about the following operations that may be performed with registry keys:

- **Access permissions change (DACL):** Change access permissions for a specific registry key.

- **Audit permissions change (SACL):** Change audit permissions for a specific registry key.

- **Change registry key owner:** Change an owner for a specific registry key.

Successful Registry Key Access Permissions Change

To audit successful registry key access permissions change operations, Success auditing must be enabled for the Write DAC advanced permission on the specific registry key.

Write DAC advanced access permission is required to modify a registry key's DACL. It depends on the application which additional permissions it is requesting for the DACL modification operation, but Write DAC permission is always requested. regedit, for example, additionally requests Read Control permission to view the current registry key's access permissions.

Listings 14-16 and 14-17 are examples of the events that are recorded in the Windows security event log after a successful registry key access permissions change operation using regedit.

Listing 14-16: Event ID 4663: An attempt was made to access an object.

```
Task Category: Registry
Keywords: Audit Success
Subject:
        Security ID:            S-1-5-21-3212943211-794299840-588279583-500
        Account Name:           Administrator
        Account Domain:         2016SRV
        Logon ID:               0x345DB
Object:
        Object Server:          Security
        Object Type:            Key
        Object Name:            \REGISTRY\MACHINE\SOFTWARE\Personal\Andrei
        Handle ID:              0x2a8
        Resource Attributes:    -
Process Information:
        Process ID:             0xc4c
        Process Name:           C:\Windows\regedit.exe
Access Request Information:
        Accesses:               %%1539 (WRITE_DAC. See tables 14-2 and 5-4)
        Access Mask:            0x40000 (See tables 14-2 and 5-4)
```

NOTE The events described in this section are available on the book's website, in the Successful Registry Key Access Permissions Change.evtx file.

The WRITE_DAC access permission type informs you that it was a DACL change operation. It is up to the application to decide which other access types to use with WRITE_DAC access, so you can see other access permissions requested in the same event along with WRITE_DAC permission.

The 4670 event (Listing 14-17) contains detailed information about the previous and new DACL values in the object's security descriptor. Both the Original Security Descriptor and New Security Descriptor fields contain information only about DACL ACEs; no owner, primary group, or SACL information is included. Values for these two fields are shown in SDDL format, which is described in Chapter 10.

Listing 14-17: Event ID 4670: Permissions on an object were changed.

```
Task Category: Registry
Keywords: Audit Success
Subject:
        Security ID:          S-1-5-21-3212943211-794299840-588279583-500
        Account Name:         Administrator
        Account Domain:       2016SRV
        Logon ID:             0x345DB
Object:
        Object Server:        Security
        Object Type:          Key
        Object Name:          \REGISTRY\MACHINE\SOFTWARE\Personal\Andrei
        Handle ID:            0x2a8
Process:
        Process ID:           0xc4c
        Process Name:         C:\Windows\regedit.exe
Permissions Change:
        Original Security Descriptor: D:AI(A;CIID;KA;;;BA)(A;CIID;KA;;;SY)
                                    (A;CIIOID;KA;;;CO)(A;CIID;KR;;;AC)
            (A;CIID;CC;;;S-1-5-21-3212943211-794299840-588279583-1000)
        New Security Descriptor: D:ARAI(A;CIID;KA;;;BA)(A;CIID;KA;;;SY)
                (A;CIIOID;KA;;;CO)(A;CIID;KR;;;AC)(A;CIID;CCDCLCSW;;;
                    S-1-5-21-3212943211-794299840-588279583-1000)
```

Unsuccessful Registry Key Access Permissions Change

To audit unsuccessful registry key access permissions change operations, `Fail` auditing must be enabled for the `Write DAC` advanced permission on the specific registry key.

The event in Listing 14-18 appears in the Windows security event log after an unsuccessful access permission change attempt on the registry key.

Listing 14-18: Event ID 4656: A handle to an object was requested.

```
Task Category: Registry
Keywords: Audit Failure
Subject:
        Security ID:          S-1-5-21-3212943211-794299840-588279583-1000
        Account Name:         Andrei
        Account Domain:       2016SRV
        Logon ID:             0xE410B1
Object:
        Object Server:        Security
        Object Type:          Key
```

```
      Object Name:              \REGISTRY\MACHINE\SOFTWARE\Personal
      Handle ID:                0x0
      Resource Attributes:      -
Process Information:
      Process ID:               0x5ec
      Process Name:             C:\Windows\regedit.exe
Access Request Information:
      Transaction ID:           {00000000-0000-0000-0000-000000000000}
      Accesses:                 %%1538 (READ_CONTROL)
                                %%1539 (WRITE_DAC)
                                %%4432 (Query key value)
                                %%4435 (Enumerate sub-keys)
                                See tables 14-2 and 5-4 for more details
      Access Reasons:           -
      Access Mask:              0x60009
         (See tables 14-2 and 5-4 for more details)
      Privileges Used for Access Check: -
      Restricted SID Count: 0
```

> **NOTE** The event described in this section is available on the book's website, in the `Unsuccessful Registry Key Access Permissions Change.evtx` file.

This `Audit Failure` event has a `WRITE_DAC` access permission type in the `Accesses` field, which is an indicator of an access permission write operation attempt.

Successful Registry Key Audit Permissions Change

No specific SACL changes are required to audit successful registry key audit permissions change operations. The "Audit Policy Change" audit subcategory must be enabled for `Success` auditing to get 4907 events.

As for audit permissions (SACL) read operations, an account must have the `SeSecurityPrivilege` privilege enabled in its session token to perform change/ write operations.

The events in Listings 14-19, 14-20, and 14-21 are generated in the Windows security event log after a successful audit permissions change operation with a registry key.

> **NOTE** The events described in this section are available on the book's website, in the `Successful Registry Key Audit Permissions Change.evtx` file.

To use the `SeSecurityPrivilege` privilege, it must be enabled in the process's access token. The 4703 event informs you that the `SeSecurityPrivilege` privilege was enabled. See Chapter 11 for more information about user privileges and logon rights.

Listing 14-19: Event ID 4703: A token right was adjusted.

```
Task Category: Token Right Adjusted Events
Keywords: Audit Success
Subject:
        Security ID:            S-1-5-21-3212943211-794299840-588279583-500
        Account Name:           Administrator
        Account Domain:         2016SRV
        Logon ID:               0x345DB
Target Account:
        Security ID:            S-1-0-0
        Account Name:           Administrator
        Account Domain:         2016SRV
        Logon ID:               0x345DB
Process Information:
        Process ID:             0x4ec
        Process Name:           C:\Windows\regedit.exe
Enabled Privileges:

                                SeSecurityPrivilege
Disabled Privileges:

                                -
```

The 4674 event informs you that some operations were performed (`Desired Access`) with the use of specific user privileges (`Privileges`).

Listing 14-20: Event ID 4674: An operation was attempted on a privileged object.

```
Task Category: Sensitive Privilege Use
Keywords: Audit Success
Subject:
        Security ID:            S-1-5-21-3212943211-794299840-588279583-500
        Account Name:           Administrator
        Account Domain:         2016SRV
        Logon ID:               0x345DB
Object:
        Object Server:          Security
        Object Type:            Key
        Object Name:            \REGISTRY\MACHINE\SOFTWARE\Personal
        Object Handle:          0x294
Process Information:
        Process ID:             0x4ec
        Process Name:           C:\Windows\regedit.exe
Requested Operation:
        Desired Access:         %%1538 (READ_CONTROL)
                                %%1542 (ACCESS_SYS_SEC)
                                %%4432 (Query key value)
                                %%4435 (Enumerate sub-keys)
                                See tables 14-2 and 5-4 for more details
        Privileges:             SeSecurityPrivilege
```

In this particular event, the most interesting part for us is the use of the `ACCESS_SYS_SEC` access right and the use of the `SeSecurityPrivilege` privilege. These two pieces together inform you that the SACL for the `\REGISTRY\MACHINE\SOFTWARE\Personal` registry key was modified. If you compare events from the "Successful Registry Key Audit Permissions Read" and current sections, you will see that some of the events are different; for example, for the Read operation it's event 4656, whereas for the Write operation it is 4674.

The event in Listing 14-21 contains more detailed information about the change to the object's SACL.

Listing 14-21: Event ID 4907: Auditing settings on object were changed.

```
Task Category: Audit Policy Change
Keywords: Audit Success
Subject:
        Security ID:            S-1-5-21-3212943211-794299840-588279583-500
        Account Name:           Administrator
        Account Domain:         2016SRV
        Logon ID:               0x345DB
Object:
        Object Server:          Security
        Object Type:            Key
        Object Name:            \REGISTRY\MACHINE\SOFTWARE\Personal
        Handle ID:              0x294
Process Information:
        Process ID:             0x4ec
        Process Name:           C:\Windows\regedit.exe
Auditing Settings:
        Original Security Descriptor:       S:AI(AU;CISAFA;WD;;;WD)
        New Security Descriptor:            S:ARAI(AU;CISAFA;WDWO;;;WD)
```

The `Subject` section contains information about the account that performed the action.

The `Object` section contains information about an object for which the SACL was changed.

The `Auditing Setting` section contains the previous and new SACL values for the object. Both the `Original Security Descriptor` and `New Security Descriptor` fields contain SACL values in SDDL format, which is described in Chapter 10. They only contain information about SACL modifications (`S:`); no information about the object's owner or DACL is included.

In the current example you see the following changes:

- SACL inheritance options (S:AI) are changed to S:ARAI, which means child objects inherit permissions from this object (AR) and inheritance is allowed (AI).

- ACE permissions were changed from WD to WDWO, which means Write DAC (WD) and Write Owner (MO).

Unsuccessful Registry Key Audit Permissions Change

If the account doesn't have `SeSecurityPrivilege`, as a result of an unsuccessful registry key audit permissions change request the event in Listing 14-22 is generated in the Windows security event log.

Listing 14-22: Event ID 4673: A privileged service was called.

```
Task Category: Sensitive Privilege Use
Keywords: Audit Failure
Subject:
        Security ID:            S-1-5-21-3212943211-794299840-588279583-1000
        Account Name:           Andrei
        Account Domain:         2016SRV
        Logon ID:               0x33F703
Service:
        Server:                 Security
        Service Name:           -
Process:
        Process ID:             0x1078
        Process Name:           C:\Program Files (x86)\Windows Resource Kits
                                                    \Tools\subinacl.exe
Service Request Information:
        Privileges:             SeTcbPrivilege
```

> **NOTE** The event described in this section is available on the book's website, in the `Unsuccessful Registry Key Audit Permissions Change.evtx` file.

There is no specific information in this event about the registry key for which the audit permissions change attempt was made.

Successful Registry Key Owner Change

To audit successful registry key ownership changes (not including DACL and SACL changes), the `Write Owner` permission must be enabled for the `Success` auditing type in the object's SACL.

The take ownership operation is allowed if at least one of the following requirements is met:

- Account has `SeTakeOwnershipPrivilege`
- Account has `SeRestorePrivilege`
- Account has "Write Owner" access permission allowed in the target object's DACL

The event in Listing 14-23 is always recorded in the Windows security event log for a successful registry key ownership change operation.

Listing 14-23: Event ID 4670: Permissions on an object were changed.

```
Task Category: Authorization Policy Change
Keywords: Audit Success
Subject:
        Security ID:            S-1-5-21-3212943211-794299840-588279583-500
        Account Name:           Administrator
        Account Domain:         2016SRV
        Logon ID:               0x345DB
Object:
        Object Server:          Security
        Object Type:            Key
        Object Name:            \REGISTRY\MACHINE\SOFTWARE\Personal\Andrei
        Handle ID:              0x274
Process:
        Process ID:             0x4ec
        Process Name:           C:\Windows\regedit.exe
Permissions Change:
        Original Security Descriptor:     O:BA
        New Security Descriptor:          O:S-1-5-21-3212943211-794299840
                                            -588279583-1000
```

> **NOTE** The event described in this section is available on the book's website, in the `Successful Registry Key Owner Change.evtx` **file.**

In this event you can see the following information:

- **Subject:** Who made a change.
- **Object:** Information about the registry key for which owner was changed.
- **Process:** Which process was used to perform owner change operation.

The `Permissions Change` section contains the original and new values of the object's security descriptor. This event does not show SACL and DACL modifications. Only the ownership section (`O:`) in the applied security descriptor is shown in the event. Both the `Original Security Descriptor` and `New Security Descriptor` fields have SDDL strings, which are described in Chapter 10.

In the current example you see that the built-in Administrators security group (BA) was changed to some other account or group (SID).

Global Object Access Auditing: Registry

Global Object Access Auditing allows you to configure a global SACL for the entire system, which will be applied to all registry keys.

The global SACL for registry objects can be defined using the following group policy setting:

```
Local Computer Policy\Computer Configuration\Windows Settings\
Security Settings\Advanced Audit Policy Configuration\System Audit
Policies - Local Group Policy Object\Global Object Access Auditing\
Registry.
```

The global SACL works in conjunction with the normal registry key object SACL. Both of them are applied at the same time.

In addition to standard registry key permissions, the following permission sets are available to be set for global SACL:

- **Read:** Includes the following advanced permissions:

  - Query Value

  - Enumerate Subkeys

  - Notify

  - Read Control

- **Write:** Includes the following advanced permissions:

  - Set Value

  - Create Subkey

  - Read Control

- **Execute:** The same as Read.

To view the applied global SACL for a local machine, use the following command: `auditpol /resourcesacl /type:Key /view`. Figure 14-3 shows an example of the output for this command:

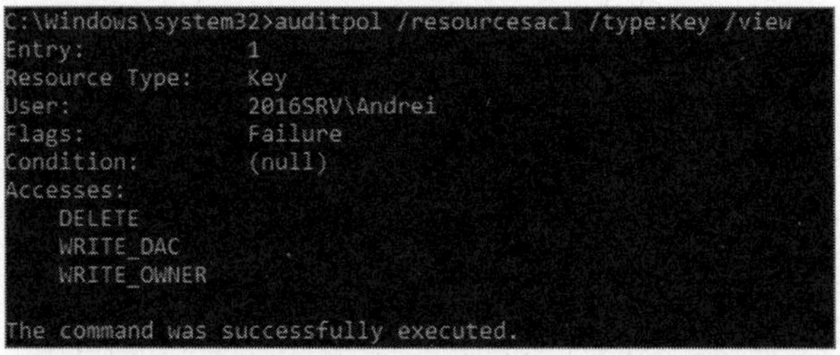

```
C:\Windows\system32>auditpol /resourcesacl /type:Key /view
Entry:              1
Resource Type:      Key
User:               2016SRV\Andrei
Flags:              Failure
Condition:          (null)
Accesses:
   DELETE
   WRITE_DAC
   WRITE_OWNER

The command was successfully executed.
```

Figure 14-3: View Global Object Access Auditing settings for registry keys using auditpol.exe command

Registry Key Integrity Levels

Integrity levels for registry keys are the same as for file system objects, as discussed in Chapter 13. And the principle of how mandatory access works is the same as discussed in Chapter 12.

There is no built-in tool available that you can use to set or view an integrity level label for a registry key, but you can use publicly available tools such as `regil` written by Mark Minasi.

By default, all unlabeled registry keys have a Medium Mandatory Level integrity level. You can verify the current integrity level for a key with `regil`. In order to view the current integrity level label for a key, use the following command: `regil REGISTRY_KEY_NAME`.

Figure 14-4 shows an example of the `regil` command output when an integrity level label is explicitly set for an object.

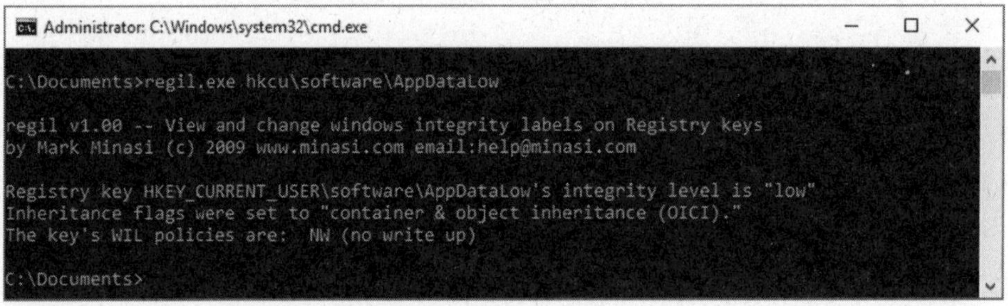

Figure 14-4: Regil output for registry key integrity level

You can see that the `HKEY_CURRENT_USER\software\AppDataLow` registry key has a Low Mandatory Level integrity label applied. You can see the list of all integrity level labels in Table 12-3 (Chapter 12).

If there is no integrity level label applied to a key, then it is considered to have a Medium Mandatory Level integrity level.

Registry Key Integrity Level Modification

You can use the same `regil` tool to modify an integrity level label for a registry key. Use the following command to perform this operation: `regil REGISTRY_KEY_NAME -i:LEVEL`, where `LEVEL` can be one of the following:

- `l`: Low Mandatory Level
- `m`: Medium Mandatory Level
- `h`: High Mandatory Level

It is not possible to set an integrity level for a registry key using this command to anything except Low, Medium, or High.

To be able to monitor for integrity label modifications, the following requirements need to be met:

- The "Authorization Policy Change" audit subcategory should be enabled for Success.

- "Take ownership" success auditing should be enabled in the object's SACL.

After an integrity label for a registry key is changed, the event in Listing 14-24 is generated in the security event log.

Listing 14-24: Event ID 4670: Permissions on an object were changed.

```
Task Category: Authorization Policy Change
Keywords: Audit Success
Subject:
        Security ID:            S-1-5-21-1913345275-1711810662-261465553-
                                                                      500
        Account Name:           Administrator
        Account Domain:         HQCORP
        Logon ID:               0x4AE47
Object:
        Object Server:          Security
        Object Type:            Key
        Object Name:            \REGISTRY\USER\S-1-5-21-1913345275-
                1711810662-261465553-500\SOFTWARE\MySoft
        Handle ID:              0xcc
Process:
        Process ID:             0xb54
        Process Name:           C:\Documents\regil.exe
Permissions Change:
        Original Security Descriptor:      S:AI(ML;OICI;NW;;;LW)
        New Security Descriptor:           S:(ML;OICI;NW;;;ME)
```

NOTE The event described in this section is available on the book's website, in the `Registry Key Integrity Level Modification.evtx` file.

Listing 14-17 discussed the 4670 event. Integrity level labels are located in the object's SACL instead of DACL.

Listing 14-24 shows that the SACL for the `\REGISTRY\USER\S-1-5-21-1913345275-1711810662-261465553-500\SOFTWARE\MySoft` registry key was changed from `S:AI(ML;OICI;NW;;;LW)` to `S:(ML;OICI;NW;;;ME)`. Here is how you can read the new SACL:

`S:(ML;OICI;NW;;;ME)`

- `S:`- SACL section

- `(ML;OICI;NW;;;ME)`

  - `ML:` ACE type is Mandatory Level (`ML`)

- **OICI**: ACE flags:

  - **OI**: child objects that are not containers inherit this ACE as an explicit ACE.

  - **CI**: child objects that are containers, such as other registry keys, inherit this ACE as an explicit ACE.

- **NW**: contains the object's integrity policy:

  - **NW**: SDDL_NO_WRITE_UP

  - **NR**: SDDL_NO_READ_UP

  - **NX**: SDDL_NO_EXECUTE_UP

    NW is a default integrity policy for all registry keys in Windows. You can read more about integrity policies in Chapter 12.

- **ME**: Medium Mandatory Level. Can also be:

  - **LW**: Low Mandatory Level

  - **HI**: High Mandatory Level

  - **SI**: System Mandatory Level

Monitoring Recommendations

Table 14-5 lists useful filesystem events to monitor.

Table 14-5: Recommended Registry Events to Monitor

SECURITY EVENT	SUBCATEGORY	EVENT TYPE
4656: A handle to an object was requested.	Registry	Audit Success
		Audit Failure
4663: An attempt was made to access an object.	Registry	Audit Success
4657: A registry value was modified.	Registry	Audit Success
4670: Permissions on an object were changed.	Authorization Policy Change	Audit Success
4907: Auditing settings on object were changed.	Audit Policy Change	Audit Success

Monitoring Scenarios

It's usually difficult to provide specific recommendations for registry monitoring, because you personally need to define which registry keys and operations are the most important to monitor and for which type of access permissions.

One of the recommendations is to define the most critical registry keys you should monitor. Some examples are:

- `HKLM\Software\Microsoft\Windows\CurrentVersion\Group Policy\Scripts\Startup`

- `HKLM\Software\Microsoft\Windows\CurrentVersion\Group Policy\Scripts\Shutdown`

- `HKLM\SYSTEM\CurrentControlSet\Control\SafeBoot\AlternateShell`

- `HKLM\SOFTWARE\Microsoft\Windows\CurrentVersion\Run`

- `HKLM\SOFTWARE\Wow6432Node\Microsoft\Windows\CurrentVersion\Run`

- `HKCU\SOFTWARE\Microsoft\Windows\CurrentVersion\Run`

- `HKCU\SOFTWARE\Microsoft\Windows\CurrentVersion\RunOnce`

- `HKLM\SOFTWARE\Microsoft\Active Setup\Installed Components`

- `HKLM\SOFTWARE\Wow6432Node\Microsoft\Active Setup\Installed Components`

- `HKLM\System\CurrentControlSet\Services`

- `HKLM\SOFTWARE\Microsoft\Windows\CurrentVersion\Explorer\SharedTaskScheduler`

- `HKLM\SOFTWARE\Wow6432Node\Microsoft\Windows\CurrentVersion\Explorer\SharedTaskScheduler`

- `HKLM\SOFTWARE\Microsoft\Windows\CurrentVersion\Explorer\ShellServiceObjects`

- `HKLM\SOFTWARE\Wow6432Node\Microsoft\Windows\CurrentVersion\Explorer\ShellServiceObjects`

- `HKLM\SOFTWARE\Microsoft\Windows\CurrentVersion\ShellServiceObjectDelayLoad`

- `HKLM\SOFTWARE\Wow6432Node\Microsoft\Windows\CurrentVersion\ShellServiceObjectDelayLoad`

- `HKLM\Software\Classes\Drive\ShellEx\ContextMenuHandlers`

- `HKLM\Software\Classes\Directory\ShellEx\ContextMenuHandlers`

- `HKLM\Software\Classes\Directory\Shellex\DragDropHandlers`

- `HKLM\Software\Classes\Directory\Shellex\CopyHookHandlers`

- HKLM\Software\Classes\Directory\Background\ShellEx\ ContextMenuHandlers

- HKLM\Software\Classes\Folder\ShellEx\ContextMenuHandlers

- HKLM\Software\Classes\Folder\ShellEx\DragDropHandlers

- HKLM\Software\Microsoft\Windows\CurrentVersion\Explorer\ ShellIconOverlayIdentifiers

- HKLM\Software\Wow6432Node\Microsoft\Windows\CurrentVersion\ Explorer\ShellIconOverlayIdentifiers

- HKLM\SOFTWARE\Microsoft\Windows NT\CurrentVersion\Winlogon\ GpExtensions

Also, some permissions are usually more important to monitor than other permissions. The most sensitive permissions to monitor are:

- Set Value
- Create Subkey
- Create Link
- Delete
- Write DAC
- Write Owner
- Read Control

CHAPTER 15

Network File Shares and Named Pipes

Network shares are designed to exchange files between hosts in the network. There are some critical network shares, such as SYSVOL on domain controllers or %systemdrive%$ on hosts. Changes to these are important to monitor.

Named pipes is a mechanism designed for communications between processes and applications within a host or over a network. In this chapter you will find information about monitoring for actions related to network file shares and named pipes.

Network File Shares

A network file share is a common mechanism to share files on a Windows host with other hosts. The Common Internet File System (CIFS) and Server Message Block (SMB) protocols are used for communications with network file shares. The CIFS protocol is considered legacy, and currently different versions of the SMB protocol are the most commonly used for network share access operations and interactions.

Network shares can be accessed via the network using, for example, Windows File Explorer, with the path format *SERVER**SHARE_NAME*, where:

- *SERVER* can be an IP address of the target host, NetBIOS name, or DNS name.

- *SHARE_NAME* represents the name of the network file share.

To get a list of shares available on the local machine, you can use the NET SHARE command. Figure 15-1 shows an example of the NET SHARE command output.

```
C:\Windows\system32>net share

Share name    Resource                      Remark

-----------------------------------------------------------------------------
C$            C:\                           Default share
IPC$                                        Remote IPC
ADMIN$        C:\Windows                    Remote Admin
Share         C:\Share
The command completed successfully.
```

Figure 15-1: Network shares list

If you see a $ character at the end of a share name, it means that this share is an administrative share. Such shares are hidden and will not be displayed when, for example, someone connects to the machine using *machine_name*\ to see the list of available shares. Administrative shares require administrative access (membership in the local Administrators security group) in order to get access to them.

Shares can also be viewed and managed using the built-in Shared Folders management snap-in (fsmgmt.msc) as shown in Figure 15-2.

Share Name	Folder Path	Type	# Client Connections	Description
ADMIN$	C:\WINDOWS	Windows	0	Remote Admin
C$	C:\	Windows	0	Default share
ccmsetup$	C:\WINDOWS\ccmsetup	Windows	0	Public Share
IPC$		Windows	0	Remote IPC
print$	C:\WINDOWS\system32\spool\drivers	Windows	0	Printer Drivers

Shared Folders (Local)
- Shares
- Sessions
- Open Files

Figure 15-2: Shared Folders management snap-in

All shared folders in Windows 10 and Windows Server 2016 have the parameters shown in Table 15-1.

Table 15-1: Network Share Parameters

PARAMETER	DESCRIPTION
Share Name	The name of the file share object. Can be different from the filesystem folder's name. If you see the $ character at the end of a share name, that means that this is an administrative share.
Folder Path	Filesystem folder path to which the share is linked.
Description	Description for the file share.

PARAMETER	DESCRIPTION
User limit: Maximum allowed	Setting for maximum allowed connections to the share. This number depends on the software's license terms.
User limit: Allow this number of users	Using this parameter you can specify the number of allowed concurrent unique users connected to the share.
Offline Settings	Allows you to configure offline access settings for a specific share. Offline access allows files from the share to be cached on the user's machine.
Share Permissions	File share access permission (different from NTFS permissions).

Each file share has one of the types described in Table 15-2.

Table 15-2: File Share Types

SHARE TYPE	CODE	DESCRIPTION
Disk Drive	0	Share located on a disk drive
Disk Drive Admin	2147483648	Administrative hidden share, which is located on a disk drive
Print Queue	1	Share for remote print operations
Print Queue Admin	2147483649	Administrative hidden share for remote print operations
Device	2	Devices shares, such as a share for a fax device
Device Admin	2147483650	Administrative hidden devices shares, such as a share for a fax device
IPC	3	Share used by inter-process communication (IPC) mechanisms
IPC Admin	2147483651	Administrative hidden share used by inter-process communication (IPC) mechanisms

Table 15-3 shows some default network file shares that exist on a system depending on which roles, hardware, and features are enabled.

Table 15-3: Default Network Shares

SHARE NAME	DESCRIPTION
DriveLetter$	Each logical disk has its own administrative hidden share enabled by default on all Windows systems
ADMIN$	Default hidden administrative share for the `%systemdrive%\Windows` folder
IPC$	Share used by inter-process communication (IPC) mechanisms

Continues

Table 15-3 (*continued*)

SHARE NAME	DESCRIPTION
NETLOGON	Domain controller network share that contains domain file objects such as domain group policy folders, scripts, and so on
SYSVOL	Domain controller network share that is used for Active Directory data replication between domain controllers
PRINT$	File share for remote print operations
FAX$	Share used for remote fax operations

Settings for manually created file shares are stored in the following registry location: HKEY_LOCAL_MACHINE\SYSTEM\CurrentControlSet\Services\ LanmanServer\Shares. Each file share has its own registry key value under the Shares key. Table 15-4 contains additional parameters that can be set in the registry key value in addition to the ones discussed previously.

Table 15-4: Additional File Share Parameters

PARAMETER	DESCRIPTION
CATimeout	Timeout settings for continuously available shares. This setting defines the minimum time the server should hold a persistent handle on a continuously available share before closing the handle if it is un-reclaimed.
	Current starting from Windows 8 and Windows Server 2012.
CSCFlags	Offline caching and file share access settings. It's a mask field that is compounded using the following numbers (the list contains the most common flags; for a complete list see the official Microsoft documentation):
	▪ 0x0: "Only the files and programs that users specify are available offline" share offline setting
	▪ 0x10: "All files and programs that users open from the shared folder are automatically available offline" share offline setting
	▪ 0x20: "All files and programs that users open from the shared folder are automatically available offline" share offline setting + "Optimize for performance" checkbox
	▪ 0x30: "No files or programs from the shared folder are available offline" share offline setting
	▪ 0x100: Disallows exclusive file opens that deny reads to an open file
	▪ 0x200: Disallows clients from opening files on the share in an exclusive mode that prevents the file from being deleted until the client closes the file

PARAMETER	DESCRIPTION
Permissions	Explains how the file share was created. Can have one of the following values: ■ **0 :** Share created using simple file sharing UI ■ **9 :** Share created using advanced file sharing UI ■ **63 :** Share created using command-line tool, like net.exe This setting is reverted to 0 each time offline caching settings for the file share are changed.
Type	File share type. See Table 15-2.

The security descriptor for each file share object is stored in the following registry key: HKEY_LOCAL_MACHINE\SYSTEM\CurrentControlSet\Services\ LanmanServer\Shares\Security. Each file share has its own registry key value under the Security key. The Get-SmbShareAccess PowerShell cmdlet can be used to read security descriptor information for a specific file share.

Network File Share Access Permissions

In addition to standard NTFS permissions, each file share object also has its own network file share permissions. Table 15-5 contains file share permissions, which can be configured for non-administrative file shares.

Table 15-5: File Share Permissions

ACCESS PERMISSION	SDDL VALUE	DESCRIPTION
Read	0x1200a9	Allows list folder content, execute files, and read files operations
Change	0x1301bf	Allows read, write, execute, delete files, and delete folders operations
Full Control	FA	Contains Read and Change permissions, plus permissions to modify file share access permissions

File share permissions are applied together with NTFS permissions. The most restrictive permission takes precedence.

File Share Creation

New file shares can be manually created (using the `net share` command, for example) or they can be created as part of the new role, feature, or software installation.

Successful File Share Creation

The event in Listing 15-1 is generated in the Windows security event log no matter what method is used to create a new file share.

Listing 15-1: Event ID 5142: A network share object was added.

```
Task Category: File Share
Keywords: Audit Success
Subject:
        Security ID:          S-1-5-21-3212943211-794299840-588279583-500
        Account Name:         Administrator
        Account Domain:       2016SRV
        Logon ID:             0x2F90A
Share Information:
        Share Name:           \\*\Documents Share
        Share Path:           C:\Documents
```

NOTE The events described in this section are available on the book's website, in the `Successful File Share Creation.evtx` file.

The `Subject` section contains information about the account that created the new file share object.

`Share Name` contains the name of the newly created share in the following format: `\\*\SHARE_NAME`.

`Share Path` contains a path for the file share's folder on a disk drive.

The 5142 event contains basic information about the newly created file share. To get more detailed information you should use registry auditing for the `HKEY_LOCAL_MACHINE\SYSTEM\CurrentControlSet\Services\LanmanServer\Shares` registry key. Configure "Set Value" `Audit Success` type auditing permission in the registry key's SACL.

The event in Listing 15-2 is generated in the Windows security event log after a new file share is created if "Set Value" `Audit Success` type auditing permission is set for the `HKEY_LOCAL_MACHINE\SYSTEM\CurrentControlSet\Services\LanmanServer\Shares` registry key.

Listing 15-2: Event ID 4657: A registry value was modified.

```
Task Category: Registry
Keywords: Audit Success
Subject:
        Security ID:          S-1-5-18
        Account Name:         2016SRV$
```

```
           Account Domain:         WORKGROUP
           Logon ID:               0x3E7
Object:
           Object Name:       \REGISTRY\MACHINE\SYSTEM\ControlSet001\Services\
                                               LanmanServer\Shares
           Object Value Name:      Documents
           Handle ID:              0x3a8
           Operation Type:         %%1904 (New registry value created)
Process Information:
           Process ID:             0x6fc
           Process Name:           C:\Windows\System32\svchost.exe
Change Information:
           Old Value Type:         -
           Old Value:              -
           New Value Type:         %%1879 (REG_MULTI_SZ (New lines are
                       replaced with *. A * is replaced with **))
           New Value: CATimeout=0*CSCFlags=0*MaxUses=10*Path=C:\Documents*
              Permissions=9*Remark=My new share*ShareName=Documents*Type=0
```

In this event you can see more details about the new file share. All file share
parameters are located in the New Value field. The new file share in this example
has the following parameters:

- CATimeout=0: No continuously available share settings were set (Table 15-4)

- CSCFlags=0: "Only the files and programs that users specify are available
  offline" share offline setting was set (Table 15-4)

- MaxUses=10: Maximum number of users that can connect to this share at
  the same time is 10

- Path=C:\Documents: File share file system folder path

- Permissions=9: Share created using advanced file sharing UI (Table 15-4)

- Remark=My new share: File share description

- ShareName=Documents: File share name

- Type=0: Share is located on a disk drive (Table 15-2)

See Chapter 14 for more information about registry auditing.

Monitoring Recommendations

Useful file share creation events to monitor are:

SECURITY EVENT	SUBCATEGORY	EVENT TYPE
5142: A network share object was added.	File Share	Audit Success
4657: A registry value was modified.	Registry	Audit Success

It's recommended to monitor for any new file share created on a machine, especially if the host is a critical or high business impact (HBI) host.

To get more detailed information about newly created file shares, collect 4657 events in addition to 5142 events.

File Share Deletion

This section contains information about monitoring for successful and unsuccessful file share deletion operations.

Successful File Share Deletion

The event in Listing 15-3 is generated in the Windows security event log no matter what method is used to delete a file share.

Listing 15-3: Event ID 5144: A network share object was deleted.

```
Task Category: File Share
Keywords: Audit Success
Subject:
        Security ID:            S-1-5-21-3212943211-794299840-588279583-500
        Account Name:           Administrator
        Account Domain:         2016SRV
        Logon ID:               0x2F90A
Share Information:
        Share Name:             \\*\Documents
        Share Path:             C:\Documents
```

NOTE   The events described in this section are available on the book's website, in the `Successful File Share Deletion.evtx` **file.**

This event shows you basic information about the deleted share. It also contains information about the account that performed this operation.

To get more detailed information about a deleted file share, enable registry auditing for "Set Value" `Audit Success` events, as explained in the "File Share Creation" section earlier in this chapter. Listing 15-4 is an example of the event that is generated when the corresponding registry key value for a file share is deleted.

Listing 15-4: Event ID 4657: A registry value was modified.

```
Task Category: Registry
Keywords: Audit Success
Subject:
        Security ID:            S-1-5-18
        Account Name:           2016SRV$
        Account Domain:         WORKGROUP
        Logon ID:               0x3E7
```

```
Object:
     Object Name:       \REGISTRY\MACHINE\SYSTEM\ControlSet001\Services\
                                              LanmanServer\Shares
     Object Value Name:    Documents
     Handle ID:            0x3a8
     Operation Type:       %%1906 (Registry value deleted)
Process Information:
     Process ID:           0x6fc
     Process Name:         C:\Windows\System32\svchost.exe
Change Information:
     Old Value Type:       %%1879 (REG_MULTI_SZ (New lines are
                  replaced with *. A * is replaced with **))
     Old Value: CATimeout=0*CSCFlags=0*MaxUses=4294967295*Path=C:\
                  Documents*Permissions=9*ShareName=Documents*Type=0
     New Value Type:       -
     New Value:            -
```

The Old Value field contains detailed information about the deleted file share parameters. See the "File Share Creation" section for more information.

Unsuccessful File Share Deletion

There is no specific indicator of an unsuccessful file share delete operation event message that I'm aware of.

Monitoring Recommendations

Useful file share deletion events to monitor are:

SECURITY EVENT	SUBCATEGORY	EVENT TYPE
5144: A network share object was deleted.	File Share	Audit Success
4657: A registry value was modified.	Registry	Audit Success

It's recommended to monitor for any file share deletions on a machine, especially if the host is a critical or HBI host.

To get more detailed information about deleted file shares, collect 4657 events in addition to 5144 events.

File Share Modification

File share settings, such as access permissions or offline access settings, can be configured using command-line applications or the built-in Windows File Explorer. This section provides information about successful and unsuccessful file share modification monitoring.

Successful File Share Modification

The event in Listing 15-5 is generated in the Windows security event log if a file share is successfully modified.

Listing 15-5: Event ID 5143: A network share object was modified.

```
Task Category: File Share
Keywords: Audit Success
Subject:
        Security ID:            S-1-5-21-3212943211-794299840-588279583-500
        Account Name:           Administrator
        Account Domain:         2016SRV
        Logon ID:               0x2F90A
Share Information:
        Object Type:            Directory
        Share Name:             \\*\Documents
        Share Path:             C:\Documents
        Old Remark:             My Share!
        New Remark:             My Modified Share!
        Old MaxUsers:           0xA
        New Maxusers:           0xF
        Old ShareFlags:         0x30
        New ShareFlags:         0x30
        Old SD:       O:BAG:S-1-5-21-3212943211-794299840-588279583-513D:
                                            (A;;0x1301bf;;;WD)
        New SD:       O:BAG:S-1-5-21-3212943211-794299840-588279583-513D:
                                            (A;;0x1200a9;;;WD)
```

NOTE The events described in this section are available on the book's website, in the `Successful File Share Modification.evtx` file.

The following changes are captured in the 5143 event:

- **File share description:** `Old Remark`, `New Remark`.

- **Maximum number of simultaneous user connections:** `Old MaxUsers`, `New MaxUsers`. This number is in hexadecimal form; you need to convert it to decimal to view a real value.

- **CSCFlags:** `Old ShareFlags`, `New ShareFlags`. See Table 15-4 for more details.

- **Security descriptor:** `Old SD`, `New SD`.

The `Old` and `New` fields will have the same values if no change occurred.

The `Old SD` and `New SD` fields contain Security Descriptor Definition Language (SDDL) expressions. You can find more information about SDDL syntax in

Chapter 10. For this example you see that the `D:(A;;0x1301bf;;;WD)` DACL ACE was changed to `D:(A;;0x1200a9;;;WD)`.

`D:(A;;0x1301bf;;;WD):`

- **`D:`** DACL ACE entry.

- **`A:`** `ACCESS_ALLOWED` ACE type.

- **`0x1301bf` (Modify) changed to `0x1200a9` (`FILE_GENERIC_READ` | `FILE_EXECUTE`):** Basically, file share permissions were changed from `Change + Read` to `Read`. See Table 15-5 for more details.

- **`WD` (Everyone/World):** This ACE is applied to the Everyone security principal.

To get more information about the change, configure "Set Value" `Audit Success` type audit permissions in the `HKEY_LOCAL_MACHINE\SYSTEM\CurrentControlSet\Services\LanmanServer\Shares` registry key's SACL. The event shown in Listing 15-6 is generated in the Windows security event log after a file share is modified if "Set Value" `Audit Success` audit permissions are set for the `HKEY_LOCAL_MACHINE\SYSTEM\CurrentControlSet\Services\LanmanServer\Shares` registry key.

Listing 15-6: Event ID 4657: A registry value was modified.

```
Task Category: Registry
Keywords: Audit Success
Subject:
        Security ID:          S-1-5-18
        Account Name:         2016SRV$
        Account Domain:       WORKGROUP
        Logon ID:             0x3E7
Object:
        Object Name:     \REGISTRY\MACHINE\SYSTEM\ControlSet001\Services\
                                        LanmanServer\Shares
        Object Value Name:    Documents
        Handle ID:            0x3f0
        Operation Type:       %%1905 (Existing registry value modified)
Process Information:
        Process ID:           0x6fc
        Process Name:         C:\Windows\System32\svchost.exe
Change Information:
        Old Value Type:       %%1879 (REG_MULTI_SZ (New lines are
                    replaced with *. A * is replaced with **))
        Old Value: CATimeout=0*CSCFlags=48*MaxUses=10*Path=C:\Documents*
               Permissions=0*Remark=My Share!*ShareName=Documents*Type=0
        New Value Type:       %%1879 (REG_MULTI_SZ (New lines are replaced
                                  with *. A * is replaced with **))
        New Value: CATimeout=0*CSCFlags=48*MaxUses=15*Path=C:\Documents*
     Permissions=0*Remark=My Modified Share!*ShareName=Documents*Type=0
```

The New Value field contains new settings applied to the "Documents" file share. See the "File Share Creation" section for more information.

Unsuccessful File Share Deletion

There is no specific event message indicator of an unsuccessful file share modification operation that I'm aware of.

Monitoring Recommendations

Useful file share modification events to monitor are:

SECURITY EVENT	SUBCATEGORY	EVENT TYPE
5143: A network share object was modified.	File Share	Audit Success
4657: A registry value was modified.	Registry	Audit Success

If you have a list of important file shares for which you should monitor all changes, such as file shares with MBI or HBI documents, you should monitor for any change to them.

All unauthorized file share access permissions changes also need to be monitored.

File Share Access

Figure 15-3 shows typical SMB negotiations for a file access attempt on a file share.

The next sections discuss successful and unsuccessful file share session connection monitoring scenarios.

Successful File Share Session Creation

After a session with a specific file share is successfully established (SMB Session Creation phase in Figure 15-3), the event in Listing 15-7 is generated in the Windows security event log.

Listing 15-7: Event ID 5140: A network share object was accessed.

```
Task Category: File Share
Keywords: Audit Success
Subject:
        Security ID:         S-1-5-21-1913345275-1711810662-261465553-1120
        Account Name:        Andrei
        Account Domain:      HQCORP
        Logon ID:            0xBAD9B
Network Information:
        Object Type:         File
```

```
      Source Address:        10.0.0.100
      Source Port:           61682
Share Information:
      Share Name:            \\*\Documents
      Share Path:            \??\C:\Documents
Access Request Information:
      Access Mask:           0x1
      Accesses:              %%4416 (ReadData (or ListDirectory))
                             See tables 5-4 and 13-4 for more details
```

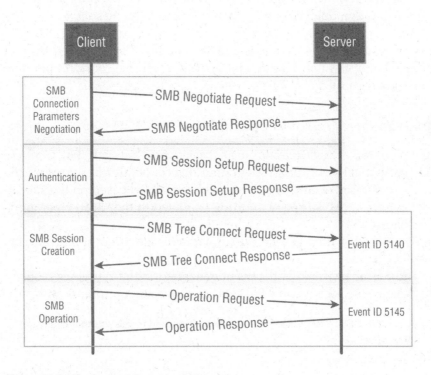

Figure 15-3: File share session negotiation steps

NOTE The event described in this section is available on the book's website, in the `Successful File Share Session Creation.evtx` **file.**

Each time a session is established with a specific file share, a 5140 event is generated. It's generated only once when the session is created; after the session is established no more 5140 events are generated.

This event is an easy way to detect new sessions established for specific file shares, but it shows you just a fact of the session being created with no details about performed actions. By default, an SMB session timeout for Windows 10 systems is 15 minutes.

The `Object Type` field always has a value of `File` for file share objects in the 5140 event.

`Source Address` may contain the IPv4 or IPv6 address of the host from which the session connection request was received.

`Share Name` contains the name of the share being accessed in the following format: **SHARE_NAME*.

`Share Path` contains the local filesystem path for the share being accessed in the following format: \\??*SHARE_PATH*. This field's value is optional and it is empty for shares that don't have a folder associated to them, such as the `IPC$` share.

The `Access Mask` and `Accesses` fields contain requested filesystem permissions. See Tables 5-4 and 13-4 for more details. For a normal tree connect operation the permission requested is always `ReadData (or ListDirectory)`.

Successful File Share File/Folder Operations

When the `Detailed File Share` auditing subcategory is enabled, "Full Control" SACL is automatically set for all filesystem objects on all file shares on the machine. The `Success` or/and `Fail` audit type is enabled based on the subcategory policy setting. This type of auditing is related to the "SMB Operation" section in Figure 15-3.

Detailed file share auditing events are similar to the filesystem auditing events discussed in Chapter 13.

Listing 15-8 is an example of the event generated in the Windows security event log when a file, located on a file share, is requested for modification.

Listing 15-8: Event ID 5145: A network share object was checked to see whether client can be granted desired access.

```
Task Category: Detailed File Share
Keywords: Audit Success
Subject:
      Security ID:          S-1-5-21-1913345275-1711810662-261465553-1120
      Account Name:         Andrei
      Account Domain:       HQCORP
      Logon ID:             0xBAD9B
Network Information:
      Object Type:          File
      Source Address:       10.0.0.100
      Source Port:          61682
Share Information:
      Share Name:           \\*\Documents
      Share Path:           \??\C:\Documents
      Relative Target Name: HBI Data.txt
```

```
Access Request Information:
     Access Mask:            0x2
     Accesses:               %%4417 (WriteData (or AddFile))
Access Check Results:
     %%4417 (WriteData (or AddFile)):   %%1801 (Granted by)
                                        D:(A;;0x1301bf;;;WD)
                See tables 5-4, 13-4 and 15-5 for more details
```

NOTE The event described in this section is available on the book's website, in the `Successful File Share File-Folder Operations.evtx` **file.**

This 5145 event is similar to the "4656: A handle to an object was requested" event for filesystem objects. It does not mean the file was modified; it only shows that access permissions were requested for a file. Usually this event can be interpreted as successful object modification.

The `Object Type` field always has a value of `File`.

`Source Address` may contain the IPv4 or IPv6 address of the host from which the operation request was received.

`Share Name` contains the name of the share being accessed in the following format: `\\*\SHARE_NAME`.

`Share Path` contains a local file path for the share being accessed in the following format: `\\??\SHARE_PATH`. This field is optional and it is empty for shares that don't have a folder associated to them, such as an `IPC$` share.

`Relative Target Name` contains the name of a file or folder for which the access/accesses were requested. The only way to differentiate between a file and folder is to check that a file extension is present in the filename. If a filename does not have a file extension, it is not possible to differentiate between a file and a folder.

The `Access Request Information` section contains information about the requested permissions. These are normal filesystem objects permissions. See Tables 5-4 and 13-4 for more details.

The `Access Check Results` field contains access check validation results for the requested access permissions. 5145 events show validation results *only* for file share permissions validation, not for filesystem (NTFS) permissions. This is important, because sometimes you can see a successful 5145 permission validation event, but the user still has no access to the file. In such cases you should use filesystem auditing events to find out why a user still got an "Access Denied" message. See Tables 5-4, 13-4, and 15-5 for more details.

It's important to understand that the 5145 event is designed to show access request validations against file share permissions, not filesystem (NTFS) permissions. This event is used mostly for file share permissions troubleshooting.

Unsuccessful Admin File Share Session Creation

If an account tries to establish a session with an administrative ($) share, but the account is not a member of the local Administrators security group, the event in Listing 15-9 is generated in the Windows security event log.

Listing 15-9: Event ID 5140: A network share object was accessed.

```
Task Category: File Share
Keywords: Audit Failure
Subject:
      Security ID:              S-1-5-21-1913345275-1711810662-261465553-1120
      Account Name:             Andrei
      Account Domain:           HQCORP
      Logon ID:                 0xCDEE8
Network Information:
      Object Type:              File
      Source Address:           10.0.0.100
      Source Port:              49746
Share Information:
      Share Name:               \\*\ADMIN$
      Share Path:               \??\C:\Windows
Access Request Information:
      Access Mask:              0x1
      Accesses:                 %%4416 (ReadData (or ListDirectory))
                                See tables 5-4 and 13-4 for more details
```

NOTE The event described in this section is available on the book's website, in the `Unsuccessful Admin File Share Session Creation.evtx` file.

Unsuccessful File Share Access - File Share Permissions

When an access attempt to a file or folder located on a file share is not successful because of insufficient file share–level permissions, multiple 5145 `Audit Failure` events are generated. The requested access permissions could be different because the application that performs the access attempts decides by itself which permissions to request. For an access attempt to a file or folder located on a file share using Windows File Explorer, the event in Listing 15-10 is generated in the Windows security event log.

Listing 15-10: Event ID 5145: A network share object was checked to see whether client can be granted desired access.

```
Task Category: Detailed File Share
Keywords: Audit Failure
Subject:
      Security ID:              S-1-5-21-1913345275-1711810662-261465553-1120
      Account Name:             Andrei
      Account Domain:           HQCORP
```

```
        Logon ID:              xF1ADD
Network Information:
        Object Type:           File
        Source Address:        10.0.0.100
        Source Port:           49746
Share Information:
        Share Name:            \\*\Documents
        Share Path:            \??\C:\Documents
        Relative Target Name: \
Access Request Information:
        Access Mask:           0x100080
        Accesses:              %%1541 (SYNCHRONIZE)
                               %%4423 (ReadAttributes)
Access Check Results:
        %%1541 (SYNCHRONIZE):     %%1802 (Denied by)  D:(D;;0x1200a9;;;WD)
        %%4423 (ReadAttributes):  %%1802 (Denied by)  D:(D;;0x1200a9;;;WD)
                               See tables 5-4, 13-4 and 15-5 for more details
```

NOTE The event described in this section is available on the book's website, in the `Unsuccessful File Share Access - file share permissions.evtx` file.

This event shows that SYNCHRONIZE and ReadAttributes access attempts were performed against the Documents (Share Name) file share root folder (Relative Target Name). This attempt failed for reasons described in the Access Check Results field.

It is important to understand that such failed access requests might be sent to any file and folder located on a share. The user might try to access another file or folder within the share, and if it has no required permissions to access it, it will generate a 5145 Audit Failure event for that specific file or folder.

Also, if the access attempt was denied at the file share level, it will not get to the filesystem level, so no success/failure filesystem auditing events are generated.

Unsuccessful File Share Access - File System Permissions

When an access attempt to a file or folder located on a file share is not successful because of insufficient filesystem (NTFS) level permissions, multiple 4656 Audit Failure events are generated. The requested access permissions could be different because the application that performs the access attempts decides by itself which permissions to request. For an access attempt to a file or folder located on a file share using Windows File Explorer, the event in Listing 15-11 is generated in the Windows security event log.

Listing 15-11: Event ID 4656: A handle to an object was requested.

```
Task Category: File System
Keywords: Audit Failure
```

```
Subject:
      Security ID:            S-1-5-21-1913345275-1711810662-261465553-1120
      Account Name:           Andrei
      Account Domain:         HQCORP
      Logon ID:               0x13EC92
Object:
      Object Server:          Security
      Object Type:            File
      Object Name:            C:\Documents
      Handle ID:              0x0
      Resource Attributes:    -
Process Information:
      Process ID:             0x4
      Process Name:
Access Request Information:
      Transaction ID:         {00000000-0000-0000-0000-000000000000}
      Accesses:               %%1541 (SYNCHRONIZE)
                              %%4423 (ReadAttributes)
      Access Reasons:
           %%1541 (SYNCHRONIZE):      %%1802 (Denied by)   D:(D;OICI;FA;;;
                          S-1-5-21-1913345275-1711810662-261465553-1120)
           %%4423 (ReadAttributes):   %%1811 (Granted by ACE on parent
                                      folder)   D:(A;OICI;0x1200a9;;;BU)
      Access Mask:            0x100080
      Privileges Used for Access Check: -
      Restricted SID Count: 0
```

NOTE The event described in this section is available on the book's website, in the `Unsuccessful File Share Access - file system permissions.evtx` file.

This event is triggered only if appropriate auditing settings are configured in the file's or folder's SACL.

You can find more information about filesystem auditing in Chapter 13.

Monitoring Recommendations

Useful file share access events to monitor are:

SECURITY EVENT	SUBCATEGORY	EVENT TYPE
5145: A network share object was checked to see whether client can be granted desired access.	Detailed File Share	Audit Success
		Audit Failure
5140: A network share object was accessed.	File Share	Audit Success
		Audit Failure
4656: A handle to an object was requested.	File System	Audit Failure

It is recommended to monitor for all unsuccessful administrative file share access attempts, especially on critical hosts. Monitor for "5140: A network share object was accessed" `Audit Failure` events.

If you have a list of important file shares located on a host/hosts, you might want to monitor for all successful and, especially, unsuccessful access attempts. Important default file share examples are `DRIVE_LABEL$` and `ADMIN$`.

Named Pipes

Named pipes is a mechanism designed for communications between processes/applications within a host or over a network.

Named pipes can be registered/created by any process and will remain available as long as at least one handle for the named pipe is open. After there are no open handles for a specific named pipe it is automatically deleted. Named pipes are memory objects, but the operating system treats them as virtual files. The `FILE_CREATE_PIPE_INSTANCE` access right is required to create a new named pipe.

All pipes are placed in the virtual named pipe file system (NPFS), which is mounted on the `\\.\pipe\` path. You can even connect to the named pipe (for example, `\\.\pipe\lsass`) using Windows File Explorer, but you will not be able to open it as a normal file.

You can get a list of all active named pipes using, for example, the free Microsoft `pipelist.exe` utility (formerly Sysinternals). An example of the `pipelist.exe` tool output is shown in Figure 15-4.

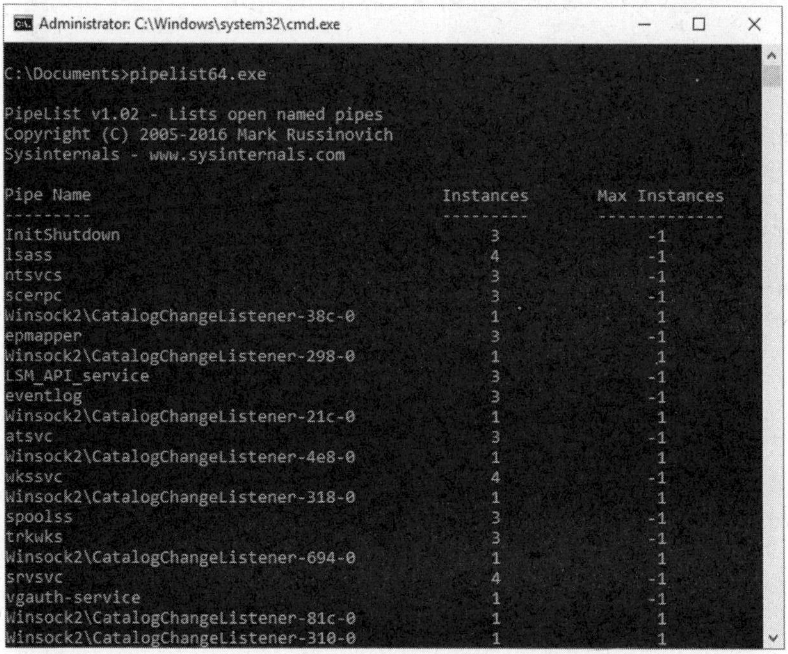

Figure 15-4: List of currently active named pipes by pipelist64.exe tool

When a named pipe is created, the application that created it applies a security descriptor for the pipe. The security descriptor contains access settings (DACL), auditing settings (SACL), and ownership information for the named pipe object. The security descriptor is applied to a pipe during its creation and is destroyed after the pipe is deleted.

By default, most named pipes don't have SACL ACEs configured, and no audit records are generated for operations with them.

There is a great free tool called Pipe Security Editor (`pipesec.exe`) by Craig Peacock that allows you to set and get security descriptors for active named pipes, and it still works under Windows Server 2016 and Windows 10.

This tool is really easy to use. If you need to view/edit permissions for a specific named pipe, you need to execute the following command: `pipesec.exe \\.\pipe\pipe_name`, where *pipe_name* is the name of the pipe you want to work with. Figure 15-5 shows an example of the `pipesec.exe` tool GUI window for the `lsass` named pipe.

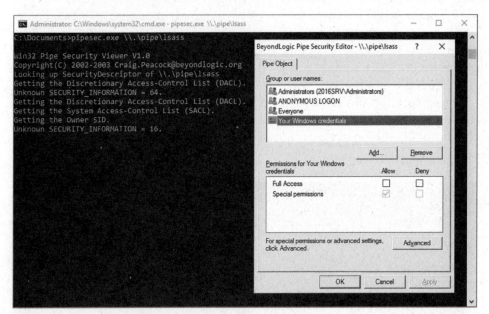

Figure 15-5: Pipesec.exe tool output for the lsass named pipe

Using `pipesec.exe` you can change DACL, SACL, and ownership information for specific named pipe.

Successful Named Pipe Auditing Settings Changes

To view and modify a named pipe object's SACL, a process must have `SeSecurityPrivilege` privilege enabled in its access token. `SeSecurityPrivilege` can be assigned by the "Manage auditing and security log" user rights group policy setting.

If named pipe auditing settings (SACL) are changed, the event in Listing 15-12 is generated in the Windows security event log.

Listing 15-12: Event ID 4907: Auditing settings on object were changed.

```
Task Category: Audit Policy Change
Keywords: Audit Success
Subject:
        Security ID:         S-1-5-21-3212943211-794299840-588279583-500
        Account Name:        Administrator
        Account Domain:      2016SRV
        Logon ID:            0x2F638
Object:
        Object Server:       Security
        Object Type:         File
        Object Name:         \Device\NamedPipe\abc
        Handle ID:           0x200
Process Information:
        Process ID:          0xc9c
        Process Name:        C:\Documents\pipesec.exe
Auditing Settings:
        Original Security Descriptor:    S:(AU;SAFA;FA;;;WD)
        New Security Descriptor:         S:AR(AU;SAFA;RC;;;WD)
```

NOTE The event described in this section is available on the book's website, in the `Successful Named Pipe Auditing Settings Changes.evtx` file.

The `Subject` section contains information about the account that performed the action.

The `Object` section contains information about the object on which the action was performed. `Object Type` is always `File` for named pipes.

`Object Name` for named pipes objects has the following format: `\Device\NamedPipe\`*pipe_name*, where *pipe_name* is the name of the named pipe being modified.

The `Auditing Setting` section contains the previous and new SACL values for the object. Both the `Original Security Descriptor` and `New Security Descriptor` fields contain SACL values in SDDL format, which described in Chapter 10. They only contain information about SACL modifications (`S:`); no information about object owner or DACL is included.

In this example you see the following changes:

- `S:` is changed to `S:AR`, which means child objects will inherit permissions from this object (`AR`).

- `FA` is changed to `RC`, which means Full Access (`FA`) was changed to Read Control (`RC`).

Unsuccessful Named Pipe Auditing Settings Changes

If the account trying to get or set a named pipe object's SACL does not have `SeSecurityPrivilege` privilege enabled, the event in Listing 15-13 is generated in the Windows security event log.

Listing 15-13: Event ID 4656: A handle to an object was requested.

```
Task Category: Kernel Object
Keywords: Audit Failure
Subject:
        Security ID:            S-1-5-21-3212943211-794299840-588279583-1001
        Account Name:           Melshar
        Account Domain:         2016SRV
        Logon ID:               0x1CCC53
Object:
        Object Server:          Security
        Object Type:            NamedPipe
        Object Name:            \abc
        Handle ID:              0x0
        Resource Attributes:    -
Process Information:
        Process ID:             0x140
        Process Name:           C:\Documents\pipesec.exe
Access Request Information:
        Transaction ID:         {00000000-0000-0000-0000-000000000000}
        Accesses:               %%1538 (READ_CONTROL)
                                %%1539 (WRITE_DAC)
                                %%1540 (WRITE_OWNER)
                                %%1541 (SYNCHRONIZE)
                                %%1542 (ACCESS_SYS_SEC)
                                %%4423 (ReadAttributes)

        Access Reasons:         -
        Access Mask:            0x11E0080
        Privileges Used for Access Check: -
        Restricted SID Count:0
See tables 5-4 and 13-4 for more details
```

> **NOTE** The event described in this section is available on the book's website, in the `Unsuccessful Named Pipe Auditing Settings Changes.evtx` **file.**

> **NOTE** To receive `Kernel Object` 4656 events, the "Audit Kernel Object" and "Audit Handle Manipulation" auditing subcategories must be enabled.

The `Subject` section contains information about the account that performed the action.

The Object section contains information about the object on which the action was performed. Object Type is always NamedPipe for named pipes in Kernel Object 4656 events.

Object Name for named pipes objects has the following format: \pipe_name, where pipe_name is the name of the named pipe being accessed.

All SACL modification or view requests must have ACCESS_SYS_SEC access permission in the list of requested accesses.

Successful Named Pipe Access Permissions Changes

To audit successful named pipe access permissions (DACL) changes, Write DAC permission should be enabled for the Success auditing type in the object's SACL.

The event in Listing 15-14 is generated in the Windows security event log if access permissions for a named pipe are successfully modified.

Listing 15-14: Event ID 4670: Permissions on an object were changed.

```
Task Category: Authorization Policy Change
Keywords: Audit Success
Subject:
        Security ID:          S-1-5-21-3212943211-794299840-588279583-500
        Account Name:         Administrator
        Account Domain:       2016SRV
        Logon ID:             0x2F638
Object:
        Object Server:        Security
        Object Type:          File
        Object Name:          \Device\NamedPipe\abc
        Handle ID:            0x200
Process:
        Process ID:           0xc9c
        Process Name:         C:\Documents\pipesec.exe
Permissions Change:
        Original Security Descriptor: D:(D;;FA;;;S-1-5-21-3212943211-
                      794299840-588279583-1001)(A;;FA;;;WD)
        New Security Descriptor:      D:AR(A;;FA;;;WD)(A;;FA;;;S-1-5-
                      21-3212943211-794299840-588279583-1001)
```

NOTE The event described in this section is available on the book's website, in the Successful Named Pipe Access Permissions Changes.evtx file.

Most fields in this event are the same as in the 4907 event discussed in the Successful Named Pipe Auditing Settings Changes section.

The Permissions Change section contains previous and new DACL values for the object. Both the Original Security Descriptor and New Security Descriptor fields contain DACL values in SDDL format, which is described in

Chapter 10. They only contain information about DACL modifications (D:); no information about object owner or SACL is included.

In this example you see the following changes:

- D: is changed to D:AR, which means "child objects will inherit permissions from this object" (AR).

- The (A;;FA;;;S-1-5-21-3212943211-794299840-588279583-1001) ACE type is changed from A (Allow) to D (Deny).

Named Pipe Access Attempts

Access attempts auditing for named pipes depends on the SACL settings of the named pipe and type of access that was requested.

Listing 15-15 is an example of a successful named pipe Read operation.

Listing 15-15: Event ID 4663: An attempt was made to access an object.

```
Task Category: File System
Keywords: Audit Success
Subject:
        Security ID:          S-1-5-21-1913345275-1711810662-261465553-500
        Account Name:         administrator
        Account Domain:       HQCORP
        Logon ID:             0x3AF8FA
Object:
        Object Server:        Security
        Object Type:          File
        Object Name:          \Device\NamedPipe\lsass
        Handle ID:            0x540
        Resource Attributes:  S:
Process Information:
        Process ID:           0x4
        Process Name:
Access Request Information:
        Accesses:             %%4416 (ReadData (or ListDirectory))
        Access Mask:          0x1
See tables 5-4 and 13-4 for more details
```

NOTE The event described in this section is available on the book's website, in the Named Pipes Access Examples.evtx file.

Named pipes access auditing is the same as file access auditing. You can read more about file access auditing in Chapter 13.

IPC$ Share Access Attempts

Named pipes can be accessed remotely and locally using the built-in IPC$ administrative file share. The Inter-Process Communication (IPC) administrative file share is used as a connection point for all named pipes located on a host.

Named pipes can be accessed via the IPC$ share in the following manner: \\ host_name\IPC$*pipe_name*.

Each connection to a named pipe through the IPC$ share generates the events in Listings 15-16 and 15-17 in the Windows security event log.

Listing 15-16: Event ID 5140: A network share object was accessed.

```
Task Category: File Share
Keywords: Audit Success
Subject:
        Security ID:            S-1-5-21-3212943211-794299840-588279583-500
        Account Name:           Administrator
        Account Domain:         2016SRV
        Logon ID:               0x2BDF6
Network Information:
        Object Type:            File
        Source Address:         fe80::3da4:40f9:dca8:8cf2
        Source Port:            49722
Share Information:
        Share Name:             \\*\IPC$
        Share Path:
Access Request Information:
        Access Mask:            0x1
        Accesses:               %%4416 (ReadData (or ListDirectory))
See tables 5-4 and 13-4 for more details
```

NOTE The events described in this section are available on the book's website, in the IPC$ Share Access Attempts.evtx file.

This event shows details for the initial session to the IPC$ file share.

Share Path for the IPC$ share is not present because the IPC$ share doesn't have any filesystem folder associated with it.

See the "Successful File Share Session Creation" section earlier in this chapter for details for the 5140 event.

Listing 15-17: Event ID 5145: A network share object was checked to see whether client can be granted desired access.

```
Task Category: Detailed File Share
Keywords: Audit Success
Subject:
        Security ID:            S-1-5-21-3212943211-794299840-588279583-500
        Account Name:           Administrator
        Account Domain:         2016SRV
        Logon ID:               0x2BDF6
Network Information:
        Object Type:            File
        Source Address:         fe80::3da4:40f9:dca8:8cf2
        Source Port:            49722
Share Information:
        Share Name:             \\*\IPC$
```

```
        Share Path:
        Relative Target Name: AndreiNamedPipe
Access Request Information:
        Access Mask:          0x12019F
        Accesses:             %%1538 (READ_CONTROL)
                              %%1541 (SYNCHRONIZE)
                              %%4416 (ReadData (or ListDirectory))
                              %%4417 (WriteData (or AddFile))
                              %%4418 (AppendData (or AddSubdirectory or
                                                      CreatePipeInstance))
                              %%4419 (ReadEA)
                              %%4420 (WriteEA)
                              %%4423 (ReadAttributes)
                              %%4424 (WriteAttributes)
Access Check Results:
                              -
See tables 5-4 and 13-4 for more details
```

The `Relative Target Name` field contains the name of the named pipe to which an access attempt was performed.

See the "Successful File Share File/Folder Operations" section earlier in this chapter for details on the 5145 event.

Monitoring Recommendations

Useful named pipes–related events to monitor are:

SECURITY EVENT	SUBCATEGORY	EVENT TYPE
5145: A network share object was checked to see whether client can be granted desired access.	Detailed File Share	`Audit Success`
5140: A network share object was accessed.	File Share	`Audit Success`
4656: A handle to an object was requested.	File System	`Audit Failure`
4663: An attempt was made to access an object.	File System	`Audit Success` `Audit Failure`
4670: Permissions on an object were changed.	Authorization Policy Change	`Audit Success`
4907: Auditing settings on an object were changed.	Audit Policy Change	`Audit Success`

Named pipes usually are hard to monitor, because most of them don't have a SACL configured by the application that created the named pipe.

You may have a list of critical named pipes that should be monitored for access attempts.

Kerberos AS_REQ, TGS_REQ, and AP_REQ Messages Ticket Options

The Kerberos `Ticket Options` field in security events 4768, 4771, 4769, and 4770 contains a bitmask with Kerberos ticket flags that were received by a Key Distribution Center (KDC) in the AS_REQ, TGS_REQ, or AP_REQ message.

The `Ticket Options` field is recorded in events in hexadecimal format, for example, `0x40810010`. To find which flags are enabled you need to convert the hexadecimal number to binary. For example:

```
0x40810010 = 01000000100000010000000000010000
```

Ticket flag bitmasks use the Most Significant Bit (MSB) 0-bit numbering format, in which bits are numbered from left to right starting from the 0 bit. So, in the preceding example bits 1, 8, 15, and 27 are enabled.

Table A-1 contains information about possible ticket flags you can find in Kerberos AS_REQ, TGS_REQ, or AP_REQ messages, as well as corresponding bits for the `Ticket Options` field.

Table A-1: Kerberos Ticket Flags

BIT	NAME	DESCRIPTION
0	Reserved	Reserved for future use.
1	Forwardable	Tells the ticket-granting service (part of a KDC role in Windows) that it can issue a new TGT based on the presented TGT with a different network address.

Continues

Table A-1 (*continued*)

BIT	NAME	DESCRIPTION
2	Forwarded	Indicates either that a TGT has been forwarded or that a ticket was issued from a forwarded TGT.
3	Proxiable	Tells the ticket-granting service (part of a KDC role in Windows) that it can issue tickets with a network address that differs from the one in the TGT.
4	Proxy	Indicates that the network address in the ticket is different from the one in the TGT used to obtain the ticket.
5	Allow-postdate	Indicates that postdated tickets are allowed.
6	Postdated	Indicates a postdated ticket.
7	Invalid	Indicates that a ticket is invalid and it must be validated by the KDC before use.
8	Renewable	Used in combination with the End Time and Renew Till fields to cause tickets with long life spans to be renewed at the KDC periodically.
9	Initial	Indicates that a ticket was issued using the authentication service (AS_REQ) exchange and not issued based on a TGT.
10	Pre-authent	Indicates that the client was authenticated by the KDC before a ticket was issued. This flag usually indicates the presence of an authenticator in the ticket. It can also flag the presence of credentials taken from a smart card logon.
11	Opt-hardware-auth	This flag was originally intended to indicate that hardware-supported authentication was used during pre-authentication. This flag is no longer recommended in the Kerberos V5 protocol.
12	Transited-policy-checked	This flag indicates that a transited policy was checked.
13	Ok-as-delegate	This flag is set if the service account is trusted for delegation.
14	Request-anonymous	Specified in the Kerberos anonymous authentication requests.
15	Name-canonicalize	Specified in the Kerberos referral ticket requests.
16-25	Unused	Reserved for future use.

BIT	NAME	DESCRIPTION
26	Disable-transited-check	By default the KDC will check the transited field of a TGT against the policy of the local realm before it will issue derivative tickets based on the TGT. If this flag is set in the request, checking of the transited field is disabled. Tickets issued without the performance of this check will be noted by the reset (0) value of the TRANSITED-POLICY-CHECKED flag, indicating to the application server that the transited field must be checked locally. KDCs are encouraged but not required to honor the DISABLE-TRANSITED-CHECK option.
27	Renewable-ok	This option indicates that a renewable ticket will be acceptable if a ticket with the requested lifetime cannot otherwise be provided, in which case a renewable ticket may be issued with a renew-till time equal to the requested end time.
28	Enc-tkt-in-skey	This option indicates that the ticket for the end server is to be encrypted in the session key from the additional ticket-granting ticket provided.
29	Unused	Reserved for future use.
30	Renew	This option indicates that the present request is for a Kerberos ticket renewal.
31	Validate	This option is used only by the ticket-granting service. It indicates that the request is to validate a postdated Kerberos ticket. Postdated tickets are not supported by the Microsoft Kerberos implementation (MS-KILE).

Kerberos AS_REQ, TGS_REQ, and AP_REQ Messages Result Codes

The Kerberos `Result Code` field exists in security event 4768. In events 4771 and 4769 it is a named `Failure Code`. It represents a hexadecimal error code.

Table B-1 contains information about possible Kerberos error codes. This information is taken from multiple Kerberos-related RFCs.

Table B-1: Kerberos Error Codes

CODE	CODE NAME	DESCRIPTION
0x0	KDC_ERR_NONE	No errors. Status OK.
0x1	KDC_ERR_NAME_EXP	Client's entry in KDC database has expired.
0x2	KDC_ERR_SERVICE_EXP	Server's entry in KDC database has expired.
0x3	KDC_ERR_BAD_PVNO	Requested Kerberos version number not supported.
0x4	KDC_ERR_C_OLD_MAST_KVNO	Client's key encrypted in old master key.
0x5	KDC_ERR_S_OLD_MAST_KVNO	Server's key encrypted in old master key.
0x6	KDC_ERR_C_PRINCIPAL_ UNKNOWN	The account name doesn't exist.

Continues

Table B-1 (*continued*)

CODE	CODE NAME	DESCRIPTION
0x7	KDC_ERR_S_PRINCIPAL_UNKNOWN	This error can occur if the domain controller cannot find the server's name in Active Directory. This error is similar to KDC_ERR_C_PRINCIPAL_UNKNOWN except that it occurs when the server name cannot be found.
0x8	KDC_ERR_PRINCIPAL_NOT_UNIQUE	This error occurs if duplicate principal names exist.
0x9	KDC_ERR_NULL_KEY	No master key was found for client or server.
0xA	KDC_ERR_CANNOT_POSTDATE	This error can occur if a client requests postdating of a Kerberos ticket. Postdating is the act of requesting that a ticket's start time be set into the future. It also can occur if there is a time difference between the client and the KDC.
0xB	KDC_ERR_NEVER_VALID	There is a time difference between the KDC and the client.
0xC	KDC_ERR_POLICY	This error is usually the result of logon restrictions in place on a user's account. For example, workstation restriction, smart card authentication requirement, or logon time restriction.
0xD	KDC_ERR_BADOPTION	Impending expiration of a TGT. The Service Principal Name (SPN) to which the client is attempting to delegate credentials is not in its Allowed-to-delegate-to list.
0xE	KDC_ERR_ETYPE_NOTSUPP	In general, this error occurs when the KDC or a client receives a packet that it cannot decrypt.
0xF	KDC_ERR_SUMTYPE_NOSUPP	The KDC, server, or client receives a packet for which it does not have a key of the appropriate encryption type. The result is that the computer is unable to decrypt the ticket.

CODE	CODE NAME	DESCRIPTION
0x10	KDC_ERR_PADATA_TYPE_NOSUPP	Smart card logon is being attempted and the proper certificate cannot be located. This can happen because the wrong certification authority (CA) is being queried or the proper CA cannot be contacted. It can also happen when a domain controller doesn't have a certificate installed for smart cards (Domain Controller or Domain Controller Authentication templates).
0x11	KDC_ERR_TRTYPE_NO_SUPP	KDC has no support for the transited type.
0x12	KDC_ERR_CLIENT_REVOKED	This might be because of an explicit disabling or because of other restrictions in place on the account. For example: account disabled, expired, or locked out.
0x13	KDC_ERR_SERVICE_REVOKED	Credentials for the server have been revoked.
0x14	KDC_ERR_TGT_REVOKED	Since the remote KDC may change its PKCROSS key while PKCROSS tickets are still active, it *should* cache the old PKCROSS keys until the last issued PKCROSS ticket expires. Otherwise, the remote KDC will respond to a client with a KRB-ERROR message of type KDC_ERR_TGT_REVOKED.
0x15	KDC_ERR_CLIENT_NOTYET	Client not yet valid—try again later.
0x16	KDC_ERR_SERVICE_NOTYET	Server not yet valid—try again later.
0x17	KDC_ERR_KEY_EXPIRED	The user's password has expired.
0x18	KDC_ERR_PREAUTH_FAILED	The wrong password was provided.
0x19	KDC_ERR_PREAUTH_REQUIRED	This error often occurs in UNIX interoperability scenarios. MIT-Kerberos clients do not request pre-authentication when they send a KRB_AS_REQ message. If pre-authentication is required (the default), Windows operating systems will send this error. Most MIT-Kerberos clients will respond to this error by giving the pre-authentication, in which case the error can be ignored, but some clients might not respond in this way.
0x1A	KDC_ERR_SERVER_NOMATCH	KDC does not know about the requested server.

Continues

Table B-1 (*continued*)

CODE	CODE NAME	DESCRIPTION
0x1B	KDC_ERR_SVC_UNAVAILABLE	A service is not available.
0x1F	KRB_AP_ERR_BAD_INTEGRITY	The authenticator was encrypted with something other than the session key. The result is that the client cannot decrypt the resulting message. The modification of the message could be the result of an attack or it could be because of network noise.
0x20	KRB_AP_ERR_TKT_EXPIRED	The smaller the value for the "Maximum lifetime for user ticket" Kerberos policy setting, the more likely it is that this error will occur. Because ticket renewal is automatic, you should not have to do anything if you get this message.
0x21	KRB_AP_ERR_TKT_NYV	The ticket presented to the server is not yet valid (in relation to the server time). The most probable cause is that the clocks on the KDC and the client are not synchronized. If cross-realm Kerberos authentication is being attempted, you should verify time synchronization between the KDC in the target realm and the KDC in the client realm, as well.
0x22	KRB_AP_ERR_REPEAT	This error indicates that a specific authenticator showed up twice—the KDC has detected that this session ticket duplicates one that it has already received.
0x23	KRB_AP_ERR_NOT_US	The server has received a ticket that was meant for a different realm.
0x24	KRB_AP_ERR_BADMATCH	This error usually represents one of the following issues: ➤ The KRB_TGS_REQ is being sent to the wrong KDC. ➤ There is an account mismatch during protocol transition.
0x25	KRB_AP_ERR_SKEW	This error is logged if a client computer sends a timestamp whose value differs from that of the server's timestamp by more than the number of minutes found in the "Maximum tolerance for computer clock synchronization" setting in Kerberos policy.

CODE	CODE NAME	DESCRIPTION
0x26	KRB_AP_ERR_BADADDR	Session tickets *may* include the addresses from which they are valid. This error can occur if the address of the computer sending the ticket is different from the valid address in the ticket. A possible cause of this could be an Internet Protocol (IP) address change. Another possible cause is when a ticket is passed through a proxy server or NAT. The client is unaware of the address scheme used by the proxy server, so unless the program caused the client to request a proxy server ticket with the proxy server's source address, the ticket could be invalid.
0x27	KRB_AP_ERR_BADVERSION	When an application receives a KRB_SAFE message, it verifies it. If any error occurs, an error code is reported for use by the application. The message is first checked by verifying that the protocol version and type fields match the current version and KRB_SAFE, respectively. A mismatch generates a KRB_AP_ERR_BADVERSION.
0x28	KRB_AP_ERR_MSG_TYPE	This message is generated when the target server finds that the message format is wrong. This applies to KRB_AP_REQ, KRB_SAFE, KRB_PRIV, and KRB_CRED messages. This error is also generated if use of UDP protocol is being attempted with user-to-user authentication.
0x29	KRB_AP_ERR_MODIFIED	This error usually represents one of the following issues: ➤ The authentication data was encrypted with the wrong key for the intended server. ➤ The authentication data was modified in transit by a hardware or software error, or by an attacker. ➤ The client sent the authentication data to the wrong server because incorrect DNS data caused the client to send the request to the wrong server. ➤ The client sent the authentication data to the wrong server because DNS data was out-of-date on the client.

Continues

Table B-1 (*continued*)

CODE	CODE NAME	DESCRIPTION
0x2A	KRB_AP_ERR_BADORDER	This event generates for KRB_SAFE and KRB_PRIV messages if an incorrect sequence number is included, or if a sequence number is expected but not present.
0x2C	KRB_AP_ERR_BADKEYVER	This error might be generated on the server side during receipt of an invalid KRB_AP_REQ message. If the key version indicated by the ticket in the KRB_AP_REQ is not one the server can use (for example, it indicates an old key, and the server no longer possesses a copy of the old key), the KRB_AP_ERR_BADKEYVER error is returned.
0x2D	KRB_AP_ERR_NOKEY	This error might be generated on the server side during receipt of an invalid KRB_AP_REQ message. Because it is possible for the server to be registered in multiple realms, with different keys in each, the realm field in the unencrypted portion of the ticket in the KRB_AP_REQ is used to specify which secret key the server should use to decrypt that ticket. The KRB_AP_ERR_NOKEY error code is returned if the server doesn't have the proper key to decipher the ticket.
0x2E	KRB_AP_ERR_MUT_FAIL	Mutual authentication failed.
0x2F	KRB_AP_ERR_BADDIRECTION	Incorrect message direction.
0x30	KRB_AP_ERR_METHOD	Obsolete.
0x31	KRB_AP_ERR_BADSEQ	Incorrect sequence number in the message.
0x32	KRB_AP_ERR_INAPP_CKSUM	When KDC receives a KRB_TGS_REQ message it decrypts it, and after that, the user-supplied checksum in the Authenticator *must* be verified against the contents of the request. The message *must* be rejected either if the checksums do not match (with an error code of KRB_AP_ERR_MODIFIED) or if the checksum is not collision-proof (with an error code of KRB_AP_ERR_INAPP_CKSUM).
0x33	KRB_AP_PATH_NOT_ACCEPTED	Desired path is unreachable.

CODE	CODE NAME	DESCRIPTION
0x34	KRB_ERR_RESPONSE_TOO_BIG	The size of a ticket is too large to be transmitted reliably via UDP. In a Windows environment, this message is purely informational. A computer running a Windows operating system will automatically try TCP if UDP fails.
0x3C	KRB_ERR_GENERIC	This error usually represents one of the following issues: ➤ Group membership has overloaded the PAC. ➤ Multiple recent password changes have not propagated. ➤ Crypto subsystem error caused by running out of memory. ➤ SPN too long. ➤ SPN has too many parts.
0x3D	KRB_ERR_FIELD_TOOLONG	Each request (KRB_KDC_REQ) and response (KRB_KDC_REP or KRB_ERROR) sent over the TCP stream is preceded by the length of the request as 4 octets in network byte order. The high bit of the length is reserved for future expansion and *must* currently be set to zero. If a KDC that does not understand how to interpret a set high bit of the length encoding receives a request with the high order bit of the length set, it *must* return a KRB-ERROR message with the error KRB_ERR_FIELD_TOOLONG and *must* close the TCP stream.
0x3E	KDC_ERR_CLIENT_NOT_TRUSTED	This typically happens when a user's smart card certificate is revoked or the root Certification Authority that issued the smart card certificate (in a chain) is not trusted by the domain controller.
0x3F	KDC_ERR_KDC_NOT_TRUSTED	The trustedCertifiers field contains a list of certification authorities trusted by the client, in the case that the client does not possess the KDC's public key certificate. If the KDC has no certificate signed by any of the trustedCertifiers, it returns an error of type KDC_ERR_KDC_NOT_TRUSTED. See RFC1510 for more details.

Continues

Table B-1 (*continued*)

CODE	CODE NAME	DESCRIPTION
0x40	KDC_ERR_INVALID_SIG	If a PKI trust relationship exists, the KDC then verifies the client's signature on AuthPack (TGT request signature). If that fails, the KDC returns an error message of type KDC_ERR_INVALID_SIG.
0x41	KDC_ERR_KEY_TOO_WEAK	If the clientPublicValue field is filled in, indicating that the client wishes to use Diffie-Hellman key agreement, the KDC checks to see that the parameters satisfy its policy. If they do not (for example, the prime size is insufficient for the expected encryption type), the KDC sends back an error message of type KDC_ERR_KEY_TOO_WEAK.
0x42	KRB_AP_ERR_USER_TO_USER_REQUIRED	In the case that the client application doesn't know that a service requires user-to-user authentication, and requests and receives a conventional KRB_AP_REP, the client will send the KRB_AP_REP request, and the server will respond with a KRB_ERROR token as described in RFC1964, with a msg-type of KRB_AP_ERR_USER_TO_USER_REQUIRED.
0x43	KRB_AP_ERR_NO_TGT	In user-to-user authentication if the service does not possess a ticket-granting ticket, it should return the error KRB_AP_ERR_NO_TGT.
0x44	KDC_ERR_WRONG_REALM	This error occurs when a client presents a cross-realm TGT to a realm other than the one specified in the TGT. Typically, this results from an incorrectly configured DNS.

SDDL Access Rights

A Security Descriptor Definition Language (SDDL) access control entry (ACE) has a section where you should define the access rights of the ACE.

Predefined constants for generic access rights (Table C-1) can be mapped to any other access rights for a securable object. For example, the GENERIC_READ access right for a filesystem object maps for the following access rights:

READ_CONTROL + SYNCHRONIZE + FILE_READ_DATA + FILE_READ_EA + FILE_READ_ATTRIBUTES.

Table C-1: Generic Access Rights

HEX	STRING	NAME
0x10000000	GA	GENERIC_ALL
0x80000000	GR	GENERIC_READ
0x40000000	GW	GENERIC_WRITE
0x20000000	GX	GENERIC_EXECUTE

There is also a set of standard access rights that are applicable to most securable objects (Table C-2).

Table C-2: Standard Access Rights

HEX	STRING	NAME
0x00010000	SD	DELETE
0x00020000	RC	READ_CONTROL
0x00040000	WD	WRITE_DAC
0x00080000	WO	WRITE_OWNER
0x00100000	-	SYNCHRONIZE
0x000F0000	-	STANDARD_RIGHTS_REQUIRED
0x01000000	-	ACCESS_SYSTEM_SECURITY
0x00250000	-	STANDARD_RIGHTS_ALL

Object-Specific Access Rights

Each securable object type may have a dedicated set of object-specific access rights associated to it.

Table C-3 contains information about Directory Service object access rights.

Table C-3: Directory Service Object Access Rights

HEX	STRING	NAME
0x1	CC	ADS_RIGHT_DS_CREATE_CHILD
0x2	DC	ADS_RIGHT_DS_DELETE_CHILD
0x4	LC	ADS_RIGHT_ACTRL_DS_LIST
0x8	SW	ADS_RIGHT_DS_SELF
0x10	RP	ADS_RIGHT_DS_READ_PROP
0x20	WP	ADS_RIGHT_DS_WRITE_PROP
0x40	DT	ADS_RIGHT_DS_DELETE_TREE
0x80	LO	ADS_RIGHT_DS_LIST_OBJECT
0x100	CR	ADS_RIGHT_DS_CONTROL_ACCESS

Table C-4 contains information about filesystem object access rights.

Table C-4: Filesystem Object Access Rights

HEX	STRING	NAME
0x0001	CC	FILE_LIST_DIRECTORY, FILE_READ_DATA
0x0002	DC	FILE_WRITE_DATA
0x0004	LC	FILE_ADD_SUBDIRECTORY, FILE_APPEND_DATA
0x0008	SW	FILE_READ_EA
0x0010	RP	FILE_WRITE_EA
0x0020	WP	FILE_EXECUTE, FILE_TRAVERSE
0x0040	DT	FILE_DELETE_CHILD
0x0080	LO	FILE_READ_ATTRIBUTES
0x0100	CR	FILE_WRITE_ATTRIBUTES
0x1F01FF	FA	FILE_ALL_ACCESS
0x120089	FR	FILE_GENERIC_READ
0x120116	FW	FILE_GENERIC_WRITE
0x1200A0	FX	FILE_GENERIC_EXECUTE

Table C-5 contains information about registry object access rights.

Table C-5: Registry Object Access Rights

HEX	STRING	NAME
0x0001	CC	KEY_QUERY_VALUE
0x0002	DC	KEY_SET_VALUE
0x0004	LC	KEY_CREATE_SUB_KEY
0x0008	SW	KEY_ENUMERATE_SUB_KEYS
0x0010	RP	KEY_NOTIFY
0x0020	WP	KEY_CREATE_LINK
0x0100	CR	KEY_WOW64_64KEY
0x0200	–	KEY_WOW64_32KEY
0x0300	–	KEY_WOW64_RES
0xF003F	KA	KEY_ALL_ACCESS
0x20019	KR	KEY_READ
0x20006	KW	KEY_WRITE
0x20019	KX	KEY_EXECUTE

Table C-6 contains information about process object access rights.

Table C-6: Access Rights for a Process

HEX	STRING	NAME
0x0001	CC	PROCESS_TERMINATE
0x0002	DC	PROCESS_CREATE_THREAD
0x0004	LC	PROCESS_SET_SESSIONID
0x0008	SW	PROCESS_VM_OPERATION
0x0010	RP	PROCESS_VM_READ
0x0020	WP	PROCESS_VM_WRITE
0x0040	DT	PROCESS_DUP_HANDLE
0x0080	LO	PROCESS_CREATE_PROCESS
0x0100	CR	PROCESS_SET_QUOTA
0x0200	-	PROCESS_SET_INFORMATION
0x0400	-	PROCESS_QUERY_INFORMATION
0x0800	-	PROCESS_SUSPEND_RESUME
0x1000	-	PROCESS_QUERY_LIMITED_INFORMATION
0x2000	-	PROCESS_SET_LIMITED_INFORMATION
0x1FFFFF	-	PROCESS_ALL_ACCESS

Table C-7 contains information about Service Control Manager (SCM) access rights.

Table C-7: Access Rights for the Service Control Manager (SCM)

HEX	STRING	NAME
0x0001	CC	SC_MANAGER_CONNECT
0x0002	DC	SC_MANAGER_CREATE_SERVICE
0x0004	LC	SC_MANAGER_ENUMERATE_SERVICE
0x0008	SW	SC_MANAGER_LOCK
0x0010	RP	SC_MANAGER_QUERY_LOCK_STATUS
0x0020	WP	SC_MANAGER_MODIFY_BOOT_CONFIG
0xF003F	-	SC_MANAGER_ALL_ACCESS

Table C-8 contains information about system service object access rights.

Table C-8: Access Rights for a Service

HEX	STRING	NAME
0x0001	CC	SERVICE_QUERY_CONFIG
0x0002	DC	SERVICE_CHANGE_CONFIG
0x0004	LC	SERVICE_QUERY_STATUS
0x0008	SW	SERVICE_ENUMERATE_DEPENDENTS
0x0010	RP	SERVICE_START
0x0020	WP	SERVICE_STOP
0x0040	DT	SERVICE_PAUSE_CONTINUE
0x0080	LO	SERVICE_INTERROGATE
0x0100	CR	SERVICE_USER_DEFINED_CONTROL
0x01FF	-	SERVICE_ALL_ACCESS

Table C-9 contains information about job object (scheduled task) access rights.

Table C-9: Access Rights for Job Object

HEX	STRING	NAME
0x0001	CC	JOB_OBJECT_ASSIGN_PROCESS
0x0002	DC	JOB_OBJECT_SET_ATTRIBUTES
0x0004	LC	JOB_OBJECT_QUERY
0x0008	SW	JOB_OBJECT_TERMINATE
0x0010	RP	JOB_OBJECT_SET_SECURITY_ATTRIBUTES
0x1F001F	-	JOB_OBJECT_ALL_ACCESS

Index